# CASEBOOK ON
# CARRIAGE OF GOODS BY SEA

To Angelika

# CASEBOOK ON

# CARRIAGE OF GOODS BY SEA

Second Edition

## A. D. Hughes
### BCL, MA (Oxon), Barrister (LI)

Former Director, External Programme in Laws,

University of London

BLACKSTONE PRESS LIMITED

First published in Great Britain 1994 by Blackstone Press Limited, Aldine Place, London W12 8AA. Telephone: (020) 8740 2277 www.blackstonepress.com

First edition, 1994
Second edition, 1999

ISBN: 1 85431 881 0

British Library Cataloguing in Publication Data
A CIP catalogue record for this book is available from the British Library.

Typeset by Montage Studios Ltd, Horsmonden, Kent
Printed by Ashford Colour Press, Gosport, Hampshire

# Contents

# Preface

As in the first edition, my aim has been to compile a selection from the many reported cases on carriage of goods by sea which will introduce the student both to the commercial background of the subject and to the fascinating art of what Lord Diplock so aptly described, in *The Maratha Envoy*, as 'judicial exegesis' of the meaning of the words used by the parties in their contracts. For reasons of space, it has been necessary to dispense with the chapters on statutory limitation of shipowners' liability and general average.

I would like to acknowledge my great debt to colleagues and students who have taken part in the LLM seminars in which I have been involved both in London and in Hong Kong and to Professor Kumchai Jongjakapun of Thammasat University, Bangkok, whose PhD thesis I had the privilege of supervising. I also gained a great deal from working on materials for the guidance of the University's external students in this subject.

Finally, I would like to express my special thanks to my daughter, Birgit, for her invaluable help in putting the manuscript into a presentable form and to my wife, Angelika, for her unfailing support and encouragement throughout.

*A. D. Hughes*
*London*
*13 June 1999*

# Acknowledgments

The publishers and author would like to thank the following for permission to reproduce extracts from the publications listed below:

Butterworths Law Publishers Ltd — The All England Law Reports, the English Reports and the Law Times.

LLP Limited — Lloyds Law Reports.

The Incorporated Council of Law Reporting for England and Wales — The Law Reports and the Weekly Law Reports.

News International Newspapers Ltd — Commercial Cases and Times Law Reports.

# Table of Cases

Page numbers relating to extracts from cases reproduced are printed in bold type. The case name is also printed in bold type.

# Table of Statutes

*Page numbers relating to extracts from statutes reproduced are printed in bold type. The statute title is also printed in bold type.*

# 1 INTRODUCTION

## SECTION 1: THE ROLE OF CONTRACT

The subject of carriage of goods by sea is concerned with the legal relations between carriers and the various parties who might be interested in the fate of the vessel and its cargo, namely a charterer of the vessel, a shipper of cargo on board her and a holder of a bill of lading in respect of part or all of the cargo to whom the right to receive the cargo has been transferred. In the nature of things, the business of carriage of goods by sea involves certain well-known risks: the cargo may arrive late, or in a damaged condition, or may not arrive at all, for reasons beyond the control of the carrier, such as storms on the voyage; in such events, will the carrier still be able to claim the agreed freight payment (or keep it if it has been paid in advance)? Will the shipper, or bill of lading holder, be entitled to compensation because the cargo has been lost, damaged or delayed? If a chartered vessel has to wait at anchor for days, or even weeks, before unloading the cargo because the port is congested and no berth is free, can the shipowner pass any of the cost of the delay on to the charterer?

As between shipowners and charterers, and as between carriers, whether they are owners or themselves charterers, and the shippers of cargo, the problems are today seen as essentially contractual in nature, that is to say that it is in principle for the parties themselves to allocate the risks by agreement, and thereby decide who shall be responsible for covering each particular risk by insurance. The underlying common law principles apply only to the extent that the parties have not modified them by the terms of the contract.

The negotiating process generally takes the form of adapting one of the many standard forms of contract to accommodate the variables of the transaction at hand. Shipping lines and frequent shippers will probably have their own forms of bills of lading; large scale charterers, such as the major oil companies, have their own standard voyage charterparties (e.g., 'SHELLVOY 5') and time charters (e.g., 'SHELLTIME 4'); many commodity trades have their own standard forms of charterparty (e.g., NORGRAIN, NIPPONORE, NUBALT-WOOD) and the forms issued by the Baltic and International Maritime Conference (BIMCO), such as 'Baltime 1939' and 'Gencon', and by the Association of Ship Brokers & Agents (USA) Inc. (ASBA), such as NYPE 93 (the New York Produce Exchange form), are widely used.

In resolving disputes arising out of such contracts, the House of Lords in particular has more than once emphasised how important it is to avoid legalistic interpretations and to give words and phrases the meaning which businessmen would expect them to bear. Certainty in such matters is also an essential support for freedom of contract, and must not be compromised by a desire for 'equitable' solutions.

### A/S Awilco v Fulvia SpA di Navigazione
### (The Chikuma)
[1981] 1 Lloyd's Rep 371 (HL)

The case concerned a clause in a time charter giving the shipowner liberty to withdraw the vessel 'failing the punctual ... payment of the hire'. The 'broad' construction of 'punctual' adopted by the Court of Appeal (Lord Denning MR, Waller and Dunn LJJ) in favour of the charterer was rejected by the House of Lords.

LORD BRIDGE OF HARWICH: My Lords, earlier exercises of judicial ingenuity to mitigate the rigours of clauses in charterparties giving the shipowners a right to withdraw their ships on failure or default in payment of hire or freight have not had a happy history. . . .

It has often been pointed out that shipowners and charterers bargain at arm's length. Neither class has such a preponderance of bargaining power as to be in a position to oppress the other. They should be in a position to look after themselves by contracting only on terms which are acceptable to them. Where, as here, they embody in their contracts common form clauses, it is, to my mind, of overriding importance that their meaning and legal effect should be certain and well understood. The ideal at which the Courts should aim, in construing such clauses, is to produce a result, such that in any given situation both parties seeking legal advice as to their rights and obligations can expect the same clear and confident answer from their advisers and neither will be tempted to embark on long and expensive litigation in the belief that victory depends on winning the sympathy of the Court. This ideal may never be fully attainable, but we shall certainly never even approximate to it unless we strive to follow clear and consistent principles and steadfastly refuse to be blown off course by the supposed merits of individual cases.

### President of India v Jebsens (UK) Ltd
### (The General Capinpin)
[1991] 1 Lloyd's Rep 1 (HL)

Here the courts had to decide the meaning of an unusual formula for the calculation of lay (i.e., loading) time: was it an 'overall' rate for the ship (which favoured the shipowners) or a rate 'per hatch' (which favoured the charterers, whose form it was). The Court of Appeal agreed with the arbitrators' award in favour of the shipowners and the House of Lords (Lord Templeman dissenting) dismissed the charterers' appeal.

LORD GOFF OF CHIEVELEY: ... [I]t must not be forgotten that a charter-party is not like legislation, forced upon parties against their wills; it is bargained for, and if any particular provision is perceived to favour one or other party, that can be taken into account when negotiating the contract consideration. Furthermore, in the commercial world contracting parties have to look after their own interests. Shipowning, and (in the case of regular charterers) chartering, are highly professional occupations; and in any event the services of brokers are available to both. It is up to them to assess the probable impact of any particular clause upon their interest, and to act accordingly when negotiating the charter.

... [O]nce a clause is embodied in a commercial contract, it has simply to be construed in its context, from the objective point of view of reasonable persons in the shoes of the contracting parties. Of course it has to be construed sensibly, and regard has to be had to its practical effect. But the objective interpretation is of paramount importance in commercial affairs; commercial men have frequently to take important decisions with some speed, and it is of great importance that they all know that they can rely on Courts and arbitrators, if any dispute should later arise, to adopt the same objective approach as they themselves have to adopt in the daily administration of their contracts.

... It is plain that what really struck the arbitrators was that the clause did indeed provide for an overall rate of discharge, and did not expressly provide for a rate per hatch, despite the existence of well-known authorities dealing with clauses which so provided. They were simply not prepared to ignore the express provision for the overall rate; they preferred to treat the reference to 'available workable hatches' not as substituting a rate per hatch for the expressly provided overall rate for the ship, but rather as imposing a qualification upon it. This was the reaction of commercial men, who must have been well aware of the practical consequences of their decision, and who must also have been well aware how charter-parties are negotiated and how they are likely to be understood by practical men in the trade. ...

*Notes and Questions*

1. Because of the doctrine of privity of contract, the position of transferees of bills of lading vis-à-vis carriers cannot be defined purely in terms of contract at common law, since they are not (or at any rate not normally) parties to the contract of carriage, but in favour of a transferee the bill of lading will be conclusive evidence of the terms of the contract and, by statute, the contract will be enforceable against the carrier by the transferee. See Chapter 6.

2. Contracts for the carriage of goods are sometimes referred to generically as contracts of 'affreightment' (see, e.g., *Scrutton on Charterparties*, 20th ed., London: Sweet & Maxwell, 1996 (hereafter referred to as Scrutton), p. 1); the term is also used at the present day to indicate a framework agreement which will be implemented by the conclusion of a series of particular contracts for the carriage of specific cargoes: see, e.g., *Sacor Maritima SA* v *Repsol Petroleo SA* [1998] 1 Lloyd's Rep 518 (QBD, Mance J).

3. Who is likely to have the stronger negotiating position: (a) shipowner or charterer, (b) carrier or shipper?

4.   Where the bargaining 'muscle' of the two parties is unequal, could the use of standard form contracts have any advantages for the 'weaker' party?

## SECTION 2: CARRIERS' LIABILITY AT COMMON LAW

Long before the appearance of the modern bill of lading and charterparty, the common law had developed principles governing the liability of carriers independently of contract. From as early as the 14th century (the *Humber Ferryman* Case (1348) YB 22 Liber Assisarum No. 41, f. 94) the law gave special protection to the customers and would-be customers of those who exercised the 'common callings' of innkeeper or common carrier. Common carriers were those who held themselves out as being willing to carry the goods of any person who could pay their charges, so long as space was available; if the goods were lost or damaged while in the carrier's care, the carrier was liable 'as an insurer'.

### *Forward* v *Pittard*
### (1785) 1 TR 27; 99 ER 953 (King's Bench)

P, a common carrier, agreed to carry 12 pockets of hops from London to Shaftesbury in Dorset. The journey involved an overnight stop at Andover. During the night a fire started accidentally at a spot 100 yards from where the hops were stored. The fire spread and destroyed the hops. The jury found that P was not negligent. The court upheld the verdict for the plaintiff.

LORD MANSFIELD: . . . The question is, whether the common carrier is liable in this case of fire? It appears from all the cases for 100 years back, that there are events for which the carrier is liable independent of his contract. By the nature of his contract, he is liable for all due care and diligence; and for any negligence he is suable on his contract. But there is a further degree of responsibility by the custom of the realm, that is, by the common law; a carrier is in the nature of an insurer. It is laid down that he is liable for every accident, except by the act of God, or the King's enemies. Now what is the act of God? I consider it to mean something in opposition to the act of man: for every thing is the act of God that happens by His permission; every thing, by His knowledge. But to prevent litigation, collusion, and the necessity of going into circumstances impossible to be unravelled, the law presumes against the carrier, unless he shows it was done by the King's enemies or by such act as could not happen by the intervention of man, as storms, lightning, and tempests.
     If an armed force come to rob the carrier of the goods, he is liable: and a reason is given in the books, which is a bad one, viz. that he ought to have a sufficient force to repel it: but that would be impossible in some cases, as for instance in the riots in the year 1780. The true reason is, for fear it may give room for collusion, that the master may contrive to be robbed on purpose, and share the spoil.
     In this case, it does not appear but that the fire arose from the act of some man or other. It certainly did arise from some act of man; for it is expressly stated not to have happened by lightning. The carrier therefore in this case is liable, inasmuch as he is liable for inevitable accident.

*Note*

The common carrier could thus escape liability for loss of or damage to the goods at common law only by showing that the cause of the loss or damage was one of the 'excepted perils'. (The excepted perils are considered in more detail in Chapter 2.)

Where a land carrier was *not* a common carrier, his liability was held to be no more than that of a bailee, that is to say a person to whom possession of goods has been given for a limited purpose. A bailee of goods, even for reward, is not treated as an insurer of them, but 'is only to do the best he can' (*per* Holt CJ in *Coggs* v *Bernard* (1703) 2 Ld Raym 909, at 918): it will therefore be a defence for the carrier to show that the goods were lost or damaged without negligence on his part, but — and this is an important qualification — the burden of proving that the goods were lost or damaged without negligence lies on the bailee (*Joseph Travers and Sons Ltd* v *Cooper* [1915] 1 KB 73 (CA), where the defendant, a wharfinger and lighterman, successfully relied on an exemption clause to cover negligence, though negligence was not specifically mentioned); *Levinson* v *Patent Steam Cleaning* [1978] QB 69, CA).

## SECTION 3: SEA CARRIERS' LIABILITY AT COMMON LAW

If the sea carrier was a common carrier it was clear that exactly the same principles of liability applied as to the common carrier by land. In most cases, however, sea carriers were not common carriers and it was, and still is, a matter of controversy what standard of liability the common law imposed in such a case. Was it, for example, merely the liability of a bailee?

### *Liver Alkali Co.* v *Johnson*
(1874) LR 9 Ex 338 (Exch Ch)

The defendant (J) owned 'flats' (i.e., barges) which he operated on the River Mersey. The plaintiffs (L) shipped a quantity of salt cake in one of J's barges for carriage from Widnes to Liverpool. The barge ran aground in fog and the salt cake was damaged. In the action by L, the jury found that J was not negligent. J argued, on appeal from the judgment of the Court of Exchequer in L's favour, that he was not a common carrier, since he did not ply between fixed termini and did not carry the goods of more than one customer at the same time, and that the absence of negligence therefore constituted a complete answer to L's claim.

The Court of Exchequer Chamber dismissed J's appeal.

BLACKBURN J: It appears by the case stated for this Court on appeal that the defendant was engaged in carrying from Widness [*sic*] to Liverpool some salt cake of the plaintiffs in a flat on the river Mersey. The goods were injured by reason of the flat getting on a shoal in consequence of a fog. This was a peril of navigation, but could in no sense be called the act of God or of the Queen's enemies.

The jury found that there was no negligence on the part of the defendant.

The question, therefore, raised is, whether the defendant was under the liability of a bailee for hire, viz., to take proper care of the goods, in which case he is not responsible for this loss, or whether he has the more extended liability of a common carrier, viz., to carry the goods safe against all events but acts of God and the enemies of the Queen.

We have purposely confined our expressions to the question, 'whether the defendant has the liability of a common carrier,' for we do not think it necessary to inquire whether the defendant is a carrier so as to be liable to an action for not taking goods tendered to him.

The rule imposing this extended liability on common carriers was originally established, as Lord Mansfield states, in *Forward* v *Pittard* 1 TR 27, at p. 33, on the ground of public policy: . . . It is too late now to speculate on the propriety of this rule, we must treat it as firmly established that, in the absence of some contract, express or implied, introducing further exceptions, those who exercise a public employment of carrying goods do incur this liability. It appears from the evidence stated that the defendant was the owner of several flats, and that he made it his business to send out his flats under the care of his own servants, different persons as required from time to time, to carry cargoes to or from places in the Mersey, but that it always was to carry goods for one person at a time, and that 'he carried for any one who chose to employ him, but that an express agreement was always made as to each voyage or employment of the defendant's flats', which means, as we understand the evidence, that the flats did not go about plying for hire, but were waiting for hire by any one. We think that this describes the ordinary employment of a lighterman, and that, both on authority and principle, a person who exercises this business and employment does, in the absence of something to limit his liability, incur the liability of a common carrier in respect of the goods he carries.

It was argued before us that the defendant could not have this liability unless he held himself out as plying between two particular places, or had put up his flat, like a general ship, to go to some particular place, and take all goods brought him for that voyage.

It was urged that in *Morse* v *Slue* 1 Vent. 190, 238 the goods were probably put on board a ship put up as a general ship. It certainly may have been so, but the count is set out in Ventris and is general, that by the law and custom of England charterers and governors of ships which go from London beyond sea are bound, &c., and the ultimate decision was that this count was proved. Hale CJ seems to have had a difficulty from the fact that the ship was bound to foreign parts, and that the shipowner would not by the civil law or the maritime law be chargeable for piracy or damnum fatale (a difficulty, it may be remarked, which does not apply to the present case, where the whole transaction is in England), but nothing is in any report said as to the ship being a general ship. And on that count no judgment could have been given on that ground.

The ultimate decision on the special verdict has always been understood to apply equally to all ships employed in commerce and sailing from England, as is shewn from the forms of charterparty and bill of lading in ordinary use in England, which always contain an engagement to deliver the goods in the same condition they were received aboard, and, when Lord Tenterden first wrote, contained only an exception of the dangers of the seas; now the exceptions in each class of instrument are much more extensive. And certainly it is difficult to see any reason why the liability of a shipowner who engages to carry the whole lading of his ship for one person should be less than the liability of one who carries the lading in different parcels for different people.

To come nearer to the particular case, we find that 'lightermen' are specially named in Bacon's Abridgment 'Carrier' (A.), and in the notes to *Coggs* v *Bernard* 1 Sm LC 6th ed. 177. In *Lyon* v *Mells* 5 East, 428 the course of business of the defendant is thus described: 'The defendant kept sloops for carrying other persons' goods for hire, and also lighters for the purpose of carrying these goods to and from his sloops, and when he had not employment for his lighters in his own business, he let them for hire to such persons as wanted to carry goods to other sloops.' If there be any difference between the employment of the now defendant, as described in this case, and the employment of the defendant in *Lyon* v *Mells* 5 East, 428, it would seem that the latter was less clearly a public employment. The great point discussed was, whether a notice limiting the liability of the defendant was, as Lord Ellenborough states it, illegal, as being 'to exempt him from a responsibility cast on him by law as a carrier of goods by water for hire', a proposition which could not well have been discussed by any one who did not think that the defendant had, but for the notice, incurred that responsibility. The point actually decided was, that the terms of the notice did not relieve the defendant from liability for furnishing an unseaworthy lighter. . . .

It is true that the point was not precisely decided in *Lyon* v *Mells* 5 East 428 and if it had been, it would not have been binding upon us in a Court of Error; but the opinion of Lord Ellenborough, and (as far as we can judge from the report) of every one concerned in the case, was that it was too clear for argument that, but for the notice, the lighterman, acting as the defendant did in that case, would have been liable to the same extent as a common carrier. . . .

We think, therefore, that the judgment below was right, and should be affirmed.

## Question

Is Blackburn J (with whose judgment Mellor, Archibald and Grove JJ concurred) deciding (a) that J was a common carrier, (b) that all sea carriers are common carriers, or (c) that lightermen are common carriers?

## Note

While agreeing with the result, one judge, a distinguished commercial lawyer, who later became Master of the Rolls, expressed the principle differently.

BRETT J: . . . I cannot come to the conclusion that the defendant in this case was liable whether he was a common carrier or not, because I conclude that he was liable, notwithstanding that I am clearly of opinion that he was not a common carrier. It seems to me that it is of the very essence of the definition of a common carrier, that he should be one who undertakes to carry the goods (not being dangerous, or of unreasonable weight or bulk) which are first offered to him — he who does not so undertake is not a common carrier. The force of the word 'common' is not that the carrier's business is a public one, or 'in common with others,' but that he undertakes to carry for all indifferently in the sense of for the first comer, i.e., 'for all in common'. It is clear to my mind that a shipowner who publicly professes to own sloops, and to charter them to any one who will agree with him on terms of charter, is not a common carrier, because he does not undertake to carry goods for or to charter his sloop to the first comer. He wants, therefore, the essential characteristic of a common carrier; he is, therefore, not a common carrier, and therefore does not incur at any time any liability on the ground of his being a common carrier. The defendant in the present case, in my opinion, carried on his business like any other owner of sloops or vessels, and was not a common carrier, and was in no way liable as such. But I think that, by a recognised custom of England, — a custom adopted and recognised by the Courts in precisely the same manner as the custom of England with regard to common carriers has been adopted and recognised by them — every shipowner who carries goods for hire in his ship, whether by inland navigation, or coastways, or abroad, undertakes to carry them at his own absolute risk, the act of God or of the Queen's enemies alone excepted, unless by agreement between himself and a particular freighter, on a particular voyage, or on particular voyages, he limits his liability by further exceptions.

I think that this liability attaches to shipowners carrying goods, by reason of recognised custom, which may be pleaded as the custom of England, just as the custom of England as to common carriers may be pleaded. But it is a custom wholly independent of the similar custom with regard to common carriers. The similarity of the two customs has occasioned phraseology to be used in some cases which has raised an inaccurate idea that shipowners are common carriers; but I am of opinion that they are not. They are not bound to carry for the first comer. I therefore hold that the defendant is liable as a shipowner, upon the custom applicable to him as such, but is not liable as a common carrier, upon the custom applicable to that business or employment.

*Note*

Two years later the issue came before the newly established Court of Appeal (the successor to the Court of Exchequer Chamber):

### *Nugent* v *Smith*
### (1876) 1 CPD 423 (CA)

COCKBURN CJ: This case involves a question of considerable importance as regards the law relating to carriers by sea, but the facts are few and simple. The plaintiff, being the owner of two horses, and having occasion to send them from London to Aberdeen, shipped them on board a steamship belonging to the company of which the defendant is the representative, plying regularly as a general ship between the two ports. The horses were shipped without any bill of lading. In the course of the voyage a storm of more than ordinary violence arose; and partly from the rolling of the vessel in the heavy sea, partly from struggling caused by excessive fright, one of the animals, a mare, received injuries from which she died. It is to recover damages in respect of her loss that this action is brought.

The jury, in answer to a question specifically put to them, have expressly negatived any want of due care on the part of the defendant, either in taking proper measures beforehand to protect the horses from the effects of tempestuous weather, or in doing all that could be done to save them from the consequences of it after it had come on. A further question put to the jury was, whether there were any known means, though not ordinarily used in the conveyance of horses by people of ordinary care and skill, by which the defendant could have prevented the injury to the mare, but to this question the jury returned no answer. The question is, whether, on this state of facts, the shipowners are liable.

For the defendant, it was insisted that the storm, which was the primary, and in a partial degree the proximate, cause of the loss, must be taken to have been an 'act of God' within the legal meaning of that term, so as, all due care having been taken to convey the mare safely, to afford immunity to the defendant's company as carriers from liability in respect of the loss complained of; and the question to be determined is, whether this contention is well founded.

The judgment of the Common Pleas Divison in favour of the plaintiff, as delivered by Mr Justice Brett, involves, if I rightly understand it, the following propositions: 1. That the Roman law relating to bailments has been adopted by our Courts as part of the common law of England; 2. That, by the Roman law, the owners of all ships, whether common carriers or not, are equally liable for loss by inevitable accident; 3. That such is the rule of English law as derived from the Roman law, and as evidenced by English authorities; 4. That, to bring the cause of damage or loss within the meaning of the term 'act of God', so as to give immunity to the carrier, the damage or loss in question must have been caused directly and exclusively by such a direct and violent and sudden and irresistible act of Nature as the defendant could not, by any amount of ability, foresee would happen, or, if he could foresee that it would happen, he could not by any amount of care and skill resist, so as to prevent its effect; 5. That, notwithstanding the inability of the jury to agree to an answer to the fifth question left to them, the defendant has in this case failed to satisfy the burden of proof cast upon him, so as to bring himself clearly within the definition, as it is impossible to say that no human ability could foresee the reasonable probability of the happening of rough weather on the voyage, and that a horse at sea might be frightened by it, or that no human ability could prevent injury to a frightened horse in such weather as occurred.

In no part of this reasoning am I able to concur. But before I proceed to deal with it, I must observe that, as the vessel by which the mare was shipped was one of a line of steamers plying habitually between given ports and carrying the goods of all comers as a general ship, and as from this it necessarily follows that the owners were common carriers, it was altogether unnecessary to the decision of the present case to determine the question so elaborately discussed in the judgment of Mr Justice Brett as to the liability of the owner of a ship, not being a general ship, but one hired to carry a specific cargo on a particular voyage, to make good loss or damage arising from inevitable accident. The question being, however, one of considerable importance — though its importance is materially lessened by the general practice of ascertaining and limiting the liability of the shipowner by charterparty or bill of lading — and the question not having before presented itself for judicial decision, I think it right to express my dissent from the reasoning of the Court below, the more so as, for the opinion thus expressed, I not only fail to discover any authority whatever, but find all jurists who treat of this form of bailment carefully distinguishing between the common carrier and the private ship. Parsons, a writer of considerable authority on this subject, defines a common carrier to be 'one who offers to carry goods for any person between certain termini and on a certain route'. 'He is bound to carry for all who tender to him goods and the price of carriage, and insures these goods against all loss but that arising from the act of God or the public enemy, and has a lien on the goods for the price of the carriage.' 'If either of these elements is wanting, we say the carrier is not a common carrier, either by land or by water'. 'If we are right in this,' he adds, 'no vessel will be a common carrier that does not ply regularly, alone or in connection with others, on some definite route, or between two certain termini.' . . . Story seems to be of a like opinion. . . .

In the absence of all common-law authority for the proposition that by the law of England every carrier by sea is subject to the same liability as the common carrier, as asserted in the judgment below, the authority of the Roman law is invoked; but this law, on which so much stress is laid in the judgment of the Court of Common Pleas, affords no support to this doctrine. In the first place, it is a misapprehension to suppose that the law of England relating to the liability of common carriers was derived from the Roman law; for the law relating to it was first established by our Courts with reference to carriers by land, on whom the Roman law, as is well known, imposed no liability in respect of loss beyond that of other bailees for reward. In the second place, the Roman law made no distinction between inevitable accident arising from what in our law is termed the 'act of God' and inevitable accident arising from other causes, but, on the contrary, afforded immunity to the carrier, without distinction, whenever the loss resulted from 'casus fortuitus', or, as it is also called, 'damnum fatale', or 'vis major' — unforeseen and unavoidable accident. . . .

After considering Roman law, French law, Scots law and the early English authorities, Cockburn CJ continued:

... The last case is that of the *Liver Alkali Co.* v *Johnson* Law Rep. 9 Ex. 338, in which the defendant was a barge owner and let out his vessels for conveyance of goods to any customers who applied to him. Each voyage was made under a separate agreement, and a barge was not let to more than one person for the same voyage. The defendant did not ply between any fixed termini, but the customer fixed in each particular case the points of arrival and departure. In an action against the defendant by the plaintiffs for not safely and securely carrying certain goods, the Court of Exchequer Chamber held, affirming the judgment of the Court of Exchequer, that the defendant was a common carrier and liable as such. Mr Justice Brett, differing from the majority, held that the defendant was not a common carrier, but, asserting the same doctrine as in the judgment now appealed from, held him liable upon a special custom of the realm attaching to all carriers by sea, of which custom, however, as I have already intimated, I can find no trace whatever. We are, of course, bound by the decision of the Court of Exchequer Chamber in the case referred to as that of a court of appellate jurisdiction, and which, therefore, can only be reviewed by a court of ultimate appeal; but I cannot help seeing the difficulty which stands in the way of the ruling in that case, namely, that it is essential to the character of a common carrier that he is bound to carry the goods of all persons applying to him, while it never has been held, and, as it seems to me, could not be held, that a person who lets out vessels or vehicles to individual customers on their application was liable to an action for refusing the use of such vessel or vehicle if required to furnish it. At all events, it is obvious that as the decision of the Court of Exchequer Chamber proceeded on the ground that the defendant in that case was a common carrier, the decision is no authority for the position taken in the Court below, that all shipowners are equally liable for loss by inevitable accident. It is plain that the majority of the Court did not adopt the view of Mr Justice Brett. Lastly, while it does not lie within our province to criticise the law we have to administer or to question its policy, I cannot but think that we are not called upon to extend a principle of extreme rigour, peculiar to our own law, and the absence of which in the law of other nations has not been found by experience to lead to the evils for the prevention of which the rule of our law was supposed to be necessary, further than it has hitherto been applied. I cannot, therefore, concur in the opinion expressed in the judgment delivered by Mr Justice Brett, that by the law of England all carriers by sea are subject to the liability which by that law undoubtedly attaches to the common carrier whether by sea or by land.

But there being no doubt that in the case before us the shipowner was a common carrier, we have now to deal with the question on which the decision really turns, namely, whether the loss was occasioned by what can properly be called the 'act of God'....

*Note*

For this aspect of the case, see Chapter 2, section 1. The other members of the Court expressed no opinion on the principle asserted by Brett J.

Subsequent cases have done little to clarify the position. In *Hill* v *Scott* [1895] 2 QB 371, Lord Russell of Killowen CJ in the QBD applied *Liver Alkali* to impose the liability of a common carrier on a party who was not a common carrier. His decision was affirmed by the Court of Appeal ([1895] 2 QB 713) without reference to this point. In *McFadden* v *Blue Star Line* [1905] 1 KB 697, Channell J stated, at pp. 703–4, without distinguishing between common carriers and others: 'If anything happens whereby the goods are damaged during the voyage, the shipowner is liable because he is an insurer except in the event of the damage happening from some cause in respect of which he is protected by the exceptions in his bill of lading.' In *Watkins* v *Cottell* [1916] 1 KB 10 (QB Divisional Ct) *Liver Alkali* was treated as a case of common carriers and Rowlatt J commented (at p. 18): 'Personally I find a difficulty in seeing that there is any distinction in substance between so assuming the liability of a common carrier and being a common carrier. The distinction seems to me to be largely a matter of words.' For good measure, Bailhache J in *Belfast Paperwork Co.* v *Buswell* [1918] 1 KB 210, 212 seems to regard *Liver Alkali* as a decision that *lightermen* have the liability of common carriers.

### Question
Given that carriers in practice deal on the basis of wide contractual exclusions of liability, does the common law position ever matter? (See Chapter 4 for the effect of deviation on the carrier's liability.)

# 2 COMMON LAW EXCLUSIONS OF LIABILITY

The liability of carriers has always been limited at common law by the principle that certain risks are excluded (the 'excepted perils'): since the turn of the 18th century it has also in principle been possible for carriers to limit their liability by contract. In this chapter we consider first the excepted perils and then some of the common contractual exemption clauses to be found in bills of lading and charterparties.

## SECTION 1: THE EXCEPTED PERILS

*A: Act of God*

### *Nugent v Smith*
### (1876) 1 CPD 423 (CA)

The facts are stated above, Chapter 1, section 3. The following definition of 'Act of God' was suggested:

JAMES LJ: ... The 'act of God' is a mere short way of expressing this proposition. A common carrier is not liable for any accident as to which he can shew that it is due to natural causes directly and exclusively, without human intervention, and that it could not have been prevented by any amount of foresight and pains and care reasonably to be expected from him. In this case the defendant has made this out.

The Chief Justice elaborated on the standard of care required of the carrier:

COCKBURN CJ: The definition which is given by Mr Justice Brett, of what is termed in our law the 'act of God' is, that it must be such a direct, and violent, and sudden, and irresistible act of Nature as could not by any amount of ability have been foreseen, or if foreseen, could not by any amount of human care and skill have been resisted. The judgment then proceeds:

> We cannot say, notwithstanding the inability of the jury to agree to an answer to the fifth question left to them, that the defendant has in this case satisfied the burden of proof cast upon him so as to bring himself clearly within the definition. It seems to me impossible to say that no human ability could foresee the reasonable probability of the happening of rough weather on the voyage, and that a horse at sea might be frightened by it, or that no human ability could prevent injury to a frightened horse in such weather as occurred.

The exposition here given appears to me too wide as regards the degree of care required of the shipowner, and as exacting more than can properly be expected of him. It is somewhat remarkable that previously to the present case no judicial exposition has occurred of the meaning of the term 'act of God', as regards the degree of care to be applied by the carrier in order to entitle himself to the benefit of its protection. We must endeavour to lay down an intelligible rule.

That a storm at sea is included in the term 'act of God', can admit of no doubt whatever. Storm and tempest have always been mentioned in dealing with this subject as among the instances of vis major coming under the denomination of 'act of God'. But it is equally true, as has already been pointed out, that it is not under all circumstances that inevitable accident arising from the so-called act of God will, any more than inevitable accident in general by the Roman and continental law, afford immunity to the carrier. This must depend on his ability to avert the effects of the vis major, and the degree of diligence which he is bound to apply to that end.

It is at once obvious, as was pointed out by Lord Mansfield in *Forward* v *Pittard* 1 TR 27, that all causes of inevitable accident — 'casus fortuitus' — may be divided into two classes — those which are occasioned by the elementary forces of nature unconnected with the agency of man or other cause, and those which have their origin either in the whole or in part in the agency of man, whether in acts of commission or omission, of nonfeasance or of misfeasance, or in any other cause independent of the agency of natural forces. It is obvious that it would be altogether incongruous to apply the term 'act of God' to the latter class of inevitable accident. It is equally clear that storm and tempest belong to the class to which the term 'act of God' is properly applicable.

On the other hand, it must be admitted that it is not because an accident is occasioned by the agency of nature, and therefore by what may be termed the 'act of God', that it necessarily follows that the carrier is entitled to immunity. The rain which fertilises the earth and the wind which enables the ship to navigate the ocean are as much within the term 'act of God' as the rainfall which causes a river to burst its banks and carry destruction over a whole district, or the cyclone that drives a ship against a rock or sends it to the bottom. Yet the carrier who by the rule is entitled to protection in the latter case, would clearly not be able to claim it in case of damage occurring in the former. For here another principle comes into play. The carrier is bound to do his utmost to protect goods committed to his charge from loss or damage, and if he fails herein he becomes liable from the nature of his contract. In the one case he can protect the goods by proper care, in the other it is beyond his power to do so. If by his default in omitting to take the necessary care loss or damage ensues, he remains responsible, though the so-called act of God may have been the immediate cause of the mischief. If the ship is unseaworthy, and hence perishes from the storm which it otherwise would have weathered; if the carrier by undue deviation or delay exposes himself to the danger which he otherwise would have avoided; or if by his rashness he unnecessarily encounters it, as by putting to sea in a raging storm, the loss cannot be said to be due to the act of God alone, and the carrier cannot have the benefit of the exception. This being granted, the question arises as to the degree of care which is to be required of him to protect him from liability in respect of loss arising from the act of God. Not only, as has been observed, has there been no judicial exposition of the meaning of the term 'act of God' as regards the degree of care to be applied by the carrier in order to entitle himself to its protection, but the text-writers, both English and American, are, for the most part, silent on the subject. . . .

After referring to Roman law, his Lordship continued:

In our own law on this subject judicial authority, as has been stated, is wanting, and the text writers, English and American, with one exception, afford little or no assistance. Story, however, in speaking of the perils of the sea, in which storm and tempest are of course included, and consequently to a great extent the instances of inevitable accident at sea which come under the term 'act of God', uses the following language:

> The phrase 'perils of the sea', whether understood in its most limited sense, as importing a loss by natural accidents peculiar to that element, or whether understood in its more extended sense as including inevitable accidents occurring upon that element, must still in either case be understood to include such losses only to the goods on board as are of an extraordinary nature or arise from some irresistible force, or from inevitable accident, or from some overwhelming power which cannot be guarded against by ordinary exertions of human skill and prudence. Hence it is that if the loss occurs by a peril of the sea which might have been avoided by the exercise of any reasonable skill or diligence at the time when it occurred, it is not deemed to be in the sense of the phrase such a loss by the perils of the sea as will exempt the carrier from liability, but rather a loss by the gross negligence of the party.

Story, it will be observed, here speaks only of 'ordinary exertion of human skill and prudence and the exercise of reasonable skill and diligence'. In my opinion this is the true view of the matter, and what Story here says of perils of the sea applies, I think, equally to the perils of the sea coming within the designation of 'acts of God'. In other words, all that can be required of the carrier is that he shall do all that is reasonably and practically possible to insure the safety of the goods. If he uses all the known means to which prudent and experienced carriers ordinarily have recourse, he does all that can be reasonably required of him; and if, under such circumstances, he is overpowered by storm or other natural agency, he is within the rule which gives immunity from the effects of such vis major as the act of God. I do not think that because some one may have discovered some more efficient method of securing the goods which has not become generally known, or because it cannot be proved that if the skill and ingenuity of engineers or others were directed to the subject something more efficient might not be produced, that the carrier can be made liable. I find no authority for saying that the vis major must be such as 'no amount of human care or skill could have resisted', or the injury such as 'no human ability could have prevented', and I think this construction of the rule erroneous. That the defendants here took all the care that could reasonably be required of them to insure the safety of the mare is, I think, involved in the finding of the jury, directly negativing negligence, and I think that it was not incumbent on the defendants to establish more than is implied by that finding.

### *Siordet* v *Hall*
(1828) 6 LJCP 137 (Common Pleas)

The bill of lading contained an exception clause for Act of God. The vessel (the *Superb*) was due to sail from London early on 11 February and, in accordance with the normal practice, the boiler was filled the night before; however, there was a hard frost and water in a pipe froze during the night. The pipe burst and when the water thawed it caused damage to the cargo. The Court of Common Pleas held that the carrier could not rely on the defence of Act of God.

BEST CJ: The question in this case, is, whether the damage which is the subject of this action, has been occasioned by the act of God, or by the negligence of the defendants. The evidence clearly shewed, that the latter was the immediate cause; for, unless the boiler had been filled with water, the frost could not have so affected the pipe; or, if it could, the bursting of the pipe would not have done the damage, unless there had been water in it. We, therefore, think, that there was negligence on the part of the defendants, in allowing the water to be placed in the boiler so long before it was absolutely necessary. The case of *Forward* v *Pittard* 1 TR 27 is a much stronger case than the present. There, it was held, that the defendant, a carrier, was liable for the loss of goods by fire, although there was no actual negligence; he being, in law, an insurer, and bound to make good all damage, unless occasioned by the act of God.

*Question*
Why is it not an Act of God if a vessel encounters thick fog and runs aground? (Cf. *Liver Alkali Co.* v *Johnson*, above.)

*B: Act of Queen's enemies*

This exception is not interpreted literally as applying only to the enemies of the British Crown, but covers the action of any forces engaged in hostilities with the *carrier's* State.

### *Russell* v *Niemann*
(1864) 17 CBNS 163; 84 ER 548 (Common Pleas)

The Duke of Mecklenburg was at war with Denmark. The vessel was a Mecklenburg ship owned by a Mecklenburg subject. She was seized by the Danes while on a voyage from Russia to England, carrying '3,325 chetverts fine Polish wheat'. Although England was not at war with Denmark, the exception applied.

WILLES J: This is an action on a bill of lading upon a ship bound from Odessa to the United Kingdom, to call at Cork or Falmouth for orders, and the declaration states that the order was given (we must now assume properly given) and that that order was disobeyed.

The defendant relies upon two points: first of all, he says, he was prevented from obeying the order given him by the act of the enemies of his sovereign the Duke of Mecklenburg-Schwerin, and he says that the bill of lading contains an exception which includes the acts of such enemies. That is the first point. . . .

As to the first point, we agree with the argument which has been addressed to the Court on the part of the defendant. It turns on the construction to be put on the words in the bill of lading 'the king's enemies'. It is necessary to take into consideration the circumstances under which the bill of lading was signed in order properly to apply those words. It appears that a bill of lading was signed at Odessa in the empire of Russia, and the shippers appear to be merchants there; otherwise, we have no account of their nationality. There is no reason for coming to the conclusion that they were either English, or Russians, or Germans; the ship was a Mecklenburg ship; her owners were Mecklenburg people. The destination of the vessel was English. You are to choose between three persons who will equally satisfy the word 'king' in the document. You have the Emperor of Russia, who strictly would not be called a king; you have the Queen of England, who strictly would not be called a king, although I believe that Queen Elizabeth in much more formal documents was more than once spoken of as a king; and you have the Duke of Mecklenburg-Schwerin, who in strictness may also be said not to be a king. But the word 'king' in these documents frequently denotes a sovereign capable of making war, or upon whom war could be made, and each of the three persons I have mentioned was equally a king in that sense. Taking into consideration the persons who made the contract, and the place where it was made, Odessa, is that any reason for saying that it is the enemies of the Emperor of Russia? Then you have the destination — England: are you, therefore, to say it must mean the Queen's enemies, although neither of the parties appears to have been an English subject? The person who signed this document and made this stipulation for himself, was a subject of the Duke of Mecklenburg-Schwerin, and that appears to be an abundantly sufficient reason why he was stipulating against dangers which might happen to him, from his own enemies rather than the enemies of other people. It expresses that by saying my king's enemies, my sovereign's enemies, the enemies of the Duke of Mecklenburg-Schwerin. I own therefore it appears to me that the good sense of the case is that 'the king's enemies' at least includes the enemies of the sovereign of the person who made this stipulation in the bill of lading.

## Note and Questions
1.  Chetverts: Russian for quarters.
2.  Would pirates come within the exception? (See Byles J in *Russell* v *Niemann*, above, at p. 174.)
3.  If, at the present day, a British ship struck a German mine left over from World War II and damage was caused to the cargo, could the carrier rely on the defence of act of the Queen's enemies?

### C: Inherent vice

The carrier is not liable for loss or deterioration caused by inherent qualities or characteristics of the goods which render them unable to withstand the ordinary, foreseeable incidents of the contemplated voyage, such as the natural deterioration of the unrefrigerated salted fish in *Albacora* v *Westcott & Laurance Line* [1966] 2 Lloyd's Rep 53 (HL) (see Chapter 7).

### D: Consignor's fault

On general principles, the carrier will not be liable if the loss or damage is attributable to the fault of the consignor. This is commonly treated as an excepted peril. One example of consignor's fault is insufficient packing of the goods: this raises the question whether the carrier can still rely on insufficient packing as a defence if the insufficiency was evident when the goods were shipped.

## *Gould v South Eastern and Chatham Railway Co.*
### [1920] 2 KB 186 (CA)

G wished to send goods, including a glass showcase, from Ramsgate to London on the defendants' railway. The person sent by the defendants to collect the goods (Perry) pointed out that the showcase was not properly packed and might be charged at a higher rate: G then asked Perry to 'do his best' for him. In purported compliance with this request Perry signed a consignment note on G's behalf at the railway station by the terms of which damageable goods 'not properly protected by packing' were carried at owner's risk. The showcase was damaged during transit. The Court of Appeal held that Perry had G's authority to make the contract for carriage at owner's risk, but also considered the issue of insufficiency of the packing.

ATKIN LJ: . . . [L]et us assume that I am wrong in holding that Perry had authority to make the special contract on the plaintiff's behalf. There remains for consideration the other point which was discussed before us — namely, whether the defendants, assuming that they carried the showcase on the terms of the liability of common carriers, are precluded from setting up as a defence that the damage was due to improper packing because they carried it with full knowledge of its condition. The county court judge held that as the carriers were aware of the condition of the packing at the time they received the article they could not disclaim their liability as insurers. That raises an important and interesting question of law. Now the rule as to the obligation of a common carrier is thus stated in *Story on Bailments*, § 492 *a*:

> Although the rule is thus laid down in general terms at the common law, that the carrier is responsible for all losses not occasioned by the Act of God, or of the King's enemies, yet it is to be understood in all cases that the rule does not cover any losses, not within the exception, which arise from the ordinary wear and tear and chafing of the goods in the course of their transportation, or from their ordinary loss, deterioration in quantity or quality in the course of the voyage, or from their inherent natural infirmity and tendency to damage, or which arise from the personal neglect, or wrong, or misconduct of the owner or shipper thereof. Thus, for example, the carrier is not liable for any loss or damage from the ordinary decay or deterioration of oranges or other fruits in the course of the voyage, from their inherent infirmity or nature, or from the ordinary diminution or evaporation of liquids, or the ordinary leakage from the casks in which the liquors are put, in the course of the voyage, or from the spontaneous combustion of goods, or from their tendency to effervescence or acidity, or from their not being properly put up and packed by the owner or shipper; for the carriers' implied obligations do not extend to such cases.

That passage is cited by Willes J in *Blower v Great Western Ry Co.* (1872) LR 7 CP 655 as an accurate statement of the law, and, being so approved, is a sufficient authority for me to act upon without more. Now does it make any difference that the faulty packing which caused the damage was manifest to the carrier at the time that the goods were delivered to him to be carried? By analogy to the exception of inherent vice it would seem that it does not. The inherent vice or natural tendency of certain kinds of goods to depreciate or become damaged may be perfectly apparent to the carrier, and in most cases would be quite apparent when he received the goods, nevertheless he is not responsible for the damage resulting from such cause, and it appears to me that there is no reason for treating the exception of damage caused by defective packing in any different way. . . .

*Note*

The decision in *Gould* was cited with approval in *Ismael* v *Polish Ocean Lines* [1976] 1 All ER 902, where the carrier was able to rely on the shipper's assurance that dunnaging was not required when stowing the cargo. It was distinguished in *Silver* v *Ocean Steamship Co.* [1930] 1 KB 416 (CA), where the shipowner was estopped, as against the indorsee of the bill of lading, from alleging that the goods were insufficiently packed, because of the statement in the bill that the goods were shipped in apparent good order and condition (see further Chapter 6).

## SECTION 2: CONTRACTUAL EXEMPTION CLAUSES

In general the common law did not permit those who exercised a common calling to contract out of their obligations. However, carriers were able from an early date to agree to carry 'excepted the casualties and dangers of the sea' (*Carre* v *Desallez* (1554) Select Pleas of Admiralty (Selden Society) vol. 2, p. 61). The possibility of more extensive exemption clauses was recognised by Lord Mansfield (*Barclay* v *Cuculla y Gana* (1784) 3 Doug 389 at p. 390), and full freedom of contract confirmed by Lord Ellenborough.

### *Leeson* v *Holt*
### (1816) 1 Stark 186; 171 ER 441 (KB)

The defendants were common carriers. In an action against them for negligence in relation to the carriage of some chairs from London to L in Nottingham, they gave evidence of a notice placed conspicuously over the door of their office, and also in the *Gazette* and *The Times* newspaper, that household furniture was 'entirely at the risk of the owners as to damage, breakage, etc'.

LORD ELLENBOROUGH: If this action had been brought twenty years ago, the defendant would have been liable, since by the common law a carrier is liable in all cases except two, where the loss is occasioned by the act of God, or of the King's enemies using an overwhelming force, which persons with ordinary means of resistance cannot guard against. — It was found, that the common law imposed upon carriers a liability of ruinous extent, and in consequence, qualifications and limitations of that liability have been introduced from time to time, till, as in the present case, they seem to have excluded all responsibility whatsoever, so that under the terms of the present notice if a servant of the carrier's had in the most wilful and wanton manner destroyed the furniture entrusted to them, the principals would not have been liable. If the parties in the present case have so contracted, the plaintiff must abide by the agreement, and he must be taken to have so contracted if he chuses to send his goods to be carried after notice of the conditions. The question then is, whether there was a special contract. If the carriers notified their terms to the person bringing the goods by an advertisement, which, in all probability, must have attracted the attention of the person who brought the goods, they were delivered upon those terms; but the question in these cases always is, whether the delivery was upon a special contract.

   Verdict for the plaintiff.

The following are among the commonest of the many contractual exemptions which have been considered and interpreted by the courts:

## A: Perils of the sea

The meaning of perils of the sea has been considered primarily in the context of marine insurance and the parallel expression 'dangers and accidents of the sea' in marine insurance policies. Some confusion was caused by the fact that the carrier's negligence is irrelevant in deciding whether the loss is covered by the policy and also by the different approach to causation in this context. The law was clarified by the House of Lords in the next two cases.

### The Xantho
#### (1887) 12 App Cas 503 (HL)

The Xantho was on a voyage from Kronstadt in Russia to Hull when she collided with the Valuta in fog and sank. In an action against them on the bills of lading, the shipowners relied on an exception for 'dangers and accidents of the sea'. Sir J. Hannen P and the Court of Appeal held, on the authority of the recent decision of the Court of Appeal in Woodley v Michell (1883) 11 QBD 47, that a collision which is brought about by the negligence of either vessel is not a peril of the sea. The House of Lords overruled Woodley v Michell and ordered a new trial.

LORD HERSCHELL: The question, What comes within the term 'perils of the sea' (and certainly the words 'dangers and accidents of the sea' cannot have a narrower interpretation), has been more frequently the subject of decision in the case of marine policies than of bills of lading. I will first notice the decision pronounced with regard to the former instrument, and then inquire how far a different interpretation is to be applied in the case of the latter.

   I think it clear that the term 'perils of the sea' does not cover every accident or casualty which may happen to the subject-matter of the insurance on the sea. It must be a peril 'of' the sea. Again, it is well settled that it is not every loss or damage of which the sea is the immediate cause that is covered by these words. They do not protect, for example, against that natural and inevitable action of the winds and waves, which results in what may be described as wear and tear. There must be some casualty, something which could not be foreseen as one of the necessary incidents of the adventure. The purpose of the policy is to secure an indemnity against accidents which may happen, not against events which must happen. It was contended that those losses only were losses by perils of the sea, which were occasioned by extraordinary violence of the winds or waves. I think this is too narrow a construction of the words, and it is certainly not supported by the authorities, or by common understanding. It is beyond question, that if a vessel strikes upon a sunken rock in fair weather and sinks, this is a loss by perils of the sea. And a loss by foundering, owing to a vessel coming into collision with another vessel, even when the collision results from the negligence of that other vessel, falls within the same category. . . .

But it is said that the words 'perils of the sea' occurring in a bill of lading, or other contract of carriage, must receive a different interpretation from that which is given to them in a policy of marine insurance; that in the latter case the causa proxima alone is regarded; whilst, in the former, you may go behind the causa proxima, and look at what was the real or efficient cause. It is on this view that the Court of Appeal acted in *Woodley* v *Michell* 11 QBD 47.

Now, I quite agree that in the case of a marine policy the causa proxima alone is considered. If that which immediately caused the loss was a peril of the sea, it matters not how it was induced, even if it were by the negligence of those navigating the vessel. It is equally clear that in the case of a bill of lading you may sometimes look behind the immediate cause, and the shipowner is not protected by the exception of perils of the sea in every case in which he would be entitled to recover on his policy, on the ground that there has been a loss by such perils. But I do not think this difference arises from the words 'perils of the sea' having a different meaning in the two instruments, but from the context or general scope and purpose of the contract of carriage excluding in certain cases the operation of the exception. It would, in my opinion, be very objectionable, unless well settled authority compelled it, to give a different meaning to the same words occurring in two maritime instruments. The true view appears to me to be presented by Willes J in his judgment in *Grill* v *General Iron Screw Collier Company* Law Rep 1 CP 600, 611. The question there arose whether, when a vessel was lost by a collision caused by the negligence of those navigating the carrying ship, the case fell within the exception of 'perils of the sea'. It was held that it did not. Reference having been made to cases on policies of insurance, and the interpretation there put upon these words, Willes J said,

I may say that a policy of insurance is an absolute contract to indemnify for loss by perils of the sea, and it is only necessary to see whether the loss comes within the terms of the contract, and is caused by perils of the sea; the fact that the loss is partly caused by things not distinctly perils of the sea, does not prevent its coming within the contract. In the case of a bill of lading it is different, because there the contract is to carry with reasonable care, unless prevented by the excepted perils. If the goods are not carried with reasonable care, and are consequently lost by perils of the sea, it becomes necessary to reconcile the two parts of the instrument, and this is done by holding that if the loss through perils of the sea is caused by the previous default of the shipowner, he is liable for this breach of his covenant.

. . . I am unable to concur in the view that a disaster which happens from the fault of somebody can never be an accident or peril of the sea; and I think it would give rise to distinctions resting on no sound basis, if it were to be held that the exception of perils of the seas in a bill of lading was always excluded when the inroad of the sea which occasioned the loss was induced by some intervention of human agency. Take the case which I put in the course of the argument, of a ship which strikes upon a rock and is lost, because the light which should have warned the mariner against it has become extinguished owing to the negligence of the person in charge. Why should this not be within the exception, whilst a similar loss arising from a vessel coming into contact with a rock not marked upon the chart admittedly would be? And what substantial distinction is there between this latter case and that of a vessel foundering through collision with a ship at anchor left at night without lights? For these reasons I have arrived at the conclusion that the case of *Woodley* v *Michell* cannot be supported.

LORD BRAMWELL: ... Was it by a peril of the sea that the defendants' ship foundered? The facts are, that the sea-water flowed into her through a hole, and flowed in such quantities that she sank. It seems to me that the bare statement shews she went to the bottom through a peril of the sea. If the hole had been small, there being a piece of bad wood, a plank starting, or a similar cause, it would be called a leak, and no one would doubt that she foundered from a peril of the sea. Does it make any difference that the hole was large, and occasioned by collision? I cannot think it does. It is admitted that if the question had arisen on an insurance against loss by perils of the sea this would have been within the policy a loss by perils of the sea. Are the words to have different meanings in the two instruments? Why should they? Different consequences may follow. The insurer may be unable to defend himself on the ground that the loss was brought about by the negligence of the crew, while the freighter may maintain an action on the ground that it was. But how is the loss a loss by perils of the sea in one case and not in the other? The argument is, that wind and waves did not cause the loss, but negligence in some one. But surely, if that were so, a loss by striking in calm weather on a sunken rock not marked on the chart would not be a loss by perils of the seas within the bill of lading; or striking on a rock from which the light had been removed, or an iceberg, or a vessel without lights. I cannot bring myself to see that such cases are not losses by perils of the sea. Is not the chance of being run against by a clumsy rider one of the perils of hunting? It would be strange if an underwriter on cargo, suing in the name of the cargo owners on the bill of lading should say, 'I have paid for a loss by perils of the sea, and claim on you because the loss was not by perils of the sea.' The Court of Appeal, with great respect, argued as though the collision caused the loss. So it did in a sense. It was a causa sine qua non, but it was not the causa causans. It was causa remota, but not causa proxima. The causa proxima of the loss was foundering. It would be strange if a plank started, and the vessel went to the bottom in consequence, that it should be held, 'Oh, the loss is not by perils of the seas, but by bad carpentering.' Let there be no doubt. I do not say that in such case the freighter might not complain that his goods were carried in an unseaworthy ship. All I say is, that the loss would be by perils of the seas.

### *Hamilton, Fraser & Co.* v *Pandorf & Co.*
### (1887) 12 App Cas 518 (HL)

P shipped rice on *The Inchrhona* from Sittwe (Burma), then known as Akyab, to Bremenhaven (*sic*: presumably Bremerhaven, though Lord Watson calls it Bremen; in the reports of the proceedings below, the only destination mentioned is Liverpool!). During the voyage rats gnawed a hole in a lead pipe connecting the bathroom with the sea and the rice was damaged by sea-water which came through the hole. In P's action for damages, the shipowners relied on an exception of 'dangers and accidents of the seas'. P succeeded in the Court of Appeal, but the judgment was reversed by the House of Lords.

(In the light of the jury's findings it was assumed that there was no negligence on the part of the shipowners.)

LORD BRAMWELL: My Lords, I am of opinion that this judgment must be reversed. This is the third case in which this House has had to consider whether a peril of the sea or other peril within the general words was shewn. The arguments and discussions in all three have been very useful in helping to a conclusion. As I have said elsewhere, I think the definition of Lopes LJ very good: 'It is a sea damage, occurring at sea, and nobody's fault.' What is the 'peril'? It is that the ship or goods will be lost or damaged; but it must be 'of the sea'. 'Fire' would not be a peril of the sea; so loss or damage from it would not be insured against by the general words. So of lightning. In the present case the sea has damaged the goods. That it might do so was a peril that the ship encountered. It is true that rats made the hole through which the water got in, and if the question were whether rats making a hole was a peril of the sea, I should say certainly not. If we could suppose that no water got in, but that the assured sued the underwriter for the damage done to the pipe, I should say clearly that he could not recover. But I should equally say that the underwriters on goods would be liable for the damage shewn in this case. Then I am of opinion that 'perils of the seas' is a phrase having the same meaning in bills of lading and charterparties as in policies of insurance. I repeat my illustration: if underwriters paid this loss as through a peril of the sea, how would they, in the name of the assured, claim from the shipowner, because it was not a peril of the sea? I do not go through the cases; I say there is none opposed to this opinion. The doubt or hesitation expressed in the case where the ship was sunk by being fired into is certainly a doubt the other way, but only a doubt.

An attempt was made to shew that a peril of the sea meant a peril of what I feel inclined to call the sea's behaviour or ill-condition. But that is met by the argument, that if so, striking on a sunken rock, on a calm day, or against an iceberg, and consequent foundering, is not a peril of the sea or its consequence.

No question of negligence exists in this case. The damage was caused by the sea in the course of navigation with no default in any one. I am, therefore, of opinion that the damage was caused by peril of the sea within the meaning of the bill of lading, that Lopes LJ was right, and that the judgment must be reversed.

*Note and Question*

1.   In yet a third case decided by the House of Lords on the same day (14 July 1887) as *The Xantho* and *Hamilton, Fraser & Co.* v *Pandorf & Co.*, above, it was held that it was not damage *ejusdem generis* with a peril of the sea within the meaning of the respondents' policy of marine insurance when a valve on a pump driven by a donkey-engine on the vessel *Inchmaree* salted up, or was left closed, with the result that the air chamber split (*Thames and Mersey Marine Insurance Co. Ltd* v *Hamilton, Fraser & Co.* (1887) 12 App Cas 484). In Lord Bramwell's words (at pp. 492–3): 'The damage to the donkey-engine was not through its being in a ship or at sea. The same thing would have happened had the boilers and engines been on land, if the same mismanagement had taken place. The sea, waves and winds had nothing to do with it.'

2.   Cargo is damaged by sea water during a storm in the Bay of Biscay. Could the carrier rely on an exception for perils of the sea? (Cf. *Great China Metal Industries Co. Ltd* v *Malaysian International Shipping Corporation Berhad (The Bunga Seroja)* [1999] 1 Lloyd's Rep 512 (High Ct of Australia).)

### *Canada Rice Mills Ltd* v *Union Marine and General Insurance Co. Ltd*
### [1941] AC 55 (PC)

Rice was damaged by heat during a voyage from Rangoon to British Columbia, when it became necessary to close the cowl ventilators and hatches because of bad weather. CRM claimed that the loss fell within their insurance against perils of the sea. The Court of Appeal of British Columbia set aside the jury's finding that the rice was damaged by a peril of the seas, but the Judicial Committee of the Privy Council allowed CRM's appeal.

LORD WRIGHT: . . . The evidence was that rice is a commodity very liable to heat if not fully ventilated while being carried in the ship's hold. It has a considerable moisture content, and has a capacity of absorbing further moisture. If this moisture is not carried off by ventilation a process of fermentation sets in and damages the grain. The heating thus caused when the ventilation was shut off would tend to develop even after full ventilation was restored. The ventilators have to be closed when water would get to the cargo if they are not closed. When the ventilators are again opened the cooler air circulating through them also sets up a condensation in the hot, moist and humid atmosphere of the hold, and precipitates moisture on the rice. If a process of fermentation is thus started it may go on for the rest of the voyage, even though the ventilators are not again closed.

. . .

Where there is an accidental incursion of seawater into a vessel at a part of the vessel, and in a manner, where seawater is not expected to enter in the ordinary course of things, and there is consequent damage to the thing insured, there is prima facie a loss by perils of the sea. The accident may consist in some negligent act, such as improper opening of a valve, or a hole made in a pipe by mischance, or it may be that sea water is admitted by stress of weather or some like cause bringing the sea over openings ordinarily not exposed to the sea or, even without stress of weather, by the vessel heeling over owing to some accident, or by the breaking of hatches or other coverings. These are merely a few amongst many possible instances in which there may be a fortuitous incursion of seawater. It is the fortuitous entry of the seawater which is the peril of the sea in such cases. Whether in any particular case there is such a loss is a question of fact for the jury. There are many deck openings in a vessel through which the seawater is not expected or intended to enter and, if it enters, only enters by accident or casualty. The cowl ventilators are such openings. If they were not closed at the proper time to prevent seawater coming into the hold, and seawater does accidentally come in and do damage, that is just as much an accident of navigation (even though due to negligence, which is immaterial in a contract of insurance) as the improper opening of a valve or other sea connection. The rush of sea water which, but for the covering of the ventilators, would have come into them and down to the cargo was in this case due to a storm which was sufficiently out of the ordinary to send seas or spray over the orifices of the ventilators. The jury may have pictured the tramp motor vessel heavily laden with 5,000 tons of rice driving into the heavy head seas, pitching and rolling tremendously and swept by seas or spray. Their Lordships do not think that it can properly be said that there was no evidence to justify their finding. On any voyage a ship may, though she need not necessarily, encounter a storm, and a storm is a normal incident on such a passage as the *Segundo* was making, but if in consequence of the storm cargo is damaged by the incursion of the sea, it would be for the jury to say whether the damage was or was not due to a peril of the sea. They are entitled to take a broad commonsense view of the whole position. . . .

There remains the second question, whether the damage which was caused not by the incursion of sea water, but by action taken to prevent the incursion, is recoverable as a loss by perils of the sea. It is curious that, so far as their Lordships know, there is no express decision on this point under a policy of marine insurance. But, in their Lordships' judgment, the question should be answered in the affirmative, as they think the jury did. The answer may be based on the view that where the weather conditions so require, the closing of the ventilators is not to be regarded as a separate or independent cause, interposed between the peril of the sea and the damage, but as being such a mere matter of routine seamanship necessitated by the peril that the damage can be regarded as the direct result of the peril. . . .

## Note

As an alternative ground for the decision the Privy Council would have held that the loss was covered by the 'general words', viz. 'all other perils, losses and misfortunes'. (It was settled by the House of Lords in *Thames and Mersey Marine Insurance Co. Ltd* v *Hamilton, Fraser & Co.* (1887) 12 App Cas 484 that these words are to be construed *ejusdem generis* with perils of the sea in this context.)

Carriers' ability to rely on an exclusion of perils of the sea is subject to performance of their 'overriding obligations'.

### *Paterson Steamship Ltd* v *Canadian Cooperative Wheat Producers*
[1934] AC 538 (PC)

LORD WRIGHT: It will therefore be convenient here, in construing those portions of the Act which are relevant to this appeal, to state in very summary form the simplest principles which determine the obligations attaching to a carrier of goods by sea or water. At common law, he was called an insurer, that is he was absolutely responsible for delivering in like order and condition at the destination the goods bailed to him for carriage. He could avoid liability for loss or damage only by showing that the loss was due to the act of God or the King's enemies. But it became the practice for the carrier to stipulate that for loss due to various specified contingencies or perils he should not be liable: the list of these specific excepted perils grew as time went on. That practice, however, brought into view two separate aspects of the sea carrier's duty which it had not been material to consider when his obligation to deliver was treated as absolute. It was recognised that his overriding obligations might be analysed into a special duty to exercise due care and skill in relation to the carriage of the goods and a special duty to furnish a ship that was fit for the adventure at its inception. These have been described as fundamental undertakings, or implied obligations. If then goods were lost (say) by perils of the seas, there could still remain the inquiry whether or not the loss was also due to negligence or unseaworthiness. If it was, the bare exception did not avail the carrier.

In the concise words of Willes J (in *Notara* v *Henderson* (1872) LR 7 QB 225, 235): 'the exception in the bill of lading . . . only exempts him [the shipowner] from the absolute liability of a common carrier, and not from the consequences of the want of reasonable skill, diligence, and care. . . .' Willes J is there referring to what may be called the specific excepted perils. . . .

But negligence and unseaworthiness of the carrying vessel might generally, by British law, be excepted by express words; in such a case, though the exception of perils of the sea (to take an instance) might not per se for the reasons stated on the facts, avail the carrier, yet he could rely on the exception of negligence or of unseaworthiness, as the case might be, when negligence or unseaworthiness had caused or contributed to the loss.

*B: Restraint of princes*

## Nobel's Explosives Co. v Jenkins & Co.
### [1896] 2 QB 326 (QBD)

MATHEW J: This was an action to recover damages for the non-delivery at Yokohama of explosives, admitted to be contraband of war, after war had been declared between China and Japan. The goods were shipped by the defendants' steamer the *Denbighshire*, under a bill of lading by which the goods were to be delivered 'at Yokohama or so near thereunto as she may safely get'. The bill of lading contained the usual exception of 'restraint of princes rulers or people', and also a special clause to which I will refer presently.

The steamer arrived in the course of her voyage at Hong Kong on August 1, 1894, when war had been declared. By the regulations of the port of Hong Kong the vessel, having explosives on board, was anchored off the government magazines at Hong Kong and was compelled to fly a red flag. There were in the port numerous revenue cruisers of the Chinese Government, and within sight from where she lay were two Chinese war-vessels. Hong Kong is near the naval station of the Southern China squadron, and there were other war-vessels about the port. The fact that the *Denbighshire* had explosives on board was generally known. The captain, in the reasonable and well founded belief that his vessel if she sailed with the plaintiffs' goods on board would be stopped and the goods confiscated, telegraphed to his owners for advice, and received from them a reply directing him to land the goods. The defendants at once informed the plaintiffs, who protested against the course proposed to be taken on the ground, as it was contended, that the goods were not contraband of war. The goods were discharged and placed in safe custody, and the vessel proceeded on her voyage on August 4 and arrived safely at Yokohama.

. . .

The main ground of defence was the exception in the bill of lading of 'restraint of princes rulers or people'. A large body of evidence was laid before me to shew that if the vessel sailed with the goods on board she would in all probability be stopped and searched. It was certain in that case that the goods would have been confiscated, and quite uncertain what course the captors would take with the ship and the rest of the cargo. I am satisfied that if the master had continued the voyage with the goods on board he would have been acting recklessly. It was argued for the plaintiffs that the clause did not apply unless there was a direct and specific action upon the goods by sovereign authority. It was said that the fear of seizure, however well founded, was not a restraint, and that something in the nature of a seizure was necessary. But this argument is disposed of by the cases of *Geipel* v *Smith* LR 7 QB 404 and *Rodoconachi* v *Elliott* LR 9 CP 518. The goods were as effectually stopped at Hong Kong as if there had been an express order from the Chinese Government that contraband of war should be landed. The analogy of a restraint by a blockade or embargo seems to me sufficiently close. The

war-ships of the Chinese Government were in such a position as to render the sailing of
the steamer with contraband of war on board a matter of great danger, though she might
have got away safely. The restraint was not temporary, as was contended by the
plaintiffs' counsel. There was no reason to expect that the obstacle in the way of the
vessel could be removed in any reasonable time. I find that the captain in refusing to
carry the goods farther acted reasonably and prudently, and that the delivery of the
goods at Yokohama was prevented by restraint of princes and rulers within the meaning
of the exception.

There was a further clause in the bill of lading upon which the defendants relied, and
which seems to me to afford a further answer to the plaintiffs' claim, which clause is as
follows: 'If the entering of or discharging in the port of discharge shall be considered by
the master unsafe by reason of war or disturbances the master may land the goods at the
nearest safe and convenient port at the expense and risk of the owners of the goods.' It
was said that this clause was only intended to apply where difficulties arose upon the
vessel's arrival at the port of destination. But I see no ground for this narrow
construction. The object was to enable the master to guard against obstacles which
might prevent his vessel from reaching her destination in due course. There is no reason
to suppose that it was intended to limit his discretion to the case where the information
reached him on his arrival off the port of destination.

But, apart from the terms of the bill of lading, it seems to me that the conduct of the
captain would be justified by reference to the duty imposed upon him to take reasonable
care of the goods entrusted to him. Whether he has discharged that duty must depend
upon the circumstances of each case, and here, if the goods had been carried forward,
there was every reason to believe that the ship would be detained and the goods of the
plaintiffs confiscated. In the words of Willes J in *Notara v Henderson* (1872) LR 7 QB
225, 'a fair allowance ought to be made for the difficulties in which the master may be
involved.... The place, the season — the opportunity and means at hand, the interests
of other persons concerned in the adventure and whom it might be unfair to delay for
the sake of the part of the cargo in peril; in short all circumstances affecting risk, trouble,
delay and inconvenience must be taken into account'. I am of opinion that the course
taken by the captain in landing the goods and landing them in safe custody was a proper
discharge of his duty. It was said that the master was not an agent for the shippers
because they had protested against the discharge of the goods. But even if this
information had reached the captain, it would not have divested him of his original
authority and discretion as agent in any emergency for the owners of the ship and the
other owners of the cargo.

*Note*

The provision in the bill of lading for carriage to Yokohama 'or as near
thereunto as she could safely get' was held not to assist the shipowners, since
the vessel did reach Yokohama.

### Watts, Watts & Co. Ltd v Mitsui & Co. Ltd
### [1917] AC 227 (HL)

On 5 June 1914, W agreed to charter a vessel (to be nominated) to M to
proceed to Marioupol, a port on the Sea of Azov, not before 1 September
1914, to load a cargo of sulphate of ammonia for carriage to Japan. The First

World War broke out at the beginning of August, and on 1 September 1914 W declared that they regarded the charterparty as cancelled, alleging that the British Government had prohibited shipping from entering the Black Sea. In fact there was no such prohibition: Turkey was still neutral and the Dardanelles remained open until 26 September 1914. The charterparty contained a cancellation clause for the event that the vessel was not ready to load by 20 September 1914.

In M's action for damages, W argued that by September there was a reasonable apprehension that Turkey would be involved in the war and that this constituted a restraint of princes. It was found as a fact that even if the vessel had arrived by the cancelling date she could not have loaded and passed through the Dardanelles before they were closed. The House of Lords affirmed the decision that W could not rely on restraint of princes.

LORD DUNEDIN: ... Restraint of princes, to fall within the words of the exception, must be an existing fact and not a mere apprehension. This was held long ago by Lord Ellenborough in *Atkinson* 10 East 530. The more recent cases cited by the appellants, such as *Geipel* LR 7 QB 404 and *Nobel's Explosives* [1896] 2 QB 326, do not in any way touch that proposition. They only show that it may be possible to invoke the exception when a reasonable man in face of an existing restraint may consider that the restraint, though it does not affect him at the moment, will do so if he continue the adventure. It would be useless to try to fix by definition the precise imminence of peril which would make the restraint a present fact as contrasted with a future fear. The circumstances in each particular case must be considered. In the present case, while there was natural and great apprehension on September 1, and while the decision of the British Government immediately after to exclude Black Sea voyages from the benefits of the Government insurance scheme might well deter British subjects from sending their ships to the Black Sea, yet it is clearly proved by the production of lists of ships which after that date and up to September 26 passed inwards and outwards through the Dardanelles that there was no such restraint as would have actually prevented the appellants presenting a ship at Marioupol before or by the appointed date of September 20. I agree on this matter with the conclusion arrived at by the Courts below.

### *Ciampa* v *British India Steam Navigation Co. Ltd*
#### [1915] 2 KB 774 (KBD)

C shipped lemons on BI's vessel the *Matiana* from Naples to London. Before proceeding to Naples the *Matiana* had called at Mombasa, where there was an outbreak of plague, and she sailed from Mombasa with a foul bill of health. From Naples she sailed to Marseilles and there, under a decree of the French Ministry of the Interior, was subjected to dératisation by sulphur fumigation because her voyage had originated in a plague affected area and she did not have a clean bill of health. The fumigation damaged the lemons. BI relied on restraint of princes as a defence to C's claim.

ROWLATT J: In my opinion the plaintiffs are entitled to succeed in this action on both of the grounds contended for by Mr Roche. His first contention is that the loss does not come within the exceptions in the bill of lading which are relied on by the defendants, namely, 'restraints of princes', and 'any circumstances beyond the shipowner's control'. The facts are that the defendants' ship had sailed from Mombassa with a foul bill of health, and therefore she would necessarily have to undergo the process of dératisation at Marseilles in accordance with the decree issued by the French Government, which decree had been in force since 1906. That decree provides in substance that a ship coming from a plague port and seeking admission into a French port is liable to the process of compulsory dératisation, except in certain circumstances which do not arise in this case. That being so, although there might be cases in which owing to the remissness of the French port authorities or by some accident a ship escaped the process, when the defendants' ship sailed from Mombassa and the other ports, including Naples, which she subsequently visited, she was beyond all doubt destined to undergo compulsorily the process of dératisation on her arrival at Marseilles. In these circumstances I do not think that the mere application at Marseilles of the French law to facts which existed before the ship sailed from Naples, which is the material transit, is a 'restraint of princes' within the meaning of the exception in the bill of lading. I am not deciding that the application of the ordinary law of a country may not in some circumstances constitute a 'restraint of princes', but I think the facts which bring that law into operation must be facts which have supervened after the ship has started on the voyage in question. When facts exist which show conclusively that the ship was inevitably doomed before the commencement of the voyage to become subject to a restraint, I do not think that there is a 'restraint of princes'.

*Notes*

1.   For the other ground of the decision in *Ciampa* v *British India Steam Navigation Co. Ltd*, see Chapter 3.
2.   In *Finlay* v *Liverpool and Great Western Steamship Co. (Ltd)* (1870) 23 LT 251, it was held that proceedings in the courts of New York, in which the master was compelled to deliver the goods to a third party from whom the indorser of the bill of lading had obtained them by fraud, did not come within restraint of princes.
3.   The common form of the exception referred (and the corresponding provision of the Hague-Visby Rules, Art. IV, r. 2(g), see Chapter 7, still refers), to restraint of 'princes, rulers or people'. In *Nesbitt* v *Lushington* (1791) 4 TR 783, it was held that 'people' meant the ruling power of the country and did not extend to a riotous mob who boarded the vessel at Elly Harbour, in Ireland, and forced the master to 'sell' part of the cargo of wheat to them at a reduced price.

*C: Strikes*

The English courts initially took a narrow view of the meaning of strike but expanded the concept to take account of changing labour practices. Some charterparties achieve the same result by the use of more flexible formulae, such as 'strike, lock-out, stoppage or *restraint* of labour' (e.g., *Shellvoy* 5, cl. 14(c)).

## *The Laga*
[1966] 1 Lloyd's Rep 582 (QBD)

Port labour at Nantes refused to unload or assist vessels carrying coal for discharge there, in order to support a strike by French miners. Other vessels continued to be unloaded. The shipowners contended that the dockworkers' action was not a 'strike' (so that laytime ran notwithstanding the charterers' inability to unload: see Chapter 9). This contention was rejected.

McNAIR J: Is it essential for the existence of a strike that the workmen who are refusing to work are attempting to obtain some solution of some industrial grievance which exists between them and their employers? If it is — if that is of the essence of a strike — then the finding of the arbitrators which I have already read is conclusive against there being such a strike. It is quite true, I think, that 100 years ago or, perhaps, even less, a strike was normally regarded as being a concerted effort by workmen either to obtain an increase in wages or to resist an attempt by employers to reduce their wages. And, indeed, it was so defined in the case of *King and Others* v *Parker* (1876) 34 LT 887 . . . Well, of course, since 1876 it is clear that we have moved a long way. Strikes in every sense of the word occur to-day which are not concerned directly with wages. They are concerned, for instance, with working conditions; and so I think one has got to bear in mind that the meaning of the term 'strike' must change with the progress (if that is the right word) of industrial history and it may have a different meaning to-day from the meaning given to it a century ago.

One stage in the development is shown in the case which is to-day generally regarded as one of the landmarks in this field. That is the case of *Williams Brothers (Hull) Ltd* v *Naamlooze Vennootschap W. H. Berghuys Kolenhandel* (1915) 21 Com Cas 253, a decision of Mr Justice Sankey. That, it will be remembered, was a case where the shipowners had difficulty in maintaining her crew at Rotterdam or engaging a new crew at Rotterdam when it became known to the old crew and to the new crew that the vessel would be sent on a voyage from Hull to Rouen when it would be exposed to the danger of the German submarine menace. The old crew refused to serve and it became impossible to obtain a new crew in Rotterdam. The question asked was: 'Was that a strike?' Mr Justice Sankey said this (*ibid.*, at p. 257):

. . . It has been said that a demand by workmen for increase of wages or a refusal by workmen to accept diminution of wages is itself a strike [— that is a reference to the case to which I have just referred —]. I think those definitions rather show the danger, if I may be allowed to say so, of attempting to give an exhaustive definition of the word 'strike', because it is obvious that since those cases were decided many circumstances have arisen which would constitute, or might be held to constitute, a strike. A strike does not depend merely upon the question of wages. At the same time I do not think it would be possible to say that abstention of a workman from mere fear to do a particular thing or perform a particular contract would necessarily constitute a strike. . . .

In parenthesis, I think possibly that Mr Justice Sankey was there referring to the refusal of the existing master to carry on. But he continues:

. . . I think the true definition of the word 'strike', which I do not say is exhaustive, is a general concerted refusal by workmen to work in consequence of an alleged grievance. . . .

And in a later passage in that same judgment, which I need not read, it is clear that Mr Justice Sankey decided in that case that there was a strike because the old crew who came out and the new crew who refused to sign on had an alleged grievance against the shipowners of this particular ship because they insisted on them going on this particular voyage. So it would seem that in 1915 at least Mr Justice Sankey was taking the view that it was necessary to have some grievance between the alleged strikers and their employers.

But I do not think the matter has rested in that stable condition since then. It may be that because since then one has had the great development of sympathetic strikes, when one has had, at any rate in this country, and, indeed, elsewhere, the general strike in which many of those out on strike had no grievance at all against an employer. And, in my judgment, it would be extremely difficult to say in a charter-party such as this that a sympathetic strike or a general strike which had the effect of causing the loss of time was not a strike within the meaning of this charter-party....

### *The New Horizon*
[1975] 2 Lloyd's Rep 314 (CA)

Dockworkers at St Nazaire customarily worked round the clock on shifts if requested, but were not legally obliged to do so. When the *New Horizon* arrived crane and sucker drivers were refusing shift work. The charterers maintained that the resulting periods when no work was done were excluded from the calculation of laytime because they were periods of strike. Ackner J and the Court of Appeal upheld this contention.

LORD DENNING MR: As I understand [the arbitrator's award] at the berth where this vessel, the *New Horizon*, came into the port of St Nazaire it would be in the normal course of events for the men to discharge her all round the clock, 24 hours in the three shifts. But in the case of this vessel the men did not work those normal hours, 24 hours round the clock. Instead, they worked only during the day time 08 30 to 12 30 and 14 00 to 18 00.

The reason they did that was because they wanted to improve their conditions of work.

It has been submitted to us by Mr Diamond that in these circumstances there was no 'strike' within the meaning of the clause. He said that these men were not in breach of any contract. They were not obliged to do a 24-hour shift. They were entitled to limit themselves to the day work. Further he said that there was not a continuous stoppage of work. There were only stoppages during the night time. The men were working perfectly properly during the day time.

There is very little guidance in the books as to the meaning of the work 'strike'. [After referring to Sankey J's definition in *William Brothers (Hull) Ltd* v *Naamlooze Vennootschap*, quoted above, Lord Denning continued:]

He took that from the *Concise Oxford Dictionary*; and ever since *Scrutton on Charterparties* has quoted those words as authoritative. If I may amplify it a little, I think a strike is a concerted stoppage of work by men done with a view to improving their wages or conditions, or giving vent to a grievance or making a protest about something or other, or supporting or sympathising with other workmen in such endeavour. It is distinct from a stoppage which is brought about by an external event such as a bomb scare or by apprehension of danger.

Applying this test, I agree with the Judge that when these men refused to work 24 hours, but only eight hours, there was a 'strike'. They did it so as to get an improvement in their terms and conditions of work. They were not in breach of contract. But it is none the less a strike. Many a strike takes place after a lawful notice; but it is still a strike. It was discontinuous. At work during the day-time, off work at night. But a strike need not be continuous. It can be discontinuous and the periods may be added up. Mr Diamond as a last resort said the employers had consented to the men not doing 24 hours, and therefore it was not a strike. But I do not read the award of the arbitrators in that sense. It seems to me that throughout the award the arbitrators and the umpire were saying that the men refused to work. The men refused to do the normal work: and they did so because of their desire to bring pressure to bear to have their terms and conditions of work improved. So it seems to me that it was a 'strike' and the charterers were entitled to an extension of laytime.

*Question*
Would the position be different (a) if the industrial action were in breach of a statutory requirement, e.g., with regard to the holding of a strike ballot, or (b) if the action is for the purpose of demonstrating opposition to the Government's foreign policy (Cf. *The Marilena P* [1969] 2 QB 641 (US)).

*Note*
The problems raised by strikes are particularly acute in the case of charterparties, since both shipowners and charterers are understandably reluctant to bear the cost of the delay. To guard against the possibility that the intended port of discharge might be strikebound on the vessel's arrival, the shipowner may reserve the right to discharge the cargo elsewhere — a so-called *Caspiana* Clause after the vessel in *Renton v Palmyra* [1957] AC 149, see Chapter 3 — and leave the cargo owner to meet the cost of getting the goods from there to the intended destination.

*D: Negligence*

There is no doubt that carriers *may* protect themselves from liability for loss or damage arising from their — or, more realistically, their employees' — negligence by appropriately worded exemption clauses. However, the difficulties which may arise in convincing a court that such protection has been achieved are graphically illustrated by the following case.

### Tor Line AB v Alltrans Group of Canada Ltd
### (The TFL Prosperity)
[1984] 1 Lloyd's Rep 123 (HL)

LORD ROSKILL: My Lords, in this appeal your Lordships' House is invited for the first time to construe cl. 13 of the well-known and widely used Baltime Uniform Time Charter. . . .
The present appeal arises in the following circumstances. The respondents ('the owners') were the charterers by demise of a vessel named *TFL Prosperity* ('the vessel'). By a time charter dated Apr. 24, 1979, the respondents in that capacity time chartered the vessel to the appellants ('the charterers') for a period of six months and 10 days upon

the terms of this charter. The version used was that amended with effect from Jan. 1, 1950. To the 25 clauses of the printed form, some of which were as is usual either deleted or amended, the parties added a massive number of typed clauses numbered 26 to 60 inclusive.

The vessel was of a type known as 'roll-on/roll-off' and the charterers required her for their 'roll-on/roll-off' liner service which they operated between Europe and the Middle East. It was no doubt for this reason that cl. 26, the first of the additional typed clauses, specified in great detail the description of certain fixed structural attributes of the vessel together with particulars of her speed and consumption. I need not set out cl. 26 in full. Reference can if necessary be made to the details set out in the report of the present case before Mr Justice Bingham at [1982] 1 Lloyd's Rep 617 at p. 620. Among the provisions of cl. 26 under the heading 'Free Heights' was 'Main Deck 6.10 m'. In fact the free height of the main deck at one critical point was only 6.05 metres. As a result a Mafi trailer double stacked with 40 ft. containers could not be loaded into the main deck. The charterers claimed damages from the owners. The damages claimed, so far as now relevant, were mainly for loss of freight but there was also a small claim for damages for delay. The owners raised various defences. One alone remains relevant, that based on cl. 13 which bears the rubric 'Responsibility and Exemption'. . . .

Mr Rokison, QC, for the charterers advanced three main submissions. First, he contended that cl. 13 upon its true construction did not in any event protect the owners against a claim for financial loss suffered by the charterers by reason of the owners' breaches of charter. This submission could not have been successfully advanced in the Courts below by reason of the decision of the Court of Appeal to which I have already referred, *Nippon Yusen Kaisha* v *Acme Shipping Corporation (The Charalambos N. Pateras)*, [1972] 1 Lloyd's Rep 1. For brevity I shall hereafter refer to that case as the '*C.N.P.* case'. The Court of Appeal there held, contrary to Mr Rokison's present submissions that cl. 13 did protect the owners against claims for financial loss.

. . .

Second, Mr Rokison urged that, even if that case were correctly decided and cl. 13 fell to be construed as the Court of Appeal had there held, it did not operate to protect the owners against a claim for damages for breach of the provisions regarding the vessel's description but only in respect of their obligations during the performance of the contractual adventure.

Third, he contended that cl. 26, being in type and specially added, must prevail over cl. 13 which was in print. Though this argument appears to have appealed to Mr Justice Bingham — see p. 627 of the report of his judgment — and to have been used by him to reinforce his conclusion that cl. 13 did not in any event protect the owners in the event of non-compliance by them with the provisions regarding the vessel's description, Mr Rokison did not seriously press this third argument.

. . .

My Lords, I propose first to consider the true construction of cl. 13 and to do so without reference to any of the decided cases to which your Lordships were referred in argument. Clause 13 reads as follows:

> Responsibility and Exemption. 13. The Owners only to be responsible for delay in delivery of the Vessel or for delay during the currency of the Charter and for loss or damage to goods on board, if such delay or loss has been caused by want of due diligence on the part of the Owners or their Manager in making the Vessel seaworthy and fitted for the voyage or any other personal act or omission or default of the Owners or their Manager. The Owners not to be responsible in any other case nor for damage or delay whatsoever and howsoever caused even if caused by the neglect or

default of their servants. The Owners not to be liable for loss or damage arising or resulting from strikes, lock-outs or stoppage or restraint of labour or vehicles (including the Master, Officers or Crew) whether partial or general.

The Charterers to be responsible for loss or damage caused to the Vessel or to the Owners by goods being loaded contrary to the terms of the Charter or by improper or careless bunkering or loading, stowing or discharging of goods or any other improper or negligent act on their part or that of their servants.

As Lord Denning, MR, pointed out in his judgment in the *C.N.P.* case, the clause contains four separate sentences. But while each sentence falls to be analysed in detail, each must also be related to the other so as to construe cl. 13 as a whole. To say that the grammar of these four sentences and indeed the drafting is in many places sadly defective and that on any view there is surplusage at various points in the clause does not solve the problems of construction but merely adds seriously to their complication. Unhappily bad grammar, bad drafting and verbal surplusage are common features in the drafting of clauses in charters. I should mention that the words 'or vehicles' in the third sentence had been added to the printed form in type no doubt because of the cargo which it was known that the charterers intended to load and carry but that addition cannot affect the construction of cl. 13 as a whole. I now turn to consider each of the four sentences in detail and I begin by breaking the first sentence down into its component parts as follows:

The owners only to be responsible (1) for delay in the delivery of the Vessel or (2) for delay during the currency of the charter and (3) for loss or damage to goods on board, if such delay or loss has been caused by (a) want of due diligence on the part of (i) the Owners or (ii) their Manager in making the Vessel seaworthy and fitted for the voyage or (b) any other personal act or omission or default of (i) the Owners or (ii) their Manager.

Three observations fall to be made upon the first sentence which I have broken down in this way. First, it is clear that it is referring to and only to two types of delay and one type of loss or damage, namely loss or damage to goods on board — a type of loss and damage which in the context is plainly intended to be physical. Second, this sentence says that the owners will 'only' be 'responsible' — that is 'legally liable' — if either of those two types of delay or that single type of loss or damage is due to one or other of the causes specified in (a) or (b) above, namely (a) want of due diligence on the part of either the owners or their manager in making the vessel seaworthy or (b) any other personal act or omission or default of either of them. In short, as is emphasized by the position at the outset of the sentence of the adverb 'only' the first sentence is directed to and only to legal liability for two particular types of delay and one particular type of physical loss or damage due to one or other of those causes. For those matters the owners expressly accept 'responsibility', that is 'legal liability'.

My Lords, it follows that the first sentence only deals with those matters for which liability will be accepted. It does not, expressly at least, deal with those other matters for which liability is to be excluded. If cl. 13 finished at the end of the first sentence, in my view the owners would not have protected themselves against 'responsibility', that is 'legal liability', for other types of delay or for other physical loss or damage due to causes other than those to which I have already referred. This further protection is therefore sought in the second sentence.

I turn to break down the second sentence in the same way as I have broken down the first.

... The owners not to be responsible (1) in any other case nor (2) for damage or delay whatsoever and howsoever caused even if caused by the neglect or default of their servants.

It will be seen at once that whereas the first sentence speaks in the same printed line (line 96) of 'loss or damage' in one place and only of 'loss' in another, the second sentence (line 99) does not mention 'loss' at all but only 'damage'. Moreover the use of the conjunction 'nor' in the second sentence is ungrammatical as a means of linking together the two parts of the second sentence. If one construes the words 'in any case' literally, the second part of the second sentence and indeed the whole of the third sentence to which I will refer shortly become surplusage because on that view there would necessarily be no other 'case', liability for which is not already excluded. Moreover such a literal construction would mean, as my noble and learned friend, Lord Brandon of Oakbrook pointed out during the argument, that the owners would be under no liability if they never delivered the vessel at all for service under the charter or delivered a vessel of a totally different description from that stipulated in the preamble.

My Lords, I cannot think that this can be right. Some limitation must be read into the first part of the second sentence. If for the moment one ignores the words beginning with 'nor', the natural construction of the phrase 'in any other case' is 'in any other case of delay in the delivery of the vessel or during the currency of the charter or of loss or damage to goods on board' or to put the same point more shortly 'in any other such case'. My noble and learned friend, Lord Keith of Kinkel, observed during the argument that the same point can equally well be made by putting a punctuation mark before the word 'nor', for example a full stop, a colon or a semicolon, without doing any violence to the language used. But what of the words from 'nor' onwards? These ensuing words suggest to my mind that the draftsman feared that if the words 'in any other case' stood alone it might be suggested that they were neither clear nor strong enough to exclude liability for damage or delay or at least when caused by the negligence of the owners' own servants. The introduction of the words 'whatsoever' and 'howsoever caused' makes use of one of the classic methods of ensuring that liability for the relevant damage or delay is intended to be excluded, especially when the words 'howsoever caused' are reinforced by the express reference to the negligence of the owners' own servants.

It is I think against this background that the word 'damage' must be construed in the second part of the second sentence. If I am right in thinking that the first part of the second sentence means 'in any such case as has been mentioned in the first sentence', then the second part of the second sentence is also directed to the same type of 'damage' or 'delay' as is referred to in the first sentence, i.e., delay in delivery or during the currency of the voyage and 'damage' (which must I think in the context of these two sentences include 'loss') to goods on board. In short the first two sentences are linked and must be related to the same subject matter of delay and loss or damage to goods on board brought about by one or more of the several causes respectively mentioned in these two sentences. Further, as Mr Rokison pointed out, if 'damage' includes financial loss or damage there is no need for the apparent dichotomy between 'delay' and 'damage' since all delay must lead to financial loss of some kind.

I turn to the third sentence. This reads:

... The Owners not to be liable for loss or damage arising or resulting from strikes, lock-outs or stoppage or restraint of labour or vehicles (including the Master, Officers or Crew) whether partial or general.

No detailed breakdown of the third sentence is required. Mr Rix relied strongly on this sentence and also on the fourth sentence as supporting his construction of 'damage' in the second part of the second sentence. The third sentence is clearly required to give the owners protection in the case of loss or damage arising or resulting from strikes, etc., these being risks which have not been excluded by the first two sentences. I unreservedly accept that 'loss or damage' in the third sentence includes financial as well as physical loss or damage.

. . .

Mr Rix pointed out that if the construction of the first two sentences and in particular of the second sentence which I have adumbrated were correct, this House would be construing the relevant phrases in a different sense in different parts of the same clause. It is of course a proper canon of construction that the same words or the same phrases should where possible be given the same meaning in the same clause but that canon must always yield to particular contexts. The crucial question is whether the words 'damage or delay' in the second part of the second sentence take their colour from the first or from the third and fourth sentences. On no view can the same meaning be given to 'loss or damage' in the third and fourth sentences as in the first sentence where the phrase is unquestionably confined to physical loss or damage to goods on board.

If I am right in thinking that the second sentence is directed to matters not covered by the first, it follows that looking at cl. 13 as a whole the more natural construction of the second sentence is to treat it as looking back to the first rather than as looking forward to the third and fourth sentences. Mr Rix is no doubt right in saying that the second sentence widens the protection given by the first since it covers matters not expressly covered by the first. But he properly conceded that no distinction could be made between 'loss' in line 96 and 'damage' in line 99. Once it has become clear that on no view can the critical phrase be given the same meaning in the first as in the third and fourth sentences and once this concession is made, any argument founded upon the need for consistent construction throughout the whole clause necessarily loses its force.

My Lords, the principles applicable to the construction of exceptions clauses in charters have long been established. I need only refer to the well known judgments of Lord Esher, MR, and of Lord Justice Bowen almost exactly one hundred years ago in *Burton & Co.* v *English* (1883) 12 QBD 218 at pp. 220 and 222. One quotation from the latter judgment will suffice.

> There is . . . another rule of construction which one would bring to bear upon this charterparty, and that is, that one must see if this stipulation which we have got to construe is introduced by way of exception or in favour of one of the parties to the contract, and if so, we must take care not to give it an extension beyond what is fairly necessary, because those who wish to introduce words in a contract in order to shield themselves ought to do so in clear words.

These are the principles I have applied to the question of construction and applying them, still without regard to any of the decided cases, I find myself unable to construe cl. 13 as a whole and in particular the second sentence as protecting the owners against liability for the breach of cl. 26 which in the umpire's and in the learned Judge's views they undoubtedly committed.

My Lords, against this background I turn to consider the decided cases. Is there anything in them which should lead to a different conclusion?

. . .

Finally I turn to the *C.N.P.* case, to which I have already referred. There the matter came first of all before Mr Justice Mocatta and then before the Court of Appeal on a motion to set aside an award for error of law on its face on the ground that the umpire had been wrong in holding that the owners were protected by 'the exemption clause in the charterparty'. That exemption clause was not set out in the award though it was admitted to be cl. 13. The charterers claimed damages for delay and also for certain expenses caused by the master wrongly refusing to enter a port in Nicaragua. The claim failed because of cl. 13. The question was whether the second sentence of cl. 13 protected the owners against claims for financial as well as for physical loss and damage. All the members of the Court of Appeal agreed with Mr Justice Mocatta that the clause did so protect the owners — see the rival arguments summarised by Lord Denning, MR, at p. 3 and by myself at p. 5 of the report.

My Lords, it is I hope always proper to admit to judicial error and I must now do so. Having had the benefit of the further detailed consideration of cl. 13 in the present case and been able closely to analyse it afresh, and having perhaps for the first time fully appreciated the significance of the position of the word 'only' in the first sentence, a point seemingly not made in argument in the Court of Appeal in the *C.N.P.* case, I accept that I reached the wrong conclusion. . . .

Having thus considered the authorities in some detail I conclude that there is nothing in any of them which would lead me to a different conclusion from that which I have reached solely upon the language of cl. 13. It follows that upon its true construction cl. 13 does not in any event afford the owners a defence to the present claim by the charterers. I therefore respectfully agree with the conclusion reached by Mr Kent and by Mr Justice Bingham and equally respectfully disagree with the conclusions of the Court of Appeal.

But, my Lords, there is a second reason why I would reach the same conclusion. I can deal with this more briefly. . . . In truth if cl. 13 were to be construed so as to allow a breach of the warranties as to description in cl. 26 to be committed or a failure to deliver the vessel at all to take place without financial redress to the charterers, the charter virtually ceases to be a contract for the letting of the vessel and the performance of services by the owners, their master, officers and crew in consideration of the payment of time charter hire and becomes no more than a statement of intent by the owners in return for which the charterers are obliged to pay large sums by way of hire, though if the owners fail to carry out their promises as to description or delivery, are entitled to nothing in lieu. I find it difficult to believe that this can accord with the true common intention of the parties and I do not think that this conclusion can accord with the true construction of the charter in which the parties in the present case are supposed to have expressed that true common intention in writing.

[Lord Diplock, Lord Fraser of Tullybelton, Lord Keith of Kinkel and Lord Brandon of Oakbrook agreed with Lord Roskill.]

*Questions*

1.   Would a clause which provided that the carrier would not be answerable for loss of or damage to the goods 'under any circumstances whatsoever' cover loss covered (a) by the negligence, or (b) by the wilful act and default of the carrier's employees? (*Cf. Taubman* v *The Pacific Steam Navigation Co.* (1872) 26 LT 704, but see also *Sze Hai Tong Bank* v *Rambler Cycle Co.* [1959] AC 576, Chapter 6.)

2.   Why are the courts so determined to thwart attempts to exclude liability for negligence? What are the *commercial* objections to such clauses?

*E: Errors of navigation*

## *The Emmanuel C*
### [1983] 1 Lloyd's Rep 310 (QBD)

The *Emmanuel C* was let on a time charter on the New York Produce Exchange form for one transatlantic round trip via the St Lawrence. Clause 16 provided an exception for 'errors of navigation'. By reason of negligent navigation the vessel grounded in the St Lawrence and became a constructive total loss. The charterers claimed damages. It was held that the shipowners were not protected by the exception.

BINGHAM J: The correct approach of the Court to exemption clauses such as cl. 16 has been the subject of authoritative guidance in a series of cases which includes *Price & Co.* v *Union Lighterage Co.* [1904] 1 KB 12; *Rutter* v *Palmer* [1922] 2 KB 87; *Alderslade* v *Hendon Laundry Ltd* [1945] 1 KB 189; *Canada Steamship Lines Ltd* v *The King* [1952] 1 Lloyd's Rep 1; *Hollier* v *Rambler Motors (AMC) Ltd* [1972] 2 QB 71; *Smith* v *South Wales Switchgear Co. Ltd* [1978] 1 WLR 165 and *The Raphael* [1982] 2 Lloyd's Rep 42. I need not make lengthy citations from these authorities because the last of them contains a most helpful distillation of the relevant principles: see Lord Justice Donaldson at pp. 44–45; Lord Justice May at pp. 47–50; and Lord Justice Stephenson at pp. 50–52. I would simply cite one paragraph from the judgment of Lord Justice May at p. 49, which provides a very succinct summary of certain important points:

> Thus, if an exemption clause of the kind we are considering excludes liability for negligence expressly, then the Courts will give effect to the exemption. If it does not do so expressly, but its wording is clear and wide enough to do so by implication, then the question becomes whether the contracting parties so intended. If the only head of liability upon which the clause can bite in the circumstances of a given case is negligence, and the parties did or must be deemed to have applied their minds to this eventuality, then clearly it is not difficult for a Court to hold that this was what the parties intended — that this is its proper construction. Indeed, to hold otherwise would be contrary to commonsense. On the other hand if there is a head of liability upon which the clause could bite in addition to negligence then, because it is more unlikely than not a party will be ready to excuse his other contracting party from the consequences of the latter's negligence, the clause will generally be construed as not covering negligence. If the parties did or must be deemed to have applied their minds to the potential alternative head of liability at the time the contract was made then, in the absence of any express reference to negligence, the Courts can sensibly only conclude that the relevant clause was not intended to cover negligence and will refuse so to construe it. In other words, the Court asks itself what in all the relevant circumstances the parties intended the alleged exemption clause to mean.

From the cases the following general conclusions in my opinion emerge:

1.   Since it is inherently improbable that one party to a contract should intend to absolve the other party from the consequences of the latter's own negligence, the Court will presume a clause not to have that effect unless the contrary is plainly shown by clear words or by implication.

2.   Statements made in one case may assist in deciding another but cannot literally determine the decision, since in each case the task is one of construction to ascertain the actual or imputed intention of the parties to the contract in question.

3.   In carrying out that task of construction the Court should not treat commercial parties as if they were law students (*The Raphael*, at p. 46, per Lord Justice Donaldson).

Often the test of what would be understood or intended by the ordinarily literate and sensible person will be appropriate: see *Hollier's* case, sub., at p. 78D per Lord Justice Salmon; *The Raphael*, at p. 51, per Lord Justice Stephenson. Picking up these references Mr Boyd for the owners suggested that the Court should adopt the standard of the intelligent layman. I accept that this will in many cases be an appropriate standard. But where a contract is made in a specialised business by two practitioners in that business I think a somewhat different standard is indicated, approximating to that of the reasonably informed practitioner in the field in question.

4.   Where the words used are wide enough to cover negligent as well as non-negligent acts or omissions but practically speaking the clause lacks substance if it is not construed as covering negligent acts or omissions, the Court may in the circumstances of a given case infer that the parties intended the clause to cover negligence (as in *The Raphael*) but it need not do so (see *Hollier's* case). All depends on the proper inference to be drawn in the instant case.

Mr Boyd contended that cl. 16 was effective to protect the owners against liability for negligence on a number of grounds of which the most important were these:

(1)   The expression 'errors of navigation' is plainly wide enough to include negligent errors. The intelligent layman would think of 'errors' primarily as negligent errors. The flavour of negligence was reflected in the *Shorter Oxford Dictionary* definition: 'Something incorrectly done through ignorance or inadvertence; a mistake'. It was a legal refinement to divide errors into those which were negligent and those which were not, and even lawyers tended to classify the latter as errors of judgment (although even those could be negligent).

(2)   It was the normal working assumption in shipping circles that liability for negligent navigation would be excepted. The exception was contained in the Harter Act (*G.E. Dobell & Co.* v *Steamship Rossmore Co. Ltd* [1895] 2 QB 408, at p. 410) s. 3, which was incorporated in this charterparty, and also in the Hague Rules which, via the USA Clause Paramount and the United States Carriage of Goods by Sea Act, were incorporated in the charterparty form as printed. Although the Harter Act did not apply to the voyage here in question, which was to Canada, and the charterparty form was amended so as to apply the USA Clause Paramount to the bills of lading but not the charterparty, it could not be supposed that by that amendment the parties intended to give 'errors of navigation' a less extended meaning than would have been sensible where the Harter Act applied or when the incorporation of the USA Clause Paramount remained unamended.

(3)   Unless 'errors of navigation' were construed to include negligent errors the reference lacked substance because it was very hard to conceive of an error of navigation which was not negligent and which would not be covered by 'dangers and accidents of the Seas'. There was, it was true, an abstruse and academic legal argument as to whether the liability of a carrier by sea was not analogous to that of a common carrier by land, making him liable for all non- or mis-performance not attributable to act of God, act of the Queen's enemies or inherent vice (see *Scrutton on Charterparties*, 18th ed., p. 198; Carver, *Carriage by Sea*, 12th ed., vol. 1, p. 4) but that was not something which the intelligent layman could credibly be thought to have had in mind. Mr Boyd reserved the right to argue hereafter that the position of a carrier by sea was not in any event analogous to that of a common carrier.

(4)   The provenance and contention of cl. 16 made it inappropriate to embark on detailed legal analysis of it. There was no common theme to be discerned in the clause and no internal consistency. It contained exceptions for the act of God and enemies,

which were unnecessary even if the common carrier analogy were valid; it would be odd if there were no exception for negligent errors of navigation, the more so since this was the one time (as compared, for example, with fire or accident) which specified not merely a result but carried one into the state of mind of the owner in pursuit of the cause.

(5)   When the United States Court of Appeals for the Second Circuit had considered the clause, it had been held that although 'dangers and accidents' could not in the absence of express provision to the contrary be held to include the results of negligence, the conclusion might have been different if the expression 'errors of steam navigation' had been used: *The Burma* 187 Fed Rep 94 (1911) at p. 97.

(6)   Although Mr Justice Staughton in *Seven Seas Transportation Ltd* v *Pacifico Union Marina Corporation* [1982] 2 Lloyd's Rep 465 had held that cl. 16 did not confer exemption in respect of negligent errors of navigation, he showed excessive subtlety in assuming that there could be liability without negligence and moreover failed to follow the three-stage process of reasoning recommended by the Privy Council in the *Canada Steamship* case, sup., at pp. 8 and 208. In any event, a number of the arguments addressed to me had not been addressed to Mr Justice Staughton.

It is plain from this summary that Mr Boyd mounted an extremely formidable argument. I embark on my consideration of it from common ground. Clause 16 contains no express reference to negligence, and no synonym for negligence. This is not, of course, fatal to the owners' argument; if it were, there would have been no need for the *Canada Steamship* formulation, and *The Raphael* could not have been decided as it was. But it does mean that the owners' task thereafter is a heavy one. This is the more so where there is not, as there is in some fields, a reluctance to describe negligence as such, and I bear in mind the arbitrator's observation in s. 0, para. 2 of his award:

In the shipping commercial world it is not unusual to see exemption clauses which clearly expressly exclude liability for negligence so that, in general, there is no, and never has been any, reluctance to use appropriate language to make it abundantly clear that negligence is being excepted.

I agree, and Mr Moore-Bick for the charterers did not argue to the contrary, that 'error' in its ordinary connotation may mean a negligent as well as a non-negligent error. I do not, however, think that the word 'error' is primarily suggestive of negligence. The arbitrator thought it to be neutral, and so do I. The O.E.D. adds to the definition quoted above, after 'mistake', the additional words 'e.g., in calculation, judgment, speech, writing, action, etc', and this reflects what I take to be the common belief, that errors in different spheres may but need not be negligent. If anything I think the intelligent layman is less ready than the lawyer to regard an error as likely to be negligent because he tends to regard negligence as something more heinous and unforgivable than the lawyer who knows how easily it can on occasions occur and (if he is honest) how universally.

It is, of course, true that in the printed form of this charterparty the Harter Act (where applicable) and the Hague Rules were incorporated, both providing protection against negligent errors of navigation. I do not, however, think that one can infer from this that cl. 16 was intended to have the same effect, nor can one ignore the fact that the form was amended to make the Hague Rules inapplicable to this charterparty. The Harter Act did not apply anyway. It may of course be that in making the amendment the parties had some other point in mind altogether, but I think more importance is to be attached to the fact of the amendment than to speculation concerning the reason for it.

Mr Moore-Bick for the charterers did not suggest examples of errors of navigation which would not be covered by 'dangers and accidents of the Seas', but instead rested his case that the reference did not lack substance if it were read as excluding negligent errors of navigation on the unresolved issue as to the extent of the sea carrier's common law liability. If the intelligent layman had never heard of that controversy, he submitted, the reasonably informed shipping man probably had, at least sufficiently to entertain doubt as to a carrier's liability, since those engaged in a shipping tended to have a greater knowledge of legal niceties than members of most other professions. I accept this submission. It matters not that a carrier might, if the issue were fully investigated, be held to have no liability for errors of navigation unless they were negligent; the important question is whether protection against the possibility of such liability could reasonably have been sought, and I conclude that it could.

It would undoubtedly be wrong to approach this charterparty form on the assumption that it represents the work of a single all-seeing creator. It is notorious that such forms contain clauses drawn from different sources, and inserted at different times, sometimes to meet special problems. Users of the form, moreover, do not take it as it stands but vary, delete and add to its contents freely. Mr Boyd is accordingly right to warn against close textual analysis of cl. 16, and indeed the clause raises problems for each of the parties. There are, I think, only two points to be made, and both help the charterers. First, while none of the events specified in the clause is clearly indicative of negligence some of them (such as act of God or restraint of princes) are plainly inconsistent with it. Secondly, on the only occasion known to me when an English Court has had to consider the meaning of a peril included in this clause which might be the result or negligence or might not, the expression was interpreted as not including the peril when it was the result of negligence: I refer to the decision in *In Re Polemis and Another and Furness, Withy & Co. Ltd* (1921) 8 Ll L Rep 351; [1921] 3 KB 560, when the meaning of 'fire' in a clause somewhat similar to this was ruled upon. It is quite true that fire is a result, whereas 'errors of navigation' carry on into the mind of the owners' servants, but that does not seem to me to advance the argument very much, save perhaps in making the lack of any express reference to negligence the more striking. The obiter, and very tentative, expression of opinion of the United States Court of Appeals in *The Burma* 187 Fed Rep 94 (1911) does not dissuade me from the conclusion to which the foregoing arguments, as it seems to me, lead.

I am naturally reassured to find that Mr Justice Staughton arrived at the same conclusion. It may be that the effect of the clause has been more fully argued in this case than it was before him, since it is the only point in this case whereas it was one of several in the other, but I find no fault in his reasoning and I do not think the additional arguments presented to me are of decisive significance.

*Notes and Question*
1.   This decision was approved by the Court of Appeal in *Seven Seas Transportation Ltd* v *Pacifico Union Marina Corporation (The Satya Kailash* and *Ocean Amity)* [1984] 1 Lloyd's Rep 586.
2.   What examples are there of errors of navigation which are *not* negligent?
3.   Contrast the provision in the Hague-Visby Rules, Art. IV, r. 2(a) (see Chapter 7).

## SECTION 3: BURDEN OF PROOF

The traditional view is that where the carrier relies on an exception as a defence, i.e., after the cargo owner has proved the loss, the burden lies on the carrier to show that the loss was caused by the excepted event or peril; it is then up to the cargo owner to show, if he can, that the cause of the loss was the carrier's negligence.

### The Glendarroch
### [1894] P 226 (CA)

The plaintiffs' cement was ruined by water when the *Glendarroch* stranded in Cardigan Bay. In an action by the plaintiffs for non-delivery the defendants relied on an exception for perils of the sea. Sir F. Jeune P ruled that the onus was on the defendants to show not merely a peril of the sea but a peril of the sea not occasioned by their negligence. The defendants appealed successfully to the Court of Appeal.

LORD ESHER MR: The exception relied upon by the defendants is that the goods were lost or damaged by a peril of the sea; and upon that, it is alleged that, even though that be true, yet that peril of the sea was the result of negligent navigation on the part of the defendants' servants.

The law is that if that be made out the defendants have no defence, and the plaintiffs are entitled to succeed, and the real question is, how is that to be made out? By which of the parties is it to be made out?

It is to be decided according to the practice of the law courts; and the question is, how is that result to be arrived at? The terms of the bill of lading as they stand on paper are, except the loss be from perils of the sea. But then it is said that, nevertheless, if the perils of the sea are produced by the negligence of the defendants' servants, then that loss cannot be relied on by the defendants. How can that be unless there be an irresistible inference that such exception does exist in the contract, though it is not written in it, so that the exception must be read into it as if it were in it? Therefore, we must try and see whether this stipulation as to negligence must be written in, or be considered as written in.

The liabilities of shipowners under a bill of lading are in that part which precedes the exceptions. Is this stipulation about the loss being the result of the negligence of the shipowners' servants — although within the terms of the exception — is that to be written in before the exceptions or not? The first thing that strikes one is that in that part of the contract it is not wanted. It is immaterial. Before you come to the exceptions the liability of the shipowner is absolute. He has contracted that he will deliver the goods at the end of the voyage. If there were no exceptions, it would be utterly immaterial whether the loss was caused by his servants or not. Even if there were no negligence whatever he would be liable. It cannot be, therefore, that this irresistible inference ought to be written into that part of the contract. It is not wanted there; therefore you must write it into that part which contains the exceptions.

When you come to the exceptions, among others, there is that one, perils of the sea. There are no words which say 'perils of the sea not caused by the negligence of the captain or crew'. You have got to read those words in by a necessary inference. How can you read them in? They can only be read in, in my opinion, as an exception upon the exceptions. You must read in, 'Except the loss is by perils of the sea, unless or except that loss is the result of the negligence of the servants of the owner.'

That being so, I think that according to the ordinary course of practice each party would have to prove the part of the matter which lies upon him. The plaintiffs would have to prove the contract and the non-delivery. If they leave that in doubt, of course

they fail. The defendants' answer is, 'Yes; but the case was brought within the exception
— within its ordinary meaning.' That lies upon them. Then the plaintiffs have a right to
say there are exceptional circumstances, viz., that the damage was brought about by the
negligence of the defendants' servants, and it seems to me that it is for the plaintiffs to
make out that second exception.

*Notes*

1.   Proof of unseaworthiness or deviation will have the same effect as proof of
negligence, always assuming that the contract does not protect the carrier even
in these events (see Chapters 3 and 4).

2.   Notwithstanding the authority of *The Glendarroch*, above, it may be
difficult for shipowners to bring themselves within some at least of the excepted
perils without showing that they were not negligent. In *Nugent* v *Smith* (1876)
1 CPD 423, above, the Court of Appeal clearly put the burden on the
shipowner to establish the absence of negligence in order to make good the
defence of Act of God, and differed from Brett J only as to the degree of care
required. In *F.C. Bradley & Sons Ltd* v *Federal Navigation Co. Ltd* (1927)
27 Ll L Rep 395, at p. 396, Lord Sumner stated:

... The bill of lading described the goods as 'Shipped in apparent good order and
condition' ... , it was common ground that the ship had to deliver what she received as
she received it, unless relieved by excepted perils. Accordingly, in strict law, on proof
being given of the actual good condition of the apples on shipment and of their damaged
condition on arrival, the burden of proof passed from the consignees to the shipowners
to prove some excepted peril which relieved them from liability, and further, as a
condition of being allowed the benefit of that exception, to prove seaworthiness at
Hobart, the port of shipment, and to negative negligence or misconduct of the master,
officers and crew ...

3.   For the position under the Hague-Visby Rules, see Chapter 7, below.

# 3 SEAWORTHINESS

In every contract for the carriage of goods by sea there is, at common law, an implied term that the carrier will provide a seaworthy vessel. Charterparties usually contain express terms governing the fitness of the vessel for the service required, and the Hague-Visby Rules impose an obligation on the carrier to make the ship seaworthy. Although these other provisions differ in some important respects from the common law implied term, the underlying concept of seaworthiness is the same throughout.

## SECTION 1: THE MEANING OF SEAWORTHINESS

*A: Definitions*

### *Kopitoff* v *Wilson*
### (1876) 1 QBD 377 (QBD)

The facts are stated in section 1E, below.

FIELD J: We hold that, in whatever way a contract for the conveyance of merchandise be made, where there is no agreement to the contrary, the shipowner is, by the nature of the contract, impliedly and necessarily held to warrant that the ship is good, and is in a condition to perform the voyage then about to be undertaken, or, in ordinary language, is seaworthy, that is, fit to meet and undergo the perils of the sea and other incidental risks to which she must of necessity be exposed in the course of the voyage. . . .

### *Virginia Carolina Chemical Co.* v *Norfolk and North American Steam Shipping Co.*
### [1912] 1 KB 229 (CA)

KENNEDY LJ: . . . [T]here is in every contract with regard to the carriage of goods by sea an absolute warranty that the carrying vessel must, at the time of sailing with the goods, have that degree of fitness as regards both the safety of the ship and also the safe carriage of the cargo in the ship which an ordinarily careful and prudent owner would require his vessel to have at the commencement of the voyage, having regard to the probable circumstances of that voyage and its nature. . . .

*Note*

For the purposes of marine insurance a ship is deemed to be seaworthy when she is reasonably fit in all respects to encounter the ordinary perils of the seas of the adventure insured (Marine Insurance Act 1906, s. 39(4)). Almost identical language was used by Lord Blackburn in *Steel* v *State Line Steamship Co.* (1877) 3 App Cas 72, at p. 90) to define seaworthiness in relation to contracts of carriage. There is no doubt, however, that seaworthiness also embraces 'cargoworthiness', i.e., fitness for the safe carriage of the cargo, as well as fitness of the ship as such: see sub-section C, below.

*B: Examples of unseaworthiness*

*(a)   Inadequate bunkers*

### McIver & Co. Ltd v Tate Steamers Ltd
[1903] 1 KB 362 (CA)

The *Patapsco* was chartered by M for one round voyage from Liverpool to the River Plate and back to the UK. Clause 2 of the charter provided that 'the charterers shall provide and pay for all coal'. When the vessel set out on the first stage of the return journey, from the River Plate to St Vincent, the chief engineer miscalculated the amount of coal in the bunkers; it then became necessary to take on coal in Brazil, which was more expensive and caused delay. M's claim for damages was upheld by Kennedy J and the Court of Appeal.

VAUGHAN WILLIAMS LJ: In my opinion the judgment of Kennedy J was right. The argument for the defendants in substance is that the terms of the charterparty relieve the shipowners from the obligation to see that the ship is seaworthy in respect of the quantity of coal on board when she first starts, and at each successive stage of the round voyage. The clause of the charterparty principally relied on for this purpose was clause 2, which is to the effect that the charterers are to provide and pay for the necessary coal. It was contended that the use of the word 'provide', as well as the words 'pay for', indicated the intention of the parties to be that it should be a matter for the charterers' discretion how much coal was required for the vessel before starting on each stage of the voyage, and that to that extent the shipowners should be relieved of the obligation of seeing that the ship was seaworthy. I cannot agree with that contention. I cannot see anything in the terms of the charterparty to relieve the shipowners from the obligation that would ordinarily be imposed upon them in this respect. It was said that, the plaintiffs having agreed to provide the coal necessary for the voyage, they could not sue for damages because they themselves had provided an insufficient amount of coal. Assuming that the plaintiffs exercised any discretion as to the quantity of coal to be provided, of which I see no evidence, it appears to me that they were placed in a position in which it was impossible for them to form a correct judgment as to the amount of coal to be provided through the default of the defendants' servants. Under the circumstances I see no reason for thinking that the judgment of Kennedy J was wrong in any respect, and I think the appeal must be dismissed.

MATHEW LJ: I agree. It is not disputed that the obligation of the shipowners to see that the ship was seaworthy was not, in terms, got rid of by this charterparty, and that the charterers in the ordinary course would be entitled to have a seaworthy ship provided by the shipowners. The argument is that, as to everything but the supply of coal, the obligation still remained on the shipowners, but as to that it was imposed on the charterers. It is only necessary, I think, to read the charterparty to see that this could not have been the intention of the parties. Having regard to the obligation, which, in my opinion, remained imposed on the shipowners, of having the ship in a seaworthy condition in respect of her supply of coal at the commencement of the different stages of the voyage, it was the duty of the captain to give the charterers correct information, to enable them to provide the requisite quantity of coal. That duty was not performed, and therefore enough coal was not provided before the ship left the River Plate. The vessel in consequence was unseaworthy for the voyage from the River Plate to St Vincent, and the loss was thereby occasioned to the plaintiffs, in respect of which the learned judge has given them damages. In my opinion his judgment was correct.

*Appeal dismissed.*

Note
In *Louis Dreyfus & Co.* v *Tempus Shipping Co.* [1931] AC 726 (HL), the coal taken on board prior to the outward voyage was unfit for the purpose and a fire broke out in the port reserve bunker early in the return voyage: the vessel was held to be unseaworthy at the commencement of the voyage.

(b)    *Incompetent or insufficient crew*

### Hongkong Fir Shipping Co. Ltd v Kawasaki Kisen Kaisha Ltd
[1962] 2 QB 26 (CA)

In December 1956, HKFS agreed to let the *Hongkong Fir* (which they were in the process of purchasing) on a 24-month time charter to K. The charter contained the usual clause (cl. 1) that the vessel was 'in every way fitted for ordinary cargo service'.

The vessel was delivered at Liverpool on 13 February 1957. She sailed in ballast for Newport News, Virginia, to load a cargo of coal for carriage to Osaka via the Panama Canal. The trip was estimated to take two months. En route she was under repair for five weeks, requiring expenditure of £21,400; after arrival in Osaka on 25 May a further £37,500 was spent on repairs lasting 15 weeks. K repudiated the charter; HKFS accepted the repudiation and claimed damages. Their action succeeded before Salmon J and in the Court of Appeal.

SELLERS LJ: During the currency of the charterparty the freight market had fallen steeply with the result that the judgment awarded the shipowners £184,743 damages.

There is no doubt that there were prolonged and aggravating delays due to breaches of contract by the shipowners, and at the outset of his argument counsel for the charterers relied strongly on the judge's findings of fact, which he submitted clearly showed the extent and the nature of the shipowners' breaches of contract and justified the charterers in terminating the charterparty.

The judge did not accept the charterers' allegations that the vessel's machinery was inefficient and defective and that the vessel was in that respect unseaworthy on delivery at Liverpool. From that finding there is no appeal, but it has been emphasised that although Salmon J held that the diesel engines and other machinery were in reasonably good condition on February 13, 1957, he found that by reason of their age the engines needed to be maintained by an experienced, competent, careful and adequate engine room staff. It was held, however, and this has been unchallenged by the shipowners in this appeal, that the engine room staff was incompetent and insufficient and in this respect the vessel was unseaworthy when handed over and on leaving Liverpool and throughout the voyage to Osaka where she was re-staffed so as to fulfil completely her requirements. She had on delivery five engineers, three fitters and seven greasers. The previous owners had employed seven engineers and eight ratings, and the judgment finds the complement of the engine room staff insufficient. If they had all been competent and efficient all might have been well notwithstanding the numerical deficiency of officers, but the chief engineer was addicted to drink and repeatedly neglected his duties. Incompetence stands out conspicuously in the events in the engine room which led to delays, and it is not surprising that the judgment finds that the owners were in breach of the obligations under clause 1 of the charter....

By clause 1 of the charterparty the shipowners contracted to deliver the vessel at Liverpool 'she being in every way fitted for ordinary cargo service'. She was not fit for ordinary cargo service when delivered because the engine room staff was incompetent and inadequate and this became apparent as the voyage proceeded. It is commonplace language to say that the vessel was unseaworthy by reason of this inefficiency in the engine room.
...

## Notes

1.  The *Hongkong Fir* case is considered further in section 5, below.
2.  In *Adamastos Shipping Co. Ltd* v *Anglo-Saxon Petroleum Co. Ltd* [1959] AC 133 (HL), the incompetence of the engine-room staff made the vessel unseaworthy, but the shipowners had exercised due diligence in the selection and appointment of the staff and were held, by a 3–2 majority in the House of Lords, to be protected by the incorporation into the charterparty of the due diligence provision of the Harter Act. (The case is considered further in Chapter 7.)

### Standard Oil Co. of New York v Clan Line Steamers Ltd
[1924] AC 100 (HL)

The *Clan Gordon* was chartered by CL to SO. She was one of seven 'turret' ships built for CL by Doxfords of Sunderland. Following the capsizing of one of these, the *Clan Ranald*, in 1909, Doxfords sent special instructions to the owners warning that these vessels had to retain water ballast when loaded with a full homogeneous cargo, but CL failed to pass these instructions to the master of the *Clan Gordon*. Soon after sailing from New York with such a load, the master ordered the ballast tanks to be emptied, with the result that the vessel keeled over and sank in calm seas.

LORD ATKINSON: It is not disputed, I think, that a ship may be rendered unseaworthy by the inefficiency of the master who commands her. Does not that principle apply where the master's inefficiency consists, whatever his general efficiency may be, in his ignorance as to how his ship may, owing to the peculiarities of her structure, behave in circumstances likely to be met with on an ordinary ocean voyage? There cannot be any difference in principle, I think, between disabling want of skill and disabling want of knowledge. Each equally renders the master unfit and unqualified to command, and therefore makes the ship he commands unseaworthy. And the owner who withholds from the master the necessary information should, in all reason, be as responsible for the result of the master's ignorance as if he deprived the latter of the general skill and efficiency he presumably possessed.

*(c)   Failure to hold necessary documents*

### Alfred C. Toepfer Schiffahrtsgesellschaft mbH v Tossa Marine Co. Ltd (The Derby)
[1985] 2 Lloyd's Rep 325 (CA)

The *Derby* was let on time charter, on the New York Produce Exchange form. She sailed under the Cypriot flag with Filipino officers and crew. She did not hold an I.T.F. blue card (to indicate that the crew's pay and conditions and manning levels met the standards laid down by the International Transport Workers Federation). The trading limits under the charter were defined to exclude areas in which the I.T.F. was known to be active, but did not exclude Portugal. While *The Derby* was discharging a cargo of logs from West Africa at the Portuguese port of Leixões (Oporto), an I.T.F. representative discovered that she did not have a blue card. This led to discharge being stopped for 21 days while the owners reached agreement with the I.T.F. Because of the delay the charterers were unable to perform a sub-charter which had been fixed, and lost profits; the sub-charter which was performed in its place caused them a loss of $32,000. The charterers claimed damages, arguing that the absence of an I.T.F. blue card meant that the owners had failed to provide a seaworthy vessel 'in every way fitted for the service' (the vessel was off-hire during the delay). Hobhouse J and the Court of Appeal held that the vessel was not unseaworthy.

KERR LJ: . . . The I.T.F. operates in different parts of the world, wherever it can or hopes to do so successfully, with the avowed objective of compelling shipowners to adopt levels of pay and conditions of employment of their crews in conformity with levels which the I.T.F. regards as acceptable. Its particular targets are ships flying 'flags of convenience' and employing 'third world' crews. The standards which it applies are not based upon the requirements of the law of the vessel's flag or of the countries in which such vessels may load or discharge. They are generally in line with the rates of pay and conditions applicable to agreements negotiated with seamen's trade unions in 'western' countries. . . . A vessel may be proof against I.T.F. intervention in a number of ways. Thus, if it is registered in a 'western' country and employs a crew on terms and conditions prevailing in such cases, including the Panhellenic Seamen's Federation form of agreement for Greek crews, which the I.T.F. recognises, the vessel is likely to be left alone. On the other hand, vessels flying flags of convenience or employing Asiatic crews may be 'blacked', either by seeking to induce the crew to go on strike or — more usually — by persuading the local stevedores or other employees in a port to boycott the vessel. In cases of vessels which have attracted the attention of the I.T.F. on a previous occasion with results satisfactory to the I.T.F., a so-called 'blue card' or 'blue certificate' may be issued to the vessel as a kind of I.T.F. pass. . . . The vessel berthed at Leixões on May 23, 1981, and discharged normally until May 28. A representative of the I.T.F. then approached the local stevedores and persuaded them to boycott or black the vessel because the rates of pay or other terms of employment of the crew did not meet I.T.F. requirements. However, instead of boycotting the vessel outright, the stevedores decided to attend the vessel on every day, but without doing any, or hardly any, work. This had the effect that the charterers nevertheless had to pay the stevedores throughout the period of the vessel's delay, while the owners were negotiating with the I.T.F. representative. These negotiations proved fruitless, and when the owners thereupon decided to make arrangements to replace the crew with a Greek crew employed on the terms of the Panhellenic Agreement, eight of the Filipino crew staged a sit-in protest. This finally caused the owners to capitulate, and they signed an agreement whereby they made substantial payments — about $55,000 — to the local I.T.F. representative. Whether these were subsequently used for the benefit of the crew is unknown. The discharge of the vessel was thereupon resumed on June 19, 1981. Although the vessel had been off-hire for all or most of the period of this delay under cl. 54 of the charter, the charterers had had to pay the stevedoring charges which were wasted in the circumstances. . . .

### After considering the arbitrator's award in detail, Kerr LJ continued:

In effect, therefore, the only parts of the arbitrator's reasons which remain supported on this appeal by the charterers are to be found in paras. 1 and 5. In these he considered the analogy between an I.T.F. 'blue certificate' and a deratisation certificate, and he concluded that in the circumstances the ship was not in every way fitted for the service, as required by line 22, 'under the expanded meaning of that phrase assigned to it by English Law as I understand it'. In this regard it was common ground that the authority uppermost in the arbitrator's mind was the decision of Mr Justice Roskill (as he then was) in *The Madeleine* [1967] 2 Lloyd's Rep 224 to which I refer below.

The learned Judge rejected this construction of line 22 and I respectfully agree with him entirely. He reviewed the authorities at pp. 640 and 641 of the report, and I can express my own reasoning for reaching the same conclusion fairly shortly. The context in which the words 'in every way fitted for the service' occur shows that these words relate primarily to the physical state of the vessel. However, the authorities also show that their scope is wider, in at least two respects. First, in *Hongkong Fir Shipping Co. Ltd* v *Kawasaki Kisen Kaisha Ltd* [1961] 2 Lloyd's Rep 478; [1962] 2 QB 26, the words 'she being in every way fitted for ordinary cargo service' in the Baltime form of time charter were treated as forming part of an express warranty that the vessel was seaworthy, and it was held that this warranty required the provision of a sufficient and competent crew to operate the vessel for the purposes of the charter service. I accept that precisely the same reasoning applies to the words 'in every way fitted for the service' in the present case. To that extent, therefore, these words go beyond the purely physical state of the vessel as such. However, I cannot see any basis for any further enlargement of the scope of these words by extracting from them a warranty that the rates of pay and conditions of employment of the crew, with which they expressly declared themselves to be satisfied, must also comply with the requirements, not of any law which is relevant to the vessel, her crew or the vessel's operation under the charter, but also of a self-appointed and extra-legal organisation such as the I.T.F. In my view this is not a meaning which these words can properly bear, let alone in the context in which they appear in the charter.

The second respect in which the scope of these words in line 22 has been held to go beyond the physical state of the vessel is that they have been held to cover the requirement that the vessel must carry certain kinds of documents which bear upon her seaworthiness or fitness to perform the service for which the charter provides. Navigational charts which are necessary for the voyages upon which the vessel may be ordered from time to time are an obvious illustration. For present purposes, however, we are concerned with certificates bearing upon the seaworthiness of the vessel. The nature of such certificates may vary according to the requirements of the law of the vessel's flag or the laws or regulations in force in the countries to which the vessel may be ordered, or which may lawfully be required by the authorities exercising administrative or other functions in the vessel's ports of call pursuant to the laws there in force. Documents falling within this category, which have been considered in the authorities, are certificates concerning the satisfactory state of the vessel which is in some respect related to her physical condition, and accordingly to her seaworthiness. Their purpose is to provide documentary evidence for the authorities at the vessel's ports of call on matters which would otherwise require some physical inspection of the vessel, and possibly remedial measures — such as fumigation — before the vessel will be accepted as seaworthy in the relevant respect. The nature or description of such certificates, which may accordingly be required to be carried on board to render the vessel seaworthy, must depend on the circumstances and would no doubt raise issues of fact in individual cases. But I do not see any basis for holding that such certificates can properly be held to include documents other than those which may be required by the law of the vessel's flag or by the laws, regulations or lawful administrative practices of governmental or local authorities at the vessel's ports of call. An I.T.F. blue card does not fall within this category, and I can therefore see no reason for including it within the scope of the words in line 22, even in their extended sense as indicated above.

Moreover, I do not consider that the words in line 22 have acquired as a matter of law, any 'expanded meaning', as the arbitrator suggests in par. 5 above. The requirement of a deratisation certificate under the laws in force in India in 1957, which was the point at issue in *The Madeleine*, (sup.) and without which the vessel could not sail to any other country, was in no way different in principle from the 'bill of health' required by the law of Sardinia, which fell to be considered in *Levy* v *Costerton* (1816) 4 Camp 389. Since a vessel chartered for a voyage from England to Sardinia could not enter and discharge in the port of Cagliari without this document, 'required from all ships even from England', and was consequently delayed by being put under quarantine by the local authorities, it was inevitably held in that case that the vessel had not been—

> ... furnished with everything needful and necessary for such a ship, and for the voyage ...

A decision about half-way in time between 1816 and the present was *Ciampa* v *British India Steam Navigation Co. Ltd* [1915] 2 KB 774. On the appeal before us there was considerable controversy whether the reason for the unseaworthiness of the vessel on arrival in Marseilles in that case was the fact that she had previously called at Mombasa, which was contaminated by a plague, or whether she had a 'foul bill of health' in the sense of some deficiency in her proper documentation. In my view this is irrelevant for present purposes. The vessel was clearly unseaworthy at Marseilles in either event, whether on the ground that the local authorities required her to be fumigated because she had recently called at Mombasa, or because she did not have any document certifying a 'clean bill of health', in the same way as the vessel in *Levy* v *Costerton*. On whichever basis that decision in 1915 falls to be considered, it is wholly in line with the other two cases decided respectively in 1816 and 1967. The same applies to the 'tonnage certificate' required by Swedish law which was in issue in *Chellew Navigation Co. Ltd* v *A.R. Appelquist Kolinport A.G.* (1933) 45 Ll L Rep 190 and (1932) 38 Com Cas 218, which the learned Judge also discussed in his judgment. In that case the umpire held, on the facts, that it was no part of the shipowners' obligation to obtain this certificate, or at any rate not by the time when the charterers had obtained it at their own expense.

I can therefore see no basis for the arbitrator's conclusion in the present case that the words in line 22 of this form of charterparty have somehow acquired an expanded meaning in our law so as to lead to the conclusion that a document in the nature of an I.T.F. blue card can nowadays be held to fall within the requirements imposed upon shipowners by virtue of these words.

## C: Cargoworthiness

### Owners of Cargo on Ship 'Maori King' v Hughes
[1895] 2 QB 550 (CA)

4,553 carcases of hard frozen mutton were shipped under a 'refrigerator bill' from Melbourne to London. Because of a breakdown of the ship's refrigerating machinery during the voyage, the meat was landed at Sydney and sold there at a loss. The plaintiffs claimed damages; the defendants relied on a clause in the bill of lading that the steamer was not to be accountable for loss or damage 'arising from failure or breakdown of machinery, insulation or other appliances'. The plaintiffs argued that there was an implied warranty of fitness of the refrigerating machinery at the commencement of the voyage, to which the exemption clause did not apply. Mathew J and the Court of Appeal found for the plaintiffs on this preliminary issue.

LORD ESHER MR: ... [T]he bill of lading is headed 'Refrigerator bill', and those words must have some meaning. In my opinion, the necessary meaning of that heading, when you know the circumstances, is, that there is refrigerating machinery on board the ship for the purpose of keeping frozen the meat which is shipped in a frozen state, for it is described in the bill of lading as '4,553 carcases of hard frozen mutton'.

An obligation, therefore, is to be implied from the bill of lading to have such machinery on board for the purpose of receiving the frozen meat; and the implication arises in the way in which all implications are made by law, and the only way in which they can be made, namely, that the Court can see that the implied obligation must have been in the contemplation and intention of both parties to the contract.

Now, the shipper who has frozen meat to send to Europe knows that, if no precaution is taken, it will be liable to decompose on the voyage. He therefore must be taken to stipulate (he would be destitute of common sense if he did not) that there shall be on board the ship the known class of machinery which will keep his meat frozen during an ordinary voyage. That is what he wants, and that is what he pays for. He does not pay the ordinary freight; he pays the higher freight which is usual for a ship with such refrigerating machinery. The shipowner, on the other hand, must know perfectly well that the shipper will not put frozen meat on board his ship, and pay him an increased freight for its carriage, unless the shipowner provides him with such machinery as will on an ordinary voyage keep the meat frozen. Therefore both parties must have contemplated, if they thought about it at all, that there should be such machinery on board the ship. If, however, the machinery will not work it is useless: it is the same thing as if there were none. Both parties must, therefore, be taken to have intended that there should be on board such machinery in proper working condition at the time when the ship is to start with the frozen meat. It by no means follows that both parties must have contemplated that, whatever accident might happen, the machinery should continue fit for its purpose during the whole voyage. The shipper, no doubt, would like to have such a stipulation made; but the shipowner would certainly not agree to it. Therefore you have no right to imply so large a contract as that, in the absence of an express stipulation for it. But the original obligation that the machinery shall at the starting of the vessel be fit for the purpose for which it is supplied, and for which payment is made, is one which the Court can see that as a matter of business both parties must have intended, and, that being so, an agreement to that effect must be inferred or implied in the bill of lading, as it would be in any other document under similar circumstances. And, if you imply a stipulation in the bill of lading, the result is the same as if it were actually written in it. The moment you can by implication insert a stipulation in a written document, it is, though not expressed, as much part of the written document as if it had been actually written in it.

The principle on which a condition or a warranty or any other stipulation is implied will apply to many other contracts; but whether that implication can be made must be determined in each case when it arises. In the present case I have no doubt that, according to the ordinary rules which govern the Court, the stipulation in question is to be implied and therefore to be introduced into the contract. But it applies only to the state of things existing at the commencement of the voyage, and not to anything which may happen after the voyage has begun.

But there are exceptions in this bill of lading just as in every bill of lading which is in the ordinary form; and, if there are in the contract express stipulations which are in terms inconsistent with the primary implication to which I have referred, that stipulation cannot be implied. In that case there would be express stipulations with regard to the condition of the machinery or the ship at starting, and when there are express stipulations as to any matter you cannot imply any others. But the exceptions here are, in my opinion, of the same kind as exceptions in ordinary bills of lading — that is, with regard to matters which may happen during the voyage. They are exceptions from the obligation of the shipowner to deliver the goods at the end of the voyage in the same condition as they were intrusted to him at its commencement. They do not apply to the primary warranty of the condition of the machinery at the time when its application is to begin. I agree, therefore, with my brother Mathew that it was an implied term in this bill of lading that the refrigerating machinery was at the time of shipment fit to carry frozen meat to Europe on an ordinary voyage made under ordinary circumstances. He made use of the term 'seaworthiness', but he did not mean the seaworthiness of the ship. He was dealing with the 'seaworthiness' of the machinery as distinct from that of the ship. In his judgment the machinery was warranted to be what might be called in nautical phraseology 'seaworthy', though it is not strictly an accurate term. But he meant that the machinery was to be at the time of shipment fit as machinery to carry frozen meat to Europe under the ordinary conditions of an ordinary voyage. I have no doubt that the learned judge was right in that respect, and therefore his judgment on the preliminary question of law must be affirmed, and the appeal must be dismisssed.

## Queensland National Bank v Peninsular and Oriental Steam Navigation Co.
### [1898] 1 QB 567 (CA)

QNB shipped 10 boxes, each containing 5,000 sovereigns, from Sydney to London on the *Oceana*. Although not expressly stated in the bill of lading, it was assumed by both parties that the cargo would be carried in the ship's bullion room. One box was stolen during the voyage. The bill of lading exempted the shipowners from liability in the event (*inter alia*) of 'loss by thefts or robberies by sea or land, and whether by persons directly or indirectly in the employment or service of the company or otherwise'. Counsel for the plaintiffs (Scrutton) argued that there was an implied warranty that the *Oceana's* bullion room was reasonably fit to resist thieves and that the exceptions in the bill of lading did not extend to breach of this warranty. Mathew J and the Court of Appeal accepted this argument on a preliminary issue.

A.L. SMITH LJ: I am of opinion that the judgment in this case should be affirmed. The action is brought for non-delivery under a bill of lading of a box containing 5,000 sovereigns. The *Oceana*, in which the gold was carried, was one of the defendant's line of steamers, and beyond all doubt on this line, and I daresay on others, bullion-rooms are provided for the stowage of gold for the purpose of obtaining this class of traffic. The bill of lading states the contract as to the carriage of the bullion in this form: 'Shipped in good order and well-conditioned by the Queensland National Bank, Limited, in the Peninsular and Oriental Steam Navigation Company's steamship *Oceana*, now at Port Jackson, ten boxes, each said to contain 5,000 sovereigns of gold, to be delivered, subject to the conditions and exceptions at foot hereof, in the like good order and well-conditioned, at the port of London, unto Lloyd's Bank, Limited.' I should add that in the bill of lading there are very large exceptions to the liability of the ship — large enough to cover almost anything that could happen as regards fixing the ship with liability.

The 5,000 sovereigns having been lost on the voyage, the action is brought; and the question which arises is whether upon this bill of lading there is an implied warranty that, when the ship sailed, the bullion-room into which the gold was to be put should be so constructed as to be reasonably fit to resist thieves. The importance of the matter is obvious, because if the plaintiffs have to rely upon the bill of lading, and not upon an implied warranty, the defendants will in all probability have an answer to the action under the exceptions to which I have referred.

It appears to me that the foundation of the judgment of the learned judge is to be found in these lines of his judgment. He says: 'In this case I assume, for the purpose of my decision, that the vessel in question, the *Oceana*, like others of her class, was furnished with a receptacle for bullion and valuables, usually called the specie-room; and that the contract in the bill of lading was entered into with the knowledge and upon the footing that this receptacle had been provided for the safe carriage of the gold mentioned in the bill of lading.' When it was pointed out to the learned counsel for the defendants that if this assumption is correct the case came within the four corners of the case of *Maori King* v *Hughes* [1895] 2 QB 550, some question was raised as to whether any such admission was made at the hearing, and whether the learned judge in making this assumption had not gone beyond anything admitted at the trial. It seems to me, from the account of what then took place, that the learned judge was justified in the assumption he made. I conclude, then, that the contract was made in relation to the carriage of the gold in a bullion-room. That room was there to secure the contents from thieves. I cannot see why, under these circumstances, it should be wrong to put the question whether the room was reasonably fit, at the time when the voyage commenced at the port of loading, to protect the gold. On the authorities, it seems to me that this is a proper question to raise, as similar questions have been raised in the case of various cargoes, such as cattle, in *Tattersall* v *National Steamship Co.* 12 QBD 297; sugar, in *Stanton* v *Richardson* (1872) LR 7 CP 421; (1874) LR 9 CP 390; frozen meat in *Maori King* v *Hughes* [1895] 2 QB 550. In some of those cases the warranty applied, as in this case, to the part of the ship appropriated for the stowage of the particular cargo. With these cases to guide me, I come to the conclusion that the decision appealed from is right, though even without them I should have come to the same conclusion. The appeal will, therefore, be dismissed.

*Notes*
1.   The bill of lading in *Queensland National Bank* drew the attention of shippers to the possibility of shipment without the exceptions upon payment of a higher rate of freight.
2.   In *Ciampa* v *British India Steam Navigation Co. Ltd* [1915] 2 KB 774, Rowlatt J, after deciding that the shipowners could not rely on 'restraint of princes' (see Chapter 2), continued:

That is a sufficient ground for deciding this case in favour of the plaintiffs, but I think that the plaintiffs are also right in saying that the ship was unseaworthy when the lemons were shipped on board at Naples. They were carried on the 'tween deck, where they became saturated with the sulphurous fumes used in the process of dératisation. They were not only spoilt in flavour, but were affected in substance also, being to a certain extent rotted. There is not much evidence as to this sort of thing having happened before, though the plaintiffs did prove that lemons belonging to them had been similarly damaged when being carried in a ship of another line about six months previously. On the other hand there is no evidence that lemons have ever passed through the ordeal of dératisation without becoming damaged; and the defendants did not appear to have carried lemons to Marseilles previously to this occasion. The only view of the evidence that I can take is that there was nothing fortuitous about the injury to the lemons on this particular occasion, and that lemons will not stand being exposed to sulphurous fumes. The defendants therefore received the lemons on board their ship for carriage, the ship being at the time free from sulphurous fumes, but circumstances existing which rendered it inevitable that the ship and cargo would in the course of the voyage be subjected to them. The ship was therefore in my opinion unfit to receive and carry the cargo. That is what is meant by unseaworthiness, quite apart from the fitness of the ship to traverse the ocean. I think, therefore, that the plaintiffs are also entitled to succeed on the ground that the ship was unseaworthy. . . .
   (Cf. *The Good Friend* [1984] 2 Lloyd's Rep 586 (QBD): holds infested by trogoderma.)

3.   In *Stanton* v *Richardson* (1874) LR 9 CP 390 (Exch Ch) (affirmed by HL: (1875) 45 LJQB 78) the ship's pumps were unable to cope with the large quantity of moisture draining from the cargo of wet sugar, though perfectly adequate in normal conditions. Held: the vessel was unseaworthy.

*D: Negligence and unseaworthiness*

It may be difficult to draw the line between the provision of an incompetent crew (section B) and negligence on the part of the crew, which is not unseaworthiness.

### *Steel v State Line Steamship Co.*
### (1877) 3 App Cas 72 (HL)

Wheat was shipped on the *State of Virginia* from New York to Glasgow. On the voyage sea-water entered through an insufficiently fastened porthole and damaged the cargo. The bill of lading, which had been indorsed to the appellants, contained an exception for perils of the sea whether arising from negligence or otherwise. The jury made no finding as to whether the vessel was seaworthy at the commencement of the voyage and the House of Lords remitted the case for a new trial.

LORD BLACKBURN: My Lords, I entirely agree in the course which is proposed to be taken, of sending the case down for a new trial, on the ground that this special verdict does not really find the cardinal fact upon which it depends whether the judgment ought to be for the Respondents or for the Appellants.

I take it my Lords, to be quite clear, both in *England* and in *Scotland*, that where there is a contract to carry goods in a ship, whether that contract is in the shape of a bill of lading, or any other form, there is a duty on the part of the person who furnishes or supplies that ship, or that ship's room, unless something be stipulated which should prevent it, that the ship shall be fit for its purpose. That is generally expressed by saying that it shall be seaworthy; and I think also in marine contracts, contracts for sea carriage, that is what is properly called a 'warranty', not merely that they should do their best to make the ship fit, but that the ship should really be fit.... 

Now, my Lords, I perfectly agree with what has been said by the noble and learned Lords who have already addressed you on the construction of this contract, that it does not provide at all for this case of an unseaworthy ship producing the mischief. The shipowners might have stipulated, if they had pleased (I know no law that would hinder them), We will take the goods on board, but we shall not be responsible at all, though our ship is ever so unseaworthy; look out for yourselves; if we put them on board a rotten ship, that is your look-out; you shall not have any remedy against us if we do. I say they might have so contracted, and perhaps in some cases they may actually so contract. I do not know. Or the shipowner might, and that would have been more reasonable, have said, I will furnish a seaworthy ship, but I stipulate that although the ship is seaworthy, and although I have furnished it, I shall only be answerable for the vitiation of your policy of insurance, if you have one, in case the ship turns out not to be seaworthy; and I will protect myself against any perils of the seas, though the loss should be produced in consequence of, or caused by, that unseaworthiness. They *might* have contracted in that way. I think that when this contract is fairly looked at it appears that they do not so contract as to apply it to this case. I think, and I agree there with the Court of Session, that they have here sufficiently expressed in the contract they will not be responsible or answerable for the consequences of a loss by perils of the seas or either of the excepted perils, even though it may be produced by the negligence of the mariners. I think that they have done that, and that is what the Court of Session appear to have thought was all that it was necessary to say.

But then, my Lords, for some reasons or other, I cannot exactly make out what, the Court below lost sight of the fact that if there was a want of seaworthiness in the ship — using the common phrase which is used as meaning if the duty or obligation to make the ship reasonably fit for the voyage had not been fulfilled — if there was a want of seaworthiness in that sense, and that want of seaworthiness caused the loss, this contract did not protect the shipowners, and therefore it was incumbent upon them to see whether there was a want of seaworthiness, and whether it did produce the loss. The point was raised on the first plea in law distinctly, and then there were several additional pleas in law in which it was not raised, and it seems to have been lost sight of; and though the issue directed was so worded as to leave this open, it is so worded as to lead me to think that those who drew the issue were not thinking of this point (no doubt it would be open upon the issue, but it is not raised by it), and when there came to be a special verdict, it was found that

one of the orlop deck ports of the said steamship was insufficiently fastened, and that in consequence the said sea water was thereby admitted to the hold after the ship had been five days at sea.

And then it was found that this port was about a foot above the water-line, and that the weather had been as is described in the mate's log.

Now, my Lords, I cannot see that this special verdict finds, either one way or the other, whether or no there was a want of seaworthiness or reasonable fitness to encounter the ordinary perils of the voyage or not. I think that is left quite ambiguous and uncertain. I quite agree with what has been said, that it was a question of fact for the jury, whether or no the vessel was made reasonably fit to encounter these ordinary perils.

I think also that there are some views of the case in which, though it would still be a question of fact for the jury, there could not be much doubt about it one way or the other. If, for example, this port was left unfastened, so that when any ordinary weather came on, and the sea washed as high as the port, it would be sure to give way and the water come in, unless something more was done — if in the inside the wheat had been piled up so high against it and covered it, so that no one would ever see whether it had been so left or not, and so that if it had been found out or thought of, it would have required a great deal of time and trouble (time above all) to remove the cargo to get at it and fasten it — if that was found to be the case, and it was found that at the time of sailing it was in that state, I can hardly imagine any jury finding anything else than that a ship which sailed in that state did not sail in a fit state to encounter such perils of the sea as are reasonably to be expected in crossing the *Atlantic*. I think, on the other hand, if this port had been, as a port in the cabin or some other place would often be, open, and when they were sailing out under the lee of the shore remaining open, but quite capable of being shut at a moment's notice as soon as the sea became in the least degree rough, and in case a regular storm came on capable of being closed with a dead light — in such a case as that no one could, with any prospect of success, ask any reasonable people, whether they were a jury or Judges, to say that that made the vessel unfit to encounter the perils of the voyage, because that thing could be set right in a few minutes, and there is always some warning before a storm comes on, so that they would have plenty of time to put it all right, and it would have been put right. If they did not put it right after such a warning, that would be negligence on the part of the crew, and not unseaworthiness of the ship. But between these two extremes, which seem to me to be self-evident cases as to what they would be, there may be a great deal of difficulty in ascertaining how it was here. It may very likely be a contested point as to how far the wheat was put against this port. That may be one of the contests, and there may be many others. I agree with what has been already said, that nothing which is said now about unseaworthiness is at all authoritative. Of course it is not laying down the opinion of the House, but what I have said is not even the expression of a final and concluded opinion formed by myself as an individual advising your Lordshps. I merely express it as being what I think might be the case.

## Note

In *International Packers London Ltd* v *Ocean Steam Ship Co. Ltd* [1955] 2 Lloyd's Rep 218, the cargo of tinned meat was damaged on the voyage from Brisbane and Melbourne to the UK when heavy seas stripped the tarpaulins from the hatch covers 48 hours after the ship left Melbourne and sea-water entered the hold. The ship was equipped with locking bars to secure the tarpaulins, but these were not in place at the time. McNair J held that the shipowners had not failed to exercise due care and diligence to make the vessel seaworthy — the test under the Hague Rules incorporated in the Australian Sea-Carriage of Goods Act 1924 — since it was for the master or other officers in charge to decide when to fit them and the weather forecast did not indicate that it would have been prudent to fit them before leaving Melbourne.

## E: Stowage and unseaworthiness

When, if ever, will bad stowage make the vessel unseaworthy?

### *Kopitoff* v *Wilson*
### (1876) 1 QBD 377 (QBD)

FIELD J: This is an action in which the plaintiff seeks to recover damages for the loss of a large number of iron armourplates and bolts, which were lost on board the defendants' ship *Walamo*, on a voyage from Hull to Cronstadt.

The cause was tried before Blackburn, J, at Guildhall, at the sittings after Hilary Term, 1875. The declaration contained several counts, and amongst them was a count alleging that the defendants had warranted that the ship should be seaworthy and reasonably fit to carry the goods in question, and alleged that, by reason of a breach of such warranty, the goods were lost. There was also a count upon the bill of lading, alleging a promise to deliver, with the exception of certain perils, &c., and a loss not within any of the exceptions. The defendants denied the warranty, and also alleged that the cause of loss was within some of the exceptions.

On the trial it appeared that the plaintiff, who was an agent of the Russian Government, had entered into a contract with the defendants, who were shipowners at Hull, by which the defendants undertook to ship for Cronstadt, from time to time, large quantities of armour-plates, which the plaintiff was having manufactured in this country, at agreed rates of freight, varying according to the season of the year. The other terms of the contract are not material to the points raised before us.

Three armour-plates of great weight, from 18 tons to 15 tons weight each, were delivered by the plaintiff to the defendants for shipment, and were by them shipped on the 15th September in the defendants' own steamship *Walamo*, under a bill of lading, containing many exceptions. The defendants themselves by their own servants stowed the ship. The armour-plates were by them placed on the top of a quantity of railway iron, and then secured there by wooden shores. There was a conflict of testimony as to whether this was or was not a proper mode of stowing them. It was not disputed that the steamship was in herself a good ship, but it was contended on behalf of the plaintiff, that the mode of stowing these plates adopted by the defendants made her unseaworthy on this voyage. On getting out to sea she encountered bad weather, the wind being high and the sea rough, and she rolled heavily. There was conflicting evidence as to the degree of this bad weather, and the cause of this rolling; the plaintiff contending that the wind and sea were no more than at that season were to be expected, and that the rolling was owing to the improper stowage of the vessel; the defendants contending that there was an unusual storm which would have made any ship, however well stowed, roll. After the ship had been out at sea for some hours, one of the armour-plates broke loose and went through the side of the ship, which, in consequence, went down in deep water and was totally lost, with all her cargo on board.

The plaintiff's contention was, that the breaking loose of the plate was, because it was improperly stowed and secured; the defendants', that it was a direct consequence of the roughness of the sea, which was a peril excepted in the bill of lading. These contentions raised questions of fact for the jury. Leave was reserved at the close of the case to enter a nonsuit if the exceptions in the bill of lading protected the defendants under the circumstances.

The case thus was left to the jury. The learned judge told the jury as a matter of law, and not as a question for them, that a shipowner warrants the fitness of his ship when she sails, and not merely that he will honestly and bona fide endeavour to make her fit, and after explaining to the jury what 'reasonably fit' meant with reference to a North Sea voyage, and the other facts in the case, left the following questions to the jury:—

Was the vessel at the time of her sailing in a state, as regards the stowing and receiving of these plates, reasonably fit to encounter the oridnary perils that might be expected on a voyage at that season from Hull to Cronstadt?

Second. If she was not in a fit state, was the loss that happened caused by that unfitness? These questions were put in writing and handed to the jury, and on that paper the judge put in writing what he had previously stated in his summing-up, that they were 'to understand (in answering this second question) that though the disaster would not have happened had there not been considerable sea, yet it is to be considered as caused by the unfitness, if they (the jury) think that the plates would not have got adrift when they did had the stowage been such as to put the ship in a fit state'.

The jury answered the first question in the negative, and the second in the affirmative. No complaint has been made as to these findings not being justified by the evidence. Upon these findings the learned judge directed a verdict to be entered for the plaintiff for the agreed amount, 6,550*l*., and in Easter term, 1875, the defendants obtained a rule to shew cause why a nonsuit should not be entered pursuant to the leave reserved, or why there should not be a new trial on the ground 'that the learned judge misdirected the jury in directing them that there was an absolute obligation on the shipowner to make his ship seaworthy as regards the stowage, and that he would be liable if, in consequence of the non-performance of that obligation, the goods should be lost'. . . .

We think that the rule must be discharged.

After defining unseaworthiness (see section A) and considering the authorities, Field J continued:

. . . It appears to us also that there are good grounds in reason and common sense for holding such to be the law. It is well and firmly established that in every marine policy the assured comes under an implied warranty of seaworthiness to his assurer, and if we were to hold that he has not the benefit of a similar implication in the contract which he makes with a shipowner for the carriage of his goods, the consequence would be that he would lose that complete indemnity against risk and loss which it is the object and purpose to give him by the two contracts taken together. Holding as we now do, the result is that the merchant, by his contract with the shipowner, having become entitled to have a ship to carry his goods warranted fit for that purpose, and to meet and struggle against the perils of the sea, is, by his contract of assurance, protected against the damage arising from such perils acting upon a seaworthy ship.

## The Thorsa
[1916] P 257 (CA)

The Nestlé and Anglo-Swiss Condensed Milk Company was the consignee of 1,838 cases of chocolate shipped at Genoa for carriage to London. A quantity of gorgonzola cheese was carried in the same hold; because of bad weather the hatches were kept on and there was insufficient ventilation, so that the cheese tainted the chocolate. An exemption clause in the bill of lading covered the shipowners against liability for damage arising from any act, neglect or default in the management, loading or stowing of the ship. Nestlé argued that bad stowage had rendered the ship unseaworthy, so that the shipowners were not entitled to rely on the exception clause. Bargrave Deane J and the Court of Appeal held that the vessel was not unseaworthy.

SWINFEN EADY LJ: ... I think the fair result of the evidence given on behalf of the plaintiffs is that the chocolate was seriously tainted by reason of its proximity to the gorgonzola cheese and that it had imbibed the taint from the cheese. That fact the plaintiffs established.

But the plaintiffs were not content with merely proving the damaged condition in which the cargo arrived; they adduced evidence to show what had occasioned the damage, and, in my opinion, it is established by the palintiffs' evidence that what occasioned the damage was the improper stowage. The exact details of the stowage are not proved. A stowage plan was produced ... it would appear that the chocolate was stowed at the bottom of the hold in question and the cheese in the upper part. In other words, it would appear that the chocolate was put on board first and the cheese was stowed over it. But in any case the plaintiffs did establish that cheese and chocolate were stowed in the same hold, and that by reason of the hatches being kept on throughout the voyage the ventilation was insufficient, and the chocolate was affected and deteriorated in quality by the proximity of the cheese....

In the present case it is not contended that the ship was in any way defective in design or in structure, or in condition or equipment, at the time when she sailed — not the ship herself. The sole point is the way in which the cargo was stowed. It is not contended that at the date when the ship was empty and prepared to receive cargo her condition was in any way defective, nor is it contended that the cargo was so stowed, or that any part of the cargo was so stowed, as to be a serious danger to the ship herself. In other words, the case is not brought within the principle of cases like *Tattersall* v *National Steamship Co.* 12 QBD 297, where the defendants had not proved the ship to be reasonably fit for the purpose of the carriage of cattle which they had contracted to take; nor is it within cases like *Kopitoff* v *Wilson* (1876) 1 QBD 377, or *Ingram & Royle Ltd* v *Services Maritimes du Tréport* [1914] 1 KB 541, where bad stowage endangered the safety of the ship. The

contention put forward really amounts to this, that if two parcels of cargo are so stowed that one can injure the other during the course of the voyage, the ship is unseaworthy. I am not prepared to accept that. It would be an extension of the meaning of 'unseaworthiness' going far beyond any reported case.
. . .

PHILLIMORE LJ: . . . The damage to this chocolate was either proved or admitted. I think — we have not heard counsel for the respondents fully on that point — that the nature of the damage was proved, at any rate, I assume it. I assume that this damage was taint of chocolate from cheese. In that case the cause of the damage was the negligent stowage of the cheese and chocolate in the same hold. . . . I take it we must suppose that it was done either by the master, the crew, the stevedores, or other servants or agents of the owners for whose negligence they have contracted not to be responsible.

The point taken in answer to that is that the stowage made the ship unseaworthy — not unseaworthy altogether, but unseaworthy quoad this parcel of cargo — unfit to carry it in the way in which it was proposed to carry it. Taking it as not proved that the cheese was there first, taking it as most probable that the cheese came there afterwards. I do not think that it made the ship unseaworthy quoad the chocolate. . . .

*Note and Question*
1.    Would it have made any difference if the cheese had been loaded first? How would the case then have differed from *Tattersall* v *National Steamship Co. Ltd* (1884) 12 QBD 297 (see section 4 below)?
2.    In *Ingram & Royle Ltd* v *Services Maritimes du Tréport Ltd* [1914] 1 KB 541, cases of metallic sodium, which was saturated with petrol, were put on deck insufficiently protected against contact with water. In the 'ordinary rough weather of the English Channel' a heavy sea came over the deck, causing the sodium to explode and ignite. There were fires in the hold and the engine room and the ship broke in two and sank. Scrutton J held that the vessel was not seaworthy and there was no appeal against the finding, though the decision was reversed on another point.

The relationship between stowage and seaworthiness was considered by the House of Lords in 1924.

### *Elder, Dempster & Co. Ltd* v *Paterson, Zochonis & Co. Ltd*
[1924] AC 522 (HL)

VISCOUNT CAVE: My Lords, the appellants Elder, Dempster & Co. Ltd, who are managers for the appellants the African Steam Ship Company and the British and African Steam Navigation Company Ltd, run to the West African ports a line of cargo steamers which carry West African produce. These vessels have their holds fitted with 'tween decks, so that goods stored in the lower part of the hold may be relieved from the weight of those stored in the upper part. The appellants Elder, Dempster & Co., requiring an additional vessel for the West African trade, chartered from the appellants the Griffiths Lewis Steam Navigation Company Ltd (whom I will refer to as 'the owners'), the steamship *Grelwen*, a ship of the Isherwood type containing deep holds but no 'tween decks. The *Grelwen* proceeded to the Sherbro River, where she loaded from the respondents Paterson, Zochonis & Co. Ltd, 297 casks or butts of palm oil, which were stowed in two or three tiers at the bottom of holds 2, 3 and 4. She also loaded there from the respondents and other shippers about 51,800 bags of palm kernels, which were stowed partly over the casks of palm oil in holds 2 and 4 (thus competely filling those holds) and partly in other parts of the ship. The vessel then proceeded to the port of Konakri, where she loaded from the respondents a further 147 butts of palm oil, which were stowed at the bottom of No. 3 hold, and also loaded from the respondents and others about 11,400 more bags of palm kernels, which were stowed partly over the palm oil in No. 3 hold (thus filling that hold) and partly elsewhere. She also loaded some piassava and other miscellaneous produce, which was stowed in the space between the main and shelter decks.

When the vessel arrived at Hull, which was her destination, it was found that the casks and butts of palm oil in holds 2, 3 and 4 had been crushed by the palm kernels stored above them, which were very heavy — it was stated in evidence that each cask had to carry 64 bags of palm kernels or nearly 6 tons in weight — and the greater part of the oil was lost or damaged. The casks must have begun to give way immediately after the palm kernels were stowed above them; for the log shows that before the vessel left the Sherbro River she had 3 feet of palm oil in the bilge well of No. 2 hold, and that before she left Konakri the same thing had happened in hold No. 3; but it is possible that the leakage continued after the vessel left port and was intensified by the rolling of the ship.

The respondents accordingly commenced this action against the appellants, claiming damages for breach of the contract entered into by the bills of lading under which the palm oil was shipped, or alternatively for negligence or breach of duty. The defendants at the trial attempted to prove that the casks and butts were frail or leaky; but this attempt failed, and it is not now denied that the damage was caused by the altogether unreasonable and excessive weight placed upon the casks. This being so, the contest resolved itself into the question whether the damage was due to bad stowage, or to the fact that the vessel was structurally unfit or unseaworthy for the carriage of the palm oil by reason of the depth of her holds and the absence of 'tween decks. It was not denied that if the damage was due to bad stowage the charterers are protected against liability by the conditions contained in the bills of lading; but if it was due to unseaworthiness, then it was contended (and I think rightly) that the charterers were not protected by any of the conditions of the bills of lading and were liable to make good the damage.

The action was tried by Rowlatt J, who held that, while the ship was well found for the purpose of traversing the sea she was 'not a ship, in the way she was prepared for this voyage, proper to carry these casks of palm oil'; and he added: 'This was a ship which was not a 'tween deck ship. It had a deep hold of a depth of 25 feet, and you cannot safely get in at the bottom of that hold casks of palm oil with any sort of cargo of dead weight or approaching dead weight of gravity on the top of it, and therefore it is a hold which you cannot put those casks in at the bottom, which is the place to put them. It could have been made proper for the stowage of such a cargo by the erection of what has been called a temporary 'tween deck or a platform, by the erection of something (to use perfectly plain and popular language) which would tend to keep the weight of the superincumbent cargo off the bilges of the barrels. That could have been done, and then the hold would have been fit to receive this cargo. That seems to me a fault which goes to the hold. It is not a fault which goes to the stowage as stowage. It is a fault which goes to the appliance for shipping the cargo safely, and makes the ship unseaworthy for the purpose of carrying this cargo on this voyage'. He accordingly gave judgment against all the defendants for damages and ordered an inquiry. On appeal the decision of the trial judge was affirmed by a majority of the Court of Appeal, consisting of Bankes LJ and Eve J; but Scrutton LJ dissented, holding that the damage was due to bad stowage. Scrutton LJ stated the principle as follows [1923] 1 KB 438: 'The ship must be fit at loading to carry the cargo the subject of the particular contract. If she is so fit, and the cargo when loaded does not make her unseaworthy, ... the fact that other cargo is so stowed as to endanger the contract cargo, is bad stowage on a seaworthy ship, not stowage of the contract cargo on an unseaworthy ship.' Thereupon the present appeal was brought.

My Lords, it was contended on behalf of the respondents that the finding of the trial judge was one of fact, and that as there was evidence to support that finding it should not now be disturbed. I do not think that this position can be maintained. The facts are not now seriously in dispute, and the question is substantially one of law — namely, what on those facts is the liability of the charterers and owners? — or at least one of mixed fact and law. I think, therefore, that the decision is open to review.

The general principles which should govern the decision are not in doubt. It is well settled that the shipowner or charterer who contracts to carry goods by sea thereby warrants, not only that the ship in which he proposes to carry them shall be seaworthy in the ordinary sense of the word — that is to say, that she shall be tight, staunch and strong, and reasonably fit to encounter whatever perils may be expected on the voyage — but also that both the ship and her furniture and equipment shall be reasonably fit for receiving the contract cargo and carrying it across the sea. . . .

Applying these principles to the present case, I have come to the conclusion that the damage complained of was not due to unseaworthiness but to improper stowage. If the fitness or unfitness of the ship is to be ascertained (as was held in *McFadden* v *Blue Star Line* [1905] 1 KB 697) at the time of loading, there can be no doubt about the matter. At the moment when the palm oil was loaded the *Grelwen* was unquestionably fit to receive and carry it. She was a well built and well found ship, and lacked no equipment necessary for the carriage of palm oil; and if damage arose, it was due to the fact that after the casks of oil had been stowed in the holds the master placed upon them a weight which no casks could be expected to bear. Whether he could have stowed the cargo in a different way without endangering the safety of the ship is a matter upon which the evidence is conflicting; but if that was impossible, he could have refused to accept some part of the kernels and the oil would then have travelled safely. No doubt that course might have rendered the voyage less profitable to the charterers, but that appears to me for present purposes to be immaterial. The important thing is that at the time of loading the palm oil the ship was fit to receive and carry it without injury; and if she did not do so this was due not to any unfitness in the ship or her equipment, but to another cause. . . .

LORD SUMNER: . . . I think that in effect the decisions in both Courts come to this. If the ship had been built on a different plan, if instead of being designed to have deep unobstructed holds she had been provided with 'tween decks or the means of erecting a substitute for 'tween decks, the oil casks would not have been crushed; but what is this except saying that if the ship had been so designed that those in charge of the stowage could not commit the particular blunder, which they did commit in stowing her, then this cargo would not have been damaged, at any rate in the particular way in which it was damaged? Of course, a ship perfectly fit to carry one cargo may be unfit to carry another and so be unseaworthy in that connection, but a ship does not become unseaworthy merely because her construction or appliances are not foolproof or because she does not carry about the world contrivances for preventing by anticipation the consequences of any want of care or skill, of which those in charge of the cargo may be guilty. If a captain, having a perfectly good hold at his disposal, puts cargo into it in the wrong way, or puts more cargo into it than is consistent with the safety of individual packages, the result is not that he makes his ship unseaworthy, but that he proves himself to be an imcompetent officer. One result of improper stowage is that damage will result thereby, and the cargo will be discharged at its destination more or less injured during the voyage, but such a loss is not caused by unseaworthiness merely because it happens during the voyage. It is the direct result of bad stowage, even though in a different ship that particular error in stowing could not have been committed.

... Bad stowage, which endangers the safety of the ship, may amount to unseaworthiness, of course, but bad stowage, which affects nothing but the cargo damaged by it, is bad stowage and nothing more, and still leaves the ship seaworthy for the adventure, even though the adventure be the carrying of that cargo.

There is a sense, but I think one sense only, in which the *Grelwen* might be said to have been unfit for the carriage of this cargo. One must distinguish between general fitness for what the nature of the trade requires and fitness to receive and carry a particular cargo or part of a cargo, tendered in the course of that trade. A ship, which in a certain trade and in certain not improbable combinations of cargo offering in the trade, has to shut out cargo and to sail less than a full ship, because if she takes the cargo offered she will thereby damage other cargo already loaded, is pro tanto an unprofitable ship. She is not as good a freight earner as she might be. For the cargo, however, that she does carry, without sacrificing it to enable her owners to carry more cargo and so earn more freight, she is perfectly fitted and quite seaworthy. All that can be said is that she might have paid better in another trade, or that another ship differently built might have paid better in the same trade. The *Grelwen* was not structurally unfitted for the West African trade, nor is that the question; but it may be that ships of another design might do better than she could. The circumstance, so much harped upon, that all Elder, Dempster & Co.'s own ships had 'tween decks is really accidental. Being better suited to the trade, they were more able to load full cargoes, however made up, but the point is not that they can carry palm-oil better than the *Grelwen*, but that they can carry palm kernels too. So far as I can see, if an entire cargo of palm kernels be assumed, the *Grelwen* is better fitted for its carriage than a 'tween deck ship would be, for, with her unencumbered holds and absence of 'tween decks to occupy cargo space, she can carry more palm kernels than a ship of the same deadweight capacity, equipped with 'tween decks. Really that is all.

Beyond all doubt, my Lords, the plaintiffs, the owners of the oil cargo, have been very badly used, and, as the oil was carried on terms which relieved the defendants from liability for bad stowage and only make them liable if the plaintiffs can show the ship to have been unseaworthy, I am very sensible of the temptation to do substantial justice by accepting a finding of unseaworthiness. The consequences of such a finding are, however, grave, since unseaworthiness affects not merely the contracts of carriage but the contracts of insurance. The unseaworthiness alleged consists in this, that a ship, unimpeached in herself, built to have holds unencumbered by transverse 'tween deck beams, is unfit to engage in the ordinary carrying trade of the West African coast, unless, in some mode or other, she is fitted with 'tween decks and so made structurally other than what she was designed and built to be. Accordingly I have thought it right to resist the impulse to take the injured plaintiffs' part and have ventured to examine the facts closely, lest I should arrive at a conclusion that would be seriously inconsistent with the way in which this class of ship is and necessarily must be employed in commerce. Ships built under the Isherwood patents are a numerous and, so far as I know, an accepted type of ship, and in their freedom from 'tween decks and 'tween deck beams, they have an advantage for carrying larger cargoes, which is part of their design. I shrink, as Scrutton LJ shrank, from saying on this evidence, that in the ordinary West African trade such a ship is an unseaworthy ship by reason of her construction and design. If the question had not been encumbered with the technicalities and refinements of modern bills of lading, it would not have occurred to any one acquainted with practical shipping to affirm that this ship was unseaworthy, or to dispute that her cargo was improperly stowed. I could have understood that it might be argued, perhaps paradoxically, that the ship was not reasonably fit to load and carry this oil, because she was in charge of a captain and mate who were without experience of such a cargo and knew their business no better than to overload the puncheons till they inevitably collapsed, but the argument, which actually has been advanced, is, I think, one which begins and ends with the circumstances that improper stowage is here the subject of an exception, unless the ship was what is called unseaworthy, whereby the loss occurred.

. . .

*Notes and Questions*
1.   Lord Carson and Lord Dunedin agreed with Viscount Cave and Lord Sumner. Viscount Finlay dissented, holding that the absence of 'tween decks made the vessel unseaworthy and that this was the cause of the damage.
2.   Why should Lord Sumner consider it 'paradoxical' to argue that the incompetence of the captain and mate might render the vessel unseaworthy?
3.   In *Smith, Hogg & Co.* v *Black Sea and Baltic General Insurance Co.* [1940] AC 997 (HL), the loading of an excessive deck cargo of timber, which caused the vessel to list during the voyage and to turn on her beam ends while bunkering, made her unseaworthy.

## SECTION 2: NATURE OF THE OBLIGATION AT COMMON LAW

At common law the obligation to provide a seaworthy vessel is 'absolute', i.e., there is a warranty that the vessel actually is fit, not merely that the owner has done his best to make her fit (see Lord Blackburn in *Steel* v *State Line Steamship Co.* (1877) 3 App Cas 72, above). The obligation attaches only to the commencement of the voyage, however, and is not a continuing obligation to maintain the vessel in a seaworthy state throughout the voyage.

### *McFadden* v *Blue Star Line*
[1905] 1 KB 697

M shipped cotton on the BS Line's vessel *Tolosa* for carriage from Wilmington to Bremen. After the cotton was loaded, the ship's engineer opened a sluice-door in a watertight bulkhead; he failed to make it watertight on closing it. He also opened a sea-cock in the ship's side to fill a ballast tank. He closed the sea-cock but, because some hard substance had got into it, water was in fact still flowing through when it appeared to be closed. This water forced a valve-chest which had been remade but inadequately packed before arrival at Wilmington. The cotton was damaged by water from the sluice-door and the valve-chest. (The bills of lading incorporated the Harter Act.)

CHANNELL J: I have to consider whether upon the facts of this case the shipowners are responsible for the damage to the plaintiff's cotton. Mr Bailhache rests his case upon a breach of the implied warranty of seaworthiness, or rather of the implied warranty that the vessel is fit for the reception of the goods and for carrying them upon the voyage in question. Now I think it is clear that, apart from the Harter Act, that warranty is an absolute warranty; that is to say, if the ship is in fact unfit at the time when the warranty begins, it does not matter that its unfitness is due to some latent defect which the shipowner does not know of, and it is no excuse for the existence of such a defect that he used his best endeavours to make the ship as good as it could be made. And there is also another matter which seems to me to be equally clear — that the warranty of seaworthiness in the ordinary sense of that term, the warranty, that is, that the ship is fit to encounter the ordinary perils of the voyage, is a warranty only as to the condition of the vessel at a particular time, namely, the time of sailing; it is not a continuing warranty, in the sense of a warranty that she shall continue fit during the voyage. If anything happens whereby the goods are damaged during the voyage, the shipowner is liable because he is an insurer except in the event of the damage happening from some cause in respect of which he is protected by the exceptions in his bill of lading. His liability for anything happening after the ship has sailed depends, not upon there being a breach of a warranty that the ship shall continue fit, but upon his position as carrier. So, too, it is clear that the warranty of the ship being fit to encounter the perils of the voyage does not attach before she sails and while she is still loading her cargo. There is, of course, no warranty at the time the goods are put on board that the ship is then ready to start on her voyage; for while she is still loading there may be many things requiring to be done before she is ready to sail. The ordinary warranty of seaworthiness, then, does not take effect before the ship is ready to sail, nor does it continue to take effect after she has sailed: it takes effect at the time of sailing, and at the time of sailing alone. But Mr Bailhache contends that the warranty with which we are here concerned, namely, that the ship was fit to receive the goods, differs in this respect from the warranty of fitness to encounter the perils of the voyage: he says that it is a continuing warranty, meaning thereby a warranty that the ship shall continue fit throughout the period of loading. Now there is very little authority about the warranty of fitness to receive the cargo; but when one comes to consider it as a matter of principle, I do not think there is much difficulty about it. In my opinion one must apply the rule which one would have to apply to the warranty of seaworthiness when the voyage is in stages. When a voyage is in stages the warranty is that the ship on starting on each particular stage is fit for that stage. Thus, if she is going to stop at an intermediate port, she must have sufficient coals to take her to that port, but she is not bound to have sufficient coals to take her the whole voyage. It is treated as a separate warranty for each stage of the voyage. I think one must apply exactly the same rule to the loading stage of a vessel whilst she remains in her port of loading. I think the warranty is that at the time the goods are put on board she is fit to receive them and to encounter the ordinary perils that are likely to arise during the loading stage; but that there is no continuing warranty after the goods are once on board that the ship shall continue fit to hold the goods during that stage and until she is ready to go to sea, notwithstanding any accident that may happen to her in the meantime. And the reason for so holding is precisely the same as that which exists with respect to the warranty of fitness to encounter the perils of the voyage; as soon as the goods are on board they are in the custody of the carrier, and he is liable for any accident which then happens because he is an insurer of them unless he is protected by some clause in his bill of lading. In that view of the matter, then, I proceed to consi̇ er whether the facts of the present case shew a breach of the warranty of fitness to rece ve the cargo. If there was such a breach, I think it is clear that the exceptions in the bill of lading would not apply to exempt the defendants from liability; for prima facie words of exception are intended to exempt the shipowner only from his liability as a carrier, and not to affect the warranty that would otherwise be implied. An intention to exclude the warranty must be indicated by express words, and there are no such express words here. Now it is suggested by the plaintiff that there was a breach of the warranty in respect of each of the three apertures through which the water came. The sluice-door in the bulkhead was left insufficiently screwed down, and if it had been left in that condition before the goods were loaded I think that that fact would have amounted to a breach of the warranty; for it was an aperture which in the ordinary state of things ought to have been closed except when it was being used, and it was imperfectly closed. It was not obviously left open, and was consequently a source of danger. Thus it is a breach of warranty of seaworthiness to go to sea with a porthole which is improperly closed but is believed to be closed, and which is in such a position that the defect cannot be remedied immediately and in time to prevent the damage being done: *Dobell* v *Steamship Rossmore Co.* [1895] 2 QB 408. But here the opening and imperfect closing of the sluice-door only took place the day before the damage happened, and long after the goods were on board. Therefore, in my opinion, it cannot amount to a breach of the warranty as I have interpreted it. The same observations apply to the insufficiently closed sea-cock. It was intended to be closed and was apparently closed, and was consequently in a dangerous condition. But that state of things also was brought about after the goods were on board, and consequently was not a breach of the warranty. Then we come to the defective packing of the valve-chest. It may be that that is a defect which points to a certain amount of negligence on the part of the man who packed the joint, but it is immaterial for the present purpose to consider whether there was negligence or not, for, as I have already said, the warranty is, apart from any consideration of the Harter Act, an absolute warranty. The result shews that in fact there was a defect, in the sense that the packing was not as good as it ought to have been. It resisted the pressure during the three hours that the tank was being hardened up, but was insufficient to resist the subsequent pressure. That defect, unlike those in the sluice-door and the sea-cock, existed before the plaintiff's goods were loaded. Whether a particular defect is sufficiently substantial to amount to a breach of the warranty must in all cases be a question of fact; but it is a question of fact which must be determined by certain rules. And the rule applicable to the present case is, I think, correctly stated in a passage in *Carver on Carriage by Sea*, s. 18, where it is said that a vessel 'must have that degree of fitness which an ordinary careful and prudent owner would require his vessel to have at the commencement of her voyage having regard to all the probable circumstances of it. To that extent the shipowner, as we have seen, undertakes absolutely that she is fit, and ignorance is no excuse. If the defect existed, the question to be put is, Would a prudent owner have required that it should be made good before sending his ship to sea had he known of it? If he would, the ship was not seaworthy within the meaning of the undertaking'. Applying that to this case, I cannot doubt tha' any prudent owner, if he had known that the joint would not resist something more than a three hours' pressure, would have at once ordered the joint to be remade. Therefore, it seems to me that I must hold that the defect was a substantial one, and that as it existed before and at the time of the loading of the goods it amounted to a breach of the warranty . . .

*Note and Questions*
1.   Channell J went on to hold that the incorporation of the Harter Act did not affect the position, but this is clearly inconsistent with the House of Lords' decision in *Adamastos Shipping Co. Ltd* v *Anglo-Saxon Petroleum Co. Ltd* [1959] AC 133 and must be regarded as wrong. On this aspect, and for the contrasting provision in the Hague-Visby Rules, see further Chapter 7.

*2.* Is Channell J's explanation for the absence of a continuing obligation convincing? Why should the shipper or charterer bear the risk of the vessel becoming unseaworthy during the voyage? What can they do about it?

*3.* For cargoworthiness the relevant time is the *commencement* of loading: the vessel must be fit at that point to receive and carry the cargo, whether or not she is seaworthy in a seagoing sense. See *A.E. Reed & Co. Ltd* v *Page, Son and East Ltd* [1927] 1 KB 743 (CA), below.

*4.* Charterparties today typically replace the common law absolute, but non-continuing, warranty of seaworthiness by continuing (non-absolute) obligations based on due diligence.

This narrow approach to the warranty of seaworthiness is modified by the doctrine of 'stages'.

### The Vortigern
### [1899] P 140 (CA)

The *Vortigern* was chartered for a voyage at a lump sum freight from the Philippines to Liverpool. She took on coal in Colombo, but the engineer miscalculated the quantity needed and it was only by burning 50 tons of copra from the cargo mixed with the remaining coal (down to the last sack!), that the *Vortigern* reached Suez, where she could obtain bunkers for the rest of the voyage. The charterers withheld part of the freight and in the owners' action for it the charterers claimed to set off the value of the copra burned and admitted liability for the balance of £20, which they paid into court. Gorell Barnes J and the Court of Appeal held that the owners were in breach of the warranty of seaworthiness and the charterers were therefore not liable for the outstanding freight.

A.L. SMITH LJ: This is an action by the owners of the steamship *Vortigern* to recover from the defendants the sum of 610*l.* 18*s.* 4*d.*, being for freight under a charterparty dated August 6, 1897. The defence is that a portion of the defendants' cargo, consisting of copra — a species of coconut — had during the voyage been burnt by the master as fuel for the ship; and that this burning of the cargo had taken place in consequence of the breach of the implied warranty of seaworthiness which attached to the contract of affreightment at the commencement of the voyage — that is, that coal necessary for the due prosecution of the voyage had not been taken on board when the ship commenced the chartered voyage, and the cargo had, therefore, to be used as fuel in the place of coal.

This defence depends upon a point of law and a question of fact.

The value of the cargo burnt equalled the freight claimed, excepting as to 20*l.*, which was paid into court by the defendants. The charterparty was in the ordinary form, and was for a voyage by the plaintiffs' steamship from Cebu, in the Philippine Islands, to Liverpool, calling at Marseilles if ordered. By the charterparty the steamship had liberty to call at any ports in any order, and by the charterparty dangers of navigation or machinery, negligence, default or error in judgment of the owners, pilot, master and crew, or other servants of the shipowner were excepted.

The question of law is what implied warranty of seaworthiness attaches to a contract of affreightment upon a voyage such as the present, when, from the necessity of the case, the ship cannot start upon the chartered voyage with an equipment of coal on board sufficient for the whole voyage, if the ship is to be a cargo-carrying vessel, which it clearly was the intention of all parties that it should be.

It cannot be denied that the implied warranty which prima facie attaches to a charterparty such as the present is that the ship shall be seaworthy for the voyage at the time of sailing, by which is meant that the vessel shall then be in a fit state as to repairs, equipment, and crew, and in all other respects, sufficient to take her in ordinary circumstances to her port of destination, though there is no warranty that the ship shall continue seaworthy during the voyage.

That coals are part of the equipment of a steamship I do not doubt, and if the voyage in this case had been an ordinary voyage, as to which there was no necessity, as regards taking in coal, for dividing it into stages, it cannot be denied that the steamship was unseaworthy when she started from Cebu on her voyage to Liverpool, for the simple reason that she had not then on board an equipment of coal sufficient to take her in ordinary circumstances to her port of destination.

To obviate this difficulty — and a great difficulty it is in cases of long voyages of cargo-carrying steamships, for it is manifest that no cargo-carrying steamship can ever be seaworthy when she starts upon such a voyage as the present, by reason of the impossibility of her having on board such an equipment of coal as will be sufficient to take her to the port of destination — it has become the practice, by reason of the necessity of the case, for cargo-carrying steamship owners to divide these long voyages into stages for the purpose of replenishing their ships with coal, and thus, as far as practicable, complying with the warranty of seaworthiness which attached when the ship commenced her voyage.

This practice was resorted to in the present case, for I find by the engineer's log that the voyage was divided into stages, and it appears from the average adjustment that the cargo owners subsequently acquiesced therein, the first stage being from Cebu to Colombo in Ceylon, the second from Colombo to Suez, and the third from Suez to Liverpool. At Colombo the ship accordingly called, and took in coal for the second stage; but the learned judge has found, and there certainly was evidence to support his finding, that the ship did not at Colombo take in a sufficiency of coal for the second stage to Suez, and thus, by reason of the coal falling short whilst passing up the Red Sea, the defendants' copra was resorted to in order to carry the ship on to Suez, where she again coaled, and so was enabled to perform her chartered voyage to Liverpool.

...

I come to the point of law, which is this: what was the implied warranty, if any — it matters not whether it is called a warranty or an absolute condition — when the ship started upon the second stage from Colombo to Suez? Was there then an implied warranty that she had a sufficiency of coal on board for this second stage, that is, that she was seaworthy for that stage? This is the real point in the case. The shipowners assert that there is no such warranty, and that the sole obligation they were then under to the cargo owners was that their master and crew should not negligently omit to take in coal at Colombo, or during the stages subsequent to the first stage, and that, although the ship might during the second stage in this case have put into Perim and obtained coal, and although it might be negligence for the master and crew not to have done so, as negligence of the master and crew is excepted by the charterparty, the shipowners are not liable to the cargo owners for having burnt up their cargo for fuel as they did.

Now, reduce this contention of the shipowners into a concrete case, to see what in practice it amounts to. Take, for instance, the case of a cargo-carrying steamship commencing a voyage of some 5,000 miles in length, and the shipowners for coaling purposes, by reason of the necessity of the case, having to divide the voyage into five stages of 1,000 miles each. The shipowners must admit that they warrant to the cargo owners that their ship has a sufficiency of coal on board for the whole voyage, when it commences that voyage; but they assert that by reason of their dividing the voyage into stages, although for their own purposes, this warranty is thus cut down to the first stage of 1,000 miles, and that as regards the residue of the stages, 4,000 miles in all, there is no warranty that the ship has a single ton of coal on board, and that the only liability they are under to the cargo owners during the residue of the voyage is for the negligence, if any, of their master and crew, for not taking coal on board when they might have done so; and as the negligence of the master and crew is excepted by the charterparty, the shipowners are under no liability whatever to the cargo owners during the transit of the 4,000 miles. I am asked to hold that this is the true meaning of the charterparty in the present case. I certainly cannot do so. On the other hand, the contention of the cargo owners is that, whether the shipowners divide the chartered voyage into stages or not for coaling purposes, that has nothing to do with them; but if, from the necessity of the case, the shipowners do so, the cargo owners in no way abandon the undoubted warranty they have at the commencement of the voyage.

The only way in which this warranty can be complied with is for the shipowners to extend the existing warranty to the commencement of each stage, and I can see no reason why such a warranty should not be implied, and I have no difficulty in making the implication, for it is the only way in which the clear intention of the parties can be carried out, and the undoubted and admitted warranty complied with. It appears to me to be no answer to say that it is a warranty subsequent to the commencement of the voyage.

In my judgment when a question of seaworthiness arises between either a steamship owner and his underwriter upon a voyage policy, or between a steamship owner and a cargo owner upon a contract of affreightment, and the underwriter or cargo owner establishes that the ship at the commencement of the voyage was not equipped with a sufficiency of coal for the whole of the contracted voyage, it lies upon the shipowner, in order to displace this defence, which is a good one, to prove that he had divided the voyage into stages for coaling purposes by reason of the necessity of the case, and that, at the commencement of each stage, the ship had on board a sufficiency of coal for that stage — in other words, was seaworthy for that stage. If he fails in this he fails in defeating the issue of unseaworthiness which prima facie has been established against him. In each case it is a matter for proof as to where the necessity of the case requires that each stage should be, and I think that in the present case the necessity for coaling places at Colombo and Suez has been established.

*Note*

The doctrine of stages has also been applied to operations which are prior to the carrying voyage in a strict sense, but are incidental to it.

### A.E. Reed & Co. Ltd v Page, Son and East Ltd
[1927] 1 KB 743 (CA)

LORD HEWART CJ: The plaintiffs employed the lightermen to lighter 500 tons of wood pulp from the steamship *Borgholm*, when it arrived at Erith Buoys, to Nine Elms, upon a journey to Farncombe. For that purpose the appellants sent three barges, named respectively the *Jellicoe*, the *May* and the *Jessie*, which between them had a carrying capacity of 500 tons and more. The persons actually engaged in discharging the cargo from the ship were in the employment of the defendant stevedore. Those responsible for the stowing of the cargo were the persons in the lighters, but they in their turn employed the stevedore to carry out the stowage on their behalf.

The first lighter to be filled was the *Jellicoe*, which had a capacity to carry 170 tons and no more. The loading of that barge was in progress on December 17, 1925. In the result, more than 170 tons were put upon the *Jellicoe*; in fact some 190 tons were loaded, and that quantity was, as the learned judge finds, and as I think is common ground, excessive. What followed was that some time before midnight the *Jellicoe* filled and sank, and her cargo of 190 tons of wood pulp was lost. It was in respect of that loss that the plaintiffs sought to recover damages.

It was made clear by the evidence, nor is it disputed, that the *Jellicoe* at all material times exhibited certain cracks, and as the process of loading went on and became completed, those cracks became, through perhaps more causes than one, both larger and more dangerous. . . .

[Roche J's decision that the barge was unseaworthy was affirmed.]

SCRUTTON LJ: There is some confusion in the authorities as to the warranty of seaworthiness, due, I think, to two causes: first, the word 'seaworthiness' is used in two senses: (1) fitness of the ship to enter on the contemplated adventure of navigation, and (2) fitness of the ship to receive the contemplated cargo, as a carrying receptacle. A ship may be unfit to carry the contemplated cargo, because, for instance, she has not sufficient means of ventilation, and yet be quite fit to make the contemplated voyage, as a ship. Secondly, the fact that there are these two meanings of seaworthiness, and that there may be different stages of seaworthiness according to different stages of the adventure, has led to some confusion in statements.

As was said in *Cohn* v *Davidson* (1877) 2 QBD 455, 461: 'Seaworthiness is well understood to mean that measure of fitness which the particular voyage or particular stage of the voyage requires.' A ship, when she sails on her voyage, must be seaworthy for that voyage, that is, fit to encounter the ordinary perils which a ship would encounter on such a voyage. But she need not be fit for the voyage before it commences, and when she is loading in port. It is enough if, before she sails, she has completed her equipment and repair. But she must be fit as a ship for the ordinary perils of lying afloat in harbour, waiting to sail. She must, in my view, be fit as a ship, as distinguished from a carrying warehouse, at each stage of her contract adventure, which may, as in *Cohn* v *Davidson* 2 QBD 455, commence before loading. And she may as a ship after loading be unfit to navigate because of her stowage, which renders her unsafe as a ship. *Kopitoff* v *Wilson* (1876) 1 QBD 377 is a good example of this. . . .

Looked at from the point of view of a ship to sail the sea the highest measure of liability will be when she starts on her sea voyage, and this is often spoken of as the stage when the warranty attaches; but what is meant is that it is the time when that highest measure of liability attaches. There are previous stages of seaworthiness as a ship, applicable to proceeding to loading port, loading, and waiting to sail when loading is completed.

On the other hand, the highest measure of liability as a cargo-carrying adventure, that is, of 'cargoworthiness', is when cargo is commenced to be loaded. It has been decided that if at this stage the ship is fit to receive her contract cargo, it is immaterial that when she sails on her voyage, though fit as a ship to sail, she is unfit by reason of stowage to carry her cargo safely. . . .

It was argued that the doctrine of stages was only a question of difference of equipment, and that overloading was not equipment. But damages unrepaired at the commencement of a new stage, collision during loading, and starting on the voyage with that damage unrepaired, may obviously be unseaworthiness at the commencement of the voyage stage. I see no reason for defining stages only by difference of equipment.

Applying the above statement of the law to the facts of the present case: the barge was sent to the ship's side to carry 170 tons, and she was fit to carry that quantity. The warranty of cargoworthiness was complied with when loading commenced. But then 190 tons were put into her, some 14 per cent more than her proper load. With that cargo in, she had a dangerously low freeboard in calm water. I think at any rate one of her gunwales was awash, and water could continuously enter through cracks, which would be only an occasional source of leakage if she were properly loaded. She had to lie so loaded for some unascertained time in the river till a tug came. The ship was not bound to let the barge lie moored to the ship's side. She might have to navigate under oars to a barge road. She was exposed to all the wash of passing vessels, and the more water she took on board, the more dangerous she would become. It is clear that she was quite unfit to lie in the river for any time exposed to the wash of passing vessels and the natural 'send' of the water. It is still clearer that she was quite unfit to be towed, and that she was in such a condition that she would soon go to the bottom. I am clearly of opinion that the barge was unseaworthy as a barge from the time loading finished, unfit to lie in the river, and still more unfit to be towed. I observe with surprise the suggestion that the surplus of 115 bales might have been put back on the ship. What possible obligation the ship which had delivered to a barge cargo which the bargeman said she could take, and had got a receipt for it, was under to hoist back by ship's steam and labour 115 bales, or 20 tons, and leave them about on the ship's deck, I cannot understand.

I accept the view of Channell J in *McFadden* v *Blue Star Line* [1905] 1 KB 697 that the warranty of cargoworthiness, if complied with at the commencement of a stage, is not continuous during the stage, but this view does not negative the position that at the commencement of a new stage of the adventure there is a renewed warranty of seaworthiness as a ship. It seems to me clear that there would be a renewed warranty when the towage started, and that this overloading would be a breach of the warranty. . . .

. . . It seems equally clear that if an overloaded barge, seaworthy in the calm waters of a dock, went out into the river to wait for a tug, there would be a renewed warranty of fitness to navigate and wait, which would be broken by overloading rendering the barge unfit to lie waiting in the river. And I think in the present case, when the loading was finished and the man in charge, apparently in the ordinary course of his business, left her unattended in the river waiting for a tug, and unfit in fact either to lie in the river or be towed, there was a new stage of the adventure, a new warranty of fitness for that stage, and a breach of that warranty which prevented the exceptions from applying.

*Note*

In *C. Wilh. Svenssons Travaruaktiebolag* v *Cliffe SS Co.* [1932] 1 KB 490 (KBD, Wright J), because the vessel (the *Headcliffe*) had a list to port while the cargo of pit props was being loaded, the last few remaining slings were put on the starboard side. The vessel then listed to starboard, the cargo shifted and carried away the bulwarks, so that a large part of the cargo shot overboard. The cargo owners contended that the vessel had passed from the stage of loading to the next stage, relying on *Reed* v *Page*. It was held that the loading stage was not complete until the cargo was stored and probably not until it was lashed as well. Accordingly, as the unfitness to receive the cargo arose after the commencement of the stage, the carriers were not liable, the vessel was seaworthy and the carrier's negligence was covered by an exemption clause.

## SECTION 3: THE BURDEN OF PROOF

The onus of proving unseaworthiness is clearly on the party alleging it: it is not for the shipowner to show that the vessel was seaworthy. How ready will the courts be to infer unseaworthiness from an unexplained casualty?

### *Fiumana Societa di Navigazione* v *Bunge and Co. Ltd*
[1930] 2 KB 47 (KBD)

B & Co. were the indorsees of the bills of lading in respect of a cargo of maize shipped on the *Alberto Fassini* in Argentina. The *Alberto Fassini* bunkered at Rotterdam for the round trip to the River Plate and back. Ten weeks after she left Rotterdam, and four days after loading of the maize began, fires broke out in the bunkers. The shipowners now claimed a general average contribution from the cargo-owners, which B & Co. resisted on the ground (*inter alia*) that the vessel was unseaworthy.

WRIGHT J: ... I think the true inference is that these fires which occurred in four different bunker spaces almost simultaneously in each pair of instances, upper and lower bunkers, were mainly governed by the common factors, the class of coal, the long voyage, the long stay at the Plate, especially in the roads at Villa Constitucion, all of which conditions had existed before loading either at Santa Fe or San Nicolas. In my judgment there was a defect in the coal at these dates of loading which did in fact result in fires, though perhaps in other similar cases no fires have occurred. I cannot regard the concurrences as a result of mere casual and sudden and sporadic conditions in coal otherwise free from any liability to spontaneous combustion. On this finding the ship was unfit to receive the cargo, and indeed, the voyage could not be proceeded with, as the claim for general average admits, until labour, time and money was expended to make her fit for the voyage. Prima facie, therefore, she was unseaworthy.
...
The onus of establishing unseaworthiness is on the defendants, but I have held that the onus is satisfied, as I understand the facts, having regard to the way these two pairs of fires occurred, their extent and the history of the coals from shipment at Rotterdam. Sir Robert Aske has contended that the mere unexplained occurrence of these fires is in itself sufficient to establish unseaworthiness on the same principles as in the case of a ship which sinks soon after leaving port with no weather or other circumstances to account for her loss. In that case unseaworthiness may be presumed: *Pickup* v *Thames and Mersey Marine Insurance Co.* (1878) 3 QBD 594, 600. In the present case nothing happened at or after loading the maize except what would normally be expected to occur. On this ground also I think that it is a reasonable presumption that it was the condition of the coal, and that alone, which caused the fires, thus arguing a defect or unfitness in the coal amounting to a breach of warranty.

*Note*
In *Aktieselskabet De Danske Sukkerfabrikker* v *Bajamar Compania Naviera SA (The Torenia)* [1983] 2 Lloyd's Rep 210 (QBD), Hobhouse J considered that the sinking of the vessel in weather conditions which were 'well within the contemplation and expectation of the vessel's owners and crew as liable to be

encountered at some stage during the voyage' raised an inference of unseaworthiness:

> Whereas in the days of wooden ships or in the days when the design of steel
> ships and their construction was less advanced or the forces they were liable
> to encounter were less well known and understood there may have been
> many instances where unexplained losses at sea gave rise to no inference of
> unseaworthiness, it will now be rare for such an inference not to arise in the
> absence of some overwhelming force of the sea or some occurrence affecting
> the vessel from outside.

*Question*
At the end of a voyage from Africa to Europe it is found that the cargo has been
damaged by seawater which entered through a leaking seam in the vessel's
plating. The leak is probably the result of an impact making an 'indent', but it
is not known whether this happened before or after the cargo was loaded. Can
the cargo-owner rely on unseaworthiness? (Cf. *The Hellenic Dolphin* [1978]
2 Lloyd's Rep 336 (QBD, Lloyd J): the plaintiffs there did not help their cause
by omitting to have the logbooks translated from the original Greek.)

## SECTION 4: UNSEAWORTHINESS AND EXCEPTION CLAUSES

The courts lean strongly against applying exception clauses to loss caused by
unseaworthiness.

### *The Christel Vinnen*
### [1924] P 208 (CA)

SCRUTTON LJ: The judgment I am about to read is to be taken as the judgment of
the Court.

The *Christel Vinnen*, a steel motor schooner built by Messrs Krupps, on her first cargo
carrying voyage sprang a leak and put back to Rio. Water entering through the leak
damaged her cargo of maize, but much less damage would have been done — the judge
finds only half the actual damage — had those on board been ordinarily careful in taking
soundings. They were negligent, and did not discover water in the hold until long after
they ought to have been aware of it.

The leak was through a rivet hole from which the rivet had dropped out. As there was
no sign of straining on any adjacent rivets, I agree with the view of the judge below that
the rivet was a defective rivet when the voyage started, and that, therefore, the ship was
unseaworthy.

The shipowner sued by the cargo owner for damage to the maize replies that he is
protected by the exceptions: 'damage occasioned by a latent defect in the hull ... even
where occasioned by the negligence of the servants of the shipowner'. It is clear law that
exceptions do not apply to protect the shipowner who furnishes an unseaworthy ship
where the unseaworthiness causes damage, unless the exceptions are so worded as
clearly to exclude or vary the implied warranty of seaworthiness. *Owners of Cargo on
board S.S. Waikato* v *New Zealand Shipping Co.* [1899] 1 QB 56, 58 is an instance of
ambiguity defeating the shipowner's probable intention: see the judgment of Collins LJ.

In *The Cargo ex Laertes* 12 PD 187 the words which protected the shipowners were 'latent defects in machinery even existing at the time of shipment'. Such words are absent in the present case and latent defects may come into existence during the voyage. In my view the shipowner here had not clearly excluded or modified the implied warranty of seaworthiness, and consequently the exception does not apply to protect him when water entering through unseaworthiness causes the damage, as is undoubtedly the case as to half the damage here. The shipowner's appeal against the judgment below, holding him liable for half the damage, therefore fails.

### *Petrofina SA of Brussels* v *Compagnia Italiana Trasporto Olii Minerali of Genoa*
### (1937) 53 TLR 650 (CA)

The cargo of benzine was found to be disoloured on delivery because of a failure to clean the tanks sufficiently. Clause 16 of the charterparty stated that the captain was 'bound to keep the tanks ... always clean', and cl. 27 provided, 'Steamer to clean for the cargo to the satisfaction of charterers' inspector'. The inspector had been satisfied and the umpire found that there was no want of due diligence on the part of the owners. Both Singleton J and the Court of Appeal found that the shipowners were in breach of the (express) warranty of seaworthiness.

LORD WRIGHT MR: We are dealing with a contract of affreightment, and it is necessary to bear in mind the well-established view which has been so often stated, that if it is sought to effect a reduction of the overriding obligation to provide a seaworthy ship, whether that is express or implied for this purpose does not matter, by other express terms of the charterparty or contract of affreightment, that result can only be achieved if perfectly clear, effective, and precise words are used expressly stating that limitation. I think that the language of clause 27 here is not sufficient. To make it sufficient I think it would need to be amplified in something like this manner. It would have to run: 'Steamer to clean for the cargo in question to the satisfaction of the charterers' inspector and if that is done that shall be treated as fulfilment of the obligations under clauses 1 and 16.' Clause 27 does not say so. I think, on the contrary, it has a much more limited effect. It gives, as I think, an added right to the charterers. They are entitled before they load the cargo to have an inspection, and to have a certificate, or whatever the form of the evidence is, that their inspector is satisfied. But, without express words, the satisfaction of the inspector cannot be relied on by the owners as a discharge and fulfilment of their obligations. From the point of view of the charterers this superadded right is something which it is worth their while to have. It gives them some sort of guarantee against their being involved in questions such as this, where, unfortunately, notwithstanding the inspection, there had been a failure to provide tanks sufficiently clean and in proper condition.

ROMER LJ: It is inherent in construction to give effect, where it is possible, to every part of a written document, none the less because the document happens to be a charterparty. In the present case, therefore, we must give effect both to clause 16 and to clause 27 of this charterparty, if it be possible. In my opinion, it is possible. In clause 16 the owner undertakes to keep the tanks, pipes, and pumps of the steamer always clean. In construing clause 27 you must do so with the knowledge of the fact that by clause 16 that obligation has been undertaken in plain terms by the owner. That being so, it is plain that the true construction of clause 27 is this — that the owner is saying: 'I have by clause 16 undertaken in plain terms the obligation of keeping the tanks clean. Not only will I keep the tanks clean, but I will keep them clean to the satisfaction of the charterers' inspector.' The result is that the owner can only discharge his obligations in respect of cleaning under the charterparty by cleaning the tanks, keeping them clean, and doing so to the satisfaction of the charterers' inspector. If he keeps them clean, and does not obtain the approval of the charterers' inspector, he has not fulfilled his contract. Nor has he fulfilled his contract if he fails to keep them clean but the charterers' inspector has expressed his approval of the state of the tanks. (© Times Newspapers Ltd 1937.)

*Notes*
1. This decision was applied recently in *Sacor Maritima SA* v *Repsol Petroleo SA* [1998] 1 Lloyd's Rep 518 (Mance, J).
2. In *Atlantic Shipping and Trading Co. Ltd* v *Louis Dreyfus & Co.* [1922] 2 AC 250, the House of Lords held that a clause requiring claims to be made within three months of final discharge did not apply to claims in respect of unseaworthiness. Lord Sumner said:

The shipowners' general liability in respect of damage due to the ship's unseaworthiness, accordingly, remains where the law places it. Underlying the whole contract of affreightment there is an implied condition upon the operation of the usual exceptions from liability — namely, that the shipowners shall have provided a seaworthy ship. If they have, the exceptions apply and relieve them; if they have not, and damage results in consequence of the unseaworthiness, the exceptions are construed as not being applicable for the shipowners' protection in such a case

and approved the decision in *Tattersall* v *The National Steamship Co. Ltd* (1884) 12 QBD 297 (QBD, Div Ct). There the plaintiff's cattle were infected with foot and mouth disease because of the failure of the defendants to clean and disinfect the ship after the previous voyage. The defendants relied on exceptions (a) that they were to be 'in no way responsible for ... disease or mortality', and (b) that 'under no circumstances [were they to] be held liable for more than £5 for each of the animals'. The clauses were construed as applying only to 'the contract so far as it refers to the carriage of goods upon the voyage' and not to anything 'before the commencement of the voyage', such as the shipowner's primary obligation to have the ship reasonably fit to receive the goods.
3. Even an exception which refers specifically to unseaworthiness will fail if it is 'so ill thought out and expressed that it is not possible to feel sure what the parties intended to stipulate': *Nelson Line (Liverpool) Ltd* v *James Nelson & Sons Ltd* [1908] AC 16, per Lord Loreburn LC at p. 19. The Earl of Halsbury added the following observation (at p. 20):

... Lord Blackburn used to say that the contest between commercial men and lawyers was that the commercial men always wished to write it short and the lawyers always wished to write it long; but a mixture of the two renders the whole thing unintelligible....

## SECTION 5: EFFECT OF BREACH OF THE OBLIGATION

### *The Europa*
[1908] P 84 (PD, Div Ct)

The *Europa* was chartered to carry sugar in bags from Stettin to Liverpool. There was an exception for 'collision'. When entering the dock at Liverpool the vessel struck the dock wall. The blow fractured a pipe and water from the pipe ran into the 'tween decks, damaging the sugar stowed there. Water from the broken pipe also passed through some old scupper holes in the 'tween decks, which had not been properly plugged after the pipes to the bilges were detached, and damaged bags of sugar in the lower hold. The shipowners admitted that the damage to the sugar in the lower hold was caused by unseaworthiness, but relied on the exception for collision in respect of the sugar in the 'tween decks. The county court judge held in favour of the cargo-owners, on the ground that breach of the obligation of seaworthiness deprived the shipowner of the benefit of all exceptions. The Divisional Court allowed the shipowners' appeal.

BUCKNILL J: We have to decide whether 'seaworthiness' is to be classed with non-deviation as a condition precedent, the non-performance of which voids the contract of affreightment, so that in the case of the *Europa*, she being unseaworthy, even though she had carried all the cargo specified in the bill of lading to the proper destination, yet could not claim exemption from liability for damage caused, not by the unseaworthiness, but by a peril of the seas or other exception in the bill of lading.

Except so far as appears in the judgment of the Court of Appeal in *The Orchis* [1907] 1 KB 660, we have not found any case where such a proposition has been enunciated, if it was, which we doubt. As between shipowner and charterer it may be that representations or promises made by the one or the other, or by both, may amount to warranties and be also conditions precedent which may give to that one who is not in default a right to treat the representation or promise of the other as a condition precedent, and to refuse to be bound to the performance of his own part of the contract. For example, if a shipowner enters into a charterparty with a merchant to go to a specified port or place and there to load a cargo, and when the ship arrives the charterer finds that the ship is not seaworthy, he may, if he be so minded, refuse to put his goods on board on the ground that the shipowner has not provided a seaworthy ship, and the shipowner could not oblige him to, because he himself had not performed on his part the condition which was precedent to his being able to oblige the charterer to load. But if the cargo was loaded and carried to its destination, even although it was damaged through the unseaworthiness, the remedy in the hands of the charterer is, in our judgment, to sue the shipowner for those damages, in answer to which he could not avail himself of the charterparty or bill of lading which, had his ship been seaworthy, would have been a protection to him. To that extent they would be useless to him.

In our opinion there must be a time when the charterer or cargo-owner has no longer a right to treat the promise or warranty of the shipowner as a condition precedent, but must rely on his breach of warranty, and must then prove that the damage sued for has been caused by the unseaworthiness of the ship at the material time.

. . .

We now come to the most anxious part of our judgment, and that is, whether Lord Collins did say in *The Orchis* [1907] 1 KB 660 that the same considerations must apply in the case of a warranty of seaworthiness in a charterparty between shipowner and charterer, as in the case of a policy of insurance on ship or goods, where such a warranty is made expressly or by implication. The conclusion to which we have come is that he neither said it, nor does it appear to us that he meant to say it. Reading his judgment as a whole, we think he had in his mind the analogy between a deviation and the warranty of seaworthiness in a policy of insurance . . .

For these reasons we are of opinion that *The Orchis* is not a case that can properly be relied on as an authority justifying the judgment of the county court judge from whose decision this appeal comes, and in our judgment the plaintiffs are only entitled to recover from the defendants such damages as directly resulted from the want of seaworthiness and not for the damage caused by the water which got into the 'tween decks through the collision between the ship and the dock wall, which was covered by the excepted perils in the charterparty, and to the protection of which the shipowner was still entitled, notwithstanding the unseaworthiness of the vessel. . . .

*Notes*
1.   *The Europa* was approved by the House of Lords in *J & E Kish* v *Charles Taylor, Sons & Co.* [1912] AC 604, 616 (Lord Atkinson, with whom the other Lords agreed).
2.   It is sufficient for the cargo-owner to establish that unseaworthiness was *a* cause of the loss: it does not have to be shown that unseaworthiness was the sole cause. *Cf. Smith, Hogg & Co. Ltd* v *Black Sea and Baltic General Insurance Co. Ltd* [1940] AC 997 (HL), where the shipowners argued that the act, neglect or default of the master was the real cause, so as to come within an exception. Lord Wright said:

. . . I can draw no distinction between cases where the negligent conduct of the master is a cause and cases in which any other cause, such as perils of the seas, or fire, is a co-operating cause. A negligent act is as much a co-operating cause, if it is a cause at all, as an act which is not negligent. The question is the same in either case, it is, would the disaster not have happened if the ship had fulfilled the obligation of seaworthiness, even though the disaster could not have happened if there had not also been the specific peril or action.

In the modern analysis the obligation to provide a seaworthy vessel is not a condition of the contract, but an 'innominate' or 'intermediate' term.

### *Hongkong Fir Shipping Co. Ltd* v *Kawasaki Kisen Kaisha Ltd*
[1962] 2 QB 26 (CA)

The facts are stated in section 1, above.

DIPLOCK LJ: Every synallagmatic contract contains in it the seeds of the problem: in what event will a party be relieved of his undertaking to do that which he has agreed to do but has not yet done? The contract may itself expressly define some of these events, as in the cancellation clause in a charterparty; but, human prescience being limited, it seldom does so exhaustively and often fails to do so at all. In some classes of contracts such as sale of goods, marine insurance, contracts of affreightment evidenced by bills of lading and those between parties to bills of exchange, Parliament has defined by statute some of the events not provided for expressly in individual contracts of that class; but where an event occurs the occurrence of which neither the parties nor Parliament have expressly stated will discharge one of the parties from further performance of his undertakings, it is for the court to determine whether the event has this effect or not.

The test whether an event has this effect or not has been stated in a number of metaphors all of which I think amount to the same thing: does the occurrence of the event deprive the party who has further undertakings still to perform of substantially the whole benefit which it was the intention of the parties as expressed in the contract that he should obtain as the consideration for performing those undertakings?

This test is applicable whether or not the event occurs as a result of the default of one of the parties to the contract, but the consequences of the event are different in the two cases. Where the event occurs as a result of the default of one party, the party in default cannot rely upon it as relieving himself of the performance of any further undertakings on his part, and the innocent party, although entitled to, need not treat the event as relieving him of the further performance of his own undertakings. This is only a specific application of the fundamental legal and moral rule that a man should not be allowed to take advantage of his own wrong. Where the event occurs as a result of the default of neither party, each is relieved of the further performance of his own undertakings, and their rights in respect of undertakings previously performed are now regulated by the Law Reform (Frustrated Contracts) Act 1943.

. . .

Once it is appreciated that it is the event and not the fact that the event is a result of a breach of contract which relieves the party not in default of further performance of his obligations, two consequences follow. (1) The test whether the event relied upon has this consequence is the same whether the event is the result of the other party's breach of contract or not, as Devlin J pointed out in *Universal Cargo Carriers Corporation* v *Citati* [1957] 2 QB 401, 434 (2) The question whether an event which is the result of the other party's breach of contract has this consequence cannot be answered by treating all contractual undertakings as falling into one of two separate categories: 'conditions' the breach of which gives rise to an event which relieves the party not in default of further performance of his obligations, and 'warranties' the breach of which does not give rise to such an event.

Lawyers tend to speak of this classification as if it were comprehensive, partly for the historical reasons which I have already mentioned and partly because Parliament itself adopted it in the Sale of Goods Act 1893, as respects a number of implied terms in contracts for the sale of goods and has in that Act used the expression 'condition' and 'warranty' in that meaning. But it is by no means true of contractual undertakings in general at common law.

No doubt there are many simple contractual undertakings, sometimes express but more often because of their very simplicity ('It goes without saying') to be implied, of which it can be predicated that every breach of such an undertaking must give rise to an event which will deprive the party not in default of substantially the whole benefit which it was intended that he should obtain from the contract. And such a stipulation, unless the parties have agreed that breach of it shall not entitle the non-defaulting party to treat the contract as repudiated, is a 'condition'. So too there may be other simple contractual undertakings of which it can be predicated that *no* breach can give rise to an event which will deprive the party not in default of substantially the whole benefit which it was intended that he should obtain from the contract; and such a stipulation, unless the parties have agreed that breach of it shall entitle the non-defaulting party to treat the contract as repudiated, is a 'warranty'.

There are, however, many contractual undertakings of a more complex character which cannot be categorised as being 'conditions' or 'warranties', if the late nineteenth-

century meaning adopted in the Sale of Goods Act 1893, and used by Bowen LJ in
*Bentsen* v *Taylor, Sons & Co.* [1893] 2 QB 274, 280; 9 TLR 552, CA be given to those
terms. Of such undertakings all that can be predicated is that some breaches will and
others will not give rise to an event which will deprive the party not in default of
substantially the whole benefit which it was intended that he should obtain from the
contract; and the legal consequences of a breach of such an undertaking, unless
provided for expressly in the contract, depend upon the nature of the event to which the
breach gives rise and do not follow automatically from a prior classification of the
undertaking as a 'condition' or a 'warranty'. For instance, to take Bramwell B's example
in *Jackson* v *Union Marine Insurance Co. Ltd* (1874) LR 10 CP 125, 142 itself, breach of
an undertaking by a shipowner to sail with all possible dispatch to a named port does not
necessarily relieve the charterer of further performance of his obligation under the
charterparty, but if the breach is so prolonged that the contemplated voyage is frustrated
it does have this effect.

In 1874 when the doctrine of frustration was being foaled by 'impossibility of
performance' out of 'condition precedent' it is not surprising that the explanation given
by Bramwell B should give full credit to the dam by suggesting that in addition to the
express *warranty* to sail with all possible dispatch there was an implied *condition precedent*
that the ship should arrive at the named port in time for the voyage contemplated. In
*Jackson* v *Union Marine Insurance Co. Ltd* there was no breach of the express warranty;
but if there had been, to engraft the implied condition upon the express warranty would
have been merely a more complicated way of saying that a breach of a shipowner's
undertaking to sail with all possible dispatch may, but will not necessarily, give rise to
an event which will deprive the charterer of substantially the whole benefit which it was
intended that he should obtain from the charter. Now that the doctrine of frustration has
matured and flourished for nearly a century and the old technicalities of pleading
'conditions precedent' are more than a century out of date, it does not clarify, but on the
contrary obscures, the modern principle of law where such an event *has* occurred as a
result of a breach of an express stipulation in a contract, to continue to add the now
unnecessary colophon 'Therefore it was an implied *condition* of the contract that a
particular kind of breach of an express *warranty* should not occur.' The common law
evolves not merely by breeding new principles but also, when they are fully grown, by
burying their progenitors.

As my brethren have already pointed out, the shipowners' undertaking to tender a
seaworthy ship has, as a result of numerous decisions as to what can amount to
'unseaworthiness', become one of the most complex of contractual undertakings. It
embraces obligations with respect to every part of the hull and machinery, stores and
equipment and the crew itself. It can be broken by the presence of trivial defects easily
and rapidly remediable as well as by defects which must inevitably result in a total loss
of the vessel.

Consequently the problem in this case is, in my view, neither solved nor soluble by
debating whether the shipowner's express or implied undertaking to tender a seaworthy
ship is a 'condition' or a 'warranty'. It is like so many other contractual terms an
undertaking one breach of which may give rise to an event which relieves the charterer
of further performance of his undertakings if he so elects and another breach of which
may not give rise to such an event but entitle him only to momentary compensation in
the form of damages. It is, with all deference to Mr Ashton Roskill's skilful argument,
by no means surprising that among the many hundreds of previous cases about the
shipowner's undertaking to deliver a seaworthy ship there is none where it was found
profitable to discuss in the judgments the question whether that undertaking is a
'condition' or a 'warranty'; for the true answer, as I have already indicated, is that it is

neither, but one of that large class of contractual undertakings one breach of which may have the same effect as that ascribed to a breach of 'condition' under the Sale of Goods Act 1893, and a different breach of which may have only the same effect as that ascribed to a breach of 'warranty' under that Act. . . .

What the judge had to do in the present case, as in any other case where one party to a contract relies upon a breach by the other party as giving him a right to elect to rescind the contract, and the contract itself makes no express provision as to this, was to look at the events which had occurred as a result of the breach at the time at which the charterers purported to rescind the charterparty and to decide whether the occurrence of those events deprived the charterers of substantially the whole benefit which it was the intention of the parties as expressed in the charterparty that the charterers should obtain from the further performance of their own contractual undertakings.

*Note*
The Court of Appeal affirmed Salmon J's decision that the breaches did not deprive the charterers of substantially the whole benefit of the contract.

*Question*
Has the *Hongkong Fir* decision made conditions less important than formerly? (*Cf. Bunge Corp* v *Tradax Export SA* [1981] 2 Lloyd's Rep 1 (HL) and *Compagnie Commerciale Sucres et Denrées* v *C. Czarnikow Ltd (The Naxos)* [1990] 3 All ER 641 (HL).)

# 4  DEVIATION

By a long-established principle of the common law, the carrier lost the protection of the excepted perils and of any contractual exception clauses if there was any unjustifiable 'deviation' from the contract voyage. The idea of deviation originated in cargo insurance, where a change in the voyage would alter the nature of the risk and invalidate the policy, and was applied by analogy to contracts of carriage. It is relevant both to voyage charterparties and to bills of lading, but not to the standard type of time charter, which does not specify a voyage.

## SECTION 1: THE CONTRACT VOYAGE

Unless the charterparty or bill of lading spells out the route to be followed from the port of loading to the port of discharge, the carrier's obligation is to follow a 'customary' or 'usual' route. This is presumed to be the direct geographical route, but the presumption may be rebutted by evidence of the practice actually adopted in a particular trade, or even by a particular shipping line.

### *Reardon Smith Line Ltd* v *Black Sea and Baltic Insurance Co.*
[1939] AC 562 (HL)

Under a charterparty of 1 September 1933, RS's vessel *Indian City* loaded a cargo of ore at the eastern Black Sea port of Poti for a voyage to Sparrow's Point, Baltimore, USA. After leaving Poti she headed for Constantza on the west of the Black Sea for bunkers. While entering Constantza she ran aground and was seriously damaged. Some of the cargo had to be jettisoned. She was unable to complete the voyage to Baltimore, but after temporary repairs discharged the remaining cargo, by agreement, at Rotterdam. The charterers withheld £1,061, the value of the undelivered cargo, from the freight.

RS claimed a general average contribution from the charterers in respect of the repairs, as well as the unpaid freight, and brought the present action on a bond entered into by the charterers as security for the satisfaction of RS's claims in order to obtain delivery of the cargo.

The charterers relied on the fact that to call at Constantza added nearly 200 miles to the length of the voyage from Poti to Baltimore and argued that this was a deviation. RS admitted that, if there was a deviation, their claims must fail, but contended that it was customary at that time for ocean-going shipping to call at Constantza for bunkers. (By the time of the proceedings the price of oil at Constantza had risen and even RS no longer took bunkers there.)

It was held, reversing the Court of Appeal that RS had not deviated, since the evidence established that the longer route via Constantza was 'a usual route'.

LORD WRIGHT: My Lords, this appeal raises an important question in the law of carriage of goods by sea which has given rise to difference of judicial opinion. Goddard J decided in favour of the appellants, but his decision was reversed by a majority of the Court of Appeal, consisting of Slesser and Clauson LJJ. Greer LJ, who dissented, agreed with Goddard J.

The appellant company at the material time owned twenty-eight vessels, of which nineteen, including the *Indian City*, were capable of being readily converted into either oil or coal burners. In 1930 cheap fuel oil for bunkers became available at Constantza in Roumania. Constantza, thereupon, became largely used as a bunkering port, in particular for vessels bound from the Black Sea on long ocean voyages. In 1932 and 1933, 114 oil-burning vessels called at Constantza for bunkering only. This figure shows the importance of the port as a bunkering port. It is not necessary to analyse closely what proportion of oil-burning vessels sailing through the Bosphorus on ocean voyages bunkered at Constantza. It is sufficient for purposes of this case to record what has been accepted on both sides, namely that 25 per cent of the whole number called and bunkered at Constantza in the three-and-a-quarter years before the casualty which overtook the *Indian City*. I emphasize these facts, because the position of Constantza as a usual and recognised bunkering port in the Black Sea seems to me to be a key point in the case.

...

This charterparty was the eighteenth charter entered into between the appellant company and the charterer in this trade. Before the voyage of the *Indian City*, the appellants made twenty-eight voyages in the trade, nineteen for the same charterer, which was a Russian State Trading Corporation, and nine for other Russian State Trading Corporations. Except on the first of these voyages, that performed in July 1930, by the *Orient City*, which bunkered at Constantza on her way to Poti to load, all the appellants' vessels bunkered at Constantza on their voyage. In each case some departure from the shortest sea route from the loading port to the Bosphorus was involved. The extra distance steamed in these cases was considerably greater where the loading ports were situated in the eastern part of the Black Sea, as were Poti, Batoum or Novorossisk. The extra distance amounted approximately to 120 miles in the case of Novorossisk, and to 193 miles in the case of Poti. Where the port of loading was in Ukrainia the extra distance to be steamed in order to bunker at Constantza was fourteen or twenty-one miles, according to the port of loading; when the loading port was in the Crimea or Sea of Azov the extra distance might be about eighty miles.

...

The appellants do not rely on the liberty to call for bunkers which is expressed in the charterparty. That liberty accordingly need not be further considered. Their case is that what was done in calling for bunkers at Constantza was not a deviation or departure from the contract voyage, but was within the contract voyage, because the vessel was pursuing a usual and reasonable commercial route for carrying out that particular adventure.... it is obvious that there will be in general various considerations, commercial or navigational, which determine what sea route is usual and reasonable. Thus in the old sailing ship days, routes were chosen in order to make use of trade winds, and varied from season to season, and between the same termini there might be several routes. In modern times in all long ocean voyages, the need to replenish bunkers (coal or oil) has to be considered. The doctrine of stages of the voyage which enables a shipowner to start with bunkers sufficient for the stage, so long as he fills up his bunkers at the next bunkering port, necessarily involves calling at that port, and also perhaps, later ports, in order to fulfil the recurring obligation to keep the vessel seaworthy in regard to bunkers. Thus to call at such ports has become an ordinary incident of the voyage. The need to do so may help to determine the general route, for instance, whether it is to be by the Cape of Good Hope or the Suez Canal. A shipowner is entitled, within certain limits determined by what is reasonable, to be guided in his choice of bunkering ports by considerations of cheapness and convenience. Thus evidence was given in this case that it is usual for a coal-burning ship bound to Australia by the Cape of Good Hope to bunker at Durban, where coal is cheaper, instead of at Cape Town, though Durban is farther off the route. Other similar instances were given in evidence. In the voyages here in question various choices are open to the shipowner when his ship is burning oil. He may fill up his bunkers for the whole voyage at Constantza on his way to the loading port. That course may be objected to by the charterer because it may reduce the quantity of cargo his ship can load, and for the same reason may be disadvantageous to the shipowner. He may decide to fill up his bunkers after sailing from the port of loading at some convenient port. He may decide to do this at Constantza, at Istanbul, or at Algiers, or at Oran, or at Ceuta, all of which are available bunkering ports, starting from the loading port with sufficient bunkers to take the ship to the next bunkering port which he decides to use. In this way he selects the stage for bunkering. The vessel must be seaworthy for that stage, but it is the shipowner's province to fix the stage, that is, to determine where he will bunker, so long as his decision is reasonable and usual. In the present case, as in the other voyages during the relevant period, the appellants selected Costantza as the bunkering port. Their case is that they had done so a great many times without objection and save in this one case without mishap. They relied on all the evidence to which I have briefly referred to support their claim that the route by Constantza is a usual route. The position therefore is that to call at some port for bunkers is no deviation, and the only question is whether Constantza is a usual and reasonable port of call for this purpose.

I agree with Greer LJ that the evidence that 25 per cent of oil-burning vessels sailing from the Black Sea on ocean voyages call at Costantza for bunkers is sufficient to show a usual route. The shipowner is not here attempting to prove a custom. To prove a custom he would have to show that it was uniform and universal in the trade, but that is not what is in question here. Nor need he show that other routes were not available, that is, that there were not alternative ports of call at which he might bunker. There are no doubt other available ports of call for this purpose, some, and perhaps all, of which would involve much less extra steaming. I think the shipowner is entitled to balance the cost to him of extra steaming against the cheapness or convenience of Constantza, so long as to do so is not unreasonable in regard to the interests of the charterer or any other persons who might be concerned. It is obvious that to put into any port to bunker involves not merely extra steaming, either more or less, but the entry into and departure from an extra port, which in itself is a separate risk however close it may be to the direct ocean route. Again it is said that the habit of bunkering at Constantza sprang up suddenly in 1930, and ceased as suddenly in 1935, at least so far as concerned the practice of the appellants. But I think a commercial habit or practice like the one claimed, may come into existence in a short time and cease as rapidly. In modern business, things are constantly changing and commercial habits may change as rapidly. That the practice of calling at Constantza for bunkers was not unreasonable is also, I think, supported by the evidence that it was well known to responsible officials who represented the charterers on the spot, and that they never objected. I refuse to believe that, if the charterers' interests had been prejudiced, they would not have objected. I refuse to believe in view of all the evidence that the practice was not well known. I do not treat this evidence as evidence of a waiver, or an agreement to vary the contract, which might raise questions of authority to vary a written contract. I merely regard it as Lord Sumner did in *Frenkel's* case [1929] AC 545 as confirming the usual and reasonable character of such a voyage, which is fairly inferred from the fact that no objection was taken.

As the necessity of using ports of call for bunkering is so obvious, I think that less evidence is needed to justify that it is usual and reasonable to use a port like Constantza for that purpose, then if the ship had gone there for purposes of trade. But I do not think it necessary to lay down any specific measure of departure from the direct sea route which may be held to be reasonable. If I am asked how far I go, I say that I go as far as the case requires. The test of what is usual and reasonable in a commercial sense may arise in very different circumstances and must be decided whenever it arises by the application of sound business considerations and by determining what is fair and reasonable in the interests of all concerned.

LORD PORTER: ... the appellants maintained that to proceed to Sparrow's Point via Constantza for bunkers was to proceed by a usual route, and that they were entitled to adduce the facts proved in evidence in support of their contention.

The law upon the matter is, I think, reasonably plain, though its application may from time to time give rise to difficulties. It is the duty of a ship, at any rate when sailing upon an ocean voyage from one port to another, to take the usual route between those two ports. If no evidence be given, that route is presumed to be the direct geographical route, but it may be modified in many cases for navigational or other reasons, and evidence may always be given to show what the usual route is, unless a specific route be prescribed by the charter party or bill of lading. In each case therefore when a ship is chartered to sail or when a parcel is shipped upon a liner sailing from one port to another, it is necessary to inquire what the usual route is. In some cases there may be more than one usual route. It would be difficult to say that a ship sailing from New Zealand to this country had deviated from her course whether she sailed by the Suez Canal, the Panama Canal, round the Cape of Good Hope or through the Straits of Magellan. Each might, I think, be a usual route. Similarly the exigencies of bunkering may require the vessel to depart from the direct route or at any rate compel her to touch at ports at which, if she were proceeding under sail, it would be unnecessary for her to call.

It is not the geographical route but the usual route which has to be followed, though in many cases the one may be the same as the other. But the inquiry must always be, what is the usual route, and a route may become a usual route in the case of a particular

line though that line is accustomed to follow a course which is not that adopted by the vessels belonging to other lines or to other individuals. It is sufficient if there is a well known practice of that line to call at a particular port.
. . .

Any doubt which I have felt in the present case has not been as to the principles applicable, but whether the evidence was sufficient to establish the voyage via Constantza as a usual route for the appellants' vessels from Black Sea ports to America and other ports to be reached by ocean voyages. Upon consideration, however, I think there was enough to enable the learned judge rightly to find that a customary route was followed, and I see no necessity for differing from the view expressed by him and by Greer LJ.

But in saying this I must not be taken to desire in any way to weaken the obligation of a shipowner to proceed by a usual course. The obligation remains, but as was recognised in *Frenkel's* case [1929] AC 545, evidence may always be adduced to show what the usual course is. It is in this, I think, that the majority of the Court of Appeal have erred. In their view evidence was not permissible; in my view, unless a specific route is laid down in the charterparty or bill of lading, it is always permissible and may be essential. No doubt prima facie the route direct from Poti to Sparrow's Point through Instanbul would be the ordinary course, but I think that in this case we have evidence sufficient to show that the route has been varied and that the practice of proceeding to Constantza to bunker after loading had become a usual one. It is true that a considerable number of vessels proceeding from Black Sea ports do not call at Constantza for bunkers, and that, if one is to take particulars of Poti and Novorossisk alone, only about one-quarter of the ships proceeding on ocean voyages call at Costantza after loading. It is true also that the journey to Constantza lengthens the voyage by some 200 miles, and that shortly after the accident to the *Indian City* the cost of oil at Constantza increased and the appellants thereafter have taken their bunkers from Algiers instead of Constantza.

All these are matters to be considered, but a short usage, particularly where the obtaining of bunkers is concerned, may still be a sufficient usage to create a usual route.

*Notes*

1.   For a useful short summary of general average, see Hodges, S., *Law of Marine Insurance*, London: Cavendish Publishing Ltd, 1996, pp. 436–449.

2.   In *Frenkel* v *MacAndrews & Co.* [1929] AC 545 F shipped barrels of olive oil on M Line's vessel *Cervantes* at Malaga under bills which specified only 'with destination to Liverpool'. M Line vessels on the service between Liverpool and Spain called at Malaga *either* on the outward *or* on the return journey. The route to be taken by each vessel from Malaga was advertised in the local papers in Malaga as 'via Levante' or 'Directo' as the case might be. The *Cervantes* sailed 'via Levante' (as F's agents knew) and the olive oil was lost in a storm between Malaga and Cartagena. Rowlatt J upheld F's argument that the *Cervantes* had deviated, but both the Court of Appeal and the House of Lords held that there was no deviation, since the *Cervantes* was on the line's customary route and therefore on the contract voyage (so that the exemption clause for perils of the sea applied: M did not have to rely on the liberty clause in the bill of lading).

3.   It is clear that an involuntary departure from the contract route, e.g., where the ship is disabled by fire and drifts off course, does not amount to deviation, so that deviation is often referred to as a *deliberate* departure from the contract

Deviation

route. Thus, in *Rio Tinto Co. Ltd* v *Seed Shipping Co.* (1926) 134 LT 764, the captain was unwell, suffering from 'indigestion' (it was not suggested that drink played any part), and, misunderstanding the pilot's directions, sailed SSE instead of SSW out of the Clyde. The steamer struck a rock and became a total loss. Roche J held that there was no deviation, because the master did not 'mean to deviate' and that it was unnecessary 'to discuss *Tait* v *Levi* as to deviation, i.e., how far involuntary deviation can be breach'. (In *Tait* v *Levi* (1811) 14 East 481, the captain sailed into Barcelona, supposing that it was Tarragona; as a result the ship was captured by French forces, but the court was divided on the question of whether this amounted to deviation.) It was, however, held by the House of Lords in *Hain Steamship Co. Ltd* v *Tate & Lyle Ltd*, below, that there was deviation where the departure from the route occurred because the master did not receive his orders in time. Did the master in *Hain* 'mean' to deviate?

## SECTION 2: WHEN IS DEVIATION JUSTIFIED?

The common law has always recognised the carrier's right to deviate in order to save life at sea. Is deviation to save property also covered?

### *Scaramanga & Co.* v *Stamp*
### (1880) 5 CPD 295 (CA)

COCKBURN CJ: This case comes before us on appeal from a judgment of Mr Justice Lindley after a trial at nisi prius. The facts are not in dispute, and lie in a very narrow compass. The steamship *Olympias*, of which the defendants are owners, having been chartered by the plaintiff to carry a cargo of wheat from Cronstadt to Gibraltar, and having started on her voyage, when nine days out, sighted another steamship, the *Arion*, in distress, and, on nearing her, found that the machinery of the *Arion* had broken down, and that the vessel was in a helpless condition. The weather was fine and the sea smooth, and there would have been no difficulty in taking off and so saving the crew; but the master of the *Arion*, being desirous of saving his ship, as well as the lives of his crew, agreed to pay 1,000*l.* to the master of the *Olympias* to tow the ship into the Texel.

Having taken the *Arion* in tow, the *Olympias*, when off the Dutch coast, on the way to the Texel, got ashore on the Terschelling Sands, and with her cargo was ultimately lost.

Under these circumstances the plaintiff claims the value of his goods, alleging that the goods were not lost by perils of the seas, so as to be within the exception in the charterparty, but were lost through the wrongful deviation of the defendant's vessel. The defendants plead that the deviation was justified, because it was for the purpose of saving the *Arion* and her cargo, and the lives of her captain and crew, the ship being in such a damaged condition that she could not be navigated.

After deciding that the English authorities were inconclusive, Cockburn CJ continued:

The case before us presents itself, therefore, so far as our Courts are concerned, as one of the first impression, on which we have to declare, or perhaps, I may say, practically, to make, the law.

I am glad to think that in doing so we have the advantage of the assistance afforded to us by the decisions of the American Courts and the opinions of American jurists, whom accident has caused to anticipate us on this question. And, although the decisions of the American Courts are of course not binding on us, yet the sound and enlightened views of American lawyers in the administration and development of the law — a law, except so far as altered by statutory enactment, derived from a common source with our own — entitle their decisions to the utmost respect and confidence on our part.

It is, however, unnecessary to go through the American decisions in any detail. The effect of them is to be found in the well known text writers, but is nowhere better stated than in the judgment of Mr Justice Sprague in the case of *Crocker* v *Jackson* Sprague R 141. The result of these authorities, immediately bearing on the question which we have here to decide, may be briefly stated.

Deviation for the purpose of saving life is protected, and involves neither forfeiture of insurance nor liability to the goods owner in respect of loss which would otherwise be within the exception of 'perils of the seas'. And, as a necessary consequence of the foregoing, deviation for the purpose of communicating with a ship in distress is allowable, inasmuch as the state of the vessel in distress may involve danger to life. On the other hand, deviation for the sole purpose of saving property is not thus privileged, but entails all the usual consequences of deviation.

If, therefore, the lives of the persons on board a disabled ship can be saved without saving the ship, as by taking them off, deviation for the purpose of saving the ship will carry with it all the consequences of an unauthorised deviation.

But where the preservation of life can only be effected through the concurrent saving of property, and the bona fide purpose of saving life forms part of the motive which leads to the deviation, the privilege will not be lost by reason of the purpose of saving property having formed a second motive for deviating.

In these propositions I entirely concur, as well as in the reasoning by which this view of the law is supported by Mr Justice Lindley in his very able judgment. The impulsive desire to save human life when in peril is one of the most beneficial instincts of humanity, and is nowhere more salutary in its results than in bringing help to those who, exposed to destruction from the fury of winds and waves, would perish if left without assistance. To all who have to trust themselves to the sea, it is of the utmost importance that the promptings of humanity in this respect should not be checked or interfered with by prudential considerations as to injurious consequences, which may result to a ship or cargo from the rendering of the needed aid. It would be against the common good, and shocking to the sentiments of mankind, that the shipowner should be deterred from endeavouring to save life by the fear, lest any disaster to ship or cargo, consequent on so doing, should fall on himself. Yet it would be unjust to expect that he should be called upon to satisfy the call of humanity at his own entire risk. Moreover, the uniform practice of the mariners of every nation — except such as are in the habit of making the unfortunate their prey — of succouring others who are in danger, is so universal and well known, that there is neither injustice nor hardship in treating both the merchant and the insurer as making their contracts with the shipowner as subject to this exception to the general rule of not deviating from the appointed course. Goods owners and insurers must be taken, at all events in the absence of any stipulation to the contrary, as acquiescing in the universal practice of the maritime world, prompted as it is by the inherent instinct of human nature, and founded on the common interest of all who are exposed to the perils of the seas. What would be the effect of such a stipulation as I have just referred to, if it existed, it is unnecessary for the purpose of the present case to consider.

Deviation for the purpose of saving property stands obviously on a totally different footing. There is here no moral duty to fulfil, which, though its fulfilment may have been attended with danger to life or property, remains unrewarded. There would be much force, no doubt, in the argument that it is to the common interest of merchants and insurers, as well as of shipowners, that ships and cargoes, when in danger of perishing, should be saved, and consequently that, as matter of policy, the same latitude should be allowed in respect of the saving of property as in respect of the saving of life, were it not that the law has provided another, and a very adequate motive for the saving of property, by securing to the salvor a liberal proportion of the property saved — a proportion in which not only the value of the property saved, but also the danger run by the salvor to life or property is taken into account, and in calculating which, if it be once settled that the insurance will not be protected, nor the shipowner freed from liability in respect of loss of cargo, the risk thus run will, no doubt, be included as an element. It would obviously be most unjust if the shipowner could thus take the chance of highly remunerative gain at the risk and possible loss of the merchant or the insurer, neither of whom derive any benefit from the preservation of the property saved. This is strikingly exemplified in the present case, in which, not content with what would have been awarded to him by the proper Court on account of salvage, the master made his own terms, and would have been paid a very large sum had the attempt to bring the *Arion* into port proved successful. It is obviously one thing to accord a privilege to one who acts from a sense of duty, without expectation of reward, another to extend it to one who neither acts from a sense of moral duty nor in obedience to what may be thought to be the policy of the law, but solely with a view to his own individual profit.

*Note*
The carrier may also deviate in an emergency, for example he may put in for repairs which are necessary for the safe and successful prosecution of the voyage. Is the deviation in such a case still justified if the need for repair arose from the unseaworthiness of the vessel?

## *J. & E. Kish* v *Charles Taylor, Sons & Co.*
### [1912] AC 604 (HL)

The *Wearside* was chartered to load a full and complete cargo of timber at Mobile and Pensacola for carriage to Europe. Because of financial embarrassment, the charterers were unable to load a full cargo. The master then obtained other cargo to fill the vessel, but because the freight for this was lower he took on board a larger quantity than he should have done. In heavy weather the cargo shifted: some cargo was lost, the vessel was damaged and the master had to put in to Halifax to restow the cargo and have the vessel repaired. On arrival, the owners sought to exercise their contractual lien for dead freight and demurrage. The holders of the bills of lading argued that the lien was lost when the vessel deviated. It was held, reversing the Court of Appeal, that the lien had not been lost.

LORD ATKINSON: . . . [I]t is not disputed that it is prima facie not only the right but the duty of the master of a ship to deviate from the course of his voyage and seek a harbour or place of safety, if that be reasonably necessary in order to save his ship and the lives of his crew from the perils which beset them. Neither is it disputed by the appellants that they are answerable in damages to every person who sustains loss or injury by reason of the breach of their warranty of the seaworthiness of their ship, and they further admit that they cannot require the owners of the cargo or any portion of it to recoup them to any extent for any loss they may have sustained or expense to which they may have been put as a result of this breach of warranty, or of any course they may have had to take in consequence of it. That voluntary or unwarranted deviation may render the contract of affreightment void ab initio was decided by the Court of Appeal in *Joseph Thorley Ltd* v *Orchis Steamship Co.* [1907] 1 KB 660, 668. What the appellants contend is, in effect, this, that justifiable deviation does not avoid the contract; that, to use the language of Lord Watson in [*Strang, Steel & Co.* v *Scott & Co.* 14 App Cas 601, at 608] 'it is the presence of the peril and not its causes' which justify it, and that it is, therefore, immaterial whether the unseaworthiness of the ship or her negligent navigation contributed directly to the peril or not. Judged by that test it is not disputed that the deviation in the present case was justifiable, and, if so, that the contract of affreightment was not void ab initio. So that the question for decision resolves itself into this: Is it the presence of the peril and not its cause which determines the character of the deviation, or must the master of every ship be left in this dilemma, that whenever, by his own culpable act, or a breach of contract by his owner, he finds his ship in a perilous position, he must continue on his voyage at all hazards, or only seek safety under the penalty of forfeiting the contract of affreightment? Nothing could, it would appear to me, tend more to increase the dangers to which life and property are exposed at sea than to hold that the law of England obliged the master of a merchant ship to choose between such alternatives.

*Notes*

1.  Where repairs become necessary, the master is not obliged to proceed merely to the nearest port: it may be reasonable for him to decide that in the circumstances he should make for a port which is further away. See *Phelps, James & Co.* v *Hill* [1891] 1 QB 605 (CA): on a voyage from Swansea to New York, following damage both to the ship and to the cargo in bad weather, the ship took refuge at Queenstown and was then sunk in a collision while heading for repair at the shipowners' yard at Bristol, rather than returning to Swansea, which would have been nearer; this was held not to be a deviation, in spite of the objection of the cargo-owners, who had not been consulted and who would have been better suited by Swansea.

2.  Deviation has also been held to be justified where it was done to avoid capture by enemy forces: *The Teutonia* (1872) LR 4 PC 171.

3.  Note the wider scope given to justified deviation under the Hague-Visby Rules, Art. IV, r. 4, considered in Chapter 7: 'saving or attempting to save life *or property* at sea or *any reasonable deviation*' (emphasis supplied).

## SECTION 3: THE EFFECT OF UNJUSTIFIED DEVIATION

### *Joseph Thorley Ltd* v *Orchis Steamship Co. Ltd*
[1907] 1 KB 660 (CA)

COLLINS MR: In this case the plaintiffs were the owners of a cargo of locust beans shipped on board the defendants' ship under a bill of lading, of which the plaintiffs became indorsees. The bill of lading described the ship as 'now lying in the port of Limassol and bound for London' and contained the usual exceptions, including an exception of loss arising from negligence of stevedores in loading or discharging the ship. When the cargo had been unloaded at the port of destination, it was found that it had been injuriously affected by being admixed with a poisonous earth called terra umber, a quantity of which was carried in the ship as ballast, and this had occurred through the negligence of those employed in discharging the cargo. Prima facie, damage occasioned by such negligence would be one of the matters covered by the exception clause in the bill of lading, but the plaintiffs contend that the defendants cannot rely upon that clause, because the ship deviated from the voyage contracted for in the bill of lading. There is no doubt that the ship did so deviate, because, instead of proceeding direct from Limassol to London, she went first to two ports in Asia Minor and thence made her way to London. The question is as to the legal effect of that deviation under the circumstances of the present case. Channell J held that it had the effect of displacing the express contract contained in the bill of lading, and so precluding the shipowners from setting up the exception clause therein contained. He based that decision upon the case of *Balian* v *Joly, Victoria Co.* 6 Times LR 345. The decision in that case, which has now stood for about seventeen years, appears to me to be in point, and, unless it can be made out that for any reason we ought not to follow it, I think it concludes the present case. In that case tobacco was shipped on board a ship for carriage from Lagos to London. By the bill of lading certain perils were excepted, and there was also a clause by which it was provided that, in the case of packages over 5*l.* each in value being shipped, the value thereof must be declared before shipment, otherwise the defendants would not be liable for more than 5*l.* per package. The tobacco, which was shipped in bales, the value of each bale being over 5*l.*, ultimately arrived in London, but by another ship and another route than that contemplated in the bill of lading. Upon its arrival it was found that a number of the bales were damaged, and an action was brought by the shippers in respect of that damage. There having been no declaration of the value before shipment, the shipowners sought to set up by way of defence the clause in the bill of lading by which, in the absence of a declaration of value, their liability was to be limited to 5*l.* in respect of each package. The Court of Appeal, consisting of Lord Esher MR, Fry LJ and Lopes LJ, held that the fact of deviation was a complete answer to the defence so set up, as having the effect of displacing the provision in the contract upon which the defendants relied and precluding them from setting it up. Upon looking at the grounds of the judgments given in that case, they appear to me to affirm a principle which is as much applicable to the present case as to that case. The principle underlying those judgments seems to be that the undertaking not to deviate has the effect of a condition, or a warranty in the sense in which the word is used in speaking of the warranty of seaworthiness, and, if that condition is not complied with, the failure to comply with it displaces the contract. It goes to the root of the contract, and its performance is a condition precedent to the right of the shipowner to put the contract in suit. It may be, no doubt, that, although that condition is broken, the circumstances are such as to give rise to an implied obligation on the part of the cargo owner to pay the shipowner the freight, and, it may be, to perform other stipulations which may be implied under the circumstances from the fact of the carriage of the cargo to its destination; but that is quite consistent with the effect of the deviation being to displace the special contract expressed in the bill of lading. This Court appears to me really to have held in *Balian* v *Joly, Victoria & Co.* that this is the true principle with regard to the effect of deviation, and therefore it is not necessary to trace the loss which has occurred to the deviation. In the case of *Balian* v *Joly, Victoria & Co.* the fact that there had been a deviation had no relation to the value of the tobacco; nor, if the damage to it was attributable to the deviation, could that fact have had any bearing upon the question whether the shipowners were entitled to set up by way of defence the particular stipulation of the bill of lading upon which in that case they were relying; and yet this Court held that the effect of the deviation was to prevent them from setting up that stipulation. It seems to me that really the only way, in point of principle, in which the decision in *Balian* v *Joly, Victoria & Co.* can be explained is that the Court regarded the deviation as amounting to failure to comply with a condition precedent, and therefore as displacing the express contract, independently of any question whether the deviation had any bearing on the particular loss complained of by the cargo owners. If that be the true principle, it is applicable, as it appears to me, to the present case. There is no connection, it is true, between the deviation and the particular negligence which in this case occasioned the loss, but that is quite immaterial if the principle underlying the decision in *Balian* v *Joly, Victoria & Co.* applies, namely, that the shipowner cannot set up the exception clause in the bill of lading contract, which only exists for his benefit, if he has not performed a condition precedent upon which his right to rely on that contract depends. I do not think that it is necessary for me to go through the authorities which have been cited, but it seems to me that the last authority to which I have referred is really consistent with all the earlier authorities on the subject as far back as the time of Lord Mansfield. I would only add that I am unable to see any reason why the doctrine admittedly applicable in the case of a contract of insurance with respect to the warranty of seaworthiness should not, as regards the undertaking not to deviate, apply equally to a contract of affreightment. It seems to me that the same considerations apply to both cases. If such a term of the contract is an absolute condition, failure to comply with which displaces the contract of insurance, it appears to me that it must be a condition in the same sense in the case of the contract of affreightment, and failure to comply with it ought in principle to produce the same results, which is the case if its effect is to displace the special contract, leaving only such terms of it surviving as may be implied from the circumstances and the conduct of the parties by way of new contract arising out of the old contract. On these grounds I think that the judgment of the learned judge was right, and this application must be dismissed.

FLETCHER MOULTON LJ: I agree. The cases shew that, for a long series of years, the Courts have held that a deviation is such a serious matter, and changes the character of the contemplated voyage so essentially, that a shipowner who has been guilty of a deviation cannot be considered as having performed his part of the bill of lading contract, but something fundamentally different, and therefore he cannot claim the benefit of stipulations in his favour contained in the bill of lading. In what position, then, does he stand? He has carried the goods to their place of destination, and is therefore entitled to some remuneration for that service, of which their owner has received the benefit. The most favourable position which he can claim to occupy is that he has carried the goods as a common carrier for the agreed freight. I do not say that in all circumstances he would be entitled as of right to be treated even as favourably as this, but in the present case the plaintiffs do not contest his right to stand in that position. That, however, still leaves him liable to the plaintiffs for the amount which they have recovered in this action.

*Note*

This approach has been applied in many cases. Thus, carriers lose not only the benefit of exemption clauses in the contract, but also the right to enforce *contractual* provisions regarding laytime and demurrage (see *United States Shipping Board* v *Bunge y Born Limitada Sociedad* (1925) 31 Com Cas 118 (HL)) or freight. It was commonly said that the contract was 'terminated' by the deviation (e.g., Lord Phillimore in *Cunard Steamship Co. Ltd* v *Buerger* [1927] AC 1, at p. 14) and although the carrier's position after deviation was often described as being that of a common carrier, the courts were reluctant to give the carrier even that much protection.

### *James Morrison & Co. Ltd* v *Shaw, Savill, and Albion Co. Ltd*
### [1916] 2 KB 783 (CA)

SWINFEN EADY LJ: . . . The plaintiffs are holders for value of two bills of lading for a quantity of wool shipped at Napier, New Zealand, for London by the defendants' steamship *Tokomaru*. This ship was torpedoed on January 30 1915, by a German submarine when between seven and eight miles from Havre, and ship and cargo were an actual total loss. The plaintiffs sue for breach of the contract evidenced by the bill of lading. The defendants, while admitting the total loss of the goods, dispute their liablity. They say that the loss occurred by an excepted peril, the King's enemies. The plaintiffs contend that the defendants are not entitled to rely upon the exception contained in the bill of lading, as they say the *Tokomaru* was deviating from the contract voyage by leaving the direct course for London and proceeding to Havre when the disaster occurred, and that the liberties contained in the bill of lading did not permit that to be done. This raises the first question, namely, whether the *Tokomaru* was deviating in proceeding towards Havre. If not deviating, there is an end of the matter, and the shipowners are protected from liability by the bill of lading. If, however the *Tokomaru* was deviating, the further question arises as to the liability of the defendants as carriers under the circumstances. The defendants contend that they incurred no greater liability than that of common carriers, and are therefore not liable for acts of the King's enemies.
. . .

The ordinary route for steamers of this line is, outwards bound, via Cape of Good Hope to New Zealand; homeward bound, from New Zealand via Cape Horn and west of the Falkland Islands to Monte Video, then to Teneriffe or Madeira, and thence direct to London.

. . . This ship was a cargo boat. Passenger ships of the same line going to and from New Zealand frequently call at Plymouth, but not so cargo boats. So far as appears from the evidence, this was the first time that a vessel of this line coming from New Zealand and bound for London had been instructed to call at Havre. The intended call was brought about in this way. A special arrangement was made to carry some frozen meat to France. At one time it was contemplated calling at Bordeaux to discharge this cargo, and in some of the bills of lading for part cargo of this ship liberty to call at Bordeaux was inserted, but on reaching Teneriffe the captain was instructed by the owners to proceed to Havre and discharge the meat cargo there. On leaving Teneriffe the course, whether for Havre or to London direct, is the same to a point about ten miles off the Casquets. There the routes diverge. From the point of divergence it is 107 miles to Havre and 118 miles Havre to Dover. Thus from the point of divergence to Dover via Havre it is 225 miles; from the point of divergence to Dover direct it is 171 miles; so by proceeding to Havre the length of the voyage would be increased by fifty-four miles. From Havre to the nearest point of the ship's ordinary route to Dover is a distance of sixty-eight miles. The direct service between New Zealand and London by the Shaw, Savill and Albion Line has been long established and is well known, and the boats always follow substantially the same route outwards or homewards, as the case may be.

After holding that the shipowners were not protected by the clause giving 'liberty on the way to London to call and stay at any intermediate port' (see section 4, below), Swinfen Eady LJ continued:

If that be so, the remaining question is whether the defendants are protected from liability as carriers by the fact that the loss occurred through the King's enemies. If they, as carriers, were duly performing their contract of carriage, they would not be liable for loss occasioned by the King's enemies. But they are breaking their contract. They are quite unable to show that the loss must have occurred in any event, and whether they had deviated or not. True it is that there had been no previous warning of danger from submarines, and that the event which occasioned the loss was wholly unexpected, but this does not assist the defendants. The answer to the argument of the defendants on this point is that given by Tindall CJ in *Davis* v *Garrett* 6 Bing 724:

> But we think the real answer to the objection is, that no wrong-doer can be allowed to apportion or qualify his own wrong; and that as a loss has actually happened whilst his wrongful act was in operation and force, and which is attributable to his wrongful act, he cannot set up as an answer to the action the bare possibility of a loss, if his wrongful act had never been done. It might admit of a different construction if he could shew, not only that the same loss *might* have happened, but that it *must* have happened if the act complained of had not been done; but there is no evidence to that extent in the present case.

. . .

PHILLIMORE LJ: ... As the accident occurred at the time and place when it did, the ship being then on her deviating course, the shipowner is responsible unless he can shew that the loss or damage would have occurred if she had been on her proper course for London. There are circumstances in which conceivably this could be proved, but it could not be and was not proved in this case. Therefore the judgment is right and must be affirmed.

*Note*
The severity of the *Orchis* view of the effect of deviation was modified in the next case.

## *Hain Steamship Co. Ltd* v *Tate & Lyle Ltd*
### [1936] 2 All ER 597 (HL)

Farr & Co chartered the *Tregenna*, which was owned by H, to load a cargo of sugar in bags from Cuba and San Domingo (the Dominican Republic) in performance of sales to T & L. After loading part of the cargo at two Cuban ports, the *Tregenna* was then sub-chartered by Farr & Co to an associated company to load at a San Domingo port. Because of the failure of a messenger to deliver the instructions for loading from the telegraph office, the master of the *Tregenna* did not receive the nomination of the San Domingo port (S. Pedro de Macoris on the south of the island); he concluded that he was not required to load at San Domingo and sailed from Cuba heading north of San Domingo on the route to Queenstown. A few hours later he was contacted by radio and changed course for S. Pedro. The remainder of the cargo was then loaded at S. Pedro, but on leaving the harbour, the *Tregenna* stranded. Some of the cargo was lost and some damaged; the rest was transhipped and brought to England on the *Baron Dalmeny*.

T & L became indorsees of the bills of lading. To obtain delivery they had to sign a Lloyd's average bond and pay a deposit against possible general average charges. After becoming aware of the deviation, T & L claimed the return of the deposit and withheld freight on the Cuban shipments. H counterclaimed for the freight and a general average contribution. The Court of Appeal found in T & L's favour. The House of Lords reversed this decision, except as to freight.

LORD ATKIN: My Lords, the effect of a deviation upon a contract of carriage by sea has been stated in a variety of cases but not in uniform language. Everyone is agreed that it is a serious matter. Occasionally language has been used which suggests that the occurrence of a deviation automatically displaces the contract, as by the now accepted doctrine does an event which 'frustrates' a contract. In other cases where the effect of deviation upon the exceptions in the contract had to be considered language is used which Sir Robert Aske argued shows that the sole effect is as it were to expunge the exceptions clause, as no longer applying to a voyage which from the beginning of the deviation has ceased to be the contract voyage. I venture to think that the true view is that the departure from the voyage contracted to be made is a breach by the shipowner of his contract, but a breach of such a serious character that however slight the deviation the other party to the contract is entitled to treat it as going to the root of the contract, and to declare himself as no longer bound by any of its terms. I wish to confine myself to contracts of carriage by sea: and in the circumstances of such a carriage I am satisfied that by a long series of decisions adopting in fact commercial usage in this respect any deviation constitutes a breach of contract of this serious nature. The same view is taken in contracts of marine insurance where there is implied an absolute condition not to deviate. No doubt the extreme gravity attached to a deviation in contracts of carriage is justified by the fact that the insured cargo owner when the ship has deviated has become uninsured. It appears to me inevitable that a breach of contract which results in such momentous consequences well known to all concerned in commerce by sea should entitle the other party to refuse to be bound. It is true that the cargo owner may, though very improbably, be uninsured: it is also true that in these days it is not uncommon for marine insurers to hold the assured covered in case of deviation at a premium to be arranged. But these considerations do not appear to diminish the serious nature of the breach in all the circumstances of sea carriage; and may be balanced by the fact that the ship can, and often does, take liberties to deviate which prevent the result I have stated. If this view be correct then the breach by deviation does not automatically cancel the express contract, otherwise the shipowner by his own wrong can get rid of his own contract. Nor does it affect merely the exceptions clauses. This would make those clauses alone subject to a condition of no deviation, a construction for which I can find no justification. It is quite inconsistent with the cases which have treated deviation as precluding enforcement of demurrage provisions. The event falls within the ordinary law of contract. The party who is affected by the breach has the right to say, I am not now bound by the contract whether it is expressed in charterparty, bill of lading or otherwise. He can, of course, claim his goods from the ship; whether and to what extent he will become liable to pay some remuneration for carriage I do not think arises in this case for reasons I will give later: but I am satisfied that once he elects to treat the contract as at an end he is not bound by the promise to pay the agreed freight any more than by his other promises. But on the other hand, as he can elect to treat the contract as ended, so he can elect to treat the contract as subsisting and if he does this with knowledge of his rights he must in accordance with the general law of contract be held bound. No doubt one must be careful to see that the acts of the cargo owner are not misinterpreted when he finds that his goods have been taken off on a voyage to which he did not agree. He could not reasonably be expected to recall the goods when he discovers the ship at a port of call presumably still intending to reach her agreed port of destination. There must be acts which plainly show that the shipper intends to treat the contract as still binding. In the present case where the charterer procured the ship to be recalled to a San Domingo port for the express purpose of continuing to load under the charter, an obligation which, of course, only existed in pursuance of the express contract, and saw that the ship did receive the cargo stipulated under the sub-charter provided by persons who had no right to load except under the sub-charter, I am satisfied that there is abundant, indeed conclusive, evidence to justify the report of Branson J that the deviation was waived by the charterers.

...

Now the position of the respondents, Messrs Tate & Lyle, has to be considered from two points of view — (a) as indorsees of the bills of lading in circumstances in which the rights and liabilities expressed in the bill of lading would devolve upon them as though the contract contained therein had been made with them (under the Bills of Lading Act); (b) as parties to Lloyd's bond.

In respect of the first, in my opinion the fact of deviation gives the bill of lading holder the rights I have already mentioned. On discovery he is entitled to refuse to be bound by the contract. Waiver by the charterer seems on principle to have no bearing upon the rights and liabilities which devolve upon the bill of lading holder under the Bills of Lading Act. The consignee has not assigned to him the obligations under the charterparty: nor in fact any obligation of the charterer under the bill of lading, for *ex hypothesi* there are none. A new contract appears to spring up between the ship and the consignee on the terms of the bill of lading. One of the terms is the performance of an agreed voyage, a deviation from which is a fundamental breach. It seems to me impossible to see how a waiver of such a breach by the party to the charterparty contract can affect the rights of different parties in respect of the breach by the same event of the bill of lading contract. I think, therefore, that a deviation would admittedly preclude a claim for contribution arising against parties to a subsisting contract of carriage, though no doubt the claim does not arise as a term of the contract: and as the bill of lading holder is entitled to say that he is not bound by the agreed term as to freight, the ship could not in the present circumstances claim against the plaintiffs either contribution or freight if they had to rely on the bill of lading alone.

After holding that the obligation under the Lloyd's bond was independent of the bill of lading, Lord Atkin continued:

On the ship's claim for the balance of freight in respect of the San Domingo sugar [sic: but Cuban must be meant] I have come to the conclusion that it must fail. That there is no claim on the express contract — the bill of lading — I have already said. An amendment to claim a *quantum meruit* was however allowed, and this has occasioned me some difficulty. I am not prepared at present to adopt the view of Scrutton LJ, that in no circumstances can a consignee, whether holder of a bill of lading or not, be liable to pay after a deviation any remuneration for the carriage from which he has benefited. I prefer to leave the matter open, and in those circumstances to say that the opinion of the Court of Appeal to the contrary in this case should not be taken as authoritative. In the present case I find that the balance of freight under the charterparty, and therefore under the bill of lading, was to be paid in New York after advice of right delivery and ascertainment of weight. The terms of the cesser clause do not affect this obligation, and consequently the charterer remained and remains still liable for that freight. In these circumstances I am not satisfied that conditions existed under which a promise should be implied whereby the shippers undertook to give to the ship a further and a different right to receive some part of what would be a reasonable remuneration for the carriage. I think, therefore, that the claim for freight fails.

LORD WRIGHT MR: ... An unjustified deviation is a fundamental breach of a contract of affreightment. Owing to the peculiar nature of a maritime adventure in which shipowner and goods owner are jointly concerned, it is a fundamental condition that in the absence of express liberties, the ship shall proceed by the ordinary and customary route: any deviation changes the adventure. It has also the serious consequences that it vitiates the goods owner's insurances. This is old law.

After quoting the passage from Fletcher Moulton LJ's judgment in *Joseph Thorley* v *Orchis*, above, Lord Wright continued:

It is on similar reasoning that a voyage policy of insurance is avoided from the moment that the vessel actually deviates. This loss of the insurance is sometimes stated as the reason why deviation is treated so drastically under a contract of affreightment. If that were all, the mischief might be remedied by means of the deviation clause which is so generally now found in policies. But the reason is more fundamental and is the same in principle in both contracts. The adventure has been changed. A contract entered into on the basis of the original adventure, is inapplicable to the new adventure. I shall later have to consider the effect of a deviation in regard to freight. But however fundamental is the condition, it may still be waived by the goods owner. For this purpose the case is like any other breach of a fundamental condition, which constitutes the repudiation of a contract by one party; the other party may elect not to treat the repudiation as being final, but to treat the contract as subsisting and to that extent may waive the breach, any right to damages being reserved. One party to a contract cannot end it by his wrongful act against the wishes of the other party. In the present case, the charterers elected to waive the breach, with the result that the charterparty was not abrogated, but remained in force. The appellants were thus entitled to the benefit of the contract conditions and in particular to rely on the exception of perils of the sea and thus vindicate any lien for contribution to general average and also enforce the charterers' liability in respect thereof. ...

I have discussed the effect of a deviation in so far as it deprives the shipowner of a right to rely on the contractual exceptions, but a deviation carries wider consequences. I think it is right to say that it abrogates the special contract entirely. By 'special' here is meant the express contract; it is thereby intended to reserve the question of there being any implied contract. But in particular the deviation destroys, as I think, the right to claim the contract freight, even if the voyage is completed and the goods delivered at the contract destination. It is curious that there is no express decision on this point. It has however been held that a deviation discharges provisions in the contract of affreightment for unloading in a fixed time — *United States Shipping Board* v *Bunge y Born* (1925) 31 Com Cas 118. Freight payable at destination under the terms of the contract must be an *a fortiori* case. But the Court of Appeal have denied the appellants' claim to any freight at all on a more fundamental ground: they have held that not only is the contract freight gone, but no freight on a *quantum meruit* can be claimed. Scrutton LJ states the proposition quite generally:

The fact that a volunteer without authority renders services to another man's property does not give him a right to remuneration, or to keep the property unless he gets remuneration. There is no authority on the question; but as a matter of logic, I think the claim for freight fails.

The 'logic' involved is also explained by Greer LJ, who thinks that after a deviation

the goods are being carried unlawfully: the shipowner is throughout in unauthorised possession of the goods of whoever may turn out to be the owner, and must deliver them up to the owner on demand without payment for a service which neither the shipper nor the owner ever asked him to perform.

During the argument I was of opinion, like your Lordships, that in the circumstances of this case the claim for freight failed. It was accordingly not necessary to hear argument on this important question of principle: it may be reserved for full argument and decision when, if ever, it arises in that simple and abstract form. I merely add a few observations to explain why as at present advised I feel difficulty about it.

I have myself in my own experience never heard of a case where a shipowner who has carried goods to their destination, but after a deviation, has been refused payment of freight. It is different if the goods have been lost after the deviation, as in *Morrison's* case [1916] 2 KB 783, or if they have been delivered at a port other than the agreed destination. But a sweeping general rule such as the Court of Appeal laid down will, if it be correct, have startling consequences. Let me put a quite possible case: A steamer carrying a cargo of frozen meat from Australia to England deviates by calling at a port outside the usual or permitted route: it is only the matter of a few hours extra steaming: no trouble ensues except the trifling delay. The cargo is duly delivered in England at the agreed port. The goods owner has had for all practical purposes the benefit of all that his contract required; he has had the advantages, of the use of a valuable ship, her crew, fuel, refrigeration and appliances, canal dues, port charges, stevedoring. The shipowner may be technically a wrongdoer in the sense that he has once deviated, but otherwise over a long period he has been performing the exacting and costly duties of a carrier at sea. I cannot help thinking that epithets like 'unlawful' and 'unauthorised' are not apt to describe such services; it may be that by the maritime law the relationship of carrier and goods owner still continues despite the deviation, though subject to the modifications consequent on the deviation. Nor can I help feeling that the court would not be slow to infer an obligation when the goods are received at destination to pay, not indeed the contract freight, but a reasonable remuneration. The observations of the Court of Appeal certainly go beyond such authority as there is.

Lord Wright quoted the passage from Fletcher Moulton LJ's judgment in *Joseph Thorley* v *Orchis*, above, and continued:

I do not think that Fletcher Moulton LJ, intended to lay down here precise rules of law. *Morrison's* case shows that the shipowner, after a deviation, cannot claim the protection afforded by law to a common carrier, nor can there be any question of the agreed freight if what is called the special contract (as distinguished from any implied contract) is displaced. Collins MR, at p. 667, says:

It may be, no doubt, that, although the condition [so not to deviate] is broken, the circumstances are such as to give rise to an implied obligation on the part of the cargo owner to pay the shipowner the freight . . . from the fact of the carriage of the cargo to its destination.

I may note that in *United States Shipping Board* v *Bunge y Born* (1925) 31 Com Cas 118 the goods owner did not contest the shipowner's right to freight, though the ship had deviated and the terms as to demurrage had gone.

I am not expressing any final opinion because I think the matter does not arise for decision in this case. Here on any view, in my opinion, all the circumstances point against the implication of an agreement to pay a *quantum meruit* freight. By the charterparty, freight was payable by the charterers in New York after delivery: there was no operative cesser clause: it was known to all parties that the charterers were liable throughout for the freight. I can find at this stage no hint that anyone was thinking that the deviation had displaced the contract. The appellants were entitled to freight from the charterers. Under these circumstances the fact that the respondents ordered the ship from the port of call to Greenock and presented the bills of lading and took delivery in the normal way without any mention of freight pointed to the view that freight was no interest of theirs. In fact they had purchased on 'arrived' terms and as against their sellers were entitled to delivery 'freight free'. . . .

*Note*

The references in *Hain Steamship Co. Ltd* v *Tate & Lyle Ltd* to 'fundamental' breach inspired a series of decisions in the 1950s and 1960s in which any sufficiently serious breach deprived the contracting party of the benefit of exception clauses, by analogy with the effect of deviation. This line of development was brought to an end by the House of Lords decisions in *Suisse Atlantique Société d'Armement Maritime SA* v *NV Rotterdamsche Kolen Centrale* [1967] 1 AC 361 and *Photo Production Ltd* v *Securicor Transport Ltd* [1980] AC 827. Neither case was concerned with deviation as such, and the question arises whether the disappearance of the doctrine of automatic cancellation of exception clauses by reason of fundamental breach, and its replacement by the principle that the continued operation of exceptions following breach is *always* a question of construction, implies any change in the law with regard to deviation. All the Law Lords in *Suisse Atlantique Société d'Armement Maritime SA* v *NV Rotterdamsche Kolen Centrale* treated deviation as being governed by the ordinary law of contract, but doubts began to emerge subsequently.

### *Photo Production Ltd* v *Securicor Transport Ltd*
[1980] AC 827

LORD WILBERFORCE: . . . I must add to this, by way of exception to the decision not to 'gloss' the *Suisse Atlantique* [1967] 1 AC 361 a brief observation on the deviation cases, since some reliance has been placed upon them, particularly upon the decision of this House in *Hain Steamship Co. Ltd* v *Tate and Lyle Ltd* (1936) LT 177 (so earlier than the *Suisse Atlantique*) in the support of the *Harbutt* doctrine. I suggested in the *Suisse Atlantique* that these cases can be regarded as proceeding upon normal principles applicable to the law of contract generally viz., that it is a matter of the parties' intentions whether and to what extent clauses in shipping contracts can be applied after a deviation, i.e., a departure from the contractually agreed voyage or adventure. It may be preferable that they should be considered as a body of authority sui generis with special rules derived from historical and commercial reasons.

*Note*

Lord Diplock in *Photo Production Ltd* v *Securicor Transport Ltd* treated deviation as governed by the ordinary principles of the law of contract (in the course of what may, without disrespect, be thought to be one of his less successful expositions of contractual principles). In *Kenya Railways* v *Antares Co. Ltd (The Antares)* [1987] 1 Lloyd's Rep 424, Lloyd LJ expressed the view (*obiter*) that 'the ordinary law of contract' should apply to deviation. The issue there was the effect of unauthorised deck carriage on the 12-month time limit for claims under the Hague-Visby Rules (see Chapter 7); it was held that the shipowners could still rely on the time limit. In view of the close analogy between unauthorised deck carriage and deviation it would be surprising if different rules applied in the two cases. The effect of deviation under the Hague-Visby Rules is considered further in Chapter 7, below.

## SECTION 4: LIBERTY CLAUSES

It is standard practice to include clauses giving the shipowner liberty to deviate. Such clauses have to be given a commercially sensible meaning and not one which would destroy the main purpose of the contract.

### *Leduc* v *Ward*
### (1888) 20 QBD 475 (CA)

3,123 bags of rape seed were shipped on the *Austria* 'now lying in the port of Fiume [Rijeka] and bound for Dunkirk, with liberty to call at any ports in any order' for delivery at Dunkirk. Instead of proceeding directly to Dunkirk the ship sailed first for Glasgow, and was lost by perils of the sea near Ailsa Craig. The shipowners argued (a) that the shippers agreed to this route, and (b) that in any event the voyage via Glasgow was covered by the liberty clause. Denman J and the Court of Appeal held that the shipowners could not rely on the liberty clause.

LORD ESHER MR: The bill of lading follows the usual form of such documents, and it seems to me clear that such form provides for a particular voyage. If the counsel for the defendants was right in his argument that there is no contract for any particular voyage in the bill of lading, just conceive what a state of things, in a business point of view, would result. The object of the carriage of the goods from port to port is that they may be sold or otherwise dealt with at the place of destination; and the person who wants them at that place for sale or use there acts upon the assumption that they will arrive there at or about a certain time in the ordinary course of a voyage there from the port of shipment. If the argument for the defendants were correct, he could not tell at what time he could calculate on having them. The indorsee of a bill of lading could not tell when he was likely to receive the goods. Business could not be carried on upon those terms. Again, with regard to the insurance of the goods, similar difficulties would arise. How could the goods be insured, if it was not known for what voyage they were to be insured? To suppose that there is no contract for a particular voyage in the bill of lading seems to me to be to disregard the whole course of mercantile business. It is obviously a most important part of the contract of carriage by sea that the route by which the goods are to be brought should be determined; and accordingly it seems to me to be provided for in the bill of lading. The ordinary form of bill of lading states that the goods are shipped on such a ship lying in the port of shipment and bound for the port of destination, and if the ship is to go to other places between those ports the names of them are inserted. Those terms appear to me to describe a voyage, and, such being the description of the voyage, what is the true effect of the document with regard to the voyage so described? A bill of lading is a common mercantile document, which has been used for hundreds of years, and I think that business men and Courts of Law have always interpreted it in one way, namely, that, if the only voyage mentioned is from the port of shipment to the port of destination, it must be a voyage on the ordinary track by sea of the voyage from the one place to the other. So here, if the description of the voyage had been merely from Fiume to Dunkirk, I think the contract would have been for a voyage on the ordinary sea track of a voyage from Fiume to Dunkirk, and any departure from that track in the absence of necessity would be a deviation. Of course when I speak of the ordinary sea track I do not mean an exact line, for it would necessarily vary somewhat according to circumstances; the ordinary track for sailing vessels would vary according to the wind; the ordinary track for a steamer, again, might be different from that for a sailing vessel; I mean the ordinary track of such a voyage according to a reasonable construction of the term. In the present case liberty is given to call at any ports in any order. It was argued that that clause gives liberty to call at any port in the world. Here, again, it is a question of the construction of a mercantile expression used in a mercantile document, and I think that as such the term can have but one meaning, namely, that the ports, liberty to call at which is intended to be given, must be ports which are substantially ports which will be passed on the named voyage. Of course such a term must entitle the vessel to go somewhat out of the ordinary track by sea of the named voyage, for going into the port of call in itself would involve that. To 'call' at a port is a well-known sea-term; it means to call for the purpose of business, generally to take in or unload cargo, or to receive orders; it must mean that the vessel may stop at the port of call for a time, or else the liberty to call would be idle. I believe the term has always been interpreted to mean that the ship may call at such ports as would naturally and usually be ports of call on the voyage named. If the stipulation were only that she might call at any ports, the invariable construction has been that she would only be entitled to call at such ports in their geographical order; and therefore the words 'in any order' are frequently added, but in any case it appears to me that the ports must be ports substantially on the course of the voyage. It follows that, when the defendants' ship went off the ordinary track of a voyage from Fiume to Dunkirk to a port not on the course of that voyage, such as Glasgow, there was a deviation, and she was then on a voyage different from that contracted for to which the excepted perils clause did not apply; and therefore the shipowners are responsible for the loss of the goods.

*Note*
*Leduc* v *Ward* is considered further in Chapter 6, with regard to the alleged agreement of the shippers to the route taken.

### *Glynn* v *Margetson & Co.*
[1893] AC 351 (HL)

LORD HERSCHELL LC: My Lords, the question raised by this appeal is the construction to be put upon a bill of lading by which the shipowners agreed to carry certain goods of the respondents. The shipowners, who are the appellants, alleged that

the Court below erred in so construing their liability under the bill of lading as to hold
that they had broken their contract by proceeding to a port called Burriana after they
had taken on board the cargo shipped by the respondents.

A cargo of oranges was shipped at Malaga, and the bill of lading is in these terms:
'Shipped in good order and condition' 'in and upon the good steamship called the *Zena*,
now lying in the port of Malaga, and bound for Liverpool. Eight third cases oranges'.
The port to which the vessel proceeded after she left Malaga was not in the direction of
Liverpool, but in the contrary direction, taking the vessel farther away from Liverpool
than she was at Malaga.

Of course it could not be disputed that, if the words which I have read to your
Lordships were the only words to be found in the bill of lading relating to the voyage,
the shipowner could not justify his act in thus deviating from the stipulated voyage and
would be liable to the shipper in respect of any damage to his goods sustained in
consequence of such deviation. In the present case, owing to the delay which took place
before the vessel arrived at Liverpool, the oranges were much damaged, and loss was
consequenty sustained. But the shipowner seeks to justify the act of proceeding to
Burriana by reason of the words which follow those which I have read, 'with liberty to
proceed to and stay at any port or ports in any rotation in the Mediterranean, Levant,
Black Sea or Adriatic, or on the coasts of Africa, Spain, Portugal, France, Great Britain
and Ireland, for the purpose of delivering coals, cargo or passengers, or for any other
purpose whatsoever'. The contention of the appellants is, that under those words the
voyage to Burriana was justified by the terms of the contract between the parties.

My Lords, it is admitted that the contention of the appellants goes this length, that
after the oranges were taken on board at Malaga upon a vessel said to be bound for
Liverpool, the ship might have been sent to any port within the limits named, or any
number of those ports in any order, staying there any time she pleased, for the purpose
of taking in cargo or delivering it at any of those ports. And it is true that if their full and
complete meaning be given to the words used, that will be the consequence of giving
them that meaning. The question is whether they ought to be so construed, or whether
there is any reason for putting a restriction upon them.

These words are printed words in a document evidently intended to be used in
relation to a variety of contracts of affreightment. The name of the particular port of
shipment, as well as the goods to be shipped, is left in blank, and the words in question
are treated as a liberty which is to attach to the particular voyage which is agreed upon
between the parties. But the main object and intent of the charterparty is the voyage so
agreed upon; and although it would not be legitimate to discard the printed words
(indeed here the shipowner requires the shipper to undertake to be bound by them as
well as by the written words), yet it is well recognised that in construing an instrument
of this sort, in considering what is its main intent and object, and what the interpretation
of words connected with that main intent and object ought to be, it is legitimate to bear
in mind that a portion of the contract is on a printed form applicable to many voyages,
and is not specially agreed upon in relation to the particular voyage.

My Lords, the main object and intent, as I have said, of this charterparty is the
carriage of oranges from Malaga to Liverpool. That is the matter with which the shipper
is concerned; and it seems to me that it would be to defeat what is the manifest object
and intention of such a contract to hold that it was entered into with a power to the
shipowner to proceed anywhere that he pleased, to trade in any manner that he pleased,
and to arrive at the port at which the oranges were to be delivered when he pleased.

Then is there any rule of law which compels the construction contended for? I think
there is not. Where general words are used in a printed form which are obviously
intended to apply, so far as they are applicable, to the circumstances of a particular

contract, which particular contract is to be embodied in or introduced into the printed form, I think you are justified in looking at the main object and intent of the contract and in limiting the general words used, having in view that object and intent. Therefore, it seems to me that the construction contended for would be an unreasonable one, and there is no difficulty in construing this clause to apply to a liberty in the performance of the stipulated voyage to call at a particular port or ports in the course of the voyage. That port or those ports would differ according to what the stipulated voyage was, inasmuch as at the time when this document was framed the parties who framed it did not know what the particular voyage would be, and intended it to be equally used whatever that voyage is. The ports a visit to which would be justified under this contract would, no doubt, differ according to the particular voyage stipulated for between the shipper and the shipowner; but it must, in my view, be a liberty consistent with the main object of the contract — a liberty only to proceed to and stay at the ports which are in the course of the voyage. In saying that I am, of course, speaking in a business sense. It may be said that no port is directly in the course of the voyage (indeed that was argued by the learned counsel for the appellants), inasmuch as in merely entering a port or approaching it nearly you deviate from the direct course between the port of shipment and the ultimate port of destination. That is perfectly true; but in a business sense it would be perfectly well understood to say that there were certain ports on the way between Malaga and Liverpool, and those are the ports at which I think the right to touch and stay is given.

Then it is said that this may be done 'in any rotation'. I do not think that that carries the matter any further. When once the conclusion which I have indicated is arrived at, if the meaning to be given to those words is that the vessel may take those ports in any order she pleases in a reasonable sense, nevertheless the ports referred to must still, in my opinion, be ports lying between Malaga and the port of destination, Liverpool, even although there might be a justification for her not touching at any particular one of those ports, or more than one of them, in the exact order in which they would come in the voyage between those two places. It is not necessary to decide what effect should be given to those words 'in any rotation'; but even giving to them the fullest possible effect they do not seem to me to enlarge the number of ports at which it would be justifiable for this vessel to touch during the course of her voyage.

My Lords, it is to be observed that the liberty which is given is not a liberty simpliciter to proceed to those ports. Purposes are mentioned; and the first which is mentioned is 'for the purpose of delivering coals, cargo or passengers'. That clause seems to me to throw light upon the construction which ought to be put upon the language used in the other part of the instrument, because the delivering of coals, cargo or passengers points to the carrying out of a voyage already determined upon in relation to a cargo already on board. . . .

LORD HALSBURY LC: My Lords, I am entirely of the same opinion. It seems to me that in construing this document, which is a contract of carriage between the parties, one must in the first instance look at the whole of the instrument and not at one part of it only. Looking at the whole of the instrument, and seeing what one must regard, for a reason which I will give in a moment, as its main purpose, one must reject words, indeed whole provisions, if they are inconsistent with what one assumes to be the main purpose of the contract. The main purpose of the contract was to take on board at one port and to deliver at another port a perishable cargo. . . .

*Notes and Question*
1.   *Leduc* v *Ward* and *Glynn* v *Margetson & Co.* were applied in *James Morrison & Co. Ltd* v *Shaw, Savill and Albion Co. Ltd* [1916] 2 KB 783, where Le Havre

was held not to be an 'intermediate port' on the voyage from New Zealand to England. Swinfen Eady LJ pointed out that Le Havre 'is

... distant sixty-eight miles from the nearest point of the route to London, and in order to reach it involves the vessel going off her course in one direction 107 miles. It is not shown to be a usual or customary port of vessels of this size and class coming from New Zealand to enter. In this particular case it was only for a special purpose, and by reason of a special bargain made after the plaintiffs' goods were shipped, that the captain was instructed to go to Havre. If the question be put, as in *Leduc* v *Ward* (1888) 20 QBD 475, Is Havre substantially a port which will be passed on the named voyage, New Zealand to London? the answer must be in the negative. If the question be put, Is Havre a port which would naturally and usually be a port of call on the named voyage? the answer must be certainly not. If the question suggested by Lord Esher's judgment in *Margetson* v *Glynn* [1892] 1 QB 343 be put, Is Havre a port in the course of the voyage, in the sense that it may be reached by the ship going slightly out of her course? the answer must again be in the negative. By slightly out of her course is meant does the ship on her course go fairly close to the port, and in order to enter the port, or call off it, would she only have to go a very short distance out of her course? Whether you take the distance in the present case as 107 miles or as sixty-eight miles only, the departure from the course of the voyage is quite substantial, and not slight.

It was emphasised that the decision is one of fact in each case.

2.   In *Stag Line Ltd* v *Foscolo, Mango & Co. Ltd* [1932] AC 328 (HL), the clause gave 'liberty to call at any ports in any order, for bunkering or other purposes, all as part of the contract voyage'. It was held that the liberty was only to call for a purpose *related to* the contract voyage. Lord Atkin said:

... What exactly the Chamber of Shipping and the Documentary Council of the Baltic and White Sea Conference (who we are told in the document adopted this form of charterparty) meant by these words I wish they could be asked. We have to struggle to find a meaning. They cannot be unlimited in scope, or they would authorise the shipowner to direct the ship to any part of the globe for any purpose he thought fit. Even if limited to port or ports on the geographical course of the voyage, as I think on authority they clearly must be, the purpose of the call must receive some limitation. The liberty could not reasonably be intended to give the right to call at an intermediate port to land or take on board friends of the shipowner for the purposes of a pleasure trip. On the other hand I find it very difficult to adopt the view which has found favour with one of your Lordships that they involve some limitation which is kindred to or associated with bunkering. Even if the purpose be extended beyond taking in motor fuel or supplies necessary for the navigation of the ship to supplies for the maintenance or comfort of passengers I find it difficult to put such a restricted meaning on the words in view of the collocation 'any ports in any order' which seems to point to some purposes other than the restricted ones suggested. Logically I find a difficulty in excluding a suggested purpose from a class until I have formed some more or less definite conception of the nature of the class. I think myself that the purposes intended are business purposes which would be contemplated by the parties as arising in carrying out the contemplated voyage of the ship. This might include in a contract other than a contract to carry a full and complete cargo a right to call at port or ports on the geographical course to load and discharge cargo for other shippers. It would probably include a right to call for orders. But I cannot think that it would include a right such as was sought to be exercised in the present case to land servants of the shipowners or others who were on board at the start to adjust machinery, and were landed for their own and their owners' convenience because they could not be transferred to any ingoing vessel. I think, therefore, the shipowner is not excused by this clause.

3.   The bill of lading in respect of a cargo of lemons shipped at Palermo for London provides:

Nothing in this bill of lading (whether written or printed) is to be read as an engagement that the said carriage shall be performed directly or without delays, the ship is to be at liberty, either before or after proceeding towards the port of delivery of the said goods, to proceed to or return to and stay at any ports or places whatsoever (although in a contrary direction to or out of or beyond the route of the said port of delivery) once or oftener in any order backwards or forwards for loading or discharging cargo passengers coals or stores or for any purpose whatsoever whether in relation to her homeward voyage or to her outward voyage or to an intermediate voyage, and all such ports places and sailings shall be deemed included within the intended voyage of the said goods.

The vessel calls at Hull before heading for London and by the time the lemons are delivered the market price has fallen. Is the shipowner liable for the loss? (*Cf. Connolly Shaw Ltd* v *Nordenfjeldske Steamship Co.* (1934) 50 TLR 418).

4.   *Glynn* v *Margetson & Co.* was distinguished in *G.H. Renton & Co. Ltd* v *Palmyra Trading Corporation of Panama* [1957] AC 149 (HL). A clause providing that 'master may discharge the cargo at port of loading or any other safe and convenient port' if it should appear that strikes would prevent the vessel from entering the port of discharge or discharging without delay was held not to be inconsistent with the main object of the contract, but a reasonable provision for an emergency. The House of Lords approved the statement by Jenkins LJ in the Court of Appeal [1956] 1 QB 462, at p. 502:

It seems to me that there is a material difference between a deviation clause purporting to enable the shipowners to delay indefinitely the performance of the contract voyage simply because they choose to do so, and provisions such as those contained in clause 45(c) and (f) in the present case, which are applicable and operative only in the event of the occurrence of certain specified emergencies. The distinction is between a power given to one of the parties which, if construed literally, would in effect enable that party to nullify the contract at will and a special provision stating what the rights and obligations of the parties are to be in the event of obstacles beyond the control of either arising to prevent or impede the performance of the contract in accordance with its primary terms. . . .

(The case is considered further in Chapter 7.)

# 5  FREIGHT

Freight is the agreed payment for the carriage of goods under a bill of lading or a voyage charterparty. (The payment under a time charter is not freight but *hire*: this is a payment for the services of the ship, not the carriage of goods, and the principles relating to freight have no application.) The rule of the common law is that delivery of the cargo at its destination is a condition precedent to the right to demand payment of the freight: freight is *calculated* (at the agreed rate) on the amount delivered and is only *earned* and *payable* on right delivery. If no cargo is delivered, no freight is payable at common law and it is immaterial *why* the carrier is unable to deliver: the rule applies even if the carrier is prevented from making delivery by circumstances beyond his control. If part only is delivered, no freight is payable in respect of the remainder.

It has always been open to the parties to vary this position and to make an agreement which places some or all of the (insurable) freight risk on the shipper, but we examine first some implications of the common law rule.

## SECTION 1: DELIVERY FREIGHT

Freight must be paid although the cargo arrives in a damaged condition. The cargo-owner's claim in respect of the damage must be asserted in a separate action, or by counterclaim, and not by way of set-off against the amount of freight.

### *Dakin v Oxley*
(1864) 15 CBNS 646; 143 ER 938 (Common Pleas)

WILLES CJ: This is an action by ship-owner against charterer to recover the freight of a cargo of coal carried from Newport to Nassau.

The first count is upon the charterparty. The second is the common count for freight. The defendant pleads that, by the fault of the master and crew, and their unskilful and negligent navigation of the vessel, the coal was damaged so as upon arrival at the port of discharge to be then there of less value than the freight, and that he abandoned it to the ship-owner. The plea, as it does not deny, admits that the cargo arrived as coal, and that it was of some value. The plaintiff demurs: and the question for us to consider is, whether a charterer whose cargo has been damaged by the fault of the master and crew so as upon arrival at the port of discharge to be worth less than the freight, is entitled to excuse himself from payment of freight by abandoning the cargo to the ship-owner. We think not: and we should not have taken time to consider, but for the general importance of the subejct, and of its having been suggested that our law was silent upon this question, and that the plea was warranted by the usage and law of other maritime countries, which, it was said, we ought to adopt.

. . .

After an extensive review of Continental writers, the Chief Justice continued:

It ought to be borne in mind, when dealing with such cases, that the true test of the right to freight is the question whether the service in respect of which the freight was contracted to be paid has been substantially performed; and according to the law of England, as a rule, freight is earned by the carriage and arrival of the goods ready to be delivered to the merchant, though they be in a damaged state when they arrive. If the ship-owner fails to carry the goods for the merchant to the destined port, the freight is not earned. If he carry part, but not the whole, no freight is payable in respect of the part not carried, and freight is payable in respect of the part carried unless the charterparty make the carriage of the whole a condition precedent to the earning of any freight, — a case which has not within our experience arisen in practice.

. . .

In the case of an actual loss or destruction by sea-damage of so much of the cargo that no substantial part of it remains; as, if sugar in mats, shipped as sugar and paying so much per ton, is washed away, so that only a few ounces remain, and the mats are worthless, the question would arise whether practically speaking any part of the cargo contracted to be carried has arrived. . . . Where the quantity remains unchanged, but by sea-damage the goods have been deteriorated in quality, the question of identity arises in a different form, as, for instance, where a valuable picture has arrived as a piece of spoilt canvas, cloth in rags, or crockery in broken shreds, iron all or almost all rust, rice fermented, or hides rotten.

In both classes of cases, whether of loss of quantity or change in quality, the proper course seems to be the same, viz. to ascertain from the terms of the contract, construed by mercantile usage, if any, what was the thing for the carriage of which freight was to be paid, and by the aid of a jury to determine whether that thing, or any and how much of it, has substantially arrived.

If it has arrived, though damaged, the freight is payable by the ordinary terms of the charterparty; and the question of fortuitous damage must be settled with the underwriters, and that of culpable damage in a distinct proceeding for such damage against the ship captain or owners. There would be apparent justice in allowing damage of the latter sort to be set off or deducted in an action for freight; and this is allowed in some (at least) of the United States, — 1. Parsons on Mercantile Law, 172, n. But our law does not allow deduction in that form; and, as at present administered, for the sake perhaps of speedy settlement of freight and other liquidated demands, it affords the injured party a remedy by cross-action only: *Davidson* v *Gwynne*, 12 East 381; *Stinson* v *Hall*, 1 Hurlst & N 831; *Sheels* (or *Shields*) v *Davies*, 4 Camp 119, 6 Taunt 65; the judgment of Parke B, in *Mondel* v *Steel*, 8 M & W 858; *The Don Francisco*, 32 Law J Adm 14, per Dr Lushington. It would be unjust, and almost absurd that, without regard to the comparative value of the freight and cargo when uninjured, the risk of a mercantile adventure should be thrown upon the ship-owner by the accident of the value of the cargo being a little more than the freight; so that a trifling damage, much less than the freight, would reduce the value to less than the freight; whilst, if the cargo had been much more valuable and the damage greater, or the cargo worth a little less than the freight and the damage the same, so as to bear a greater proportion to the whole value, the freight would have been payable, and the merchant have been put to his cross-action. Yet this is the conclusion we are called upon by the defendant to affirm in his favour, involving no less than that that damage, however trifling, if culpable, may work a forfeiture of the entire freight, contrary to the just rule of our law, by which each party bears the damage resulting from his own breach of contract, and no more.

The extreme case above supposed is not imaginary; for, it has actually occurred on many occasions, and notably upon the cessation of war between France and England in 1748, which caused so great a fall in prices that the agreed freight in many instances exceeded the value of the goods. The merchants in France sought a remission of freight or the privilege of abandonment, but in vain. (2 Boulay-Paty, Cours de Droit Commercial, 485, 486.)

It is evident enough from this review of the law that there is neither authority nor sound reason for upholding the proposed defence. The plea is naught, and there must be judgment for the plaintiff.

*Question*
Can this rule still be justified as a matter of policy?

*Note*
The practical difference between permitting set-off and forcing the cargo-owner to rely on a counterclaim is shown by the next case, where the House of Lords declined to overrule the authorities on which the principle is based.

### *Aries Tanker Corporation* v *Total Transport Ltd*
### *(The Aries)*
[1977] 1 Lloyd's Rep 334 (HL)

LORD WILBERFORCE: My Lords, this appeal arises out of the carriage of a cargo of petroleum from the Arabian Gulf to Rotterdam under a voyage charterparty. The respondents, a Liberian corporation, are the owners of the vessel *Aries* which is a Greek ship; the appellants, a Bermuda company, are the charterers; the contract was made in Paris and is expressed to be governed by English law. Since, on the view which I take, the case turns upon the terms of the contract, I must first refer to its essential provisions.

The charterparty, dated Mar. 21, 1973, was on a standard (B.P.) voyage charter form. The vessel was to proceed to a port or ports in the Arabian Gulf as ordered by the charterers, and was there to load a full and complete cargo of petroleum. It was then to proceed to a port or ports in the United Kingdom or Europe as ordered by the charterers — in fact Rotterdam was nominated — and there to deliver the cargo in consideration of the payment of freight. The freight payable was specified in cl. 6 by a formula which, it is not disputed, meant that it was to be calculated upon the intaken quantity of cargo. Clause 7 provided that freight was to be payable after completion of discharge — the currency and place of payment was stated — in cash without discount. Clause 30 provided as follows:

> The provisions of Articles III (other than Rule 8), IV and VIII of the Schedule to the Carriage of Goods by Sea Act, 1924, of the United Kingdom shall apply to this Charter and shall be deemed to be inserted *in extenso* herein. This Charter shall be deemed to be a contract for the carriage of goods by sea to which the said articles apply and Owners shall be entitled to the protection of the said articles in respect of any claim made hereunder . . .

Article III, r. 6, of the schedule (the Hague Rules) contains the following vital words:

> . . . in any event the carrier and the ship shall be discharged from all liability in respect of loss or damage unless suit is brought within one year after delivery of the goods or the date when the goods should have been delivered . . .

The vessel duly loaded a cargo of regular gasoline and premium gasoline in April, 1973. It arrived in Rotterdam in May, 1973, and there discharged. On measurement of the quantity discharged, it was found that there was a short delivery in respect of each product, the value of which is claimed by the appellants to be U.S. $30,000. In or about June, 1973, the appellants paid, as provided in the charterparty, the amount due for freight but they did so subject to deduction of $30,000: the respondents made it clear that they did not accept the validity of this deduction.

On Oct. 17, 1974, the respondents issued in the Queen's Bench Division a specially endorsed writ for £11,753.18, being the then sterling equivalent of $30,000 as unpaid freight. On Feb. 21, 1975, the appellants served a defence and counterclaim in which they admitted that they had withheld $30,000 from the freight, but claimed that they were entitled to set off against the freight the loss claimed on the cargo and that they were not liable for $30,000. They also counterclaimed for $30,000.

The respondents proceeded under R.S.C., O.14 for summary judgment. It was not disputed that the appellants had a triable case in respect of a claim for short delivery, and that the appellants had not instituted suit within 12 months of discharge. Mr Justice Donaldson refused the appellants leave to defend and gave judgment in favour of the respondents for £11,753.18 with interest, subject to a stay pending appeal. His judgment was affirmed by the Court of Appeal (see [1976] 2 Lloyd's Rep 256).

After holding that the time limit of 12 months under the Hague Rules was not merely procedural but had the substantive effect of extinguishing the claim, his Lordship turned to the question of set-off (at p. 337):

> Then the appellants sought by argument to show that the law, as it is, or alternatively, as it ought to be declared by this House, allows claims in respect of short delivery of cargo to operate by way of reduction of the freight, so that, in their contention, the owner can only sue for a reduced amount, viz., the freight contracted for less a deduction for short delivery. It was to this argument that their major effort was directed both here and in the Court of Appeal. It involved, in effect, a contention that the case of *Henriksens Rederi A/S* v *T.H.Z. Rolimpex (The Brede)* [1973] 2 Lloyd's Rep 33; [1974] QB 233 — a case indistinguishable on its facts from the present — was wrong and should be over-ruled.
>
> . . .
>
> That a claim in respect of cargo cannot be asserted by way of deduction from the freight, is a long established rule in English law. It dates at least from *Sheels* v *Davies*

(1814) 4 Camp 119: it received authoritative approval in 1864 from an eminent Court in *Dakin* v *Oxley* (1864) 15 CB (NS) 646, and again from the same court in *Meyer* v *Dresser* (1864) 33 Law J Rep CP 289, where the rule was called 'settled law'. As a rule it has never been judicially doubted or questioned or criticized; it has received the approval of authoritative text books. It could have been attacked, but was not, by eminent commercial counsel in *Bede Steam Shipping Co. Ltd* v *Bunge y Born* (1927) 27 Ll L Rep 410 (incidentally a case of a time bar). It was reaffirmed after full consideration by the Court of Appeal in *The Brede* (u.s.), and though it has not the full authority of this House, it was referred to by Lord Atkinson as the law in *Kish* v *Taylor* [1912] AC 604 at p. 612.

It is said to be an arbitrary rule — and so it may be, in the sense that no very clear justification for it has ever been stated and perhaps also in the sense that the law might just, or almost, as well have settled for a rule to the opposite effect. But this does not affect its status in the law. A rule is none the less capable of being a rule of law, though no reason can be given for it: as Lord Sumner said, an established rule does not become questionable merely because different conjectural justifications of it have been offered, or because none is forthcoming that is not fanciful (*Admiralty Commissioners* v *S.S. Amerika* [1917] AC 38 at p. 56). In commercial matters it is all the more important that established rules, unless clearly wrong, should not be disturbed by the Courts (see *Atlantic Shipping and Trading Co.* v *Dreyfus* (1922) 10 Ll L Rep 707; [1922] 2 AC 250 at pp. 707 and 257 per Lord Dunedin). It is said to be inconsistent with the rule laid down in relation to the sale of goods and contracts for work as to which an eminent Court in 1841 laid down that claims amounting to a breach of warranty can be asserted by way of deduction — *Mondel* v *Steel* (1841) 8 M & W 858, a rule which, as regards the sale of goods was validated by statute (Sale of Goods Act 1893, s. 53). And your Lordships were asked to assimilate the rule in the present case to that. There are two answers to this: first, the two rules have been running in parallel for over a century without difficulty, and indeed in *Mondel* v *Steel* itself Baron Parke specifically referred to the existence of a separate rule as regards freight. In this House, that the rule of deduction, or abatement, is one confined to contract for the sale of goods or for work and labour and does not extend to contracts generally, was recognised in *Gilbert-Ash (Northern) Ltd* v *Modern Engineering (Bristol) Ltd* [1974] AC 689 at p. 717, per Lord Diplock. There is no case of its having been extended to contracts of any kind of carriage. The rule against deduction in cases of carriage by sea is, in fact, as well settled as any common law rule can be. As to the argument from inconsistency with the rule prevailing in relation to the sale of goods, it is no part of the functions of this House, or the Judges, to alter a well established rule or, to put it more correctly, to say that a different rule is part of our law, for the sake of harmonisation with a rule operating in a different field — not unless there is an intrinsic case, I would say a strong case, for altering the former rule. To quote again from Lord Sumner:

> Nor does it follow, in the case of a legal system such as ours, that a principle can be said to be truly a part of the law merely because it would be a more perfect expression of imperfect rules which, though imperfect, are well established and well defined. (loc. cit).

To do this would be to macro-architecture of the law and would be for a particular type of reformer.

But beyond all this there is a decisive reason here why this House should not alter the rule approved in *The Brede* by reversing it. That is that the parties in this case have, I think beyond doubt, contracted upon the basis and against the background that the established rule is against deduction. Such a case as this, in fact, marks out very decisively the possible limits of judicial intervention: for it would be undesirable in this, or in any other case where the same question arose, for the Courts to declare that a rule, clearly shown to exist, and shown to be the basis of the contract before the Court, ought to be replaced by a different rule which would have to operate on the contract in question. However convinced the Courts might be of the latter's merits, to substitute it could be no part of a judicial process. This is all the less so since the parties themselves, if they dislike the rule, can perfectly well provide otherwise in their contract.

I am therefore firmly of the opinion that the rule against deduction has to be applied to this charterparty so that the charterers' claim for short delivery cannot be relied on by way of defence. On any view, therefore, of the time bar, and even assuming the latter to be only procedural, it must defeat the claim.

. . .

*Notes*

1. Lord Simon (at p. 340) drew attention to the contrast between the rule regarding freight and other cases of defective performance, where set-off came to be allowed early in the 19th century: 'Freight, representing the original rule, stands uneroded, like an outcrop of pre-Cambrian amid the detritus of sedimentary deposits'.

Other members of the House considered that no apology for the rule was needed. Lord Salmon said:

This rule of law which was fathered by such masters of the law as Baron Parke, Baron Alderson, Chief Justice Erle and Mr Justices Willes and Byles has been generally accepted for well over 100 years and never judicially questioned. It has been confirmed in the original and every succeeding edition of Scrutton on Charterparties and Carver, Carriage of Goods by Sea. It was adopted in Lord Atkinson's speech, with which Lord Macnaghten and Earl Loreburn LC, concurred in *Kish* v *Taylor* [1912] AC 604, and recently by the Court of Appeal in *The Brede* [1973] 2 Lloyd's Rep 333; [1974] 1 QB 233. A rule of law, particularly a rule of commercial law which has stood so long and upon the faith of which many thousands of contracts of carriage have been made and are daily being made containing a provision that the contract shall be governed by the law of England, cannot now be successfully challenged in our Courts. The fact that English law may not in this respect coincide with the laws of the USA, see e.g., *Pennsylvania R. Co. Ltd* v *Miller* 124 Fed 2nd 160, is beside the point; so is the fact that neither the reason nor the justification for this rule of English law has ever been defined. I am, however, by no means satisfied that no reason or justification exists. It may well be, e.g., that the whole incidence of insurance cover in respect of freight is based upon the rule. However this may be, it is a rule so well recognised and accepted as the law of England that if it is to be altered, it can, in my view be altered by Parliament alone. If it were to be altered by statute it would presumably not be altered retrospectively and the alteration would therefore apply only to contracts made after the statute came into operation.

2. The House of Lords in *The Aries* also rejected an argument by the charterers that the deduction for short delivery might be based on an *equitable* set-off. This point had not been argued at all in *The Brede* [1974] QB 233, when the Court of Appeal affirmed the *Dakin* v *Oxley* principle. It was given a more extensive airing in *Colonial Bank* v *European Grain & Shipping Ltd (The*

*Dominique*) [1989] 1 Lloyd's Rep 431 (HL) and was again rejected. *The Dominique* is considered further in relation to advance freight, below.

3.  The principle of no set-off against freight applies also to domestic carriage by land: *United Carriers Ltd* v *Heritage Food Group (UK) Ltd* [1995] 4 All ER 95 (QBD).

4.  It is of course open to the parties to agree that cargo claims may be set-off against freight: Cf. *Protank Shipping Inc* v *Total Transport Corp. (The Protank Orinoco)* [1997] 2 Lloyd's Rep 42 (QBD, Thomas J). There the charterparty provided: 'In the event that any cargo remains on board upon completion of discharge, charterers shall have the right to deduct from freight an amount equal to the FOB port of loading value of such cargo plus freight due with respect thereto, provided that the volume of cargo remaining on board is liquid and pumpable and reachable by vessel's pumps (or would have been liquid and pumpable and reachable by vessel's pumps, but for the fault or negligence of the owners, master, vessel or her crew, including incorrect trim procedure) as determined by an independent surveyor whose estimate shall be final and binding'. On the facts, no such determination had taken place: in particular the provision for a final and binding determination (which is not found in standard cargo retention clauses) meant that the surveyor should be one appointed *jointly* by shipowner and cargo owner.

Freight is not payable if the goods delivered are no longer the cargo contracted for.

### Asfar & Co. v Blundell
### [1896] 1 QB 123 (CA)

A & Co. chartered the *Govino* for a voyage from the Persian Gulf to London at a lump sum freight of £3,900. A & Co. then took on board cargo from various shippers. The total freight due under the bills of lading was £4,690. A & Co. insured their profit on the charter with B for £2,000.

While the *Govino* was sailing up the Thames she was hit by another vessel and filled with water, remaining almost entirely submerged for two days before she could be raised and docked. The cargo included a quantity of dates which were then found to be saturated with sewage and fermenting, although still mostly retaining the appearance of dates. They were condemned as unfit for human consumption and could not be landed; they were, however, sold for £2,400 for distillation into spirit, transhipped and exported.

A & Co. claimed on their freight insurance and succeeded before Mathew J. B appealed.

LORD ESHER MR: I am of opinion that this appeal should be dismissed. The first point taken on behalf of the defendants, the underwriters, is that there has been no total loss of the dates, and therefore no total loss of the freight on them. The ingenuity of the argument might commend itself to a body of chemists, but not to business men. We are dealing with dates as a subject-matter of commerce; and it is contended that, although these dates were under water for two days, and when brought up were simply a mass of pulpy matter impregnated with sewage and in a state of fermentation, there had been no change in their nature, and they still were dates. There is a perfectly well known test which has for many years been applied to such cases as the present — that test is whether, as a matter of business, the nature of the thing has been altered. The nature of a thing is not necessarily altered because the thing itself has been damaged; wheat or rice may be damaged, but may still remain the things dealt with as wheat or rice in business. But if the nature of the thing is altered, and it becomes for business purposes something else, so that it is not dealt with by business people as the thing which it originally was, the question for determination is whether the thing insured, the original article of commerce, has become a total loss. If it is so changed in its nature by the perils of the sea as to become an unmerchantable thing, which no buyer would buy and no honest seller would sell, then there is a total loss. That test was applied in the present case by the learned judge in the Court below, who decided as a fact that the dates had been so deteriorated that they had become something which was not merchantable as dates. If that was so, there was a total loss of the dates. What was the effect of this upon the insurance? If they were totally lost as dates, no freight in respect of them became due from the consignee to the person to whom the bill of lading freight was payable — that is, to the charterers — and there was a total loss of the bill of lading freight on these dates.

. . .

LOPES LJ: I am of the same opinion. The first point taken was that there was no total loss of the dates. But the facts shew that they had been submerged for two days, and that when they were again seen they were a mixture of date pulp and sewage and were in a state of fermentation and putrefaction; they had clearly lost any merchantable character as dates. In my judgment, it is idle to suggest that there was not a total loss of the dates, and that the plaintiffs were not entitled to recover as for a total loss of their freight....

*Question*
Did the Court of Appeal here give sufficient weight to the fact that the cargo was received at the contemplated destination and could be resold for a substantial sum? If the shippers/consignees choose to take the cargo should they not pay the freight?

*Note*
It is enough to sustain the right to freight if the cargo delivered satisfies in commercial terms the description in the contract of carriage.

### *Montedison SpA* v *Icroma SpA*
### *(The Caspian Sea)*
### [1980] 1 Lloyd's Rep 91 (QBD)

DONALDSON J: *Caspian Sea* was chartered to carry a part cargo of crude oil and/or dirty pertroleum products from Punta Cardon to Genoa. Freight was payable 'upon delivery of the cargo'. The oil in fact shipped was 'Bachaquero Crude', a Venezuelan crude whose special value lies in the fact that it is free of paraffin and is therefore suitable for the production of lubricating oils of high quality and value. The charterers took delivery of the oil on discharge, but allege that what was discharged contained paraffinic products derived from the residues of a previous cargo of low sulphur fuel oil which had not been removed from the vessel's tanks before loading. I am asked to assume that the charterers' allegations are correct.

In arbitration proceedings the owners claimed payment of the freight and the charterers counterclaimed damages for breach of contract. However, the owners contended that they were entitled to an immediate interim award covering the full amount of the freight, because a claim for damage to cargo cannot be set off against a claim for freight (*Aries Tanker Corporation* v *Total Transport Ltd* [1977] 1 Lloyd's Rep 334; [1977] 1 WLR 185). The charterers retorted that there was no *immediate* right to freight, because what was delivered was not merchantable as 'Bachaquero Crude' or alternatively was not commercially identical with the cargo loaded. This contention was unarguable and has rightly been abandoned by Mr Rix who has appeared for the charterers. The charterers' current contention is different. It is that in these circumstances there is no right to freight now or at any other time, because there was no 'delivery of the cargo' and accordingly no freight was ever earned.

. . .

Mr Sumption for the owners submits that the shipowner will be entitled to full freight unless the goods are a total or constructive total loss in insurance terms and that their identity must not only be changed, they must be worthless to the consignee. He also submits that whatever the state of the goods at the port of discharge, the consignee is obliged to pay the freight if he takes delivery of those goods.

*Scrutton on Charterparties* (18th ed.) art. 163 at p. 339 states the law as follows:

The shipowner will be entitled to full freight:

(1) If he is ready to deliver in substance at the port of destination the goods loaded, though in a damaged condition. The freighter will not be entitled to make a deduction from the freight for the damage, but will have a separate cause of action or counterclaim for the damage, unless caused solely by excepted perils or by the vice of the goods themselves. The question is whether the substance delivered is identical commercially with the substance loaded, though it may have deteriorated in quality.

This statement of the law seems to me to be fully supported by the authorities and indeed to be the obvious conclusion apart from authority. The freight clause specifies the circumstances in which freight becomes payable, namely, 'upon delivery of the cargo'. If there is no delivery of anything or if what is delivered is not 'the cargo', no freight is payable. But the mere fact that goods are delivered in a damaged state does not necessarily, or even usually, involve the proposition that they are not 'the cargo'. The real problem is to determine the point at which the damage to, or transformation of, the goods which were shipped is such as to render them incapable of being any longer so described.

After referring to the earlier authorities, including *Duthie* v *Hilton* (1868) LR 4 CP 138, where cement in bags solidified after being submerged and was held no longer to be cement, Donaldson J continued:

The most recent, and in my view the most helpful, authority is *Asfar & Co.* v *Blundell* (1896) 1 QB 123. There a vessel carrying a cargo of dates was sunk during the voyage. She was raised, but the dates were 'affected', to use a neutral term, by seawater and sewage. Although the dates were unmerchantable as dates, and were not allowed to be landed in London, a large proportion retained the appearance of dates and they had considerable value abroad as the raw material for distillation into spirit. They were in

fact transhipped and sold for this purpose. The claim was brought upon a policy insuring the freight and it was held that the right to the freight had been lost.
. . .

Donaldson J quoted the passage from the judgment of Lord Esher MR, set out above, and continued:

Lord Justice Lopes at p. 130 held that the dates were totally lost and Lord Justice Kay at p. 132 held that while the substance of the dates still remained, it was sufficient that there had been a total destruction of their mercantile character.

The learned editors of Scrutton have expressed doubt as to the correctness of this decision, because the consignees took the cargo and sold it. With the greatest respect, I do not share this doubt. The consignees took what was their property, but it had been so damaged as to cease to be 'the cargo' and there was a total failure by the shipowners to perform the contract for which the freight was payable, namely, the carriage and delivery of the cargo at the port of destination. But however that may be, the decision is binding upon me.

I therefore turn to the question of law posed in the award. The mere fact that the oil as delivered was not identical commercially with the cargo loaded does not, in my judgment, deprive the owners of their right to freight. Undamaged or uncontaminated goods can rarely be considered to be identical commercially with damaged or contaminated goods, but it is well settled that damage or contamination is not, as such, a bar to the right to freight. Nor do I accept the argument that the test is to be found in the amended definition of 'merchantable quality' in s. 62(1A) of the Sale of Goods Act 1893. Again I get no assistance by considering the law of insurance and the concept of a constructive total loss of goods. I also reject the argument that the consignee having accepted goods tendered by the shipowner, the shipowners necessarily are entitled to be paid the freight.

The owners will be entitled to the freight if what they delivered could in commercial terms, bear a description which sensibly and accurately included the words 'Bachaquero Crude', e.g., 'Bachaquero Crude contaminated with paraffin or low sulphur oil residues'. The question is whether an honest merchant would be forced to qualify the description applicable to the goods on shipment to such an extent as to destroy it. If the qualification destroys the description, no freight has been earned because 'the cargo' has not been delivered. If the description is merely qualified, 'the cargo' has been delivered, albeit damaged or as the case may be contaminated. This, in my judgment, is what Lord Esher meant by the test of merchantability or of the nature of the goods being so altered as to become for business purposes something else.

I can best illustrate this by examples. If one takes a carboy of sulphuric acid and adds a limited quantity of water — an experiment which should only be conducted with extreme care and with knowledge of the likely consequences — the resulting liquid will still be sulphuric acid, albeit dilute sulphuric acid. But if one adds enough water, the point will be reached at which the liquid is more properly described as water contaminated with acid than as dilute acid. This is the dividing line. Of course, some descriptions of goods are such that any damage or contamination contradicts the description, e.g., 'pure water' or 'sterile dressings'. The arbitrators will have to consider what is meant by the description 'Bachaquero Crude'. Does it mean a paraffin free crude? If it does, 'Bachaquero Crude contaminated by paraffin' is a contradiction in terms and the owners will not be entitled to freight. Or does it mean 'a crude from the Bachaquero region which in its natural state contains no paraffin'? If so, there is no necessary contradiction in 'Bachaquero Crude contaminated by paraffin'. In that event, the fact of contamination will not of itself deprive the owners of their right to freight. However, the arbitrators would have to consider the degree of contamination. They would have to ask themselves the question 'Is the oil so contaminated that it has ceased to be even contaminated Bachaquero Crude?' If so, the right to freight has gone. No doubt a relevant factor will be the cost and practicability of extracting the paraffin, but there may well be other criteria. These are matters of fact which are for the arbitrators as the tribunal of fact.

The award will be remitted to the arbitrators in order that they may make such further award or awards as is appropriate in the light of this judgment.

No freight is payable if the cargo is not carried to the agreed destination, unless the carrier can show an agreement (express or implied) to pay for the carriage which has actually taken place.

### *Metcalfe* v *Britannia Ironworks Company*
### (1877) 2 QBD 423 (CA)

The *Meredith*, owned by M, was chartered by B to load a cargo of railway iron at Middlesborough for carriage to Taganrog at the north of the Sea of Azov in Russia. The *Meredith* arrived at the port of Kerch, at the entrance to the Sea of Azov, in mid-December and found that the Sea was ice-bound for the winter. The charterer's agent would not accept delivery at Kerch (which was 300 miles from Taganrog by sea and *700* miles by land), but the captain discharged the cargo and delivered it to the custom-house authorities. Soon afterwards an agent for the consignees, a Russian railway company, produced the bills of lading and obtained possession from the authorities without payment of the freight. M brought this action against the charterers for the freight. The action failed, but Cockburn CJ, dissenting, thought that M was entitled to freight pro rata. The Court of Appeal affirmed the majority decision.

BRETT LJ: The shipowner here claims full freight, or, if not, freight pro rata, but it appears to me that he is not entitled to either. The charterparty is in the ordinary form, which has often been construed, and we must hold, as a condition precedent to the recovery of anything as freight under the charterparty, that the goods shall have been carried to the port of destination, or as near thereto as the ship can safely get. Nothing, therefore, can be recovered under this charterparty unless the agreement has been performed, or the performance has been waived by the charterers or by some one authorised by them. Now, construing this charterparty as well as we can, it is obvious that the condition has not been fulfilled; nor was it waived by the charterers, nor, for reasons already given, can we hold that it was waived by the consignees. It seems to me clear that the consignees only took the goods because the captain had left them, and had declared that he would not carry them any farther. It is true that the consignees were not obliged to treat this declaration as final, but they had a right so to treat it. And even if they had believed that they had a right to waive the performance of the charterparty, they would not have bound the charterers so as to make them liable. The consignees were not the agents of the charterers, and could not bind them. They might, if they chose, accept the goods at a place short of the port of destination, and possibly in that case the charterer could not bring an action against the shipowners for not having duly carried the goods; but it does not follow that the shipowner earns his freight because the consignee takes the cargo. If the consignee does take delivery at another port, the question depends upon the terms on which he has taken it. He may have bound himself to the shipowner, but that is a new contract between them, and not with the charterer. The only thing which can make the charterer liable is a substantial fulfilment of the charter, or a waiver by the charterer or his authorised agent. It appears to me that the charterers here are not liable, and that even if the consignees had waived the full performance, that would not bind the charterers and make them liable.

As to the claim for freight pro rata, the Lord Chief Justice seems to think that the case of *Luke* v *Lyde* 2 Burr 882 determines that, by a principle of maritime commercial law, apart from any contract between the parties, the merchant is bound to pay freight pro rata, if he accepts the delivery at any place short of the destination when, without any default on the part of the shipowner, but through the operation of a vis major, he is prevented from carrying the goods farther. The Lord Chief Justice, having extracted that propositon, proceeds to shew that the other cases bear out that conclusion, or can be distinguished. But I cannot say that by the law of England liability to pro rata freight can arise, except on a new contract. If it is necessary to make a new contract, that may be made between the owner and the charterer, or between the owner and the consignee, and may be express or implied. But here there was no express contract between the charterers and the shipowner to pay pro rata freight, and there are no facts from which any such contract can be inferred. Neither is there any express contract between the shipowner and the consignees, and, for the reasons which have been already given, I think there are no facts, as between the shipowner and the consignees, from which any contract for pro rata freight could be implied according to the ordinary doctrine in such cases. Therefore the plaintiff has no contract with any one. But if such a contract could have been implied between the plaintiff and the consignees, it would not have enabled the plaintiff to sue the charterers. The consignees were no more the agents of the charterers to bind them to pay freight pro rata than they were to waive the charterparty altogether. If therefore the plaintiff is entitled to pro rata freight, that is as between him and the consignees, and not as between him and these defendants; as between him and them he cannot be allowed to recover the charterparty freight because he has not performed the conditions precedent. I am therefore of opinion that the judgment of the majority of the Court below was right, and ought to be affirmed.

*Notes and Questions*
1.   In the proceedings in the lower court it had in fact been assumed that Kerch and Taganrog were merely 30 miles apart, and the true situation only came out on the appeal.
2.   Pro rata freight means freight *pro rata itineris*, i.e., calculated on the proportion of the voyage which has been performed. The Court of Appeal could scarcely have found that the charterers had agreed to pay freight pro rata, and they also seemed decidedly unsympathetic to the idea that the bill of lading holders might have been found liable on an implied contract. Nevertheless, the railway company did receive the cargo at its ultimate destination (eventually), and what else could the master have done?
3.   If the master had decided to leave the cargo on board and take it back to England, could the shipowner have claimed *back* freight? (*Cf. Cargo ex Argos* (1873) LR 5 PC 134.)

4.   The full freight is payable on delivery short of the agreed destination if the action of the cargo-owner prevents the completion of the voyage: *Cargo ex the Galam* (1863) 33 LJ Ad 97, at p. 100.

## SECTION 2: LUMP SUM FREIGHT

The parties may agree on a freight expressed as a single sum which does not vary with the quantity of cargo shipped. (*Cf. Asfar & Co.* v *Blundell,* above.) The effect of such an agreement is that the whole sum is payable even though the whole cargo is not delivered, provided that the carrier has the benefit of an exception in respect of any part of the cargo which is not delivered.

Lump sum freight was sometimes described as being payment for a voyage, but this explanation does not fit the decision of the House of Lords in the next case.

### *William Thomas & Sons* v *Harrowing Steamship Co.*
### [1915] AC 58 (HL)

VISCOUNT HALDANE LC: My Lords, if I entertained any doubt about this case I should ask your Lordships to take time to consider it, but it seems to me, both upon the facts and upon the law, a plain case. It arises between the owners of the cargo, who are the appellants, and the owners, who are the respondents, of the ship which was chartered by the appellants. The charterparty was made on September 1, 1911, and its purport was this. The steamer was to carry a full and safe deck load at charterers' risk, not exceeding what she could reasonably stow and carry, over and above her tackle, apparel, provisions, and furniture, and being so loaded was to proceed to Port Talbot dock as ordered, or so near thereunto as she could safely get, and deliver the same, always afloat, on being paid freight as follows. Then it was provided that a lump sum of 1,600*l.* was to be the freight 'in full of all port charges and pilotages, in consideration of which owners place at charterers' disposal the full reach of steamer, on and under decks, including spare bunkers, if any.' Then there is the usual clause excepting perils of the sea, and then there is, finally, the only other clause I need read, clause 9: 'The freight to be paid in cash without discount (less freight advance, if any) on unloading and right delivery of the cargo.' That is a not unimportant clause.

Now, my Lords, what happened was this. The steamer sailed from the port of loading and she proceeded to Port Talbot, where she arrived on October 29, but she could not get into dock on that day, and before she could get into dock her anchors dragged, and her cables parted owing to perils of the sea, and in consequence she drove ashore on the north side of the breakwater at Port Talbot and there she remained. Then for the rest of what happened I turn to the judgment of Pickford J, because he has found the facts, and the learned judges in the Court of Appeal in substance concurred in his finding. He says that what happened was this (Appendix, p. 13): 'Her cargo consisted partly of deck cargo, and that deck cargo was swept off; some of it was stranded on the beach and some of it was not recovered at all. The rest of the cargo was washed out and was washed out because it was assisted in being washed out by holes being cut or blasted in the side of the ship in order to enable the cargo to get out.' It is not very clear what were the circumstances under which these holes were cut or blasted, but that does not matter. There was a Mr Jenkins who appears to have acted at first on the instigation of the

Salvage Association, and afterwards by arrangement with the captain, and the learned judge finds the facts as to what happened.

I think the result of that was this, that the master agreed, on behalf of his owners, to be the other contracting party with regard to this offer which was made by Mr Jenkins, and I do not think any difference is made by the fact that some of the work had been done before the master signed that document, and done, perhaps, by Mr Jenkins under the impression that he was doing it under agreement with the Salvage Association. I think the result of it really was this, if you put it into legal language, that the master promised that in consideration of his going on to perform the services mentioned in his offer, he, on behalf of his owner, would pay for the whole of the contract, what had been done and what remained to be done.

The effect of that was that with the assistance of Mr Jenkins it became possible for the shipowner to see that the cargo got into the hands of the cargo owners, who obtained delivery of some two-thirds or three-fourths of it as the result of what I have described.

Now, my Lords, the question which is argued, the main question, is this. It is said that this was what is called a lump sum contract, and that, as the ship did not arrive alongside the quay in Port Talbot and deliver in the ordinary way, the freight is not payable. It is an action for freight. The shipowners were plaintiffs; they are now respondents, but they were plaintiffs in the Court of first instance, and they sued for their freight. The answer made was, 'No, you have not performed your contract, which was an entire contract as shown by the nature of the consideration. You were to proceed to Port Talbot with your ship; your ship never got there; you have not performed your contract, and you are not entitled to the consideration stipulated for.' But, my Lords, I do not think that the question whether the freight is a lump sum freight is in the least decisive of the character of the contract. There may be contracts, as the learned judge has said, and as Kennedy LJ afterwards said, in which the stipulation is simply for the use of a ship, for the hiring of a ship, which is to proceed to a certain port for a lump sum; and in that case it may be, if you get such a contract, that there is no right to freight unless the voyage is completed literally. We have not to do with a contract like that; we have to deal with this contract, and as regards this contract I entirely agree with what the learned judge said, that the meaning of the contract in this case is that it is the ordinary and regular charter for the services of a ship to carry a particular cargo to a particular port. The substance of the contract is the carrying of the cargo, and the ship (reading the contract as a whole) is the instrument by means of which the cargo is to be carried, and considerations relating to the ship are subordinate to considerations relating to the cargo.

My Lords, in that state of facts the law which seems to me to apply is the law which was laid down by Lord Ellenborough in *Hunter* v *Prinsep* 10 East 378 to this effect:

The ship owners undertake that they will carry the goods to the place of destination, unless prevented by the dangers of the seas, or other unavoidable casualties: and the freighter undertakes that if the goods be delivered at the place of their destination he will pay the stipulated freight; but it was only in that event, viz. of their delivery at the place of destination, that he, the freighter, engages to pay anything. If the ship be disabled from completing her voyage, the ship owner may still entitle himself to the whole freight, by forwarding the goods by some other means to the place of destination.

Now the learned judge has held here that what took place was equivalent to that transhipment of which Lord Ellenborough speaks. It does not matter that it was not done in lighters; it was done by getting the pit props brought out to the beach where they were delivered. It does not matter that wind and waves played a large part in the process; the point is that they arrived there and everybody was anxious that they should arrive and was doing his best to secure that they should arrive. Under those circumstances the learned judge has held that the facts are facts which amount to a transhipment of the goods, or at any rate have the same effect in law, and that, consequently, there was delivery of two-thirds of the cargo, and as to the rest of the cargo it came within the clause excepting perils of the sea.

My Lords, I entirely concur in the judgment of Pickford J and the reasoning of the learned Lords Justices in the Court of Appeal who took the same view. I therefore move your Lordships that the appeal be dismissed with costs.

*Question*
What would the position be if some of the cargo had been lost for a reason which did not fall within any of the exceptions?

Even a freight which is related to the quantity of the cargo shipped may produce the effect of a lump sum freight in making freight payable on more cargo than is actually delivered.

### *Shell International Petroleum Ltd* v *Seabridge Shipping Ltd*
### *(The Metula)*
[1978] 2 Lloyd's Rep 5 (CA)

LORD DENNING MR: In July, 1974, a huge super tanker called the *Metula* loaded in the Persian Gulf a cargo of Arabian light oil. It was to be carried to Chile. The amount of the cargo loaded — the intake quantity — was measured, and an inspector's certificate was given, making it come to 190,415 long tons. Unfortunately, as the vessel went through the Magellan Strait, she stranded, and a large quantity of the oil was lost. One-third of it was lost: two-thirds was transferred to other tankers and carried through to the destination in Chile.

When the oil was landed in Chile, the total amount was 138,195.3 long tons. Thereupon the shipowners claimed that they were entitled under the terms of the charterparty to the full amount of the freight on the intaken quantity. The freight was on the World Scale of $7.64 a ton. On that basis on the intaken quantity of 190,000-odd long tons, they were entitled to £625,170 sterling. But the charterers said, 'No; we are not going to pay on the intake quantity. We are only going to pay on that which was delivered', and they paid only £446,567 sterling. Thereupon the shipowners claimed the balance. They claimed £178,602 sterling, because they said they were entitled to be paid on the intaken quantity. They said they were not liable for the stranding or the loss because they were protected by the exceptions.

This issue depends on the interpretation of the charterparty and one or two clauses in it. It is on the Exxonvoy form for a tanker voyage charterparty. It is a form in use both in New York and in London — providing for arbitration in either place according to where the parties choose. So it is very desirable that the interpretation of this charterparty should be the same whether it is being considered in New York or in London. It is for four consecutive voyages. There is a provision in part I for freight on the World Scale. Clause 2 of the printed form reads as follows:

> Freight shall be at the rate stipulated in Part I and shall be computed on intake quantity (except dead-freight as per Clause 3) as shown on the Inspector's Certificate of Inspection . . .

So it is clear that it is computed on the intake quantity as shown on the inspector's certificate. That sentence deals with computation. The next sentence reads:

... Payment of freight shall be made by Charterer without discount upon delivery of cargo at destination, less any disbursements or advances made to the Master or Owner's agents at ports of loading and/or discharge and cost of insurance thereon ...

That sentence deals with payment. There is to be payment upon delivery of cargo at destination. The third sentence reads:

... No deduction of freight shall be made for water and/or sediment contained in the cargo. [— That contemplates that some of the oil which was put on board also contained water or sediment. There is to be no deduction of freight on that account. The fourth sentence reads: —] The services of the Petroleum Inspector shall be arranged and paid for by the charterer who shall furnish the Owner with a copy of the Inspector's Certificate.

So the charterer has to get it and then furnish the owner with the certificate.

Clause 3 deals with deadfreight. The first sentence reads:

Should the Charterer fail to supply a full cargo, the Vessel may, at the Master's option, and shall, upon request of the Charterer, proceed on her voyage, provided that the tanks in which cargo is loaded are sufficiently filled to put her in seaworthy condition. [— The second sentence reads: —] In that event, however, deadfreight shall be paid at the rate specified in Part I hereof on the difference between the intake quantity and the quantity the Vessel would have carried if loaded to her minimum permissible freeboard for the voyage.

That deadfreight provision makes it quite clear that the owners stipulate that they are to be paid the full amount on the full intake quantity even though the charterers do not fuel [sic] her to that extent.

Those are the sentences to be considered. The argument for the owners is that the freight — although not a lump sum freight it has many characteristics similar to it — is computed on the intake quantity and it is to be paid on the delivery of cargo at the destination. It does not mean the full cargo has to be delivered or that if it is short-delivered they get less. The full payment has to be made when cargo is delivered. Of course, if more [sic] of it is delivered, they may not be entitled to their freight; but if some is delivered, they are entitled to the full quantity even though short.

The question in this case seems to me to be simply one of construction of this charterparty. (I may say that bills of lading were issued, but they do not affect this case and I need not further refer to them.) We have been referred, as usual, to other cases on similar clauses. We have been referred in particular to a case in the United States: *Christie* v *Davis Coal & Coke Co.* (1899) 95 Fed Rep 837. That case went to the Court of Appeals, and was affirmed straightaway. The principal English case which was cited to us was the decision of Lord Alverstone in *London Transport Co. Ltd* v *Trechmann Bros.* [1904] 1 QB 635, and which is more fully reported, including the judgment of Mr Justice Walton in 90 LT 132.

I do not propose to analyse all the words in those cases or the distinctions which can be taken from them. I put this question in the course of the argument:

If the freight is payable only on such part of the cargo as is delivered, why is special provision made in this charterparty that it has been computed on the intake quantity?

I never received any satisfactory answer to that question. It seems to me the very purpose of having the computation being made on the intake quantity is that freight should be ascertained then, although payable later when the ship gets to its destination. There is no provision whatsoever for subsequent adjustment or calculations being made at the port of destination. Furthermore, as Mr Hallgarten pointed out such a structure would involve very difficult calculations which could arise both as to temperature and specific gravity, and goodness knows what else in order to assess the sum payable at the port of destination.

    ... [I]n my opinion on the true construction of this clause, although this is not a lump sum freight properly so-called, it has the characteristics of a lump sum in that the freight is computed on the intake quantity. When the cargo is delivered, it is to be paid on that intake quantity. Even though there is a shortage, that full freight has to be paid.

I think the Judge was right, and I would therefore dismiss the appeal.

ROSKILL LJ: The question which has to be answered is whether on the true construction of cl. 2 of this charterparty in the events which have happened the charterers are liable to pay the balance of freight claimed to the owners notwithstanding that the owners have failed to deliver about 50,000 or 60,000 tons of the oil which was shipped on this super tanker in the Persian Gulf some years ago. The learned Judge has held that that balance of freight is due because of the construction he put on the clause. He held that non-delivery of the whole cargo did not preclude recovery of the whole of the freight which would have been due had the whole of the cargo been delivered.

If the question in the present case were whether the present freight can properly be labelled 'a lump sum freight' as that phrase has been understood for at least 150 years, if not longer, I would have no hesitation in saying that it was not a lump sum freight. If the question were, as it sometimes is, whether the freight was due under a clause such as appears in the Shell form of bill of lading, which was used by the parties in the present case, although it never operated as a contract of affreightment:

    ... Freight shall be deemed to be earned on commencement of loading and shall be payable vessel and/or cargo lost or not lost ...

again I would unhesitatingly say that cl. 2 does not have the same effect as that clause. But in his argument Mr Hallgarten submitted that this clause was a very special clause. He submitted that the clause did not go so far as to entitle the shipowners to the freight on the whole quantity loaded in the Persian Gulf if the ship had been totally lost with the cargo. He did not go as far as that. Whether that concession was rightly made or not, I do not stop to enquire. That does not have to be decided. But what he did submit was that under this very special clause, which I regard as unlike the clauses in the other cases which have come before the Courts either of this country or, as far as I know, of the United States, in the events which happened the charterers were liable for the whole of the balance of the freight. That, as I said a moment ago, must depend on the construction of this clause.

I hope it is not out of place to say that this clause might have been more clearly expressed, but we have to deal with it as it is. When one turns to the clause as it has been broken down into separate sentences for our benefit, one finds that the opening sentence of cl. 2 first of all describes what the rate of the freight is and how it should be computed; it is clear that that freight has to be computed on the intake quantity. When one comes to the second sentence of cl. 2, one finds:

    ... Payment of freight shall be made by Charterer without discount upon delivery of cargo at destination.

and the only question we have to decide, as I see it, is whether that means that payment of the entirety of the freight upon the whole of the intake quantity of the cargo is conditional upon the delivery of that cargo at destination, in this case Chile.

It seems to me very curious — and Mr Hallgarten rightly put this point in the forefront of his argument — that, if it were intended that the entitlement of the shipowners to the freight should be dependent upon the quantity delivered at the port of discharge, not one single word should appear in this clause providing for the ascertainment of the weight or the volume of that which is delivered on discharge. After all, a shipowner who is suing his charterer or the consignee under the bill of lading for freight due on delivery cannot claim to be entitled to recover the freight merely because he delivers everything that was in the ship. He has to quantify his claim and, when quantifying that claim, he has to prove the weight or volume of that which he has delivered; otherwise his monetary claim cannot be suitably quantified. Yet, if one looks at this clause, one finds no provision made for quantifying the weight or volume of that which is delivered. I find that a curious omission if the appellants be right, although it is not conclusive against them, for of course that weight or that volume could always be ascertained in point of fact even though there were no contractual provision for that to be done. But it does seem, when one looks at the first sentence in cl. 2, that the whole burden of this clause is directed to what is taken on board at the port of loading. That provision is not there, as I see it, simply for the purpose of computing what will become due if and when the whole cargo is delivered. It is there to determine what the freight is which is going to be for all purposes the freight due under the charterparty, and I think Mr Hallgarten was right when he said that the word 'freight' in the second sentence of cl. 2 is to be equated with the amount ascertained in accordance with the first sentence of the clause. It is that sum which has to be paid and no other.

I think further support is given to that conclusion by the deadfreight clause. As I pointed out during the argument this morning, the deadfreight clause seems quite conclusively against this freight being a lump sum freight properly so-called. But it is not irrelevant because when one looks at cl. 3 one sees that that which is described as deadfreight is to be calculated by reference to the difference between the intake quantity and the quantity the vessel would have carried if loaded to her minimum permissible freeboard for the voyage. That seems to me to reinforce that part of Mr Hallgarten's argument on cl. 2 which emphasised that the whole weight of these provisions, whether in regard to freight or to deadfreight, is directed to the port of loading where special provision is made in order to avoid disputes either as to the weight or volume loaded of the type which so often used to arise with regard to the determination of what was on board at the time of loading. Thus it is provided that the inspector's certificate of inspection is to determine what the intake quantity is.

Therefore I have come to the conclusion on the construction of this clause that the learned Judge was right.

*Questions*
What result do you think the intaken quantity clause was intended to achieve? If you were advising the charterers, what amendment of the clause would you suggest?

## SECTION 3: ADVANCE FREIGHT

Except in the case of tankers chartered by oil companies, it is no longer usual for freight to be payable entirely on (or even after) delivery. If the contract provides for freight to be payable in advance of delivery, even at common law such advance freight was not recoverable, whatever happened to the cargo. This was explained by Brett J, in *Allison* v *Bristol Marine Insurance Co*. (1876) 1 App Cas 209, at p. 226, as having originated in the long voyages to India and the difficulty for the shipowner of borrowing in the meantime on the security of freight owed. This rule is reinforced by express provisions in modern contracts. However, as freight is still only *earned* on delivery, the right to payment will be lost if the contract is frustrated, e.g., by the sinking of the vessel, before the time for payment has arrived.

### *Compania Naviera General SA* v *Kerametal Ltd* *(The Lorna I)* [1983] 1 Lloyd's Rep 373 (CA)

Under a freight contract between the shipowners and the charterers, the vessel *Lorna I* was nominated to carry a cargo of ore from Durres in Albania to a Rumanian port. Freight was payable, as to 75 per cent, within five days after Master signed bills of lading, and the balance after right and true delivery of the cargo. Bills of lading were signed on 6 December 1977. The vessel sailed the next day, but on 11 December she encountered a severe storm in the Black Sea and was lost with all hands. The advance freight had not been paid and the charterers refused to pay it. The Court of Appeal affirmed Goff J's decision in favour of the charterers.

SIR JOHN DONALDSON MR: This appeal concerns the liability for advance freight where the goods are lost during the voyage. The general rule, as stated in *Scrutton on Charterparties* (18th ed.) art. 159, p. 332, is that:

> If it is an advance of freight, it must be paid, though the goods are, after the due date of payment, but before payment, lost by excepted perils, and it will not be recoverable from the shipowner if the goods are after payment so lost.

In the instant appeal voyage charterparty freight was payable pursuant to the following clause:

> 16. Freight non returnable cargo and/or vessel lost or not lost to be paid telegraphically at owners' expense, free of discount in U.S. Dollars, to the Owners, Messrs. COMPANIA NAVERIA [*sic*] GENERAL S.A. c/o BANCO DI ROMA PER LA SVIZZERA — LUGANO as follows: 75% (Seventy Five per cent) within 5 (Five) days after Master signed Bills of Lading and the balance after right and true delivery of the cargo and receipt of documents from discharging ports.

...

Mr Anthony Clarke QC, for the appellant owners, submits, rightly I think, that his clients' rights depend upon the construction to be placed upon cl. 16. He goes on to submit that upon its true construction either the freight is earned or deemed to be earned on shipment or signing bills of lading or, alternatively, that the liability to make payment of advance freight survives the catastrophe which overtook ship and cargo. For my part I am unable to accept either construction.

Freight is the consideration payable for the carriage of the goods to and their delivery at the destination. In the absence of special contractual provisions, it is earned only upon the delivery of the goods at their destination. Forms of words appropriate to alter this position are well known, e.g., 'Freight to be considered earned on shipment'.

As Mr Nicholas Phillips, QC, who has appeared for the charterers, pointed out, a liability to pay advance freight does not per se affect the time when freight is earned. It is simply an obligation to make a payment on account of freight at a time when it has not yet been earned. However that obligation is subject to a customary incident, capable of being varied or confirmed by express stipulation, that advance freight paid pursuant to the contract is not returnable or recoverable should the contract be frustrated before the freight can be earned (see *Fibrosa Spolka Akcyjna* v *Fairbairn Lawson Combe Barbour* (1942) 73 Ll L Rep 45; [1943] AC 32 at pp. 50 and 43 per Viscount Simon LC). If, in breach of contract, there is a failure to pay the advance freight before the occurrence of the frustrating event, the accrued liability to pay it continues. This is because frustration excuses further performance of the contract, not prior non-performance.

In the present case cl. 16 contains no words appropriate to produce the result that any part of the freight is earned, or deemed to be earned, upon shipment or on signing bills of lading. That route is accordingly not open to the shipowners.

The alternative approach involves construing cl. 16 in such a way as to make the liability to pay advance freight survive the sinking. In theory this could be achieved either by an obligation to pay before the sinking occurred or by an obligation to pay afterwards, notwithstanding the sinking. Mr Clarke espouses both approaches.

As to the first, he submits that on the true construction of cl. 16 there is an obligation to pay advance freight which arises as soon as the bills of lading are signed, this obligation being coupled with an option to postpone payment for up to five days, but no longer, 'cargo and/or vessel lost or not lost'. As to the second, he submits that even if there is no obligation to pay the advance freight arising before the expiration of the five-day period, the words 'Freight non-returnable cargo and/or vessel lost or not lost to be paid' are to be construed as importing an obligation to pay the 75 per cent. advance freight even if the vessel be lost. The argument does not, of course, apply to the balance of the freight which is only payable 'after right and true delivery'.

For my part I am unable to accept either submission. In my judgment on the true construction of cl. 16, there was no obligation to make any payment of or on account of freight until the expiration of the five-day period and before that occurred the contractual basis of the obligation had been undermined by the loss of the cargo and of the vessel and the frustration of the contract. As to the other approach, this involves a separation of the words 'non-returnable' from 'cargo and/or vessel lost or not lost' which does not grammatically exist. The ordinary meaning of the words is that advance freight, if paid, is non-returnable whether or not the cargo and/or vessel is subsequently lost, thereby confirming the customary incident of a contract for the payment of advance freight. To achieve any other construction would require much clearer words....

*Note*
Contrast with that the decision in the next case.

### *Oriental Steamship Co.* v *Tylor*
[1893] 2 QB 518 (CA)

Under a charterparty freight was to be paid 'one-third on signing bills of lading, less 3 per cent for interest, insurance, etc.' and bills of lading were to be signed by captain or agents as presented to him within 24 hours of loading. The ship left the quay but sank (within 24 hours of loading) before reaching the dock gates, having holed her side by fouling her anchor. The charterers refused to present bills of lading or pay any freight. Pollock B found for the charterers and the shipowners appealed.

BOWEN LJ: ... It is inconceivable that the rights which are given to the shipowner on signing bills of lading can be delayed by the act of the charterers in not presenting bills of lading for signature. It is obvious that there must be an implied term in the charterparty, in order to make the contract effectual, that the charterers should present bills of lading to the captain or agent for signature within a reasonable time, so as to give effect to the rights of the shipowner. The case comes within the well-known rule that where the contract as expressed in writing would be futile, and would not carry out the intention of the parties, the law will imply any term obviously intended by the parties which is necessary to make the contract effectual. That being so, the only question that remains is, can the charterers say that the obligation to present bills of lading ceases if the ship is lost? In my opinion no such excuse for the non-performance of that obligation can be properly put forward, for the loss of the ship is not a circumstance which affects, as between these parties, the validity or commercial importance of the bills of lading. The bills of lading do not contain the contract to carry. They are the evidence of the receipt of the goods; and in this case they are something more than that, because their signature is made the event upon which the shipowner is to be entitled to enforce certain of his rights. They are part of the machinery upon which the rights of the parties depend ... here there is a right, conditional, no doubt, on the signing bills of lading, but, subject to that, an absolute right, to be paid advance freight, which is never lost so long as the bills of lading can be presented for signature and signed. The loss of the ship did not prevent the bills of lading being presented and signed. The charterers have broken the implied contract to present bills of lading, and, though the advance freight cannot be recovered as such, the measure of damages for breach of that contract is in this case the amount of the advance freight. The appeal must accordingly be allowed.

*Question*
Why were the charterers not allowed the full 24 hours before being held in breach of their obligation to present the bills for signature?

*Note*
To avoid the difficulty illustrated by *The Lorna I*, freight clauses frequently provide that freight is not merely *payable* in advance of delivery, but also *earned* in advance, e.g., on loading. Problems may still arise if subsequent events do not follow their expected course.

### *Vagres Compania Maritima SA* v *Nissho-Iwai American Corporation (The Karin Vatis)*
[1988] 2 Lloyd's Rep 330 (CA)

LLOYD LJ: On or about Nov. 16, 1985 *Karin Vatis* sank, shortly after passing Suez. She was in the course of a voyage from Liverpool to India, with a cargo of shredded scrap. The charter is dated Oct. 9, 1985 and is on the Gencon form. The printed form of the Gencon charter provides for the cargo to be delivered at the contractual destination on being paid freight on the delivered/intake quantity at the charterparty rate of freight. But the words 'on being paid freight' have been struck out from the present charterparty, and the rate of freight clause has been left blank. In its place there is an addendum which provides for: (i) a lump sum freight of $715,000; (ii) freight to be deemed earned as the cargo is loaded; (iii) 95 per cent. of the freight to be paid within three banking days after completion of loading; and (iv) the balance of 5 per cent to be settled within 20 days after completion of discharge.

The first tranche of freight was duly paid by the charterers before the vessel sank. There is no question of the charterers seeking to recover that part of the freight. But they say that they are not obliged to pay the second tranche of freight, that is to say the balance of 5 per cent, because the time for payment never came. They concede that the debt in repect of that part of the freight became due as the cargo was loaded. But they say that they were not obliged to pay that part of the freight until 20 days after completion of discharge. The debt had accrued due before the vessel sank, but it was not yet payable.

The owners, on the other hand, say that they are entitled to 100 per cent of the freight under the terms of the clause, even though the vessel never arrived.

In due course the owners claimed arbitration. Each side appointed an arbitrator, and the two arbitrators so chosen appointed a third, Mr Bruce Harris. It is clear from their reasons that they did not find the point an easy one. They say that their minds fluctuated in the course of the hearing and their final conclusion was reached very much on balance. In the event they accepted the charterers' argument and dismissed the owners' claim.

The Judge upheld the arbitrators' award (see [1987] 2 Lloyd's Rep 361). There is now an appeal to this Court.

We in this Court are always reluctant to disturb the unanimous award of experienced arbitrators as to the meaning of a few ill-drawn provisions in a charterparty, especially when their award has been upheld by the Commercial Judge. But in this case I find myself taking a different view from the arbitrators and the Judge. Before explaining why, I should first set out the clause on which the case turns verbatim. It provides as follows:

> Freight, when due, is payable at the rate of:
> Lumpsum Seven Hundred Fifteen Thousand Dollars ($715,000.00) basis one load and one discharge port.
> Freight payable in US currency in New York. Freight deemed earned as cargo loaded. Ninety-five (95%) Percent of freight to be paid within three (3) banking days after completion of loading and surrender of signed Bills of Lading marked: 'FREIGHT PREPAID', discountless and non-returnable, vessel and/or cargo lost or not lost. Balance of freight demurrage/despatch to be settled within twenty (20) days after completion of discharge and Owners' presentation of Laytime Statements from load/discharge ports. Charterers' privilege to deduct undisputed despatch and maximum 3.75% brokerage from ninety-five (95%) freight payment.

The ordinary rule, in the absence of express or implied provision to the contrary, is that freight under a voyage charter is not payable until the cargo is delivered or tendered for delivery. That rule, which is reflected in the language of the printed form of the Gencon charterparty and elsewhere, does not depend on considerations which are in any way peculiar to voyage charters. It is common to all types of contract where the consideration is entire. The shipowner promises to deliver the goods at the contractual destination. If he fails to do so he has failed to earn his contractual freight. It matters not that the vessel and cargo have been lost by an excepted peril.

Now there are many ways in which that rule can be excluded but the commonest is to provide for freight to be earned on shipment. The arbitrators in their reasons note that in the present case the clause provides for freight to be '*deemed* earned' on shipment, or as cargo is loaded, not 'earned'. They evidently attached significance to this verbal distinction. With respect, I do not think there is any difference between 'earned' and 'deemed earned' or 'considered as earned'. They all mean the same, namely that the shipowners have done all they have to do to earn their freight once the cargo has been loaded. Of course they have other contractual obligations to perform. But the failure to perform such other obligations will sound in damages. It does not affect the shipowners' accrued right to freight. . . .

What, then, is the effect of a provision postponing the date of payment, where the freight is deemed to be earned on shipment? The Judge has held that the contractual date of payment is an essential part of the owners' cause of action. Since, on the facts of the present case, the date in question can never arrive, the owners' cause of action must remain for ever incomplete. I quote from the judgment:

> No means was suggested in argument by which the requirements of (a) unloading, (b) the presentation of laytime statements, or (c) the lapse of 20 days after those events could be dispensed with. The events never happened. The balance, including the outstanding freight, never became payable. No cause of action arose in respect of the 5 per cent.

Mr Veeder, in support of the Judge's conclusion, submitted that the completion of discharge and the other requirements mentioned by the Judge were conditions precedent to the charterers' obligation to pay.

The difficulty with Mr Veeder's argument, as he frankly conceded, is that in relation to the 5 per cent it gives no effect, or virtually no effect, to the provision that freight is deemed earned as cargo loaded. The layout of the clause, and in particular the full stop at the end of the crucial sentence, makes it clear beyond doubt that the 'deemed earned' provision applies to the entire lump sum freight, not just to 95 per cent payable within three days of completion of loading. That being so, I am unwilling to give the provision no effect, or virtually no effect, in relation to the 5 per cent unless compelled by the clearest language. The provision that freight is deemed to be earned as cargo loaded is, to my mind, the paramount or controlling provision. It is well understood by commercial men. It casts the risk in relation to freight on to the charterers. It excludes the ordinary rule of construction, whereby freight is only earned and therefore only payable on delivery. The charterers' construction would mean reintroducing the ordinary rule in relation to the 5 per cent. Indeed, as Mr Johnson pointed out, it would make the owners' position worse. For, under the ordinary rule, the shipowner is entitled to freight when the goods are delivered, or tendered for delivery. If the charterers' argument is correct, they would only be entitled to freight 20 days thereafter. I am unwilling to hold that that is what these parties can have intended.

So how are the provisions to be reconciled? The answer must surely be that the concluding part of the clause is dealing with the manner of payment, not the obligation to pay. It provides a formula for ascertaining the date of payment, and for insuring that loading and discharging port demurrage or despatch, as the case may be, and the balance of freight are all settled at the same time. If instead of 20 days after completion of discharge, the parties had named a day certain for settlement of the amount due, or if they had calculated the length of the voyage and the time for discharging and had then stipulated for settlement of mutual debts, let us say, 60 days after completion of loading instead of 20 days after completion of discharge, the problem in the present case would never have arisen. The owners would have recovered the balance of freight due on the day certain, or at the expiry of the 60 days, as the case might be. Instead of taking that course, the parties have provided a formula based on the completion of discharge. I cannot believe that by so doing they were intending to introduce a speculative element into the owners' right to recover freight. They were assuming that the vessel would discharge in normal course. It might perhaps have been different (it is unnecessary to decide) if the clause had read 20 days after *safe arrival*. In that event it might have been argued that the parties had given their minds to the possibility of the vessel sinking, or the cargo being lost. Mr Veeder accepted that his case would have been so much the stronger if that had been what the clause provided. Even so, it would be difficult to see why the obligation to pay demurrage or despatch at the loading port should depend on the safe arrival of the vessel. But it is unnecessary to pursue these thoughts any further. The clause does not provide for the freight to be paid 20 days after safe arrival, but 20 days after completion of discharge. The reference to completion of discharge is, in my judgment, neutral. It connotes nothing more than a point of time, in the course of the expected performance of the contract, for ascertaining the date of payment.

I would therefore reject Mr Veeder's argument that the completion of discharge is a condition precedent to the owners' right to recover 5 per cent. such a construction would be inconsistent with the main thrust and purpose of the clause. If the formula for ascertaining the date of payment is unworkable, because the vessel never completes her discharge, then some other way of arriving at the date of payment must be found. I do not have the same difficulty, as did the Judge, in 'dispensing with' the requirements to which he refers, once those requirements have become unworkable.

But something must be substituted. The question is what. In the Court below Mr Cooke submitted three alternatives. The Judge regarded the very existence of these three alternatives as indicating the weakness of the owners' case. Before us Mr Johnson suggested two alternatives. I need not refer to them since the answer to my mind is clear. Once the formula has been displaced, the Court substitutes a reasonable time. There is nothing strange or heroic in the Court taking that course.

There is, indeed, a useful analogy in the field of sale of goods. In *Alexander* v *Gardner* (1835) 1 Bing N Cas 671 there was a contract for the sale of butter f.o.b. London. Payment was to be made by bill of exchange two months from the date of landing. The vessel sank in the course of the voyage. The sellers brought an action for the price of goods bargained and sold. It was argued, inter alia, just as it has been argued here, that the landing of the goods was a condition precedent. The Court rejected that argument. Chief Justice Tindall said at p. 677:

> The third objection to the Plaintiffs' recovery is, that the butters were to be paid for by a bill at two months after landing. But the object of that stipulation was, merely to fix the time of payment, and not to make the landing a condition precedent. For that point it is enough to refer to the decision in *Fragano* v *Long*.

...

In *Fragano* v *Long* (1825) 4 B & C 219, where goods were to be paid for three months after arrival, it was held that, if they did not arrive, the buyers 'would be bound to pay in a reasonable time after the arrival became impossible'.

Mr Veeder argued that the sale of goods is a dangerous analogy, since voyage freight is subject to its own special rules. I would not accept that argument. There are, of course, many differences. But in one sense the analogy is quite close, since payment of the price and delivery of the goods are concurrent conditions in the sale of goods unless otherwise agreed, just as payment of the freight and delivery of the goods are concurrent conditions, unless otherwise agreed, in a contract for carriage by sea under a voyage charter.

*Notes*
1. Slade LJ (at p. 336) described the provisions relating to the time for payment as 'intended merely to provide the machinery for payment based on the parties' expectations of the normal course of events' and not to alter the allocation of risk intended by the 'freight deemed earned' provision.
2. Provisions for freight to be payable and deemed earned in advance have been held to apply even if the shipowner repudiates the contract after freight has accrued.

### *Colonial Bank* v *European Grain & Shipping Ltd* *(The Dominique)*
[1989] 1 Lloyd's Rep 431 (HL)

LORD BRANDON OF OAKBROOK: My Lords, the subject matter of this appeal is a claim by the appellants ('the bank') as assignees of the owners of the m.v. *Dominique* ('the owners') to recover from the respondents ('the charterers') advance freight which the bank alleges became payable by the charterers under a voyage charterparty relating to that vessel made between the owners and the charterers in June, 1982. The charterers dispute that any such freight became payable, but it is agreed between the parties that, if it did, the amount of it was US$223,676.

The bank's claim was referred to arbitration by three arbitrators in London, who by a reasoned award made on Feb. 12, 1986 decided in favour of the charterers and dismissed the claim. The bank appealed with leave to Mr Justice Hobhouse in the Commercial Court [1987] 1 Lloyds Rep 239, who by an order dated Oct. 24, 1986 allowed the appeal and awarded to the bank the full amount of their claim. The charterers appealed to the Court of Appeal (Fox, Croom-Johnson and Mustill LJJ) [1988] 1 Lloyd's Rep 215; [1988] 3 WLR 60, which by an order dated Dec. 21, 1987, as amended on Jan. 14 and Apr. 11, 1988 allowed the appeal, set aside the order of Mr Justice Hobhouse and restored the arbitrators' award. The bank now brings a further appeal from the decision of the Court of Appeal with the leave of your Lordships' House.

The facts found by the arbitrators are as follows. By an assignment under seal dated Apr. 14, 1982 the owners assigned absolutely to the bank all the earnings of *Dominique* including all freight. By a charterparty dated June 16, 1982 the owners chartered *Dominique* to the charterers to proceed to Kakinada, in India, and there load a cargo of agricultural products in bulk for carriage to European ports. Under that charterparty *Dominique* loaded at Kakinada between June 28 and July 13, 1982 various parcels of cargo, in respect of which bills of lading were signed between those dates and on July 14, 1982. On that date *Dominique* left Kakinada bound for Colombo for bunkers. At about the same time the bank received notice that the vessel's club entry would be cancelled with effect from June 28, 1982, and they accordingly gave to the charterers written notice of the assignment referred to earlier. On July 19, 1982 *Dominique* arrived at Colombo and was arrested by previous suppliers of bunkers to her. *Dominique* remained under arrest and it became apparent to both the charterers and the bank that the owners had no funds of their own with which to procure her release and that the club would not assist them. By a telex from the charterers to the owners dated July 22, 1982 the charterers justifiably elected to treat the owners' conduct as a repudiation of the charterparty. By July 26, 1982 all the bills of lading previously signed had been surrendered, which I take to mean delivered, to the shippers. On Aug. 12 1982 the charterers obtained the leave of the Court in Colombo to discharge the cargo from *Dominique*. During September, 1982 the cargo, following such discharge, was transhipped to another vessel. That vessel then on-carried the cargo to European ports where it was discharged during November, 1982. *Dominique* was later sold by order of the Court in Colombo.

The cost to the charterers of discharging and transhipping the cargo at Colombo, and having it on-carried to European ports and discharged there, exceeded the amount of the advance freight claimed from them by the bank.

The charterparty was on the Gencon form with typed alterations, a series of additional typed clauses and an addendum, and was governed by English law. The essential provision relating to the payment of advance freight was cl. 16 of the additional typed clauses, which was in these terms:

> 16. Freight shall be prepaid within five days of signing and surrender of final bills of lading, full freight deemed to be earned on signing bills of lading, discountless and non-returnable, vessel and/or cargo lost or not lost and to be paid to [a named bank].

The charterers disputed their liability to pay the advance freight claimed by the bank on two grounds. The first ground was that the charterers, by accepting the owners' repudiation of the charterparty, had lawfully brought the charterparty to an end before the owners' right to be paid freight under cl. 16 had accrued. The second ground was that, if, contrary to the first ground, the owner's right to be paid freight under cl. 16 had accrued before the charterparty was brought to an end, the charterers were entitled to set off against the bank's claim to freight the damage suffered by them as a result of the owners' repudiation.

Mr Justice Hobhouse considered, rightly in my view, that the grounds for disputing liability relied on by the charterers raised four questions for decision. Using my own words, I would formulate those four questions as follows: (1) Had the owners' right to advance freight accrued before the charterparty was terminated by the charterers' acceptance of the owners' repudation of it? (2) If such right had so accrued, did it survive such termination? (3) If so, would the charterers, had the owners not assigned their right to freight to the bank, have been entitled to set off against such right the damage suffered by the charterers as a result of the owners' repudiation of the charterparty? (4) If not, are the charterers nevertheless entitled to such set-off as against the bank claiming as assignees?

*Question (1): Accrual of owners' right to advance freight*
The answer to this question depends on two matters. The first matter is the sequence of the relevant events as found by the arbitrators. The second matter is the true construction of cl. 16 of the charterparty.

So far as the firt matter is concerned the arbitrators found the sequence of the relevant events to have been as follows: (i) on July 14, 1982 the signing of the bills of lading was completed; (ii) on July 22, 1982 the charterparty was terminated by the charterers' acceptance of the owners' repudiation of it; and (iii) by July 26 all the bills of lading had been surrenderd to the shippers. The expression 'by 26 July', used by the arbitrators in relation to event (iii) above, is in a sense equivocal, in that, on a literal interpretation, it might refer to any date not later than July 26, including a date earlier than July 22. The inference which I would draw, however, is that, while the arbitrators were unable to fix the date with certainty, they were satisfied that it was later than July 22. In any case, in so far as it would be to the advantage of the bank to have had a finding that the surrender of the bills of lading was completed before the termination of the charterparty on July 22, they failed to obtain such finding.

So far as the second matter is concerned, it was recognised by both Courts below that cl. 16 of the charterparty is confusingly drawn and because of that difficult to interpret. The main difficulty arises from the apparent conflict between the first phrase of the clause, which reads 'freight shall be prepaid within five days of signing and surrender of final bills of lading', and the second phrase, which reads 'full freight deemed to be earned on signing bills of lading'. For the bank it was contended that the effect of the two phrases taken together was that the owner's right to the freight accrued on completion of the signing of all the bills of lading, but payment was postponed until five days after the bills of lading, having been signed, were delivered to the shippers. On this basis the owners' right to freight accrued on July 14, 1982, well before the termination of the charterparty on July 22. For the charterers it was contended that their obligaton to pay the freight and the corresponding right of the owners to be paid the freight were both governed, and governed only, by the first phrase. On that basis the owners' right to be paid the freight accrued after July 22, 1982.

While the matter is far from easy, I consider that the contention for the bank is to be preferred to that for the charterers. The reason why I take that view is that the contention for the charterers gives no effect to the second phrase of cl. 16 'full freight deemed to be earned on signing bills of lading', whereas the contention for the bank does. This conclusion accords with the decision of the Court of Appeal on a different but comparable clause in a charterparty in *Vagres Compania Maritima SA v Nissho-Iwai American Corporation* [1988] 2 Lloyds Rep 330.

I would therefore answer question (1) by saying that the owners' right to freight accrued before the termination of the charterparty.

*Question (2): Effect of charterparty being terminated*
The principles of law applicable when a contract is terminated by the acceptance by one party to it of a repudiation by the other party to it are not in doubt. They were clearly and simply stated by Mr Justice Dixon In *McDonald v Dennys Lascelles Ltd* (1933) 48 CLR 457 at pp. 476–77, where he said:

> When a party to a simple contract, upon a breach by the other contracting party of a condition of the contract, elects to treat the contract as no longer binding upon him, the contract is not rescinded as from the beginning. Both parties are discharged from further performance of the contract, but rights are not divested or discharged which have already been unconditonally acquired. Rights and obligations which arise from the partial execution of the contract and causes of action which have accrued from its breach alike continue unaffected.

That statement of the relevant principles was expressly approved and adopted by Lord Wilberforce in *Johnson v Agnew* [1980] AC 367 at p. 396. Applying those principles to the facts of the present case it is necessary to consider whether the owners' right to the freight had been 'unconditionally acquired' by them before the termination of the charterparty. The circumstance that, by reason of the first phrase of cl. 16, the charterers' obligation to pay the freight was postponed until after the termination of the charterparty does not, in my view, mean that the owners' prior acquisition of the right to the freight was conditional only. The postponement of payment was an incident attaching to the right acquired, but it was not a condition of its acquisition. It follows that, in accordance with the principles of law referred to above, the owners' right to the freight, having been unconditionally acquired before the termination of the charter-party, was not divested or discharged by such termination.

I would therefore answer question (2) by saying that the owners' right to the freight survived the termination of the charterparty.

...

*Note*
Lord Brandon went on also to reject the alternative argument based on set-off. The other Lords agreed with Lord Brandon and the bank's appeal was allowed.

*Questions*
1.   Where was the justice in making the charterers pay freight, for carriage which was not performed, in return for a worthless claim for damages against the carrier?
2.   What do you think of a clause which provides for the balance of freight to be paid 'after completion of discharge and settlement of demurrage/despatch'? (See *Antclizo Shipping Corporation* v *Food Corporation of India (The Antclizo) (No. 2)* [1992] 1 Lloyd's Rep 558 (CA).)

## SECTION 4: LIABILITY TO PAY FREIGHT

### *Cho Yang Shipping Co. Ltd* v *Coral (UK) Ltd*
[1997] 2 Lloyd's Rep 641 (CA)

HOBHOUSE LJ:

*Introduction*
In this action the plaintiff shipowners, *Cho Yang Shipping Co. Ltd* of Seoul, Korea, seek to recover freight from the defendants, Coral (UK) Ltd of London W1, under three bills of lading issued in Hamburg for the carriage of containers containing sugar from Hamburg and Bremerhaven to Dubai and Mina Qaboos. Each bill of lading was issued in Hamburg by EOS Europa-Overseas Schiffahrtsargentur GmbH (EOS), the plaintiffs' German agents, and related to the carriage of 20 containers.

The action was tried in the Central London County Court by Judge Hallgarten, QC. Documentary and oral evidence was adduced. In February, 1996 he gave judgment for the plaintiffs against Coral. Coral have appealed to this Court.

The three shipments were — June 25, 1993 per *DRS Rostock*; June 30, 1993 per *Cho Yang Success*; July 16, 1993 per *St. Petersburg Senator*. Only the second of these vessels was owned by the plaintiffs but they were all sailing as part of the liner service operated by the plaintiffs and the bills of lading were issued by EOS on their behalf. It is accepted that, apart from one point which can be left on one side until later in this judgment, all three shipments raise the same question and that it suffices to refer to the second shipment on *Success*.

*The bill of lading*
The *Success* bill of lading was (like the others) on the plaintiffs' form for issue by EOS. It was dated Hamburg Juni 30 [i.e. June], 1993. It named Coral as the shippers and consigned the goods to their order. The port of loading was Bremerhaven and the discharge port was Mina Qaboos. In the box headed 'Particulars Furnished by Shipper' there appeared, besides the marks and description of the goods, the words 'Freight

Prepaid' and 'Clean on Board'. Before it was issued there was added — it must have been by EOS — the stamped words 'Freight Prepaid as Arranged' as well as 'Shipper's Load, Stow and Count' and 'Shipped on Board 30 Juni 1993'. (This statement was not correct as to the knowledge of EOS the containers were not in fact shipped on board until July 8; but nothing turns on this in the present case.) The form used stated that freight was payable at Hamburg. The box providing for 'Freight Rates Charges' was left blank save for two stipulations that certain charges at the discharge port should be paid by the consignee. The back of the bill of lading contained typical liner clauses. The definitions of 'merchant' and 'charges' included respectively the shipper and freight. Charges were deemed to be fully earned on receipt of the goods to be paid non-returnable in any event. There was a wide lien clause. There was no further clause dealing with freight as such; there was a clause which referred to the plaintiffs' tariff but no reliance has been placed on this and it was not in evidence. The wording of the bill of lading was all in the English language. It was expressly made subject to Korean law and jurisdiction.

### The legal context

In the absence of some other consideration, the shipper is contractually liable to the carrier for the freight (Scrutton, 20th ed., art. 172). This is because the carriage is for reward and the personal liability to pay the reward is a contractual liability (whether the carriage was as a common carrier or pursuant to a 'special' contract). The personal liability is that of the person with whom the performing carrier has contracted to carry the goods. This person is normally the shipper. (*Dommett* v *Beckford* (1883) 5 B & Ad 521.) But the shipper may be shipping as the agent of the consignee in which case the contract will be with the consignee (e.g., *Fragano* v *Long* (1825) 4 B & C 219, *Dickenson* v *Lano* (1860) 2 F & F 188). A contract to pay the freight will not always be implied from the fact of shipment and the issue of a bill of lading. (*Smidt* v *Tiden* (1874) LR 9 QB 446.) It is possible for there to be more complex contractual schemes; the performing carrier may be in contractual relations with others as well, as, for example, where there is a voyage or time charter; this can affect the position.

In English law the bill of lading is not the contract between the original parties but is simply evidence of it.

. . . Therefore, as between shipper and carrier, it may be necessary to inquire what the actual contract between them was; merely to look at the bill of lading may not in all cases suffice. It remains necessary to look at and take into account the other evidence bearing upon the relationship between the shipper and the carrier and the terms of the contract between them. (Scrutton, art. 33). The terms upon which the goods have been shipped may not be in all respects the same as those actually set out in the bill of lading. It does not necessarily follow in any given case that the named shipper is to be under a personal liability for the payment of the freight.

As will be readily appreciated, the inclusion of the words 'freight prepaid' in the bill of lading does not of itself show that the shipper is not to be under any liability for the freight if it has not in fact been paid (e.g., *The Nanfri* [1979] 1 Lloyd's Rep 201; [1979] AC 757). Such words are not, in English law, words of contract (e.g., *Compania Naviera Vascongada* [*sic*] v *Churchill* [1906] 1 KB 237) and their insertion in the bill of lading does not without more serve to negative a pre-existing, undischarged, contractual liability to pay the freight. Indeed, a request to the carrier that he issue a freight pre-paid bill of lading before the freight has in fact been paid would normally imply a personal undertaking by the person making the request that it would be paid (cf. the implied indemnity where a charterer requests the master to sign bills of lading: *The Caroline P.* [1984] 2 Lloyd's Rep 466). Thus, in the present case, the mere inclusion of those words in the bill of lading does not preclude a liability of Coral for the freight but it is part of the evidence to be taken into account when considering whether or not Coral were under a contractual liability to the plaintiffs for the freight.

The parties have argued this case solely upon the basis of English law. No foreign law has been pleaded nor has any evidence of it been adduced. There is a certain artificiality about this. The shipment was at a German port and the bill of lading was issued in Germany. In German law a bill of lading has a different contractual status. A German Court has already considered a similar claim by the shipowners against another shipper, a German company.

*The facts of this case*
The primary facts are not now in dispute: the findings of the Judge are accepted. In this case the shipment of the containers of Coral's sugar on *Success* arose from a chain of contractual relations. Coral contracted with Nortrop Speditions-und Schiffahrtsgesell-schaft mbH of Hamburg. Nortrop contracted with Interport Speditions-und Befrach-tungskontor Stoob GmbH also of Hamburg. Interport contracted with EOS the Hamburg agents of the plaintiffs acting on their behalf. The relevant contracts related to other shipments besides those concerned in this case. The communications relevant to the making of the various contracts extended back to the preceding September, 1992. It is not necessary to trace the steps by which the contracts came about. They seem to have originated from a long term contract between Interport and Nortrop. The Judge held that in all the relevant transactions the parties were dealing with each other as principals and not as agents (apart from EOS).

The contracts were not mere booking contracts; they were contracts *for* the carriage of certain numbers of containers during stated periods from German ports to Gulf ports at stated freights. It is not now in dispute that as a result of each of these contracts the one party became liable to pay to the other, for each shipment made, the freight which those two parties had agreed upon between them. Thus Coral became liable to pay to Nortrop US$1,010 per container, Nortrop to pay to Interport US$1,000 and Interport to pay to EOS (as the agents of the plaintiffs) US$980 less 2½ per cent. commission. At all material times Coral had no knowledge of the existence of Interport and had no dealings with them; similarly they had no knowledge of any freight rate other than the US$1,010 to which they had agreed. Nortrop had no authority to impose any liability upon Coral to pay freight to the performing carrier (whoever it might be). The agreement between Coral and Nortrop was that Coral would pay Nortrop the freight they had agreed, not any one else. Nortrop gave no authority to Interport to contract on behalf of Coral; Nortrop did not disclose to Interport the identity of the goods owners.

It was also part of each contract that an owner's freight prepaid liner bill of lading would be issued. At the relevant times in Hamburg there was an association of forwarding agents, shipping companies and shipping agencies, the Frachten-Ausschuß, of which EOS, the plaintiffs and, at the material time, Interport were members. Members of the association were entitled to be issued with freight prepaid bills of lading and be given credit for the payment of the freight due on the shipment. The purpose was to enable the relevant member to collect payment from its customer before having to pay the carrier; this is how it was put by the witness called by the plaintiffs from EOS, Mr Müller, in his statement.

We were provided with a copy of the relevant document ('Letter of Responsibility') signed by Interport in favour of the other members of the association including EOS which, in translation, included the following:

> 1. I herewith commit myself with regards to the liner agents ... with whom I am effecting export shipments, or will effect in future, to settle the payable freight within

a period of 15 working days (except Saturday) after the date mentioned in the Bill of Lading for all shipments for which I receive Bills of Lading from the liner agents which are payable at the port of loading, especially those, accepted under the conditions 'FREIGHT PAID' respectively 'FREIGHT PREPAID' without prior freight payment irrespective of whether these Bills of Lading are issued in my name or in the name of third parties and/or if I am acting on my behalf or as representative of a third party. Furthermore this is unaffected by the responsibility for the freight payment of third parties.

The Bill of Lading clause 'FREIGHT PREPAID' or a remark with the same meaning does not symbolise a 'receipt' of the freight payment for me. Therefore I remain responsible for the burden of proof for freight payment.

2. This declaration does not justify the responsibility for the liner agents to deliver Bills of Lading without cash payment of freight. It is rather within the liner agents' discretion if they are ready to make a concession to me.

This concession can be cancelled at any time, especially on default of my payments. It is also within the liner agents' discretion to generally decide cash against documents or a prompt cash payment in future, especially if they are instructed by the shipping line or by the conference.

. . .

The remaining paragraphs of the document gave EOS remedies against Interport should it fail to pay within the period of credit.

It was this procedure that was followed for the relevant shipment. Coral had sold the sugar on c. & f. terms; Coral gave Nortrop instructions what particulars Coral required the bill of lading to contain. These were incorporated in what the witnesses called a 'matrix' being a blank document with the requested wording appropriately positioned so that when EOS prepared the actual bill of lading for issue on behalf of the plaintiffs this 'matrix' could simply be inserted. The 'matrix' was sent by Nortrop direct to EOS, presumably with the knowledge and concurrence of Interport. The wording requested by Coral included the words 'Freight Prepaid'. Unlike the Judge, I consider that the clear inference is that it was pursuant to the Frachten-Ausschuß agreement and the practice above referred to that EOS additionally stamped the bill of lading 'FREIGHT PREPAID AS ARRANGED'. This can only have been a reference to their arrangement with Interport. When EOS released the bill of lading, they sent an invoice to Interport for the freight (at US$980 per container, less 2½ per cent. Commission). Interport invoiced Nortrop and were paid by Nortrop (at US$1,000). Nortrop invoiced Coral and were paid by Coral (at US$1,010).

At the time the containers were shipped and the bill of lading issued, EOS were apparently still treating Interport as creditworthy. Interport were still fully effective members of the Frachten-Ausschuß. What went wrong was that Interport were in fact in financial difficulties (having accepted more commitments than they could fulfil) and when the time came for Interport to pay EOS they failed to do so and, being insolvent, have not done so since. It was under these circumstances that EOS on behalf of the plaintiffs on August 28 (some two months after the date of the bill of lading) wrote a letter to Coral demanding that they pay the freight, sending them a back-dated invoice (at US$980).

*The Judge's judgment*

The trial was primarily taken up with resolving the disputes regarding whether any of the intermediaries were the agents of the plaintiffs or the defendants and who were the parties to the relevant bills of lading. He held that all the intermediaries were acting as principals. He also held that the shipper of the goods and therefore the party to the bills of lading contracts was Coral.

Having thus answered the question who were the parties to the contracts evidenced by the bills of lading, he went on to ask himself whether 'the terms of such contracts preclude recovery of the bill of lading freight?' Presumably he was referring to recovery from Coral of the freight EOS had agreed with Interport. He answered this question by considering in turn the clauses 'freight prepaid' and 'freight prepaid as arranged'. As regards the former he said:

> ... In my view the basic commercial function of a 'freight prepaid' clause is to assure the notify party or other consignee that as between him and the shipowner no liability for freight can be asserted. In my view, the expression 'freight prepaid' serves in no way to affect the basic liability of the shipper if freight has not in fact been prepaid: Cf. *The Constanza M.* [1980] 1 Lloyd's Rep 505 per Mr Justice Lloyd at p. 514 [p. 12].

(Neither party before us founded any argument upon *The Constanza M.*) The Judge excluded any entitlement of Coral to rely upon an estoppel; he had earlier refused an application by the defendants for leave to amend to raise such a plea.

As regards the other clause he rejected the submission that there was any significance in what he described as the 'vague and cryptic' words *as arranged*.

. . .

He therefore held Coral liable to the plaintiffs for the bill of lading freight; but he said that the plaintiffs must give Coral credit for the commission of 2 ½ per cent. to which Interport would have been entitled had they paid the freight.

*Conclusion*

In my judgment the Judge came to the wrong conclusion and asked himself the wrong question. He did not ask himself whether it was to be inferred that Coral had agreed to pay freight to the plaintiffs. He did not take adequate account of the fact that the bill of lading is only evidence of the contract between the shipper and the carrier which has been made before the goods were shipped nor of what terms and what agreement were to be inferred from what had happened prior to shipment. He asked himself the question whether there was anything in the bill of lading to *preclude* liability. He should have asked whether having regard to the facts of this particular shipment it is to be inferred that Coral were undertaking to the plaintiffs that they would pay freight to them.

In a situation such as that which occurred in this case the question can only be answered by looking at all the relevant evidence not just the fact that Coral owned the sugar at the time it was shipped and were named as the shippers in the bill of lading. As I have explained earlier in this judgment it is correct that the inference that the shipper is agreeing to pay the freight is the usual inference but it is not a necessary inference and a different inference may in a particular case be appropriate. Here the plaintiffs and EOS had their own agreement with Interport as principals and extended credit to them. Whatever agreement Coral had made about freight with Nortrop was unknown to the plaintiffs and EOS. EOS never agreed or attempted to agree any freight with Coral or Nortrop. All EOS knew was that Coral required a freight prepaid bill of lading. EOS had an agreement with Interport which provided for the issue of freight prepaid bills of lading against Interport's undertaking to pay the freight within the agreed period of credit and they contemplated that during that period the shipper would, directly or indirectly, have paid Interport (as indeed occurred). The inference that Coral did not agree to pay freight to the plaintiffs is in my judgment inescapable.

There are a number of difficulties about the case of the plaintiffs as accepted by the Judge. The bill of lading does not say what the freight was. The freight sued for was a freight agreed to solely between EOS and Interport. When did Coral agree to pay that freight? If it is alleged that an agent made that agreement on Coral's behalf, did that agent have their authority to do so? These questions cannot be satisfactorily answered. In the present case the freight agreed to by Coral was higher than that agreed to by the other parties up the line but that need not have been the case. Where each of the parties is dealing as a principal, each is taking the risk of profit or loss on the freight transaction. It is possible that Coral might have been able at the time they made their contract with Nortrop to obtain more favourable terms than Interport obtained from EOS. As with a hierarchy of charter-parties, the freight rate risk was separated from the carriage risk. The plaintiffs argued before us that Coral were liable for the freight and that if Interport defaulted it was for Coral to sue Nortrop for failing to procure that Interport had paid the freight and to indemnify them against the consequences of Interport's default. This argument might have been persuasive if the intermediaries had been acting as agents but, as the Judge held, they were not.

In my judgment the correct inference in the present case is that there was no agreement by Coral to pay freight to the plaintiffs. The Judge should have dismissed the plaintiff's claim. The appeal should be allowed.

*Notes*

1.   In *Cory Brothers Shipping Ltd* v *Baldan Ltd* [1997] 2 Lloyd's Rep 58, Judge Diamond QC found that 'a usage that forwarding and shipping agents who book cargo space on a vessel but are known to be acting for a shipper whose name is not disclosed, incur personal liability for the freight' was clearly established. Moreover, it was 'so well-known in the forwarding industry in the United Kingdom that those who conduct business in that market contract with that usage in mind' and was entirely reasonable.

Of course, it is open to the parties to exclude this liability by the terms of the contract.

2.   The common law gives the shipowner a lien on the cargo, i.e., a right to retain possession of it, to secure payment of freight due on delivery, for recovery of a general average contribution from cargo and for expenses incurred in protecting the cargo.

Charterparties take the concept much further: see, e.g., *Gencon*, cl. 8, which provides 'The Owners shall have a lien on the cargo and on all sub-freights payable in respect of the cargo, for freight, deadfreight, demurrage, claims for damages and for all other amounts due under this Charter Party including costs of recovering same.' Clauses providing that the charterer's liability is to cease on cargo being shipped ('cesser clauses') are construed to take effect only 'to the extent that the owners have an alternative remedy by way of lien on the cargo' (per Donaldson J in *The Sinoe* [1971] 1 Lloyd's Rep 514, at 516 — see also Pearson LJ in *Fidelitas Shipping* v *V/O Exportchleb* [1963] 2 Lloyd's Rep 113, at 122.

Effective incorporation of the charterparty clauses into the bill of lading is essential to avoid problems with the doctrine of privity of contract: on incorporation, see Chapter 6, below.

# 6   BILLS OF LADING

In this chapter we deal with the three functions of the bill of lading, namely to act as a receipt for the goods shipped, to serve as evidence of the contract of carriage, and to operate as a transferable ('negotiable') document of title to the goods. Historically, these three functions evolved at entirely different periods. The practice of using bills of lading as documents of title gained legal recognition only with the verdict of the special jury in *Lickbarrow* v *Mason* (1794) 5 TR 683, centuries after bills of lading were first devised, but it has been the catalyst for most of the development in relation to the other functions as well. The reason is obvious: most disputes arise not between the carrier and the shipper, but between the carrier and an indorsee of the bill of lading. The provisions of the Carriage of Goods by Sea Act 1971 (hereafter COGSA 1971), which incorporated the Hague-Visby Rules into English law, will be considered separately in Chapter 7.

## SECTION 1: THE BILL OF LADING AS A RECEIPT FOR GOODS SHIPPED

The first step in any claim against the carrier for short delivery or cargo damage is proof that the cargo was shipped in good condition and in the quantity alleged. The bill of lading is an acknowledgement by the master or other agent of the shipowner of the goods shipped (or 'received for shipment' as the case may be). It will contain statements as to the apparent condition of the goods, the quantity (weight, volume, number of bags, etc.), any markings and various other matters. In favour of the shipper such statements are generally prima facie evidence of the facts stated but no more; in favour of an indorsee of the bill of lading, however, they normally give rise to an estoppel against the carrier and thus become conclusive evidence of the facts stated.

*A: Apparent good order and condition*

It will usually be vitally important for shippers to obtain a 'clean' bill of lading in order to fulfil their obligations under contracts of sale and to satisfy the terms of documentary credits. A clean bill was stated by Salmon J in *British Imex Industries Ltd* v *Midland Bank Ltd* [1958] 1 QB 542, at p. 551, to be 'one that does not contain any reservation as to the apparent good order or condition of the goods or the packing'. Where a clean bill is issued the shipowner is estopped from asserting, as against an indorsee of the bill of lading, that the goods were damaged at the time of shipment unless the damage would not have been apparent on reasonable examination at that time.

### *Silver* v *Ocean Steamship Co. Ltd*
[1930] 1 KB 416 (CA)

S was the indorsee of bills of lading issued at Shanghai in respect of 21,334 cans of frozen eggs 'shipped in apparent good order and condition for delivery subject to conditions' in London. The cans were rectangular and of thin metal and each held 42 lbs. On arrival a large number were dented or perforated, some perforations being gashes, others being merely pinholes. The bills of lading incorporated the Hague Rules. The shipowners asserted that some of the damage occurred prior to shipment and that the cans were insufficiently packed. The Court of Appeal held that they were estopped from raising these defences.

SCRUTTON LJ: ... The liquid content of the eggs was contained in metal cases holding 42 lbs each, cases of a rectangular shape, and, therefore, with twelve right-angled edges. The cases were not covered with any cloth, fibre or cardboard covering. The contents were frozen and the cases carried in refrigerated holds. The more usual method of conveyance was either in rectangular cases covered with some kind of covering, or in circular drums which were sometimes uncovered. In this case the rectangular cases of the size in fact used were used at the request of London purchasers for reasons connected with their own business. They were probably uncovered for cheapness. As to shape, rectangular cases were obviously better for the ship's stowage, as cylindrical cases wasted room in stowage. But the right-angled edges were probably more likely to damage other goods even in careful stowage and handling; and were certainly more likely to do so if there was negligent handling. There was in the whole transit from shippers' warehouse to store very considerable damage to the cases. None of it was due to failure of refrigeration. But out of 21,334 cases shipped, 10,982 cases were damaged in their metal coverings, so that London purchasers rejected them ... the bills of lading by which the shipowner acknowledges the receipt of goods are for 16,000 and 5,334 cases respectively, in apparent good order and condition, 'for delivery subject to conditions and exceptions hereinafter mentioned', and the first condition mentioned is 'This bill of lading is subject to the Rules contained in the Schedule to the statute of the United Kingdom of Great Britain and Northern Ireland entitled the Carriage of Goods by Sea Act, 1924, hereinafter referred to as "the Rules".' Though the Act does not apply to this bill the parties have apparently by agreement made the rules in the Schedule to the Act conventional terms of the bill of lading. Rule 3 of Art. III of the Schedule requires the carrier to issue a bill of lading showing the apparent order and condition of the goods, which by r. 4 is to be prima facie evidence of the receipt of goods as described.

Two questions seem to arise at this stage. First, under the law prior to the Carriage of Goods by Sea Act 1924, a shipowner who received goods which he signed for 'in apparent good order and condition' to be delivered in the like good order and condition, and who delivered them not in apparent good order and condition, had the burden of proving exceptions which protected him for the damage found. The present bill of lading runs 'Shipped in apparent good order and condition of delivery subject to Conditions', etc. Has any difference been made in the old law by this wording? In my opinion no difference has been made. I agree with the view expressed by Wright J in *Gosse Millerd* v *Canadian Government Merchant Marine* [1927] 2 KB 432, 436, 437, on similar words, that there is still an obligation to deliver in the like apparent good order and condition unless the shipowner proves facts bringing him within an exception covering him. Lord Sumner in *Bradley & Sons* v *Federal Steam Navigation Co.* 27 Ll L Rep 395, 396 appears to express the same view.

The second point of law is this. It has been decided by Channell J in *Compañia Naviera Vasconzada* v *Churchill & Sim* [1906] 1 KB 237, and affirmed by the Court of Appeal in *Brandt* v *Liverpool, Brazil and River Plate Steam Navigation Co.* [1924] 1 KB 575, that the statement as to 'apparent good order and condition' estops (as against the person taking the bill of lading for value or presenting it to get delivery of the goods) the shipowner from proving that the goods were not in apparent good order and condition when shipped and therefore from alleging that there were at shipment external defects in them which were apparent to reasonable inspection. Art. III, r. 4, of the Carriage of Goods by Sea Act, 1924, which says the bill shall be prima facie evidence (not prima facie evidence *only*, liable to be contradicted), can hardly have been meant to render the above decisions inapplicable. For the information relates to the shipowner's knowledge; he is to say what is 'apparent', that is, visible by reasonable inspection to himself and his servants, and on the faith of that statement other people are to act, and if it is wrong, act to their prejudice.

I am of opinion that r. 4 of Art. III has not the effect of allowing the shipowner to prove that goods which he has stated to be in apparent good order and condition on shipment were not really in apparent good order and condition as against people who accepted the bill of lading on the faith of the statement contained in it. Apparent good order and condition was defined by Sir R. Phillimore in *The Peter der Grosse* (1875) 1 PD 414, 420 as meaning that 'apparently, and so far as met the eye, and externally, they were placed in good order on board this ship'. If so, on the *Churchill & Sim* decision the shipowner is not allowed to reduce his liability by proving or suggesting contrary to his statement in the bill that the goods in respect of matters externally reasonably visible were not in good condition when shipped.

Now what was reasonably apparent to the shipowner's servants loading at Shanghai at night but under clusters of electric lights? The ultimate damage was classed by the surveyors as (1) serious damage where the tins were gashed or punctured, damage easily discernible in handling each tin; (2) minor damage, pinhole perforations, which on tins covered with rime were not easily discernible but which were found when the tins were closely examined. I have considered the evidence and I find that the first class of damage was apparent to reasonable examination; the second, having regard to business conditions, was not apparent. The result of this is that the shipowner is estopped against certain persons from proving or suggesting that there were gashes or serious damage when the goods were shipped. He may raise the question whether there was not minor or pin-prick damage at that time, but having regard to the small quantity of goods rejected for visible damage I should not estimate the amount of such minor damage at shipment as very high.

The question whether the shipowner is prevented by the statement as to 'apparent good order and condition' from relying on the allegation or exception of 'insufficiency of packing', one of the exceptions under the Rules in the Schedule to the Act, is more difficult. The shipowners' contention is that there was insufficiency of packing, because (a) the eggs were packed in uncovered tins, and, therefore, were difficult to handle when frozen and had less protection than if the tins were covered; (b) the tins had sharp edges and corners and were therefore dangerous to each other; and (c) that the tins were of too thin plating to stand the wear and tear of contact with other tins. Now the facts that the tins were (1) uncovered and (2) with rectangular edges were obvious on shipment. If this was insufficient packing the insufficient packing was obvious. I cannot think that a shipowner who receives, say, a wooden case broken open at one corner or side can describe it as 'in apparent good order and condition' and afterwards prove the opposite. And if the insufficiency of the packing is obvious, again I think it cannot be described as in 'apparent good order and condition'. In truth the rectangular uncovered packages are not 'insufficiently packed' but may be dangerous to other cases and are difficult to handle, each matter being obvious to external inspection. Some suggestion is made that the metal containers were too thin, and they were obviously too thin to resist the treatment they received. But it appears from the letter of August 26, 1927, that the metal was of the same thickness as the Union Cold Storage Company's usual tins. I do not see why rectangular tins carefully stowed should damage each other and they are obviously better for the ship in stowage in that they waste less space than round tins, while their lack of covering is apparent.

I am therefore of opinion that against the proper person the shipowners are estopped by their statement that the cans were shipped in apparent good order and condition from proving that they were insufficiently packed, or in fact seriously gashed, but that they may prove or suggest pinholes on shipment as not being reasonably apparent. . . .

Whether the consignee is entitled to rely on the statement as to apparent good order depends on whether he relied on the statement without knowledge of its untruth to his prejudice. It was argued that as he ordered square tins and uncovered tins he must have known they were insufficiently packed. He certainly ordered square tins, but had certainly no knowledge of the make of the edges, which were said to be unusually sharp. The statement that he ordered uncovered tins is based on his telegram of May 18 ordering 'plain' tins. But this, I think, clearly relates only to absence of mark, as the letter of June 21 contrasting 'plain tins' with tins branded 'Superegg' shows. In my view the consignee in London had no knowledge of any facts that showed that the tins were not in apparent good order and condition. The last objection was that the witness did not say he relied on the bill of lading being a clean bill of lading by reason of the statement as to good order and condition. The mercantile importance of clean bills of lading is so obvious and important that I think the fact that he took the bill of lading, which is in fact clean, without objection, is quite sufficient evidence that he relied on it.

*Note*

The decision in *Silver* v *Ocean Steamship Co. Ltd* removes the need for positive proof of reliance on the statement in the bill which had weighed rather heavily on Channell J in *Compañia Naviera Vasconzada* v *Churchill & Sim* [1906] 1 KB 237, the first decision to give effect to the estoppel. The damage there was apparent (timber badly stained by petroleum); Scrutton KC, counsel for the shipowners, relied (*inter alia*) on the further clause in the bill of lading 'quality and measure unknown' to negative any representation. As to this Channell J said:

... It seems to me that while in reference to some things and to some defects in them 'condition' and 'quality' may mean the same thing, yet that they do not either necessarily or even usually do so. I think that 'condition' refers to external and apparent condition, and 'quality' to something which is usually not apparent, at all events to an unskilled person. I think a captain is expected to notice the apparent condition of the goods, though not the quality. He may qualify or (except perhaps when the Harter Act applies) erase the words 'good order and condition'; but if he leaves them in he does not, in my opinion, get rid of the admission as to condition (meaning thereby apparent condition) by saying that the quality is unknown. It is probably unnecessary for him to protect himself as regards quality, which it is not his business to know anything about, except perhaps when the description of the goods set out in the bill of lading contains words importing a statement as to the quality. . . .

There will be no estoppel if the statement is not sufficiently clear and unqualified.

### Canada and Dominion Sugar Co. Ltd v Canadian National (West Indies) Steamships Ltd
#### [1947] AC 46 (PC)

LORD WRIGHT: The appellants claimed in the action as holders of a bill of lading in respect of a quantity of sugar shipped at Demerara on the respondents' steamship *Colborne* for delivery at Montreal. In due course the appellants, who had purchased the sugar on c.i.f. terms, took up the bill of lading against payment of 95 per cent of the purchase price when it was presented to them in accordance with the terms of the contract, and thereupon became owners of the sugar and duly thereafter paid the balance of the price. The sugar was found to be damaged. In the action it was alleged, in addition to the claim on estoppel, that the damage had been sustained during the voyage and that the respondents as shipowners were liable either for failure to carry with due care or for bad stowage. On the appeal before this Board the primary issue on which the appellants claimed to succeed was on estoppel based on the terms of the bill of lading which, it was contended, contained an unqualified statement that the sugar had been received in apparent good order and condition for shipment on the *Colborne*; the appellants, it was said, accepted the bill of lading on presentation at Montreal and paid for the sugar on the faith of the statement and were entitled to recover accordingly for the resulting loss. The trial judge upheld the claim, but the Supreme Court of Canada dismissed it on the ground that the statement of good order and condition was qualified by the other terms of the bill of lading.

The two further contentions of fact on which the appellants originally relied, namely, want of due care on the voyage and bad stowage, did not succeed either before the judge or before the Supreme Court and need not here be further considered. Their Lordships agree that the contentions failed.

The bill of lading, dated at Georgetown, B.G., on June 13, 1938, and signed by the agents of the shipowners (the respondents) was a 'received for shipment' not a 'shipped' bill of lading. The loading of the sugar in question was completed on June 13, and the ship's receipt was signed on that date. It is not clearly established whether the signing of the bill of lading was before or after the actual completion of the loading, but as the bill of lading bore on its face an endorsement 'Signed under guarantee to produce ship's clean receipt' it would seem reasonable to infer that the ship's receipt had not reached the agents' office when they signed the bill. As will be shown later, this particular point is not material in the final stage of the argument. Evidence was given, and not questioned, that there was a practice at the port to issue bills of lading before the completion of the loading and the issue of the mate's receipt in order to facilitate the shippers' business arrangements by enabling them to catch an earlier mail for the port of destination, so that the document could be presented to the buyer for acceptance and payment before the carrying vessel's arrival. In the present case the *Colborne* did not arrive until July 3, 1938, but the bill of lading was taken up against payment at Montreal on June 29, 1938.

It was not disputed that the sugar, which had been lying for some time at the wharf at Georgetown, had suffered some damage before shipment. From this resulted the damage found on arrival at Montreal. The voyage had been made under favourable weather conditions, and there was nothing to account for the wet condition of part of the cargo except exposure during the rainy season while waiting for shipment. The ship's receipt, signed on Jun 13, 1938, by the chief tally clerk acting for Booker Bros McConnell and Co. Ltd, who were the shippers and sellers, and by the same company as agents for the shipowners, had the notation 'Many bags stained, torn and resewn'. This state of things would be sufficient to explain the damage found at Montreal on unloading, though that damage would not involve an inference of bad stowage, as on the evidence the Supreme Court, rightly, in their Lordships judgment, found.

The third point, estoppel, depends primarily on whether the bill of lading contained an unqualified statement that the sugar was received by the ship 'in apparent good order and condition'. . . .

The crucial question is what is the true construction of the bill of lading in regard to the matters relevant to this case. The issue is here between the shipowners and the indorsees of the bill, and has to be decided as between these parties on the basis of what appeared on the face of the bill when it was presented at Montreal to the respondents. Their rights and liabilities would not, in a case like this, be affected by what happened at the port of shipment as between the shippers and the shipowners, except in so far as appeared from the bill of lading. Authority for that proposition (if authority be needed at this time of day) is afforded by *Evans v James Webster and Bros. Ltd* (1928) 34 Com Cas 172, where it was held that an innocent indorsee for value of a bill of lading is entitled to act on the statements contained in the bill of lading unless he has at the material time clear and definite knowledge from other sources that the statements in the bill are untrue. Any other view would affect the value of a bill of lading as a document of title on the faith of which shipowners and indorsees deal. If the statement at the head of the bill, 'Received in apparent good order and condition', had stood by itself, the bill would have been a 'clean' bill of lading, an expression which means, at least in a context like this, that there was no clause or notation modifying or qualifying the statement as to the condition of the goods. But the bill did in fact on its face contain the qualifying words, 'Signed under guarantee to produce ship's clean receipt': that was a stamped clause clear and obvious on the face of the document, and reasonably conveying to any business man that if the ship's receipt was not clean the statement in the bill of lading as to apparent order and condition could not be taken to be unqualified. If the ship's receipt was not clean, the bill of lading would not be a clean bill of lading, with the result that the estoppel which could have been set up by the indorsee as against the shipowner if the bill of lading had been a clean bill of lading, and the necessary conditions of estoppel had been satisfied, could not be relied on. That type of estoppel is of the greatest importance in this common class of commercial transactions; it has been upheld in a long series of authoritative decisions, of which their Lordships need only cite one, *Silver v Ocean Steamship Company* [1930] 1 KB 416, where the rules applicable to cases in which bills of lading are dealt with as between shipowners and indorsees or other holders for value are laid down. But if the statement is qualified, as in the opinion of their Lordships and the judges of the Supreme Court it was, the estoppel fails.

... Their Lordships in so deciding are not in any way weakening the rule that a shipowner who issues a clean bill of lading is bound by the statement in it that the goods are shipped in good or in apparent good order and condition: if the statement turns out to be untrue the shipowner is estopped from alleging its falsity as against a purchaser who relies on the statement at its face value and acts on it to his detriment. This is a rule which may be applied any day in the case of c.i.f. contracts. To cast doubts on it would be to weaken the whole course of dealing between business men in regard to bills of lading in their character of documents of title used in connexion with overseas shipments of goods. It is true that the unqualified statement is only one step in the establishment of the estoppel. Estoppel is a complex legal notion, involving a combination of several essential elements, the statement to be acted on, action on the faith of it, resulting detriment to the actor. Estoppel is often described as a rule of evidence, as, indeed, it may be so described. But the whole concept is more correctly viewed as a substantive rule of law. The purchaser or other transferee must have acted on it to his detriment, as, for instance, he did in this case when he took up the documents and paid for them. It is also true that he cannot be said to rely on the statement if he knew that it was false: he must reasonably believe it to be true and therefore act on it. Estoppel is different from contract both in its nature and conseqeunces. But the relationship between the parties must also be such that the imputed truth of the statement is a necessary step in the constitution of the cause of action. But the whole case of estoppel fails if the statement is not sufficiently clear and unqualified. That, in their Lordships' judgment, is the position in this case. ...

*Notes*

1.   In the case of *Evans* v *James Webster and Bros. Ltd* (1928) 34 Com Cas 172, timber was shipped under a clean bill of lading, but on arrival the quantity was less than stated and some of the timber was stained and damaged. Before the defendants paid they were made aware that the loss and damage were the subject of protests by the shipper and the master, and L, their representative, saw copies of the protests. Wright J held nevertheless that the defendants could rely on the estoppel. It was not clear that the master's protest referred to the defendants' cargo, but even if it did, the result would have been the same. Wright J stated the position as follows:

... The statement in the bill of lading is quite clear and unambiguous. By mercantile usage is it essential that every bill of lading should state the condition, or apparent condition, of the goods shipped. The master can always qualify the statement by a clause stating that some of the goods are damaged, or dirty, or whatever may be the appropriate description. But every master signing a bill of lading must know that he is signing a document which may be in the ordinary course of commerce transferred against value, and will be acted upon as a document of title. It seems to me therefore that a shipowner ought not to be heard to say that the bill of lading holder, the indorsee who has taken the bill according to its face value, is not entitled to rely on it, unless there is before him information contradicting the bill of lading which is of at least equal value with the statement in the bill itself. I do not say there may not be cases where an indorsee for value of a bill of lading may not be estopped from saying that he took the bill according to its face value; there may be cases where he has independent knowledge of such a character that he knows quite clearly that the statement in the bill of lading is inaccurate.

But I think such cases must be very rare. Persons to whom bills of lading are tendered to implement a contract like the present ought to be entitled as against the shipowner to take the bills at their face value unless, as I have said, the contrary evidence in their possession is of conclusive and overwhelming importance. Any other view would tend to diminish the value of bills of lading in commerce, and would also tend to promote carelessness, if not fraud, on the part of a shipmaster.

In this case I do not think that the information before the defendants was of such a character as to justify them in rejecting the bills of lading as not representing the true facts. The material date is August 17, the date of the acceptance of the bills of exchange. The acceptance was an act done to their prejudice by the defendants in reliance on the bill of lading. They had, on the one hand, the clean bill of lading, and on the other hand, the protests. The shipper's protest I disregard, because it was a peculiar circumstance which in itself might puzzle and raise suspicion; but taking the master's protest, the position was that they had, on the one hand, the bill of lading signed by the master, an authoritative document under his signature; and they had, on the other hand, his protest. The protest cannot be regarded as of greater value than the bill of lading; and these two documents signed by the master contradicted each other. In view of that contradiction I think that the defendants would have been entitled to rely upon the statement in the bill of lading even if there had been no ambiguity in the protest. . . .

2. In *The Peter Der Grosse* (1875) 1 PD 414, bales of down and feathers were shipped from St Petersburg to London under clean bills of lading, but arrived stained and with an offensive smell. The shipowners sought to rely on a clause in the bills of lading: 'Weight, contents and value unknown.' It was held by Sir Robert Phillimore (and affirmed by the Court of Appeal: (1876) 34 LT 749) that the bills of lading were still prima facie evidence that *externally* the bales were in good condition when shipped and that the shipowners had failed to rebut that evidence.

3. See also *The Tromp* [1921] P 337: 'All that appears to the eye upon a shipment of potatoes in bags is the state of the packages' (per Sir Henry Duke P, at p. 348). Potatoes shipped in wet bags arrived in a rotted condition. The bill of lading stated that they were shipped in good order and condition, but that 'weight, quality, condition and measure' were unknown. The 'condition unknown' clause referred to *internal* condition or quality and the carriers were accordingly estopped from denying that the bags were wet when shipped, which was the cause of the rotting.

4. Because of the commercial importance to shippers of having bills of lading to which purchasers and banks will raise no objection, pressure is put on carriers to issue clean bills, in return for an indemnity, even where the carrier has doubts about the condition of the goods. In *Brown Jenkinson & Co. Ltd* v *Percy Dalton (London) Ltd* [1957] 2 QB 621, a clean bill was issued by the plaintiffs, in return for an indemnity, in respect of 100 barrels of orange juice known by all parties to be old, frail and leaking at the time of shipment. The Dutch purchasers had resold to a firm in Hamburg: they described the cargo on arrival in Hamburg as being

. . . a hopeless mess only. The orange juice was streaming like water out of the barrels, and when Rotmans should not have taken immediately action to put some men to work and to fix the iron belts of the barrels firmer the damage should have been much bigger.

All the barrels have to be washed with water, to clean them, for they were laying in a bath of orange juice, which barrels have been closed by special men as we said above, and when the goods were weighed the loss in weight was about 10 per cent.

Morris and Pearce LJJ held that the indemnity was illegal because the consideration for it was the making of a representation of fact known to be false, with intent that it should be acted upon. Pearce LJ had this to say:

The plaintiffs issued a clean bill of lading in respect of goods contained in barrels that were to their knowledge faulty. Thereby they made a representation of fact that they knew to be false. They knew that the purpose of the representation was to procure payment by bankers, who are very often not prepared to provide the money if the bill of lading is not clean. The bankers paid the money relying, no doubt, on the plaintiffs' representation. Others besides the bankers were affected by the representation, since subsequent purchasers were entitled to rely on the bills of lading.

I find it difficult to see what answer the plaintiffs would have had if the purchasers had sued them in fraud. The fact that the damage was subsequently made good seemed to the judge to change the quality of their act. But it does not, in my opinion, alter the fact that the plaintiffs, by making a representation of fact that they knew to be false, with intent that it should be acted on (as in fact it was), were committing a tort. They are now seeking to recover on the indemnity in consideration of which they committed the tort. Had they been actively intending that someone should be defrauded by their misrepresentation, their case would have been unarguable.

The real difficulty that arises in the case is due to the fact that the plaintiffs, whatever may have been the defendants' intentions, appear from the evidence not to have contemplated that anybody would ultimately be defrauded. Theirs was a slipshod and unthinking extension of a known commercial practice to a point at which it constituted fraud in law. In the last 20 years it has become customary, in the short-sea trade in particular, for shipowners to give a clean bill of lading against an indemnity from the shippers in certain cases where there is a bona fide dispute as to the condition or packing of the goods. This avoids the necessity of rearranging any letter of credit, a matter which can create difficulty where time is short. If the goods turn out to be faulty, the purchaser will have his recourse against the shipping owner, who will in turn recover under his indemnity from the shippers. Thus no one will ultimately be wronged.

This practice is convenient where it is used with conscience and circumspection, but it has perils if it is used with laxity and recklessness. It is not enough that the banks or the purchasers who have been misled by clean bills of lading may have recourse at law against the shipping owner. They are intending to buy goods, not law suits. Moreover, instances have been given in argument where their legal rights may be defeated or may not recoup their loss. Trust is the foundation of trade; and bills of lading are important documents. If purchasers and banks felt that they could no longer trust bills of lading, the disadvantage to the commercial community would far outweigh any conveniences provided by the giving of clean bills of lading against indemnities.

The evidence seemed to show that, in general, the practice is kept within reasonable limits. In trivial matters and in cases of bona fide dispute, where the difficulty of ascertaining the correct state of affairs is out of proportion to its importance, no doubt the practice is useful. But here the plaintiffs went outside those reasonable limits. They did so at the defendants' request without, as it seems to me, properly considering the implications of what they were doing. They thought that they could trust the defendants' agreement to indemnify them. In that they were in error.

Lord Evershed MR dissented on the ground that, since the plaintiffs' conduct was not really 'dishonest', as the parties did not intend any other person to suffer damage ultimately, public policy did not require that the plaintiffs should be deprived of the benefit of the indemnity, an approach which is no longer tenable since the House of Lords decision in *Tinsley* v *Milligan* [1994] 1 AC 340. In *Standard Chartered Bank* v *Pakistan National Shipping Corporation* [1998] 1 Lloyd's Rep 684, Cresswell J said: 'Antedated and false bills of lading are a cancer in international trade. A bill of lading is issued in international trade with the purpose that it should be relied upon by those into whose hands it properly comes — consignees, bankers and endorsees. A bank, which receives a bill of lading signed by or on behalf of a shipowner (as one of the documents presented under a letter of credit), relies upon the veracity and authenticity of the bill. Honest commerce requires that those who put bills of lading into circulation do so only where the bill of lading, as far as they know, represents the true facts.'

## B. Statements as to quantity

The principle of estoppel was not applied at common law to statements of the quantity shipped. The claim of an indorsee for value of a bill of lading stating 'shipped . . . 100 bales of jute' who received only 50 bales could be met by proof that the other 50 had never in fact been put on board. This extraordinary rule was drawn from a perceived limitation on the master's authority to bind the shipowner.

### Grant v Norway
#### (1851) 10 CB 665; 138 ER 263 (Common Pleas)

The facts found by the jury were as follows:

The plaintiffs, during the year 1846, and thence hitherto, had carried on business as merchants, at Calcutta, under the firm of Gladstone & Co.

During the month of April, 1846, the defendants were possessed of, and owners of, the 'Belle', then lying in the river Hooghley, at Calcutta, bound for London, by charterparty for the conveyance of goods for freight; Henry Tillman being the master appointed by the defendants.

On the 17th of April, in that year, Henry Tillman, being such master, and professing to act as such, signed and delivered to Biale, Koch & Co., in the declaration mentioned, being merchants and traders then in credit and carrying on business in Calcutta, a bill of lading, in the usual form, as follows, and numbered in the margin:

> Shipped, by the grace of God, in good order and well conditioned, upon the good ship 'Belle', whereof is master for this present voyage Henry Tillman, and now riding at anchor in the Hooghley, and bound for London, twelve bales of silk, numbered as in the margin, to be delivered in the like good order at London, the act of God, the Queen's enemies, &c., excepted, unto order or assigns, he or they paying freight 5*l*. per ton, &c.

In witness whereof the said master hath affirmed to three bills of lading, all of this tenor and date, the one of which being accomplished, the other two to stand void. Dated this 17th day of April, 1846. Contents unknown.

(Signed) 'H. TILLMAN'.

The bill of lading was indorsed 'Biale, Koch & Co'.

The bill of lading was deposited with the plaintiffs and indorsed to them, but the goods were never shipped.

JERVIS CJ: This case was argued before my brothers Cresswell and Williams and myself. It arises upon a special verdict, and presents a question of considerable importance, both to those who take bills of lading on the faith of their representing property which passes by the transfer of them, and to the ship-owner, whom it is attempted to bind by all bills of lading which his captain may think fit to sign. The point presented by the several pleas is substantially one and the same, viz. whether the master of a ship, signing a bill of lading for goods which have never been shipped, is to be considered as the agent of the owner in that behalf, so as to make the latter responsible. The authority of the master of a ship is very large, and extends to all acts that are usual and necessary for the use and enjoyment of the ship; but is subject to several well-known limitations. He may make contracts for the hire of the ship, but cannot vary that which the owner has made. He may take up money in foreign ports, and, under certain circumstances, at home, for necessary disbursements, and for repairs, and bind the owners for repayment; but his authority is limited by the necessity of the case, and he cannot make them responsible for money not actually necessary for those purposes, although he may pretend that it is. He may make contracts to carry goods on freight, but cannot bind his owners by a contract to carry freight free. So, with regard to goods put on board, he may sign a bill of lading, and acknowledge the nature and quality and conditions of the goods. Constant usage shews that masters have that general authority; and, if a more limited one is given, a party not informed of it is not affected by such limitation.... Is it then, usual, in the management of a ship carrying goods on freight, for the master to give a bill of lading for goods not put on board? for, all parties concerned have a right to assume that an agent has authority to do all which is usual. The very nature of a bill of lading shews that it ought not to be signed until goods are on board; for, it begins by describing them as shipped. It was not contended that such a course is usual. In *Lickbarrow v Mason* 2 TR 75, Buller J says: 'A bill of lading is an acknowledgment by the captain, of having received the goods on board his ship: therefore, it would be a fraud in the captain to sign such a bill of lading, if he had not received the goods on board; and the consignee would be entitled to his action against the captain for the fraud.'

It is not contended that the captain had any real authority to sign bills of lading, unless the goods had been shipped: nor can we discover any ground upon which a party taking a bill of lading by indorsement, would be justified in assuming that he had authority to sign such bills, whether the goods were on board or not.

If, then, from the usage of trade, and the general practice of ship-masters, it is generally known that the master derives no such authority from his position as master, the case may be considered as if the party taking the bill of lading had notice of an express limitation of the authority; and, in that case, undoubtedly, he could not claim to bind the owner by a bill of lading signed, when the goods therein mentioned were never shipped....

*Question*
The bill of lading in *Grant* v *Norway* included a 'contents unknown' clause:
would this have prevented an estoppel from arising anyway?

*Notes*
1.   The decision was, to say the least, difficult to reconcile with the House of
Lords decision in *Lloyd* v *Grace, Smith & Co.* [1912] AC 716, though it was not
overruled: see the comments of Sheen J in *The Nea Tyhi* [1982] 1 Lloyd's Rep
606, at pp. 610–11, subsection D, below.
2.   *Grant* v *Norway* prompted the enactment of s. 3 of the Bills of Lading Act
1855, which made the statement in the bill that goods had been shipped on
board *conclusive* evidence of shipment in favour of the consignee or indorsee of
the bill for valuable consideration (unless he had actual notice when receiving
the bill of lading that the goods had not been shipped), but only as against *the
master or other person signing* the bill. Contrary to the view apparently expressed
by no lesser an authority than Scrutton LJ (in *New Chinese Antimony Co. Ltd* v
*Ocean Steamship Co. Ltd* [1917] 2 KB 664, at p. 672), the section was held to
create no estoppel, and therefore no remedy, against the *shipowner* (except in
the rare case where the bill of lading was signed by the latter personally, or by
his clerk in a purely ministerial capacity: see *V/O Rasnoimport* v *Guthrie & Co.
Ltd* [1966] 1 Lloyd's Rep 1, per Mocatta J, at pp. 17–18). It was thus, for
practical purposes, largely ineffective and has now been repealed by the
Carriage of Goods by Sea Act 1992 (COGSA 1992), s. 6(2).
3.   Where the bill of lading is subject to COGSA 1971 (as to which see
Chapter 7, section 1), Art. III, r. 4 of the Hague-Visby Rules makes the
statement of receipt conclusive evidence against the carrier in favour of a
transferee of the bill of lading acting in good faith. (See further subsection E,
below.) Where the bill of lading was issued on or after 16 September 1992, s. 4
of COGSA 1992 will apply:

**4.   Representations in bills of lading**
A bill of lading which—
     (a)   represents goods to have been shipped on board a vessel or to have been
received for shipment on board a vessel; and
     (b)   has been signed by the master of the vessel or by a person who was not the
master but had the express, implied or apparent authority of the carrier to sign bills of
lading,
shall, in favour of a person who has become the lawful holder of the bill, be conclusive
evidence against the carrier of the shipment of the goods or, as the case may be, of their
receipt for shipment.

For the definition of 'lawful holder', see s. 5(2) below.
     See also COGSA 1992, s. 5(5), giving priority to COGSA 1971: to avoid
conflict between s. 4 of COGSA 1992 and Art. III, r. 4 of the Hague-Visby Rules,
the statement in the bill of lading can never be conclusive in favour of the shipper.

Although not conclusive at common law, the statement that the goods had
been shipped was strong prima facie evidence. If the shipowner could not

explain how part (or all) of the cargo came to be missing on arrival the cargo-owner's claim succeeded.

### Henry Smith & Co. v Bedouin Steam Navigation Co. Ltd
### [1896] AC 70 (HL)

A cargo of jute was shipped from Calcutta to Dundee, but on arrival 12 bales were missing from the 1,000 stated to have been shipped. The shipowners argued that the tallymen, who were local labour, probably made a mistake, since there was no way that the bales, which each weighed 400 lbs, could have been removed from the ship after loading. The House of Lords held that the shipowners (the respondents) had not done enough to defeat the inference from the bill of lading.

LORD SHAND: ... The onus is clearly on the respondents to prove the alleged short shipment, not only because of the bill of lading, but because it has been proved that the quantity of bales there acknowledged was fixed after the number and marks on the bales shipped had been carefully checked by tallymen employed by the shipowners under the superintendence of the chief mate, and after the mate had himself granted receipts to the lightermen representing the shippers corresponding as to quantities with the tallymen's notes. These detailed notes — the mate's receipts and the bills of lading — all evidence of acts by servants of the shipowners, form a strong and consistent body of proof that the shipment acknowledged under the captain's hand was actually made, and impose a heavy onus on the shipowner who alleges that nevertheless there was a deficiency, through non-shipment, in the quantity of goods shipped. What is the extent of this onus? Proof must be met by counter-proof, and that counter-proof will be insufficient if it be not strong enough to displace the consistent and clear evidence of the acts of the shipowners' own servants or employees. It will not be sufficient to shew that fraud may have been committed, or to suggest that the tallymen may have made errors or mistakes, in order to meet a case of positive proof on the other side. It must be shewn that there was in point of fact a short shipment — that is, the evidence must be sufficient to lead to the inference not merely that the goods may possibly not have been shipped, but that in point of fact they were not shipped. Any proposition short of this would appear to me to give less effect to the evidence of the shippers than that evidence ought to have, and unwarrantably to diminish the onus which that evidence has thrown on the shipowner.

*Note*
To avoid being caught in this way, shipowners have long resorted to the practice of issuing bills of lading which say as little as possible about the goods, but rely on non-committal phrases such as 'weight unknown' and 'said to be'. The effectiveness of this device was confirmed in the next case.

### New Chinese Antimony Co. Ltd v Ocean Steamship Co. Ltd
### [1917] 2 KB 664 (CA)

The bill of lading stated 'shipped ... on board the steamship *Tientsin* ... nine hundred and thirty-seven (937) tons antimony oxide ore in bulk, being marked and numbered as per margin ...'; in the margin there was a typed note 'No mark. A quantity said to be nine hundred and thirty-seven tons', and the bill also contained the (printed) clause 'weight, measurement, contents and value (for purpose of estimating freight) unknown'. The ore was put on the *Tientsin* at Hankow [now Wuhan] for carriage to Shanghai, where it was transhipped and taken to London and from there in coasters to Newcastle. On arrival the ore weighed only 861 tons. Sankey J attributed 53 tons of this loss to natural wastage and held the shipowners liable for the remaining 23 tons. The Court of Appeal held that the defendants were not responsible for any of the loss.

VISCOUNT READING CJ: The plaintiffs bring their action to recover the difference in value between 861 and 937 tons, and on the facts proved the learned judge had before him a body of evidence for the defendants, which he accepted to the effect that the cargo was of a particularly wasting nature; the antimony ore in wet weather stuck to the baskets in which it was placed, and when it dried the moisture evaporated, and it became very friable and was easily blown away by the wind. I may add that the cargo was shipped in bulk, which was very unusual, as it is usually shipped in bags, which is far less wasteful. As a result the shippers have lost, after allowing for wastage, according to the view of the learned judge, 23 tons of ore.

The question for us is whether Sankey J was right in his view that the defendants are responsible for the 23 tons. The defendants called evidence to show that all the antimony put on board had been carried to Newcastle. The question is very largely one of fact, and if I could come to the conclusion that the judgment of Sankey J depended solely on the view which he took of the evidence and did not depend on any view of law, I should not feel justified in differing from him. But after a careful examination of his judgment as a whole, and after consideration of the evidence, I have come to the conclusion that he had in mind that there was a presumption against the shipowner because of the statement in the bill of lading that 937 tons had been shipped and that he did not pay regard to the words 'weight unknown', and I think that for this reason only he has allowed the 23 tons against the defendants. He has taken the view that the shipowners have not discharged themselves of the onus put upon them by what he considered was the prima facie case that 937 tons had been received by them.... If there is such a presumption in this case, it would be easily displaced. But on a broader ground this judgment cannot stand. Where in a bill of lading, which is prepared by the shippers for acceptance by the defendants' agent, the agent accepts in the margin a quantity 'said to be 937 tons', and in the body of the bill of lading there is a clause 'weight, &c., unknown', there is no prima facie evidence that 937 tons have been shipped. Sankey J in my judgment omitted to give proper effect to the words 'weight, &c., unknown'. He based his judgment on the decision in *Smith & Co. v Bedouin Steam Navigation Co.* [1896] AC 70, but he omitted to notice that in that case a definite quantity was given in the bill of lading and that there were no qualifying words such as 'said to be' or 'weight unknown'. I think that the true effect of this bill of lading is that the words 'weight unknown' have the effect of a statement by the shipowners' agent that he has received a quantity of ore which the shippers' representative says weighs 937 tons but which he does not accept as being of that weight, the weight being unknown to him, and that he does not accept the weight of 937 tons except for the purpose of calculating freight and for that purpose only....

*Notes*
1. *New Chinese Antimony Co. Ltd* v *Ocean Steamship Co. Ltd* was applied in *Noble Resources Ltd* v *Cavalier Shipping Corporation (The Atlas)* [1996] 1 Lloyd's

Rep 642 (Longmore J) and *Agrosin Pte Ltd* v *Highway Shipping Co. Ltd (The Mata K)* [1998] 2 Lloyd's Rep 614 (Clarke J): a 'weight unknown' clause has the same effect as the expression 'said to be' and prevents the bill from representing the quantity for the purposes of s. 4 of COGSA 1992, above.

2. *New Chinese Antimony Co. Ltd* v *Ocean Steamship Co. Ltd* was distinguished in *A-G of Ceylon* v *Scindia Steam Navigation Co. Ltd* [1962] AC 60 (PC). There the bill of lading stated that 100,652 bags of rice had been shipped (at Rangoon for carriage to Colombo), 'weight contents and value when shipped unknown'. On outturn there was short delivery of 235 bags. It was held that the 'weight . . . unknown' clause did not qualify the statement as to the *number* of bags, which was strong prima facie evidence of the number supplied. Further, it was held that although the bill of lading was not even prima facie evidence of the contents of the missing bags, it was a reasonable inference that they each contained about 160 lbs of rice, since this was the average of the bags delivered, and that the plaintiff had therefore proved his loss.

3. In *Ace Imports Pty Ltd* v *Companhia de Navegaçao Lloyd Brasileiro (The Esmeralda I)* [1988] 1 Lloyd's Rep 206, a sealed container with 437 boxes of cutlery, posters and leaflets was sent from Brazil to Australia. When the container was opened at the plaintiffs' premises about a quarter of the boxes were missing. The bill of lading was marked 'FCL/FCL', meaning that the container was packed by the shipper, sealed and unpacked by the importer. The bill was also stamped 'said to contain — packed by shippers'. Yeldham J, in the Commercial Division of the Supreme Court of New South Wales, held that the bill contained no representation by the carrier that the number of boxes stated actually was in the container on shipment.

### C. Statements as to marks

Where the marks stated in the bill of lading do not correspond to the marks on the cargo tendered for delivery, the carrier is not precluded from showing that the cargo tendered is in fact the cargo received, thereby avoiding liability to the holder of the bill of lading for non-delivery.

### Parsons v New Zealand Shipping Co.
[1901] 1 QB 548 (CA)

Frozen lamb carcases were shipped from Timaru to London. The marks noted in the margin of the bills of lading included 'Sun Brand 488 X' in respect of 226 carcases and 'Sun Brand 622 X' in respect of 608 carcases. On arrival it was found that the ship did not have the stated number of carcases with these marks, but she did have 21 carcases marked 'Sun Brand 388 X' and 101 marked 'Sun Brand 522 X' which were not covered by any other bill of lading. The defendants tendered these as part of the delivery to the plaintiff, but the plaintiff refused to take them and claimed damages for non-delivery. (The market price had fallen since the plaintiff bought the lamb.) It was proved that the first figure of the mark had no commercial significance to buyers but was merely a record, for the shippers' own purposes, of the day of slaughter. It was also proved that the only tally at Timaru was of the number of carcases and no attempt was, or could be, made to check the marks. Kennedy J held that the defendants had proved that the carcases in question were part of the quantity included in the bills of lading and that the plaintiff's claim failed. The Court of Appeal affirmed this decision, rejecting the plaintiff's argument that he could rely on an estoppel created by s. 3 of the Bills of Lading Act 1855.

COLLINS LJ: . . . It is obvious that, where marks have no market meaning and indicate nothing whatever to a buyer as to the nature, quality, or quantity of the goods which he is buying, it is absolutely immaterial to him whether the goods bear one mark or another . . . the goods which the bill of lading represents as shipped continue to be the same goods, whichever out of any number of merely arbitrary marks are put on them, and will remain the same whether the marks were on them before shipment or are rubbed off or changed after shipment. In other words, they go to the identification only, and not the identity. The goods represented by the bill of lading to have been shipped have been shipped, and a mistaken statement as to marks of this class merely makes identification more difficult; it does not affect the existence or identity of the goods. It seems to me, therefore, that, both on the strict wording of the section, and having regard to the mischief to which it was addressed, the plaintiff has failed to bring his case within the estoppel which it creates. . . .

*Notes*
1.   *Parsons* v *New Zealand Shipping Co.* is unusual in that it was assumed without question that their agent's signature would bind the defendants for the purposes of s. 3. No reference was made to *Thorman* v *Burt* (1886) 54 LT 349 (CA), which is clear authority to the contrary. See also subsection B, above.
2.   In *Cox, Patterson & Co.* v *Bruce & Co.* (1856) 18 QBD 147, the Court of Appeal applied the principle of *Grant* v *Norway* (above, subsection B) to a statement of quality marks, holding that the master has no authority to indicate the quality of the goods and that the carriers were therefore not estopped from proving that goods of the quality indicated had not in fact been shipped. In *Compania Importadora de Arroces Collette y Kamp SA* v *P & O Steam Navigation Co.* (1927) 28 Ll L Rep 63, Wright J held that, though not conclusive, the statements as to marks were still prima facie evidence of the shipment of goods bearing those marks and put the onus on the shipowner to establish 'by clear and sufficient evidence' that the bill of lading was not correct.

*D. Other statements in bills of lading*

It would seem to follow from the authorities considered so far that any statement in the bill of lading which is of commercial significance to an indorsee of the bill may give rise to an estoppel against the shipowner. The contrary argument will rely heavily on the assertion that *Grant* v *Norway*, above, extends to the kind of statement in question.

## *The Nea Tyhi*
[1982] 1 Lloyd's Rep 606 (QBD, Admiralty Court)

The plaintiffs were indorsees of the bills of lading in respect of a cargo of plywood carried on the *Nea Tyhi* from Port Kelang in Malaysia to Newport. The bills of lading stated that the plywood was 'shipped under deck', as plywood must be, but in fact the cargo was carried on deck and was badly damaged by rain water. It was held that the charterers' agents had ostensible, though not actual, authority to sign the bills of lading and therefore to establish contractual liability against the carriers. The judge had this to say about *Grant* v *Norway*:

SHEEN J: ... To those who are not familiar with the law relating to the carriage of goods by sea, but who are familiar with general principles of agency and, in particular, with the decision of the House of Lords in *Lloyd* v *Grace, Smith and Co.* [1912] AC 716 the decision in *Grant* v *Norway* may come as a surprise. But that decision has survived for 130 years and has been quoted with approval in the Court of Appeal and House of Lords; see *Kleinwort, Sons & Co.* v *Associated Automatic Machine Corporation Ltd* (1934) 151 LT 1. Accordingly I am bound by it. The decision in *Grant* v *Norway* and the cases which followed it were fully considered in the judgment of Mr Justice Mocatta in *V/O Rasnoimport* v *Guthrie and Co. Ltd* [1966] 1 Lloyd's Rep 1 at pp. 8–10. It is unnecessary for me to repeat in this judgment all that Mr Justice Mocatta stated in that case. It is however noticeable that, in order to achieve a result which did justice in that case without declining to follow the decision in *Grant* v *Norway*, Mr Justice Mocatta was driven to complex and tortuous reasoning. I confess that I find it impossible to reconcile the decision in *Lloyd* v *Grace Smith and Co.* with the decision in *Grant* v *Norway*, and yet the earlier case cannot have been overlooked by the House of Lords when giving judgment in the later one. *Lloyd* v *Grace Smith* was decided at first instance by Mr Justice Scrutton, with a special jury at Liverpool Assizes and he gave judgment for the plaintiff. Only two years earlier he had been counsel in *Russo-Chinese Bank* v *Li Yan San* [1910] AC 174, in which case he had successfully relied upon *Grant* v *Norway*. The Court of Appeal by a majority, namely Lord Justice Farwell and Lord Justice Kennedy, allowed the appeal. In the judgment of Lord Justice Farwell the decision in *Grant* v *Norway* and *Russo-Chinese Bank* v *Li Yan San* played a prominent part. In the House of Lords no mention is made of the decision in *Grant* v *Norway* in any of the speeches. The main speech was made by Lord Macnaghten, who was a member of the Privy Council in the *Russo-Chinese Bank* case, and who also wrote the principal speech in *George Whitechurch Ltd* v *Cavanagh* [1902] AC 117 in which *Grant* v *Norway* was approved. I can only conclude that the decision in *Grant* v *Norway* is to be regarded as an exception and not as laying down a general principle. Indeed in *Uxbridge Permanent Benefit Building Society* v *Pickard* [1939] 2 KB 248 Lord Justice MacKinnon sought to rationalise the distinction between the liability of the principal in *Lloyd* v *Grace Smith* and the non-liability of the principal in *Grant* v *Norway* with the words—

... anyone dealing with the captain of a ship must be taken to know that he has, and can only have, authority to sign a bill of lading for goods which have been in fact shipped, and therefore he can have no ostensible authority to sign a bill of lading for goods which have not been shipped.

I do not understand how the conclusion follows from the premise.

The decision in *Grant* v *Norway* is the first stepping stone in the submissions of Mr Colman. In this Court it gives him a firm foothold. But his next step is to say that the misdescription of the shipment, the erroneous statement that the plywood was under deck, is an act of such gravity of quality between shipowner and shipper that it is similar to a statement that goods have been shipped when in fact they have not been shipped. Mr Colman says that accordingly it should be treated in a similar manner and that no liability should fall on the shipowner. In order to tempt me to extend the protection to shipowners which is afforded by the decision in *Grant* v *Norway*, Mr Colman submitted that I have to decide which of two innocent parties should suffer and where the line should be drawn.

In the light of the comments which I have already made about the decision in *Grant* v *Norway* it must already be clear that I can see no justification for extending that protection. Furthermore there is a distinction between the case of a master issuing a bill of lading in respect of goods which have not in fact been shipped and the case of a master issuing a bill of lading which states that the goods are under deck when in truth they are on deck. In the former case the shipper ought to know that his goods have not been shipped, whereas in the latter case there is not necessarily any reason for the shipper to know that there is an erroneous statement on the bill of lading. If the shipper does know of the error in the bill of lading he has no right to endorse it to a purchaser for value. As to Mr Colman's submission that one of two 'innocent' parties must suffer, if I had to choose whether the shipowner or the endorsee of a bill of lading should be the loser I would have no hesitation in saying that there is more reason that he who contracts with the charterer and puts trust and confidence in him to the extent of authorising the charterers' agent to issue and sign bills of lading should be a loser, than a stranger. This principle was stated by Chief Justice Holt in *Hern* v *Nichols* Holt 462 in 1701.

In my judgment the charterers' agents had ostensible authority to sign the bills of lading on behalf of the master. Accordingly that signature binds the shipowners as principals to the contract contained in or evidenced by the bills of lading. . . .

*Notes*
1.   Sheen J had a further opportunity to consider *Grant* v *Norway* in *The Saudi Crown* [1986] 1 Lloyd's Rep 261, where it was held that the incorrect dating of bills of lading was an act within the ostensible authority of the shipowners' agents: the indorsees were awarded damages for the loss of the opportunity to reject the bills of lading because of the fraudulent misrepresentation of the date of the bills.
2.   For the shipper's right to demand a bill of lading containing specified particulars when the Hague-Visby Rules apply, see Chapter 7.

## SECTION 2: THE BILL OF LADING AS A CONTRACT

Although, as we have seen in the previous section, estoppel plays an important part in enabling indorsees of a bill of lading to assert their rights against a carrier, the fact remains that the legal relationship between carrier and cargo-owner is essentially contractual and we turn now to examine the role of the bill of lading in establishing the terms of the contract of carriage. COGSA 1992, adopting a traditional formulation, defines a contract of carriage (s. 5(1)) as 'the contract *contained in or evidenced by*' the bill of lading, thereby highlighting the two possibilities — the bill of lading may *contain* the contract, or it may merely be *evidence* of it, subject to contradiction by other evidence.

Further complications arise where the vessel is under charter: these are considered separately in subsection B, below.

*A: Contained in or evidenced by*

The Bills of Lading Act 1855, s. 1, spoke of 'the contract contained in the bill of lading'. In *Sewell* v *Burdick* (1884) 10 App Cas 74, at p. 105, Lord Bramwell, after criticising the wording of another part of the Act, said:

> There is, I think, another inaccuracy in the statute, which indeed is universal. It speaks of the contract contained in the bill of lading. To my mind there is no contract in it. It is a receipt for the goods, stating the terms on which they were deliverd to and received by the ship, and therefore excellent evidence of those terms, but it is not a contract. That has been made before the bill of lading was given. . . .

The significance of this distinction is shown by the next case.

### *SS Ardennes (Cargo Owners)* v *SS Ardennes (Owners)*
### [1951] 1 KB 55 (KBD)

The plaintiffs shipped 3,000 cases of mandarin oranges at Cartagena for carriage to London. They received an oral undertaking from the shipowners' agent that the vessel would proceed directly to London. The bill of lading contained liberty to call at other ports, however, and instead of sailing to London the ship went first to Antwerp (where some of the mandarin oranges were left behind). The resulting delay meant that the plaintiffs had to pay a higher rate of import duty, which was increased annually on 1 December, and secured a lower price because of the arrival of other cargoes in the meantime. (Even so they obtained a price of marginally over £1 for 10 kilos — a not insubstantial sum in 1947.) It was held that they were entitled to damages for the extra duty paid and the fall in the market price.

LORD GODDARD CJ: . . . The defences raised were in substance that there was no oral agreement, and reliance is placed on one of the conditions in the bill of lading. I have no hesitation in finding that there was a promise made to the shippers' representative that the ship should go direct to London, and that they shipped in reliance on that promise. I therefore have now to consider the defence which arises out of the terms of the bill of lading. [His Lordship read it.] Sir Robert Aske contended that the second of these clauses is a complete defence and, indeed, that evidence of any other bargain or promise is not admissible; and that seems to me to be the main question which falls for decision in this case.

It is, I think, well settled that a bill of lading is not in itself the contract between the shipowner and the shipper of goods, though it has been said to be excellent evidence of its terms: *Sewell* v *Burdick* (1884) 10 App Cas 74, 105, *per* Lord Bramwell and *Crooks* v *Allan* 5 QBD 38. The contract has come into existence before the bill of lading is signed; the latter is signed by one party only, and handed by him to the shipper usually after the goods have been put on board. No doubt if the shipper finds that the bill contains terms with which he is not content, or does not contain some term for which he has stipulated, he might, if there were time, demand his goods back; but he is not, in my opinion, for that reason, prevented from giving evidence that there was in fact a contract entered into before the bill of lading was signed different from that which is found in the bill of lading or containing some additional term. He is no party to the preparation of the bill of lading; nor does he sign it. It is unnecessary to cite authority further than the two cases already mentioned for the proposition that the bill of lading is not itself the contract; therefore in my opinion evidence as to the true contract is admissible.

*Leduc & Co.* v *Ward* (1888) 20 QBD 475, on which Sir Robert Aske so strongly relied, was a case between shipowner and endorsee of the bill of lading, between whom its terms are conclusive by virtue of the Bill of Lading Act 1855, so that no evidence was admissible in that case to contradict or vary its terms. Between those parties the statute makes it the contract. In any case, the representation that the ship would sail direct to London would amount to a warranty, for it was in consequence of that representation that the goods were shipped, both parties being fully aware of its high importance in the circumstances; or, as it might be put, it was a promise that the shipowner would not avail himself of a liberty which otherwise would have been open to him.

*Notes*

1. The distinction is also important in determining who is liable to pay the freight: see *Cho Yong Shipping Co. Ltd* [1997] 2 Lloyd's Rep 641, above, Chapter 5.

2. The shipper will not be bound by any unusual clause of which he was not aware and which the carrier took no steps to draw to his attention.

### *Crooks & Co.* v *Allan*
### (1879) 5 QBD 38 (QBD)

LUSH J: The plaintiffs are the shippers of goods on board the *Sardinian*, a steamer belonging to the defendant company, for conveyance from Liverpool to Montreal. In the course of the voyage a fire broke out in the hold which made it necessary to scuttle the ship in order to protect the whole from destruction. The water materially damaged the plaintiffs' goods and occasioned a general average loss. The ship returned to Liverpool; the cargo was discharged and handed over by the defendants to the Liverpool Salvage Association, to be distributed and disposed of as might be most for the benefit of the parties concerned. The complaint against the defendants is that they refused to give any assistance to enable either the association, or the underwriters, or the persons whose goods were so damaged, to get an average statement made out, or to take any steps to enable the plaintiffs to recover contribution. They delivered up the cargo without taking the usual security from any of the owners of cargo, and the plaintiffs were not only without the benefit of such security, but without the means of ascertaining in what proportions the several cargo owners were liable to contribute, or even who, besides the defendants, were the contributing parties. The defendants' reason for adopting so unusual a course avowedly was because they considered the ship not liable to contribution; and they based their claim to immunity from general average on a clause in the bill of lading.

By this instrument, the defendants undertake to deliver the goods at the port of Montreal (unless prevented by certain specified perils), unto the Grand Trunk Railway, by them to be forwarded 'upon the conditions before and after expressed', thence per railway to the station nearest to Toronto, and at the said station delivered to the consignees at a through tonnage freight. Then follow a number of minute stipulations and exemptions, amongst which is the following: 'The shipowner or railway company are not to be liable for any damage to any goods which is capable of being covered by insurance; ...'

It was stated by the counsel for the defendants in the course of the argument, that these words were introduced ... to relieve the shipowner from general average contribution. If the words fairly bore that construction, another and a more serious question would have arisen; a question which might equally have arisen if the claim was one strictly within the meaning of this clause. The long list of excepted perils and the much longer list of exemptions and qualifications of which the clause in question is one, and which seem designed to exonerate the shipowners from all liability as carriers, and to reduce them substantially to the condition of irresponsible bailees, are printed in type so minute, though clear, as not only not to attract attention to any of the details, but to be only readable by persons of good eyesight. The clause in question comes in about the middle of thirty closely packed small type lines, without a break sufficient to attract notice. If a shipowner wishes to introduce into his bill of lading so novel a clause as one exempting him from general average contribution — a clause which not only deprives the shipper of an ancient and well understood right, but which might avoid his policy and deprive him also of recourse to the underwriter, he ought not only to make it clear in words, but also to make it conspicuous by inserting it in such type and in such a part of the document as that a person of ordinary capacity and care could not fail to see it. A bill of lading is not the contract, but only the evidence of the contract; and it does not follow that a person who accepts the bill of lading which the shipowner hands him, necessarily and without regard to circumstances, binds himself to abide by all its stipulations. If a shipper of goods is not aware when he ships them, or is not informed in the course of the shipment that the bill of lading which will be tendered to him will contain such a clause, he has a right to suppose that his goods are received on the usual terms, and to require a bill of lading which shall express those terms. Notwithstanding the concluding sentence of these small typed thirty lines, which says, 'In accepting this bill of lading, the shipper, or other agent of the owner of the property carried, expressly accepts and agrees to all its stipulations, exceptions, and conditions, whether written or printed', I should have thought it right if the stipulation in question bore the meaning contended for to give the plaintiffs an opportunity of supplying by means of an official inquiry, information as to the circumstances under which the goods were shipped and the bill of lading was taken, and whether the special clauses of this remarkable document were brought to their notice, or were read by them before they accepted it. It is unnecessary in the present case to ascertain these facts, because the clause has not the meaning which the defendants ascribe to it, and the only question is the liability of the ship to contribute.

*Questions*
If the bill of lading is issued after a contract has already been made, at what point of time *is* the contract made? Is it when space is booked? Or when the goods are put on board? See *Heskell* v *Continental Express Ltd* (1950) 83 Ll LR 438, per Devlin J at pp. 448–9. In the highly unusual circumstances of that case a bill of lading was issued although no contract of carriage had been made, and nearly 18 months passed before it was established that the goods had never left the warehouse: without a contract of carriage the bill of lading was simply a nullity (*ibid.* at p. 455). Contrast *Ngo Chew Hong Edible Oil Pte Ltd* v *Scindia Steam Navigation Co. Ltd (The Jalamohan)* [1988] 1 Lloyd's Rep 443 (QBD, Hirst J), where the fixture note was held to be the contract, and validly

incorporated a 'demise clause' in the bill of lading: on this aspect, see further subsection D, below.)

## Leduc v Ward
### (1888) 20 QBD 475 (CA)

The facts are stated above, Chapter 4. It was held that the indorsee of the bill of lading was not affected by the alleged agreement between the shippers and the carriers that the ship would proceed via Glasgow.

LORD ESHER MR: ... The plaintiffs were clearly indorsees of the bill of lading to whom the property passed by reason of the indorsement; and, therefore, by the Bills of Lading Act, the rights upon the contract contained in the bill of lading passed to them. The question, therefore, arises what the effect of that contract was. It has been suggested that the bill of lading is merely in the nature of a receipt for the goods, and that it contains no contract for anything but the delivery of the goods at the place named therein.... Where there is no charterparty, as between the grantee of the bill of lading and the shipowner, the bill of lading is no doubt a receipt for the goods, and as such, like any other receipt, it is not conclusive, for it may be controverted by evidence shewing that the goods were not received; the question whether it will be more than a receipt as between the shipper and shipowner depends on whether the captain has received the goods, for he has no authority to make a contract of carriage to bind the shipowner, except in respect of goods received by him. If the goods have not been received, the bill of lading cannot contain the terms of a contract of carriage with respect to them as against the shipowner. But, if the goods have been received by the captain, it is the evidence in writing of what the contract of carriage between the parties is; it may be true that the contract of carriage is made before it is given, because it would generally be made before the goods are sent down to the ship: but when the goods are put on board the captain has authority to reduce that contract into writing: and then the general doctrine of law is applicable, by which, where the contract has been reduced into a writing which is intended to constitute the contract, parol evidence to alter or qualify the effect of such writing is not admissible, and the writing is the only evidence of the contract, except where there is some usage so well established and generally known that it must be taken to be incorporated with the contract....

*Question*
How would Lord Esher have decided *The Ardennes*?

*B: Bill of lading in the hands of a charterer*

Charterers do not necessarily intend to ship their own goods, but if they do a bill of lading will usually be issued to them, thereby giving them a dual role as shippers and charterers. It is well settled that in this case the *charterparty* is the contract, and the bill of lading is a receipt and document of title only.

## Rodocanachi, Sons & Co. v Milburn Brothers
### (1886) 18 QBD 67 (CA)

R chartered M's ship for carriage of a cargo of cotton seed from Alexandria to the UK. The charterparty provided that the master was to sign bills of lading 'at any rate of freight and as customary at port of lading'. The bill of lading issued to R contained a clause exempting M from liability for the act, neglect or default of the master. The charterparty had no such clause. The cargo was lost by the negligence of the master. M were held liable for non-delivery.

LOPES LJ: ... The main question in this case is whether the charterparty or the bill of lading is to govern the liability of the defendants. There is an exception in the latter which is not contained in the former, the bill of lading exempting the shipowners from loss occasioned by the negligence of their servants. It is urged that the charterparty must be read as incorporating the terms of the bill of lading; and the defendants rely on a supposed custom at Alexandria to insert such an exception in the bill of lading, though not contained in the charterparty. According to my construction of the charterparty, no such contention can be made on the terms of the 10th clause. I am inclined to believe that all that is meant by 'as customary at the port of lading' is 'as usual', and that the clause must be construed as subject to the condition that the bill of lading is to be signed without prejudice to the stipulation as to freight and other terms of the charterparty. But I will assume that more was intended, and that it was intended that the master should sign the bill of lading in the form in which this bill of lading was signed. Even then I am clear that, unless there is a distinct expression of intention to the contrary, in such a case the charter must prevail. I believe the law to be that, when there is a charterparty, as between charterers and shipowners, the bill of lading operates prima facie as a mere receipt for the goods, and a document of title which may be negotiated, and by which the property is transferred, but does not operate as a new contract, or alter the contract contained in the charterparty.

*Note*
If the shipper is not the charterer, then clearly the relevant contract can only be the bill of lading contract. A neat legal conundrum arises if such a shipper later indorses the bill of lading to the charterer: does the charterer *now* hold on the bill of lading terms, or does the charterparty still govern? The answer was given in 1916, but overlooked for more than 50 years.

### *President of India v Metcalfe Shipping Co. Ltd*
[1970] 1 QB 289 (CA)

LORD DENNING MR: In 1961 the Government of India bought a quantity of fertiliser from sellers in Italy. They chartered a British ship, the *Dunelmia*, to carry the fertiliser from Ancona to Madras. The Italian sellers loaded the fertiliser onto the ship and took a bill of lading to order. They indorsed it in blank. They presented it in due course to the Government of India, who paid the price, took the bill of lading, and obtained delivery of the goods. But they claimed that there was a shortage on delivery and asked for arbitration in accordance with a clause in the charterparty. The shipowners refused. They said that the carriage was governed, not by the charterparty, but by the bill of lading, which did not contain an arbitration clause. So the question is: which is to govern? The charterparty? or the bill of lading?

Four contracts fall for consideration: first, the contract of sale. . . .

The second contract is the charterparty of June 6, 1961, under which the shipowners agreed that the *Dunelmia* would proceed to an Italian port and there load at a safe berth a cargo of 8,000 metric tons . . . urea in bags . . . [and] being so loaded the vessel shall proceed with all convenient speed to Madras . . . and there deliver the cargo at a safe berth on being paid freight . . . 70s. net.

I need not go through all the clauses of the charter. Suffice it to mention clause 7, which says:

The master or his agent shall sign bills of lading at any rate of freight required by the charterers or their agents, without prejudice to this charterparty, but at not less than the chartered rate. [And clause 17]: Any dispute arising under this charter shall be settled in accordance with the provisions of the Arbitration Act 1950 in London.

In pursuance of their charterparty, the *Dunelmia* went to Ancona, and loaded these 8,000 tons of fertiliser.

The third contract is the bill of lading of July 11, 1961. The master signed a bill of lading which was on a printed form of the sellers, the A.N.I.C. company. It says:

Shipped by A.N.I.C. on the *Dunelmia* to be conveyed to Madras Port (India) and on safe arrival to be delivered unto order.

The goods are described, and then comes this clause: 'All conditions and exceptions as per charterparty stipulated at London on June 6, 1961'. It was issued to the shipper, A.N.I.C.

The fourth contract is the indorsement and delivery of the bill of lading. A.N.I.C. indorsed it in blank and sent it forward with the invoice to the representative of the Government of India in London. The price was paid. The bill of lading was released to the Government of India, who sent it to Madras, and took delivery of the goods.
. . .

The Government of India said that there was a shortage of cargo delivered. In 1963 they wished to refer the dispute to arbitration in accordance with the clause in the charterparty; but the shipowners said the goods were carried on the terms of the bill of lading, which contained no arbitration clause. The bill of lading said: '. . . all conditions and exceptions as per charterparty'; but that did not bring in the arbitration clause: see *T.W. Thomas & Co. Ltd* v *Portsea Steamship Co. Ltd* [1912] AC 1. If the shipowners are right, it means that the charterers have to sue at law: but it is too late to do so, because the Statute of Limitations has run.

So the charterers rely on the charterparty. The shipowners rely on the bill of lading. Which is the governing contract? The shipowners pray in aid some passages in the textbooks. First, *Scrutton on Charterparties*, 17th ed. (1964), article 18, says, at p. 45:

Where, however, a bill of lading is issued to a shipper, other than the charterer, differing in terms from the charter, and the charterer subsequently becomes indorsee of the bill of lading, the later is bound by its terms and cannot assert against the shipowner that in his hands the bill of lading is a mere receipt and the charter the only effective contract

—for which is cited *Calcutta S.S. Co.* v *Andrew Weir & Co.* [1910] 1 KB 759, and *Hogarth S.S. Co.* v *Blyth, Greene, Jourdain & Co. Ltd* [1917] 2 KB 534.

Second is *Carver, Carriage by Sea, British Shipping Laws,* Vol. 2, 11th ed. (1963), article 405, p. 340:

Where on the other hand bills of lading are given to a shipper, not being the charterer or his agent, and he indorses them to the charterer, the bills of lading become the governing documents in a claim by the charterer against the shipowners for damage to the goods.

And the same two cases are cited.

Are these statements right? I will first consider the matter on principle. It seems to me that whenever an issue arises between the charterer and the shipowner, prima facie their relations are governed by the charterparty. The charterparty is not merely a contract for the hire of the use of a ship. It is a contract by which the shipowners agree to carry goods and to deliver them. If the shipowners fail to carry the goods safely, that is a breach of the contract contained in the charterparty; and the charterers can claim for the breach accordingly, unless that contract has been modified or varied by some subsequent agreement between the parties. The signature by the master of a bill of lading is not a modification or variation of it. The master has no authority to modify or vary it. His authority is only to sign bills of lading 'without prejudice to the terms of the charterparty'. There is a long list of cases on this 'without prejudice' clause.

. . .

It is sometimes said that the 'without prejudice' clause is put in for the benefit of the shipowners only. But that is not correct. It is for the benefit of both shipowners and charterers. In *Turner* v *Haji Goolam Mahomed Azam* [1904] AC 826, Lord Lindley, giving the judgment of the Privy Council said, at p. 837:

> The words, 'without prejudice to this charter' means that the rights of the shipowners against the time charterers, *and vice versa*, are to be preserved.

In this case, therefore, the bill of lading did not modify or vary the charter. And there is nothing else. So the charter governs.

I now turn to *Calcutta S.S. Co. Ltd* v *Andrew Weir & Co.* [1910] 1 KB 759, 15 Com Cas 172, which is said to decide the contrary. The *Calcutta* was chartered to go from Bombay to Busreh and load a cargo of lawful merchandise. She was put up at Busreh as a general ship. A man called Noats shipped 1,031 boxes of dates on the ship on the terms of a bill of lading. The bill of lading contained a number of exceptions which were not in the charterparty. While the goods were afloat, Mr Noats borrowed some money. He borrowed it from the charterers. Noats indorsed the bill of lading to them as security for the advance they made. They eventually took delivery of the dates but alleged that they were not in good order and condition. The charterers sought to sue the shipowners for the damage to the dates. The charterers said that they were 'shipped under the charterparty' which did not contain exceptions. But the shipowners said that the goods were shipped under the bill of lading which contained exceptions. The question was: which contract was to govern?

Hamilton J said that the allegation 'shipped under the charterparty' had not been proved in fact. The dates were not shipped under the charterparty but under the bill of lading. So the remedy was only under the bill of lading. As I understand it, Hamilton J regarded the bill of lading as a separate contract, which was made by the shipowners with Noats, independent of the charterparty. The goods were shipped under the bill of lading only. And when the charterers took the bill of lading as security for an advance, they took over that contract, just the same as any third person who lent money on the faith of it. They were in no better position than Noats himself.

Contrast that case with the present. The bill of lading here was not separate or severable from the charterparty. It was issued in pursuance of it. The Italian sellers A.N.I.C. had already contracted to sell the fertiliser to the Government of India: and the government had chartered the ship to carry it. The bill of lading was a mere instrument to carry out those contracts. It did not evidence any separate contract at all. As between charterers and shipowners, it was only a receipt for the goods.

This view is supported by a case in the House of Lords, for which we are indebted to Mr Hobhouse. It does not appear in any textbooks and was newly found for this court. It is the Scottish case of *Love and Stewart Ltd* v *Rowtor Steamship Co. Ltd* 1916 SC 223, and [1916] 2 AC 527. Love and Stewart contracted to buy a large parcel of pit props from a gentleman named Grankull in Finland for delivery f.o.b. Kristinestad in Finland. The purchasers chartered a steamship to go to Kristinestad and load the pit props and carry them to Newport in South Wales. The charterparty allowed 13 days for loading and 13 days for discharging. In point of fact, Grankull managed to load the pit props in nine days, thus saving four days in loading. By the terms of the charterparty those days were 'reversible', that is, the four days saved in the loading could be added on to the 13 days for discharging, making altogether 17 days allowable for discharging. The master issued a bill of lading for those pit props, making them deliverable to Grankull's order, but in the margin of the bill of lading were written the words, apparently by agreement between the parties: '13 days used for loading' whereas in fact only nine days had been used. (Those words were untrue but were inserted in an endeavour to say that only 13 days were allowable for discharging instead of 17 days.) Grankull indorsed the bill of lading in blank; he presented it with an invoice to the charterers, Love and Stewart, while the goods were still afloat. They paid the invoice, got the bill of lading, and on arrival of the ship, they took delivery. It took 17½ days to discharge the pit props. The shipowners claimed for four and a half days demurrage excess over 13 days. The charterers said that they were only liable for half a day demurrage (excess over 17 days). The shipowners said the charterers were bound by the words in the bill of lading: '13 days used for loading'. The Court of Session upheld this contention. The Lord Justice Clerk relied on *Calcutta S.S. Co. Ltd* v *Andrew Weir & Co.* . . . But the House of Lords reversed the Court of Session. It was held that the shipowners could only claim for half a day demurrage. they were bound by the 'reversible' clause in the charterparty, and could not rely on the '13-day' clause in the bill of lading. Lord Sumner himself, giving the only judgment, made it clear that the position was governed by the charterparty and not by the bill of lading. He said [1916] 2 AC 527, 540:

> Furthermore, in presenting the bill of lading the defenders [charterers] merely did what they must needs do in order to get delivery of their cargo. They received it from Grankull [seller] under the contract of sale as the symbol of the delivery of goods while afloat. Nothing had occurred by which any contract for the carriage of the goods arose between them and the shipowners other than the charter itself. No new bargain had been made, under which the pursuers [shipowners] carried for the defenders [charterers] under a bill of lading instead of a charter. The freight earned was chartered freight and the bill of lading in the defenders' [charterers] hands was only the ship's receipt for the goods. This is the ordinary effect of documents such as these under such circumstances, and the cases cited do not bear upon them.

Clearly Lord Sumner thought that *Calcutta S.S. Co. Ltd* v *Andrew Weir & Co.* had no relevance to that case.

I see no difference between the House of Lords case and this case. In each there is: — (i) a contract of sale; (ii) a charter taken out in order to implement that sale; (iii) a bill of lading taken by the seller; and (iv) soon afterwards an indorsement over to the charterer.

. . .

My conclusion is that the statements in the textbooks are wrong. They must be revised in the light of the decision of the House of Lords and of our present case. The writers of textbooks suffer under the impediment that they do not have the full argument and discussion which we have. After full consideration, I am prepared to hold that in a case such as this the relations between shipowner and charterer are governed by the charterparty. Even though the charterer is not the shipper and takes as indorsee of a bill of lading, nevertheless their relations are governed by the charter, at any rate when the master is only authorised to sign bills of lading without prejudice to the charter. I think that Megaw J was right. I would dismiss the appeal.

## C: Incorporation of charterparty terms in bills of lading

Where the vessel is on charter, carriers naturally want the bill of lading contracts to follow the terms of the charterparty as closely as possible. (The form of bill of lading to be used is often prescribed and annexed to the charterparty.) As charterparties tend to be rather lengthy documents and it is inconvenient to set them out in full — not least because many of the provisions in them are not appropriate in a bill of lading anyway — shipowners have resorted to the device of incorporation by reference, i.e., incorporation by a general formula which does not involve setting out the exact provisions of the charterparty. The usual battle ground has been the alleged incorporation into the bill of lading of an arbitration clause from the charterparty. There are two stages in this process. The first is to show that the words of incorporation are wide (and particular) enough to include the arbitration clause. The second is to show that the words of the arbitration clause are apt for inclusion in the bill of lading.

### T.W. Thomas & Co. Ltd v Portsea Steamship Co. Ltd
### [1912] AC 1 (HL)

T & Co. were the holders of the bill of lading for a cargo of timber. The bill provided for 'other conditions as per charterparty' and also had a marginal note, 'Deck load at shipper's risk, and all other terms and conditions and exceptions of charter to be as per charterparty'. P brought an action in the county court claiming £200 demurrage and T & Co. argued that the proceedings should be stayed, relying on an arbitration clause in the charterparty. It was held, affirming the Court of Appeal, that the arbitration clause was not incorporated in the bill of lading.

LORD ATKINSON: I think it would be a sound rule of construction to adopt that when it is sought to introduce into a document like a bill of lading — a negotiable instrument — a clause such as this arbitration clause, not germane to the receipt, carriage, or delivery of the cargo or the payment of freight, — the proper subject-matters with which the bill of lading is conversant, — this should be done by distinct and specific words, and not by such general words as those written in the margin of the bill of lading in this case.

## Note

In *The Merak* [1965] P 223, the Court of Appeal held by a majority that a clause in the bill of lading incorporating 'all the terms, conditions, clauses and exceptions, including clause 30, contained in the said charterparty' *was* effective to incorporate the arbitration clause from the charterparty, although this was clause 32, not 30. The proceedings by writ were accordingly stayed (and it was too late for the plaintiffs to start arbitration proceedings). Subsequent authorities seem to suggest that this decision will be confined to its own special facts.

### Federal Bulk Carriers Inc v C. Itoh & Co. Ltd
### (The Federal Bulker)
[1989] 1 Lloyd's Rep 103 (CA)

The bills of lading in respect of a cargo of soya beans stated, 'all terms conditions and exceptions as per charterparty ... to be considered as fully incorporated herein as if fully written'. The arbitration clause in the charterparty referred to 'all disputes arising out of this contract'. The cargo-owners commenced arbitration proceedings over a claim for damage to the cargo; the shipowners successfully sought a declaration that the arbitration clause was not incorporated in the bills of lading.

BINGHAM LJ: It is common ground that the Court is concerned with the construction of the contract contained in or evidenced by the bills of lading, that is, the contract of carriage between the shipowners and the cargo-owners. The Court's task is to ascertain the intention of those parties as expressed in the written document and the Court is not in any way concerned to construe the charterparty or ascertain the intentions of the parties to that contract save in so far as the terms of the charterparty have been effectively incorporated in the bill of lading contract. That, I think, is clearly stated in *The Varenna* [1983] 2 Lloyd's Rep 592 by Sir John Donaldson MR at p. 594 col. 1.

Generally speaking, the English law of contract has taken a benevolent view of the use of general words to incorporate by reference standard terms to be found elsewhere. But in the present field a different, and stricter, rule has developed, especially where the incorporation of arbitration clauses is concerned. The reason no doubt is that a bill of lading is a negotiable commercial instrument and may come into the hands of a foreign party with no knowledge and no ready means of knowledge of the terms of the charterparty. The cases show that a strict test of incorporation having, for better or worse, been laid down, the Courts have in general defended this rule with some tenacity in the interests of commercial certainty. If commercial parties do not like the English rule, they can meet the difficulty to spelling out the arbitration provision in the bill of lading and not relying on general words to achieve incorporation.

The importance of certainty in this field was emphasised by Lord Denning MR in *The Annefield* [1971] 1 Lloyd's Rep 1 at p. 3, col. 2; [1971] P 168 at p. 183G, by Sir John Donaldson MR in *The Varenna* at p. 594, col. 2, and by Lord Justice Oliver in the same case at p. 597 col. 2. This is indeed a field in which it is perhaps preferable that the law should be clear, certain and well understood than that it should be perfect. Like others, I doubt whether the line drawn by the authorities is drawn where a modern commercial lawyer would be inclined to draw it. But it would, I think, be a source of mischief if we were to do anything other than try to give effect to settled authority as best we can.

The first question for decision is whether the language used in this bill of lading is effective to incorporate the arbitration clause set out in cl. 11 of the charterparty. I deal at the outset with a point strongly made by Mr Hirst for the cargo-owners in reliance on the words in the bill of lading 'as if fully written'. Those are words not found, I think, in any of the decided cases and it was submitted by Mr Hirst that their presence strengthened the case for incorporation.

For my part I cannot agree. It is clear beyond argument, whether expressly stated in the bill of lading or not, that any provision which is incorporated is to be treated as if fully written. But an express statement to this effect does not, in my judgment, assist in determining what is to be incorporated and what is not.

Mr Hirst accepted, obviously rightly, that the arbitration clause was not an 'exception' in the charterparty. So he gained no help from this expression.

It was clearly decided by this Court in *The Varenna*, affirming a clear and comprehensive judgment of Mr Justice Hobhouse reported in [1983] 1 Lloyd's Rep 416, that an arbitration clause was not a condition. So Mr Hirst placed reliance on the expression 'terms' and argued that even if the arbitration clause in the contract was not a condition or an exception, it was on any ordinary commonsense construction a term of the charterparty and so was incorporated into the bill of lading by the reference to 'terms' in the charterparty.

There is obvious force in this submission, but in my judgment it runs counter to House of Lords authority decided over 75 years ago and never, to my knowledge, doubted. The authority in question is *T.W. Thomas & Co. Ltd* v *Portsea Steamship Co. Ltd* [1912] AC 1....

I do not think this authority can be distinguished on grounds that the words in question were used in a different context nor on the ground that arbitration clauses were in 1911 viewed with less favour than they are today. It seems to me that this is clear authority, binding on us, that general language of the kind used here is not sufficient to incorporate an arbitration clause.

In *The Varenna* the bill of lading made reference to conditions and not terms. Sir John Donaldson considered *T.W. Thomas & Co. Ltd* v *Portsea Steamship Co. Ltd* and concluded that it was clear authority on the true construction of the expression 'conditions simpliciter'. Had the expression 'terms' been in issue he would, I think, have been bound to reach the same conclusion.

...

I think that *Thomas v Portsea* is authority binding on us and, as I understand, it is the case that in no reported decision has the language employed here proved effective to incorporate an arbitration clause in a charterparty. The nearest that Mr Hirst can get is *The Merak* [1964] 2 Lloyd's Rep 527; [1965] P 223.... Mr Justice Scarman, as he then was, at first instance and the Court of Appeal considered the effect of the incorporating words which, as I have indicated, included the expression 'clauses' not found here. The Court of Appeal considered the incorporating language to be very comprehensive. Lord Justice Sellers at pp. 531, col. 2 and 205E described the incorporating words as 'clear and wider'. Lord Justice Davies, at pp. 533, col. 1 and 253D described them as 'all-embracing' and Lord Justice Russell, at pp. 536, col. 2 and 269G described the language as 'of the most ample width possible to imagine'.

*The Merak* was perhaps an unusual case, as Lord Justice Phillimore in *The Annefield* described it at pp. 5, col. 2 and 186B. But it is authority for the proposition that reference to 'clauses' is enough at this first stage to permit incorporation of an aptly drafted arbitration clause. Mr Hirst, understandably and strongly, relies on this decision and contends that it is offensive to commonsense if a reference to 'clauses' is sufficient to incorporate an arbitration clause, but a reference to 'terms' is not.

I have some sympathy with that submission but, as it seems to me, that is where, reading *Thomas v Portsea* and *The Merak* together, the line has been drawn. I do not think it is open to us, nor do I think it in all the circumstances desirable, that we should give to the expression 'terms' a meaning which *Thomas v Portsea* denied.

If that conclusion is right, it is enough to decide this appeal in the shipowners' favour, upholding the decision of the Judge. . . .

In case, however, my conclusion on the first question is wrong, I should turn to consider the second which is whether, on reference to the charterparty, it clearly appears that the arbitration clause itself is apt to be incorporated in the bill of lading.

In a number of the decided cases, as in *Thomas* v *Portsea*, the arbitration clause refers to 'disputes arising under this charter' and such language is obviously inapt for incorporation in a bill of lading. In other cases such as *The Merak*, reference is to —

. . . disputes arising out of this charterparty or any bill of lading issued under it.

Language of that kind is plainly apt for incorporation in the bill of lading if the incorporating language is otherwise sufficient.

In the present case the reference is to 'this contract'. That language imports in itself no obvious inconsistency. If the term were to be incorporated into the bill of lading the term would plainly be understood to mean 'this bill of lading contract'. But equally the clause contains within itself no express reference on which the cargo-owners can rely since there is no reference to the bill of lading in terms within it.

Looking at the incorporating words and cl. 11 alone, this Court is I think bound to conclude that the cargo owners cannot show that cl. 11 should be incorporated, because the incorporating words and the arbitration clause in the charterparty are exactly the same as those in *The Annefield* where the Court of Appeal held affirming Mr Justice Brandon, that the arbitration clause was not incorporated. Lord Denning MR said at pp. 4, col. 1 and 184E:

. . . I would follow the test laid down by Lord Justice Russell in *The Merak* [1965] P 223 at p. 260; [1964] 2 Lloyd's Rep 527 at p. 537 but I would adapt it slightly. I would say that a clause which is directly germane to the subject-matter of the bill of lading (that is to the shipment, carriage and delivery of goods) can and should be incorporated into the bill of lading contract, even though it may involve a degree of manipulation of the words in order to fit exactly the bill of lading. But if the clause is one which is not thus directly germane, it should not be incorporated into the bill of lading contract unless it is done explicitly in clear words either in the bill of lading or in the charterparty.

Applying this test, it is clear that an arbitration clause is not directly germane to the shipment, carriage and delivery of goods. That appears from the decision of the House of Lords in *T. W. Thomas & Co. Ltd* v *Portsea S.S. Co. Ltd* [1912] AC 1. It is, therefore, not incorporated by general words in the bill of lading. If it is to be incorporated, it must either by express words in the bill of lading itself (for example, if there were added in this case: 'including the arbitration clause as well as the negligence clause'), or by express words in the charterparty itself (as indeed happened in *The Merak* where the words were: 'Any dispute arising out of this charter or any bill of lading issued hereunder'). If it is desired to bring in an arbitration clause, it must be done explicitly in one document or the other. As Lord Loreburn LC, said in *T. W. Thomas & Co. Ltd* v *Portsea Steamship Company Ltd* [1912] AC 1 at p. 6:

. . . If it is desired to put upon the holders of a bill of lading an obligation to arbitrate because that obligation is stated in the charterparty, it must be done explicitly.

In this case the words in the charterparty are 'any disputes under this contract'. Those words, in this context, meant :*'under this charterparty contract'*. They do not include the bill of lading contract. In any case they are not so explicit as to bring in disputes under the bill of lading.

*Note*
The suggestion made by Lord Denning MR in *The Annefield* [1971] P 168, that some 'verbal manipulation' is in order where the clause is 'directly germane' to the shipment, carriage and delivery of goods, came under scrutiny by the House of Lords in the next case.

### *Miramar Maritime Corp.* v *Holborn Oil Trading Ltd*
[1984] 1 AC 676 (HL)

M let their tanker *Miramar* to a Singaporean company on a voyage charter on the Exxonvoy 1969 form. Clause 8 of the form provided 'Charterer shall pay demurrage' at a specified rate. The bill of lading form stipulated for use with the charterparty provided that 'all terms whatsoever of the charter except the rate and payment of freight ... apply to and govern the rights of the parties concerned in this shipment'. The charterers failed to pay demurrage which was owing after discharge at Trincomalee and were now insolvent. M claimed that the consignees, H, were liable to pay the demurrage by virtue of the incorporation of the charterparty terms in the bill of lading. It was held, affirming the Court of Appeal, that the consignees were not liable.

LORD DIPLOCK: ... Although the amount of the demurrage in issue is of the order of US$250,000, the principal purpose of the parties in pursuing the appeal from that part of Mustill J's judgment that held that the consignees were not liable to the owners for demurrage, was to obtain an authoritative ruling on the question whether the holder of a bill of lading in the form ('the Exxonvoy bill of lading') annexed to a charterparty in the Exxonvoy 1969 standard form, if he were not himself the charterer, was nevertheless personally liable to the shipowner for the full amount of demurrage payable by the charterer under the terms of the charterparty. Neither party has contended either in the Court of Appeal or in this House that the answer to this question depended upon the particular fact that in the instant case there was only one bill of lading and this covered a complete cargo of petroleum products carried in the Miramar from Singapore to Trincomalee in 1980. Exxonvoy 1969 contemplates that, at charterer's option, there may be more than one loading port and more than one discharging port and that separate bills of lading may be issued, and must be issued if the charterer so requests, for shipments forming parts of the complete cargo loaded, it may be, at different loading ports for carriage to different discharging ports. The words in the Exxonvoy bill of lading upon which the appeal turns are the same irrespective of whether it is issued in respect of a complete or a part of the cargo, received on board at the first or any subsequent loading port for carriage to and discharge at the last or any previous discharging port. There must be ascribed to the words a meaning that would make good commercial sense if the Exxonvoy bill of lading were issued in *any* of these situations, and not some meaning that imposed upon a transferee to whom the bill of lading for goods afloat was negotiated, a financial liability of unknown extent that no business man in his senses would be willing to incur.

The Court of Appeal [1984] 1 Lloyd's Rep 142 in a judgment delivered by Sir John Donaldson MR upheld Mustill J's rejection of the personal liablity of the consignees to the owners for demurrage although the reasons preferred by him for so doing differed somewhat, at any rate in emphasis, from those of Mustill J.

Both judgments, however, took as their starting point what had been said by Russell LJ in *The Merak* [1965] P 223, 260, and restated by Lord Denning MR in *The Annefield* [1971] P 168, 184. Those two cases were concerned with whether or not the presence of a clause expressed to incorporate the terms of the charterparty in the bill of lading annexed, in *The Merak* to a charterparty in the Newbaltwood [sic] standard form, and in *The Annefield* in the Centrocon standard form, was effective to make the arbitration clause in the charterparty binding upon a holder of the bill of lading other than the charterer himself. . . .

In strictness, what was said by Russell LJ and Lord Denning MR in *The Merak* [1965] P 223 and *The Annefield* [1971] P 168 was obiter as respects the correct approach to the extent to which incorporation clauses in bills of lading issued in standard forms annexed to charterparties are effective to impose upon the bill of lading holder personal liability for non-performance of obligations undertaken by the charterer that are contained in clauses of the charterparty, other than an arbitration clause. Nevertheless, those dicta drew a clear distinction as respects incorporation in the bill of lading between an arbitration clause in the charterparty and a clause therein 'which is directly germane to the shipment, carriage and delivery of goods'. A clause that falls within this latter category, it was said, is to be treated as incorporated in the bill of lading even though it may involve a degree of 'manipulation' of the words in order to fit exactly a bill of lading.

The manipulation in the instant case for which the owners argued was of the words 'charterer' in the demurrage clause (clause 8) of Exxonvoy 1969, so as to substitute for it 'consignee' or 'bill of lading holder' when clause 8 was incorporated in the Exxonvoy bill of lading. Mustill J and Sir John Donaldson MR were able to find reasons for holding such substitution impermissible notwithtanding that a demurrage clause is one which is germane to the shipment, carriage and delivery of goods.

The owners' application for leave to appeal from the Court of Appeal's judgment was refused by that court, but was subsequently granted by an appeal committee of this House. As was explained to the petitioners at the hearing of the petition, leave was granted not because their Lordships had, at that stage, reached a state of prima facie doubt as to the correctness of the result reached by the Court of Appeal, but in order to give this House an opportunity of dealing with the extent, if any, to which it is permissible to indulge in what in the dicta to which I have referred was described as 'verbal manipulation' of clauses in charterparties in order, by means of an incorporation clause in a bill of lading, to impose upon the holder of the bill of lading personal liability for non-performance of obligations which under the express terms of the charterparty are undertaken by 'the charterer' under that designation alone and are not therein referred to as being obligations of any other persons interested in the shipment.

. . .

The incorporation clause in the Exxonvoy bill of lading, it is argued for the owners, requires one to treat the bill of lading as if it included the provisions contained in clause 8 of Exxonvoy 1969, not verbatim as they appear in that clause itself, but with the substitution by verbal manipulation of 'consignee under a bill of lading issued in respect of the whole or any part of the cargo' in place of the word 'charterer'.

My Lords, before I come to any refinements of semantics, I draw attention to the various combinations of circumstances affecting the using up of laytime and the accrual of liablity to pay demurrage in which a bill of lading for some part of the cargo may be issued by the master on behalf of the owners or after having been issued may be negotiated by the holder of the bill. Laytime may have been exhausted and the vessel may already be on demurrage before any cargo has been shipped at the first loading port, let alone subsequent loading ports if the charterparty gives an option for more than one. After completion of loading of the full cargo any unused laytime will start running again on arrival at the first discharging port and will continue to run until either (i) the cargo has been completely discharged there or at subsequent discharging ports if there be more than one, or (ii) the laytime is exhausted and liability for demurrage starts to accrue.

So if the owners are right in their contention as to the construction of the incorporation clause in the Exxonvoy bill of lading, clause 8 read in conjunction with clauses 5 to 7 of Exxonvoy 1969, has the effect that every consignee to whom a bill of lading covering any part of the cargo is negotiated, is not only accepting personal liability to pay to the owners freight, as stated in the bill of lading, but is also accepting blindfold a potential liability to pay an unknown and wholly unpredictable sum for demurrage which may, unknown to him, already have accrued or may subsequently accrue without any ability on his own part to prevent it, even though that sum may actually exceed the delivered value of the goods to which the bill of lading gives title.

My Lords, I venture to assert that no business man who had not taken leave of his senses would intentionally enter into a contract which exposed him to a potential liability of this kind; and this, in itself, I find to be an overwhelming reason for not indulging in verbal manipulation of the actual contractual words used in the charter-party so as to give to them this effect when they are treated as incorporated in the bill of lading. I may add that to do so would raise a whole host of questions as to how the liability is to operate as between different consignees of different parts of the cargo, to which question no attempt has been made to vouchsafe any answer, let alone a plausible one. To give some examples: is any personal liability for demurrage incurred by consignees of cargo which has been discharged before the expiry of laytime? If the discharge of a consignee's cargo takes place after the vessel is on demurrage is his liability to pay demurrage limited to the amount of demurrage accrued after the expiry of laytime and up to the time when the discharge of his part of the cargo is complete? Is each consignee liable for all demurrage accrued while his cargo remains on board? Is the liability of each consignee to pay demurrage several? If the shipowner chooses to sue one consignee of part of the cargo for the full amount of demurrage has that consignee any right of contribution against consignees of other parts of the cargo and, if so, against which of them and upon what basis?

...

I turn now to the terms of Exxonvoy 1969 which it is provided by the incorporation clause in the Exxonvoy bill of lading, are to 'apply to and govern the rights of the parties concerned in this shipment'. As there is no cesser clause in Exxonvoy 1969 such parties include the charterers until completion of discharge of the vessel, as well as the holders of the Exxonvoy bill of lading as consignees.

Exxonvoy 1969 comprises a preamble which states the parties, described as 'owner' and 'charterer' respectively, and the vessel's name. This is followed by Part I in which particulars of the chartered voyage are to be inserted including, what is most directly relevant to the instant appeal, total laytime in running hours and the rate of demurrage. Part II, which is in standard printed form, consists of 26 numbered clauses to which there is annexed the Exxonvoy bill of lading.

The obligation on the master to sign bills of lading in this form is referred to in clause 1, and is expressly imposed by clause 20 'Insurance and terms of bills of lading,' which sets out in seven sub-paragraphs specific terms commonly included in bills of lading including the clause paramount. Clause 20 goes on to provide:

(b) *The carriage of goods under this charterparty and under all bills of lading issued for the cargo* shall be subject to the statutory provisions and other terms specified in sub-paragraphs (i) through (vii) of this clause and such terms shall be incorporated verbatim or be deemed to be incorporated by reference in any such bill of lading.

The seven sub-paragraphs comprise (i) a clause paramount; (ii) a Jason clause; (iii) a general average clause; (iv) a 'both to blame' clause; (v) a limitation of liability clause; (vi) a war risks clause, and (vii) a deviation clause. There is nothing here to impose upon a consignee or bill of lading holder any personal liability for demurrage: and parenthetically I draw attention to the fact that the passage in paragraph (b) of clause 20, for which I have myself supplied the emphasis, draws a distinction between carriage under the charterparty and carriage under bills of lading. It recognises the co-existence of a plurality of contracts for the carriage of the same goods in the vessel; the charterparty is one, a bill of lading issued for those goods after it has been negotiated is the other.

. . .

I see no justification for resort to the maxim of construction falsa demonstratio non nocet cum de corpore constat, such as induced this House in *Adamastos Shipping Co. Ltd v Anglo-Saxon Petroleum Co. Ltd* [1959] AC 133, to treat the words 'This bill of lading' as if they were 'This charterparty'. This part of the *Adamastos* case, upon which, unlike other issues in the same case the House was unanimous, provided as good an elementary text-book example of the application of this Latin maxim as the classic one in which the intended corpus which is 'Blackacre' is, by an obvious mistake described as 'Whiteacre'. In the instant case, however, every reference to 'the charterer' by that designation in Exxonvoy 1969 although it would not necessarily affect directly legal obligations as between the owner and the consignee would nevertheless make perfectly good sense, when incorporated verbatim in the Exxonvoy bill of lading, if it meant the person designated as 'the charterer' in the charterparty and no-one else.

If further reasons were needed (and for my part I do not think that any are) for treating 'the charterer' as meaning only the person referred to in the preamble to Exxonvoy 1969 as the charterer and no-one else, a good semantic reason may be found in the fact that in four clauses in Part II, of which one is clause 8, the demurrage clause itself, and the other three are: clause 10 'Pumping in and out', clause 14 'Ice', and clause 19 'General exceptions clause', there are specific references to 'consignee' under that express designation in the very same sentence as a separate reference to 'the charterer'.

## Questions

1.   Shipowners let their vessel to charterers for 13 years' consecutive voyages, the charterparty providing for arbitration in respect of all disputes between owner and charterer. Charterers later sub-chartered for a single voyage from Ras Tanura to Sweden on the Asbatankvoy form, which provided for arbitration in London in respect of 'all differences and disputes arising out of this charter'. The bill of lading held by the Swedish consignees incorporated all terms conditions and exceptions in the charterparty (not specifying which charterparty was meant), 'including the arbitration clause'.

(a)   Was the incorporation clause in the bill of lading effective to incorporate the arbitration clause? (See *Daval Aciers d'Usinor et de Sacilor* v *Armare SRL (The Nerano)* [1996] 1 Lloyd's Rep 1 (CA), not following *The Nai Matteini* [1988] 1 Lloyd's Rep 452, Gatehouse J.)

(b)   If so, was the arbitration clause from the head charterparty or from the sub-charter incorporated? (See *Pacific Molasses Co.* v *Entre Rios CN (The San Nicholas)* [1976] 1 Lloyd's Rep 8, and *Bangladesh Chemical Industries* v *Henry Stephens Shipping Co. (The SLS Everest)* [1981] 2 Lloyd's Rep 389.)

2.   What other clauses might be considered 'directly to the shipment, carriage and delivery of goods'?

3.   In *India Steamship Co.* v *Louis Dreyfus Sugar Ltd (The Indian Reliance)* [1997] 1 Lloyd's Rep 52, bills of lading issued to sub-charterers were marked 'FREIGHT PAYABLE AS PER CHARTER PARTY'. The (sub-) charter-party provided for payment to a nominated account in Geneva. Although referred to as the owners' account, it was in fact that of Cosemar Schiffahrts Transport GmbH, the time charterers; after the bill of lading freight was paid into the account, Cosemar went into liquidation having failed to pay the charter hire. Rix J rejected the argument by Mr Glennie QC for the owners that only the provisions relating to the *rate* of freight were incorporated and held that the sub- charterers did not have to pay again.

### D: The identity of the carrier

Where the vessel is under charter the bill of lading holder needs to know whether the contract is with the charterer or with the shipowner. Pursuing the wrong defendant if the cargo is lost or damaged is not only a waste of money, but will probably lead to fatal delay in commencing proceedings against the proper party where the 12-month time limit under the Hague-Visby Rules applies. Unfortunately, it is sometimes far from clear whether the charterer or the shipowner is the carrier under the bill of lading contract.

The normal understanding, however, is that, except in the case of a demise charter, bills of lading are signed by the master as agent for the shipowner.

### *Sandeman* v *Scurr*
### (1866) LR 2 QB 86 (QBD)

COCKBURN CJ: The action is brought against the defendants, who are the owners of the ship *The Village Belle*, for damage and loss occasioned by bad stowage, to certain goods shipped in that vessel by the plaintiffs. The facts upon which the case turns are as follows:

*The Village Belle* went to Oporto under a charterparty entered into between her master, on behalf of the owners, and a Mr Hodgson, by which the master contracted to load at Oporto from the factors of the affreighter a full cargo of wine or other merchandise, and to carry the same to a safe port in the United Kingdom. Should the cargo consist of wine, the freight was to be 18*s.* per tun of 252 gallons; should other goods than wine be shipped, the freight was to be at the same rate on the quantity of wine the vessel would have carried, the quantity to be ascertained by a stevedore to be appointed by the charterer's agents and the master. The cargo was 'to be brought to and taken from alongside the vessel at the merchant's risk and expense'. The captain was to 'sign bills of lading at any rate of freight, without prejudice to the charter'. The ship was 'to be addressed to the charterer's agents at Oporto on usual terms'.

The ship accordingly proceeded to Oporto, consigned to the agents of the charterer. She was by them put up as a general ship, but without it being at all made known that the vessel was under charter. The plaintiffs delivered their goods on board without any knowledge that the ship was not entirely at the disposition of the owner. Bills of lading for the goods in question were signed by the master in the usual form. The cargo was stowed by stevedores employed and paid by the charterer's agents, but the amount so paid by the latter was repaid to them by the master.

The goods having been damaged by reason of improper stowage, the plaintiffs have brought their action against the defendants, as owners of the vessel; and the question is, whether the defendants, under the circumstances stated, are liable. We are of opinion that they are liable, and that the action against them lies.

On the argument, it was contended on behalf of the defendants', that, as the use of the ship had been made over to Hodgson, the charterer, and the ship had been put up as a general ship by his agents, and the bill of lading had been given by the captain in furtherance of a contract for freight of which the charterer was to have the benefit, the captain must be considered as having given the bill of lading as the agent of the charterer, and the contract as having been made with the latter, and not with the defendants, the owners of the vessel; and that, consequently, the charterer was alone responsible for the negligent stowing of the goods in question.

It is unnecessary to decide whether the charterer would or would not have been liable, if an action had under the circumstances been brought against him. Our judgment proceeds on a ground, wholly irrespective of the question of the charterer's liability, and not inconsistent with it, namely, that the plaintiffs, having delivered their goods to be carried in ignorance of the vessel being chartered, and having dealt with the master as clothed with the ordinary authority of a master to receive goods and give bills of lading on behalf of his owners, are entitled to look to the owners as responsible for the safe carriage of the goods.

The result of the authorities ... is to establish the position, that in construing a charterparty with reference to the liability of the owners of the chartered ship, it is necessary to look to the charterparty, to see whether it operates as a demise of the ship itself, to which the services of the master and crew may or may not be superadded, or whether all that the charterer acquires by the terms of the instrument is the right to have his goods conveyed by the particular vessel, and, as subsidiary thereto, to have the use of the vessel and the services of the master and crew.

In the first case, the charterer becomes for the time the owner of the vessel, the master and crew become to all intents and purposes his servants, and through them the possession of the ship is in him. In the second, notwithstanding the temporary right of the charterer to have his goods loaded and conveyed in the vessel, the ownership remains in the original owners, and through the master and the crew, who continue to be their servants, the possession of the ship also. If the master, by the agreement of his owners and the charterer, acquires authority to sign bills of lading on behalf of the latter, he nevertheless remains in all other respects the servant of the owners; in other words, he retains that relation to his owners out of which by the law merchant arises the authority to sign bills of lading by which the owner will be bound.

It appears to us clear that the charterparty in the present instance falls under the second of the two classes referred to. There is here no demise of the ship itself, either express or implied. It amounts to no more than a grant to the charterer of the right to have his cargo brought home in the ship, while the ship itself continues, through the master and crew, in the possession of the owners, the master and crew remaining their servants.

It is on this ground that our judgment is founded. We think that so long as the relation of owner and master continues, the latter, as regards parties who ship goods in ignorance of any arrangement whereby the authority ordinarily incidental to that relation is affected, must be taken to have authority to bind his owner by giving bills of lading. We proceed on the well known principle that, where a party allows another to appear before the world as his agent in any given capacity, he must be liable to any party who contracts with such apparent agent in a matter within the scope of such agency. The master of a vessel has by law authority to sign bills of lading on behalf of his owners. A person shipping goods on board a vessel, unaware that the vessel has been chartered to another, is warranted in assuming that the master is acting by virtue of his ordinary authority, and therefore acting for his owners in signing bills of lading. It may be that, as between the owner, the master, and the charterer, the authority of the master is to sign bills of lading on behalf of the charterer only, and not of the owner. But, in our judgment, this altered state of the master's authority will not affect the liability of the owner, whose servant the master still remains, clothed with a character to which the authority to bind his owner by signing bills of lading attaches by virtue of his office. We think that until the fact that the master's authority has been put an end to is brought to the knowledge of a shipper of goods, the latter has a right to look to the owner as the principal with whom his contract has been made.

*Notes*
1.   In *Wehner* v *Dene Steamship Co.* [1905] 2 KB 92, Channell J pointed out the difficulty of accounting for the shipowner's lien on sub-freights if the bill of lading contract is made with the charterer. See Chapter 5, above.
2.   This understanding of the position is commonly reinforced by charterparty provisions requiring the master to sign bills of lading 'as presented' by the charterer, and the corresponding right of the shipowner to be indemnified by the charterer if larger liabilities are incurred to the bill of lading holder than was contemplated in the charterparty: see *Krüger & Co. Ltd* v *Moel Tryvan Ship Co. Ltd* [1907] AC 272 (HL), in Chapter 10.
3.   The normal understanding will not be displaced by provisions in the charterparty making the master the agent of the charterers, unless the bill of lading holder has *actual* notice of them: *Manchester Trust* v *Furness* [1895] 2 QB 539 (CA). Knowledge of the existence of the charterparty does not fix the bill of lading holder with (constructive) notice of its contents.

The bills of lading may be charterers' bills, however, if signed, with authority, on their behalf.

## The Rewia
[1991] 2 Lloyd's Rep 325 (CA)

A claim was made in respect of a cargo of nutmeg and mace shipped from St George's, Grenada, to Rotterdam, when several containers were lost overboard. One of the issues in the case was whether the bills of lading were charterers' or shipowners' bills.

LEGGATT LJ: The plaintiffs adopt the Judge's approach, contending that it is strongly arguable that the bills of lading were charterers' bills. They argue that the bills were issued by or in the name of a container line of which the first defendants were operators. There was nothing in the bills, which were their documents, to limit or qualify an assumption of personal liability of the first defendants. The bills contained no clause identifying any person other than the first defendants as 'carriers'. The absence of any provision identifying the 'carriers' should lead to the inference, the plaintiffs argue, that the first defendant were liable as the persons in whose name the bills were issued.

. . .

The inspiration of the plaintiffs' argument on this issue appears to be *Scrutton on Charterparties*, 19th ed. pp. 68–9, where in art. 38 it is stated first that:

> When a bill of lading is issued for goods on a chartered ship, the question whether the bill of lading, in the hands of a shipper other than the charterer or of a bona fide holder for value is a contract with the shipowner or the charterer is one of some difficulty and it is difficult to lay down general rules.

For this proposition is cited:

> Per Walton J in *Samuel* v *West Hartlepool Co.* (1906) 11 Com Cas 115 at page 125.

What the judge in fact said at that page was this:

> Upon this point many cases were cited, and to some extent the authorities appear conflicting. But since the question is really a question of fact depending upon the documents and circumstances in each case, it may be that the apparent conflict arises mainly from the fact that the documents and circumstances are different in different cases.

At p. 126 Mr Justice Walton added, after referring to an example of an owners' bill:

> But even in cases of this kind it is scarcely safe, in my opinion, to lay down a hard and fast rule. The circumstances and terms of the documents may differ in different cases belonging to this class. And between the two types of classes which I have described there is a great variety of intermediate cases, of which the present case is an example. If there was any decision upon documents and facts substantially or in all material respects similar to those in the present case, I should, of course, follow it.

After referring to a demise charter, the editors of Scrutton continue at p. 69:

> If the charter is not a demise a bill of lading signed by the master or by the charterer as authorised agent of the master is usually a contract with the shipowner.

For that among many other authorities is cited the dictum of Mr Justice Channell in *Wehner* v *Dene Steamship Co.* [1905] 2 KB 92 at p. 98:

> In ordinary cases, where the charterparty does not amount to a demise of the ship, and where possession of the ship is not given up to the charterer, the rule is that the contract contained in the bill of lading is made, not with the charterer, but with the owner . . .

There then follows in Scrutton the sentence that has given rise to controversy:

> However, although the master is the owner's servant, his signature may in some cases bind the charterer and not the owner.

When the original editor wrote the sentence he may be supposed to have cited as authority only *Harrison* v *Huddersfield Steamship Co.* (1903) 19 TLR 386. An agreement had been made between shipowner and charterer that the captain was to be the agent of the charterer and to have no authority to make contracts by bills of lading on behalf of the shipowner. The words 'as Master' which were printed on the bills of lading had been struck out and the words 'as agent for time charterers' substituted in writing. The captain gave evidence that he received express instructions not to sign bills of lading for owners but only as agent for time charterers. Mr Justice Walton held that:

... if the master had signed as master he would have been making a contract for the shipowners. But he did not do so. Under the whole circumstances of the case, the contract by the bills of lading was not made for the shipowners, nor did the master propose to act for the shippers, nor had he apparent authority.

It followed that the shipowners were not liable.

For reasons that are not clear, to footnote 79 in which *Harrison* v *Huddersfield* (sup.) is cited the following passage has since been added:

... see too *Wehner* v *Dene SS Co.* ... *Wilston SS Co.* v *Andrew Weir & Co.* (1925) 31 Com Cas 111; *Paterson Zochonis* v *Elder Dempster* (1922) 12 Ll L Rep 69, 71; *Zwilchenbart* v *Henderson* (1854) 9 Ex 722; *The Venezuela* [1980] 1 Lloyd's Rep 393.

Taking those cases in chronological order, *Zwilchenbart* v *Henderson* (sup.) depended on the fact that there was no evidence of a contract between the master and the consignee, and was not relied on in the present case by either Counsel. To *Wehner* v *Dene SS Co.* (sup.) I have already referred; the bills were owners' bills. *Paterson Zochonis & Co.* v *Elder Dempster & Co.* (1922) 12 Ll L Rep 69, concerned a claim for cargo damage which occurred on a vessel chartered for use in the Elder Dempster Line. The bills of lading were issued in the name of the first three defendants, of whom African Shipping Co. were the time charterers. The question of liability on the bills was dealt with only in passing, Mr Justice Rowlatt observing:

... it seems to me that there is a contract with the African Shipping Co. on this bill of lading. This is a case where a well-known line of ships found it necessary to supplement its fleet by getting in another upon a time charter; and people in the commercial world who use the line know nothing at all about that. They think they are shipping by this line; and unless it is clear to the contrary the contract should be regarded as being made with the line. In this case the mate's receipt — as the bill of lading itself which goes just as far — it is the more material document — proclaims to the people who took the bill of lading that those who are going to carry the goods are the African Steamship Co; and there is the signature at the bottom which may be the signature of the master without qualification. Therefore, I think, in these circumstances it is a bill of lading with the African Steamship Co.

...

In essence the plaintiffs' argument depends on the use of liner forms of bills of lading, coupled with their ignorance of the fact that the vessel was chartered. But on the present state of the evidence there is nothing to detract from the bills of lading which on their true construction were signed for the master by agents to whom he was empowered to give authority and must be taken to have done so, since he was required to sign them as presented. The master was in fact the servant of the shipowners....

It is common ground that the charter in the present case is a time charter, not amounting to a demise. It appears to me that the law was correctly stated by Mr Justice Channell in the passage from *Wehner* v *Dene SS Co.* which I have cited earlier. That formulation has never been doubted.... The text in *Scrutton on Charterparties* to which note 79 is appended is now misleading, and in context only the first of the cases there referred to is helpfully cited. If Mr Justice Walton had had the benefit in 1905 of the cases subsequently decided, he would have been unlikely to regard them as 'to some extent... conflicting'. They are all of a pattern. In my judgment they support the conclusion that a bill of lading signed for the master cannot be a charterers' bill unless the contract was made with the charterers alone, and the person signing has authority to sign, and does sign, on behalf of the charterers and not the owners. Accordingly, the bills of lading in this case were owners' bills.

*Note*

The editors of the 20th edition of *Scrutton* have amended the controversial sentence by adding (p. 76): 'although this will only be the case where the master has authority to sign and does sign the bill of lading on behalf of the charterer and not the shipowner'. The offending footnote has also been returned to its original form. In any event, the decision is likely to be finely balanced.

***Sunrise Maritime Inc v Uvisco Ltd***
*(The Hector)*
[1998] 2 Lloyd's Rep 287 (QBD)

RIX J: This action arises out of the financial failure of time charterers at the very outset of a voyage for the carriage of a cargo of steel from Tuapse in Russia to Guatemala. The voyage sub-charterers and f.o.b. buyers of the steel have paid freight under their voyage charter to or for the account of the time charterers, and the owners of the vessel are concerned about the prospect of having to undertake the voyage without payment for it. Their vessel, *Hector*, is still in the Black Sea. They have commenced this action as plaintiffs, to assert their claim that they have no obligation to go to Guatemala with the cargo. The defendants are the sub-charterers, who say that they are the holders of a freight prepaid bill of lading which obliges the vessel to complete the voyage. Neither the shippers, nor the time charterers, nor the ultimate contemplated receivers of the cargo in Guatemala are parties to the action, although they have, I am told, been informed about it.

. . .

On Feb. 8, 1998 *Hector* completed loading a part cargo of 5,268.329 tonnes of rolled steel billets at Tuapse. The vessel had been chartered by her owners, Sunrise Maritime Inc. of Liberia ('owners'), to U.S. Express Lines of Pennsylvania U.S.A. ('USEL') under a time charter fixed on Jan. 21/22, 1998. USEL in turn had sub-chartered her on Jan. 22/23, 1998 to Uvisco Ltd., an English company ('Uvisco'). Neither charter-party has as yet been drawn up, but the time charter was fixed on amended NYPE terms, and the voyage sub-charter was fixed on amended Gencon terms.

Following loading, the vessel was delayed at Tuapse for reasons which are not entirely clear to me but which I suspect were connected with the fact that USEL were running short of funds and were unable for a while to clear the vessel for departure. On Feb. 11, a further instalment of hire fell due and went unpaid. By Feb. 17, USEL informed the owners that they were unable to complete the voyage due to cash flow problems. USEL invited the owners to speak to Uvisco (or their agents) direct. On Feb. 18, the owners (i.e., Mr Edward Ross of Zodiac Maritime Agencies Ltd, their London managers: but I will short-circuit detail of that sort whenever possible and speak simply of owners, USEL, Uvisco etc.) spoke to Uvisco in an (unsuccessful) attempt to intercept any freight payments under the voyage charter. The owners also made enquiries of the Tuapse port agents, Kobos Shipping Agency ('Kobos'), as to the existence of any bill of lading, and were told that they, Kobos, had not signed or issued any. On Feb. 19, owners withdrew the vessel from the time charter. The vessel sailed from Tuapse on the same day, but only to a nearby port to obtain bunkers.

Also on Feb. 19, owners learned for the first time of the existence of a bill of lading: a copy of it had been faxed from Uvisco's solicitors, Messrs. Ince & Co., to owners' solicitors, Messrs. Mischon de Reya, together with a copy of a fax dated Feb. 12, from USEL to 'Withersfield Attn: Chris Greengrass' stating that USEL were in receipt of freight and were authorising the release of the bill of lading. Other than that no information was forthcoming from Uvisco. The bill of lading was dated Feb. 5, three days before completion of loading on Feb. 8, even though the bill was in 'shipped' form. The owners considered that the only party who had been authorised to issue a bill of lading on their behalf had been Kobos, under a letter of authority issued by the master to Kobos on completion of loading. On Feb. 23, owners therefore commenced this action against Uvisco, claiming the following relief:

. . .

2.    A declaration that the Plaintiff is not obliged or otherwise bound to the Defendant to carry the part-cargo of 5,268.329 mts steel billets from Tuapse to Puerto Barrios.

The parties came before me on Feb. 26 and I gave direction for an expedited trial. The trial took place on Mar. 10/11. I rendered my decision on Mar. 13, and am now giving my reasons for it.

. . .

The bill of lading on which Uvisco relied was in the following form. It was a Conline bill and was headed 'LINER BILL OF LADING'. The shipper was on this occasion given as Uvisco themselves. The consignee and notify party were in each case given as Aceros Suarez S.A. (to whom Uvisco had on-sold the steel). The port of discharge was again given as Puerto Barrios, Guatemala. Towards the top of the bill, in a prominent position on the right hand side, appeared the typed words 'CARRIER: U.S. EXPRESS LINES'. The bill was in standard 'SHIPPED' bill form, ending—

IN WITNESS whereof the Master of the said Vessel has signed the number of original Bills of Lading stated below . . .

In the signature box appeared the following:

FOR AND ON BEHALF OF THE MASTER — MR V. ILNITSKY
WITHERSFIELD LIMITED
AS AGENTS

Freight was said to be prepaid, and the bill was dated 'London 05.02.98', i.e., it was a predated bill, as I have mentioned above.

On the reverse appear the standard Conline bill clauses. There was a general paramount clause (cl. 2), and an identity of carrier clause (cl. 17). The latter read as follows:

The Contract evidenced by this Bill of Lading is between the Merchant and the Owner of the vessel named herein (or substitute) and it is therefore agreed that said Shipowner only shall be liable for any damage or loss due to any breach or non-performance of any obligation arising out of the contract of carriage, whether or not relating to the vessel's seaworthiness. If, despite the foregoing, it is adjudged that any other is the Carrier and/or bailee of the goods shipped hereunder, all limitations of, and exonerations from, liability provided for by law or by this Bill of Lading shall be available to such other.

It is further understood and agreed that as the Line, Company or Agents who has executed this Bill of Lading for and on behalf of the Master is not a principal in the transaction, said Line, Company or Agents shall not be under any liability arising out of the contract of carriage, nor as Carrier nor bailee of the goods.

Consistently with that clause, the bill's clauses are all drafted in terms of the merchant and the carrier.

...

Although each case must ultimately turn on the terms of the bill of lading in question and upon its own circumstances, it has for long been well established in English law that a bill of lading signed for the master is very likely to be an owner's bill: see, for instance, *The Rewia* [1991] 2 Lloyd's Rep 325, where the earlier authorities were fully investigated. There the Court of Appeal approved the statement in Scrutton on Charterparties, now found in its 20th ed., 1996, at p. 80.

...

In the present case, the vessel was not demised but in the possession of her owners, the bill was expressly signed 'for and on behalf of the master', and for good measure the bill contained an identity of carrier clause, cl. 17, which emphasized in express terms that the contract evidenced by the bill was with the vessel's owners. Those are the matters relied on by Mr Eder for submitting that this is another case within the general rule.

On behalf of the owners, however, Mr Tomlinson QC has relied upon the express stipulation on the face of the bill 'CARRIER: U.S. EXPRESS LINES'. He submits that in the circumstances the form of signature is ambiguous, and that the typed stipulation on the face of the bill must be given precedence over the printed clause on its back. He also prays in aid the context, as he submits it to be, that the bill was not in fact authorised by the owners (because it was not signed by Kobos under the master's letter of authority, nor signed in conformity with the mate's receipt, as the time charter required, and was in any event a predated bill) but was in fact authorised by USEL; as well as the evidence that Uvisco themselves intended to contract with USEL rather than the owners.

It is uncertain to me on the authorities whether the question of whether a bill of lading is an owner's or a charterer's bill is a pure question of construction, or depends on all the circumstances of the case. Of course, even questions of construction must be set in their context or matrix: but that is usually limited to matters which are either known or ought to be known to both parties to the contract. That factor is complicated, however, where the question which has to be answered is which of two alternative parties is privy to the contract. It is further complicated, it seems to me, where the question is concerned with a negotiable document like a bill of lading. Such documents are relied on by third parties, far removed from the original circumstances of the bill's creation. That should mean that the rule should either be a matter of construction in its purest form, to be decided on the face (the two faces) of the bill itself, or that the position may well be different depending on whether the issue is joined between immediate parties to the creation of the bill or after negotiation to a third party. The question is still further complicated by the existence of an issue as to the owners' authority. Of course, subject to rules relating to usual or ostensible authority, it is always open to a party to any (purported) contract to show by extrinsic evidence that he did not authorise it. That, however, is a different question from the question whether a valid bill is one entered into by an owner or a charterer: but, the two questions may become interconnected when the issue of construction (for instance as to the meaning of the language in the signature box) cannot be separated from the underlying facts as to who authorised what.

...

In *The Ines* [1995] 2 Lloyd's Rep 144 Mr Justice Clarke decided that issue as a matter of construction (at p. 150), but also tested his conclusion against a consideration of the surrounding circumstances (ibid.), and accepted the submission of Counsel (at p. 149) that—

... in order to ascertain who the true contracting parties were it is necessary to examine the whole document and indeed to consider the whole context in which it came into existence.

These are interesting questions, but the exigencies of time under which this action has been prepared, argued and decided have not been conducive for their careful elucidation. In the circumstances it seems to me that I should adopt the approach of Mr Justice Clarke and seek to determine first, if I can, as a matter of construction what the bill of lading means, and then go on to consider whether the surrounding circumstances support or detract from that conclusion.

As a matter of construction, then, I have found the issue an intriguing one, largely I think because of the pressure created by the general rule that a bill of lading signed by the master is an owner's bill. There is also of course the powerful pointer of cl. 17. However, I have not been able to satisfy myself that the stipulation that the carrier is USEL is to be shrugged off as ambiguous. What does it mean, and why has it been inserted, unless it is intended to have effect as the definition of the carrier? The term 'carrier' is a critical term. It is not like an expression which might merely indicate that USEL was the operator of the vessel or the owner of the line. 'Carrier' is the expression in which the party with the obligations to carry out the bill of lading contract is clothed. That is made clear by the bill of lading terms as a whole, and by cl. 17 in particular. It is also made clear by the Hague rules, to which the bill of lading was made subject by cl. 2. Thus art. I(a) defines 'Carrier' as including 'the owner or charterer who enters into a contract of carriage with the shipper'. The bill of lading therefore stipulates that the carrier under the bill of lading is USEL. Although the master may be the servant of the owners, and cl. 17 say that the owners are the carriers, the only party which is identified expressly by name in the bill of lading as the carrier is USEL. For all that anyone reading the bill of lading knows USEL are owners, and there is no conflict between the stipulation that USEL are the carrier on the one hand and the signature for the master and cl. 17 on the other. I accept that that does not apply to Uvisco, who were aware that USEL were not the owners, but only the charterers of the vessel: but that is to go beyond a matter of pure construction on the face of the bill.

In my judgment, therefore, the matter can be looked at in two ways. Either the three elements of the bill — the USEL stipulation, the signature and cl. 17 — can be regarded as being consistent with one another, on the basis that because it is stipulated that USEL are the carrier, it must therefore follow that they are owners too; or the typed stipulation of USEL as carrier on the face of the bill must be regarded as superseding the printed provisions of cl. 17. After all, that clause does at least contemplate that, despite its terms, someone other than the owners may be adjudged to be carrier. In the latter case, the signature for the master will take effect on the basis that the owners have authorised the agents who have signed for the master to contract in those terms. If the owners have authorised it, then the fact that the bill is signed by agents for the owners' servant, their master, cannot compel the bill to be construed as an owners' bill. The rule is only that in the ordinary way a bill signed by or for the master will be an owner's bill, not that it must be.

It seems to me that this conclusion is consistent with the authorities. I do not know of any identical case, where the carrier is defined by name by a separate and special stipulation on the front of the bill: but the two closest cases in my judgment are *The Venezuela* [1980] 1 Lloyd's Rep 393 and *The Ines*, sup. *The Venezuela* is the only case cited before me where a bill of lading signed for the master was held to be a charterer's bill; it is therefore of particular interest. The bill there was 'signed by or on behalf of the master' by NYK as 'general agents and as agents for the master'. NYK were the agents of sub-time charterers C.A.V.N., who ran a line. The vessel, in fact *Samjohn Governor*, was owned by Panamanian owners and time chartered to Chinese time charterers. NYK had authority from the Chinese owners to sign bills for the master, under both head and sub-charters. The question was whether the bill took effect as a contract with the Panamanian owners or with C.A.V.N., the sub-charterers. There was nothing on the front of the bill to indicate that the contract was other than with owners. However, the reverse of the bill contained a clause which defined the carrier as either C.A.V.N. or (its joint venturer) FMG, depending on which of the two was operating the vessel. There were other arguments raised on the precise terms of the bill, but Mr Justice Sheen regarded the identity of carrier clause as critical, and held that it was C.A.V.N.'s bill. He said (at p. 397):

> It seems to me that if C.A.V.N. did not wish to contract as the 'carrier', then the bill of lading issued by C.A.V.N. should at least have made it clear with which company the shipper was entering into the contract of carriage. Until the shipper or holder of the bill of lading was told that *Samjohn Governor* was on time charter for the voyage in question there was nothing on either side of the bill of lading which indicated that anyone other than C.A.V.N. was contracting as carrier.

It seems to me that what Mr Justice Sheen was there saying was that without the knowledge that the vessel was on charter, a third party holder of the bill of lading such as the shipper only knew what he was told in the bill: he would therefore suppose that there was no conflict between a bill signed for the master and a bill under which C.A.V.N. was the designated carrier. If, however, the bill had expressly stipulated that the Panamanian owners were the carriers, then that would or might have been different. It seems to me that that is directly applicable to the case before me. In this case, there is nothing on the face of the bill to say who the owners (and therefore the carrier) are, save for the clause stipulating that USEL are the carrier. That, therefore, becomes the critical provision. *The Venezuela* was dealt with by *The Rewia* at p. 331 on the basis that it was a straightforward case. At the very least it shows that a signature for the master is not determinative.

. . .

   I conclude, therefore, that as a matter of construction, the bill of lading contract is with USEL not owners.

. . .

*Notes*
1.   Rix J then examined the surrounding circumstances and found that they strongly supported his conclusion on construction. See also *Fetim BV v Oceanspeed Shipping Ltd (The Flecha)* [1999] 1 Lloyd's Rep 612 (Adm, Moore-Bick J).
2.   One device used in an attempt to clarify the situation is the so-called 'demise clause' in the bill of lading. This provides that if the company, e.g., the shipping line, by which the bill is issued is not the owner or demise charterer of the ship, the bill is to take effect only as a contract with the owner or demise charterer. See *The Berkshire* [1974] 1 Lloyd's Rep 185 (QBD, Adm Div). Does this tell bill of lading holders what they need to know? (Some European legal systems hold such clauses to be ineffective as against the bill of lading holder: see Tetley, W., *Marine Cargo Claims*, 3rd ed., Blais, 1988, p. 1011 (Belgium). *Cf* for German Law, Prüßmann, H/Rabe, D, *Seehandelsrecht* [The Law of

Maritime Trade], 3rd edn, Munich: CH Beck'sche Verlagsbuchhandlung, 1992, pp. 614–616.)

*E: Bills of lading and third parties*

One of the difficulties facing the shipowners in *Elder, Dempster & Co. Ltd* v *Paterson, Zochonis & Co. Ltd* [1924] AC 522, was that the bills of lading were charterers' bills. The House of Lords held nevertheless, upholding the dissenting judgment of Scrutton LJ in the Court of Appeal, that the shipowners had the benefit of the exception for bad stowage. In *Scruttons Ltd* v *Midland Silicones Ltd* [1962] AC 446 this decision was described as 'an anomalous and unexplained exception to the general principle that a stranger cannot rely for his protection on provisions in a contract to which he is not a party' (per Lord Reid, at p. 479). (It was applied by Devlin J in *Pyrene Co. Ld* v *Scindia Navigation Co. Ltd* [1954] 2 QB 402 to enable the fob seller to sue on the contract of carriage made by the buyer.) However, although the House of Lords in *Scruttons Ltd* v *Midland Silicones Ltd* refused to extend the benefit of the bill of lading limitation of liability to the stevedores who negligently dropped the drum of chemicals during the unloading operation, a series of decisions of the Judicial Committee of the Privy Council has now confirmed that third parties can be given the benefit of provisions in the bill of lading. In the latest case, the Privy Council had to consider whether the principle extended to an exclusive jurisdiction clause.

### *The Mahkutai*
[1996] 2 Lloyd's Rep 1 (PC)

LORD GOFF OF CHIEVELEY: There is before their Lordships an appeal by the appellants, the owners of the Indonesian vessel *Mahkutai* ('the shipowners'), from a decision dated July 2, 1993 of the Court of Appeal of Hong Kong [1994] 1 H.K.L.R. 212, who by a majority (Litton JA and Mayo J., Bokhari JA dissenting) reversed an order by Mr Justice Sears granting the shipowners a stay of proceedings brought in Hong Kong by the respondents, the owners of cargo lately laden on the vessel ('the cargo owners'), on the ground that the proceedings had been brought in contravention of an exclusive jurisdiction clause under which any dispute was to be determined in the Courts of Indonesia.

. . .

The main issues . . . are concerned with the question whether the shipowners, who were not parties to the bill of lading contract, can invoke as against the cargo-owners the exclusive jurisdiction clause contained in that contract, the bill of lading being a charterers' bill issued by their agents to the shippers. The ship-owners claim to be able to do so, either under a Himalaya clause incorporated into the bill, on the principles established by the Privy Council in *The Eurymedon* [1974] 1 Lloyd's Rep 534; [1975] AC 154 and *The New York Star* [1980] 2 Lloyd's Rep 317; [1981] 1 WLR 138, or alternatively on the principle of bailment on terms, which originated in the speech of Lord Sumner in *Elder Dempster & Co. Ltd* v *Paterson Zoochonis & Co. Ltd* (1924) 18 Ll L Rep 319; [1924] AC 522.

. . .

*The facts of the case*

By a time charter dated Oct. 11, 1989 the shipowners chartered the vessel for a period of 12 months, later extended by a further 12 month period, to another Indonesian corporation, PT Rejeki Sentosa ('Sentosa'). By a voyage charter evidenced by a fixture note dated Jan. 15, 1991 Sentosa, as disponent owners, sub-chartered the vessel to Indonesian timber exporters called PT Jabarwood ('the shippers') for the carriage of a cargo of plywood from Jakarta to Shantou in the People's Republic of China. On Jan. 17, 1991 a shipping order was issued by Gesuri Lloyd (Sentosa's general agents) directing the vessel to receive the cargo of plywood from the shippers for carriage to Shantou subject to the provisions of 'the Companies' Bill of Lading ', i.e., Sentosa's form of bill. The shipping order was signed by the master, stating that the cargo had been received in good order, and as so signed no doubt constituted a mate's receipt for the goods. It provided that:

For further terms and conditions the clauses as stipulated in the B/L will apply.

On the following day, Jan. 18, the master issued an authorisation letter to Gesuri Lloyd, authorising them to sign the bill of lading 'in accordance with Mate's receipts and relevant Charter Party'. Accordingly on Jan. 19 a bill of lading was issued in Sentosa's form, signed by Gesuri Lloyd as agents for Sentosa, the disponent owners of the vessel. Among the bill of lading clauses were the following:

1.  CONDITIONS IN THIS BILL OF LADING

Carrier means the P.T. REJEKI SENTOSA SHIPPING and/or subsidiary companies on whose behalf the Bill of Lading has been signed.

'Vessels' includes the ship named herein and any ship or craft to which and from which transhipment may be made in the performance of the contract . . .

4.  SUB-CONTRACTING

(i)    The Carrier shall be entitled to sub-contract on any terms the whole or any part of the carriage, loading, unloading, storing, ware-housing, handling and any and all duties whatsoever undertaken by the Carrier in relation to the Goods.

(ii)    The Merchant undertakes that no claim or allegation shall be made against any servant, agent or sub-contractor of the Carrier, including but not limited to stevedores and terminal operators, which imposes or attempts to impose upon any of them or any vessel owned by any of them any liability whatsoever in connection with the Goods and, if any such claim or allegation should nevertheless be made, to indemnify the Carrier against all consequence thereof. Without prejudice to the foregoing, every such servant, agent and sub-contractor shall have the benefit of all exceptions, limitations, provision, conditions and liberties herein benefiting the carrier as if such provisions were expressly made for their benefit, and, in entering into this contract, the Carrier, to the extent of these provisions, does so not only on as [*sic*] own behalf, but also as agent and trustee for such servants, agents and sub-contractors. The Carrier shall be entitled to be paid by the Merchant on demand any sum recovered or recoverable by such Merchant from any such servant, agent or sub-contractor of the Carrier for any loss, damage, delay or otherwise.

(iii)    The expression 'Sub-Contractor' in this clause shall include direct and indirect sub-contractors and their respective servants and agents.

19.  JURISDICTION CLAUSE

The contract evidenced by the Bill of Lading shall be governed by the law of Indonesia and any dispute arising hereunder shall be determined by the Indonesian Courts according to that law to the exclusion of the jurisdiction of the courts of any other country.

The vessel, laden with the cargo of plywood, then sailed for Shantou where she arrived on Feb. 16, 1991, following a call for repairs at Manila Bay. A cargo survey was carried out at Shantou, and as a result the cargo-owners claimed that plywood in one of the holds had been damaged by seawater. On completion of discharge at Shantou the vessel proceeded to Hong Kong for the discharge of other cargo.

On arrival of the vessel at Hong Kong the cargo-owners issued a writ claiming damages arising from damage to the cargo by reason of breach of contract, breach of duty or negligence, and caused the vessel to be arrested. To obtain the release of their vessel, the shipowners then provided security for the cargo-owners' claim in the form of a bank guarantee, reserving the right to seek a stay of the Hong Kong proceedings.

On Dec. 5, 1991 the shipowners issued a summons seeking a stay of proceedings, either on the ground of breach of cl. 19 (the exclusive jurisdiction clause) in the bill of lading, or on the ground of forum non conveniens. Mr Justice Sears ... ordered that the Hong Kong proceedings be stayed, ... the Court of Appeal [1994] 1 HKLR 212 (by a majority — Litton JA at pp. 214–228 and Mayo, J at p. 231) allowed the cargo-owners' appeal....

*The pendulum of judicial opinion*
The two principles which the shipowners invoke are the product of developments in English law during the present century. During that period, opinion has fluctuated about the desirability of recognising some form of modification of, or exception to, the strict doctrine of privity of contract to accommodate situations which arise in the context of carriage of goods by sea, in which it appears to be in accordance with commercial expectations that the benefit of certain terms of the contract of carriage should be made available to parties involved in the adventure who are not parties to the contract. These cases have been concerned primarily with stevedores claiming the benefit of exceptions and limitations in bills of lading, but also with shipowners claiming the protection of such terms contained in charterers' bills. At first there appears to have been a readiness on the part of Judges to recognise such claims, especially in *Elder Demptster & Co. Ltd* v *Paterson Zochonis & Co. Ltd* (1924) 18 Ll L Rep 319; [1924] AC 522, concerned with the principle of bailment on terms. Opinion however hardened against them in the middle of the century as the pendulum swung back in the direction of orthodoxy in *Scruttons Ltd* v *Midland Silicones Ltd* [1961] 2 Lloyd's Rep 365; [1962] AC 446, but in more recent years it has swung back again to recognition of their commercial desirablity, notably in the two leading cases concerned with claims by stevedores to the protection of the Himalaya clause — *New Zealand Shipping Co. Ltd* v *A.M. Satterthwaite & Co. Ltd (The Eurymedon)* [1974] 1 Lloyd's Rep 534; [1975] AC 154 and *Port Jackson Stevedoring Pty. Ltd* v *Salmond and Spraggon (Australia) Pty. Ltd (The New York Star)* [1980] 2 Lloyd's Rep 317; [1981] WLR 138.

In the present case shipowners carrying cargo shipped under charterers' bills of lading are seeking to claim the benefit of a Himalaya clause in the time charterers' bills of lading, or in the alternative to invoke the principle of bailment on terms. However, they are seeking by these means to invoke not an exception or limitation in the ordinary sense of those words, but the benefit of an exclusive jurisdiction clause. This would involve a significantly wider application of the relevant principles; and, to judge whether this extension is justified, their Lordships consider it desirable first to trace the development of the principles through the cases.

*The Elder Dempster case*
The principle of bailment on terms finds its origin in the *Elder Dempster* case (1924) 18
Ll L Rep 319; [1924] AC 522. That case was concerned with a damage to cargo claim
in respect of a number of casks of palm oil which had been crushed by heavy bags of
palm kernels stowed above them in a ship with deep holds but no 'tween decks to take
the weight of the cargo stowed above. The main question in the case was whether such
damage was to be classified a damage arising from unseaworthiness of the ship due to
absence of 'tween decks, or as damage arising from bad stowage; in the latter event, no
claim lay under the bills of lading, which contained an exception excluding claims for
bad stowage. The bills of lading were time charterers' bills, the vessel having been
chartered in by the time charterers as an additional vessel for their West African line.
The House of Lords (on this point differing from a majority of the Court of Appeal) held
that the damage was to be attributed to bad stowage, and as a result the time charterers
were protected by the bill of lading exception; but the cargo-owners had also sued the
shipowners in tort, and the question arose whether the shipowners too were protected
by the exception contained in the bill of lading, to which they were not parties.

In the Court of Appeal (1922) 13 Ll L Rep 513 at pp. 516-517; [1923] 1 KB 420 at
pp. 441-442 Lord Justice Scrutton (who alone considered that the damage was to be
attributed to bad stowage rather than unseaworthiness) rejected the claim against the
shipowners on a suggested principle of vicarious immunity. This principle was relied on
by the shipowners in argument before the House of Lords, and was accepted (at p. 321;
p. 534) by Viscount Cave (with whom Lord Carson agreed), and apparently also (at
p. 327; p. 548) by Viscount Finlay. But the preferred reason given (at p. 333; p. 564) by
Lord Sumner (with whom Lord Dunedin and Lord Carson agreed) was that:

> ... in the circumstances of this case the obligations to be inferred from the reception
> of the cargo for carriage to the United Kingdom amount to a bailment upon terms,
> which include the exceptions and limitations of liability stipulated in the known and
> contemplated form of bill of lading.

*The Midland Silicones case*
This was a test case in which it was sought to establish a basis upon which stevedores
could claim the protection of exceptions and limitations contained in the bill of lading
contract. Here the stevedores had negligently damaged a drum of chemicals after
discharge at London, to which the goods had been shipped from New York under a bill
of lading incorporating the US Carriage of Goods by Sea Act 1936, which contained the
Hague Rules limitation of liability to US$500 per package or unit. The stevedores
sought to claim the benefit of this limit as against the receivers. They claimed to rely on
the principle of bailment on terms derived from the *Elder Dempster* case. But they also
sought a contractual basis for their contention on various grounds — that they had
contracted with the receivers through the agency of the shipowners; that they could rely
on an implied contract independent of the bill of lading; or that they could as an
interested third party take the benefit of the limit in the bill of lading contract. All these
arguments failed. The principle of bailment on terms was given a restrictive treatment;
and the various contractual arguments foundered on the doctrine of privity of contract,
Viscount Simonds in particular reasserting that doctrine in its orthodox form (at pp.
370-371, pp. 467-468). For present purposes, however, three features can be selected
as important.

First, the case revealed, at least on the part of Viscount Simonds (here reflecting the
view expressed by Mr Justice Fullagar in *Wilson* v *Darling Island Stevedoring and
Lighterage Co. Ltd* [1956] 1 Lloyd's Rep 346 at p. 364; (1956) 95 CLR 43 at p. 78), a

remarkable shift from the philosophy which informed the decision in the *Elder Dempster* case. There the point in question was treated very briefly by the members of the Appellate Committee, apparently because it seemed obvious to them that the cargo-owners' alternative claim against the shipowners should fail. It was perceived, expressly by Viscount Finlay (at p. 327; p. 548) and, it seems, implicitly by the remainder, that:

> ...It would be absurd that the owner of the goods could get rid of the protective clauses of the bill of lading, in respect of all stowage, by suing the owner of the ship in tort.

By contrast Mr Justice Fullagar, in the *Darling Island* case at p. 357; p. 71, condemned—

> ... a curious, and seemingly irresistible, anxiety to save grossly negligent people from the normal consequences of their negligence ...

a sentiment to be echoed by Viscount Simonds in the concluding sentence of his speech in the *Midland Silicones* case [1961] 2 Lloyd's Rep 365 at p. 373; [1962] AC 446 at p. 472.

Second, the *Elder Dempster* case was kept within strict bounds. Viscount Simonds (at p. 372; p. 470) quoted with approval the interpretation adopted by Mr Justice Fullagar (with whom Dixon, CJ agreed) in the High Court of Australia in the *Darling Island* case, where he said (at p. 364; p. 78):

> In my opinion, what the *Elder Dempster* case decided, and all that it decided is that in such a case, the master having signed the bill of lading, the proper inference is that the shipowner, when he receives the goods into his possession, receives them on the terms of the bill of lading. The same inference might perhaps be drawn in some cases even if the charterer himself signed the bill of lading, but it is unnecessary to consider any such question.

This approach is consistent with that of Lord Sumner. In the *Midland Silicones* case Lord Keith of Avonholm (at p. 378; p. 481) and Lord Morris of Borth-y-Gest (at p. 386; p. 494) spoke in similar terms. Lord Reid (at p. 377; p. 479) treated the decision on the point as—

> ... an anomalous and unexplained exception to the general principle that a stranger cannot rely for his protection on provisions in a contract to which he is not a party.

Lord Denning dissented (at pp. 379-384; pp. 481-492).

It has to be recognised that this reception did not enhance the reputation of the *Elder Dempster* case, as witness certain derogatory descriptions later attached to it, for example by Mr Justice Donaldson in *Johnson Matthey & Co. Ltd* v *Constantine Terminals Ltd* [1976] 2 Lloyd's Rep 215 at p. 219 — 'something of a judicial nightmare', and by Lord Justice Ackner in *The Forum Craftsman* [1985] 1 Lloyd's Rep 291 at p. 295 — 'heavily comatosed, if not long-interred'.

Third, however, and most important, Lord Reid in *Midland Silicones* case, while rejecting the agency argument on the facts of the case before him, nevertheless indicated how it might prove successful in a future case. He said (at p. 374; p. 474):

> I can see a possibility of success of the agency argument if (first) the bill of lading makes it clear that the stevedore is intended to be protected by the provisions in it which limit liability, (secondly) the bill of lading makes it clear that the carrier, in addition to contracting for these provisions on his own behalf, is also contracting as agent for the stevedore that these provisions should apply to the stevedore, (thirdly)

the carrier has authority from the stevedore to do that, or perhaps later ratification by the stevedore would suffice, and (fourthly) that any difficulties about consideration moving from the stevedore were overcome.

It was essentially on this passage that the Himalaya clause (called after the name of the ship involved in *Adler* v *Dickson* [1954] 2 Lloyd's Rep 267; [1955] 1 QB 158) was later to be founded.

*The pendulum swings back again*
In most recent years the pendulum of judicial opinion has swung back again, as recognition has been given to the undesirability, especially in a commercial context, of allowing plaintiffs to circumvent contractual exception clauses by suing in particular the servant or agent of the contracting party who caused the relevant damage, thereby undermining the purpose of the exception, and so redistributing the contractual allocation of risk which is reflected in the freight rate and in the parties' respective insurance arrangements. Nowadays, therefore, there is a greater readiness, not only to accept something like Lord Justice Scrutton's doctrine of vicarious immunity (as to which see, e.g., art. IV bis of the Hague-Visby rules scheduled to the Carriage of Goods by Sea Act 1971) but also to rehabilitate the *Elder Dempster* case itself, which has been described by Lord Justice Bingham in *Dresser U.K. Ltd* v *Falcongate Freight Management Ltd* [1991] 2 Lloyd's Rep 557 at p. 562, col. 1; [1992] QB 502 at p. 511F as 'a pragmatic legal recognition of commercial reality'. Even so, the problem remains how to discover, in circumstances such as those of the *Elder Dempster* case, the factual basis from which the rendering of the bailment subject to such a provision can properly be inferred. At all events the present understanding, based on Lord Sumner's speech, is that in the circumstances of that case the shippers may be taken to have impliedly agreed that the goods were received by the shipowners, as bailees, subject to the exceptions and limitations contained in the known and contemplated form of bill of lading; see *The Pioneer Container* [1994] 2 Lloyd's Rep 593 at p. 600, cols. 1 and 2; [1994] 2 AC 324 at pp. 339D-340B. Their Lordships will however put on one side for later consideration the question how far the principle of bailment on terms may be applicable in the present case, and will turn first to consider the principle developed from Lord Reid's observations in the *Midland Silicones* case, in *The Eurymedon* and *The New Year Star*.

*The Eurymedon* and *The New York Star*
Their Lordships have already quoted the terms of cl. 4 (the Himalaya clause) of the bill of lading in the present case. For the purposes of this aspect of the case, the essential passage reads as follows:

> Without prejudice to the foregoing, every such servant, agent and sub-contractor shall have the benefit of all exceptions, limitations, provision, conditions and liberties herein benefiting the Carrier as if such provisions were expressly made for their benefit, and, in entering into this contract, the Carrier, to the extent of these provisions, does so not only on [his] own behalf, but also as agent and trustee for such servants, agents and sub-contractors.

The effectiveness of a Himalaya clause to provide protection against claims in tort by consignees was recognised by the Privy Council in *The Eurymedon* and *The New York Star*. In both cases, stevedores were sued by the consignees for damages in tort, in the first case on the ground that the stevedores had negligently damaged a drilling machine in the course of unloading, and in the second on the ground that they had negligently allowed a parcel of goods, after unloading onto the wharf, to be removed by thieves without production of the bill of lading. In both cases, the bill of lading contract incorporated a one year time bar, and a Himalaya clause which extended the benefit of defences and immunities to independent contractors employed by the carrier. The stevedores relied upon the Himalaya clause to claim the benefit of the time bar as against the consignees.

In *The Eurymedon* the Privy Council held, by a majority of three to two, that the stevedores were entitled to rely on the time bar. The leading judgment was delivered by Lord Wilberforce (at pp. 537-540; pp. 164-169). He referred to cl. 1 of the bill of lading under which the carrier stipulated for certain exemptions and immunities among them the one year time bar in art. III, r. 6, of the Hague Rules, and in addition (in the Himalaya clause) the carrier, as agent for (among others) independent contractors, stipulated for the same exemptions. Referring to Lord Reid's four criteria in the *Midland Silicones* case [1961] 2 Lloyd's Rep 365 at p. 374; [1962] AC 446 at p. 474, he considered it plain that the first three were satisfied, the only question being whether the requirement of consideration was fulfilled. He was satisfied that it was. He observed (at p. 539, col. 1; p. 167B) that—

> . . . If the choice, and the antithesis, is between a gratuitous promise and a promise for consideration . . . there can be little doubt which, in commercial reality, this is.

He then proceeded to analyse the transaction in a way which showed a preference by him for what is usually called a unilateral contract, though he recognised that there might be more than one way of analysing the transaction.

In *The New York Star*, the Privy Council again upheld (on this occasion unanimously) the efficacy of a Himalaya clause to confer upon the stevedores the benefit of defences and immunities contained in the bill of lading, including a one year time bar. The judgment of the Judicial Committee was again given by Lord Wilberforce. In the course of his judgment, he stressed (at p. 321, col. 2; p. 143F-G) that:

> . . . It may indeed be said that the significance of *Satterthwaite's* case lay not so much in the establishment of any new legal principle, as in the finding that in the normal situation involving the employment of stevedores by carriers, accepted principles enable and require the stevedore to enjoy the benefit of contractual provisions in the bill of lading.

He continued (at p. 321, col. 2; p. 144A-B):

> Although, in each case, there will be room for evidence as to the precise relationship of carrier and stevedore and as to the practice at the relevant port, the decision does not support, and their Lordships would not encourage, a search for fine distinctions which would diminish the general applicability, in the light of established commercial practice, of the principle.

Lord Wilberforce in particular expressed the Board's approval of the reasoned analysis of the relevant legal principles in the judgment of Barwick CJ, which in his opinion substantially agreed with, and indeed constituted a powerful reinforcement of, one of the two possible bases put forward in the Board's judgment in *The Eurymedon*. In his judgment in the Court below (the High Court of Australia), Barwick CJ (see [1979] 1 Lloyd's Rep 298 at pp. 304–305) saw no difficulty in finding that the carrier acted as the authorised agent of the stevedores in making an arrangement with the consignor for the protection of the stevedores. By later accepting the bill of lading the consignee became party to that arrangement. He could not read the clauses in the bill of lading as an unaccepted but acceptable offer by the consignor to the stevedores. However, the consignor and the stevedores were ad idem through the carrier's agency, upon the acceptance by the consignor of the bill of lading, as to the protection the stevedores should have in the event that they caused loss of or damage to the consignment. But that consensus lacked consideration. He continued (at p. 305):

> To agree with another that, in the event that the other acts in a particular way, that other shall be entitled to state a protective provision only needs performance by the doing of the specified act or acts to become a binding contract . . . The performance of the act or acts at the one moment satisfied the test for consideration and enacted the agreed terms.

Such a contract Barwick CJ was prepared, with some hesitation, to describe as a bilateral contract.

### Critique of the Eurymedon principle

In *The New York Star*, Lord Wilberforce (at p. 321; p. 144) discouraged—

> . . . a search for fine distinctions which would diminish the general applicability, in the light of established commercial practice, of the principle.

He was there, of course, speaking of the application of the principle in the case of stevedores. It has however to be recognised that, so long as the principle continues to be understood to rest upon an enforceable contract as between the cargo-owners and the stevedores entered into through the agency of the shipowner, it is inevitable that technical points of contract and agency law will continue to be invoked by cargo-owners seeking to enforce tortious remedies against stevedores and others uninhibited by the exceptions and limitations in the relevant bill of lading contract. Indeed, in the present case their Lordships have seen such an exercise being legitimately undertaken by Mr Aikens QC on behalf of the respondent cargo-owners. In this connection their Lordships wish to refer to the very helpful consideration of the principle in Palmer on Bailment, 2nd ed. (1991) at pp. 1610–1625, which reveals many of the problems which may arise, and refers to a number of cases, both in England and in Commonwealth countries, in which the Courts have grappled with those problems. In some cases, notably but by no means exclusively in England, Courts have felt impelled by the established principles of the law of contract or of agency to reject the application of the principle in the particular case before them. In others, Courts have felt free to follow the lead of Lord Wilberforce in *The Eurymedon*, and of Lord Wilberforce and Barwick CJ in *The New York Star*, and so to discover the existence of a contract (nowadays a bilateral contract of the kind identified by Barwick CJ) in circumstances in which lawyers of a previous generation would have been unwilling to do so.

Nevertheless there can be no doubt of the commercial need of some such principle as this, and not only in cases concerned with stevedores; and the bold step taken by the Privy Council in *The Eurymedon*, and later developed in *The New York Star*, has been widely welcomed. But it is legitimate to wonder whether that development is yet complete. Here their Lordships have in mind not only Lord Wilberforce's discouragement of fine distinctions, but also the fact that the law is now approaching the position where, provided that the bill of lading contract clearly provides that (for example) independent contractors such as stevedores are to have the benefit of exceptions and limitations contained in that contract, they will be able to enjoy the protection of those terms as against the cargo-owners. This is because (1) the problem of consideration in these cases is regarded as having been solved on the basis that a bilateral agreement between the stevedores and the cargo-owners, entered into through the agency of the shipowners, may, though itself unsupported by consideration, be rendered enforceable by consideration subsequently furnished by the stevedores in the form of performance of their duties as stevedores for the shipowners; (2) the problem of authority from the stevedores to the shipowners to contract on their behalf can, in the majority of cases, be solved by recourse to the principle of ratification; and (3) consignees of the cargo may be held to be bound on the principle in *Brandt* v *Liverpool Brazil and River Plate Steam Navigation Co. Ltd* (1923) 17 Ll L Rep 142; [1924] 1 KB 575. Though these solutions are now perceived to be generally effective for their purpose, their technical nature is all too apparent; and the time may well come when, in an appropriate case, it will fall to be considered whether the Courts should take what may legitimately be perceived to be the final and perhaps inevitable, step in this development, and recognise in these cases a fully-fledged exception to the doctrine of privity of contract, thus escaping from all the technicalities with which Courts are now faced in English law. It is not far from their Lordships' minds that, if the English Courts were minded to take that step, they would be following in the footsteps of the Supreme Court of Canada (see *London Drugs Ltd* v *Kuehne & Nagel International Ltd* (1992) 97 DLR (4th) 261) and, in a different context, the High Court of Australia (see *Trident General Insurance Co. Ltd* v *McNiece Bros. Pty Ltd* (1988) 165 CLR 107). Their Lordships have given consideration to the question whether they should face up to this question in the present appeal. However, they have come to the conclusion that it would not be appropriate for them to do so, first, because they have not heard argument specifically directed towards this fundamental question, and second because, as will become clear in due course, they are satisfied that the appeal must in any event be dismissed.

*Application of the Eurymedon principle in the present case*
Their Lordships now turn to the application of the principle in *The Eurymedon* to the facts of the present case. Two questions arose in the course of argument which are specific to this case. The first is whether the shipowners qualify as 'sub-contractors' within the meaning of the Himalaya clause (cl. 4 of the bill of lading). The second is whether, if so, they are entitled to take advantage of the exclusive jurisdiction clause (cl. 19). Their Lordships have come to the conclusion that the latter question must be answered in the negative. It is therefore unnecessary for them to answer the first question; and they will proceed to address the question of the exclusive jurisdiction clause on the assumption that the shipowners can be regarded as sub-contractors for this purpose.

*The exclusive jurisdiction clause*
The Himalaya clause provides that, among others, sub-contractors shall have the benefit of 'all exceptions, limitations, provision, conditions and liberties herein benefiting the Carrier as if such provisions were expressly made for their benefit'. The question therefore arises whether the exclusive jurisdiction clause (cl. 19) falls within the scope of this clause.

In *The Eurymedon* (at p. 540; p. 169) and *The New York Star* (at p. 321; p. 143) Lord Wilberforce stated the principle to be applicable, in the case of stevedores, to respectively 'exemptions and limitations' and 'defences and immunities' contained in the bill of lading. This is scarcely surprising. Most bill of lading contracts incorporate the Hague-Visby rules, in which the responsibilities and liabilities of the carrier are segregated from his rights and immunities, the latter being set out primarily in art. IV, rr. 1 and 2, exempting the carrier and the ship from liability or responsibility for loss of or damage to the goods in certain specified circumstances; though the limitation on liability per package or unit is to be found in art. IV, r. 5, and the time bar in art. III, r. 6. Terms such as these are characteristically terms for the benefit of the carrier, of which sub-contractors can have the benefit under the Himalaya clause as if such terms were expressly made for their benefit.

It however by no means follows that the same can be said of an exclusive jurisdiction clause, here incorporating, as is usual, a choice of law provision relating to the law of the chosen jurisdiction. No question arises in the present case with regard to the choice of law provision. This already applied to the bill of lading contract itself, and may for that reason also apply to another contract which comes into existence, pursuant to its terms, between the shipper and a sub-contractor of the carrier such as the shipowners in the present case. But the exclusive jurisdiction clause itself creates serious problems. Such a clause can be distinguished from terms such as exceptions and limitations in that it does not benefit only one party, but embodies a mutual agreement under which both parties agree with each other as to the relevant jurisdiction for the resolution of disputes. It is therefore a clause which creates mutual rights and obligations. Can such a clause be an exception, limitation, provision, condition or liberty benefiting the carrier within the meaning of the clause?

First of all, it cannot in their Lordships' opinion be an exception, limitation, condition or liberty. But can it be a provision? That expression has, of course, to be considered in the context of the Himalaya clause; and ... the question is whether an exclusive jurisdiction clause is a provision benefiting the carrier, of which servants, agents and sub-contractors of the carrier are intended to have the benefit, as if the provision was expressly made for their benefit. Moreover, the word 'provision' is to be found at the centre of a series of words, viz. 'exceptions, limitations ... conditions and liberties', all of which share the same characteristic, that they are not as such rights which entail correlative obligations on the cargo-owners.

In considering this question, their Lordships are satisfied that some limit must be placed upon the meaning of the word 'provision' in this context. In their Lordships' opinion the word 'provision' must have been inserted with the purpose of ensuring that any other provision in the bill of lading which, although it did not strictly fall within the description 'exceptions, limitations, ... conditions and liberties', nevertheless benefited the carrier in the same way in the sense that it was inserted in the bill for the carrier's protection, should enure for the benefit of the servants, agents and sub-contractors of the carrier. It cannot therefore extend to include a mutual agreement, such as an exclusive jurisdiction clause, which is not of that character.

Their Lordships draw support for this view from the function of the Himalaya clause. That function is, as revealed by the authorities, to prevent cargo-owners from avoiding the effect of contractual defences available to the carrier (typically the exceptions and limitations in the Hague-Visby Rules) by suing in tort persons who perform the contractual services on the carrier's behalf. To make available to such a person the benefit of an exclusive jurisdiction clause in the bill of lading contract does not contribute to the solution of that problem. Furthermore to construe the general words of the Himalaya clause as effective to make available to servants, agents or sub-contractors a clause which expressly refers to disputes arising under the contract evidenced by the bill of lading, to which they are not party, is not easy to reconcile with those authorities (such as *Thomas & Co. Ltd* v *Portsea Steamship Co. Ltd* [1912] AC 1) which hold that general words of incorporation are ineffective to incorporate into a bill of lading an arbitration clause which refers only to disputes arising under the charter.

Furthermore, it is of some significance to observe how adventitious would have been the benefit of the exclusive jurisdiction clause to the shipowners in the present case. Such a clause generally represents a preference by the carrier for the jurisdiction where he carries on business. But the same cannot necessarily be said of his servants, agents or sub-contractors. It could conceivably be true of servants, such as crew members, who may be resident in the same jurisdiction; though if sued elsewhere they may in any event be able to invoke the principle of forum non conveniens. But the same cannot be said to be true of agents, still less of sub-contractors. Take, for example, stevedores at the discharging port, who provide the classic example of independent contractors intended to be protected by a Himalaya clause. There is no reason to suppose that an exclusive jurisdiction clause selected to suit a particular carrier would be likely to be of any benefit to such stevedores; it could only conceivably be so in the coincidental circumstance that the discharging port happened to be in the country where the carrier carried on business. Exactly the same can be said of a shipowner who performs all or part of the carrier's obligations under the bill of lading contract, pursuant to a time or voyage charter. In such a case, the shipowner may very likely have no connection with the carrier's chosen jurisdiction. Coincidentally he may do so, as in the present case where the shipowners happened, like Sentosa, to be an Indonesian corporation. This of course explains why the shipowners in the present case wish to take advantage of the exclusive jurisdiction clause in Sentosa's form of bill of lading; but it would not be right to attach any significance to that coincidence.

In the opinion of their Lordships, all these considerations point strongly against the exclusive jurisdiction clause falling within the scope of the Himalaya clause. However in support of his submission that the exclusive jurisdiction clause fell within the scope of the Himalaya clause in the present case, Mr Gross QC, for the shipowners, invoked the decision of the Privy Council in *The Pioneer Container* [1994] 1 Lloyd's Rep 593; [1994] 2 AC 324. That case was however concerned with a different situation, where a carrier of goods sub-contracted part of the carriage to a shipowner under a 'feeder' bill of lading, and that shipowner sought to enforce an exclusive jurisdiction clause contained in that bill of lading against the owners of the goods. The Judicial Committee held that the shipowner was entitled to do so, because the goods owner had authorised the carrier so to sub-contract 'on any terms', with the effect that the shipowner as sub-bailee was entitled to rely on the clause against the goods owner as head bailor. The present case is however concerned not with a question of enforceability of a term in a *sub-bailment* by the sub-bailee against the head bailor, but with the question whether a sub-contractor is entitled to take the benefit of a term in the *head contract*. The former depends on the scope of the *authority* of the intermediate bailor to act on behalf of the head bailor in agreeing on his behalf to the relevant term in the *sub-bailment*; whereas the latter depends on the scope of the *agreement* between the head contractor and the sub-contractor, entered into by the intermediate contractor as agent for the sub-contractor, under which the benefit of a term in the *head contract* may be made available by the head contractor to the sub-contractor. It does not follow that a decision in the former type of case provides any useful guidance in a case of the latter type; and their Lordships do not therefore find *The Pioneer Container* of assistance in the present case.

In the event, for the reasons they have already given, their Lordships have come to the conclusion that the Himalaya clause does not have the effect of enabling the shipowners to take advantage of the exclusive jurisdiction clause in the bill of lading in the present case.

*Application of the principle of bailment on terms in the present case*
In the light of the principle stated by Lord Sumner in the *Elder Dempster* case at p. 333; p. 564, as interpreted by Mr Justice Fullagar in the *Darling Island* case at 364; p. 78, the next question for consideration is whether the shipowners can establish that they received the goods into their possession on the terms of the bills of lading, including the exclusive jurisdiction clause.

. . .

Their Lordships feel able to deal with this point very briefly, because they consider that in the present case there is an insuperable objection to the argument of the shipowners. This is that the bill of lading under which the goods were shipped on board contained a Himalaya clause under which the shipowners as sub-contractors were expressed to be entitled to the benefit of certain terms in the bill of lading but, as their Lordships have held, those terms did not include the exclusive jurisdiction clause. In these circumstances their Lordships find it impossible to hold that, by receiving the goods into their possession pursuant to the bill of lading, the shipowners' obligations as bailees were effectively subjected to the exclusive jurisdiction clause as a term upon which they implicitly received the goods into their possession. Any such implication must, in their opinion, be rejected as inconsistent with the express terms of the bill of lading.

...

### Question

A container holding the plaintiff's goods is in the container park at the docks awaiting arrival of the ship on which it is to be loaded. While discharging another vessel an employee of the dock company negligently drives into a container holding a corrosive chemical; the chemical escapes and damages the plaintiff's goods. Could the dock company rely on a Himalaya clause in the plaintiff's contract of carriage? (See *Raymond Burke Motors Ltd* v *The Mersey Docks and Harbour Co.* [1986] 1 Lloyd's Rep 155, per Leggatt J.)

## SECTION 3: THE BILL OF LADING AS A DOCUMENT OF TITLE

When used as a 'negotiable' document of title, the bill of lading enables the shipper to sell and transfer ownership of the cargo during the voyage, makes it possible for the owner to raise finance on the security of the goods while in transit and provides the carrier with a safe and straightforward system that will eliminate the risk of liability for misdelivery at the port of discharge.

### *Sanders Brothers* v *Maclean & Co.*
### (1883) 11 QBD 327 (CA)

Bills of lading in respect of a cargo of old iron flange rails from the Black Sea to Philadelphia were issued in a set of three. The shipper, in St Petersburg, forwarded two bills to the buyers and retained the third in his possession. The buyers rejected the documents, insisting that they were entitled to receive the whole set. The third bill was tendered later, but the buyers still rejected it.

BOWEN LJ: I am of opinion that the first tender of the 3rd of August was perfectly good.

The law as to the indorsement of bills of lading is as clear as in my opinion the practice of all European merchants is thoroughly understood. A cargo at sea while in the hands of the carrier is necessarily incapable of physical delivery. During this period of transit and voyage, the bill of lading by the law merchant as universally recognised as its symbol, and the indorsement and delivery of the bill of lading operates as a symbolical delivery of the cargo. Property in the goods passes by such indorsement and delivery of the bill of lading, whenever it is the intention of the parties that the property should pass, just as under similar circumstances the property would pass by an actual delivery of the goods. And for the purpose of passing such property in the goods and completing the title of the indorsee to full possession thereof, the bill of lading, until complete delivery of the cargo has been made on shore to some one rightfully claiming under it, remains in force as a symbol, and carries with it not only the full ownership of the goods, but also all rights created by the contract of carriage between the shipper and the shipowner. It is a key which in the hands of a rightful owner is intended to unlock the door of the warehouse, floating or fixed, in which the goods may chance to be.

The above effect and power belong to any one of the set of original bills of lading which is first dealt with by the shipper. Except in furtherance of the title so created of the indorsee, the other originals of the set are, as against it, perfectly ineffectual and have no efficacy whatever, unless they are fraudulently used for the purposes of deceit. By inveterate practice among most of the commercial nations of Europe, bills of lading have long been drawn by the shipowner in sets of three or more. Sometimes one of the set is retained by the captain, the others being transferred by the captain to the shipper. Sometimes the whole of the set are handed, upon shipment, to the merchant, the captain retaining a copy only. This practice of drawing bills of lading in triplicate may be at the present day, and under the altered conditions of communication between one part of the world and another, less valuable than it was when originally introduced. But it certainly had its distinct uses in the early stages of European commerce, and it still survives. If it survives it is probably that the commercial world still finds it more convenient or less troublesome to preserve it than to change it.

And it is plain that the purpose and idea of drawing bills of lading in sets — whatever the present advantage or disadvantage of the plan — is that the whole set should not remain always in the same hands. The possibility of its separation is intentionally devised for the purpose not of fraud, but of protecting honest dealing. The separation may conceivably afford opportunities of fraud, if the holders chose to be dishonest, but on the whole the commercial world is satisfied to run the risk of this contingency for the sake of the compensating advantages and conveniences which merchants rightly or wrongly have, till lately at all events, believed to be afforded by the system of triplicates or quadruplicates. The shipper or his vendees may prefer to retain one of the originals for their own protection against loss, or to transfer it to their correspondents. In such cases they are in the habit of treating the remainder of the set as the effective documents and as sufficient for all purposes of negotiating the goods comprised in the bill of lading. The question we have to decide is whether the tender to the vendee of the only effective originals of the set is a sufficient tender under their contract, notwithstanding the absence of a third original, which is outstanding in the hands of the shipper; but which it is admitted in the present case has been in no way dealt with by him, and which has always remained in his hands as an ineffective and innocent triplicate.

If we were to hold that such a tender is not adequate, we must, as it appears to me, deal a fatal blow at this established custom of merchants, according to which, time out of mind, bills of lading are drawn in sets, and one of the set is habitually dealt with as representing the cargo independently of the rest. If the set, for purposes of contracts like the present, must always be kept together, the whole object, be it wise or unwise, of drawing bills of lading in triplicate is frustrated. For if one of the set were lost, or had been forwarded by the shipper or any subsequent owner of the cargo to his correspondent by way of precaution, the cargo becomes unsaleable. The only possible object of requiring the presentation of the third original must be to prevent the chance, more or less remote, of fraud on the part of the shipper or some previous owner of the goods. But the practice of merchants, it is never superfluous to remark, is not based on the supposition of possible frauds. The object of mercantile usages is to prevent the risk of insolvency, not of fraud; and any one who attempts to follow and understand the law merchant will soon find himself lost if he begins by assuming that merchants conduct their business on the basis of attempting to insure themselves against fraudulent dealing. The contrary is the case. Credit, not distrust, is the basis of commercial dealings; mercantile genius consists principally in knowing whom to trust and with whom to deal, and commercial intercourse and communication is no more based on the supposition of fraud than it is on the supposition of forgery.

*Notes*

1.   The risks for buyers such as those in *Sanders Brothers* v *Maclean & Co.* are brought out by the decision of the House of Lords in *Glyn Mills Currie & Co.* v *The East and West India Dock Co.* (1882) 7 App Cas 591. There the merchants pledged one bill of the set (marked 'First') to the appellant bank; they subsequently used the bill marked 'Second' to authorise the respondents to deliver the cargo to a purchaser. The merchants being insolvent, the bank presented their bill and demanded delivery. It was held that, in accordance with the traditional phrase in the bills, 'one of which bills being accomplished, the others to stand void', the cargo belonged to the first holder of a bill to obtain delivery and the bank had no rights in the cargo, the respondents having acted bona fide and without notice of the bank's claim.

2.   Whether a bill of lading is a transferable document of title depends upon the intention of the parties: if it is issued as a 'non-negotiable' document it will not be a document of title, even if used in the relevant trade as such: *Kum* v *Wah Tat Bank Ltd* [1971] 1 Lloyd's Rep 439 (PC), see Chapter 7.

Because of the doctrine of privity of contract, however, the common law was faced with a much more intractable problem in finding a basis for claims by a transferee of the bill of lading against the carrier and vice versa. A partial solution was provided by the Bills of Lading Act 1855, under which the transfer of rights to consignees and indorsees and the creation of liabilities was linked to the passing of property in the goods 'upon or by reason of such consignment or endorsement' (s. 1). After the inadequacies of this approach were demonstrated in a series of well-known decisions, notably *The Aramis* [1989] 1 Lloyd's Rep 213 (CA), *Enichem Anic SpA* v *Ampelos Shipping Co. Ltd (The Delfini)* [1990] 1 Lloyd's Rep 252 (CA) and *The Aliakmon* [1986] AC 785 (HL), the Law Commission proposed new legislation (Law Com No. 196). The draft bill was enacted as the Carriage of Goods by Sea Act 1992, and to this we now turn.

## Carriage of Goods by Sea Act 1992

*An Act to replace the Bills of Lading Act 1855 with new provision with respect to bills of lading and certain other shipping documents.*                                                   [16 July 1992]

1.   Shipping documents etc. to which Act applies
   (1)   This Act applies to the following documents, that is to say—
      (a)   any bill of lading;
      (b)   any sea waybill; and
      (c)   any ship's delivery order.

(2)   References in this Act to a bill of lading—

(a)   do not include references to a document which is incapable of transfer either by indorsement or, as a bearer bill, by delivery without indorsement; but

(b)   subject to that, do include references to a received for shipment bill of lading.

(3)   References in this Act to a sea waybill are references to any document which is not a bill of lading but—

(a)   is such a receipt for goods as contains or evidences a contract for the carriage of goods by sea; and

(b)   identifies the person to whom delivery of the goods is to be made by the carrier in accordance with that contract.

(4)   References in this Act to a ship's delivery order are references to any document which is neither a bill of lading nor a sea waybill but contains an undertaking which—

(a)   is given under or for the purposes of a contract for the carriage by sea of the goods to which the document relates, or of goods which include those goods; and

(b)   is an undertaking by the carrier to a person identified in the document to deliver the goods to which the document relates to that person.

(5)   The Secretary of State may by regulations make provision for the application of this Act to cases where a telecommunication system or any other information technology is used for effecting transactions corresponding to—

(a)   the issue of a document to which this Act applies;

(b)   the indorsement, delivery or other transfer of such a document; or

(c)   the doing of anything else in relation to such a document.

(6)   Regulations under subsection (5) above may—

(a)   make such modifications of the following provisions of this Act as the Secretary of State considers appropriate in connection with the application of this Act to any case mentioned in that subsection; and

(b)   contain supplemental, incidental, consequential and transitional provision;

and the power to make regulations under that subsection shall be exercisable by statutory instrument subject to annulment in pursuance of a resolution of either House of Parliament.

*Note*

The provisions of the Act apply not only to transferable bills of lading, including 'received for shipment' bills, but also to (non-transferable) sea waybills and ship's delivery orders. Sea waybills are frequently used for containers and any shipment where there is no need for dealing with the goods while in transit. Ship's delivery orders are important in dealing with parcels of a bulk cargo. Note the power to extend the Act, by regulations, to paperless transactions.

## Carriage of Goods by Sea Act 1992

### 2.   Rights under shipping documents

(1)   Subject to the following provisions of this section, a person who becomes—

(a)   the lawful holder of a bill of lading;

(b)   the person who (without being an original party to the contract of carriage) is the person to whom delivery of the goods to which a sea waybill relates is to be made by the carrier in accordance with that contract; or

(c)   the person to whom delivery of the goods to which a ship's delivery order relates is to be made in accordance with the undertaking contained in the order,
shall (by virtue of becoming the holder of the bill or, as the case may be, the person to whom delivery is to be made) have transferred to and vested in him all rights of suit under the contract of carriage as if he had been a party to that contract.

(2)   Where, when a person becomes the lawful holder of a bill of lading, possession of the bill no longer gives a right (as against the carrier) to possession of the goods to which the bill relates, that person shall not have any rights transferred to him by virtue of subsection (1) above unless he becomes the holder of the bill—

(a)   by virtue of a transaction effected in pursuance of any contractual or other arrangements made before the time when such a right to possession ceased to attach to possession of the bill; or

(b)   as a result of the rejection to that person by another person of goods or documents delivered to the other person in pursuance of any such arrangements.

(3)   The rights vested in any person by virtue of the operation of subsection (1) above in relation to a ship's delivery order—

(a)   shall be so vested subject to the terms of the order; and

(b)   where the goods to which the order relates form a part only of the goods to which the contract of carriage relates, shall be confined to rights in respect of the goods to which the order relates.

(4)   Where, in the case of any document to which this Act applies—

(a)   a person with any interest or right in or in relation to goods to which the document relates sustains loss or damage in consequence of a breach of the contract of carriage; but

(b)   subsection (1) above operates in relation to that document so that rights of suit in respect of that breach are vested in another person,
the other person shall be entitled to exercise those rights for the benefit of the person who sustained the loss or damage to the same extent as they could have been exercised if they had been vested in the person for whose benefit they are exercised.

(5)   Where rights are transferred by virtue of the operation of subsection (1) above in relation to any document, the transfer for which that subsection provides shall extinguish any entitlement to those rights which derives—

(a)   where that document is a bill of lading, from a person's having been an original party to the contract of carriage; or

(b)   in the case of any document to which this Act applies, from the previous operation of that subsection in relation to that document;
but the operation of that subsection shall be without prejudice to any rights which derive from a person's having been an original party to the contract contained in, or evidenced by, a sea waybill and, in relation to a ship's delivery order, shall be without prejudice to any rights deriving otherwise than from the previous operation of that subsection in relation to that order.

*Notes*

*1.*   The lawful holder is defined in s. 5(2), below.

*2.*   Section 2(1) embodies the major change made by the Act, by vesting contractual rights against the carrier in the lawful holder of the bill of lading irrespective of the passing of property (and similarly for the person to whom delivery is to be made under non-negotiable documents). Does this not expose carriers to additional claims (in tort) by persons who are not holders of a bill of lading, but in whom the property in the goods is still vested?

3.   Section 2(2) is dealing with situations in which a bill of lading comes into the hands of a lawful holder after delivery of goods by the carrier to the person entitled to them. Rights of action are transferred to the holder only in the two situations specified. (In a chain of sales, bills of lading often take a long time to find their way down the chain and delivery without the bills of lading — against suitable indemnities — is in everybody's interest.)

4.   Section 2(4) was inserted in order to overcome the reluctance of the courts to allow full damages to be recovered by one person for the benefit of another.

5.   Under s. 2(5), when s. 2(1) has effected a transfer of rights, the rights of the original shipper and of any previous transferees under a bill of lading are extinguished. The subsection is, however, 'without prejudice to' the rights of the sea waybill shipper and the person entitled under the contract for which a ship's delivery order was issued, so that these rights are not taken away automatically. This was done to accommodate the practice under sea waybills of reserving to the shipper a right of disposal, i.e., to change the delivery instructions, until delivery has actually been made.

## Carriage of Goods by Sea Act 1992

### 3.   Liability under shipping documents

(1)   Where subsection (1) of section 2 of this Act operates in relation to any document to which this Act applies and the person in whom rights are vested by virtue of that subsection—

(a)   takes or demands delivery from the carrier of any of the goods to which the document relates;

(b)   makes a claim under the contract of carriage against the carrier in respect of any of those goods; or

(c)   is a person who, at a time before those rights were vested in him, took or demanded delivery from the carrier of any of those goods,

that person shall (by virtue of taking or demanding delivery or making the claim or, in a case falling within paragraph (c) above, of having the rights vested in him) become subject to the same liabilities under that contract as if he had been a party to that contract.

(2)   Where the goods to which a ship's delivery order relates form a part only of the goods to which the contract of carriage relates, the liabilities to which any person is subject by virtue of the operation of this section in relation to that order shall exclude liabilities in respect of any goods to which the order does not relate.

(3)   This section, so far as it imposes liabilities under any contract on any person, shall be without prejudice to the liabilities under the contract of any person as an original party to the contract.

*Note*

The right to receive the goods may carry with it responsibility for outstanding charges such as freight and demurrage. Under the Bills of Lading Act 1855, this was also linked to the passing of 'the property' in the goods. In *Sewell* v *Burdick* (1884) 10 App Cas 74, the House of Lords held, reversing the Court of Appeal, that where bills were indorsed in blank and pledged to the bank as security for a loan, the bank did not acquire 'the' property so as to make it liable for outstanding freight. Instead it acquired only 'a special property' which did not fall within the Act. The problem of the bank's liability for charges if it took possession of the goods (which was not possible in *Sewell* v *Burdick*, as the cargo had been sold by the Russian customs for a sum which just covered duty and charges!) was solved by the process of implying a contract, usually known as a *Brandt* v *Liverpool* contract after *Brandt* v *Liverpool, Brazil and River Plate Steam Navigation Co. Ltd* [1924] 1 KB 575. Section 3 of COGSA 1992 is in substance to the same effect.

Section 3 does not spell out the position of an intermediate holder of a bill of lading (i.e., a person who having become holder subsequently transfers the bill to another) with regard to liabilities. The Court of Appeal was divided on the issue in the next case.

### *Borealis AB* v *Stargas Ltd*
### *(The Berge Sisar)*
[1998] 2 Lloyd's Rep 475 (CA)

MILLETT LJ: A bill of lading is both a document of title to goods and evidence of the contract of carriage. Before the Bills of Lading Act 1855 ('the 1855 Act') property in the goods was transferable by endorsement of the bill of lading but the contractual rights of the consignor under the contract of carriage were not. Liability for freight and other liabilities under the contract of carriage, on the other hand, were not transferable, but the consignee or final holder of the bill who took delivery of the goods was considered to be subject to such liabilities. This was not by virtue of the original contract of carriage or endorsement of the bill of lading, but by virtue of a new contract implied from his acceptance of the goods: see *Smurthwaite* v *Wilkins* (1862) 11 CB (NS) 842. The result was that the consignor remained liable under the express contract of carriage, the consignee or final holder of the bill who accepted delivery of the goods became subject to the same liabilities under a separate but implied contract, and intermediate holders of the bill of lading were not liable at all.

As appeared from the preamble to the 1855 Act, one of the purposes of the Act was to make the rights under the contract of carriage pass with the property in the goods. Section 1 of the Act provided:

> 1.   Every consignee of goods named in a bill of lading, and every endorsee of a bill of lading to whom the property in the goods therein mentioned shall pass, upon or by reason of such endorsement, shall have transferred to and vested in him all rights of suit, and be subject to the same liabilities in respect of such goods as if the contract contained in the bill of lading had been made with himself.

The section has been considered in a number of cases, most recently by the House of Lords in *Effort Shipping Co. Ltd* v *Linden Management SA* [1998] 1 Lloyd's Rep 337; [1998] 2 WLR 206. Lord Lloyd pointed out that s. 1 dealt with the rights and the liabilities under the contract of carriage differently. Whereas the rights were transferred with the property in the goods, the liabilities were not. They were vested directly in the endorsee by force of the section, not by assignment. The consignor remained liable, and the holder of the bill of lading came under the same liability as the consignor. His liability was by way of addition, not substitution.

Lord Lloyd said nothing, however, to case doubt on Chief Justice Erle's decision in *Smurthwaite* v *Wilkins* (sup.) that the 1855 Act did not work the 'most glaring injustice' of leaving the liabilities with the intermediate holder of the bill of lading after he had parted with the property in the goods. In this respect the law was unchanged by the 1855 Act. The liability of an endorsee was by way of addition to that of the consignor but by way of substitution for that of a previous endorsee. Although different mechanisms were employed in relation to the vesting of rights and liabilities, they were closely linked; it was only the consignee or endorsee who had the rights of suit who was subject to liabilities.

The 1992 Act was enacted to give effect to the Report of the Law Commission and the Scottish Law Commission 1991 on Rights of Suit in respect of Carriage of Goods by Sea (Law Com. No. 196; Scot. Law Com. No. 130) and is in the terms of the draft Bill annexed to the report. One of the main defects in the pre-existing law to which the recommendations of the Law Commissions were directed was that the rights under the contract of carriage were transferred by endorsement of the bill of lading only where the property in the goods was also transferred. The rights were not transferred if no property passed by reason of the endorsement or if the property passed independently of the endorsement. This had the beneficial consequence that banks and others holding the bill of lading by way of security could not be made liable for freight, demurrage and other charges: *Sewell* v *Burdick* (1884) 10 App Cas 74. But it also meant that they could not sue the carrier under the 1855 Act when they were enforcing their security.

The two Law Commissions recommended that the transfer of contractual rights should be separated from the passing of the property. Rights of suit should be made transferable by endorsement of the bill of lading regardless of the passage of property in the goods to which the bill related. Extension of the rights of suit in this way without more, however, would expose banks and other persons holding the bill by way of security to liability for freight, demurrage and other charges. This would reverse the decisions of the House of Lords in *Sewell* v *Burdick* (sup.) and would be commercially undesirable.

Accordingly the Commissions were compelled to reconsider the link between rights and liabilities. They rejected the extreme view that the link should be broken and opted for a solution which kept the link between rights and liabilities intact but stipulated that only the holder who enforced any rights conferred on him under the contract of carriage should be liable under the contract.

Recommendation (4) was in the following terms:

> (4)    Where the holder of a bill of lading, or any other person entitled to sue under our recommendations, takes or demands delivery of the goods, or otherwise makes a claim under the contract of carriage against the carrier, he should become subject to any contractual liabilities as if he had been a party to the contract of carriage, without prejudice to the liabilities under the contract of carriage of the original shipper.

Rights of suit are dealt with by s. 2 of the 1992 Act. Section 2(1) provides:

> (1)    Subject to the following provisions of this section, a person who becomes —
> (a) the lawful holder of a bill of lading shall (by virtue of becoming the holder of the bill . . .) have transferred to and vested in him all rights of suit under the contract of carriage as if he had been a party to that contract.

This re-enacts that part of s. 1 of the 1855 Act which dealt with rights while separating the transfer of rights of suit from the passing of the property in the goods. The important point for present purposes is that it retains the mechanism of transfer.

Section 2(1) is subject to s. 2(5) which provides:

(5)    Where rights are transferred by virtue of the operation of subsection (1) above in relation to any document, the transfer for which that subsection provides shall extinguish any entitlement to those rights which derives — (a) ... from a person's having been an original party to the contract of carriage; or (b) ... from the previous operation of that subsection ...

It may be doubted whether para. (b) is strictly necessary, since it is the inevitable consequence of the mechanism of transfer. Rights which are transferred to a transferee (and not simply vested in him without a transfer) are not retained by the transferor.

Liabilities are dealt with by s. 3. This gives effect to recommendation (4) which I have quoted above. Section 3(1) and (3) are in the following terms:

3(1)    Where subsection (1) of section 2 of this Act operates in relation to any document to which this Act applies and the person in whom rights are vested by virtue of that subsection — (a) takes or demands delivery from the carrier of any of the goods to which the document relates; (b) makes a claim under the contract of carriage against the carrier in respect of any of those goods; or (c) is a person who, at a time before those rights were vested in him, took or demanded delivery from the carrier of any of those goods, that person shall (by virtue of taking or demanding delivery or making the claim or, in a case falling within paragraph (c) above, of having the rights vested in him) become subject to the same liabilities under that contract as if he had been a party to that contract.

(3)    This section, so far as it imposes liabilities under any contract on any person, shall be without prejudice to the liabilities under the contract of any person as an original party to that contract.

The question for decision is whether the lawful holder of a bill of lading who has taken one of the steps specified in s. 3(1) in relation to any goods and afterwards endorses the bill of lading and transfers the goods to a third party is thereby discharged from liability under the contract of carriage. This question was not considered by the Law Commissions. They drew no distinction between a claim or demand for delivery of the goods, which may be withdrawn or abandoned, and actual delivery of the goods which, once taken, is irreversible.

In my opinion he is. Intermediate holders of a bill of lading remain potentially liable under the contract of carriage, and become actually liable if they take any of the steps mentioned in s. 3(1). But unless and until they take actual delivery of the goods their position is not irreversible; they may, for example, withdraw the claim or demand and endorse the bill to a third party purchaser instead. If he then demands or takes delivery of the gods it is appropriate that he should become subject to the liabilities under the contract of carriage. But there is no good reason why his liability should be additional to instead of in substitution for the liability of the previous holder of the bill; or why the latter should remain liable merely because he made a claim or demand which he has since withdrawn. The Law Commissions did not recommend the reversal of the decision in *Smurthwaite* v *Wilkins* and it was no part of the purpose of the 1992 Act to do so.

The report of the Law Commissions, and the structure of the 1992 Act, show that the provisions of paras (a), (b) and (c) of s. 3(1) are intended to limit the class of persons who are subject to liability under the contract of carriage, not to extend it. Formerly limited to holders of the bill of lading who had the property in the goods, the class is now limited to holders of the bill who take steps to enforce rights under the contract of carriage. But the class never included intermediate, that is to say previous, holders of the bill, who drop out when a later holder takes delivery. In my judgment, a holder of the bill who is entitled to the contractual rights under the contract of carriage, and who fulfils the additional conditions for liability, does not become irrevocably liable under the contract of carriage, but is in the same position as a holder for the time being of the bill was under the 1855 Act, that is to say, liable unless and until he endorses the bill to someone who also fulfils the conditions of liability.

This conclusion can be reached by a simple process. If the words which limit the class by imposing additional conditions for liability are omitted, the section reads:

> Where subsection (1) of section 2 of this Act operates in relation to any document to which this Act applies . . . that person shall . . . become subject to the same liabilities under that contract as if he had been a party to that contract.

This, in effect, re-enacts that part of s. 1 of the 1855 Act which dealt with liabilities. It employs the same mechanism of direct vesting and describes the consequences in the same terms. Likewise it contains nothing to exonerate the holder of the bill who has once become subject to liability. Yet under the 1855 Act the liability did not remain irrevocably with the holder, if he transferred the goods by endorsement it attached to the transferee in exoneration of the transferor. The position is, in my opinion, the same under the 1992 Act. Liability does not remain irrevocably with the holder of the bill who takes any of the steps mentioned in the section unless, of course, the nature of those steps precludes any further dealing with the goods. If not, and the holder endorses the bill in favour of a third party who becomes liable, the previous holder is exonerated.

It was argued that the absence of any divesting provision in s. 3 corresponding to s. 2(5) led to the opposite conclusion. But in my judgment the divestment operates automatically. Section 3(1) imposes liability only upon those holders of the bill who have contractual rights vested in them by virtue of s. 2(1). Save in the case of the original consignor, such rights are vested by transfer from the previous holder, who does not retain the rights which he is taken to have transferred (a result which is confirmed by s. 2(5) to which s. 2(1) is expressly made subject). After endorsement of the bill, the endorser no longer qualifies as a person in whom the liabilities are vested by the opening words of s. 3(1). The fact that he did so previously and at a time when he satisfied the further conditions of liability specified in s. 3(1) subjected him to liability but, in my opinion, only until he transferred the rights to a new holder.

*Notes*
1.   Schiemann LJ agreed with Millett LJ. Sir Brian Neill took the opposite view.
2.   The House of Lords has now confirmed that the shipper's liability after transfer is the same under the Bills of Lading Act 1885 as under s. 3(3) of COGSA 1992: *Effort Shipping Co.* v *Linden Management Co. (The Giannis NK)* [1998] 1 Lloyd's Rep 337.

For s. 4, see above, section 1B.

## Carriage of Goods by Sea Act 1992

### 5.   Interpretation, etc.
   (1)   In this Act—
   'Bill of lading', 'sea waybill' and 'ship's delivery order' shall be construed in accordance with section 1 above;

'the contract of carriage'—

(a)   in relation to a bill of lading or sea waybill, means the contract contained in or evidenced by that bill or waybill; and

(b)   in relation to a ship's delivery order, means the contract under or for the purposes of which the undertaking contained in the order is given;

'holder', in relation to a bill of lading, shall be construed in accordance with subsection (2) below;

'information technology' includes any computer or other technology by means of which information or other matter may be recorded or communicated without being reduced to documentary form; and

'telecommunication system' has the same meaning as in the Telecommunications Act 1984.

(2)   References in this Act to the holder of a bill of lading are references to any of the following persons, that is to say—

(a)   a person with possession of the bill who, by virtue of being the person identified in the bill, is the consignee of the goods to which the bill relates;

(b)   a person with possession of the bill as a result of the completion, by delivery of the bill, of any indorsement of the bill or, in the case of a bearer bill, of any other transfer of the bill;

(c)   a person with possession of the bill as a result of any transaction by virtue of which he would have become a holder falling within paragraph (a) or (b) above had not the transaction been effected at a time when possession of the bill no longer gave a right (as against the carrier) to possession of the goods to which the bill relates;

and a person shall be regarded for the purposes of this Act as having become a lawful holder of a bill of lading wherever he has become the holder of the bill in good faith.

(3)   References in this Act to a person's being identified in a document include reference to his being identified by a description which allows for the identity of the person in question to be varied, in accordance with the terms of the document, after its issue; and the reference in section 1(3)(b) of this Act to a document's identifying a person shall be construed accordingly.

(4)   Without prejudice to sections 2(2) and 4 above, nothing in this Act shall preclude its operation in relation to a case where the goods to which a document relates—

(a)   cease to exist after the issue of the document; or

(b)   cannot be identified (whether because they are mixed with other goods or for any other reason);

and references in this Act to the goods to which a document relates shall be construed accordingly.

(5)   The preceding provisions of this Act shall have effect without prejudice to the application, in relation to any case, of the rules (the Hague-Visby Rules) which for the time being have the force of law by virtue of section 1 of the Carriage of Goods by Sea Act 1971.

## 6.   Short title, repeal, commencement and extent

(1)   This Act may be cited as the Carriage of Goods by Sea Act 1992.

(2)   The Bills of Lading Act 1855 is hereby repealed.

(3)   This Act shall come into force at the end of the period of two months beginning with the day on which it is passed; but nothing in this Act shall have effect in relation to any document issued before the coming into force of this Act.

(4)   This Act extends to Northern Ireland.

*Notes and Questions*
1. The definition of contract of carriage follows that in COGSA 1971, s. 1(6)(a).
2. Could the holder in good faith of a forged bill of lading claim under the Act?
3. Could the original shipper either (a) be, or (b) become the lawful holder of the bill of lading?
4. For a helpful short account of the Act, see Reynolds, F.M.B., 'The Carriage of Goods by Sea Act 1992', [1993] LMCLQ 436.

# 7 THE CARRIAGE OF GOODS BY SEA ACT 1971

One of the principal functions of the contract of carriage is to determine which of the parties bears the risk of accidental damage to, or loss of, the goods during the voyage. Although this is ultimately a question of insurance, and freight calculations will take into account the incidence of liability to pay the insurance premiums, by the end of the 19th century the cargo-owning nations were becoming increasingly dissatisfied with the way the shipowning countries, such as England, allowed carriers to exclude virtually all responsibility for anything that happened to the goods during the voyage.

The first step towards a 'fairer' regime for cargo interests was taken by the US, with the enactment of the Harter Act in 1893; similar legislation followed in Australia, New Zealand and Canada before the First World War and the basic ideas were embodied in a draft set of rules by the International Law Association's Maritime Law Committee (CMI) at The Hague in 1921. These Hague Rules eventually became a draft Convention, signed at Brussels in 1924 and incorporated into English law, with minor variations, by the Carriage of Goods by Sea Act 1924.

The current COGSA 1971 came into force on 23 June 1977 and adopts the Hague Rules as amended in the 1960s and now known as the Hague-Visby Rules (after the Swedish town of Visby, where the CMI met to adopt the proposed amendments in 1963).

We will refer to the Hague-Visby Rules as 'the Rules' and to the 1924 version as 'the 1924 Hague Rules'.

## SECTION 1: THE INCORPORATION OF THE RULES INTO ENGLISH LAW

The international Convention has no binding force as such in English law and only becomes part of English law to the extent that a statute makes it so. The

1924 Act required 'every bill of lading, or similar document of title, issued in
Great Britain or Northern Ireland which contains or is evidence of any contract
to which the Rules apply . . . [to] contain an express statement that it is to have
effect subject to the provisions of the said Rules as applied by this Act' (s. 3).
Under this provision the Rules became implied terms of the contract of
carriage. COGSA 1971 adopts an entirely different approach.

## Carriage of Goods by Sea Act 1971

### 1. Application of Hague Rules as amended

(1)   In this Act, 'the Rules' means the International Convention for the unification
of certain rules of law relating to bills of lading signed at Brussels on 25 August 1924, as
amended by the Protocol signed at Brussels on 23 February 1968 [and by the protocol
signed at Brussels on 21 December 1979]

(2)   The provisions of the Rules, as set out in the Schedule to this Act, shall have the
force of law.

(3)   Without prejudice to subsection (2) above, the said provisions shall have effect
(and have the force of law) in relation to and in connection with the carriage of goods by
sea in ships where the port of shipment is a port in the United Kingdom, whether or not
the carriage is between ports in two different States within the meaning of Article X of
the Rules.

### *The Hollandia*
### [1983] 1 AC 565 (HL)

The facts are stated in section 5, below.

LORD DIPLOCK: The provisions in section 1 [(1)–(3)] . . . appear to me to be free
from any ambiguity perceptible to even the most ingenious of legal minds. The
Hague-Visby Rules, or rather all those of them that are included in the Schedule, are to
have the force of law in the United Kingdom: they are to be treated as if they were part
of directly enacted statute law. But since they form part of an international convention
which must come under the consideration of foreign as well as English courts, it is, as
Lord Macmillan said of the Hague Rules themselves in *Stag Line Ltd* v *Foscolo, Mango
and Co. Ltd* [1932] AC 328, 350:

> desirable in the interests of uniformity that their interpretation should not be rigidly
> controlled by domestic precedents of antecedent date, but rather that the language of
> the rules should be construed on broad principles of general acceptance.

They should be given a purposive rather than a narrow literalistic construction,
particularly wherever the adoption of a literalistic construction would enable the stated
purpose of the international convention, viz., the unification of domestic laws of the
contracting states relating to bills of lading, to be evaded by the use of colourable devices
that, not being expressly referred to in the Rules, are not specifically prohibited.

. . . I must return in a brief postscript to an argument based on certain passages in an
article by a distinguished commentator, Dr F.A. Mann, 'Statutes and the Conflict of
Laws' which appeared in (1972–73) 46 B.Y.I.L. 117. . . . The passages to which our
attention was directed by Counsel for the carriers I find myself (apparently in
respectable academic company) unable to accept. They draw no distinction between the

Act of 1924 and the Act of 1971 despite the contrast between the legislative techniques adopted in the two Acts, and the express inclusion in the Hague-Visby Rules of article X (absent from the Hague Rules), expressly applying the Hague-Visby Rules to every bill of lading falling within the description contained in the article, which article is given the force of law in the United Kingdom by section 1(2) of the Act of 1971. The Act of 1971 deliberately abandoned what may conveniently be termed the 'clause paramount' technique employed in section 3 of the Act of 1924 ...

*Notes*

1.   Since many of the provisions in the Rules date back to the 1924 Hague Rules (and, beyond, to the Harter Act), decisions from before 1977 are often referred to, but it is always necessary to ask whether they might be affected by the change in legislative technique.

2.   Note that s. 1(3) applies the Rules, as a matter of English law, to certain contracts which do not fall within the Convention proper: see section 2, below.

## SECTION 2: CONTRACTS TO WHICH THE RULES APPLY

In general, the Rules apply to bills of lading which (a) relate to 'contracts of carriage' as defined in Art. I, and (b) satisfy the further conditions of Art. X. They do not apply, as such, to charterparties or to non-negotiable documents such as sea waybills.

### Carriage of Goods by Sea Act 1971

SCHEDULE
THE HAGUE RULES AS AMENDED BY THE BRUSSELS PROTOCOL 1968

**Article I**

In these Rules the following words are employed, with the meanings set out below—

(a)   'Carrier' includes the owner or the charterer who enters into a contract of carriage with a shipper.

(b)   'Contract of carriage' applies only to contracts of carriage covered by a bill of lading or any similar document of title, in so far as such document relates to the carriage of goods by sea, including any bill of lading or any similar document as aforesaid issued under or pursuant to a charter party from the moment at which such bill of lading or similar document of title regulates the relations between a carrier and a holder of the same.

(c)   'Goods' includes goods, wares, merchandise, and articles of every kind whatsoever except live animals and cargo which by the contract of carriage is stated as being carried on deck and is so carried.

(d)   'Ship' means any vessel used for the carriage of goods by sea.

(e)   'Carriage of goods' covers the period from the time when the goods are loaded on to the time they are discharged from the ship.

**Article X**

The provisions of these Rules shall apply to every bill of lading relating to the carriage of goods between ports in two different States if;

(a)   the bill of lading is issued in a contracting State,
or

(b)    the carriage is from a port in a contracting State,

or

(c)    the contract contained in or evidenced by the bill of lading provides that these Rules or legislation of any State giving effect to them are to govern the contract, whatever may be the nationality of the ship, the carrier, the shipper, the consignee, or any other interested person.

*Note*

The requirement of carriage 'between ports in two different States' renders the Rules inapplicable to British coastal shipping, but s. 1(3), above, removes this limitation if the contract would otherwise fall within the Rules. (In practice, this will probably not be the case in any event, since the contract may well not provide 'for the issue of a bill of lading': see s. 1(4), in section 2A below.)

*Question*

Why is nationality irrelevant under Art. X?

*Note*

The principal issues which arise on the interpretation of these provisions are: what does 'covered by' mean, what is a 'similar' document of title, when does a contract provide that the Rules or legislation giving effect to them shall 'govern' it, and can the carrier avoid the provisions of the Rules by simply not issuing bills of lading?

*A: Covered by a bill of lading*

Can a contract of carriage be 'covered by' a bill of lading if no bill of lading has actually been issued?

### Pyrene Co. Ltd v Scindia Navigation Co. Ltd
[1954] 2 QB 402 (QBD)

P were the f.o.b. sellers of several fire tenders. They delivered the tenders to the dock for loading on to S's ship the *Jalazad*, the vessel nominated by the buyers. As one of the tenders was being lifted by the ship's tackle, and before it had crossed the ship's rail, it was dropped on to the quayside and damaged. When the bill of lading was issued in respect of the shipment, the damaged tender was deleted from it. In P's action to recover £966, the cost of repairing the tender, S admitted liability but relied on the 1924 Hague Rules to limit their liability to £200. In reply, P argued, *inter alia*, that the contract was not 'covered by' a bill of lading and that the 1924 Hague Rules were therefore inapplicable.

DEVLIN J: The next contention on behalf of the plaintiffs is that the rules are incorporated in the contract of carriage only if a bill of lading is issued. The basis for this is in the definition of article 1(b) of 'contract of carriage'; I have already quoted it, and it 'applies only to contracts of carriage covered by a bill of lading'. The use of the word 'covered' recognises the fact that the contract of carriage is always concluded before the bill of lading, which evidences its terms, is actually issued. When parties enter into a contract of carriage in the expectation that a bill of lading will be issued to cover it, they enter into it upon those terms which they know or expect the bill of lading to contain. Those terms must be in force from the inception of the contract; if it were otherwise the bill of lading would not evidence the contract but would be a variation of it. Moreover, it would be absurd to suppose that the parties intend the terms of the contract to be changed when the bill of lading is issued: for the issue of the bill of lading does not necessarily mark any stage in the development of the contract; often it is not issued till after the ship has sailed, and if there is pressure of office work on the ship's agent it may be delayed several days. In my judgment, whenever a contract of carriage is concluded, and it is contemplated that a bill of lading will, in due course, be issued in respect of it, that contract is from its creation 'covered' by a bill of lading, and is therefore from its inception a contract of carriage within the meaning of the rules and to which the rules apply. There is no English decision on this point; but I accept and follow without hesitation the reasoning of Lord President Clyde in *Harland & Wolff Ltd* v *Burns & Laird Lines Ltd* [1931] SC 722; 40 Ll L Rep 286.

*Notes*

1.  *Pyrene Co. Ltd* v *Scindia Navigation Co. Ltd* is one of the few cases in which counsel is recorded as having based an argument on the original French text of the Convention. (Unusually, in 1924 the French text was the *only* authentic version: for the Hague-Visby Rules, the English text is now also authentic, as provided by the concluding words of the Brussels Protocol of 23 February 1968.) Counsel for the plaintiffs (John Megaw QC) objected, but Devlin J allowed it, warning however that it was of limited use without expert evidence from a French lawyer. Ironically, the French text does seem, on the face of it, to support the plaintiffs' argument. Article 1(b) reads '"Contrat de transport" s'applique uniquement au contrat de transport constaté par un connaissement' and 'constaté' (literally, 'confirmed') appears to imply that the bill of lading actually exists. However, there can be little doubt that Devlin J's interpretation is not only commercially sensible, but also gives greater internal consistency to the Rules — the shipper's right to *demand* a bill of lading under Art. III, rr. 3, 7 creates a logical difficulty otherwise. Devlin J's view is also confirmed by the wording of s. 1(4): 'Subject to subsection (6) below, nothing in this section shall be taken as applying anything in the Rules to any contract for the carriage of goods by sea, unless the contract expressly or by implication provides for the issue of a bill of lading or any similar document of title.' Other European systems appear to avoid the problem by applying the equivalent rules to contracts made without a bill of lading. If there is no bill of lading, the shipper may demand one, but the absence of a bill of lading does not relieve the carrier of the responsibilities laid down in the Rules. See, for German law, Prüßmann, H/Rabe, D, *op cit*, pp. 611–612; for French law, see Rodière, R/du Pontavice, E, Droit Maritime [Maritime Law], 11th edn, Paris: Dalloz, 1991, pp. 255, 268.

2.  Although the distinction between a shipped bill and a received for shipment bill is important in some contexts (see, e.g., *Diamond Alkali Export Corporation* v *Fl. Bourgeois* [1921] 3 KB 443, per McCardie J), it is clear that

the Rules must apply to both: Art. III, r. 7 for instance assumes that there can be a contract of carriage where the bill is not a shipped bill.

*B: A similar document of title*

### Kum v Wah Tat Bank Ltd
[1971] 1 Lloyd's Rep 439 (PC)

It was established that in trade between Sarawak and Singapore the normal commercial practice was to deal with mate's receipts, marked 'non-negotiable', as equivalent to bills of lading. The Judicial Committee of the Privy Council held that the mate's receipts were not in law documents of title.

LORD DEVLIN: If the mate's receipt had been a bill of lading, the legal position would be beyond dispute. Not only is the bill of lading a document of title, but delivery of it is symbolic delivery of the goods. But the mate's receipt is not ordinarily anything more than evidence that the goods have been received on board. This is so firmly settled by *Hathesing* v *Laing* (1873) LR 17 Eq 92 and *Nippon Yusen Kaisha* v *Ramjiban Serowgee* [1938] AC 429, that the respondents have not sought to argue otherwise. Their contention is that a mate's receipt must in this case be treated as a document of title equivalent to a bill of lading by virtue of a custom in the trade in which it was issued.

. . .

Their Lordships can see no reason in principle why a document of title should not be created by local custom.

. . .

In speaking of a custom of merchants the law has not in mind merchants in the narrow sense of buyers and sellers of goods. A mercantile custom affects transactions either in a particular trade or in a particular place, such as a market or a port, and binds all those who participate in such transactions, whatever the nature of their callings. It is true that a document relating to goods carried by sea and said to be negotiated through banks could hardly be recognised as a document of title if the evidence did not show it to be treated as such by shipowners, shippers and bankers. But the limits of the custom, if it be established, are not to be defined by reference to categories of traders or professional men; if established, it binds everyone who does business in whatever capacity. To describe a custom as belonging to particular callings diverts attention from its true character which consists in its attachment to a trade or place.

Universality, as a requirement of custom, raises not a question of law but a question of fact. There must be proof in the first place that the custom is generally accepted by those who habitually do business in the trade or market concerned. Moreover, the custom must be so generally known that an outsider who makes reasonable enquiries could not fail to be made aware of it. The size of the market or the extent of the trade affected is neither here nor there. It does not matter that the custom alleged in this case applies only to part of the shipping trade within the State of Singapore, so long as the part can be ascertained with certainty, as it can here, as the carriage of goods by sea between Sarawak and Singapore.

. . . Thus the custom in this case, if proved, takes effect as part of the common law of Singapore. As such it will be applied by any Court dealing with any matter which that Court treats as governed by the law of Singapore. In this sense it is binding not only in Singapore but on anyone anywhere in the world.

The common law of Singapore is in mercantile matters the same as the common law of England, this being enacted in the Laws of Singapore (1955) cap. 24, sect. 5(1). Accordingly, the question whether the alleged custom, if proved in fact as their Lordships hold that it is, is good in law must be determined in accordance with the requirements of the English common law. These are that the custom should be certain, reasonable and not repugnant. It would be repugnant if it were inconsistent with any express term in any document it affects, whether that document be regarded as a contract or as a document of title.

In their Lordships' opinion the custom alleged is neither uncertain nor unreasonable. . . .

Up to this stage their Lordships find themselves entirely in agreement with the judgment of the Chief Justice. The factor that in the end compels them to differ from his conclusion is the presence on the mate's receipt of the words 'NOT NEGOTIABLE'.

These words are part of the printed form. Their presence on a mate's receipt which is to be used simply as such may be superfluous, but it is not incongruous. The only meaning, whether it be a popular or a legal meaning, that can be given to this marking is that the document is not to pass title by endorsement and delivery. Unfortunately businessmen frequently do not trouble themselves about such points. These documents were from the beginning of the practice, which goes back at least 40 years, handled just as if they were negotiable and transferable by endorsement. In 1959, that is, two years or less before the events which the Board is considering, a third shipping line went into the Singapore/Sarawak trade which up to then had been divided between two shipping companies. The manager of this third line, understanding that it was customary in the Sarawak trade to effect delivery on a mate's receipt, omitted the words 'not negotiable' from the top copy which was given to the shipper. There is no evidence as to what proportion of the mate's receipts subsequently in circulation was issued by this line, but it is clear that the custom had already been established entirely in relation to documents marked 'not negotiable'.

Nearly all the witnesses were asked their view of this marking. The minority, who did not treat the mate's receipt as a document of title, naturally found the marking appropriate. Those in the majority expressed their view in different words which all amounted to much the same thing — that they had never considered what the marking meant, that they paid no attention to it, that it meant nothing, that it was unimportant: and one witness said that the words had lost all significance and were purposeless. The Chief Justice found 'that everybody connected with this trade has ignored these printed words'.

The question is whether a Court of law can also ignore them. The Courts are well aware of the tendency of businessmen to retain in the documents they use inapplicable or outmoded expressions; and they endeavour, albeit with reluctance since the retention is inevitably a source of confusion — to give effect to what they take to be the true nature of the document. There are well established rules of construction which permit the Court to disregard printed words when they are inconsistent with written words or with the paramount object which the document appears from its language to be designed to achieve. But these rules can be used only when there is a conflict between one part of the document and another or between the effect of a part and the effect of the whole. They are rules for reconciling different expressions in or of the document itself. They cannot be used to introduce into the document, either by implication or by force of custom, what is outisde it. The rule is plain and clear that inconsistency with the document defeats the custom. If this document had 'Negotiable' printed in the right hand corner and 'Not negotiable' in the left, the argument could begin. But if the right-hand corner is blank, custom cannot be used to fill it. Whichever way the argument for the respondents is put, it amounts in the end to a submission that the force of custom should expel from the document words that are on it: this is not permissible by law.

*Note*
The bank succeeded on the ground that delivery of the goods to the ship made the carrier a bailee for the bank, so that delivery without production of the mate's receipts — which the bank held as security — amounted to conversion of the goods.

*C: When does the contract provide that legislation giving effect to the Rules shall 'govern'?*

### Hellenic Steel Co. v Svolamar Shipping Co. Ltd
### (The Komninos S)
### [1991] Lloyd's Rep 370 (CA)

H shipped a cargo of steel coils on S's vessel the *Komninos S* at Thessaloniki for carriage to Ravenna and Ancona. The cargo discharged at Ravenna was found to have been damaged by water. Leggatt J held that the damage was caused by unseaworthiness (inadequately cleaned holds) and negligent failure to pump the bilges during the voyage. The bills of lading contained exceptions which, if valid, relieved the shipowners of liability and provided that all disputes were 'to be referred to the British Courts'. The exceptions were void by Greek domestic law, but the Court of Appeal accepted the shipowners' submission that the proper law of the contracts was not Greek law, but English law. Under English law the exceptions were valid unless the Hague-Visby Rules applied. As Greece was not a contracting State under the Convention, neither (a) nor (b) of Art. X was satisfied. Leggatt J and the Court of Appeal held that Art. X(c) was not satisfied either, so that the Rules did not apply.

BINGHAM LJ: If, contrary to his submission, English law was the proper law of these contracts, Mr Collins argued that English law included the Hague-Visby Rules and accordingly invalidated the exemption clauses on which the shipowners relied. The Judge rejected this submission (which on his primary conclusion did not of course arise) and I agree with him.

The Hague-Visby rules were given the force of law by the Carriage of Goods by Sea Act 1971. By virtue of the Act and the Rules themselves the Rules apply (1):

> ... in relation to and in connection with the carriage of goods by sea in ships where the port of shipment is a port in the United Kingdom [s. 1(3) of the Act].

(2) without prejudice to Art. X(c) of the Rules—

> ... in relation to any bill of lading if the contract contained in or evidenced by it expressly provides that the Rules shall govern the contract [s. 1(6)(a) of the Act]

or if such express provision is contained in a non-negotiable receipt (s. 1(6)(b) of the Act); and (3):

> ... to every bill of lading relating to the carriage of goods between ports in two different States if (a) the bill of lading is issued in a contracting State, or (b) the carriage is from a port in a contracting State, or (c) the contract contained in or evidence by the bill of lading provided that these Rules or legislation of any State giving effect to them are to govern the contract, whatever may be the nationality of the ship, the carrier, the shipper, the consignee or any other interested person [Art. X of the Rules].

Since the shipment was from Greece, s. 1(3) plainly had no application. It was not suggested that these bills expressly provided that the Rules should govern the contract so as to trigger the application of s. 1(6). Greece was not a contracting state, so the bills of lading were not issued in a contracting state and the carriage was not from a port in a contracting state, and Art. X(a) and (b) accordingly had no application. There was thus no question of the United Kingdom legislation applying automatically. It had to be incorporated. So the argument centred on Art. X(c). Here again Mr Collins did not, I think, argue that the bills provided that the Rules should govern the contracts. The question was whether, assuming the choice of an English forum showed an intention that English law should govern the contracts, the bills of lading 'provided' that the legislation of the United Kingdom giving effect to the Rules should govern the contracts. Mr Collins submitted that this test was satisfied on the facts here, Mr Aikens that it was not.

The French text (which uses the expressions 'prévoit' and 'législation') gives no assistance. We were referred to no relevant English authority. Nor had the researches of Counsel unearthed any foreign authority, which if it existed would be of obvious importance in interpreting an international convention. For this purpose one must eschew any approach to interpretation peculiar to this jurisdiction. In this context it is relevant to bear in mind that in many civil law systems, as I think, much stricter rules govern incorporation by reference than are accepted here. One must also, of course, bear in mind that these bills are negotiable instruments which may bind parties remote from the original contracts. Interpreting Art. X(c) as best I can, I find it impossible to conclude that 'All dispute[s] to be referred to British Courts' amounted to a provision that the legislation of the United Kingdom giving effect to the Rules should govern the contract. The cargo-owners' insurers evidently thought otherwise or there would have been no need to seek an extension [i.e., of time for claiming]. But I see no escape from this conclusion.

The consequence of concluding, as I do, that the Hague-Visby rules were not incorporated is that the exemption clauses in the bills of lading protect the shipowners and the cargo-owners are unable to recover. Given the undoubted negligence of the shipowners' servants or agents, this is at first blush an unattractive result. I do not, however, think that in a purely commercial dispute of this kind one should strive to reflect a superficial view of the merits. The fact is that the cargo-owners contracted on terms which expressly relieved the shipowners, their master and crew, of responsibility for any act, error, neglect or default in the management, stowage, navigation or preparation of the vessel or otherwise. This judgment gives effect, for better or worse, to what the parties expressly agreed....

*Question*
What words are needed to satisfy Art. X(c)? Would it be enough to say 'the contract is governed by English law'?

*D: No bill of lading contemplated*

There are many shipments from British ports to ports in other contracting States for which the shipper does not require a bill of lading. If disposal of the goods during the course of transit is not intended, or not even practicable in the case of very short crossings, it is commercially feasible to use documents other than bills of lading to 'evidence or contain' the contract of carriage. Are the Rules excluded in this event?

### Harland & Wolff Ltd v Burns & Laird Lines Ltd
### (1931) 40 Ll L Rep 286

H & W shipped machinery made by them in Glasgow for carriage on B & L's ship *Lairdselm* to their (H & W's) ship-building yard in Belfast. The contract was for carriage 'at owner's risk' and was subject to the conditions in B & L's 'sailing bills', which excluded the shipowner's liability for unseaworthiness 'before, at, or after the commencement of the voyage'. The vessel sank on the voyage and H & W claimed damages of £50,000, alleging that the vessel was unseaworthy. The Scottish Court of Session held that the Carriage of Goods by Sea Act 1924 did not apply and that B & L were protected by the exceptions.

THE LORD PRESIDENT (LORD CLYDE): It is common ground between the parties that the contract of affreightment in this case was not a charterparty. Accordingly, in at least one view of it, the whole case turns on the question whether the defenders were 'carriers' under a 'contract of carriage' within the meaning of Art. I (Definitions (a) and (b)) of the Schedule of the Act of 1924, so as to bring them under the provisions of that Act and of the Rules in the Schedule thereto. In Art. I the expression 'contract of carriage' has assigned to it the following meaning, that is to say, it

applies *only* to contracts of carriage *covered* by a bill of lading or any similar document of title . . .

Unless this definition is to be loosely regarded in construing the Act and Schedule, the effect of it is materially to restrict the application of the Act. No bill of lading was asked, given, or (I think I may safely add) thought of, in connection with the contract of affreightment in the present case. A bill of lading is not itself a contract of affreightment or carriage. The contract of affreightment or carriage must be precedent to, or at any rate independent of, the mere fact of the shipment of the goods. The bill of lading may be, and often is, in practice, given after shipment in exchange for the 'mate's receipt', or even after the vessel has sailed. Nevertheless, it vouches and identifies the conditions of the pre-existing or independent contract, whose terms normally follow the custom of merchants in the particular trade in the course of which the shipment takes place. In this way the bill of lading 'covers' the contract of affreightment of carriage made between the shipper and the shipowner.

As appears from the correspondence above referred to, the contract of affreightment in the present case was a highly special one. It was not only not actually 'covered' by a bill of lading, but a bill of lading (as that document is known and used in the custom of merchants) was alien to its purpose. That purpose was not mercantile — for the goods were neither sold nor for sale — but was limited to the transport of the machinery, which

the pursuers had made in their Glasgow shops at Finnieston for a particular ship they were building in their Belfast yard, from Finnieston to that yard. I do not see what contractual part a bill of lading capable of being used as a document of title could have played in such a contract of affreightment, nor how the contract of carriage in this case could have been 'covered' by a bill of lading. Further, I do not think that the defenders, under the special terms of this contract, could have been required by the pursuers to undertake the responsibilities to third parties implied by giving the pursuers a bill of lading. For instance, the pursuers were to supply their own cranage at Belfast.
. . .

But the pursuers presented, in addition to this, a much wider and more important argument. They maintained that the Act, on a construction of its provisions as a whole, should be read (1) as applying to all contracts of affreightment except such as take the form of charterparties; (2) as making the issue of a bill of lading compulsory in all such contracts (with the effect of applying Rule 1 of Art. III of the Schedule to them); and (3) as admitting of no exception to its application to such contracts except that provided in Art. VI. The defenders did not dispute that, if this contention is sound, the acknowledgement which they granted after the vessel and her cargo were lost did not comply with the provisions of Art. VI in respect that it was not marked 'non-negotiable', and would not therefore give them the benefit of the exception therein provided.

The pursuers' argument is founded on the terms of Rule 3 of Art. III, and on the generality of the terms of Art. VI. It is not altogether easy to read Rule 3 of Art. III consistently with the definition of 'carrier' and 'contract of carriage' in Art. I. Applying the definition of 'carrier' in Art. I to the construction of Rule 3 of Art. III, the obligation imposed by that rule to issue a bill of lading can only come into force with reference to a contract of affreightment which is 'covered' by a bill of lading; and if the expression 'covered' necessarily implies the *prior* issue of such a bill the rule is reduced to confusion. But I doubt if this is necessarily so. Contracts of affreightment are often made by the signature of a simple freight note, or some similar mercantile writing, and may even be made without writing at all; and, in these cases, the conditions of the contract are accepted as being those which in the particular trade are subsequently incorporated in the bill of lading usual in that trade, that is to say, in the bill which, at or after shipment of the goods, the shipper becomes entitled to demand from the master or shipowner. In such cases, the contract of affreightment is truly 'covered' by that bill not necessarily issued contemporaneously with the conclusion of the contract. Notwithstanding that the bill is not issued contemporaneously with the conclusion of the contract of affreightment, it is none the less *pars negotii* and usually contains the only express formulation of the conditions of the contract. If, then, the word 'covered' may be read as including cases of this kind, the difficulty of reading Rule 3 of Art. III consistently with the definitions of the word 'carrier' and the expression 'contract of carriage' employed in it disappear; and the statute operates by requiring, in the wide class of cases referred to, that the bill of lading (which the master or shipowner is in any view bound to issue) shall contain the particulars specified in (a), (b), and (c) of Rule 3 of Art. III, and shall impose on the 'carrier' (by force of the statute) the obligations set forth in Rule I of that article. See also Rule 8. But all this has no relevancy to a contract of affreightment such as the present, in which a bill of lading plays no part and has indeed no part to play.

Apart from the specialities attending this particular contract of affreightment, there are in the coasting trade and in the trade between this country and Ireland manifold instances in which bills of lading are neither used not practicable — the conditions of carriage being those which are published in the shipowner's sailing bills. In these instances there is no 'carrier' and no 'contract of carriage' within the meaning of the Act, and, if I am right, the Act does not apply to them.

*Notes*
1.   The scope of Art. VI is considered below.
2.   The decision in *Harland & Wolff Ltd* v *Burns & Laird Lines Ltd* was followed in *Hugh Mack & Co. Ltd* v *Burns & Laird Lines Ltd* (1944) 77 Ll L Rep 377 (CA, Northern Ireland) and approved by the Privy Council in *Vita Food Products Inc.* v *Unus Shipping Co. Ltd* [1939] AC 277. In *Browner International Ltd* v *Monarch Shipping Co. Ltd (The European Enterprise)* [1989] 2 Lloyd's Rep 185, at p. 188, Steyn J said that 'shipowners, if they are in a strong enough bargaining position, can escape the application of the rules by issuing a notice to shippers that no bills of lading will be issued by them in a particular trade'.
3.   Referring to the right to demand a bill of lading under Art. III, r. 3, Wilson maintains (Wilson, J.F., *Carriage of Goods by Sea*, 3rd edn, Financial Times Management, 1998, pp. 174–5) that Art. X(b) contains a 'latent ambiguity' and suggests that 'the most logical interpretation' is to hold the Rules applicable to all outward shipment from the UK unless the shipper was not 'entitled to demand' a bill of lading or other document of title because that was 'not in accordance with the custom of a particular trade or the intention of the parties'. The suggested ambiguity disappears, however, when the words of Art. X(b) are read, as they must be, in the context of the opening lines of Art. X: there must be a 'bill of lading relating to the carriage of goods', and it is submitted that it is always open to the parties to contract on the basis that no bill of lading will be issued. The shipper will then have no right to demand a bill of lading, because the Rules will not apply anyway.

*Question*
Given the policy of the Rules against contracting out (see section 5, below), is it not paradoxical that they can be avoided altogether by a simple change of contractual document?

## SECTION 3: INCORPORATION OF THE RULES INTO OTHER DOCUMENTS

The technique of incorporating documents by reference is a familiar one in English law and there has never been any suggestion that COGSA 1971 restricts the parties' freedom in this respect. On the contrary, the Act enlarges the scope of incorporation by providing that the parties may give the full force of law to the Rules in relation to any bill of lading, including one which would not otherwise fall within the Rules, and also to non-negotiable documents.

### Carriage of Goods by Sea Act 1971

**1.   Application of Hague Rules as amended**
    (6)   Without prejudice to Article X(c) of the Rules, the Rules shall have the force of law in relation to—
        (a)   any bill of lading if the contract contained in or evidenced by it expressly provides that the Rules shall govern the contract, and

(b) any receipt which is a non-negotiable document marked as such if the contract contained in or evidenced by it is a contract for the carriage of goods by sea which expressly provides that the Rules are to govern the contract as if the receipt were a bill of lading,

but subject, where paragraph (b) applies, to any necessary modifications and in particular with the omission in Article III of the Rules of the second sentence of paragraph 4 and of paragraph 7.

*Note*

If a non-negotiable transport document states that the Rules 'shall apply', is that enough to satisfy s. 1(6)(b)? The authorities are conflicting.

## *McCarren & Co. Ltd v Humber International Transport Ltd and Truckline Ferries (Poole) Ltd (The Vechscroon)*
### [1982] 1 Lloyd's Rep 301

LLOYD J: This case arises out of the carriage of 293 sides of pork from Poole to Cherbourg in January 1978, on a vessel called *Vechscroon* under a document described as a commercial vehicle movement order.

The facts, told briefly, are that the vehicle in which the goods were being carried on board the vessel overturned in the course of the voyage. The vehicle was refrigerated. The refrigeration had to be turned off in order to minimise the risk of fire. A a result when the goods reached Cherbourg they were condemned. McCarren & Co. were the owners of the goods. They claimed against the defendants, Humber International Transport Services Ltd, under a through contract of carriage for the goods from Ireland to Paris. The defendants have settled the plaintiffs' claim for £15,000 plus costs. The defendants now seek to recover that sum from the third parties, Truckline Ferries (Poole) Ltd as owners of the vessel.

. . .

Clause 1 to 3 of the conditions of carriage read as follows:

1.   The terms, exceptions and immunities contained in the Brussels International Convention of the 25th August 1924 and any subsequent amendment thereto shall apply to this contract subject as hereinafter mentioned and with the exception that no bill of lading shall be issued it being agreed by the parties hereto that the provisions of Article VI of the said Convention are applicable to this transaction.

2.   Any vehicle and/or trailer and/or flat and/or container attached to the vehicle and goods loaded therein or thereon shall be deemed for all purposes to constitute, including the carrier's limitation of liability, one package or unit.

3.   The sea-carrier's liability is limited to F.2,000 per package or unit whether or not any value in excess of these sums be stated in this document or otherwise declared to the sea-carrier, his agent or the master of the vessel.

It is not disputed that the Hague-Visby Rules — that is to say, the rules as amended by the Protocol signed at Brussels on Feb. 23, 1968 — were an amendment to the International Convention signed at Brussels on Aug. 25, 1924. The 1971 Act came into force on June 23, 1977, which was some six months before the contract of carriage was made in this case and before the commercial vehicle movement order was issued. It is clear, therefore, that when cl. 1 of the conditions of carriage refers to 'the Brussels

Convention and any subsequent amendment thereto', it is referring to the rules as amended in 1968 and as scheduled to the 1971 Act.

Having held that the defendants' claim against the third party was, by virtue of Art. III, r. 6 (below, section 9), not time barred, although proceedings had not been commenced within one year of delivery, his Lordship continued:

The question whether the third parties are entitled to rely on the limit of F.2,000 per package or unit as set out in cl. 3 of the conditions of carriage is much more difficult. Mr Gee conceded in the course of his argument that that limit should be read as if it were F.10,000 per package or unit not F.2,000, for reasons which I need not go into; for they do not affect the point which I have to decide. It is only if the defendants can rely on the alternative limitation based on weight introduced for the first time by the Hague-Visby Rules that they can recover more than a very small proportion of their loss in this case. Whereas under the old Art. IV, r. 5 there was a single limit per package or unit, the amended Art. IV, r. 5 provides:

> ... neither the carrier nor the ship shall in any event be or become liable for any loss or damage to or in connection with the goods in an amount exceeding the equivalent of 10,000 francs per package or unit or 30 francs per kilo of gross weight of the goods lost or damaged, whichever is the higher.

The goods in the present case weighed 17,601 kilos. The limit based on that weight works out at £23,585, which is well in excess of the defendants' loss, whereas the unit or package limitation is very much less. The question for decision, therefore, is whether the weight limitation introduced by the amended Art. IV, r. 5 of the Hague-Visby Rules and incorporated by cl. 1 of the conditions of carriage overrides the package or unit limitation set out in cl. 3 of the conditions of carriage.

...

Mr Malins' argument was simple. He submitted that the commercial vehicle movement order is a non-negotiable receipt marked as such. It provides, by cl. 1 of the conditions of carriage printed on the back, that the rules are to govern. That can only mean the Hague-Visby Rules. Accordingly, the Hague-Visby Rules have the force of law by virtue of s. 1(6)(b) of the 1971 Act, and insofar as cl. 3 of the conditions of carriage purports to lessen the third parties' liability it is void under Art. III, r. 8.

Mr Gee had two answers to that simple argument. First, he draws attention to the words 'as if the receipt were a bill of lading'. Even if a non-negotiable receipt expressly provides that the rules are to govern, nevertheless if the words that I have just mentioned are omitted, the rules do not have the force of law. Since there is no mention in cl. 1 of the conditions of carriage that the rules are to govern the contract 'as if the receipt were a bill of lading', the rules can have no more than contractual force.

I cannot accept that argument. I can think of no sensible reason why Parliament should have intended to draw any distinction between a document which says 'this non-negotiable receipt shall be governed by the Hague-Visby Rules' and a document which says this non-negotiable receipt shall be governed by the Hague-Visby rules as if it were a bill of lading'; neither could Mr Gee.

He rightly referred to a learned and influential article by Mr Anthony Diamond QC, on the Hague-Visby Rules, which appears in Lloyd's Maritime and Commercial Law Quarterly for May 1978, at p. 225. At p. 261 Mr Diamond is dealing with the non-negotiable receipt and he says this:

It is moreover curious to note as another limiting factor the paramount clause must by section 1(6)(b) state that the Rules are to govern as if the receipt were a bill of lading. If those words are missing from the paramount clause, is the application of the Rules to be statutory or only contractual? The answer would seem to be the latter.

With great respect to Mr Diamond, I would take the opposite view. It seems to me that the purpose of the words is, as Mr Malins submitted, quite simply to equate non-negotiable receipts, which are expressly governed by the rules, with bills of lading which are expressly governed by the rules. Since non-negotiable receipts are never mentioned as such in the amended rules, it was natural, though not perhaps strictly necessary, to include the words I have mentioned in s. 1(6)(b). Obviously there was no need to include the words in s. 1(6)(a). Otherwise I can see no difference between the two paragraphs. I would hold that their effect is, and was intended to be, the same.
...

I find I get no real assistance in the construction of cl. 1 of the conditions of carriage by the reference in that clause to Art. VI. In the end, it seems to me, the case comes back to the single question: does cl. 1 of the conditions of carriage expressly provide that the rules are to *govern* this contract? I have come to the conclusion that the answer is 'Yes', despite the words 'subject as hereinafter mentioned'. I note that these words are themselves not altogether clear, although I am prepared to assume that they are to be taken as meaning 'subject to the remaining clauses of these Conditions of Carriage'. Even so, it seems to me that the contract is, as a whole, *governed* by the rules. The language of s. 1(6)(b) of the 1971 Act is perfectly general. It does not provide that the contract must be exclusively governed by the rules for the rules to have the force of law. Nor does it provide that the contract is to be governed by the rules without condition or qualification. It is not a case, as was suggested in argument, of the rules, the whole rules and nothing but the rules. Mr Gee submitted that the only function of the rules in the present contract was, as it were, to fill in the gaps left by the other clauses in the conditions of carriage. I do not think that can be right. As a matter of ordinary language I would hold that the contract was expressly governed by the rules and that, as a consequence, the rules have the force of law by virtue of s. 1(6)(b) of the Act.

## *Browner International Ltd* v *Monarch Shipping Co. Ltd*
### *(The European Enterprise)*
### [1989] 2 Lloyd's Rep 185 (QBD)

STEYN J: This matter raises questions of pure law regarding the interpretation of the Carriage of Goods by Sea Act 1971, and the Hague-Visby Rules, which are set out in a schedule to the Act. The first point relates to the proper construction of s. 1(6)(b) of the Carriage of Goods by Sea Act 1971. The second involves the correct interpretation of Art. IV, r. 5(c) [*sic*: but r. 5(e) is clearly meant], of the Hague-Visby Rules.

The briefest outline of the background will be sufficient. The plaintiffs are freight hauliers, and they used a refrigerated tractor and trailer unit ('the goods') in their business. In January 1985 the plaintiffs agreed to carry a consignment of meat from Cork to inland destinations in France. In order to carry out their obligations under the agreement with plaintiffs entered into a contract of carriage with the defendants, the owners of the ferry *European Enterprise*, in terms of which the defendants agreed to carry the goods from Dover to Calais. On Jan. 6, 1985 the goods were embarked on the vessel. The goods were loaded on the upper deck of the vessel. At 18 00 hours that day during heavy weather the vessel entered Calais harbour. The goods overturned and sustained damage.

It is the invariable practice of all English cross channel operators not to issue bills of lading for the cross channel Ro-Ro ferry trade. Instead, they issue commercial non-negotiable receipts. That is what happened in the present case. The goods were carried by the defendants under a contract contained in or evidenced by the defendants' consignment note/waybill which was signed at Dover on Jan. 6, 1985. Paragraph 3, in so far as it is relevant, of the conditions of the consignment note/waybill, reads as follows:

> The good are received loaded stowed carried discharged and otherwise handled and kept by the Carrier under and subject to:— (a) the Rules (commonly known as the Hague-Visby Rules and hereinafter called 'the Rules') set out in the Schedule to the Carriers [sic] of Goods by Sea Act 1971, save as follows:— (i) each vehicle (whether consisting of a single unit, an articulated unit or a trailer or semi trailer) together with any container(s) flat(s) pallet(s) package(s) or other equipment and together with their respective contents (if any) shall be deemed to be one package or unit for the purposes of Art. IV, para. 5(a) of the Rules; (ii) the Carrier shall be entitled to limit its liability to 10,000 frs. per package or unit, and par. 5(a) shall be read as though the words 'or 30 frs. per kilo of gross weight of the goods lost or damaged, whichever is the higher' were deleted; (iii) the value of a franc shall be as defined in the Sterling Equivalents Order made by the Secretary of State pursuant to Sec. 1(5) of the Carriage of Goods by Sea Act 1971 in force at the time the loss or damage occurs; (iv) Art. IV, para. 5(c) [sic] of the Rules shall be deleted.

Paragraph 3 of the condition of carriage therefore purports to replace the limitation provision under Art. IV, r. 5, of the Hague-Visby Rules, with the substantially less generous limitation provisions under para. 3. To this extent it purports to lessen the carrier's liability as provided in the Hague-Visby Rules.

The defendants have admitted liability under Art. III, r. 2, of the Hague-Visby Rules. That is of course, a reference to the provision that—

> ... the carrier shall properly and carefully load, handle, stow, carry, keep, care for and discharge the goods carried.

If the defendants are entitled to limit their liability, under their conditions of carriage, it is agreed the plaintiffs are entitled to judgment only in the sum of £566.03 (exclusive of interest and costs). If the defendants are not entitled to limit their liability, it is agreed the plaintiffs are entitled to judgment in the sum of IR£32,673.99 and £1,117.79 (exclusive of interest and costs).

...

The defendants contend that they can limit their liability under par. 3(a)(i)–(iv) of their conditions of carriage. The plaintiffs contend that the defendants cannot so limit their liability because the Hague-Visby Rules have statutory force in relation to this contract and par. 3, in so far as it lessens the defendants' liability, is void under Art. III, r. 8, of the Hague-Visby Rules. Article III, r. 8, renders null and void and of no effect inter alia any clause in the contract of carriage relieving the carrier of liability under Art. III, r. 2, or lessening liability under it. The issue turns on whether the Hague-Visby Rules were incorporated as a matter of contract (as the defendants contend) or have the force of law (as the plaintiffs contend).

The Hague-Visby Rules are set out in a schedule to the 1971 Act. Section 1(2) of the 1971 Act provides that the rules shall have the force of law. In this context 'force of law' means more than enforceable at law as a matter of contract: it denotes mandatory statutory force. Section 1(3) reads as follows:

Without prejudice to subsection (2) above, the said provisions shall have effect (and have the force of law) in relation to and in connection with the carriage of goods by sea in ships where the port of shipment is a port in the United Kingdom, whether or not the carriage as between ports in two different States within the meaning of Article X of the Rules.

Section 1(4) provides as follows:

(4)   Subject to subsection (6) below, nothing in this section shall be taken as applying anything in the Rules to any contract for the carriage of goods by sea, unless the contract expressly or by implication provides for the issue of a bill of lading or any similar document of title.

This provision is in line with the definition of 'contract of carriage' in Art. 1 of the rules as applying only to contracts of carriage 'covered by a bill of lading or any similar document of title'. The primary statutory (as opposed to consensual) application of the 1971 Act is therefore so restricted. And in the present case the contract expressly provided that no bill of lading would be issued. The consignment note is described as a non-negotiable receipt note, which is not a document of title.

The only gateway to the statutory application of the rules is therefore s. 1(6)(b) of the 1971 Act....

The plaintiffs argue that the receipt in the present case fulfils the requirements of s. 1(6)(b), and that the rules therefore have the force of law. The defendants contend that the receipt fails to conform to the requirements of s. 6(b) in two material respects, namely — (a) the receipt does not expressly provide that the rules are to govern the contract *as if the receipt were a bill of lading*; (b) the receipt does not provide that the 'Rules' are to govern the contract but in effect provides for a partial incorporation of the 'Rules'. These submissions run counter to the judgment of Mr Justice Lloyd (now Lord Justice Lloyd) in *The Vechscroon* [1982] 1 Lloyd's Rep 301 to which I will have to turn in some detail. I have, however, been invited not to follow that decision. In the absence of binding authority, and in the light of full argument challenging the reasoning in *The Vechscroon*, I am obliged to reconsider the issues afresh.

Mr Anthony Diamond QC, who appeared on behalf of the defendants, emphasised the juridical status of a receipt which complies with the requirements of s. 1(6)(b) of the 1971 Act. Article 1(b) of the amended Convention defines 'contract of carriage' as applying only to 'contracts of carriage covered by a bill of lading or any other similar documents of title'. This refers to a contract under the terms of which the shipper is *entitled* at or after shipment to demand a bill of lading. See *Harland & Wolf* v *Burns & Laird* (1931) 40 Ll L Rep 286. Moreover s. 1(4) of the 1971 Act makes clear that, subject to s. 1(6), the Act does not apply to shipments where the shipper has no right to demand a bill of lading or other document of title. Section 1(6) is therefore dealing with a situation when a carrier *voluntarily* incorporates a clause into a non-negotiable receipt which provides that the rules are to govern the contract. The effect of s. 1(6) was neatly summarised in *The Hollandia* (sub nom *The Morviken*), [1982] 2 Lloyd's Rep 325 at p. 330, col. 1; [1982] 1 QB 872 at p. 885G, by Sir Sebag Shaw in the following terms:

The consensual tie is reinforced by this provision which, in effect, confers on the primary contractual bond a statutory binding character.

This is the substance of the legal analysis which Mr Diamond placed before me. While the correctness of the analysis was not conceded, the cornerstone of it, viz the clear terms of s. 1(4), proved an insurmountable obstacle to any effective challenge to it. In my judgment it is clearly correct to approach the issues to the interpretation of s. 1(6)(b) on the basis that the purpose of the sub-section was to confer on a voluntary contractual tie a statutory binding character. It follows that shipowners, if they are in a strong enough bargaining position, can escape the application of the rules by issuing a notice to shippers that no bills of lading will be issued by them in a particular trade. Subject to the limited restriction introduced by the Unfair Contract Terms Act 1977 in favour of carriage for consumers (as to which see ss. 2(2), 12 and Schedule 1, par. 2(c)), the position is that freedom of contract prevails. Section 1(6)(b) can only be activated by contracting into the statutory regime in the appropriate contractual form. This is an inevitable result of the structure of the 1971 Act. Against this background I now turn to the two grounds on which the defendants contend that the non-negotiable receipt in the present case does not meet the requirements of s. 1(6).

(a) *The omission of the words 'as if the receipt were a bill of lading'*: The words 'as if the receipt were a bill of lading' do not appear in the receipt in the present case. Prima facie s. 1(6)(b) can only apply if the receipt expressly provides that 'the Rules are to govern the contract as *if the receipt were a bill of lading*' or contains similar wording. Mr Simon, who appeared for the plaintiffs, argued that the words 'as if the receipt were a bill of lading' are words of supposition dealing with the effect of the express terms, and are not a formal requirement. It is therefore sufficient, he submits, that par. 3(a) of the receipt states that the goods are carried 'subject to the rules'. He suggested that s. 1(6)(b) should be read as if a comma appeared immediately before the words 'as if the receipt were a bill of lading'. The fact is, however, that there is no comma. And this interpretation treats the words in question as devoid of legislative effect. The correct interpretation seems to me that the legislature laid down two formal requirements, viz (a) that the receipt, which is a non-negotiable document, must be marked as such and (b) that the contract must expressly provide that the rules are to govern the contract as if the receipt were a bill of lading. Only if these formal requirements are fulfilled, does s. 1(6)(b) confer on a voluntary contractual tie the statutory force which is ordinarily only applicable in the case of bills of lading. This is an interpretation which is supported by commentators in two important articles: See M.J. Mustill QC, The Carriage of Goods by Sea Act 1971, Art. IV for Sjorett, vol II, issue 4–5, 1972, at p. 697; A. Diamond QC, The Hague-Visby Rules, (1978) 2 LMCLQ, at p. 37. (It is only right that I should add that I expressly invited Mr Diamond to refer me to his article which, if I may say so, is a seminal work.) This view is also supported by the editors of the last two editions of *Scrutton on Charterparties*: 18th ed. (1974), at p. 452; 19th edn. (1984) pp. 415–16. Indeed, a cryptic reference to *The Vechscroon* in the latest edition of this work (at pp. 415–16) reveals that the editors were not persuaded by Mr Justice Lloyd's contrary view. This body of opinion therefore reinforces the view already expressed.

... Reluctantly, I have come to the conclusion that I must differ from Mr Justice Lloyd on this point. It seems to me that I have had the benefit of fuller argument, and that I must give effect to my opposite view. A significant factor not argued before Mr Justice Lloyd is the fact that the purpose of s. 1(6)(b) was to confer on a voluntary consensual tie a statutory binding character. That affords an explanation for the formal requirements of s. 1(6)(b), which were no doubt designed to bring clearly to the mind of parties what documents will attract the statutory regime ordinarily reserved for bills of lading or similar documents of title. In any event s. 1(6)(a) and (b) require different express provisions, and there seems no warrant as a matter of ordinary language to treat the additional words 'as if the receipt were a bill of lading' as having no legislative force. For these reasons I decline to follow *The Vechscroon*, and I rule that the receipt in this case fails to comply with s. 1(6)(b).

(b) *Does a partial incorporation of the rules result in the statutory application of all the rules?* In the present case the non-negotiable receipt does not incorporate the rules en bloc. Mr Simon emphasised that cl. 3(a) of the contract states the goods are carried 'subject to the rules'. In his submission that is sufficient. But para. 3(a) then carves out of the scope of the incorporating clause important exceptions. Is it still correct to say that the contract provides that 'the Rules' are to govern the contract? This question was also considered by Mr Justice Lloyd in *The Vechscroon*. And Mr Simon adopted the reasoning of Mr Justice Lloyd.... For my part I would say that the ordinary meaning of the statute is contrary to this construction. Section 1(6) stipulates on any view that as a formal requirement the contract must expressly provide that the 'Rules' are to govern the contract. 'The Rules' are by s. 1(1) defined as—

> ... the International Convention for the unification of certain rules of law relating to bills of lading signed at Brussels on 25th August 1924, as amended by the Protocol signed at Brussels on 23rd February 1968, and by the Protocol signed at Brussels on December 21st, 1979.

Prima facie therefore it is only when the receipt expressly provides that the whole Convention, as amended by the Protocol, is to govern the contract, that s. 1(6)(b) comes into operation. And that initial impression is reinforced by the consideration that the Convention, as amended by the Protocol, is a pragmatic but coherent compromise between shipowning interests and cargo interests. It is to be viewed as an integrated package. This consideration makes it difficult to treat a provision to the effect that 'the Rules shall apply save for the following Rules which are deleted ...' as complying with the requirement of s. 1(6)(b) of an express provision that the 'rules' are to govern. And Mr Simon was unable to suggest any test, let alone a test with a statutory foundation, for deciding what degree of incorporation will be sufficient. Leaving aside de minimis arguments, it seems to me that any test designed to decide which partial incorporations of the rules will or will not be sufficient will in practice be unworkable.

But there is yet another reason of substance militating against the plaintiffs' submissions. Mr Diamond said, and I agree, that it would be curious if a voluntary paramount clause, which effected only a partial incorporation of the rules, had the result that a statutory binding character was given to *all* the rules, even when there was no primary contractual bond. It must be right that in enacting s. 1(6)(b) the legislation did not intend to override the agreement of the parties when the parties had freedom of choice whether or not to incorporate the rules into their contract.

For all these reasons, and not following *The Vechscroon*, I rule that in relation to the present contract the partial incorporation of the rules did not comply with s. 1(6)(b)....

## Question

Which of the alternative interpretations of s. 1(6)(b) gives better effect to the intention of the parties?

## Notes

1. Where the Rules apply to a contract by virtue of s. 1(6), the normal exclusion of deck cargo and live animals does not apply: see s. 1(7), section 10, below.

2. The Rules, or one of the many enactments around the world giving effect to them, are often incorporated consensually not only into bills of lading, but

also into charterparties. This can create serious problems of interpretation unless great care is taken with the drafting.

### Adamastos Shipping Co. Ltd v Anglo-Saxon Petroleum Co. Ltd
### [1959] AC 133 (HL)

The respondent oil company chartered the appellants' tanker for 18 months' consecutive voyages. A typed slip was attached to the charterparty, reading:

'Paramount clause. This bill of lading shall have effect subject to the Carriage of Goods by Sea Act of the United States ... 1936, which shall be deemed to be incorporated herein, and nothing herein contained shall be deemed a surrender by the carrier of any of its rights or immunities or an increase of any of its responsibilities or liabilities under said Act. If any term of this bill of lading be repugnant to said Act to any extent, such term shall be void to that extent, but no further.

The United States Act states that its provisions are not applicable to charterparties. Moreover, it applies only to cargo-carrying voyages to and from United States ports. It requires the carrier to exercise due diligence to make the ship seaworthy before and at the beginning of the voyage. Clause 1 of the charterparty contained an unqualified undertaking by the shipowner that the tanker was, and would be maintained, in a seaworthy state, 'tight, staunch and strong and every way fitted for the voyage'. Following a series of breakdowns it was necessary to determine whether the finding that the shipowners had exercised due diligence provided a defence (a) in relation to US port cargo-carrying voyages, and (b) in relation to other voyages. Devlin J held that the United States Act was incorporated into the charterparty, but did not apply to non-cargo carrying voyages. The Court of Appeal held that the Act was not incorporated. The House of Lords allowed the shipowners' appeal and held the United States Act to be incorporated. They also held, Lord Morton of Henryton and Lord Reid dissenting, that the provisions of the Act extended to all voyages under the charterparty.

VISCOUNT SIMONDS: ... [A] broadside attack was made upon the owners' claim to rely on the paramount clause. In the context of this charterparty, it was said, the clause is insensible and must be rejected. It opens with the words 'This bill of lading', and it purports to incorporate the provisions of an Act of the United States which itself enacts that it shall not apply to charterparties. It is therefore ex facie inapplicable to this charterparty. My Lords, I must confess that this is to me an attractive approach and I would willingly adopt it. For it is not agreeable to find a business transaction of some importance carried through in a manner which Devlin J, as I think, too indulgently described as 'slapdash'. But I do not think that I can do so. I can entertain no doubt that the parties, when they agreed by clause 52 of the charter that the 'paramount clause ... as attached' should be incorporated in their agreement, and proceeded physically to attach the clause which I have set out, had a common meaning and intention which compels me to regard to opening words 'This bill of lading', as a conspicuous example of the maxim 'falsa demonstratio non nocet cum de corpore constat'. There can be no doubt what is the corpus. It is the charterparty to which the clause is attached. Nor, pursuing this main line of attack, can I be driven to a wholesale rejection of the clause because the Act, whose provisions are in turn deemed to be incorporated, itself enacts that its provisions shall not apply to charterparties. I cannot attribute to either party an intention to incorporate a provision which would nullify the total incorporation.

My Lords, I should have come to this conclusion without the aid of any external circumstance. But I am confirmed in it by the notorious fact, to which both the learned judge and the editors of the 16th edition of Scrutton on Charterparties refer, that the parties to a charterparty often wish to incorporate the Hague Rules in their agreement: and by that I do not mean, nor do they mean, that they wish to incorporate the ipsissima verba of those rules. They wish to import into the contractual relation between owners and charterers the same standard of obligation, liability, right and immunity as under the rules subsists between carrier and shipper: in other words, they agree to impose upon the owners, in regard, for instance, to the seaworthiness of the chartered vessel, an obligation to use due diligence in place of the absolute obligation which would otherwise lie upon them.

Here, then, my Lords, is the agreement that the parties have made, an original printed document with sundry erasures and typed additions, a complex of attached clauses and an Act of the United States of America whose provisions are deemed to be incorporated. How shall it be construed? The same sort of problem has arisen before, and I agree with Devlin J that the procedure should be followed here which was laid down in *Hamilton & Co.* v *Mackie & Sons* (1889) 5 TLR 677, and approved in this House in *T.W. Thomas & Co. Ltd* v *Portsea Steamship Co. Ltd* [1912] AC 1.... It is obvious that there is much in the Act which in relation to this charterparty is insensible, or, as I would rather say, inapplicable, and must be disregarded. But in regard to the matters with which the questions now to be answered are concerned there has been acute controversy.

First, the Act, being an Act of the United States, is geographically confined to its own jurisdictional limits.... Therefore, it is said, let it be granted that the incorporation of the Act is not altogether insensible, and that the statutory standard of obligation is contractually imported into the charterparty. Yet why should it extend beyond the limits prescribed by the Act itself? Why should it apply to any other voyages than those to or from ports of the United States? I do not think that there is a clearer answer to this question than that given by the learned judge. The contract between the parties is of worldwide scope: the area of State jurisdiction is necessarily limited, and, because it is limited, the Act is given a restricted operation. No reason has been suggested, nor, as for as I am aware, could be suggested, why a similar restriction should be imported into the contract. On the contrary, to do so would from the commercial point of view make nonsense of it. I find it easy, therefore, as did the learned judge, to construe this contract as making the substituted standard of obligation coterminous with the enterprise.

The second and perhaps more difficult question relates to the non-cargo carrying voyages. The learned judge, though he felt the weight of the argument to the contrary, decided that to such voyages the express warranty of seaworthiness in clause 1 of the charterparty must apply. It is with great diffidence that I come to the opposite conclusion.
. . .

My Lords, it is, I think, permissible in a consideration of this commercial transaction to ask what possible difference it makes to the charterers whether the delay, to which their loss is due, occurs when the ship is in ballast or is loaded with a cargo of oil or of water. It matters not for this purpose whether the charterparty was for a single voyage, as the original document seemed to contemplate, or for a number of consecutive voyages. The contractual subject-matter was the whole period during which the vessel was under charter, and it is, in my opinion, to this whole period that the parties agreed that the statutory standard of obligation and immunity should relate. I think that the learned judge might have come to the same conclusion but for the fact that he thought that it might lead to an unreasonable and unnecessary burden being placed upon the owner. For it appeared to him that it would or might impose upon him an obligation under s. 3(1)(c) of the incorporated Act to exercise due diligence to 'Make the holds, refrigerating and cooling chambers, and all other parts of the ship in which goods are carried, fit and safe for their reception, carriage, and preservation' even at a time when the vessel was leaving in ballast for her port of loading. I do not feel myself qualified, in the absence of any evidence, to say how serious a burden this would be. But I would, with great respect, doubt whether the obligation under s. 3(1)(c) arises until the vessel arrives at the port of loading, though it may be convenient substantially to perform it at an earlier stage. I do not, in any case, find in this consideration a sufficient counterweight to the fact that from a commercial point of view it is unlikely that owner and charterer will adopt a shifting standard of obligation between cargo carrying and non-cargo carrying voyages. It does not appear to me that the fact that voyage charterparties often contain a cesser clause offers a useful analogy.

Upon this part of the case it was further argued that non-cargo carrying voyages could not be brought within the scope of the diminished obligation because the Act is an Act dealing with the carriage of goods by sea under bills of lading, and in almost every section deals with obligations, liabilities, rights and immunities in respect of goods so carried. Therefore, it was said, the incorporated provisions could have no application to a voyage in which no goods were carried. But this seems to me merely to restate the problem in other words. The question remains what is the meaning and effect of a commercial agreement which contemplates voyages with or without cargo and introduces by reference to the United States Act a qualified standard of obligation. I have already stated my opinion and would only add that I find it difficult upon a broad consideration of the case to make any distinction between non-cargo carrying voyages and voyages to or from other than United States ports. A narrow interpretation would exclude, a generous one include, both of them in the substituted standard of obligation.
. . .

My Lords, this has not been an easy case to decide. Of that the difference of opinion in the courts below of learned judges well versed in this branch of the law is proof enough. Lord Bramwell, in a phrase which the learned editors of *Scrutton on Charterparties*, 16th ed., at p. 186, have done well to preserve, described a certain class of case as 'cases where no principle of law is involved, but only the meaning of careless and slovenly documents'. This is such a case. No doubt there are rules or canons of construction applicable to careless and slovenly, as to other, documents. I have tried to apply them, resolute, on the one hand, to construe commercial agreements broadly and not to be astute to find defects in them or reject them as meaningless and, on the other, not to make a contract for the parties which they have not thought fit to make for themselves. Nor have I forgotten that it is only by sufficiently clear words that an exception to an obligation (whether arising at common law or under the contract itself) can be established: see *Glynn v Margetson & Co.* [1893] AC 351; 9 TLR 437, *Nelson Line (Liverpool) Ltd v James Nelson & Sons Ltd* [1908] AC 16; 24 TLR 114, *Hillas & Co. Ltd v Arcos Ltd* (1932) 147 LT 503, *Petrofina SA of Brussels v Compagnia Italiana Trasporto Olii Minerali of Genoa* (1937) 53 TLR 650 and *Golodetz v Kersten, Hunik & Co.* (1926) 24 Ll L Rep 374 the last-named case being a particularly interesting example of the way in which the court will strive to give a sensible effect to a commercial document. These, no doubt, are the familiar principles applied by the Court of Appeal from whose conclusions I reluctantly differ. I think that the point of difference lies in this, that, looking at the documents as a whole and bearing in mind what the learned judge described as 'a general practice, well known to those sitting and practising in this court', I have no difficulty in seeing the broad purpose and intent of the parties. I must reject, if I can, the unattractive argument urged by the charterers through their counsel that the agreement to which they put their hands meant nothing at all. It is true that at a certain stage it was suggested that the paramount clause was intended to refer to bills of lading issued under the charterparty, but this suggestion has been rightly rejected for the conclusive reasons given by Parker LJ. If it did not mean that but did mean something, what did it mean? I think the parties intended, as I have already said, to introduce as a term governing their relationship as owners and charterers the limited measure of responsibility prescribed by the American Act. This seems to me so plain that I should properly be regarded as unduly astute if I turned my eye away from it. If this initial step is taken, it does not seem to me difficult to make commercial sense of the agreement, though I would not dissent from Parker LJ's description of it as a 'jumble of provisions'.

*Notes and Question*

1. The decision in *Adamastos Shipping Co. Ltd* v *Anglo-Saxon Petroleum Co. Ltd* was applied by the Court of Appeal in *Seven Seas Transportation Ltd* v *Pacifico Union Marina Corporation (The Satya Kailash and Ocean Amity)* [1984] 1 Lloyd's Rep 586, to give the shipowner the benefit of the immunities in the United States statute in respect of negligent navigation off the Indian port of Tuticorin which caused damage to the charterers' own vessel, the *Ocean Amity*. (The chartered ship was employed to lighten the *Ocean Amity* to enable her to enter the port.)

2. In *Noranda Inc.* v *Barton (Time Charter) Ltd (The Marinor)* [1996] 1 Lloyd's Rep 301 (QBD), Colman J said (at pp. 310–311) 'If the effect of incorporation of the rules by general words is to enable the shipowner to rely on the protection of Art. IV to the extent enunciated in *Adamastos* and *The Satya Kailash*, then there can, in my judgment, be no reason in principle why the protection provided to the shipowner by Art. III, r. 6 should not apply to an equally broad spectrum of claims, provided always that it is possible to identify a date when goods sufficiently relevant to the claim were delivered or should have been delivered. To restrict claims covered by the Art. III, r. 6 protection to those based on a factual foundation which would involve a breach by the owners of their obligations as carriers under the rules in the context of a bill of lading contract would be inconsistent with the reasoning in those two cases. Thus liability 'in respect of goods' (the words of Art. III, r. 6) is not to be construed in the context of a periodic time charter as meaning a liability arising from facts which found a claim by a cargo-owner under the Hague or Hague-Visby Rules in the context of a bill of lading contract but rather as meaning a liability based on facts involving a particular cargo or intended cargo and, in the absence of physical loss or damage, sufficiently closely involving that cargo for it to be said that the financial loss sustained was referable to what was done with that cargo or was directly associated with it.

Accordingly, the approach which in my judgment, is established by the authorities which I have considered is that where there is incorporation by general words into a time charter of legislation enacting the Hague Rules or Hague-Visby Rules, the shipowners will be entitled to rely on the protection of the time bar against claims for breach of any of the terms of the charter, even if not co-extensive with obligations under the rules, provided that (i) those claims assert (a) a liability involving physical loss of or damage to goods or (b) a liability for financial loss sustained in relation to goods and (ii) the goods in question were either shipped or were intended to be shipped pursuant to the charter.'

3.  Clause 13 of a charterparty reads: 'The provisions of Art. III of the Australian Sea Carriage of Goods Act 1924 shall apply to this charterparty and be deemed to be inserted in extenso herein.' Article III, r. 6 is the usual one-year time limit on claims. Clause 24 of the charterparty is an arbitration clause requiring the claimant's arbitrator to be appointed within six months of delivery in the event of a dispute. Nine months after delivery the charterers made a claim in respect of the cargo and appointed an arbitrator. The shipowners say it is now too late to make the claim. Are they right? (See *Sabah Flour and Feedmills Sdn Bhd* v *Comfez Ltd* [1988] 2 Lloyd's Rep 18 (CA).)

4.  Attempts to reconcile the incorporated Rules with other (inconsistent) provisions of the incorporating document can lead to tortuous drafting and intractable problems of interpretation: see *Finagra (UK) Ltd* v *OT Africa Line Ltd* [1998] 2 Lloyd's Rep 622 (QBD), where Rix J said (at p. 629) 'Clear words are required for a time bar, so that in a case of doubt or ambiguity the conflict must be resolved in favour of the longer time limit'.

In general, however, the provisions of the incorporating document, if clear, will take precedence over the wording incorporated: *Metalfer Corporation v Pan Ocean Shipping Co. Ltd* [1998] 2 Lloyd's Rep 632 (QBD, Longmore J: 30 day arbitration time limit applied notwithstanding incorporation of the Hague Rules).

## SECTION 4: CONTRACTS EXCLUDED FROM THE RULES

In two cases the application of the Rules is excluded, even for carriage between ports in different contracting States.

*A: Deck cargo and live animals*

### Carriage of Goods by Sea Act 1971

#### SCHEDULE

**Article I**

(c)  'Goods' includes goods, wares, merchandise, and articles of every kind whatsoever except live animals and cargo which by the contract of carriage is stated as being carried on deck and is so carried.

## *Svenska Traktor Aktiebolaget* v *Maritime Agencies (Southampton) Ltd*
### [1953] 2 QB 295 (QBD)

ST were the consignees of 50 tractors shipped on the *Glory* from Southampton to Stockholm. M were the charterers of the vessel, but it was agreed that they were to be treated as the carriers and that references in the bill of lading to the shipowners were references to them. Sixteen of the tractors were carried on deck and one was washed overboard during the voyage. In answer to ST's claim for damages, M relied on a clause in the bill of lading: 'Steamer has liberty to carry goods on deck and shipowners will not be responsible for any loss damage or claim arising therefrom.' It was held that the clause was ineffective to exclude the carriers' responsibility.

PILCHER J: It was submitted on behalf of the defendants that while there was admittedly no specific statement on the face of the bill of lading that any of these tractors were being carried on deck, the clause in the bill of lading giving liberty to the vessel to carry goods on deck, amounted to an agreement between the parties that the steamer was entitled so to carry goods, and, it being common ground that the particular tractor which was lost was in fact shipped on deck, the clause giving liberty to ship on deck amounted in all the circumstances to a statement that the tractor was in fact shipped on deck sufficient to satisfy Article 1(c) of the Schedule, and thus to exclude the tractor in question from the definition of 'goods' to which the Act applies. In my view that submission is quite untenable. The intention of the Act and Schedule in relation to deck cargo appears to me to be reasonably clear. At common law a shipowner is only authorised to stow goods on deck in certain circumstances: the principle is set out accurately in *Scrutton on Charter Parties*, 15th ed., at p. 157, as follows:

> The shipowner or master will only be authorised to stow goods on deck; (1) by a custom binding in the trade, or port of loading, to stow on deck goods of that class on such a voyage; or (2) by express agreement with the shipper of the particular goods so to stow them. The effect of deck stowage not so authorised will be to set aside the exceptions of the charter or bill of lading and to render the shipowner liable under his contract of carriage for damage happening to such goods.

The policy of the Carriage of Goods by Sea Act 1924, was to regulate the relationship between the shipowner and the owner of goods along well-known lines. In excluding from the definition of 'goods', the carriage of which was subject to the Act, cargo carried on deck and stated to be so carried, the intention of the Act was, in my view, to leave the shipowner free to carry deck cargo on his own conditions, and unaffected by the obligations imposed on him by the Act in any case in which he would, apart from the Act, have been entitled to carry such cargo on deck, provided that the cargo in question was in fact carried on deck and that the bill of lading covering it contained on its face a statement that the particular cargo was being so carried. Such a statement on the face of the bill of lading would serve as a notification and a warning to consignees and indorsees of the bill of lading to whom the property in the goods passed under the terms of section 1 of the Bill of Lading Act 1855, that the goods which they were to take were being shipped as deck cargo. They would thus have full knowledge of the facts when accepting the documents and would know that the carriage of the goods on deck was not subject to the Act. If, on the other hand, there was no specific agreement between the parties as to the carriage on deck, and no statement on the face of the bill of lading that goods carried on deck had in fact been so carried, the consignees or indorsees of the bill of lading would be entitled to assume that the goods were goods the carriage of which could only be performed by the shipowner subject to the obligations imposed on him by the Act. A mere general liberty to carry goods on deck is not in my view a statement in the contract of carriage that the goods are in fact being carried on deck. To hold otherwise would in my view do violence to the ordinary meaning of the words of Article I(c). I hold, accordingly, that the plaintiffs' tractors were being carried by the shipowners subject to the obligations imposed upon them by Article III, r. 2, of the Act.

The next question is: Was the shipowner in those circumstances entitled to carry the tractors or any of them on deck? The clause in the bill of lading at line 76 which purports to grant to the shipowner a liberty to ship goods on deck is in two parts, and in my view it is reasonably clear that the second part of the clause offends and must offend against Article III, r. 8, of the Schedule to the Act and cannot be relied upon by the shipowner.... Counsel for the defendants argued that the clause should be read disjunctively, and that, inasmuch as the first portion did not offend against the Act it should be allowed to remain, and that, consequently, it could not be said that, in shipping some tractors on deck, the owners had committed such a fundamental breach of their obligation under the contract of carriage as to disentitle them from relying on any of the statutory exceptions, and in particular on the exception of perils of the seas. The two portions of the clause under consideration are connected by the conjunction 'and' without any stop. The second part offends against the Act and the first part does not. While, in the view which I take of the facts, the point in this case has not any practical importance, I am inclined to think that Mr Brandon is right and I proceed upon the assumption that the shipowners had liberty to ship cargo on deck, subject always to their obligations under Article III, r. 2, properly and carefully to load, handle, stow, carry, keep and care for the goods in question.

*Notes and Question*

1.   Pilcher J went on to hold that the carriers had not brought themselves within the exception of perils of the seas: the tractor was lost because it was inadequately secured and there was 'no evidence of fortuitous or unexpected peril'. See further section 8E, below, as to the burden of proof.

2.   Containers are carried both on and below deck. Does this mean that the Rules are excluded with respect to the containers on deck? If not, why not?

3.   Unauthorised deck carriage is a serious breach by the carrier. It used to be thought that such a breach deprived the shipowner of the protection of the charterparty or bill or lading because the effect of it was 'to set aside the exceptions' (Scrutton, 19th ed. p. 167). The Court of Appeal has now rejected this view.

### *Kenya Railways* v *Antares Co. Pte Ltd*
### *(The Antares)*
### [1987] 1 Lloyd's Rep 424 (CA)

LLOYD LJ: In December 1983, machinery was shipped at Antwerp on board the vessel *Antares* under two bills of lading dated Dec. 20, 1983. The bills of lading provided for carriage to Mombasa. They were subject to the Hague Rules or alternatively the Hague-Visby rules. Unusually, they contained an arbitration clause. When the cargo was discharged at Mombasa on Feb. 17, 1984 it was discovered that part of the machinery had been loaded on deck and had been seriously damaged in the course of the voyage. Naturally, the bill of lading holders, Kenya Railways, turned their minds to claiming damages. The bill of lading was on the form of Mediterranean Shipping Co. SA (to whom I shall refer as 'MSC'). MSC were, however, not the owners of the vessel. They operated a liner service between Europe and East Africa. MSC had chartered the vessel from Antares Pte. Ltd, a company registered in Singapore, pursuant to a time charter on the New York Produce Exchange form dated Apr. 20, 1983. Antares were the owners of the vessel and I shall refer to them simply as 'the owners'.

Those acting on behalf of Kenya Railways assumed that MSC were the owners of the vessel. They overlooked the demise clause printed on the back of the bill of lading. That made it clear that MSC might not be the owners of the vessel even though the bill of lading was issued on their form.

After referring to the view expressed in Scrutton, Lloyd LJ continued:

That passage has appeared in identical terms in successive editions of Scrutton, going back, we are told, to the last edition for which Lord Justice Scrutton was himself responsible. But with great respect to the editors of the current edition it no longer represents the law. The doctrine of fundamental breach on which Mr Nicholls relies, that is to say the doctrine that a breach of contract may be so fundamental as to displace the exceptions clauses altogether, no longer exists. The death knell sounded in *Suisse Atlantique Société d'Armement Maritime SA* v *Rotterdamsche Kolen Centrale* [1966] 1 Lloyd's Rep 529; [1967] 1 AC 361. The corpse was buried in *Photo Production Ltd* v *Securicor Transport Ltd* [1980] 1 Lloyd's Rep 545; [1980] AC 827. It is sufficient to quote a single sentence from Lord Wilberforce's speech in the latter case at pp. 549 and 842 where, after referring to *Suisse Atlantique*, he said:

... I have no second thoughts as to the main proposition that the question whether, and to what exent an exclusion clause is to be applied to a fundamental breach, or a breach of a fundamental term, or indeed to any breach of contract, is a matter of construction of the contract ...

It is sometimes said that the so-called 'deviation cases' may have survived the abolition of the doctrine of fundamental breach. Mr Nicholls argues that, by analogy with the deviation cases, the rule relating to deck cargo as set out in Scrutton has also survived.

In *Suisse Atlantique* Lord Wilberforce suggested that the deviation cases should be regarded as proceeding on ordinary principles applicable to contract generally. In *Photo Production* v *Securicor* he said that it might be preferable to regard them as a body of authority sui generis with special rules derived from historical and commercial reasons. Whatever may be the position with regard to deviation cases strictly so called (I would myself favour the view that they should now be assimilated into the ordinary law of contract), I can see no reason for regarding the unauthorised loading of deck cargo as a special case.

The sole question therefore is whether, on its true construction, art. III, r. 6 applies. It is clear that it does. It provides that the carrier shall in any event be discharged from all liability whatsoever unless suit is brought within one year. This is even wider language than the old art. III, r. 6, which omitted the word 'whatsoever'. In the current edition of Scrutton it is said, at p. 440, that the edition [*sic*] of the word 'whatsoever' makes it clear that the time limit applies even where the carrier has committed a deviation. Whether that be true of a deviation strictly so called, it is certainly true of the unauthorised carriage of goods on deck. By their amended originating summons the plaintiffs seek a declaration that the defendants are barred from relying on art. III, r. 6, by reason of their fundamental breach of contract. For the reasons I have given they are not entitled to that declaration.

*Note*

Although the decision was apparently not referred to in *The Antares*, the Judicial Committee of the Privy Council had already rejected as 'unsound' and 'unreal' a similar post-*Photo Production* attempt to use 'fundamental breach' to overcome the one-year limit in the Hague Rules: *Salmond & Spraggon (Australia) Pty Ltd* v *Port Jackson Stevedoring Pty Ltd (The New York Star)* [1980] 2 Lloyd's Rep 317, at p. 322. See section 9A below.

## *Wibau Maschinenfabric Hartman SA* v *Mackinnon Mackenzie & Co. (The Chanda)*
### [1989] 2 Lloyd's Rep 494 (QBD)

W sold an asphalt drying and mixing plant to f.o.b. buyers in Saudi Arabia. Being several storeys high when assembled, the plant was transported in parts. W shipped part of the plant, including the control cabin, on the *Chanda* at Bremen for carriage to Jeddah. The bill of lading contained a paramount clause incorporating the Hague Rules 'as enacted in the country of shipment', but also provided for the court in London to have exclusive jurisdiction and for English law to apply 'except as provided elsewhere herein'. By German law, at the relevant time, the 1924 Hague Rules still applied and the carriers' liability under those Rules was limited to DM 1,250 per package. Without authority, the control cabin (which contained delicate electronic equipment) was stowed on deck on No. 1 hatch, i.e., in the most exposed position on the ship. After sailing from Bremen in December 1981, the *Chanda* encountered severe weather in the Bay of Biscay (winds force 9 and 10). The control cabin was so severely damaged that it had to be replaced. The insurers having paid for a total loss (around £85,000) now claimed by subrogation against the carriers, who sought to limit their liability to DM 1,250. It was held that they were liable for the full amount.

HIRST J: [The cases rest on a principle of construction] that clauses which are clearly intended to protect the shipowner provided he honours his contractual obligation to stow goods under deck do not apply if he is in breach of that obligation. This same principle seems to me to be reflected in the passage cited above from Lord Wilberforce's speech in the *Suisse Atlantique* case, and in particular in the quotation from the judgment of Lord Justice Scrutton in *Gibaud* v *Great Eastern Railway* [1921] 2 KB 426. As Lord Wilberforce said, this rule is quite clearly based on contractual intention.

I am satisfied that the package limitation clause falls fairly and squarely within this category, since it can hardly have been intended to protect the shipowner who, as a result of the breach, exposed the cargo in question to such palpable risk of damage. Otherwise the main purpose of the shipowners' obligation to stow below deck would be seriously undermined (compare *Evans'* case [i.e., *Evans (J) & Sons (Portsmouth) Ltd* v *Andrea Merzario* [1976] 2 Lloyd's Rep 165 (CA)]).

In my judgment there is nothing in the *Antares* case which conflicts with this view. The exception at issue there (the one year limitation clause) not only had statutory force by virtue of the terms of the 1971 Act (unlike the present clause), but was also not of a nature which in any way undermined the purpose of the shipowners' obligation to stow below deck.

As a result I hold that the package limitation clause, being repugnant to and inconsistent with the obligation to stow below deck, was inapplicable.

If, however, I am wrong, and the proper approach is, as Mr Macdonald submits, a matter of pure construction within the four walls of the bill of lading itself, then in my judgment, on the proper construction of the bill of lading as a whole, cl. 10 lays down a complete and comprehensive code for transportation on deck.

. . . Thus, even if I accepted Mr Macondald's basic approach, I should still have held that the package limitation did not apply.

## Note and Questions

1. Why did Hirst J not apply COGSA 1971?
2. Does the principle of construction apply to contracts governed by COGSA 1971? In *Nelson Pine Industries Ltd* v *Seatrans New Zealand Ltd (The Pembroke)* [1995] 2 Lloyd's Rep 290, Ellis J in the New Zealand High Court considered that *The Chanda* applied both to the Hague Rules and the Hague-Visby Rules, but also relied on art. IV, r. 5(e) to exclude the package or weight limitation: see below, Section 9.

*B: Shipments which justify a special agreement*

## Carriage of Goods by Sea Act 1971

### SCHEDULE

**Article VI**
Notwithstanding the provisions of the preceding articles, a carrier, master or agent of the carrier and a shipper shall in regard to any particular goods be at liberty to enter into any agreement in any terms as to the responsibility and liability of the carrier for such goods, and as to the rights and immunities of the carrier in respect of such goods, or his obligation as to seaworthiness, so far as this stipulation is not contrary to public policy, or the care or diligence of his servants or agents in regard to the loading, handling, stowage, carriage, custody, care and discharge of the goods carried by sea, provided that in this case no bill of lading has been or shall be issued and that the terms agreed shall be embodied in a receipt which shall be a non-negotiable document and shall be marked as such.

Any agreement so entered into shall have full legal effect.

Provided that this article shall not apply to ordinary commercial shipments made in the ordinary course of trade, but only to other shipments where the character or condition of the property to be carried or the circumstances, terms and conditions under which the carriage is to be performed are such as reasonably to justify a special agreement.

### *Harland & Wolff Ltd* v *Burns & Laird Lines Ltd*
(1931) 40 Ll L Rep 286 (Court of Session)

The facts are stated in section 2D above. Reliance was placed on Art. VI.

LORD PRESIDENT (LORD CLYDE): The terms of Art. VI were also founded on by the pursuers in support of the wide construction of the Act which they contended for. But, in form at least, that article does no more than provide in favour of a 'carrier' under a 'contract of carriage covered by a bill of lading' exemption in certain circumstances from the provisions of the Act and Schedule.

By Sect. 4 of the Act, Art. VI is made to apply to 'goods of any class' carried between this country and Ireland; and the reference to 'particular goods' in Art. VI may therefore be disregarded. By the same section of the Act, the proviso to Art. VI is excluded from applying to goods so carried.

The pursuers, however, argued, with much force, that the terms of Art. VI are suggestive of a context containing a universal prohibition against all limitations of liability in any contract of affreightment other than those contained in a charterparty or permitted by the Act and Schedule. But, to adopt this view, it would be necessary not only to give the word 'carrier' in Art. VI a meaning inconsistent with the definition of that word in Art. I — in other words, to read it as meaning a carrier under a contract of carriage whether 'covered' by a bill of lading or not — but also to put out of account the significant facts: (1) that in the preamble to the Act the object of the rules in the Schedule is stated to be neither more nor less than to establish 'the responsibilities, liabilities, rights and immunities attaching to carriers *under bills of lading*'; and (2) that the title of the Schedule itself is: 'Rules relating to *Bills of Lading.*' Moreover, I do not think the actual context discloses any prohibition so comprehensive as that suggested by the pursuers as the meaning of the Act and Schedule as a whole. If I may hazard an attempt to define the object of Art. VI — consistently with the definitions in Art. I and with the meaning I have already attributed to the word 'covered' occurring therein — I should say that it is to allow a 'carrier' under a 'contract of carriage covered by a bill of lading' (that is to say, a contract of carriage which entitles the shipper, according to the custom of the particular trade, to demand at or after shipment a bill of lading setting forth the terms of the contract) to limit his responsibilities by agreement with the shipper in any way 'not contrary to public policy'; provided that the bill of lading (which would otherwise have been issued at or after shipment with the agreed-on limitations embodied in it) shall not be issued, but that instead thereof a non-negotiable receipt, marked as such and embodying the limitations, shall be used. This interpretation, if sound, would leave ample scope for the application of the exemption, and would do no violence either to the definitions or to what is apparently the general scope of the Act.

*Notes*
1. Section 4 of COGSA 1924, which extended the scope of Art. VI in its application to 'non-Convention' cases of carriage between British or from British to Irish ports, has no counterpart in COGSA 1971.
2. Contrary to the Lord President's view, the reference to public policy is confined to the obligation as to seaworthiness: *Hugh Mack & Co. Ltd* v *Burns & Laird Lines Ltd* (1944) 77 Ll L Rep 377, at p. 384 per Andrews LCJ (NI). In any event, public policy has nothing to do with it — 'it is simply a question as to which of the parties is to insure the goods' (ibid.).

*Questions*
1. Under what circumstances will a 'special agreement' be reasonably justified? (If the word 'reasonably' were omitted — as in the French text — would it be implied?) When is a commercial shipment not an 'ordinary' one? Would Art. VI have applied in *The Chanda* above?

2. Article VI appears to have been drafted on the assumption that carriers do not have a choice whether to issue bills of lading or not. If the authorities permitting that choice are correct (see section 2D above), is Art. VI now otiose? The contrary view is argued by Tetley, *op cit*, pp. 944 *et seq*.

## SECTION 5: CONTRACTING OUT

It is a fundamental principle of the Rules that there shall be no contracting out. If the Rules apply, they apply *in toto*.

### Carriage of Goods by Sea Act 1971

SCHEDULE

**Article III**
(8)   Any clause, covenant, or agreement in a contract of carriage relieving the carrier or the ship from liability for loss or damage to, or in connection with, goods arising from negligence, fault, or failure in the duties and obligations provided in this article or lessening such liability otherwise than as provided in these Rules, shall be null and void and of no effect. A benefit of insurance in favour of the carrier or similar clause shall be deemed to be a clause relieving the carrier from liability.

### *The Hollandia*
### [1983] 1 AC 565 (HL)

The plaintiffs shipped a road-finishing machine at Leith in Scotland for carriage to Bonaire in the Netherlands Antilles. The machine was taken first to Amsterdam on one of the carriers' own ships and then transhipped onto the *Morviken*, a Norwegian flag vessel on charter to the carriers. The plaintiffs claimed that the machine suffered damage amounting to £22,000 during discharge at Bonaire and commenced an Admiralty action *in rem* against the *Hollandia*, owned by the carriers, the Royal Netherlands Steamship Co. The carriers asked for the proceedings to be stayed, relying on condition 2 of the bill of lading:

Law of application and jurisdiction. The law of the Netherlands in which the Hague Rules, as adopted by the Brussels Convention of August 25, 1924, are incorporated — with the exception of article 9 — shall apply to this contract. The maximum liability per package is D.fl. 1,250. For goods loaded or discharged at a Belgian port, the rules of article 91 of Chapter 2 of the Belgian Commercial Code shall apply.

Whenever the carrier is not the owner or demise charterer of the ocean vessel, the owner or demise charterer of such vessel shall, nevertheless, be entitled to avail himself of every exemption, limitation, condition and liberty herein contained and every right, exemption from liability, defence and immunity of whatsoever nature applicable to the carrier or to which the carrier is entitled hereunder as if this bill of lading had been issued by the said owner or demise charterer in his own name and on his own behalf.

All actions under the present contract of carriage shall be brought before the Court of Amsterdam and no other court shall have jurisdiction with regard to any such action unless the carrier appeals to another jurisdiction or voluntarily submits himself thereto.

The Netherlands had not at the time adopted the Hague-Visby Rules and a Dutch court would have applied the package limit of D.fl 1,250. Under the Hague-Visby Rules the limit would be based on the weight of the goods (9,906 kg) and would have amounted to about £11,000. Sheen J granted the stay, but the Court of Appeal and the House of Lords held that the action could proceed.

LORD DIPLOCK: The bill of lading issued to the shippers by the carriers upon the shipment of the goods at the Scottish port of Leith was one to which the Hague-Visby Rules were expressly made applicable by article X; it fell within both paragraph (a) and paragraph (b); it was issued in a contracting state, the United Kingdom, and it covered a contract for carriage from a port in a contracting state. For good measure, it also fell directly within section 1(3) of the Act of 1971 itself.

The first paragraph of condition 2 of the bill of lading, prescribing as it does for a per package maximum limit of liability on the part of the carriers for loss or damage arising from negligence or breach of contract instead of the higher per kilogram maximum applicable under the Hague-Visby Rules, is ex facie a clause in a contract of carriage which purports to lessen the liability of the carriers for such loss or damage otherwise than is provided in the Hague-Visby Rules. As such it is therefore rendered null and void and of no effect under article III, paragraph 8. So much indeed was conceded by counsel for the carriers, subject to a possible argument to the contrary which was briefly mentioned but not elaborated upon. I shall have to revert to this argument later, but can do so with equal brevity.

The first paragraph of clause 2 of the bill of lading down to the first full stop is ambiguous. It may mean that the general law of the Netherlands (including its private international law) relating to carrige of goods by sea is adopted as the 'proper law' of the contract of carriage or it may mean, as the absence of a comma between 'Netherlands' and 'in which' might suggest, that only that part of the law of the Netherlands which incorporates the Hague Rules is to be applicable to the contract which, in other respects, is to be governed by what the court seized of any claim under the contract would treat as being its 'proper law'. In the case of a contract made in Scotland for the carriage of goods from a port in Scotland, the 'proper law' would, prima facie at any rate, be Scots Law, and this, so far as contracts of carriage of goods by sea are concerned, is in all relevant respects the same as English law. But whether the first paragraph of condition 2 of the bill of lading be given the wider or the narrower meaning, in so far as it purports to lessen, as it expressly does, the liability of the carriers for which article IV, paragraph 5 of the Hague-Visby Rules provides, it unquestionably contravenes article III, paragraph 8 and by that rule is deprived of any effect in English or Scots law.

The Court of Appeal [1982] QB 872 were unanimous in so holding and counsel for the carriers has not argued to the contrary in this House, at any rate so far as the paragraph limits the maximum liability of the carriers to 1,250 Dutch florins instead of the higher maximum for which the Hague-Visby Rules provide. Sheen J, at first instance (sub nom. *The Morviken* [1981] 2 Lloyd's Rep 61), found it unnecessary to decide this point because he regarded the three paragraphs of clause 2 as severable, since they deal with separate subject matters. Indeed, the second paragraph does not deal with choice of law, whether substantive or curial, at all. It was on the third paragraph of condition 2, which deals only with choice of forum that the learned judge based his judgment granting the stay. This he felt able to do notwithstanding the fact that, although on the face of the third paragraph it deals only with the choice of curial law which (as was held by this House in *Compagnie Tunisienne de Navigation SA* v *Compagnie d'Armement Maritime SA* [1971] AC 572) may be a different law from that chosen as the 'proper law' of the contract, it was common ground between the parties that to give effect to the choice of the Court of Amsterdam as the forum would have the same consequences in limiting the carriers' liability as would the application of the first paragraph of the clause, since the Court of Amsterdam would treat as the applicable substantive law that substantive law for which the first paragraph of condition 2 provides.

Counsel for the carriers sought to justify the judge's decision on this point by putting a narrow literalistic interpretation on article III, paragraph 8 of the Hague-Visby Rules. A choice of forum clause, he contended, is to be classified as a clause which only prescribes the procedure by which disputes arising under the contract of carriage are to be resolved. It does not ex facie deal with liability at all and so does not fall within the description 'Any clause, covenant, or agreement in a contract of carriage . . . lessening . . . liability,' so as to bring it within article III, paragraph 8; even though the consequence of giving effect to the clause will be to lessen, otherwise than is provided in the Hague-Visby Rules, the liability of the carrier for loss or damage to or in connection with the goods arising from negligence, fault or failure in the duties and obligations provided in the Rules.

My Lords, like all three members of the Court of Appeal, I have no hesitation in rejecting this narrow construction of article III, paragraph 8, which looks solely to the form of the clause in the contract of carriage and wholly ignores its substance. The only sensible meaning to be given to the description of provisions in contracts of carriage which are rendered 'null and void and of no effect' by this rule is one which would embrace every provision in a contract of carriage which, if it were applied, would have the effect of lessening the carrier's liability otherwise than as provided in the Rules. To ascribe to it the narrow meaning for which counsel contended would leave it open to any shipowner to evade the provisions of article III, paragraph 8 by the simple device of inserting in his bills of lading issued in, or for carriage from a port in, any contracting state a clause in standard form providing as the exclusive forum for resolution of disputes what might aptly be described as a court of convenience, viz., one situated in a country which did not apply the Hague-Visby Rules or, for that matter, a country whose law recognised an unfetterd right in a shipowner by the terms of the bill of lading to relieve himself from all liability for loss or damage to the goods caused by his own negligence, fault or breach of contract.

My Lords, unlike the first paragraph of condition 2 a choice of forum clause, such as that appearing in the third paragraph, does not ex facie offend against article III, paragraph 8. It is a provision of the contract of carriage that is subject to a condition subsequent; it comes into operation only upon the occurrence of a future event that may or may not occur, viz.: the coming into existence of a dispute between the parties as to their respective legal rights and duties under the contract which they are unable to settle by agreement. There may be some disputes that would bring the choice of forum clause into operation but which would not be concerned at all with negligence fault or failure by the carrier or the ship in the duties and obligations provided by article III; a claim for unpaid freight is an obvious example. So a choice of forum clause which selects as the exclusive forum for the resolution of disputes a court which will not apply the Hague-Visby Rules, even after such clause has come into operation, does not necessarily always have the effect of lessening the liability of the carrier in a way that attracts the application of article III, paragraph 8.

My Lords, it is, in my view, most consistent with the achievement of the purpose of the Act of 1971 that the time at which to ascertain whether a choice of forum clause will have an effect that is proscribed by article III, paragraph 8 should be when the condition subsequent is fulfilled and the carrier seeks to bring the clause into operation and to rely upon it. If the dispute is about duties and obligations of the carrier or ship that are referred to in that rule and it is established as a fact (either by evidence or as in the instant case by the common agreement of the parties) that the foreign court chosen as the exclusive forum would apply a domestic substantive law which would result in limiting the carrier's liability to a sum lower than that to which he would be entitled if article IV, paragraph 5 of the Hague-Visby Rules applied, then an English court is in my view commanded by the Act of 1971 to treat the choice of forum clause as of no effect.

The rule itself speaks of a proscribed provision in a contract of carriage as a 'clause, covenant, or agreement in a contract of carriage' and describes the effect of the rule on the offending provision as being to render it 'null and void and of no effect'. These pleonastic expressions occurring in an international convention (of which the similarly pleonastic version in the French language is of equal authenticity) are not to be construed as technical terms of legal art. It may well be that if they were to be so construed the most apt to be applied to a choice of forum clause when brought into operation by the occurrence of a particular dispute would be the expression 'of no effect', but it is no misuse of ordinary language to describe the clause in its application to the particular dispute as being pro tanto 'null' or 'void' or both.

*Notes*

1.  In *Australasian United Steam Navigation Co. Ltd* v *Hunt* [1921] 2 AC 351 (PC), H shipped bananas from Fiji to Australia under bills of lading which provided that any claim for loss or damage must be made in writing within seven days from the date when the cargo was or should have been landed. The bananas were damaged by the unseaworthiness of the vessel, but the claim was not made within seven days of landing. The relevant Fiji Ordinance, following the Australian Sea-Carriage of Goods Act 1904, made void any clauses which weakened, lessened or avoided the shipowner's obligation to make and keep the refrigerating chambers fit for the cargo. It was held that the seven-day limit was void and the claim succeeded.

2.  In *Studebaker Distributors Ltd* v *Charlton Steam Shipping Co. Ltd* [1938] 1 KB 459, Goddard J held that a clause making a surveyor's certificate conclusive evidence of proper stowage was null and void under the corresponding provision of the Harter Act. He also held that an 'agreed value' clause was not contrary to the Act, but this seems questionable, at least if the agreed value is less than the actual value: see *Nabob Foods Ltd* v *Cape Corso (Owners)* [1954] 2 Lloyd's Rep 40 (Exch. Ct of Canada).

## SECTION 6: THE PERIOD COVERED BY THE RULES

When do the carrier's obligations begin and end? How far do the Rules apply to anything done before or after the actual voyage?

## Carriage of Goods by Sea Act 1971

### SCHEDULE

**Article I**
(e)   [See above, section 2.]

**Article II**
Subject to the provisions of Article VI, under every contract of carriage of goods by sea
the carrier, in relation to the loading, handling, stowage, carriage, custody, care and
discharge of such goods, shall be subject to the responsibilities and liabilities, and
entitled to the rights and immunities hereinafter set forth.

**Article VII**
Nothing herein contained shall prevent a carrier or a shipper from entering into any
agreement, stipulation, condition, reservation or exemption as to the responsibility and
liability of the carrier or the ship for the loss or damage to, or in connection with, the
custody and care and handling of goods prior to the loading on, and subsequent to the
discharge from, the ship on which the goods are carried by sea.

## *Pyrene Co. Ltd* v *Scindia Navigation Co. Ltd*
### [1954] 2 QB 402 (QBD)

The facts are stated in section 2A, above. The principal argument advanced
by the plaintiffs was that the Rules do not apply until the goods have crossed
the ship's rail.

DEVLIN J: Mr Megaw's argument turns upon the meaning to be given to article 1(e),
which defines 'carriage of goods' as covering 'the period from the time when the goods
are loaded on to the time when they are discharged from the ship'. Mr Megaw says that
these goods never were loaded *on* to the ship. In a literal sense obviously they were not.
But Mr Megaw does not rely on the literal sense; there are rules which could hardly be
made intelligible if they began to operate only after the goods had been landed on deck.
He treats the word 'on' as having the same meaning as in 'free on board'; goods are
loaded on the ship as soon as they are put across the ship's rail, which the tender never
was. He submits that the rule (which, of course, has effect in English law only by virtue
of its place in the Schedule to the Carriage of Goods by Sea Act, 1924) must be
construed in accordance with English principles. He relies upon *Harris* v
*Best, Ryley & Co.* (1892) 68 LT 76 and *Argonaut Navigation Co. Ld* v *Ministry of Food*
[1949] 1 KB 572 which lay down the rule that loading is a joint operation, the shipper's
duty being to lift the cargo to the rail of the ship (I shall refer to that as the first stage of
the loading), and the shipowner's to take it on board and stow it (I shall refer to that as
the second stage).

Mr Megaw contends, therefore, that the accident occurred outside the period
specified in article 1(e)....

In my judgment this argument is fallacious, the cause of the fallacy perhaps lying in
the supposition inherent in it that the rights and liabilities under the rules attach to a
period of time. I think that they attach to a contract or part of a contract. I say 'part of a
contract' because a single contract may cover both inland and sea transport; and in that
case the only part of it that falls within the rules is that which, to use the words in the
definition of 'contract of carriage' in article 1(b), 'relates to the carriage of goods by sea'.

Even if 'carriage of goods by sea' were given by definition the most restricted meaning possible, for example, the period of the voyage, the loading of the goods (by which I mean the whole operation of loading in both its stages and whichever side of the ship's rail) would still *relate* to the carriage on the voyage and so be within the 'contract of carriage'.

Article 2 is the crucial article which for this purpose has to be construed. It is this article that gives the carrier all his rights and immunities, including the right to limit his liability. He is entitled to do that 'in relation to the loading' and 'under every contract of carriage'. Now I shall have to consider later the meaning of 'loading' in article 2 and whether it is such as to exclude what I have called the first stage, that is, the operations on the shore side of the ship's rail. For the moment I am concerned only to see whether its meaning is cut down by the definition in article 1(e) on which Mr Megaw relies. The only phrase in article 2 that can cut it down is the one I have quoted: 'under every contract of carriage'; it is only in so far as article 1(e) operates through the definition of 'contract of carriage' that it can have any effect on article 2. I have already sought to demonstrate that, however limited the period in article 1(e) may be, the loading in both its stages must still *relate* to it and so be within the definition of contract of carriage. A precise construction of article 1(e), while not irrelevant, is in no way conclusive of the point I have to decide, which turns, I think, upon the meaning of 'loading' in article 2.

But before I try to elucidate that, let me state my view of article 1(e). For, as I have said, though not dominant, it is not irrelevant; in construing 'loading' in article 2 you must have regard to similar expressions throughout the rules, article 1(e) included. In my judgment, no special significance need be given to the phrase 'loaded *on*'. It is not intended to specify a precise moment of time. Of course, if the operation of the rules began and ended with a period of time a precise specification would be necessary. But they do not. It is legitimate in England to look at section 1 of the Act, which applies the rules not to a period of time but 'in relation to and in connexion with the carriage of goods by sea'. The rules themselves show the same thing. The obligations in article 3, r. 1, for example, to use due diligence to make the ship seaworthy and man and equip her properly are independent of time. The operation of the rules is determined by the limits of the contract of carriage by sea and not by any limits of time. The function of article 1(e) is, I think, only to assist in the definition of contract of carriage. As I have already pointed out, there is excluded from that definition any part of a larger contract which relates, for example, to inland transport. It is natural to divide such a contract into periods, a period of inland transport, followed perhaps by a period of sea transport and then again by a period of inland transport. Discharging from rail at the port of loading may fall into the first period; loading on to the ship into the second. The reference to 'when the goods are loaded on' in article 1(e) is not, I think, intended to do more than identify the first operation in the series which constitutes the carriage of goods by sea; as 'when they are discharged' denotes the last. The use of the rather loose word 'cover', I think, supports this view.

There is another reason for thinking that it would be wrong to stress the phrase 'loaded on' in article 1(e). It is no doubt necessary for an English court to apply the rules as part of English law, but that is a different thing from assuming them to be drafted in the light of English law. If one is inquiring whether 'loaded *on*' in article 1(e) has a different meaning from 'loaded' or 'loading' in other parts of the rules, it would be mistaken to look for the significant distinction in the light of a conception which may be peculiar to English law. The idea of the operation being divided at the ship's rail is certainly not a universal one. It does not, for example, apply in Scotland: *Glengarnock Iron and Steel Co. Ltd* v *Cooper & Co.* (1895) 22 R 672 per Lord Trayner. It is more reasonable to read the rules as contemplating loading and discharging as single operations. It is no doubt possible to read article 1(e) literally as defining the period as being from the completion of loading till the completion of discharging. But the literal interpretation would be absurd. Why exclude loading from the period and include discharging? How give effect to the frequent references to loading in other rules? How reconcile it with article 7 which allows freedom of contract 'prior to the loading on and subsequent to the discharge from'? Manifestly both operations must be included. That brings me back to the view that article 1(e) is naming the first and last of a series of operations which include in between loading and discharging, 'handling, stowage, carriage, custody and care'. This is, in fact, the list of operations to which article 2 is by its own terms applied. In short, nothing is to be gained by looking to the terms of article 1(e) for an interpretation of article 2.

I think, therefore, that article 1(e), which was the spearhead of Mr Megaw's argument, turns out to be an ineffective weapon. But that still leaves it necessary to consider the meaning of 'loading' in article 2. Just how far does the operation of loading, to which article 2 grants immunity, extend? Now I have already given reasons against presuming that the framers of the rules thought in terms of a divided operation, and in the absence of such a presumption the natural meaning of 'loading' covers the whole operation. How far can that be pressed? Article 3, rule 2, for example, provides: 'the carrier shall properly and carefully load', etc. If 'load' includes both stages, does that oblige the shipowner, whether he wants to or not, to undertake the whole of the loading? If so, it is a new idea to English lawyers, though perhaps more revolutionary in theory than in practice. But if not, and 'load' includes only the second stage, then should it not be given a similar meaning in article 2 with the result that immunity extends only to the second stage?

There is, however, a third interpretation to article 3, r. 2. The phrase 'shall properly and carefully load' may mean that the carrier shall load and that he shall do it properly and carefully: or that he shall do whatever loading he does properly and carefully. The former interpretation perhaps fits the language more closely, but the latter may be more consistent with the object of the rules. Their object as it is put, I think, correctly in *Carver's Carriage of Goods by Sea*, 9th ed. (1952), p. 186, is to define not the scope of the contract service but the terms on which that service is to be performed. The extent to which the carrier has to undertake the loading of the vessel may depend not only upon different systems of law but upon the custom and practice of the port and the nature of the cargo. It is difficult to believe that the rules were intended to impose a universal rigidity in this respect, or to deny freedom of contract to the carrier. The carrier is practically bound to play some part in the loading and discharging, so that both operations are naturally included in those covered by the contract of carriage. But I see no reason why the rules should not leave the parties free to determine by their own contract the part which each has to play. On this view the whole contract of carriage is subject to the rules, but the extent to which loading and discharging are brought within the carrier's obligations is left to the parties themselves to decide.

I reject the interpretation of loading in article 2 as covering only the second stage of the operation. Such authority as there is against it. If loading under the rules does not begin before the ship's rail, by parity of reasoning discharging should end at the ship's rail; but so to hold would be contrary to the decision of Roche J in *Goodwin, Ferreira & Co. Ltd* v *Lamport & Holt Ltd* (1929) 141 LT 494.

Since the shipowner in this case in fact undertook the whole operation of loading it is unnecessary to decide which of the other two interpretations is correct. I prefer the more elastic one, that which I have called the third. There appears to be no binding authority on the point. I have noted the view expressed in Carver; on the other hand, *Temperley's*

*Carriage of Goods by Sea Act, 1924,* 4th ed. (1932), p. 26, and *Scrutton on Charterparties and Bills of Lading,* 15th ed. (1948), p. 160, consider that the carrier is responsible for the whole of the loading. However, it is sufficient for me to say that on the facts of this case the rights and immunities under the rules extend to the whole of the loading carried out by the defendants and, therefore, Mr Megaw's first point fails.

I think, if I may so put it, that it is a good thing that it should fail. There must be many cases of carriage to which the rules apply where the ship undertakes the whole of the loading and discharging; and it would be unsatisfactory if the rules governed all but the extremities of the contract. It so happens that in this case (rather unusually) the exemption of the extremities would benefit the shipper. For the form of bill of lading which would have applied is made subject to the rules simpliciter, and does not set out the traditional mass of clauses which the rules have rendered generally ineffective. If they were there the shipper would probably fare worse under them than under the rules. It would certainly be a triumph for the innate conservatism of those who have not scrapped their small print if, though only on the outer fringes, it was to come into its own. But the division of loading into two parts is suited to more antiquated methods of loading than are now generally adopted and the ship's rail has lost much of its nineteenth-century significance. Only the most enthusiastic lawyer could watch with satisfaction the spectacle of liabilities shifting uneasily as the cargo sways at the end of a derrick across a notional perpendicular projecting from the ship's rail.

## The Arawa
### [1977] 2 Lloyd's Rep 416 (QBD, Admiralty)

BRANDON J: These are claims for damage to parts of a cargo of frozen meat carried from ports in New Zealand to London in the ship *Arawa* in 1970. The plaintiffs are various meat merchants, who were the receivers of the cargo. The defendants are Shaw Savill & Albion Co. Ltd, who were the owners of the *Arawa.* The latter was a passenger and refrigerated cargo vessel running on a scheduled service between New Zealand and England. I shall refer to the plaintiffs and the defendants as 'the cargo-owners' and 'the shipowners' respectively, and to the *Arawa* as 'the ship'.

The cargo in respect of which the claims are made consisted of carcasses of lamb, hogget and wethers, cartons of ewe legs, cartons of ox thick flanks, chucks, silversides, topsides and clods, and cartons of beef livers. It was carried in refrigerated compartments and intended to be delivered in a frozen condition similar to that in which it had been shipped.

The cargo was carried under contracts of carriage contained in or evidenced by 24 bills of lading in the shipowners' then standard form for such carriage, entitled 'Shaw Savill Line New Zealand Homeward Joint Bill of Lading 1969 Refrigerated Cargo'. . . .

The cargo was shipped in good order and condition at Opua on Apr. 5, and at Auckland between Apr. 15 and 18, 1970. The voyage proceeded normally and the ship was expected to arrive at London and berth at no. 5 shed, King George V dock, on May 23, 1970. That day was a Saturday, and the following Monday, May 25, was the Spring Bank Holiday. It follows that discharge could not be expected to begin until Tuesday, May 26. This created a problem for the shipowners, because the ship was in part a passenger ship, with a published schedule to keep, and delay in discharge would interfere with such schedule.

It would have been usual for the ship to discharge the whole of her cargo onto the quay, where it would have been sorted and then delivered to the various receivers. This procedure, however, if followed on this occasion, would have taken too long to allow the ship to keep her schedule. The shipowners accordingly arranged for all cargo in no. 2 hold and 'tween decks, amounting to some 1,100 tons, to be discharged overside into lighters at the same time as the rest of the cargo in other holds was being discharged onto the quay, and for the lighters to carry the goods so discharged up river to Chambers Wharf, where they would be first sorted and then received into the cold store for later collection by the cargo-owners from there.

The shipowners made this arrangement by means of a contract with Chambers Wharf. Under such contract Chambers Wharf undertook to effect the lighterage of the cargo concerned from the ship's side to their wharf; to land and sort it there; to receive it into their cold store; and to store it there for up to 28 days from the date of discharge from the ship. In consideration of Chambers Wharf doing these various things in respect of the cargo, the shipowners were to pay them a comprehensive rate of £8 per ton.

Chambers Wharf in turn sub-contracted the lighterage part of their contract with the shipowners to Humphrey and Grey Ltd, owners and operators of Thames river barges, including refrigerated and insulated barges suitable for the lightering of frozen goods.
. . .

The discharge of the *Arawa* generally, and the lighterage of cargo from no. 2 hatch to Chambers Wharf in particular, took place in unusually hot summer weather, with day temperatures of 80 deg. F. or more. Thirteen barges were used for the lighterage, of which three were of the refrigerated and the other 10 of the insulated kind. One of the refrigerated barges and two of the insulated barges performed two trips each, so that there were 16 movements of cargo in all.
. . .

The goods were landed from the barges onto the roof of the Chambers Wharf cold store, and there sorted. They were then moved by means of trolleys, conveyor belts and lifts into various compartments of the cold store and stacked there. Later, on different dates, the various parcels of goods were collected from the cold store by the cargo-owners entitled to them.

When the cargo-owners collected their goods from the cold store in this way, it was found that part of them had suffered considerable damage from defrosting and softening. A schedule containing particulars of the damage to each parcel concerned is annexed to the statement of claim, and shows that the total loss attributable to the damage was £16,731.80, including survey fees. These particulars are admitted by the shipowners, without prejudice to the questions of causation of and liability for the damage and loss concerned.

I am satisfied, on the evidence which was put before me, that the main cause of the damage particularised in the schedule was delay in the landing of the goods from the barges at Chambers Wharf. It would normally be expected that frozen goods lightered in circumstances such as these would not remain in insulated barges for more than about 3 or 4 days inclusive. The details set out above, however, show that some of the goods spent as much as 7, 8, 9, 12 and 13 days inclusive in such lighters. Other goods spent up to 20 days inclusive in refrigerated barges, and, although these goods should not in theory have suffered damage by reason of such delay, it is to be inferred that, owing to some unexplained inadequacy in the refrigeration, perhaps connected with the prolonged hot weather, they did in fact do so.

I am further satisfied, on the evidence, that the cause of this delay in landing the goods from the lighters at Chambers Wharf was industrial action taken by the dock workers employed there, in the form of a deliberate go-slow and refusal to work overtime. That industrial action was taken by the workers concerned in connection with the further reorganisation of labour in the docks under what is generally known as Devlin Phase 2, their purpose being to make it appear, in order to increase their rates of remuneration under the new scheme about to be introduced, that their work took much longer to perform than it really did.

After holding that the Chambers Wharf arrangement (to which the cargo-owners had not objected) was not on the terms of the bill of lading, Brandon J considered the possible effect of the Hague Rules if the bill of lading did apply.

... the question which arises in the present case is whether the discharge of the goods was completed, so that the sea carriage ended, when the goods were transferred from the ship into the lighters; or whether the lighterage was all part of the operation of discharge, so that the sea carriage did not end until the goods had been carried in the lighters to Chambers Wharf and landed there.

While there is no direct English authority on the matter, and it is treated in *Scrutton on Charterparties*, 18th ed., pp. 419–20, as an open point, I am of opinion that the former of the two views, namely, that discharge was completed, so that the sea carriage ended, when the goods were transferred from the ship to the lighters, is the correct one. This view seems to me to accord with the ordinary and natural meaning of the words 'when they are discharged from the ship' as used in definition (e) of art. I. The other view, that the lighterage was all part of the operation of discharge, so that the sea carriage did not end until the goods had been carried in the lighters to Chambers Wharf and landed there, would involve giving an unnaturally extended meaning to the words referred to, and I do not see any good reason for doing so.

While there is, as I have said, no direct English authority on the point, such authority as there is tends to support the interpretation of the rules which I have indicated that I prefer. In *Goodwin* v *Lamport and Holt* (1929) 34 Ll L Rep 192, it was held by Mr Justice Roche that, when goods were discharged from the carrying ship into a lighter provided by the carrier, discharge within the meaning of the rules was not complete before the lighter had been fully loaded with all the goods intended to be put into it. While it was not necessary to decide whether discharge would then have been complete, it seems a reasonable inference from the judgment that Mr Justice Roche thought that it would. It follows that the case, while not an authority for the proposition that discharge in such circumstances is completed when a lighter is fully loaded, is entirely consistent with that view.

In the USA the view which I prefer is supported by two authorities on substantially the same question arising out of the Carriage of Goods by Sea Act of the United States, 1936 (COGSA). These are *Amerlux Steel Products Corporation* v *Motor Vessel Houffalize and ors* 1958 AMC 567 and *Remington Rand Inc. and ors.* v *American Export Lines Inc* 1955 AMC 1789. It is to be observed that both these decisions were adverse to the carrier, who was seeking to rely on the protection afforded to him by COGSA, and for this purpose contended unsuccessfully that such protection continued after the goods concerned had been transferred from the carrying ship to lighters provided by him at the port of discharge. In my view, however, this circumstance does not weaken the force of the decisions as persuasive authority on the question of interpretation involved.

The other view of the matter was taken by a Canadian Court in *Falconbridge Nickel Mines Ltd* v *Chimo Shipping Ltd* [1969] 2 Lloyd's Rep 277. This case can, however, in my view, be distinguished on two grounds. The first ground is that the craft into which the goods were transferred from the carrying ship for conveyance to the shore was a scow which was part of the equipment of such ship. The second ground is that the Canadian statute giving effect to the Hague Rules is the Canadian Water Carriage of Goods Act 1936, which applies to carriage of goods by water of any description, and not only by sea, and contains in art. I of the rules scheduled to it definitions of 'contract of carriage' and 'ship' which reflect this wider scope. If the case cannot properly be distinguished on these grounds, or one or other of them, I would with respect be unwilling to follow it.

*Note and Question*

1.   Brandon J's decision was reversed by the Court of Appeal ([1980] 2 Lloyd's Rep 135), who held that there was a new contract for the Chambers Wharf arrangement on the terms of the bill of lading. They did not consider the Hague Rules point.

2.   Where the bill of lading covers a voyage during which the goods will be transhipped, do the Rules apply during the interval between discharge from the first ship and loading on to the second?

### *Mayhew Foods Ltd* v *Overseas Containers Ltd*
[1984] 1 Lloyd's Rep 317 (QBD)

BINGHAM J: This is a claim by Mayhew Foods Ltd (Mayhew) as shippers against Overseas Containers Ltd (OCL) as carriers. It arises out of the carriage of a cargo of food which was found on arrival at its destination to be unfit to eat. OCL accept that the food became unfit and that they are liable for its deterioration, but seek to limit the damages recoverable against them in reliance on the terms of a standard clause in their bill of lading. Mayhew claim that the relevant carriage was subject to the Carriage of Goods by Sea Act 1971, and the Hague-Visby Rules scheduled thereto and that, accordingly, the contractual limitation of damage clause is of no effect. Whether OCL are entitled to limit their damages in reliance on the contract or whether the contract is superseded by the statutory provisions is the major issue I have to determine.

On about Nov. 27, 1981, Mayhew and OCL made an oral contract for the carriage by OCL of a refrigerated container of Mayhew's products from Mayhew's premises at Uckfield in Sussex to Jeddah in Saudi Arabia. The products in question consisted of 1,100 cartons (weighing 8,685 kilogrammes) of chicken and turkey portions, some cooked, some uncooked, and a few breaded drumsticks which were coated but uncooked. In order that these products should remain in good condition, it was necessary that they should be deep frozen at minus 18 dec. C. It was envisaged that the goods would be carried in a refrigerated container on the vessel *Benalder*. The cartons were collected from Mayhew's premises at Uckfield and stuffed into a refrigerated container on Dec. 3. They were then, it seems, taken to Shoreham and were, on Dec. 5, carried from Shoreham to Le Havre on a vessel named *Voline*, arriving in Le Havre very early on the 6th. The container was discharged and remained in Le Havre until it was loaded on *Benalder* on Dec. 11 or 12. *Benalder* arrived in Jeddah on Dec. 21, but permission to discharge this container was refused because the contents had decayed and offensive juices were reported to be dripping from it. The reason for this was that the temperature control on the container, instead of being set at minus 18 deg. C., as it should have been, had been set at plus 2 deg. C. to plus 4 deg. C. Far from being deep frozen, the goods had been subject to some heating while in the container. OCL accept that, as a result of this failure properly to refrigerate the goods in the container, they were in breach of their contract and of their duty as bailees and at law in failing to take reasonable care of the goods and to carry, keep and care for the same properly and carefully.

When the state of the cargo was discovered and discharge at Jeddah refused, the contents of the container were deep frozen to the required temperature and the container remained aboard the vessel as it continued its journey to the Far East. A cursory inspection of the contents was made in Malaya, but no detailed survey was made until the container was returned to Mayhew on Feb. 25, 1982. The food was then found to be unfit for human consumption and was sold at 2p per pound for animal food.

OCL's bill of lading showed Mayhew as the shipper. The consignee was to order. The notify party was United Foods Ltd, Jeddah. The place of receipt of the goods was shown as Mayhew's Uckfield premises; the place of delivery as a numbered berth in Jeddah. The intended vessel and voyage number were shown as '*Benalder* 0418'. The 'intended port of loading' was Southampton; the 'intended port of discharge' Jeddah. The place and date of issue were entered as 'London 08 12 81'. The bill bore a signature on behalf of OCL and a stamp which read—

> Shipped on board per ocean vessel *Benalder* on 12 December 1981 for Overseas Containers Ltd. . . .

followed by a further signature.

The conditions on the reverse of the bill differed in their application depending on whether combined transport shipment or port to port shipment was being undertaken. It is common ground that this was combined transport shipment and I need not refer to the other conditions, save to note that a different scheme applied. Clause 6 provided:

> Carrier's Responsibility — Combined Transport 1/ The Carrier shall be liable for loss or damage to the Goods occurring between the time when he receives the Goods for transportation and the time of delivery.

There follow exceptions irrelevant for present purposes. Clause 7 specified how any compensation recoverable should be calculated and specified an upper limit of—

> . . . US $2 per kilo of gross weight of the Goods lost or damaged.

It is this provision, entitling Mayhew to US $17,370, on which OCL rely to limit Mayhew's damages. Clause 8 was a long and involved condition, the effect of which, for present purposes, was to make cl. 7 subject to the Hague Rules or any national law or international convention having mandatory effect in respect of the relevant damage. Clause 21, so far as relevant, provided:

> Methods and Routes of Transportation 1/ The Carrier may at any time and without notice to the merchant:— a/ use any means of transport or storage whatsoever. b/ transfer the Goods from one conveyance to another including transhipping or carrying the same on another vessel than the vessel named overleaf or on any other means of transport whatsoever . . . d/ load and unload the Goods at any place or port (whether or not any such port is named overleaf as the Port of Loading or Port of Discharge) and store the Goods at any such place or port. 2/ The liberties set out in sub-clause 1/ may be invoked by the Carrier for any purpose whatsoever . . . and anything done in accordance with sub-clause 1 or any delay arising therefrom shall be deemed to be within the contractual carriage and shall not be a deviation.

In seeking to limit the damages recoverable against OCL to the measure prescribed by cl. 7 of the bill, Mr Flaux on their behalf submitted: (1) that the 1971 Act and the Hague-Visby Rules did not apply to this carriage until the goods were shipped aboard *Benalder* at Le Havre on Dec. 11 or 12, 1981: (2) that even if the Act and the rules did apply during the period of carriage by sea from Shoreham to Le Havre, they did not apply when the goods were lying ashore at Le Havre before shipment aboard *Benalder*: (3) that during any period when the Act and the rules did not apply, OCL were entitled to limit their damage in accordance with cl. 7 of the bill of lading: (4) that by the time the goods were loaded aboard *Benalder* at Le Havre on Dec. 11 or 12, from which time the 1971 Act and the Hague-Visby Rules admittedly did apply, the goods had already deteriorated to such an extent that Mayhew thereafter suffered no loss and damage as a consequence of OCL's failure to refrigerate.

The first of these submissions rested on the contention that the bill of lading related to shipment on *Benalder* as shown by the reference to the intended vessel and to the stamp. That shipment occurred at Le Havre. No bill of lading was issued in respect of the sea leg from Shoreham to Le Havre and this bill did not cover it. Mayhew could not rely on the Act and the rules before loading aboard the vessel nominated in the bill to undertake the sea carriage.

I cannot accept this submission. As Mr Justice Devlin pointed out in *Pyrene Co. Ltd* v *Scindia Navigation Co. Ltd* [1954] 1 Lloyd's Rep 321; [1954] 2 QB 402, at pp. 329 and 415, the rights and liabilities under the rules attach to a contract or part of a contract. The contract here was for carriage of these goods from Uckfield to the numbered berth at Jeddah. The rules did not apply to inland transport prior to shipment on board a vessel, because under s.1(3) of the 1971 Act, they are to have the force of law only in relation to and in connection with the carriage of goods by sea in ships. But the contract here clearly provided for shipment at a United Kingdom port, intended to be Southampton but in the event Shoreham, and from the time of that shipment, the Act and the rules plainly applied. It does not matter that the vessel on which the container left this country was not *Benalder*, because OCL had liberty to substitute vessels or tranship and *Benalder* was only the intended vessel. Nor does it matter that the bill of lading was issued some days after the goods had arrived in Le Havre showing *Benalder* and Southampton as the intended vessel and port of shipment. The parties clearly expected and intended a bill of lading to be issued and when issued it duly evidenced the parties' earlier contract. Since this bill was issued in a contracting state and provided for carriage from a port in a contracting state, I think it plain that the rules applied once the goods were loaded on board the vessel at Shoreham.

OCL's second submission took as its starting point fact already noted that the Act and the rules only apply—

... in relation to and in connection with the carriage of goods by sea in ships ...

It was accordingly argued that even if the statutory provisions governed carriage from Shoreham to Le Havre, they did not apply while the goods were lying ashore at Le Havre any more than they applied before the goods were loaded at Shoreham or after they were discharged at Jeddah. In short, it was said that the interval of storage at Le Havre was not carriage by sea and so not covered by the rules. As persuasive authority for this submission, Counsel relied on *Captain* v *Far Eastern Steamship Co.* [1979] 1 Lloyd's Rep 595, where a shipowner seeking to rely on the Hague Rules scheduled to the Canadian Carriage of Goods by Water Act was held disentitled to do so because the damage to the cargo had occurred during a lengthy period of storage ashore between two voyages. I do not, however, think that this decision gives much assistance, because the shipper there was told when the contract was made that there would be transhipment and there were separate bills of lading for the two legs of the journey. The present case is factually different. The answer to this problem is again to be found in the principle that the rights and liabilities under the rules attach to a contract. They do not apply to carriage or storage before the port of shipment or after the port of discharge, because that would be inland and not sea carriage. But between those ports the contract was, despite the wide language of cl. 21, for carriage by sea. If, during that carriage, OCL chose to avail themselves of their contractual right to discharge, store and tranship, those were, in my judgment, operations 'in relation to and in connection with the carriage of goods by sea in ships', to use the language of the Act, or were 'within the contractual carriage', to use the language of cl. 21(2) of the bill of lading conditions. It would, I think, be surprising if OCL could, by carrying the goods to Le Havre and there storing the goods before transhipment, rid themselves of liabilities to which they would have been subject had they, as contemplated, shipped the goods at Southampton and carried them direct to Jeddah, the more so since Mayhew had no knowledge of any voyage to Le Havre. My conclusion is that the rules, having applied on shipment at Shoreham, remained continuously in force until discharge at Jeddah.

## SECTION 7: THE CARRIER'S DUTIES UNDER THE RULES

We are here concerned with the carrier's responsibilities and liabilities 'in relation to the loading, handling, stowage, carriage, custody, care and discharge' of the goods (Art. II) and the duty to issue a bill of lading (Art. III, r. 3).

*A: Seaworthiness*

While it may be assumed that the basic concept of seaworthiness is the same under the Rules as at common law, there are significant differences in the treatment of the obligation.

### Carriage of Goods by Sea Act 1971
### SCHEDULE

**Article III**
(1)   The carrier shall be bound before and at the beginning of the voyage to exercise due diligence to—
   (a)   Make the ship seaworthy.
   (b)   Properly man, equip and supply the ship.
   (c)   Make the holds, refrigerating and cool chambers, and all other parts of the ship in which goods are carried, fit and safe for their reception, carriage and preservation.

**Article IV**
(1)   Neither the carrier nor the ship shall be liable for loss or damage arising or resulting from unseaworthiness unless caused by want of due diligence on the part of the carrier to make the ship seaworthy, and to secure that the ship is properly manned, equipped and supplied, and to make the holds, refrigerating and cool chambers and all other parts of the ship in which goods are carried fit and safe for their reception, carriage and preservation in accordance with the provisions of paragraph 1 of Article III. Whenever loss or damage has resulted from unseaworthiness the burden of proving the exercise of due diligence shall be on the carrier or other person claiming exemption under this article.

*Note*
These provisions are reinforced by s. 3 of the Act:

## Carriage of Goods by Sea Act 1971

### 3.  Absolute warranty of seaworthiness not to be implied in contracts to which Rules apply

There shall not be implied in any contract for the carriage of goods by sea to which the Rules apply by virtue of this Act any absolute undertaking by the carrier of the goods to provide a seaworthy ship.

(a)  *'before and at the beginning of the voyage'*

### *Maxine Footwear Co. Ltd* v *Canadian Government Merchant Marine Ltd*
### [1959] AC 589 (PC)

Three crates and a drum of shoe leather and 'findings' were loaded at Halifax, Nova Scotia, for carriage to Kingston, Jamaica. Loading of all cargo was completed on Friday, 6 February 1942, at around 8.15 p.m. and the vessel was due to sail the next day.

On the Friday morning some scupper pipes had been found to be blocked by ice and the master gave instructions for them to be thawed out. The officer in charge of this operation used a shore-based firm, whose employee thawed out the pipes with an acetylene torch.

The heat from the torch started a fire in the cork insulation round the pipes which was not noticed until 11.30 p.m. The fire then spread and early next morning the ship had to be scuttled, with the loss of the cargo. The shipowners accepted that the officer was negligent.

It was held by the Privy Council, reversing the Supreme Court of Canada, that the shipowners were in breach of Art. III, r. 1.

LORD SOMERVELL OF HARROW: Before proceeding to consider the arguments it is convenient to state certain conclusions which appear plain to their Lordships. From the time when the ship caught on fire she was unseaworthy. This unseaworthiness caused the damage to and loss of the appellants' goods. The negligence of the respondents' servants which caused the fire was a failure to exercise due diligence.

Logically, the first submission on behalf of the respondents was that in cases of fire article III never comes into operation even though the fire makes the ship unseaworthy. All fires and all damage from fire on this argument fall to be dealt with under article IV, r. 2(b). If this were right there was at any rate a very strong case for saying that there was no fault or privity of the carrier within that rule, and the respondents would succeed.

In their Lordships' opinion the point fails. Article III, r. 1, is an overriding obligation. If it is not fulfilled and the non-fulfilment causes the damage the immunities of article IV cannot be relied on. This is the natural construction apart from the opening words of article III, r. 2. The fact that that rule is made subject to the provisions of article IV and rule 1 is not so conditioned makes the point clear beyond argument.

The further submissions by the respondents were based, as they had to be, on the construction of article III, r. 1. It was submitted that under that article the obligation is only to exercise due diligence to make the ship seaworthy at two moments of time, the beginning of the loading and the beginning of the voyage.

It is difficult to believe that this construction of the word 'before' could have been argued but for the fact that this doctrine of stages had been laid down in relation to the absolute warranty of seaworthiness in English law.

It is worth, therefore, bearing in mind words used by Lord Mcmillan with reference to the English Carriage of Goods by Sea Act 1924, which embodied the Hague Rules, as does the present Act.

It is important to remember that the Act of 1924 was the outcome of an International Conference, and that the rules in the Schedule have an international currency. As these rules must come under the consideration of foreign courts it is desirable in the interests of uniformity that their interpretation should not be rigidly controlled by domestic precedents of antecedent date, but rather that the language of the rules should be construed on broad principles of general acceptation. (*Stag Line Ltd* v *Foscolo, Mango & Co.* [1932] AC 328, 350; 48 TLR 127)

In their Lordships' opinion 'before and at the beginning of the voyage' means the period from at least the beginning of the loading until the vessel starts on her voyage. The word 'before' cannot in their opinion be read as meaning 'at the commencement of the loading'. If this had been intended it would have been said. The question when precisely the period begins does not arise in this case, hence the insertion above of the words 'at least'.

On that view the obligation to exercise due diligence to make the ship seaworthy continued over the whole of the period from the beginning of loading until the ship sank. There was a failure to exercise due diligence during that period. As a result the ship became unseaworthy and this unseaworthiness caused the damage to and loss of the appellants' goods. The appellants are therefore entitled to succeed.

It becomes therefore unneccessary to consider whether the Supreme Court were justified in holding that the appellants' goods were not stowed until after the commencement of the fire.

It is also unnecessary to consider the earlier cases as to 'stages' under the common law. The doctrine of stages had its anomalies and some important matters were never elucidated by authority. When the warranty was absolute it seems at any rate intelligible to restrict it to certain points of time. It would be surprising if a duty to exercise due diligence ceased as soon as loading began, only to reappear later shortly before the beginning of the voyage.

*Notes and Question*
1.   The unsuccessful attempt to limit the scope of the Rules by importing into them concepts derived from the common law is by no means unique.
2.   In *A. Meredith Jones & Co. Ltd* v *Vangemar Shipping Co. Ltd (The Apostolis)* [1997] 2 Lloyd's Rep 241 (CA), Phillips LJ commented (at p. 257), but without further explanation, that he has 'always found that [i.e., *Maxine Footwear*] a difficult decision'.

*(b)   'exercise due diligence'*

### Riverstone Meat Co. Pty Ltd v Lancashire Shipping Co. Ltd
### (The Muncaster Castle)
[1961] 1 Lloyd's Rep 57 (HL)

RM's cargo of 150 cases of ox tongues was damaged when sea water entered the hold on the voyage from Sydney to London. The water entered through inspection covers on storm valves because the nuts had not been properly tightened by the fitter after the covers were removed by reputable ship-repairers in the course of surveyors' inspection. McNair J and the Court of Appeal held that, although the vessel was unseaworthy, the shipowners had exercised due diligence and were not liable for the damage to the cargo. The House of Lords allowed the cargo-owners' appeal.

LORD RADCLIFFE: My Lords, I have no doubt that this case is important in its implications and that it has merited the full consideration that it has received at all its hearings. Nevertheless, it appears to me that the answer to be returned to the problem it raises depends upon a very short question: What kind of obligation is imported by the words 'shall be bound ... to exercise due diligence to make the ship seaworthy' that appear in Art. III, r. 1, of the Rules scheduled to the Australian Sea-Carriage of Goods Act, 1924? As we know, these are in fact the Hague Rules. Read them in one way, the answer must necessarily be for the appellants, the cargo-owners: read them in another, it must be for the respondents, the carriers.

The relevant facts are of the simplest. Cargo has been damaged in the course of a voyage and it was damaged because the ship on which it was carried was unseaworthy. The unseaworthiness was caused by the carelessness of a fitter employed by skilled repairers working for the carriers. The work that they were doing was in connection with the ship's No. 2 special survey and annual load-line survey, in other words, work which was reasonably required in order to keep the ship in a seaworthy condition.

Now, I am quite satisfied that, treating the carriers as a legal person, a limited company whose mind, will and actions are determined by its officers and servants, they did nothing but what they should have done as responsible and careful persons in the carrying business. They were not themselves in the repairing business and there is no reason why they should have been, but they were mindful of their duty to have their ship in good order for its voyage or voyages and they not only entrusted her to a ship-repairing company of repute for reception in dry dock, but also employed an experienced and competent marine superintendent to act on their behalf. He, in his turn, acted with more than usual caution in requiring all the ship's storm valves to be opened up for inspection and, although it was the carelessness of one of the repairers' fitters that left one of these valves ineffectively closed, it was ordinary prudent practice to entrust the work of closing up to a fitter and not to subject such work to an independent inspection.

I see no ground, therefore, for saying that the carriers themselves were negligent in anything that they did. If the content of their obligation is that they should, as a legal person, observe the standard of reasonable care that would be required at common law in a matter of this sort, which involves skilled and technical work, and if there is nothing more in their obligation than that, then I should not regard them as in default or, consequently, as liable to the cargo-owners. Full and instructive as are the several judgments of the members of the Court of Appeal, I do not think that, in the end, they amount to more than an acceptance of this standard of obligation and a drawing of the necessary conclusion from the facts.

But there is, on the other hand, a way of looking at the intrinsic nature of the obligation that is materially different from this. It is to ask the question, when there has been damage to cargo and that damage is traceable to unseaworthiness of the vessel, whether that unseaworthiness is due to any lack of diligence in those who have been implicated by the carriers in the work of keeping or making the vessel seaworthy. Such persons are then agents whose diligence or lack of it is attributable to the carriers. An inquiry on these lines is not concerned with distinctions between carelessness on the part of officers or servants of the carriers or their supervising agents on the one hand and carelessness on the part of their contractors or those contractors' contractors on the other. The carriers must answer for anything that has been done amiss in the work. It is the work itself that delimits the area of the obligation, just as it is the period 'before or at the beginning of the voyage' that delimits the time at which any obligation imputed to the carriers can be thought to begin. If these last points are borne in mind I think that the difficulties about 'an almost unlimited retrogression' (see *W. Angliss & Co. (Australia) Pty Ltd* v *Peninsular and Oriental Steam Navigation Company* [1927] 2 KB 456, at p. 461; (1927) 28 Ll L Rep 202, at p. 213) tend to disappear: for there is a point in each case at which defective work is not the work of any agent of the carrier and the duty to be diligent is no more than a duty to be skilled and careful in inspection. But the inspection that is relevant in such a case is not merely the carrier's inspection of his contractor's work: it is inspection on the part of anyone working for the carrier who is concerned to make sure that he does not accept defective materials or use defective tools.

If one had to choose between these two alternatives without any background in the way of previous authority or opinion with regard to the interpretation of this section of the Hague Rules, I think it would be very difficult to know which way one ought to turn. The natural meaning of the words does not seem to me to accord well with either reading. Whatever the responsibility is, it is imposed on the carrier and no one else — that is clear — but it is equally clear that no one would regard the carrier as being in the wrong merely because he gets whatever requires to be done, inspection, survey or work, done for him by someone else. If the respondents' reading is adopted, the one that has commended itself to Mr Justice McNair and the Court of Appeal, one must treat the words 'due diligence to make the ship seaworthy' as if they were equivalent to 'due diligence to see that the ship is made seaworthy' and that is not the same thing. On the other hand, the reading for which the appellants contend is not, in truth, consistent with the grammatical meaning of the words they have to rely upon, for the exercise of due diligence to which the carrier would be held would include the performance or omission of acts that were not in law the acts of the carrier at all.

Such general considerations as occur to me appear to favour the cargo-owner's claim. He is not in any sense behind the scenes with regard to what is done to the vessel or how or when it is done. His concern with it begins and ends with the loading and discharge of his goods. The carrier on the other hand must have some form of ownership of the vessel and some measure of responsibility for seeing that it is fit and in proper condition for the carriage undertaken. He may qualify that responsibility by stipulation, if the law allows him to; or the law may write out the terms of his responsibility for him; but within those limits the responsibility is there. I should regard it as unsatisfactory, where a cargo-owner has found his goods damaged through a defect in the seaworthiness of the vessel, that his rights of recovering from the carrier should depend on particular circumstances in the carrier's situation and arrangements with which the cargo-owner has nothing to do; as for instance, that liability should depend upon the measure of control that the carrier had exercised over persons engaged on surveying or repairing the ship or upon such questions as whether the carrier had or could have done whatever was needed by the hands of his own servants or had been sensible or prudent in getting it done by other hands. Carriers would find themselves liable or not liable, according to circumstances quite extraneous to the sea carriage itself.

What I think should determine this appeal, however, is what we know of the history of these words 'due diligence to make the ship seaworthy' in connection with sea carriage of goods and what I regard as the settled interpretation of their significance which has been alluded to from time to time in the English Courts. These sources seem to me to be wholly in favour of the appellants' claim. We have, to begin with, the common learning that the words in question were adopted by international convention in the Hague Rules at a time when they had been for many years familiar in the Harter Act 1893, of the United States. We know what content successive decisions of American Courts had given those words: that the carrier was responsible to the cargo-owner unless due diligence in the work had been shown by every person to whom any part of the necessary work had been entrusted, no matter whether he was the carrier's servant, agent or independent contractor. 'Merely employing agents of good repute' was not enough [Per Brown J, in *The Colima* (1897) 82 Fed 665 at p. 678.]

*Note*

The decision in *The Muncaster Castle* finally brought English law into line with the interpretation adopted under the Harter Act as long ago as 1897 in *The Colima* 82 Fed 665. Given that the onus is on the shipowner to prove due diligence (Art. IV, r. 1), is there any practical difference between the position under the rules and the 'absolute' common law obligation? (*Cf.* Lord Keith of Avonholm in *The Muncaster Castle*, at p. 87.)

However, in the next case the House of Lords tempered the severity of the rule: lack of due diligence is not shown merely by proving that some further steps could have been taken to discover and remedy the cause of the unseaworthiness.

### Union of India v NV Reederij Amsterdam
### (The Amstelslot)
[1963] 2 Lloyd's Rep 223 (HL)

LORD DEVLIN: My Lords, the appellants are shipowners who in 1957 contracted to carry grain for the respondents from Portland (Oreg.) to Bombay. In September, 1957, in the course of the voyage the engines of the vessel broke down because of a fracture of part of the reduction gear. The grain was eventually transhipped at the expense of the respondents. The respondents sue for damage and the appellants counterclaim for a general average contribution.

Both these issues turn on what is now a short question. The fracture was due to a fatigue crack in the after helix tyre of the main gear drum. It is admitted that the crack, although unknown at the commencement of the voyage, must then have been there and, accordingly, that the ship was unseaworthy. The unchallenged evidence makes it probable that the crack, whether visible or invisible, was there when the ship was last surveyed in July, 1956. The question is whether the appellants have shown that it was not then discoverable by due diligence. If they have, they win; and if they have not, they lose. This is pure fact. . . .

The survey of July, 1956, which included the examination of the reduction gear, was conducted in Amsterdam by two surveyors, one the Amsterdam surveyor to Lloyd's Register of Shipping and the other the appellants' engineer superintendent. The Judge described them both as impressive witnesses whose veracity was not challenged. There is, therefore, no dispute about what they did nor that as a result of it they did not see the crack or anything which should have caused them to suspect its existence. It was at one time suggested — indeed it was the respondents' main case at the trial — that the fatigue crack was caused by a loose rim, which is something that should have been discovered on inspection. But that theory was negatived by the Judge, whose finding on this point was not thereafter challenged. It was also at one time suggested that a magnaflux test should have been used. This is a process in which oil impregnated with iron particles is spread over the gears and then charged with an electric current, which will produce a visible line of particles at any crack. But this suggestion also was negatived by the learned Judge and has not been pursued.

It was, therefore, in the end, accepted that the proper sort of examination of the gear was a visual examination in which cracks should be looked for among other possible defects. No one can say for certain whether a visual examination, however thorough, would have discovered the crack in July, 1956. It may or may not have been detectable by then. But it is for the appellants to prove that the surveyors they employed made as thorough an examination as, in the circumstances, they could reasonably be expected to make and that it revealed revealed nothing suspicious. It is not disputed that the examination was conducted efficiently and that it revealed nothing. The question to be decided is whether, in the circumstances, it was thorough enough. The Judge thought that it was. It would not have been surprising if, after his careful and exhaustive analysis of the evidence, the matter had ended there. But it was taken to appeal and as there was a division of opinion in the Court of Appeal, the majority reversing the finding of the learned Judge, the matter has naturally come before your Lordships.

The plaintiffs' case, on appeal, was that there were three precautions that could have been taken by the surveyors which would have increased their chances of discovering any crack. These precautions were:

(a)   to remove the upper housing of the gears for the purpose of the examination;
(b)   to wipe the teeth of the gears clean of oil before examining them; and
(c)   to examine the teeth of one helix at a time instead of the teeth of four helices simultaneously.

Your Lordships are not invited to say that these were the sort of precautions that were obviously necessary, whatever the experts might think. The respondents must rely on qualified witnesses who are prepared to criticise the survey as inadequate in one or more of the above respects. I do not think that this is a case in which the Judge has to keep it constantly in mind that the burden of proof of due diligence lies on the defendant. Proof of unseaworthiness fulfils, as Mr Brandon says, the same function in this type of case as *res ipsa loquitur* does in the ordinary case of negligence. But where, as here, the defendant meets the *prima facie* case against him by calling two surveyors of unchallenged reputation who are found by the Judge to be impressive and who say what they did and why they did it and why they did not do more, then, unless they can be successfully criticised for their omissions, a Judge is entitled to say that due diligence was exercised. No doubt he must remember that if, in the end, he is unable to make up his mind whether or not the criticisms are weighty enough to disturb his confidence in the surveyors' judgment, he must find for the plaintiff and not for the defendant. But that is not the sort of situation that often arises.

It is important to get clear the point to which criticism must be directed. There is here no lack of care and no lack of skilled knowledge. The surveyors were quite familiar with the three methods of examination which it is said that they should have adopted; and they could easily have followed them if they had chosen to do so. What is said against them is that by deciding in effect that these methods were not appropriate to the sort of examination they were conducting, they made an error of judgment which a competent surveyor ought not to have made. Lack of due diligence is negligence; and what is in issue in this case is whether there was an error of judgment that amounted to professional negligence.

My Lords, speaking with great respect to the judgments of Lord Denning MR, and of Lord Justice Donovan in the Court of Appeal, I cannot find anything in the evidence of the qualified witnesses that goes that far. Apart from the two surveyors themselves, four professional witnesses were called — two consulting engineers, a naval architect and Mr Siggers, the principal engineer surveyor of Lloyd's Register of Shipping. Mr Siggers is the one best qualified to speak about how a survey of this sort should be conducted; and he is the one on whose evidence the Court of Appeal reversed the finding of the trial Judge. He was asked in respect of each of the three suggested precautions whether there was 'a better chance' of the crack being found if it had been adopted; and he answered in each case that there was. Some of the other three witnesses gave a similar answer to one or more of the precautions suggested.

My Lords, I fully accept these answers which were the only answer that on the facts of this case could have been made to such a question. After all, there would be a better chance of avoiding road accidents if everyone drove at five miles an hour. This line of questioning is quite legitimate for the purpose of laying a foundation, but it does no more than that. The ultimate question is not whether there was a better chance of discovering the crack, but whether, on balance, one or more of the precautions ought to have been taken. What has to be balanced is in the one scale the extreme unlikelihood of there being any crack to be found and in the other scale the serious damage and loss that could occur if there were a crack. The balance that is so struck will determine whether or not a prudent surveyor should have felt it necessary to do more than these surveyors did. . . .

On this question of whether the balance should have been struck, which is the cardinal question in this case, there are in the mass of evidence only two answers which are directly probative. They are in Mr Siggers's evidence and I quote them together with the preceding question that leads up to and explains them ([1962] 2 Lloyd's Rep, at p. 342).

Q.: I am suggesting if all these three things are done — if you take off the housing, look at one helix at a time, and remove the oil — you have got a much better chance of finding a crack than if you do not? A.: Yes, I agree.

Q.: I further suggest there would be nothing unreasonable in asking people to do that once every four years. A.: No, not unreasonable.

Q.: And it would be a reasonable precaution against the type of casualty that occurred in this case? A.: Yes, I think so.

My Lords, I do not think that these answers go far enough for the respondents' purpose. They show what Mr Siggers considered a reasonable precaution to take, but not necessarily that he considered that anyone who thought differently would be incompetent. When one reads his evidence as a whole — it was generally in favour of the appellants whose witness he was — I strongly doubt whether he would have gone as far as that. Certainly he was not specifically asked to do so. If, on the basis of these two answers, the trial Judge had found a lack of due diligence, it might have been difficult, slender though they are, for an appellate Court to have reversed him. I do not know. But I am quite sure it would be wrong for an appellate Court to allow two answers of this character to cast doubt on the finding of the trial Judge who heard the witnesses give their evidence and weighed it as a whole and found due diligence proved.

I would allow the appeal.

*Note*

In spite of the clear message from the House of Lords that the issue is one of fact only, there is still a small but steady flow of reported decisions on due diligence.

In deciding whether due diligence has been exercised, much will depend on the credibility of the master and other witnesses for the shipowner: compare *Phillips Petroleum Co.* v *Cabaneli Naviera SA (The Theodegmon)* [1990] 1 Lloyd's Rep 52 (QBD) with *The Hellenic Dolphin* [1978] 2 Lloyd's Rep 336 (QBD, Adm Ct). See also *The Toledo* [1995] 1 Lloyd's Rep 40 (QBD, Adm Ct): owners failed to discharge the burden — they were complacent, and did not follow their own system for reporting damage. Although the carrier has the burden of showing due diligence, the cargo owner must first establish that the vessel was unseaworthy: see *Empresa Cubana Importada de Alimentos 'Alimport'* v *Iasmos Shipping Co SA (The Good Friend)* [1984] 2 Lloyd's Rep 586 (QBD), at p. 588 (Staughton J).

*B: Care of the cargo*

## Carriage of Goods by Sea Act 1971

### SCHEDULE

**Article III**
  (2)   Subject to the provisions of Article IV, the carrier shall properly and carefully load, handle, stow, carry, keep, care for, and discharge the goods carried.

*Note*
What, if anything, does 'properly' add to the obligation to take care?

### *Albacora SRL* v *Westcott & Laurance Line Ltd*
[1966] 2 Lloyd's Rep 53 (HL)

1,200 cases of wet salted ling fillets were consigned from Glasgow to A in Genoa on W & L's vessel, the *Maltasian*. On arrival the fish was found to have been damaged by halophilic bacteria because the temperature in the hold had been above the critical level of 5°C. Neither the shippers nor the carriers realised that refrigeration was necessary and the contract did not provide for it. A claimed damages and argued that W & L were in breach of Art. III, r. 2 since the fish could only be 'properly' carried in refrigeration. The Court of Session and House of Lords held that the shipowners were not in breach of Art. III, r. 2.

LORD REID: ... There was no suggestion that the voyage took longer than it should have done. The appellants accept the finding that there was no negligence and do not suggest that the result in any other similar unrefrigerated ship would have been any better.
    The appellants' argument is that the respondents were in breach of Art. III, r. 2 ... of the Schedule to the Carriage of Goods by Sea Act 1924, which was incorporated in the bill of lading:

Subject to the provisions of Article IV, the carrier shall properly and carefully load, handle, stow, carry, keep, care for and discharge the goods carried.

The argument is that in this Article 'properly' means in the appropriate manner looking to the actual nature of the consignment, and that it is irrelevant that the shipowner and ship's officers neither knew nor could have discovered that special treatment was necessary. The obligation under the Article is to carry goods properly and if that is not done there is a breach of contract. So it is argued that in the present case it is proved that the only proper way to carry this consignment on this voyage was in a refrigerated hold, and there the obligation of the respondents was to do that, even if the appellants' agents who were parties to the contract were aware that there was no refrigeration in this ship.

This construction of the word 'properly' leads to such an unreasonable result that I would not adopt it if the word can properly be construed in any other sense. The appellants argue that, because the article uses the word 'properly' as well as 'carefully', the word 'properly' must mean something more than carefully. Tautology is not unknown even in international conventions, but I think that 'properly' in this context has a meaning slightly different from 'carefully'. I agree with Viscount Kilmuir, LC, that here 'properly' means in accordance with a sound system (*G.H. Renton & Co. Ltd* v *Palmyra Trading Corporation of Panama* [1957] AC 149, at p. 166; [1956] 2 Lloyd's Rep 379, at p. 388) and that may mean rather more than carrying the goods carefully. But the question remains by what criteria it is to be judged whether the system was sound.

In my opinion, the obligation is to adopt a system which is sound in light of all the knowledge which the carrier has or ought to have about the nature of the goods. And if that is right, then the respondents did adopt a sound system. They had no reason to suppose that the goods required any different treatment from that which the goods in fact received.

LORD PEARCE: The real point in this case, therefore, is the pursuers' contention that the carriers' obligation under Art. III, r. 2, that they shall 'properly and carefully load, handle, stow, carry, keep, care for' the cargo imports a duty to carry in the most appropriate manner, that is to say to carry in a refrigerator a cargo which is found to have needed a refrigerator and that an unrefrigerated ship automatically breaks its contract when it carries a cargo, such as that in question, which could not possibly support the journey without refrigeration. In my opinion, such a proposition is not maintainable and would lead to injustice and absurdity.

The word 'properly' presumably adds something to the word 'carefully'. In *G.H. Renton & Co. Ltd* v *Palmyra Trading Corporation of Panama* [1957] AC 149, this House construed it as meaning 'upon a sound system'. A sound system does not mean a system suited to all the weaknesses and idiosyncrasies of a particular cargo, but a sound system under all the circumstances in relation to the general practice of carriage of goods by sea. It is tantamount, I think, to efficiency. To accept the pursuer's contention would be to import into the Hague Rules a revolutionary departure from the scheme of the common law. Viscount Sumner said in *F.C. Bradley & Sons Ltd* v *Federal Steam Navigation Company Ltd* (1927) 27 Ll L Rep 395, at p. 399:

> ... When the common law makes the ship bear the risks of the voyage and of all that may happen to the cargo in the course of it, but excepts the act of God, the King's enemies and inherent vice, the scheme is evident. Neither party can wholly guard against the act of God and the King's enemies, so the loss lies where it falls. For the rest, the carrier answers for his ship and men, the cargo-owner for his cargo. The carrier has at least some means of controlling his crew and has full opportunity of making his ship seaworthy, but of the cargo he knows little or nothing and, as the shipper has the advantage over him in this respect, he must bear the risks belonging to the cargo.

Was it intended that the Hague Rules should make a radical departure from the common law, and impose on the ship an obligation to use the best possible means of carriage, suited to the weakness of the cargo, even if those means were not within the competence of the ship? Was it intended that if a cargo had only the strength to endure a quick passage in the *Queen Mary*, but not the slower and rougher passage in a tramp steamer, then the tramp steamer, which without any prior information as to its weakness agreed to carry it, was automatically liable for its deterioration during the voyage? Such an intention would produce a novel and unfair result. And such an intention would certainly have been expressed in clear language. It would not have been left in ambiguity dependent on the one word 'properly'.

*Notes*
*1.* Lord Pearson referred to the French text for guidance ('*de façon appropriée*') and defined 'properly' as 'the manner appropriate to be adopted in all the circumstances of the case', which included the fact that the shipowners had no reason to know or suspect that refrigeration was necessary.
*2.* In *Balli Trading Ltd* v *Afalona Shipping Co. Ltd (The Coral)* [1993] 1 Lloyd's Rep 1, at 5, Beldam LJ said: 'It is now settled that Art. III, r. 2 does not impose upon the carrier an obligation to load, handle, stow, carry, keep, etc., the goods carried' and referred to *Pyrene Co. Ltd* v *Scindia Navigation Co. Ltd*, above, and *G. H. Renton & Co.* v *Palmyra Trading Corporation of Panama*, below. With respect, there is a world of difference between saying that the contract determines who shall load and where the goods shall be carried to, and holding that the whole of Art. III, r. 2 is subject to contrary agreement. (The case itself concerned stowing, which is indistinguishable for this purpose from loading).

*C. Issue of bills of lading*

When the Rules apply, the shipper has the right to demand a shipped bill of lading containing the specified particulars. The shipper in turn guarantees the accuracy of the information supplied by him as to marks, etc.

## Carriage of Goods by Sea Act 1971

### SCHEDULE

**Article III**
    (3)    After receiving the goods into his charge the carrier or the master or agent of the carrier shall, on demand of the shipper, issue to the shipper a bill of lading showing among other things—
    (a)    The leading marks necessary for identification of the goods as the same are furnished in writing by the shipper before the loading of such goods starts, provided such marks are stamped or otherwise shown clearly upon the goods if uncovered, or on the cases or coverings in which such goods are contained, in such a manner as should ordinarily remain legible until the end of the voyage.
    (b)    Either the number of packages or pieces, or the quantity, or weight, as the case may be, as furnished in writing by the shipper.
    (c)    The apparent order and condition of the goods.

Provided that no carrier, master or agent of the carrier shall be bound to state or show in the bill of lading any marks, number, quantity, or weight which he has reasonable ground for suspecting not accurately to represent the goods actually received, or which he has had no reasonable means of checking.

(4)   Such a bill of lading shall be prima facie evidence of the receipt by the carrier of the goods as therein described in accordance with paragraph 3(a), (b) and (c). However, proof to the contrary shall not be admissible when the bill of lading has been transferred to a third party acting in good faith.

(5)   The shipper shall be deemed to have guaranteed to the carrier the accuracy at the time of shipment of the marks, number, quantity and weight, as furnished by him, and the shipper shall indemnify the carrier against all loss, damages and expenses arising or resulting from inaccuracies in such particulars. The right of the carrier to such indemnity shall in no way limit his responsibility and liability under the contract of carriage to any person other than the shipper.

(6)   ...

(7)   After the goods are loaded the bill of lading to be issued by the carrier, master, or agent of the carrier, to the shipper shall, if the shipper so demands, be a 'shipped' bill of lading, provided that if the shipper shall have previously taken up any document of title to such goods, he shall surrender the same as against the issue of the 'shipped' bill of lading, but at the option of the carrier such document of title may be noted at the port of shipment by the carrier, master, or agent with the name or names of the ship or ships upon which the goods have been shipped and the date or dates of shipment, and when so noted if it shows the particulars mentioned in paragraph 3 of Article III, shall for the purpose of this article be deemed to constitute a 'shipped' bill of lading.

*Notes*

1.   For Art. III, r. 6, see section 9, below.
2.   In *Compania Importadora de Arroces Collette y Kamp SA* v *P & O Steam Navigation Co.* (1927) 28 Ll L Rep 63, Wright J held that 'leading marks' was not a term of art and covered quality marks as well as identification marks. It seems clear, however, that in para. 3(a) it is being used in the narrow sense of identification marks only, as opposed to quality marks.

What is the effect of Art. III, r. 3 on a bill of lading which contains a 'weight unknown' or 'said to be' notation?

### *Agrosin Pte Ltd* v *Highway Shipping Co. Ltd*
### *(The Mata K)*
### [1998] 2 Lloyd's Rep 642 (QBD)

CLARKE J: The plaintiffs were the charterers of the defendants' motor vessel *Mata K* under a voyage charter dated Dec. 17, 1996 in an amended Fertivoy 88 form for the carriage of 25,000 tonnes (10 per cent. more or less in owners' option) of muriate of potash from one safe berth Ventspils to 1/2 safe berth(s) each two safe ports South Korea 1/2 safe berth(s) each 1/2 safe port(s) Japan. A cargo of potash was shipped at Ventspils under three bills of lading each dated Dec. 31, 1996. The total tonnage referred to in the bills of lading was 24,024.70 tonnes. I am, however, concerned with only one of the three bills, No. SVJ-0187/96. It is in the Congenbill form. The plaintiffs are named as shippers and the goods were consigned to order but the notify address is that of Mitsui and Co. in Tokyo ('Mitsui'). The bill of lading is signed by the plaintiffs on behalf of the defendants as carriers. The port of loading is described as Ventspils, Latvia and the port of discharge as Japanese port(s). In the box marked 'Shipper's description of goods' the goods are described as 'Muriate of Potash In Bulk' and under 'Gross weight' there appears the figure '11,000 MT'. The box marked 'SHIPPED' includes the following:

Weight, measure, quality, quantity, condition, contents and value unknown.

It is common ground that the carriage was governed by the Hague Rules. Clause 1 of the conditions of carriage on the back of the bill of lading provides:

All terms and conditions, liberties and exceptions of the Charter Party, dated as overleaf, including the Law and Arbitration Clause, are herewith incorporated.

It is common ground that the charter-party referred to in the clause is the charter-party between the plaintiffs and the defendants to which I have already referred.

After loading, the vessel proceeded to discharge at Ulsan and Chinhae in Korea. She then proceeded to Japan where she discharged the remainder of her cargo at Ishinomaki and Sodeguara. It is alleged that on final discharge at Sodeguara it was discovered that there was a shortfall of about 2705 tonnes as compared with the total of the cargo stated in the three bills of lading, namely 24,024.7 tonnes. I do not know how the outturn figure were arrived at at the four discharge ports, but it appears that Mitsui made a claim in respect of the alleged shortage. They appear to have made a claim as buyers against the plaintiffs as sellers under an alleged contract of sale, although I have seen very little of the relevant documentation in that regard. They also made a claim as holders or indorsees of the bill of lading which I have described against the defendants as carriers. The plaintiffs reached a settlement with Mitsui, who assigned their rights against the defendants to them. This action is brought by the plaintiffs as assignees of Mitsui's rights against the defendants arising out of the bill of lading.

. . .

The defendants deny the alleged shortage. They say that all the cargo shipped was discharged and that, if less than the total bill of lading quantity was discharged, the explanation is that the total bill of lading was not shipped. The plaintiffs say that the defendants are bound by the bill of lading quantity and that it is not open to them to say that the whole quantity was not shipped. The plaintiffs have issued a summons under RSC, O. 14A for the determination of the following question (as slightly amended), namely whether the defendants are bound by the quantity of goods stated in the bill of lading by reason of the terms of the bill of lading and/or by reason of the incorporation of cl. 46 of the charter-party. I think that it is agreed that I should determine that question under RSC, O. 14A and that for that purpose I should assume that the facts alleged by the plaintiffs are true.

After holding that the bill of lading did not satisfy s. 4 of COGSA 1992 (see Chapter 6) Clarke J continued:

Mr Davey submits, however, that the Court should disregard or treat as null and void and of no effect the expression 'weight . . . unknown' by reason of the provisions of art. III, rr. 3 and 8 of the Hague Rules. Article III, rr. 3, 4 and 8 provide, so far as material, as follows:

3. After receiving the goods into his charge, the carrier, or the master or agent of the carrier, shall, on demand of the shipper, issue to the shipper a bill of lading

showing among other things — . . . (b) either the number of packages or pieces, or the quantity, or weight, as the case may be, as furnished in writing by the shipper,
. . . provided that no carrier, master or agent of the carrier, shall be bound to state or show in the bill of lading any marks, number, quantity, or weight which he has reasonable grounds for suspecting not accurately to represent the goods actually received, or which he has had no reasonable means of checking.

4.    Such a bill of lading shall be prima facie evidence of the receipt by the carrier of the goods as therein described in accordance with paragraphs (a), (b) and (c).
. . .

8.    Any clause, covenant or agreement in a contract of carriage relieving the carrier or the ship from liability for loss or damage to or in connection with goods arising from negligence, fault or failure in the duties and obligations provided in this Article or lessening such liability otherwise than as provided in these rules, shall be null and void and of no effect.

If I have understood it correctly, Mr Davey's argument is to this effect. The plaintiffs as shippers demanded the issue of a bill of lading showing the weight of the cargo. The defendants failed to comply with that demand when the plaintiffs issued the bill of lading on their behalf containing the provision 'weight . . . unknown'. That provision is null and void and of no effect under art. III, r. 8. It follows that the bill of lading should be read as if the 'weight . . . unknown' provision was not included with two results. The first is that the bill of lading 'shows' the weight within the meaning of art. III, r. 3 and is thus prima facie evidence of the weight against the defendants under art. III, r. 4. The second is that it 'represents' the weight within the meaning of s. 4 of the Carriage of Goods by Sea Act 1992 and is conclusive evidence of the weight in favour of Mitsui as lawful holders of the bill. It further follows that it is conclusive evidence that 11,000 tonnes of cargo were shipped in favour of the plaintiffs as assignees of Mitsui.

A similar argument was rejected by Mr Justice Longmore in *The Atlas* namely that the effect of the Hague Rules was to make any bill of lading prima facie evidence of quantity shipped, because (i) it was contrary to art. III, r. 3 or r. 8 for the ship-owners to include or rely on clauses such as 'said to be' or 'weight unknown' and (ii) art. III, r. 4 provided for the statements in the bill to be prima facie evidence. Mr Justice Longmore rejected that argument both as a matter of language and as a matter of authority. He put it thus at p. 646:

Do the Russian bills show the number of packages or weight 'as furnished in writing by the shipper'? In one sense it can be said they do, because the bills have figures which were in fact provided by the shipper in writing. But if the bills provide 'Weight . . . number . . . quantity unknown' it cannot be said that the bills 'show' that number or weight. They 'show' nothing at all because the shipowner is not prepared to say what the number or weight is. He can, of course, be required to show it under art. III, r. 3 but, unless and until he does so, the provisions of art. III, r. 4 as to prima facie evidence cannot come into effect.

This seems to me to be right as a matter of language but there is authority to the same effect.

Mr Justice Longmore then referred to *Canadian and Dominion Sugar Co. Ltd* v *Canadian National (West Indies) Steamship Ltd* (1946) 80 Ll L Rep 113; [1947] AC 46 and *Attorney General of Ceylon* v *Scindia Steam Navigation Co. Ltd* [1961] 2 Lloyd's Rep 173; [1962] AC 60.

On the facts of the instant case it would not be sufficient for Mr Davey to persuade the Court that, contrary to the views of Mr Justice Longmore, this bill of lading 'shows' the shipment of 11,000 tonnes of muriate of potash. That is because, for the reasons which I have already given, it does not 'represent' the shipment of that weight of potash and, if it does not represent such shipment, Mitsui could not rely upon s. 4(a) of the Carriage of Goods by Sea Act 1992. I note in passing that the position would be different if such a bill of lading did show the weight shipped and the carriage were governed by the Hague-Visby Rules, because art. III, r. 4 of those rules includes the following sentence:

> However, proof to the contrary shall not be admissible when the bill of lading has been transferred to a third party acting in good faith.

In order to succeed under this head Mr Davey must persuade the Court that the provision 'weight . . . unknown' must be disregarded or treated as null and void and of no effect under art. III, r. 8. That involves establishing both that it was the duty of the defendants to include in the bill of lading an unqualified statement of the weight of the cargo and that the provision 'weight . . . unknown' is a:

> . . .clause, covenant or agreement . . . relieving the carrier or the ship from liability for loss or damage to or in connection with goods arising from negligence, fault or failure in the duties and obligations provided in this Article or lessening such liability . . .

within the meaning of art. III, r. 8. I shall consider those requirements in turn.

Mr Turner submits that there was no such duty because there was no relevant demand of the shippers within the meaning of art. III, r. 3. I accept the submission that in order to succeed the plaintiffs would, as a first step, have to prove that they demanded a bill of lading showing the weight of the goods as furnished in writing by them: *Canada and Dominion Sugar Co. Ltd* v *Canadian National (West Indies) Steamships Ltd* (1946) 80 Ll L Rep 13 at p. 18; [1947] AC 46 at p. 57 per Lord Wright, giving the judgment of the Judicial Committee of the Privy Council. The question is whether there was such a demand on the facts here. There is no suggestion or evidence that the plaintiffs asked the defendants to issue a bill of lading showing the shipment of 11,000 tonnes without the qualification 'weight . . . unknown'. The only evidence relied upon is the bill of lading itself. I do not however think that it is a fair inference from the form of the bill of lading that the plaintiffs made such a request. On the contrary the natural inference is that the shippers were content with a bill of lading in standard Congenbill form, which includes the provision 'weight . . . unknown' as part of its printed form. The plaintiffs signed the bill of lading on behalf of the defendants. They were surely happy with it. If they had wanted a bill of lading in a different form they would surely have drafted one.
. . .

In all the circumstances I have reached the conclusion that, on the allegations made by the plaintiffs and on the facts set out in the material before the Court, there was no demand such as would satisfy art. III, r. 3 of the Hague Rules. It follows that there is no basis on which the 'weight . . . unknown' provision could be treated as null and void and of no effect under art. III, r. 8. It also follows that art. III, r. 4 has no application because the bill of lading is not 'such a bill of lading' (that is a bill of lading of the kind referred to in art. III, r. 3) so that the bill is not prima facie evidence of the receipt of 11,000 tonnes of cargo under r. 4. Finally (and crucially on the facts of this case) it follows that the bill of lading does not represent that 11,000 tonnes were shipped so as to be conclusive evidence against the defendants under s. 4 of the Carriage of Goods by Sea Act 1992.

The above conclusions make it unnecessary for me to consider the further questions that were argued. I shall not therefore do so, save to this limited extent. First, it occurred to me during my consideration of this judgment that it might be said that a bill of lading in this form does 'show' the quantity of cargo shipped within the meaning of art. III, r. 3 of the Hague or Hague-Visby Rules even though it does not 'represent' it within the meaning of s. 4 of the Carriage of Goods by Sea Act 1992. As Mr Justice Longmore said in the passage quoted above, in one sense it can be said that it does. Moreover if it does not, it seems that bills of lading which do not comply with art. III, r. 3 have commonly been in circulation for very many years since 1924.

However, I respectfully agree with Mr Justice Longmore on this point. Although I recognise that his conclusion is doubted by Yates on Contracts on the Carriage of Goods at par. 1.6.8.3.31, it appears to have been approved by Scrutton on Charterparties, 20th ed., pp. 112 and 433.

It seems to me that it would make little sense to hold that a bill of lading in this form 'shows' the quantity of cargo shipped within the meaning of art. III, r. 3 but that it does not 'represent' the quantity of cargo shipped within the meaning of s. 4 of the Carriage of Goods by Sea Act 1992. That view is I think reinforced by the sentence added to art. III, r. 4 in the Hague-Visby Rules. That addition has the effect that, where the bill of lading shows the quantity within the meaning of art. III, r. 3, proof to the contrary shall not be admissible against the lawful holder of the bill. If the reasoning in *The Atlas* were rejected, the result would be that the bill of lading did not 'represent' the quantity of cargo within the meaning of s. 4 of the Carriage of Goods by Sea Act 1992 so that it would not be conclusive evidence against the carrier under that section but that it did 'show' the quantity shipped within the meaning of art. III, r. 3 and in effect be conclusive evidence against him under art. III, r. 4. In my judgment it is likely that s. 4 of the Carriage of Goods by Sea Act 1992 was intended to lead to the same result as art. III, r. 4 of the Hague-Visby Rules.

Finally, some reliance is placed by Mr Davey upon a dictum of Lord Justice Scrutton in the *New Chinese Antimony* case, where he said at p. 673:

It is pressed upon as that our view is very inconvenient to shippers; but the answer is that some nations have by statute provided for such a state of things, as the United States has done by section 4 of the Harter Act and Canada in the Dominion of Canada Act 1910.

Lord Justice Scrutton does not there explain what he meant, but, in any event, in my judgment the position is as stated by Mr Justice Longmore. It appears that the reasons that bills of lading in this form are still in common use is that shippers and carriers are content with them and that in practice shippers do not demand the issue of a bill of lading which shows the weight of the cargo.

Secondly, there is no support in the authorities for the conclusion that where a demand is made under art. III, r. 3, but a bill of lading is issued in, say, the Congenbill form a provision such as 'weight . . . unknown' is null and void under art. III, r. 8. That suggestion was rejected (albeit implicitly) by Mr Justice Longmore in *The Atlas*. It is true, as Mr Davey points out, that neither of the two cases to which he refers expressly considered art. III, r. 8, but they both proceeded on the basis that under the Hague Rules (as at common law) the bill of lading must be construed in accordance with its terms. As he put it, in the *Canadian and Dominion Sugar* case there was a statement in the bill of lading qualifying the words 'apparent good order and condition', but the Privy Council held that there was—

. . . no reason under the rules or otherwise for refusing effect to the bill of lading according to its construction (per Lord Wright at p. 18; p. 57).

Although this conclusion is not necessary for my decision in the instant case, as I see it at present, even if shippers make a demand within the meaning of art. III, r. 3, if the carriers then introduce a provision such as 'weight . . . unknown' that provision would not be a—

> . . . clause, covenant or agreement . . . relieving the carrier or the ship from liability for loss or damage to or in connection with goods arising from negligence, faulty [*sic*] or failure in their duties and obligations provided in the Article or lessening such liability . . .

within the meaning of art. III, r. 8. The 'liability' referred to must in this context be liability arising for breach of the obligations in art. III, rr. 1 and 2. The inclusion of the provision 'weight . . . unknown' does not have the effect of relieving the carrier from such a liability or lessening such liability. It merely means (as Mr Justice Longmore pointed out) that the provisions of art. III, r. 4 as to prima facie evidence cannot come into effect.

In any event, for the reasons which I have tried to give, in my judgment the question posed under this head must be answered No.

*D: Deviation*

## Carriage of Goods by Sea Act 1971

### SCHEDULE

**Article IV**
(4) Any deviation in saving or attempting to save life or property at sea or any reasonable deviation shall not be deemed to be an infringement or breach of these Rules or of the contract of carriage, and the carrier shall not be liable for any loss or damage resulting therefrom.

*Question*
Apart from the specific case of saving or attempting to save property, does this add anything to the common law?

### *Stag Line Ltd* v *Foscolo, Mango & Co. Ltd*
[1932] AC 328 (HL)

LORD BUCKMASTER: My Lords, the appellants are the owners of the steamship *Ixia*, of 4,300 tons dead weight exclusive of bunkers, which they chartered to the respondents, Foscolo, Mango & Co. Ltd, under a charterparty dated June 14, 1929, made between the appellant and the second respondents, who acted as agents for the charterers. The vessel was chartered to carry a cargo of coal sold by the second respondents to the first not exceeding 4,350 tons nor less than 4,100 tons, and to proceed from Swansea, where the coal was to be loaded with all possible despatch, to Constantinople. The terms of the charterparty were incorporated in the bills of lading. The charterparty contained a clause (clause 6) giving the vessel liberty 'to call at any ports in any order for bunkering or other purposes or to make trial trips after notice'. The usual and customary route for the voyage was from Swansea, south of Lundy, from thence in a straight line to a point about five miles off Pendeen, on the north coast of Cornwall, and then with a slight alteration to the east to Finisterre and so on.

The ship had been fitted with a heating apparatus designed to make use of the heat which might otherwise be wasted as steam and so to diminish the bill for fuel. This apparatus had not been working satisfactorily, and the owners therefore arranged to send representatives of the engineers to make a test when the vessel started on her next voyage. Two engineers accordingly joined the boat, the intention being that they should leave the ship with the pilot somewhere off Lundy.

The firemen on board the ship were not in possession of their full energies when the boat started at 1.45 in the morning on June 31, 1929, owing to excessive drinking before they joined the ship. The result was that a proper head of steam necessary for making the test was not got up in time to enable the test to be made before the pilot was discharged. Accordingly they proceeded on the voyage until the ship was off St Ives, when the ship was turned about five miles out of its course to enter the St Ives harbour in order that the engineers might be landed. After landing them, the ship did not go straight back to the recognised route that she ought to have pursued, but hugged too closely the dangerous coast of Cornwall, and ran on a rock called the Vyneck rock, with the result that the vessel and cargo were totally lost though, fortunately, there was no loss of life. The accident took place at about 3.20 p.m., there was a moderate wind from E.N.E., the weather was cloudy, but visibility was moderately good up to six miles.

The respondents sought to recover damages for loss of their cargo upon the ground that there had been an unlawful deviation from the contracted course. The appellants made three answers to this claim: first, they set up the clause of the charterparty to which reference has been made; and, secondly, they said by the Carriage of Goods by Sea Act 1924, the rules in the Schedule must be regarded as incorporated in the contract and, by those rules, they were entitled to make the deviation which led to the disaster.
. . .

The appellants' argument upon the statute is, firstly, that the accident was a peril of the sea; and, secondly, that the deviation in question was a reasonable deviation and consequently was not an infringement of the contract of carriage.

. . . [T]he first point can, I think, be disregarded. It involves the view that perils and accidents of the sea are not qualified by the provisions as to deviation, and that such perils exempted the shipowner from responsibility for damage if they arise from or in the course of deviation, whether such deviation be reasonable or not. In my opinion clause 4 must be given its full effect without rendering it to a large extent unnecessary by such an interpretation, for it would follow from the arguments that a peril encountered by deviation, wholly unreasonable and wholly unauthorised, would be one for which the shipowner would be exempted from loss. In other words, the reasonable deviation would then only apply to questions of demurrage whatever the deviation might be.

The real difficulty in this case, and it is one by which I have been much oppressed, is whether in the circumstances the deviation was reasonable. It hardly needed the great authority of Lord Herschell in *Hick v Raymond* [1893] AC 22 to decide that in construing such a word it must be construed in relation to all the circumstances, for it is obvious that what may be reasonable under certain conditions may be wholly unreasonable when the conditions are changed. Every condition and every circumstance must be regarded, and it must be reasonable, too, in relation to both parties to the contract and not merely to one. But if, when full consideration has been given to this fact, two Courts have decided that a set of circumstances are reasonable, unless it can be shown that the learned judges have misdirected themselves in reaching their conclusion, or have overlooked any important consideration or introduced considerations that did not deserve notice, it would not, I think, be in accordance either with good sense or the comity of the Courts to decide that what they thought was reasonable other people did not. In this case three judges have decided that the deviation here could not be so regarded — and Greer LJ has agreed for a slightly different reason, because he thought the original deviation was permissible to St Ives but not afterwards — but I think that all of them have really considered the facts that were necessary for the purpose, and I am not prepared to differ from the conclusions that they have reached. I do not think elaborate definitions, whether contained in dictionaries or judgments, are of much use in determining the value of a word in common use which means no more in this context than a deviation which where every circumstance has been duly weighed commends itself to the common sense and sound understanding of sensible men.

I notice that Scrutton LJ also supports his judgment upon the view that the rules in the Schedule did no more than incorporate in a codified form the permissible limits of deviation which had previously been stated in *The Teutonia* (1872) LR 4 PC 171, 179. Upon the view I take it is unnecessary to consider the soundness of this conclusion and I express no opinion upon it. Nor again is it necessary to determine whether Greer LJ was right in assuming that the deviation became unreasonable after St Ives, but I think there is much to be said in support of his reasoning. The deviation had not ended at the port. It continued until the contracted line of route was resumed, and to deviate by going along the coast, though it may be regarded as bad seamanship, might none the less be an unreasonable deviation.

For these reasons I think the appeal should be dismissed.

LORD ATKIN: There remains the provision of Art. IV, r. 4, of the Schedule to the Carriage of Goods by Sea Act, which with the other Rules in the Schedule is incorporated expressly in the bill of lading pursuant to s. 3 of the Act.... In approaching the construction of these rules it appears to me important to bear in mind that one has to give the words as used their plain meaning, and not to colour one's interpretation by considering whether a meaning otherwise plain should be avoided if it alters the previous law. If the Act merely purported to codify the law, this caution would be well founded. I will repeat the well known words of Lord Herschell in the *Bank of England* v *Vagliano Brothers* [1891] AC 107, 144. Dealing with the Bills of Exchange Act as a code he says:

> I think the proper course is in the first instance to examine the language of the statute and to ask what is its natural meaning, uninfluenced by any considerations derived from the previous state of the law, and not to start with inquiring how the law previously stood, and then, assuming that it was probably intended to leave it unaltered, to see if the words of the enactment will bear an interpretation in conformity with this view.... The purpose of such a statute surely was that on any point specifically dealt with by it, the law should be ascertained by interpreting the language used instead of, as before, by roaming over a vast number of authorities in order to discover what the law was.

He then proceeds to say that of course it would be legitimate to refer to the previous law where the provision of the code was of doubtful import, or where words had previously acquired a technical meaning or been used in a sense other than their ordinary one. But if this is the canon of construction in regard to a codifying Act, still more does it apply to an Act like the present which is not intended to codify the English law, but is the result (as expressed in the Act) of an international conference intended to unify certain rules relating to bills of lading. It will be remembered that the Act only applies to contracts of carriage of goods outwards from ports of the United Kingdom: and the rules will often have to be interpreted in the courts of the foreign consignees. For the purpose of uniformity it is, therefore, important that the Courts should apply themselves to the consideration only of the words used without any predilection for the former law, always preserving the right to say that words used in the English language which have already in the particular context received judicial interpretation may be presumed to be used in the sense already judicially imputed to them.

Having regard to the method of construction suggested above, I cannot think that it is correct to conclude, as Scrutton LJ does, that r. 4 was not intended to extend the permissible limits of deviation as stated in *The Teutonia* (1872) LR 4 PC 171, 179. This would have the effect of confining reasonable deviation to deviation to avoid some imminent peril. Nor do I see any justification for confining reasonable deviation to a deviation in the joint interest of cargo owner and ship, as MacKinnon J appears to hold, or even to such a deviation as would be contemplated reasonably by both cargo owner and shipowner, as has been suggested by Wright J in *Foreman and Ellams Ltd* v *Federal Steam Navigation Co.* [1928] 2 KB 424, 431, approved by Slesser LJ in the present case. A deviation may, and often will, be caused by fortuitous circumstances never contemplated by the original parties to the contract; and may be reasonable, though it is made solely in the interests of the ship or solely in the interests of the cargo, or indeed in the direct interest of neither: as for instance where the presence of a passenger or of a member of the ship or crew was urgently required after the voyage had begun on a matter of national importance; or where some person on board was a fugitive from justice, and there were urgent reasons for his immediate appearance. The true test seems to be what departure from the contract voyage might a prudent person controlling the voyage at the time make and maintain, having in mind all the relevant circumstances existing at the time, including the terms of the contract and the interests of all parties concerned, but without obligation to consider the interests of any one as conclusive. I think this view conforms to that of Greer LJ, the only criticism of whose test I would make is that it appears unnecessary to introduce the reasonable cargo owner into the discussion. The decision has to be that of the master or occasionally of the shipowner; and I conceive that a cargo owner might well be deemed not to be unreasonable if he attached much more weight to his own interests than a prudent master having regard to all the circumstances might think it wise to do.

Applying then this test, was this deviation reasonable? I do not discuss the facts except to say that I see no ground for suggesting that the deviation was due to some default of the shipowner in respect of the firemen. In the absence of evidence directed to that issue it does not seem right to impute blame to the owners in that respect. I desire to refrain from expressing an opinion whether the question of whether a deviation is reasonable is a question of law or fact. In the present case we are judges both of law and of fact; and if the question is of fact the concurrence of the learned judges below seems to me to lose some of its value when regard is had to the meaning they attributed to the issue they were determining. I think that Greer LJ is plainly right in applying the test of reasonableness to the deviation as a whole. It could not, however, be laid down that as soon as the place was reached to which deviation was justified, there was an obligation to join the original course as directly as possible. A justified deviation to a port of refuge might involve thereafter a shorter and more direct route to the port of destination compared with a route which took the shortest cut to the original course. On the other hand, though the port of refuge was justifiably reached, the subsequent voyage might be so conducted as to amount to an unreasonable deviation. Taking all the facts into account I am pressed with the evidence which the learned judge accepted, that after St Ives the coasting course directed by the master was not the correct course which would ordinarily be set in those circumstances. It is obvious that the small extra risk to ship and cargo caused by deviation to St Ives, was vastly increased by the subsequent course. It seems to me not a mere error of navigation but a failure to pursue the true course from St Ives to Constantinople which in itself made the deviation cease to be reasonable. For these reasons I agree that this appeal should be dismissed.

*Note*
Lord Warrington of Clyffe and Lord Russell of Killowen had no doubt that the
reasonableness or otherwise of a deviation was a question of fact (at p. 338 and
p. 346 respectively). Lord Macmillan thought (at p. 349) that it was 'in general
a conclusion of fact . . . an inference of fact from a given set of facts'.

## *G.H. Renton & Co. Ltd* v *Palmyra Trading Corporation of Panama* *(The Caspiana)*
## [1957] AC 149 (HL)

Timber was shipped in British Columbia on the *Caspiana* for carriage to
London under three bills of lading, and to Hull under a fourth bill of lading.
While the *Caspiana* was on the voyage to London a strike of dock workers began
there, and the shipowners ordered the vessel to continue to Hamburg. The
London cargo was discharged at Hamburg and then the Hull cargo also, since
the strike had by then spread to Hull. On the day discharge was completed the
strike came to an end. The shipowners demanded payment of the full freight,
which was done under protest; they left the bill of lading holders to make (and
pay for) all arrangements for forwarding the cargo to London and Hull.
    In the appellants' action for damages, the respondent shipowners relied on
the following clauses in the bills of lading:

    14.(c)  Should it appear that epidemics, quarantine, ice, — labour
troubles, labour obstructions, strikes, lockouts, any of which onboard or
on shore — difficulties in loading or discharging would prevent the vessel
from leaving the port of loading or reaching or entering the port of
discharge or there discharging in the usual manner and leaving again, all
of which safely and without delay, the master may discharge the cargo at
port of loading or any other safe and convenient port. . . .
    (f)   The discharge of any cargo under the provisions of this clause shall
be deemed due fulfilment of the contract. If in connexion with the exercise
of any liberty under this clause any extra expenses are incurred, they shall
be paid by the merchant in addition to the freight, together with return
freight if any and a reasonable compensation for any extra services
rendered to the goods.

In reply, the appellants argued that these clauses were repugnant to the
main purpose of the contract and also void under the Hague Rules because
they (a) relieved the shipowners of the obligation to 'carry' the cargo, and (b)
permitted deviation contrary to Art. IV, r. 4. The House of Lords affirmed
the Court of Appeal's decision in favour of the shipowners on all points.

LORD SOMERVELL OF HARROW: My Lords, in my opinion, the appellants fail, for
the reasons given by the Court of Appeal. The first question is whether the printed
provisions as to strikes in clause 14(c) and (f) defeat or are repugnant to the typewritten
words, which describe the voyage as one to a named destination.

Under clause 14 the master has, in my opinion, to act reasonably and, in particular, in deciding what is a convenient port, he must have regard to the consignee's convenience as well as the ship's. So construed, I think it is in no way repugnant to the typewritten words. I would adopt the distinction between the clauses which have in whole or in part come within the principle applied in *Glynn* v *Margetson & Co* [1893] AC 351 and the present clause drawn by Jenkins LJ in the passage which has already been cited by my noble and learned friend the Lord Chancellor.

The general ambit of the Hague Rules is to be found in article III, r. 2, which has already been cited. It is, in my opinion, directed and only directed to the manner in which the obligations undertaken are to be carried out. Subject to the later provisions, it prohibits the shipowner from contracting out of liability for doing what he undertakes properly and with care. This question was considered by Devlin J in *Pyrene Co. Ltd* v *Scindia Navigation Co. Ltd* [1954] 2 QB 402, 417–418 in relation to the words 'shall properly and carefully load'. I agree with his statement, which has already been cited.

Prima facie, therefore, the rules leave the parties free to contract in the terms in question here. They do not prohibit Hamburg as a destination in the events which happened, but they apply on that voyage as they would have done on the voyage to and discharge at London if there had been no strike.

The appellants submitted that even if they had to accept this view as the prima facie ambit of the rules, the strike clause in these bills of lading was invalidated because it provided for the possibility of the port of loading being the safe and convenient port for discharge. In such an event, it was argued, there was no carriage and a provision under which the ship need not carry at all must be bad. I accept neither the premises not the conclusion. Once goods have been loaded there is, I think, 'carriage' in the sense in which the word is used in these rules. This is reinforced by the definition in article 1(e). Even if it could be said that a discharge at the port of loading as a result of war, ice, strikes, etc., prevented there being any carriage, I would not regard a provision to this effect as thereby invalidated by article III, r. 2. Such a provision is outside its scope.

An argument was also based on the wording of article IV, r. 4. It was submitted that the words there used assume that a deviation would be a breach of the rules; therefore, it is said, the rules are concerned with the course of the voyage; therefore they prohibit the provision for a substituted safe and convenient port as this amounts to a deviation.

This final step in the argument is, I think, plainly wrong if, as I have held, the appellants fail on the 'repugnancy' point. The voyage to Hamburg was not a deviation. It was, in the circumstances which arose, the contractual voyage. I agree that the words of the rule assume that a deviation would or might be a breach of the rules. Deviation is a breach of the shipowners' undertaking, implied if not expressed, to proceed by a usual and reasonable route. Assuming the contractual voyage is from A to B, the undertaking as set out certainly could be and, I think, would be treated as a 'term' on which the service — that is, the voyage from A to B — was to be performed. A deviation would, therefore, be a failure properly and carefully to carry. If this were only a possible view, it would be sufficient to explain the presence of the words in the rule.

The respondents submitted that the words in article III, r. 8, 'loss or damage to or in connexion with goods', covered physical damage only; that the damage here was not physical, as the goods were undamaged though in the wrong place; and that, therefore, the rules did not apply. The Court of Appeal did not decide this point. In one sense it is not necessary to do so. On the other hand, if right, it is a complete and short answer to the claim. It is unnecessary to decide whether there are heads of damage which might be outside the words, about I am myself clear that the appellants' loss or damage in the present case was 'to or in connexion with goods'.

I would dismiss the appeal.

*Note*

It is still uncertain how far deviation will deprive the carrier of the benefit of other provisions in the Rules. In *Stag Line Ltd* v *Foscolo, Mango & Co. Ltd* [1932] AC 328, Lord Atkin said:

... I find no substance in the contention faintly made by the defendants that an unauthorised deviation would not displace the statutory exceptions contained in the Carriage of Goods by Sea Act. I am satisfied that the general principles of English law are still applicable to the carriage of goods by sea except as modified by the Act: and I can find nothing in the Act which makes its statutory exceptions apply to a voyage which is not the voyage the subject of 'the contract of carriage of goods by sea' to which the Act applies....

See, however, *Kenya Railways* v *Antares Co. Ltd (The Antares)* [1987] 1 Lloyd's Rep 424 (CA), above, and the common law position discussed in Chapter 4.

## SECTION 8: THE CARRIER'S DEFENCES

The carrier's duties under Art. III, r. 2 in relation to the cargo are expressly made subject to the provisions of Art. IV. In general terms these follow the pattern of the common law excepted perils and the more usual contractual exceptions. Apart from r. 2(a), they cover events which happen without the fault of the carrier or those for whom he is responsible.

### Carriage of Goods by Sea Act 1971

#### SCHEDULE

**Article IV**

(2)    Neither the carrier nor the ship shall be responsible for loss or damage arising or resulting from—

(a)    Act, neglect, or default of the master, mariner, pilot, or the servants of the carrier in the navigation or in the management of the ship.

(b)    Fire, unless caused by the actual fault or privity of the carrier.

(c)    Perils, dangers and accidents of the sea or other navigable waters.

(d)    Act of God.

(e)    Act of war.

(f)    Act of public enemies.

(g)    Arrest or restraint of princes, rulers or people, or seizure under legal process.

(h)    Quarantine restrictions.

(i)    Act or omission of the shipper or owner of the goods, his agent or representative.

(j)    Strikes or lockouts or stoppage or restraint of labour from whatever cause, whether partial or general.

(k)    Riots and civil commotions.

(l)    Saving or attempting to save life or property at sea.

(m)    Wastage in bulk or weight or any other loss or damage arising from inherent defect, quality or vice of the goods.

(n)    Insufficiency of packing.

(o)    Insufficiency or inadequacy of marks.

(p)   Latent defects not discoverable by due diligence.

(q)   Any other cause arising without the actual fault or privity of the carrier, or without the fault or neglect of the agents or servants of the carrier, but the burden of proof shall be on the person claiming the benefit of this exception to show that neither the actual fault or privity of the carrier nor the fault or neglect of the agents or servants of the carrier contributed to the loss or damage.

(3)   The shipper shall not be responsible for loss or damage sustained by the carrier or the ship arising or resulting from any cause without the act, fault or neglect of the shipper, his agents or his servants.

...

## A: Act, neglect, or default in the navigation or management of the ship

Error of navigation is a well-understood concept, but it is less clear what 'management' of the ship covers.

### Gosse Millerd Ltd v Canadian Government Merchant Marine Ltd
### [1929] AC 223 (HL)

LORD HAILSHAM LC: Under a bill of lading dated February 6, 1925, 5,808 boxes of tinplates belonging to the appellants were shipped at Swansea for carriage to Vancouver by the *Canadian Highlander*. The whole of these tinplates were stowed in No. 5 lower hold, which is the aftermost hold in the ship. After loading these tinplates the *Canadian Highlander* proceeded to Liverpool in order to discharge inward cargo and to load further outward cargo. On February 9 certain lumber, forming part of the inward cargo, was unloaded from the No. 5 'tween decks at Liverpool. During the discharge of this lumber through the hatchway of No. 5 hold there was heavy rain. On February 10, whilst undocking, the *Canadian Highlander* collided with a pier and damaged her stern. As a result, it became necessary to dry-dock the vessel and to do extensive repairs. During the course of the repairs it was discovered that the tail shaft liner was cracked and it became necessary to remove the tail shaft in order that a new liner might be fitted to it; for this purpose it was necessary to shift some of the cargo in the No. 4 hold and to remove the tail shaft liner through a door leading from the tunnel recess into No. 5 hold. The repairs continued until April 4, when the *Canadian Highlander* was undocked and proceeded to Glasgow, and thence to Vancouver, where she arrived on May 17. On her arrival it was found that the appellants' tinplates had sustained serious damage by fresh water. The learned judge came to the conclusion that during the vessel's stay in dry dock there was carelessness in moving and replacing the tarpaulins which were supposed to cover the No. 5 hold when work was being done there, and that in consequence rain got into the No. 5 hold and did the damage; and that probably there was also carelessness with regard to the use of the tarpaulins on February 9 when the lumber was being unloaded and that on that occasion also some rain was admitted. The learned judge seems to have acquitted the ship's officers of any lack of care, and there was no evidence to enable him to decide who were the persons responsible for the negligence which occasioned the damage. From time to time the hold seems to have been entered by the stevedores' men, by members of the crew, by surveyors, and by the men employed by the repairers; and it is easy to understand that one or more of these persons may not have been sufficiently scrupulous in replacing the tarpaulins on their entrance to, or exit from, the hold, or in preventing the water which had accumulated on the tarpaulins from finding its way into the hold.

...

From the statement of the facts as found by the learned judge it could not be disputed that the respondents had failed properly and carefully to carry, keep and care for the goods carried. But the respondents pointed out that the obligation imposed upon them was expressly made subject to the provisions of Art. IV, and they claimed that the loss or damage complained of resulted from the act, neglect or default of their servants in the management of the ship. The argument at the bar turned mainly upon the meaning to be placed upon the expression 'management of the ship' in that rule. The words in question first appeared in an English statute in the Act now being considered; but nevertheless they have a long judicial history in this country. The same words are to be found in the well known Harter Act of the United States, and as a consequence they have often been incorporated in bills of lading which have been the subject of judicial consideration in the Courts in this country. I am unable to find any reason for supposing that the words as used by the Legislature in the Act of 1924 have any different meaning to that which has been judicially assigned to them when used in contracts for the carriage of goods by sea before that date; and I think that the decisions which have already been given are sufficient to determine the meaning to be put upon them in the statute now under discussion.

In the year 1893, in the case of *The Ferro* [1893] P 38, 44, 46, certain oranges had been damaged by the negligent stowage of the stevedore. It was held by the Divisional Court that the negligent stowage of the cargo was not neglect or default in the management of the ship. Gorell Barnes J says: 'I think it is desirable also to express the view which I hold about the question turning on the construction of the words "management of the ship". I am not satisfied that they go much, if at all, beyond the word "navigation".' Sir Francis Jeune says: 'It would be an improper use of language to include all stowage in such a term' (i.e., 'mismanagement of the ship'). 'It is not difficult to understand why the word "management" was introduced, because, inasmuch as navigation is defined as something affecting the safe sailing of the ship . . . it is easy to see that there might be things which it would be impossible to guard against connected with the ship itself, and the management of the ship, which would not fall under navigation. Removal of the hatches for the sake of ventilation, for example, might be management of the ship, but would have nothing to do with the navigation.'

In the case of *The Glenochil* [1896] P 10, 15, 16, 19 the same two learned judges, sitting as a Divisional Court, held that the words did protect the shipowner for damage done by pumping water into the ballast tank in order to stiffen the ship without ascertaining that a pipe had become broken, and thereby let the water into the cargo. Gorell Barnes J says:

> There will be found a strong and marked contrast in the provisions which deal with the care of the cargo and those which deal with the management of the ship herself; and I think that where the act done in the management of the ship is one which is necessarily done in the proper handling of the vessel, though in the particular case the handling is not properly done, but is done for the safety of the ship herself, and is not primarily done at all in connection with the cargo, that must be a matter which falls within the words 'management of the said vessel'.

Sir Francis Jeune says: 'It seems to me clear that the word "management" goes somewhat beyond — perhaps not much beyond — navigation, but far enough to take in this very class of acts which do not affect the sailing or movement of the vessel, but do affect the vessel herself.' And referring to his own judgment in *The Ferro*, he says: 'It may be that the illustration I gave in that case, as to the removal of the hatches for the sake of ventilation, was not a very happy one; but the distinction I intended to draw then, and intend to draw now, is one between want of care of cargo and want of care of the vessel indirectly affecting the cargo.'

... In the case of *Hourani* v *Harrison* 32 Com Cas 305 the Court of Appeal had to consider the meaning to be attached to the words of Art. IV, r. 2, in a case in which loss was caused by the pilfering of the stevedore's men whilst the ship was being discharged. The Court held that this did not fall within the expression 'management of the ship'; but both Bankes LJ and Atkin LJ (as he then was) discussed the meaning to be placed on the expression. Bankes LJ reviews the authorities both in this country and in the United States; he points out that the principle laid down in *The Glenochil* has been accepted in the Supreme Court of the United States as being correct, and he adopts and applies that principle to the case which he is then considering. The learned judge expresses the distinction as being between 'damage resulting from some act relating to the ship herself and only incidentally damaging the cargo, and an act dealing, as is sometimes said in some of the authorities, solely with the goods and not directly or indirectly with the ship herself'. Atkin LJ says: 'that there is a clear distinction drawn between goods and ship; and when they talk of the word "ship", they mean the management of the ship, and they do not mean the general carrying on of the business of transporting goods by sea'.

My Lords, in my judgment, the principle laid down in *The Glenochil* and accepted by the Supreme Court of the United States in cases arising under the American Harter Act, and affirmed and applied by the Court of Appeal in the *Hourani* case under the present English statute, is the correct one to apply. Necessarily, there may be cases on the border-line, depending upon their own particular facts; but if the principle is clearly borne in mind of distinguishing between want of care of cargo and want of care of vessel indirectly affecting the cargo, as Sir Francis Jeune puts it, there ought not to be very great difficulty in arriving at a proper conclusion....

My Lords, it appears to me plain that if the test which I have extracted from the earlier cases is the correct one, it follows that the appellants are entitled to recover in the present case. It is clear that the tinplates were not safely and properly cared for or carried; and it is for the respondents then to prove that they are protected from liability by the provisions of Art. IV, and that the damage was occasioned through the neglect or default of their servants in the management of the ship. In my judgment they have not even shown that the persons who were negligent *were* their servants; but even if it can be assumed that the negligence in dealing with the tarpaulins was by members of the crew, such negligence was not negligence in the management of the ship, and therefore is not negligence with regard to which Art. IV, r. 2(a), affords any protection. It follows that the judgment of the majority of the Court of Appeal was wrong, that the appeal must be allowed with costs here and below, and that the judgment of the trial judge must be restored; I move your Lordships accordingly.

### *International Packers London Ltd* v *Ocean Steam Ship Co. Ltd*
[1955] 2 Lloyd's Rep 218 (QBD)

The facts are stated in Chapter 3. A further argument advanced by the shipowners was that the failure to use the locking bars was default in the management of the ship.

McNAIR J: ... The next question is whether the defendants are excused from liability for this failure by the exceptions of 'act, neglect, or default of the master, mariner ... or the servants of the carrier ... in the management of the ship' in Art. IV, r. 2(a), of the scheduled Rules. The fact that in the *Gosse Millerd case* [1929] AC 223, the failure of the ship's crew to close the hatches while repairs were being effected in port was held to be within the exceptions [*sic*: a 'not' has clearly dropped out after 'held'], does not, I think, assist in the solution of the present case; for, as Lord Sumner observes (at pp. 239 and 97 of the respective reports),

> it is never wise to try to decide case B because the part of the ship mishandled is 'like' the part mishandled in case A.

In any event, the dissimilarity between the position of a ship in port and at sea is self-evident. In that case Lord Hailsham LC, with whom Lord Atkin agreed, accepted as accurate the principle to be applied in determining this issue as stated by Sir Francis Jeune in *The Glenochil* [1896] P 10, and followed by the decisions of the Supreme Court of the United States, as being that a distinction must be drawn between 'want of care of cargo and want of care of the vessel indirectly affecting cargo', and observed, possibly rather optimistically, that if this distinction is observed 'there ought not to be great difficulty in arriving at a proper conclusion'. Lord Sumner (at pp. 237 and 97) stated that the Legislature by the use of these words which comprise the exception,

> has ... shown a clear intention to continue and enforce the old clause as it was previously understood and regularly construed by the Courts of law

and concluded (at pp. 240 and 98), on the facts of that case, that

> the particular use of the tarpaulin, which was neglected, was a precaution solely in the interest of the cargo.

In the course of the judgment he expressed approval of the dissenting judgment of Lord Justice Greer in the case under appeal, during the course of which the learned Lord Justice is reported in [1928] 1 KB 717, at p. 749; (1927) 29 Ll L Rep 190, at p. 200, as summarising the position as follows:

> If the cause of the damage is solely, or even primarily, a neglect to take reasonable care of the cargo, the ship is liable, but if the cause of the damage is a neglect to take reasonable care of the ship, or some part of it, as distinct from the cargo, the ship is relieved from liability; but if the negligence is not negligence towards the ship, but only negligent failure to use the apparatus of the ship for the protection of the cargo, the ship is not so relieved.

The Load Line Rules, 1941, which, as I have already said, were amended in 1946, contain elaborate provisions which have to be complied with before a load line certificate can be issued. These provisions deal with the height of the hatch coamings, the carriers or sockets for hatchway beams, the cleats, battens, wedges and tarpaulins, clearly taking the view that the whole of the appliances which go to make up a properly secured hatch in an exposed position are to be regarded as part of the mechanism for securing the safety of the ship. It would, in my view, be in the highest degree artificial to say that tarpaulins and wedges are primarily intended for the protection of the cargo, whereas hatchway beams and hatch covers are intended primarily for the protection of the ship.

In my judgment, on the facts of this case, the failure on the part of the ship's officers which caused the admission of sea water into the ship falls within the exception, notwithstanding that the amount of water which in fact entered did not endanger the ship as such. This failure resulted in the failure of one of the ship's main defences against the entry of sea water. This, in my judgment, is, to use the language of Lord Justice Greer, a 'neglect to take reasonable care of the ship or some part of it as distinct from the cargo'; or, to use the language of Sir Francis Jeune, 'a want of care of the vessel indirectly affecting the cargo'.

*Note and Questions*
1.  Why should the cargo-owner bear the risk of the carrier's negligence?
2.  In *Caltex Refining Co. Pty Ltd v BHP Transport Ltd (The Iron Gippsland)* [1994] 1 Lloyd's Rep 335, (NSW Supreme Court, Adm, Carruthers J) it was held that although inert gas systems were installed on tankers fundamentally for the protection of the vessel, 'the purpose of the inert gas system is primarily to manage the cargo not only for the protection of the cargo but for the ultimate protection of the vessel from adverse consequences associated with that cargo'. Accordingly, failure in the use of the system was not covered by r. 2(a).
3.  A cargo of butter is carried in the same refrigerated chamber as the ship's provisions. The temperature setting is too high and the butter deteriorates. Can the carrier rely on Art. IV, r. 2(a)? (*Cf. Rowson v Atlantic Transport Co.* [1903] 2 KB 666 (CA).)

*B: Inherent defect or vice of the goods*

### *Albacora SRL* v *Westcott & Laurance Line Ltd*
[1966] 2 Lloyd's Rep 53 (HL)

The facts are stated in section 7B above. The shipowners also argued that the damage was due to inherent vice.

LORD REID: Art. IV, r. 2(m) provides that the carrier shall not be responsible for damage arising from 'inherent defect, quality, or vice of the goods'. A number of authorities were cited, and perhaps the most concise statement is that of Mr Justice Gorell Barnes in *The Barcore* [1896] P 294, at p. 297:

> ... This cargo was not damaged by reason of the shipowner committing a breach of contract, or omitting to do something which he ought to have done, but it was deteriorated in condition by its own want of power to bear the ordinary transit in a ship.

By 'the ordinary transit' I would understand the kind of transit which the contract requires the carrier to afford. I agree with the Lord President, Lord Clyde, when he says ([1965)] 2 Lloyd's Rep, at p. 56):

> ... Art. IV, Rule 2(m), is, in my opinion, intended to give effect to the well-settled rule in our law that if an article is unfitted owing to some inherent defect or vice for the voyage which is provided for in the contract, then the carrier may escape liability when damage results from the activation of that inherent vice during the voyage. ...

It follows that whether there is an inherent defect or vice must depend on the kind of transit required by the contract. If this contract had required refrigeration there would have been no inherent vice. But as it did not there was inherent vice because the goods could not stand the treatment which the contract authorised or required.

*C: Latent defects*

Whereas Art. IV, r. 2(m) refers to defect of the goods, r. 2(p) is dealing with defects in the vessel. It raises difficult questions of proof.

### *The Antigoni*
[1991] 1 Lloyd's Rep 209 (CA)

STAUGHTON LJ: In August 1986, a number of parcels of cargo were loaded on board *Antigoni* at Antwerp, Ipswich and Le Havre for carriage to Tema and Lagos in West Africa. The defendants and appellants were the owners of the vessel; the plaintiffs and respondents owned the cargo. In practice I suppose that the dispute is between the insurers of cargo on the one hand and a protection and indemnity association as liability insurers of the shipowners on the other. Damage to cargo cases very rarely come to trial these days, still less to the Court of Appeal. We were told that some issue of principle was thought to be involved, but I cannot for my part detect any novel question of law in what we have to decide.

The vessel was engaged on a regular service between Northern Europe and West Africa. Bills of lading were issued. However, it has not proved necessary to look at them, still less to read the small print, since it is agreed that the contracts of carriage incorporated the Hague-Visby Rules, which are to be found in the Schedule to the Carriage of Goods by Sea Act 1971....

On Sept. 16, 1986, while the vessel was at sea and some 110 miles west of Freetown, there was a major breakdown in the engine-room. Attempts were made to repair the engine at sea, but these were unsuccessful, and salvage services were obtained from another vessel, which towed the *Antigoni* to Las Palmas. After her arrival there on Oct. 1 the main engine was eventually replaced and she continued on her voyage, reaching Lagos on Jan. 31, 1987.

These misfortunes did not, so far as we are aware, result in any physical damage to the cargo; but there was considerable expense. The award payable to the salvors totalled £145k, of which the share attributed to cargo was some £83k. That has been paid by the cargo-owners or their insurers, and they seek to recover it from the shipowners in this action as damages for breach of contract. In addition there was other general average expenditure. The proportion attributable to cargo comes to £269k, but that figure must include (as it seems to me) the share of the salvage reward which the cargo has already paid. The shipowners counterclaim for a declaration that the balance of the cargo's contribution in general average is payable.

The action was tried by Mr Anthony Diamond QC, sitting as a Deputy Judge of the Admiralty Court. He gave judgment for the cargo-owners on their claim and dismissed the shipowners' counterclaim (see [1990] 1 Lloyd's Rep 45). The shipowners now appeal.

*The engine*
*Antigoni* was built in 1977, and was equipped with an 18-cylinder V form diesel engine of a kind that had been in service since 1969. Attached to the crankshaft were 10 counterweights, designed to ensure smooth running and reduce vibration. These were large and heavy blocks of steel, roughly in the shape of the space between two concentric circles for about one-sixth of their circumference. At each end of their inner circumference there were shoulders or lugs which would slide into grooves in the crankshaft, thus holding the counterweight in place.

The centre of each counterweight was pierced by a bolt which penetrated to the crankshaft. This was not the type of bolt which holds two objects together, but rather one that forces them apart. It was threaded near the head and smooth for the rest of its length. Screwing the bolt into the counterweight until it reached the crankshaft would have the effect of forcing the counterweight away from the crankshaft. That process would continue until one side of the shoulders or lugs on the counterweight was hard against one side of the grooves in the crankshaft. Then the bolt would be tight, and the counterweight firmly held in place.

A problem would arise if one or more of the bolts became loose. It was not that a counterweight could fly off the crankshaft, propelled by centrifugal force, and penetrate the engine casing and possibly the ship as well. The shoulders on the counterweight would prevent that. But if a bolt was loose the counterweight could pivot round it, and might obstruct the path of another moving part in the engine with disastrous consequences.

. . .

To meet these problems the engine builders recommend that the counterweight bolts should be checked, and tightened if necessary, after every 5,000 running hours. Two circulars were issued by the engine builders, setting out details as to how this should be done. These came to the notice of the shipowners and the vessel's chief engineer. One of the two critical questions in this case is whether a bolt could become loose, in either of the ways that I have described, after significantly less than 5,000 running hours.

*The casualty*

Investigations after the breakdown revealed that the two counterweights in No. 9 unit, on the aft end of the crankshaft, were loose and able to pivot. One of those two counterweights had come into contact with the connecting rod in one of the two cylinders which together form the V in No. 9 unit. In the result both connecting rods and both pistons penetrated the engine casing. The engine was ruined beyond repair.

. . .

It was, or became, common ground at the trial that the vessel was unseaworthy before and at the beginning of the voyage, in terms of art. III, r. 1 and art. IV, r. 1. The cargo-owners said that she was unseaworthy because the counterweight bolts in No. 9 unit were not then properly tightened; the shipowners, because although properly tightened, the bolts had a propensity to become loose before they would next be checked. Either way, as I have said, the vessel was unseaworthy and the casualty was caused by unseaworthiness. It was then for the shipowners to establish a defence to the claim.

*The burden and method of proof*

The shipowners relied at the trial on two defences under art. IV of the Hague-Visby Rules. The first was in r. 1, that the casualty (or rather the unseaworthiness of the vessel) was not caused by want of due diligence on their part to make the ship seaworthy; the second, under r. 2(p), that the casualty was caused by a latent defect not discoverable by due diligence. In either case the burden of proof lay on the shipowners — under r. 1, because the rule says so, and under r. 2 by virtue of the common law principle that he who seeks to rely upon an exception in his contract must bring himself within it.

However, the two defences were alternatives. The shipowners could succeed if they established either one of them, and did not need to establish both. Mr Crookenden on their behalf complains that the Judge misunderstood the law, and imposed a duty on them to establish both defences. Mr Anthony Diamond QC has immense experience of the Hague-Visby Rules. But it is possible for even the most experienced to err; and the relationship between art. IV, r. 1 and r. 2(p) is not wholly apparent at first sight.

*Scrutton on Charterparties*, 19th Edition, p. 446, has this passage in connection with r. 1:

> Seeing that due diligence must be exercised not only by the shipowner himself but also by his servants or agents, the protection given by the rule in relation to the physical condition of the ship protects, in effect, only against latent defects.

The emphasis there must be on the words 'in effect'. Of course a Judge may be so impressed by the evidence of those whose task it was to exercise due diligence as to find that they did so, even though he is totally mystified as to how the vessel still became unseaworthy; he may think it right to believe that evidence, while not being able to identify any possible latent defect which they can reasonably have overlooked. There may, indeed, be cases where a Judge has reached such a result. But in practice the shipowner will wish, if he can, to lead evidence of such a latent defect, and the Judge must necessarily have regard to that evidence before deciding whether due diligence has been exercised. If he concludes that there is no possibility of a latent defect which could be overlooked in the exercise of due diligence, he will find it very difficult to accept that due diligence was in fact exercised, if not wholly impossible. If the evidence points to no more than 'purely scientific hypotheses' (*cf. Moore v R. Fox & Sons* [1956] 1 QB 596 at p. 607) as to the existence of some explanation which is consistent with the exercise of due diligence, the Judge is entitled and bound to take into account the plausibility of that explanation. There is not imposed on the shipowner in law any burden to establish a latent defect if he seeks to rely on art. IV, r. 1. But he will find it much easier to establish due diligence if he can point to the likelihood of a latent defect, and much more difficult if he can suggest none, or only one which is wholly implausible.

Mr Crookenden referred us to a number of cases on the maxim res ipsa loquitur. I am not myself convinced that that is in all respects a wholly analogous case. However, I would refer to the speech of Lord Simonds in the case of *Woods v Duncan* [1946] AC 401 at p. 439, where he said of a defendant against whom that maximum applied:

> This does not mean that he must prove how and why the accident happened; it is sufficient if he satisfies the court that he personally was not negligent. It may well be that the court will be more easily satisfied of this fact if a plausible explanation which attributes the accident to some other cause is put forward on his behalf; but this is only a factor in the consideration of the probabilities. The accident may remain inexplicable, or at least no satisfactory explanation other than his negligence may be offered: yet, if the court is satisfied by his evidence that he was not negligent, the plaintiffs' case must fail.

On that view of art. IV, r. 1, it might be thought that the exception in r. 2(p) of latent defects not discoverable by due diligence is superfluous. That would not necessarily be an obstacle, since the rules were the product of an international Convention and have to be applied in many countries throughout the world, which may not have the same predilection for avoiding surplusage. But Scrutton (p. 450) points to a case where r. 2(p) would be important:

> Another possible meaning for these words resulting in their giving the shipowner an immunity additional to that provided in Rule 1 of this Article is that they cover defects which would not have been discovered by the exercise of due diligence even though the shipowner could not show that he had in fact exercised such diligence.

That view had the support of Mr Justice Branson in *Corporation Argentina de Productores de Carnes* v *Royal Mail Lines Ltd* (1939) 64 Ll L Rep 188 at p. 192.

*The facts*

So I turn to consider the shipowners' two defences, and to see how they stand on that analysis of the law, taking first the defence of latent defect not discoverable by due diligence within r. 2(p). If one leaves aside the evidence relating to *Antigoni* in this case, there is nothing more than the speculation of experts and a meagre account of other casualties. The latent defect, to be relevant, must be a propensity of counterweight bolts in this type of engine to become loose in some period of less than 5,000 running hours since they were last tightened. I limit the definition in that way, because the shipowners were warned that there was a possibility that bolts might become loose in a longer period, and due diligence required at least that after 5,000 hours they should be checked.

...

The most that can be said on that evidence is that there is a theoretical possibility that the bolts have a propensity to become loose after less than 5,000 running hours. It is true that this may actually have happened in five cases, and that in others bolts may have become loose without any damage to the engine. There is some rather vague evidence of other loose counterweights. But the tiny proportion of casualties which might be attributed to this cause, notwithstanding the fact that the engine builders have only ever recommended checking and tightening after 5,000 hours, persuades me that the Judge was fully entitled to find that the supposed latent defect was not made out on the evidence as to other vessels. I do not see what other conclusion he could have reached.

...

The evidence of Mr Misiek, the chief engineer, was that the practice was for two engineers to inspect the crankshaft every two to two-and-a-half months, after approximately 1,000 running hours of the engine. Inspection included checking the counterweight bolts, and tightening them if necessary. He had been part of the team in January and April, 1986, and had himself checked the bolts on July 2, 1986, which was some 900 to 950 running hours before the casualty. If that evidence had been accepted by the Judge due diligence would have been made out, whether or not the Judge was also able to make a finding of latent defect. There was some confirmation of Mr Misiek's evidence in his own work book and in the engine-room log, although the entries were somewhat cryptic and in some cases written in Polish.

The Judge formed the view that Mr Misiek was in general a reasonably capable and conscientious ship's engineer. I find support for that view in Mr Misiek's statement, where he says that when he heard an unusual noise in the engine he ran down two decks from his cabin to the engine-room in 10–15 seconds. Some 30 years ago I recall old Mr Casebourne (to distinguish him from the present Mr Casebourne) saying in evidence that a good chief engineer listened to his engines whether awake or asleep, and that in the event of major trouble could be expected to reach the engine-room platform before the engineer on watch had had time to shut down the engine.

Nevertheless, the Judge did not accept Mr Misiek's evidence ... the heart of the Judge's reasoning is to be found, as it seems to me, in two passages. The first is where he said that the shipowners' expert witness—

... failed to give any adequate technical explanation as to how, if the counterweight bolts had been properly checked and/or tightened on 2nd July 1986, they could have lost their tightness only 900 to 950 engine hours later.

In another passage he said:

I was unable to see how the casualty could have occurred if the counterweights had been properly inspected and maintained.

The Judge was there carrying out the task which I have mentioned earlier in this judgment and which is referred to by Lord Simonds in *Woods* v *Duncan*. Before deciding whether he should accept the evidence of Mr Misiek, he considered what alternative explanation of the casualty there might be other than lack of due diligence. He could find none. In those circumstances, he was fully entitled not to accept the evidence as to due diligence, unless he thought it so convincing as to override all other considerations. Evidently he did not do so. He concluded:

I have to say that, after weighing all the evidence before me, I am left in no doubt that the ship's engineers failed properly to carry out the very clear and detailed procedures described in [the engine builders' circulars].

Once the Judge decided not to accept the evidence of Mr Misiek, it followed that due diligence was not proved. It also followed that latent defect was not proved, since the meagre evidence of other casualties on other vessels could not establish latent defect on its own.

I would dismiss this appeal.

*Question*
Why is Art. IV, r. 1 not sufficient on its own?

*D: Any other cause*

Since the burden of disproving fault is on the carrier, there has, not surprisingly, been little use made of this general exception in the reported cases. It was, however, successfully relied upon by the carrier in the next case.

## Leesh River Tea Co. Ltd v British India Steam Navigation Co. Ltd
### [1967] 2 QB 250 (CA)

The plaintiffs shipped chests of tea from Calcutta to London, Hull and Amsterdam on the defendants' vessel, *The Chyebassa*. During the course of discharging and loading other cargo, when the vessel called at Port Sudan, a stevedore or stevedores stole the brass cover plate of a storm valve near No. 2 hold. As a result of the removal of the plate, seawater entered the hold on the remainder of the voyage and damaged the tea. McNair J awarded the plaintiffs damages, but the Court of Appeal allowed the shipowners' appeal. The Hague Rules as enacted in India were the same as in England.

SELLERS LJ: ... 'Any other cause' would clearly include theft of part of or malicious damage to the ship, and, if the loss is not to be held to be a loss by perils of the sea, it must be attributed to the removal and theft of the cover plate which gave rise to the unseaworthiness which allowed the sea to come in.

The shipowners established that the theft was without their actual fault or privity and they have to establish also that it was without the fault or neglect of their agents or servants. *R.F. Brown & Co. Ltd* v *T. & J. Harrison* (1927) 43 TLR 633; *sub nom. R.F. Brown & Co. Ltd* v *Harrison, Hourani* v *Harrison*, 32 Com Cas 305, CA held that 'and' has to be substituted for 'or'.

The Red Sea Stevedore Co. Ltd were the agents of the shipowners for the discharge and loading of cargo and its handling and stowing at Port Sudan. The thief (I disregard that there may have been more than one, similarly employed) was the servant of the stevedoring company, by whom no doubt he was engaged and paid. Both the agents and their servants selected by them for the work were performing, in the task for which they were engaged, the ship's work, that is, they were carrying out the shipowners' obligations under the contract of carriage. It is beyond question, I think, that the shipowners could not have escaped liability if the stevedores' men in the performance of the work in hand had damaged or stolen the cargo they had to handle. But the men involved did not damage the cargo which they were handling and did not steal any of it. They took the opportunity to remove a very small part of the ship itself in order to steal it and in so doing so damaged the ship that seawater could enter.

The removal was not ship's work. It was not in the ship's interest and did not purport to be. It was in no way incidental to or a hazard of the process of discharge and loading. If a complete stranger had entered the hold unobserved and removed the plate, sub-clause (q) would, I think, apply if the shipowner could prove that it was a stranger who removed the cover and reasonable care had been taken to prevent strangers getting aboard the ship and due diligence generally had been exercised. In the present case the act of the thief ought, I think, to be regarded as the act of a stranger. The thief in interfering with the ship and making it, as a consequence, unseaworthy was performing no duty for the shipowners at all, neither negligently nor deliberately nor dishonestly. He was not in fact their servant and no question, therefore, strictly arises of his acting outside the scope of his employment. The shipowners were liable for his acts only when he, as a servant of the stevedores, was acting on behalf of the shipowners in the fulfilment of the work for which the stevedores had been engaged. Without that the shipowners were in no relationship at all with the thief.

The circumstances here seem to create one of the perhaps rare occasions when article IV(2)(q) can be invoked. The thief was not in fact the servant of the shipowners and could only be regarded as one — or more correctly as an agent of the shipowners — in so far as he was performing a task for and on their behalf.

In dealing with the ship's structure the thief was not acting or purporting to act for the shipowners and ought not in such circumstances to be held to be their agent. So to hold seems to me a fair interpretation and application of sub-paragraph (q) not involving any peculiarities of our English law, if indeed scope of employment is a feature peculiar to it.

### E: Burden of proof

It is uncertain how far the common law analysis exemplified in *The Glendarroch* [1894] P 226 (CA) (see Chapter 2) applies to the Rules, where the Rules themselves do not expressly deal with the matter. In *Svenska Traktor Aktiebolaget v Maritime Agencies (Southampton) Ltd* [1953] 2 QB 295, above, Pilcher J put the burden generally on the carrier to 'prove affirmatively (i) that he has taken reasonable care of the goods while they were in his custody and (ii) that the loss or damage falls within one of the immunities specified in Article IV, r. 2' (approving the statement in Carver's *Carriage of Goods by Sea*, 9th ed., p. 185). However, in *Albacora SRL v Westcott & Laurance Line* [1966] 2 Lloyd's Rep 53, above, Lord Pearce doubted a similar statement of Wright J (*Gosse Millerd Ltd v Canadian Government Merchant Marine Ltd* [1927] 2 KB 432) in relation to Art. IV, r. 2(m). In *Aktieselskabet De Danske Sukkerfabrikker v Bajamar Compania Naviera SA (The Torenia)* [1983] 2 Lloyd's Rep 210,

Hobhouse J described the question as 'a highly controversial issue' which it was not necessary for him to resolve. Any remaining doubt disappears, however, if the opening words of Art. III, r. 2 are taken at face value: the carrier's duties are 'subject to the provisions of Article IV' and the carrier has a complete answer to the claim if the case is brought within one of the Art. IV, r. 2 defences.

## SECTION 9: LIMITS ON LIABILITY

The Rules limit the carrier's liability in two ways: by imposing a time limit for the commencement of proceedings which is short by English, though perhaps not by Continental European, standards, and by setting financial limits on liability. The time limit of 12 months has remained unchanged since 1924; the financial limits, on the other hand, have varied considerably over the years — the current provisions are much more favourable to cargo-owners than the earlier ones.

*A: The time limit*

### Carriage of Goods by Sea Act 1971

SCHEDULE

**Article III**

(6) Unless notice of loss or damage and the general nature of such loss or damage be given in writing to the carrier or his agent at the port of discharge before or at the time of the removal of the goods into the custody of the person entitled to delivery thereof under the contract of carriage, or, if the loss or damage be not apparent, within three days, such removal shall be prima facie evidence of the delivery by the carrier of the goods as described in the bill of lading.

The notice in writing need not be given if the state of the goods has, at the time of their receipt, been the subject of joint survey or inspection.

Subject to paragraph 6*bis* the carrier and the ship shall in any event be discharged from all liability whatsoever in respect of the goods, unless suit is brought within one year of their delivery or of the date when they should have been delivered. This period may, however, be extended if the parties so agree after the cause of action has arisen.

In the case of any actual or apprehended loss or damage the carrier and the receiver shall give all reasonable facilities to each other for inspecting and tallying the goods.

(6*bis*) An action for indemnity against a third person may be brought even after the expiration of the year provided for in the preceding paragraph if brought within the time allowed by the law of the Court seized of the case. However, the time allowed shall be not less than three months, commencing from the day when the person bringing such action for indemnity has settled the claim or has been served with process in the action against himself.

### *Aries Tanker Corp* v *Total Transport Ltd*
### *(The Aries)*
[1977] 1 Lloyd's Rep 334 (HL)

The facts are stated in Chapter 5, section 1.

LORD WILBERFORCE: My Lords, if this case is to be decided on the terms of the
contract it would appear to me to be a comparatively simple one. There is an obligation
to pay freight, calculated upon the amount of cargo intaken, which obligation arises
upon discharge. There is no dispute as to the amount: it is a liquidated claim. The
contract contemplates the possibility of a crossclaim by the charterers in respect of loss
or damage to the cargo and it expressly provides by incorporation of art. III(6) of the
Hague Rules that the carrier and the ship *shall be discharged* unless suit is brought within
one year after the date of delivery or the date when delivery should have been made. This
amounts to a time bar created by contract. But, and I do not think that sufficient
recognition to this has been given in the Courts below, it is a time bar of a special kind,
viz., one which extinguishes the claim (cf. art. 29 of the Warsaw Convention, 1929) not
one which, as most English statutes of limitation (e.g., the Limitation Act 1939, the
Maritime Conventions Act 1911) and some international conventions (e.g., the
Brussels Convention on Collisions, 1910 art. 7) do, bars the remedy while leaving the
claim itself in existence. Therefore, arguments to which much attention and refined
discussion has been given, as to whether the charterer's claim is a defence, or in the
nature of a cross action, or a set off of one kind or another, however relevant to cases to
which the Limitation Act 1939, or similar Acts apply, appear to me, with all respects, to
be misplaced. The charterers' claim after May 1974, and before the date of the writ, had
not merely become unenforceable by action, it had simply ceased to exist, and I fail to
understand how a claim which has ceased to exist can be introduced for any purpose
into legal proceedings, whether by defence or (if this is different) as a means of reducing
the respondents' claim, or as a set off, or in any way whatsoever. It is a claim which, after
May 1974, had no existence in law, and could have no relevance in proceedings
commenced, as these were in October 1974. I would add, though this is unnecessary
since the provision is clear in its terms, that to provide for the discharge of these claims
after 12 months meets an obvious commercial need, namely, to allow shipowners, after
that period, to clear their books.

*Note*
In general, the time limit applies whatever the nature of the breach alleged.

### Salmond and Spraggon (Australia) Pty Ltd v Port Jackson Stevedoring Pty ltd
### (The New York Star)
[1980] 2 Lloyd's Rep 317 (PC)

LORD WILBERFORCE: The action was brought by the respondent in respect of a
consignment of razor blades in 37 cartons, shipped from Canada to Australia on the
Blue Star Line. The relevant bill of lading dated Mar. 27, 1970, was issued in Montreal,
Quebec; the port of loading was St John, New Brunswick; and the port of discharge was
Sydney. The shipper, named in the bill of lading was Schick Safety Razor Co. Division
of Eversharp of Canada Ltd; the respondent was named as consignee. The bill of lading
was issued to the consignor and was transmitted to and accepted by the consignee.

The appellant carried on business as stevedore in the port of Sydney. Forty nine per
cent of its capital was owned by Blue Star Line Australia Ltd and it commonly acted as
stevedore in Sydney for the Blue Star Line.

*New York Star* arrived at Sydney on May 10, 1970. On her arrival — and there was
evidence that this was in accordance with the normal practice in the port — the packages

of razor blades were discharged from the ship and placed by the stevedore in part of a shed (called 'the dead house') on the wharf which was under its control. Later the goods were stolen from the wharf, having been delivered by servants of the stevedore to persons who had no right to receive them, so that when the consignee presented the bill of lading they were unavailable. The consignee brought this action against the stevedore and against the ship's agent — Joint Cargo Services Pty Ltd — alleging negligence in failing to take proper care of the goods, delivery of the goods to an unauthorised person and non-delivery to the consignee. The action against the ship's agent failed at first instance and has not been the subject of appeal. The trial Judge however found that the stevedore had been negligent in the care of the goods and that there had been a misdelivery: these findings have not been disputed.

The bill of lading contained a 'Himalaya clause' extending the benefit of defences and immunities conferred by the bill of lading upon the carrier to independent contractors employed by the carrier, and also a time bar (similar to that contained in The Hague Rules) barring any action if not brought within one year after the delivery of the goods or the date when the goods should have been delivered: this action was not so brought. . . .

Thirdly, as to 'fundamental breach'. The proposition that exemption clauses may be held inapplicable to certain breaches of contract as a matter of construction of the contract, as held by the House of Lords in *Suisse Atlantique SA* v *NV Rotterdamsche Kolen Central* [1966] 1 Lloyd's Rep 529; [1967] 1 AC 361 and *Photo Production Ltd* v *Securicor Transport Ltd* [1980] 1 Lloyd's Rep 545; [1980] 2 WLR 283 and endorsed in Australia by Mr Justice Windeyer in *Thomas National Transport* v *May & Baker* (1966) 115 CLR 353 at p. 376 was not disputed. But Mr Hobhouse QC, for the respondent put forward a special, and ingenious argument that, because of the fundamental nature of the breach, the appellants had deprived themselves of the benefit of cl. 17 of the bill of lading — the time bar clause. A breach of a repudiatory character, which he contended that the breach in question was, entitles the innocent party, unless he waives the breach, to claim to be released from further performance of his obligations under the contract — so far their Lordships of course agree. One of these obligations, learned Counsel proceeded to argue, was to bring any action upon the breach within a period of one year, and the innocent party was released from this obligation. An alternative way of putting it was that the bringing of suit within one year was a condition with which the innocent party was obliged to comply: the repudiatory breach discharged this condition. A further point made was that cl. 17 applied at most to actions for breach of contract: the appellant's negligence as bailee, however, gave rise to an action in tort which was not governed by the time bar.

Their Lordships' opinion upon these arguments is clear. However adroitly presented, they are unsound, and indeed unreal. Clause 17 is drafted in general and all-embracing terms:

> In any event the Carrier and the ship shall be discharged from all liability in respect of loss or damage unless suit is brought within one year after the delivery of the goods or the date when the goods should have been delivered. Suit shall not be deemed brought until jurisdiction shall have been obtained over the Carrier and/or the ship by service of process or by an agreement to appear.

The reference to delivery of the goods shows clearly that the clause is directed towards the carrier's obligations as bailee of the goods. It cannot be supposed that it admits of a distinction between obligations in contract and liability in tort — 'all liability' means what it says.

Moreover it is quite unreal to equate this clause with those provisions in the contract which relate to performance. It is a clause which comes into operation when contractual performance has become impossible, or has been given up: then, it regulates the manner in which liability for breach of contract is to be established. In this respect their Lordships find it relevantly indistinguishable from an arbitration clause, or a forum clause, which, on clear authority, survive a repudiatory breach (*Heyman* v *Darwins* (1942) 72 Ll L Rep 65; [1942] AC 356, *Photo Production Ltd* v *Securicor Transport Ltd* [1980] 1 Lloyd's Rep 525; [1980] 2 WLR 283, at pp. 553 and 295). Mr Hobhouse appealed for support to some observations by Lord Diplock in *Photo Production Ltd* v *Securicor Transport Ltd* (u.s. at pp. 553 and 294–295) where reference is made to putting an end 'to all primary obligations remaining unperformed'. But these words were never intended to cover such 'obligations' to use Lord Diplock's word, as arise when primary obligations have been put an end to. There then arise, on his Lordship's analysis, secondary obligations which include an obligation to pay monetary compensation. Whether these have been modified by agreement is a matter of construction of the contract. The analysis, indeed, so far from supporting the respondent's argument, is directly opposed to it. Their Lordships are of opinion that, on construction and analysis, cl. 17 plainly operates to exclude the respondent's claim.

*Notes*
1.   The time limit has been held to apply in the case of unauthorised deck carriage: *Kenya Railways* v *Antares Co. Pte Ltd (The Antares)* [1987] 1 Lloyd's Rep 424 (CA), see section 4A above. For deviation, see section 7C above.
2.   One of the commonest mistakes made in practice seems to be to commence proceedings against the wrong party: after the year has passed it will not be possible to retrieve the situation by starting fresh proceedings against the correct party. An attempt to circumvent the time limit in this situation by joining the correct party as a defendant in the existing proceedings was unsuccessful in *Zainalabdin Payabi* v *Armstel Shipping Corp Ltd (The Jay Bola)* [1992] 2 Lloyd's Rep 62 (QBD). Joinder is equally ineffective on the plaintiff's side if the timeous proceedings have been brought by the wrong party: *Transworld Oil (USA) Inc.* v *Minos Compania Naviera SA (The Leni)* [1992] 2 Lloyd's Rep 48 (QBD).

*B: Financial limits*

The traditional limit was based on an amount per package or unit: in the Hague-Visby Rules an alternative limit based on the gross weight of the goods has been introduced.

### Carriage of Goods by Sea Act 1971

SCHEDULE

**Article IV**
   (5)(a)   Unless the nature and value of such goods have been declared by the shipper before shipment and inserted in the bill of lading, neither the carrier nor the ship shall in any event be or become liable for any loss or damage to or in connection with the goods in an amount exceeding 666.67 units of account per package or unit or 2 units of account per kilogramme of gross weight of the goods lost or damaged, whichever is the higher.

(b)   The total amount recoverable shall be calculated by reference to the value of such goods at the place and time at which the goods are discharged from the ship in accordance with the contract or should have been so discharged.

The value of the goods shall be fixed according to the commodity exchange price, or, if there be no such price, according to the current market price, or, if there be no commodity exchange price or current market price, by reference to the normal value of goods of the same kind and quality.

(c)   Where a container, pallet or similar article of transport is used to consolidate goods, the number of packages or units enumerated in the bill of lading as packed in such article of transport shall be deemed the number of packages or units for the purpose of this paragraph as far as these packages or units are concerned. Except as aforesaid such article of transport shall be considered the package or unit.

(d)   The unit of account mentioned in this Article is the special drawing right as defined by the International Monetary Fund. The amounts mentioned in sub-paragraph (a) of this paragraph shall be converted into national currency on the basis of the value of that currency on a date to be determined by the law of the court seised of the case.

(e)   Neither the carrier nor the ship shall be entitled to the benefit of the limitation of liability provided for in this paragraph if it is proved that the damage resulted from an act or omission of the carrier done with intent to cause damage, or recklessly and with knowledge that damage would probably result.

(f)   The declaration mentioned in sub-paragraph (a) of this paragraph, if embodied in the bill of lading, shall be prima facie evidence, but shall not be binding or conclusive on the carrier.

(g)   By agreement between the carrier, master or agent of the carrier and the shipper other maximum amounts than those mentioned in sub-paragraph (a) of this paragraph may be fixed, provided that no maximum amount so fixed shall be less than the appropriate maximum mentioned in that sub-paragraph.

(h)   Neither the carrier nor the ship shall be responsible in any event for loss or damage to, or in connection with, goods if the nature or value thereof has been knowingly mis-stated by the shipper in the bill of lading.

*Note and Question*
1.   For the position with regard to containers under the 1924 Hague Rules, see *The River Gurara* [1998] 1 Lloyd's Rep 225 (CA).
2.   Does r. 5(e) refer to recklessness of the carrier in person, or does it include the recklessness of the carrier's servants or agents?

### *Browner International Ltd v Monarch Shipping Co. Ltd*
### *(The European Enterprise)*
[1989] 2 Lloyd's Rep 185

The facts are stated above, see section 3.

STEYN J: The received view is that r. 5(e) refers to the carrier himself, and does not include his servants or agents, except in so far as employees are to be regarded as constituting part of the alter ego of the company on the basis of the principle enunciated in *Lennard's Carrying Co. Ltd* v *Asiatic Petroleum Co. Ltd* [1915] AC 705, at pp. 713–715 and reaffirmed in *Grand Champion Tankers* v *Norpipe A/S (The Marion)* [1984] 2 Lloyd's Rep 1; [1984] AC 563. In the literature there is considerable support for this view. See

Mustill, op. cit., at p. 701; Diamond, op. cit, pp. 20–21; *Scrutton on Charterparties*: 18th ed. (1974), at p. 463; 19th ed. (1984), at p. 456.

It is, however, of the first importance that Judges, and notably Judges in specialist Courts, should be prepared to re-examine conventional wisdoms. But, having listened with care to Mr Simon's argument, I found nothing in it to induce in me any scepticism about the generally held view. Concentrating on the language of r. 5(e) it seems to me clear that the opening words of this provision that 'Neither the carrier nor the ship shall be entitled . . .' must refer to the liability of the carrier himself. If that is so, it would be rather infelicitous to use the word 'carrier' in a different and more extensive sense in the same sub-rule. Mr Simon urged that there is no sensible reason why the carrier should not be responsible for the acts or omissions of their servants for the purposes of art. IV, r. 5(e), just as they are liable for such acts or omissions under other provisions of the rules. He referred me to *Riverstone Meat Co. Pty Ltd* v *Lancashire Shipping Co. Ltd* [1961] 1 Lloyd's Rep 57; [1961] AC 807. But art. IV, r. 5(e), does not impose on a carrier a non-delegable duty. And, contrary to the plaintiffs' contentions, there are respectable commercial arguments in favour of a restrictive meaning of the word 'carrier' in art. IV, r. 5(e). Firstly, and looking at the matter as between the parties to a contract of carriage, one must bear in mind that once an ocean voyage has commenced the carrier has rather limited control over the acts and omissions of his servants and agents. Taking a broad view of the matter, this factor alone would have provided a rational justification for a narrow view of what constitutes a 'carrier' under a provision allowing the limitation to be broken. Secondly, there is another reason why a narrower view of 'carrier' would have appealed to those who drafted the 1968 Protocol. That is the consideration that, although limitation provisions are often viewed with scepticism by lawyers, the undoubted advantage of limitation provisions such as those contained in art. IV, r. 5(e), is that it makes it easier and less expensive to obtain the insurance vital to the conduct of the shipping trade. A fairly narrow breaking of limitation provision, predicated on the misconduct or recklessness of the carrier himself, therefore serves a rational commercial purpose.

But there is another factor which reinforces the restrictive interpretation. Article 25 of the amended Warsaw Convention provides as follows:

> The limits of liability specified in Article 22 shall not apply if it is proved that the damage resulted from an act or omission *of the carrier, his servants or agents*, done with intent to cause damage or recklessly and with knowledge that damage would probably result; provided that, in the case of such act or omission of a servant or agent, it is also proved that he was acting within the scope of his employment. [Emphasis supplied.]

See Schedule 1 to the Carriage by Air Act, 1961. This is the very provision which the parties to the 1968 Protocol had before them. They adopted the ipsissima verba of art. 25 of the amended Warsaw Convention with one notable change: they deleted the words 'his servants or agents'. That tends to indicate that a restrictive view of what is comprehended by 'carrier' prevailed. This is, of course, no more than an external aid to construction, which could not prevail in the face of convincing contrary internal indicia. But it is part of the legislative setting, which it would be wrong to ignore. In my judgment, it reinforces my view that 'carrier' should be given the narrower meaning.

*Conclusion*
It follows that I have come to the conclusion:— (a) that the limitation provisions of par. 3(a) of the contract are not invalidated by s. 1(6)(b) of the 1971 Act; and (b) art. IV, r. 5(e), of the Hague-Visby Rules, refers only to the misconduct or recklessness of the carrier himself or his alter ego.

*Note*
In *Nelson Pine Industries Ltd* v *Seatrans New Zealand Ltd (The I*
2 Lloyd's Rep 290 (NZ High Ct) Ellis J held that r. 5(e) referre
and knowledge on the part of the master.

## SECTION 10: SHIPMENT OF DANGEROUS GOODS

### Carriage of Goods by Sea Act 1971

### Schedule

Article IV(6): 'Goods of an inflammable, explosive or dangerous nature to the shipment whereof the carrier, master or agent of the carrier has not consented with knowledge of their nature and character, may at any time before discharge be landed at any place, or destroyed or rendered innocuous by the carrier without compensation and the shipper of such goods shall be liable for all damages and expenses directly or indirectly arising out of or resulting from such shipment. If any such goods shipped with such knowledge and consent shall become a danger to the ship or cargo, they may in like manner be landed at any place, or destroyed or rendered innocuous by the carrier without liability on the part of the carrier except to general average, if any.'

The interpretation of this provision, and in particular the relationship between it and Art. IV, r. 3 ('The shipper shall not be responsible for loss or damage sustained by the carrier or the ship arising or resulting from any cause without the act, fault or neglect of the shipper, his agents or his servants'), was settled by the House of Lords in the next case. The speeches display interesting differences of approach to the wider aspects of the process of interpreting the Rules.

### *Effort Shipping Co. Ltd* v *Linden Management SA*
### *(The Giannis NK)*
### [1998] 1 Lloyd's Rep 337 (HL)

LORD LLOYD OF BERWICK: The relevant facts are all agreed. On Nov. 18, 1990 the appellant shipped a cargo of ground-nut extractions at Dakar, Senegal, for carriage to Rio Haina in the Dominican Republic. The ground-nut cargo was loaded in No. 4 hold of the respondents' vessel *Giannis NK* under a bill of lading which incorporates the Hague Rules. It is agreed that the ground-nut cargo was infested with Khapra beetle at the time of shipment. But this was unknown to the appellant shippers as well as the respondent carriers.

The vessel had previously loaded a cargo of wheat pellets in Nos. 2 and 3 holds for carriage to San Juan, Puerto Rico and Rio Haina. There was no danger of the beetle infestation spreading from the ground-nut cargo in No. 4 hold to the wheat cargo in Nos. 2 and 3 holds. But the beetle infestation in No. 4 hold nevertheless rendered the vessel and its cargo (including the wheat cargo) subject to exclusion from the countries where the cargo was to be discharged.

After discharging part of the wheat cargo at San Juan, the vessel proceeded to Rio Haina where she was placed in quarantine after the discovery of insects in No. 4 hold. It thought that the insects might be Khapra beetles. The vessel was fumigated twice. But it did not eradicate the insects. Accordingly on Dec. 21 the vessel was ordered to leave port with all her remaining cargo.

Meanwhile the vessel had been arrested by the receivers. It was only when the arrest was lifted on an undertaking given by the vessels P. & I. club that the vessel was able to leave port. She returned to San Juan, in an attempt to find a purchaser for the cargo, in accordance with the club's undertaking. But when she arrived at San Juan, the U.S. authorities identified a Khapra beetle and a Khapra beetle larva, both dead, in No. 4 hold. On Jan. 3, 1991 the U.S. authorities issued a notice requiring the carrier to return the cargo to its country of origin, or to dump it at sea, but at all events to leave U.S. ports. It is common ground that in those circumstances the carrier had no practical alternative but to dump the whole of the cargo at sea, including the wheat cargo. The vessel sailed on Feb. 3, and the cargo was dumped between Feb. 4 and 12.

When the vessel returned to San Juan after dumping her cargo there was a further inspection. Eighteen live Khapra beetles and Khapra beetle larvae were found in No. 4 hold. There was a further fumigation. The vessel was eventually cleared to load under her next charter, at Wilmington, North Carolina after a delay of two-and-a-half months. The question is who is to pay for the delay?

Mr Johnson QC, on behalf of the shippers, submits that the loss should lie where it falls. Mr Schaff, on behalf of the carriers, submits that the carriers are entitled to recover damages for delay to the vessel, and the cost of the fumigations, either under art. IV, r. 6 of the Hague Rules, or by virtue of an implied term at common law. Mr Justice Longmore decided all questions in favour of the carriers, and so did the Court of Appeal. The shippers now appeal to the House by leave of your Lordships.

*Dangerous goods and the Hague Rules*
[After setting out art. IV, r. 6, Lord Lloyd continued:] It is convenient to get two preliminary points out of the way. They are not in dispute.

First, it has been settled law since *Chandris* v *Isbrandtsen-Moller Co. Inc* (1950) 83 Ll L Rep 385; [1951] 1 KB 240 that the word 'dangerous' in the expression 'goods of . . . [a] dangerous nature' must be given a broad meaning. Dangerous goods are not confined to goods of an inflammable or explosive nature, or their like. . . .

Secondly, goods may be dangerous within the meaning of art. IV, r. 6 if they are dangerous to other goods, even though they are not dangerous to the vessel itself.

What then is the meaning of the word 'dangerous' in this context? Mr Schaff argues that 'dangerous' means, or at any rate includes, cargo which is physically dangerous to other cargo. Even though there was no risk of the infestation spreading from the ground-nut cargo in No. 4 hold to the wheat cargo in Nos. 2 and 3 holds, nevertheless the ground-nut cargo was physically dangerous to the wheat cargo because the dumping of the wheat cargo at sea was 'a natural and not unlikely consequence' of shipping the ground-nut cargo infested with Khapra beetle: see par. 7(1) of the agreed statement of facts.

Mr Johnson, on the other hand, while conceding that the ground-nut cargo caused physical damage to the wheat cargo in that sense, submits that there was no *direct* physical damage to the wheat cargo. Cargo is only dangerous within the meaning of art. IV, r. 6 if it causes, or is likely to cause, direct damage to other cargo by its own physical operation, for example, by overheating or leakage. Here, the only physical damage to the wheat resulted from the decision to dump the cargo at sea. That was a decision which was taken for commercial reasons. No doubt the decision was sensible, and perhaps unavoidable. But at the time the wheat was dumped it was sound. It had not been affected in any way by the inherent characteristics of the ground-nut cargo.

I prefer Mr. Schaff's argument. I can see no reason to confine the word 'dangerous' to goods which are liable to cause direct physical damage to other goods. It is true that goods which explode or catch fire would normally cause direct physical damage to other cargo in the vicinity. But there is no need to qualify the word 'dangerous' by reading in the word 'directly', which is what Mr Johnson's argument in effect requires. Indeed the reference to 'all damages or expenses directly or indirectly arising out of or resulting from such shipment' point in the other direction.

Mr Justice Longmore, in an admirably clear and succinct judgment ([1994] 2 Lloyd's Rep 171), found that the ground-nut cargo was of a dangerous nature on shipment, on the ground that it was liable to give rise to the loss of other cargo loaded on the same vessel by dumping at sea. This finding was upheld by Lord Justice Hirst in the Court of Appeal: [1996] 1 Lloyd's Rep 577. I find myself in complete agreement with their reasoning. Accordingly it is unnecessary to consider a further argument that goods may be of a dangerous nature even though they do not present any physical danger to ship or cargo, but are 'legally' dangerous in the sense that they are liable to cause delay to ship and cargo through the operation of some local law.

What are the consequences of the finding that the ground-nut cargo was physically dangerous to the wheat cargo? Since the carriers did not consent to the shipment of the ground-nut cargo with knowledge of its dangerous character, the shippers are prima facie liable for all damages and expenses suffered by the carriers. But this brings me to the second question. Mr Johnson argues that the shippers' liability under art. IV, r. 6 is qualified by the provisions of art. IV, r. 3. That rule provides:

> The shipper shall not be responsible for loss or damage sustained by the carrier or the ship arising or resulting from any cause without the act, fault or neglect of the shipper, his agents or his servants.

It cannot have been intended, says Mr Johnson, that shippers should incur unlimited liability for the shipment of dangerous goods when they did not know, and had no means of knowing, that the goods were infested. Shippers should only be liable in case of some fault or neglect on their part.

Mr Schaff, on the other hand, argues that art. IV, r. 6 is a free-standing provision, covering the specific subject matter of dangerous goods. If the shippers' liability under art. IV, r. 6 was to be governed by art. IV, r. 3 one would have expected this to be made clear by the inclusion in art. IV, r. 6 of some expression such as 'subject to Article IV, r. 3'.

Mr Justice Longmore and the Court of Appeal rejected Mr Johnson's argument, and so would I. The very breadth of art. IV, r. 3 ('shall not be responsible for loss or damage ... arising or resulting from any cause ...') makes it unlikely that it was intended to qualify the specific provisions of art. IV, r. 6: generalia specialibus non derogant. If art. IV, r. 3 was intended to have overriding effect, the framers of the rule had appropriate language to hand: see art. II which is expressly made subject to art. VI, and art. VI, which applies 'notwithstanding the provisions of the preceding Articles'. No such qualifying language is found in either art. IV, r. 6 or in art. III, r. 5.

But there is a more fundamental reason for rejecting Mr Johnson's argument. The first half of the first sentence of art. IV, r. 6 gives the carrier the right to destroy or render innocuous dangerous goods which have been shipped without his knowing their dangerous nature. Obviously that right cannot be dependent in any way on whether the shipper has knowledge of the dangerous nature of the goods. Yet the sentence continues, without a break, 'and the shipper of such goods shall be liable ...'. It is natural to read the two halves of the first sentence as being two sides of the same coin. If so, then the shippers' liability for shipping dangerous goods cannot be made to depend on the state of his knowledge. His liability is not confined to cases where he is at fault.

Mr Johnson rightly drew our attention to the law on this point in the United States. . . . [but] there appear to be no U.S. cases in which the relationship between art. IV, r. 3 and art IV, r. 6 has fallen for decision, as indeed Mr Johnson conceded. I am not forgetting that in *The Athanasia Comninos* [1990] 1 Lloyd's Rep 277 Mr Justice Mustill considered that the U.S. cases to which I have referred answered the point in issue in favour of the shippers. But with respect I do not regard that as a correct reading of those cases.

Mr Johnson pointed out how important it is that provisions of an international convention should, so far as possible, be given the same construction by the Courts of different countries: see *Riverstone Meat Co. Pty Ltd* v *Lancashire Shipping Co. Ltd* [1961] 1 Lloyd's Rep 57 at p. 70; [1961] AC 807 at p. 840 per Viscount Simonds. This is an argument which would carry great weight with me, if there were what Viscount Simonds called 'prevailing harmony' on the other side of the Atlantic. But such is not the case. There is no generally prevailing view on the precise point in issue, either in the U.S. or in Canada: see *Heath Steel Mines Ltd* v *The Erwin Schroder* [1970] Ex Cr 426. Nor were we referred to any cases decided in other maritime jurisdictions.

Turning to the English cases, Mr Justice Mustill in *The Athanasia Comninos* [1990] 1 Lloyd's Rep 277 expressed the view, obiter, that art. IV, r. 6 is not qualified by art. IV, r. 3. In *Mediterranean Freight Services Ltd* v *BP Oil International Ltd (The Fiona)* [1993] 1 Lloyd's Rep 257 Judge Diamond, QC, sitting as a Deputy Commercial Court Judge, with all his great experience of this branch of the law, expressed the same view. I agree with those views, and accept Mr Schaff's formulation as a correct statement of the law. Article IV, r. 6 is a free-standing provision dealing with a specific subject matter. It is neither expressly, nor by implication, subject to art. IV, r. 3. It imposes strict liability on shippers in relation to the shipment of dangerous goods, irrespective of fault or neglect on their part.

If I am right so far, it becomes unnecessary to consider the meaning of the word 'act' in the phrase 'act fault or neglect of the shipper' in art. IV, r. 3. In *The Fiona* Judge Diamond held that the shipment of dangerous goods is an act of the shipper, whether or not the shipment of such goods was due to his fault or neglect. This would, if correct, afford an alternative ground for a decision in favour of the carriers in this case. However, in the United States it has been said that COGSA is a negligence statute, and not a strict liability statute, and that fault is therefore a prerequisite for recovery: see *Sea-Land Service Inc.* v *The Purdy Co. of Washington*, A.M.C. 1593 [1982] cited with approval in *Excel Shipping Corporation* v *Seatrain International SA*, 584 F. Supp 734 [1984] at p. 748. On this view the shipment of dangerous goods would not be an 'act' of the shipper unless accompanied by fault or neglect. I prefer not to express an opinion as to which of these two views is correct. Since I have held that art. IV, r. 6 is not in any event subject to art. IV, r. 3, the point does not arise for decision.

. . .

LORD STEYN: My Lords, the answers to important questions arising in this case have been a matter of controversy in this country and elsewhere for many years. Moreover a divergence in approach between the Courts of this country and the Courts of the United States in regard to art. IV, r. 6 of the Hague Rules has emerged. In these circumstances I propose to explain the reasons for my conclusions.

. . .

*Does art. IV, r. 6 provide a free-standing bundle of rights to carriers?*
The question to be resolved is whether art. IV, r. 6 provides a free-standing bundle of rights and obligations or whether those rights and obligations are qualified by art. IV, r. 3. The answer to this question is far from obvious.

Counsel for the shippers said that it is wrong to focus on art. IV, r. 6 in isolation and to form a presumptive view of its nature and scope on that basis. I agree. Like Mr Justice Longmore and Lord Justice Hirst I proceed to consider art. IV, r. 6 and art. IV, r. 3 in the context in which they appear. Article IV, r. 3 is cast in negative form. It provides for an immunity in favour of the shipper for loss sustained by carrier 'from any cause without the act, fault or neglect of the shipper'. It is a general provision. Article IV, r. 6 is a very specific provision. It falls into three parts. The first part allows the carrier to land, destroy or render innocuous goods of a dangerous nature to the shipment of which the carrier has not consented. The carrier may exercise this liberty without incurring any liability to pay compensation. The second part makes the shipper liable for all expenses directly or indirectly *arising from such shipment*. The words which I have emphasised seem to be a reference back to a shipment as described in the first part. The third part concerns shipment of goods to which the carrier has consented with knowledge of their nature and character but which become a danger to the ship or cargo. Again the carrier is allowed to land, destroy or render innocuous the goods without incurring any liability 'except to general average, if any'. In such cases, however, the shipper is not liable in damages to the carrier.

That brings me directly to the competing arguments. Counsel for the owners said that art. IV, r. 6 is not expressed to be 'subject to Article IV, r. 3' and suggested that this omission is significant. Counsel for the shippers put forward the counter argument that art. IV, r. 6 could have been introduced as applying 'Notwithstanding Article IV, r. 3'. Judged simply as language that could have been used, but was not used, I regard these points as self cancelling makeweights. Counsel for the owners also drew attention to art. IV, r. 5 which provides that the shipper shall be deemed to have guaranteed to the carrier the accuracy at the time of shipment of the marks, number, quantity and weight, as furnished by him. Plainly this provision imposes a free-standing and absolute obligation on shippers. The owners pointed out that art. IV, r. 3 is not expressly made subject to art. IV, r. 5. They argued that this factor supports the argument that art. IV, r. 3 also does not qualify art. IV, r. 6. This is a type of argument that might have some attraction in the construction of a conveyancing document. But in the interpretation of a multi-lateral trade convention it is a rather insubstantial point on which I would not wish to put any weight. The search ought to be for more secure footholds on which to make a judgment in regard to the meaning of provisions in the Hague Rules.

This much we know about the broad objective of the Hague rules: it was intended to reign in the unbridled freedom of contract of owners to impose terms which were 'so unreasonable and unjust in their terms as to exempt from almost every conceivable risk and responsibility' ((1992) 108 LQR 501, at p. 502); it aimed to achieve this by a pragmatic compromise between interests of owners and shippers; and the Hague Rules were designed to achieve a part harmonisation of the diverse laws of trading nations at least in the areas which the convention covered. But these general aims tells us nothing about the meaning of art. IV, r. 3 or art. IV, r. 6. One is therefore remitted to the language of the relevant parts of the Hague Rules as the authoritative guide to the intention of the framers of the Hague Rules.

Counsel for the owners relied on two factors of substance in support of his submission that art. IV, r. 6 is a free-standing provision. First, the immunities provided for in art. IV, r. 3 are expressed in language of generality. On the other hand art. IV, r. 6 spells out a specific bundle of rights in respect of the shipment of goods which may become a danger to the ship or cargo. Counsel for the owners relied on the generalia specialibus non derogant principle which informs the drafting techniques of English Parliamentary draftsmen. The point can, however, be put on a broader basis. In our daily lives we do not necessarily regard general instructions as impinging on specific instructions.

Similarly, in the construction of documents we may proceed on an initial premise that a general provision does not necessarily qualify a specific provision in the same document. That common sense consideration also applies to international conventions. But it is not a mechanical rule. Everything depends on the context. And ultimately the matter is one of judgment. In the present case my view is that the contrast between the generality of art. IV, r. 3 and the specificity of art. IV, r. 6 goes some way to supporting the proposition that the latter ought to be construed as free-standing. But I am not saying that on its own this is a decisive factor in favour of the interpretation put forward by the owners. The second point of substance is the argument that art. IV, r. 6 in its three different parts points in a similar direction. The right given in the first and third parts to the carrier to land, etc., dangerous cargo cannot sensibly depend on whether the shippers knew or ought to have known of the dangerous nature of the cargo. That would be impractical: the carrier must be able to land, etc., dangerous cargo irrespective of his shippers' actual or constructive knowledge. Counsel for the shippers did not dispute this proposition. But he said that this liberty to land dangerous cargo already existed under the common law. That is no answer: pro tanto the Hague Rules upon their enactment displaced the common law. It follows that the liberty to land dangerous cargo under the first and third parts derives exclusively from art. IV, r. 6. And in respect of the first and third parts it exists irrespective of the actual or constructive knowledge of the shippers. If one were now to accept the shippers' argument there would be this difference between the first and third parts as contrasted with the second part: only in respect of the second part would the rights of the owners be conditional upon the actual or constructive knowledge, or due diligence, of the shippers. But this is prima facie implausible because the rights to land, etc., dangerous cargo, and to claim damages seem to arise in the same circumstances. Indeed the second part in imposing liability for damage resulting from 'such shipment' refers back the 'shipment' of dangerous cargo, etc., in the first part. The natural construction is therefore that in neither the first nor the second parts (or for that matter the third part) are the rights of owners conditional upon the actual or constructive knowledge, or due diligence, of shippers. This is a point of some weight.

Cumulatively, the two factors identified in the last paragraph point to art. IV, r. 6 being of a free-standing nature. But now I have to set against this initial impression three matters upon which Counsel for the shippers relied. First there are the decisions of the Courts of the United states to which my noble and learned friend Lord Lloyd of Berwick has referred. Counsel for the owners criticised the reasoning in some of those cases. For my part I regard it as unnecessary to discuss these cases in detail. I have found the analysis of the position in the United States in Wilford, Coghlin and Kimball, *Time Charters*, 4th ed. (1995), at pp. 169 and 173-176, of assistance. Mr Kimball is the senior partner of a New York law firm and a distinguished maritime lawyer. No doubt he was responsible for the separate discussions of United States law in this book. It is stated in this book that the Courts in the United States have taken the view that art. IV, r. 3 qualifies art. IV, r. 6: at p. 169. Like Mr Justice Mustill in *The Athanasia Comninos* [1990] 1 Lloyd's Rep 277 I am satisfied that this is the established position in the United States. That is a weighty factor against my initial view that art. IV, r. 6 contains a bundle of free-standing rights in favour of the owners. In the construction of an international convention an English Court does not easily differ from a crystallised body of judicial opinion in the United States.

That brings me to the argument for the shippers based on the *travaux preparatoires* of the Hague Rules. Those materials are now readily accessible: see Michael F. Sturley, *The Legislative History of the Carriage of Goods by Sea Act* and *The Travaux Preparatoires of the Hague Rules* (1990) vols. 1-3. Although the text of a convention must be accorded primacy in matters of interpretation, it is well settled that the *travaux preparatoires* of an international convention may be used as 'supplementary means of interpretation': compare art. 31, Vienna Convention the Law of Treaties, Vienna, May 23, 1969. Following *Fothergill* v *Monarch Airlines Ltd* [1980] 2 Lloyd's Rep 295; [1981] AC 251, I would be quite prepared, in an appropriate case involving truly feasible alternative interpretations of a convention, to allow the evidence contained in the *travaux preparatoires* to be determinative of the question of construction. But that is only possible where the Court is satisfied that the *travaux preparatoires* clearly and indisputably point to a definite legal intention: see *Fothergill* v *Monarch Airlines Ltd*, per Lord Wilberforce, at p. 202, col. 1; p. 278C. Only a bull's eye counts. Nothing less will do. In the present case the shippers relied on the fact that on Oct. 11, 1922 at the London Conference the chairman stated with reference to art. IV, r. 3 his view that 'the words framed have been designed to give the shipper the largest protection that could be devised for him' and that the conference agreed. Neither this passage nor any other exchanges reflected in the *travaux preparatoires* thrown any light on the question whether art. IV, r. 6 was intended as a free-standing provision. The statement that art. IV, r. 3 was designed to give the shipper 'the largest protection that could be devised for him' was undoubtedly intended to give comfort to shippers but it is singularly uninformative even as to the scope of art. IV, r. 3. It was no more than a statement that under art. IV, r. 3 shippers get the largest protection that in a practical world could be afforded to them. In context the chairman's statement can be seen to be weasel words. The resort to the *travaux preparatoires* provided nothing worthy of consideration in the process of the interpretation of art. IV, r. 3 and art. IV, r. 6.

Counsel to the shippers also relied on evidence given by Lord Justice Scrutton before the Joint Committee on the Carriage of Goods by Sea Act in June 1923 at the time when the United Kingdom had already decided that effect should be given to the Hague Rules: see 1923 V Parliamentary Papers, June 27, 1912, par. 442, at p. 94. Lord Justice Scrutton offered the view that the committee should consider whether art. IV, r. 3 'would in any way limit the shippers and others as to shipping dangerous goods.' But, as Lord Roskill pointed out in an elegant piece in the law Quarterly Review Lord Justice Scrutton, notwithstanding a changing order in regard to world trade, was a passionate protagonist of the freedom of owners to dictate their terms: (1992) 108 LQR 501-505. Referring to the evidence of Lord Justice Scrutton and Frank MacKinnon QC before the committee Lord Roskill observed, at p. 502:

> The criticism of Scrutton and MacKinnon was then concentrated upon their language. They gave dire and in the event wholly unwarranted warnings of the problems which would arise as to their construction with uncertainty and endless litigation replacing what they saw as the clarity of the existing law based upon freedom of contract. In truth, as every commercial lawyer knows, it is remarkable how few cases there have been in this country upon the construction of the Rules.

Lord Justice Scrutton's observation was the outcome of an hostility to the very concept of a multilateral trade convention. His tentative observation on art. IV, r. 6 is of no value.

That leaves the overall position that the language of art. IV, r. 6, read with art. IV, r. 3, tends to suggest that art. IV, r. 6 was intended to be a free-standing provision. I have already described the two pointers in that direction. As against that there is the fact that the United States Courts have interpreted art. IV, r. 3 as qualifying art. IV, r. 6. Given the desirability of a uniform interpretation of the Hague Rules, the choice between the competing interpretations is finely balanced. But there is a contextual consideration which must also be weighed in the balance. It is permissible to take into account the legal position in the United Kingdom and in the United States regarding the shipment of dangerous cargo before the Hague Rules were approved. It is relevant as part of the contextual scene of the Hague rules: *Riverstone Meat Co. Pty. Ltd* v *Lancashire Shipping Co. Ltd* [1961] 1 Lloyd's Rep 57 at p. 68; [1961] AC 807 at p. 836 per Viscount Simonds. In *Brass* v *Maitland* (1856) 6 E & B 470 the majority held that under a contract of carriage there is a term implied by law that a shipper will not ship dangerous goods without notice to the carrier; the obligation is absolute. The same view prevailed in the Court of Appeal in *Bamfield* v *Goole and Sheffield Transport Co. Ltd* [1910] 2 KB 94 and in *Great Northern Railway Co.* v *L.E.P. Transport and Depository Ltd* [1922] 2 KB 742. This view was controversial. It was disputed in a strong minority judgment in *Brass* v *Maitland* and in *Bamfield* v *Goole and Sheffield Transport Co. Ltd*; see also *Mitchell Colts & Co.* v *Steel Brothers & Co.* [1916] 2 KB 610, per Mr Justice Atkin at pp. 613-614; and *Abbot on Merchant Ships and Seamen*, 13th ed. (1892) at p. 522. Nevertheless, the law of England was as held by the majority in *Brass* v *Maitland*. That view probably would have been regarded as authoritative in most countries in what was then the British Empire. In 1861 a Court in the United States adopted the majority holding in *Brass* v *Maitland* as a sound rule on the policy grounds viz. that 'It throws the loss on the party who generally has the best means of informing himself of the character of the article shipped:' *Pierce* v *Winsor*, 2 Sprague 35; see also Parsons, a *Treatise of the Law of Shipping* (1869) vol. 1 at pp. 265-266. That remained the legal position in the United States until the conferences that led to the adoption of the Hague Rules. The United States was then already a great maritime power. Its shipping law was a matter of great importance. The British Empire was in decline but collectively the trading countries under its umbrella controlled a considerable proportion of ocean-going world trade. That means that at the time of the drafting of the Hague Rules the dominant theory in a very large part of the world was that shippers were under an absolute liability not to ship dangerous goods. This circumstance must have been known to those who drafted and approved the Hague Rules. No doubt they also knew that there was an alternative theory namely that the shipper of dangerous goods ought only to be liable for want of due diligence in the shipment of dangerous goods. If this contextual scene is correctly described, and I have not understood it to be disputed, one is entitled to pose the practical question: What would the framers of the Hague Rules have done if collectively they had been minded to adopt the step of reversing the dominant theory of shipper's liability for the shipment of dangerous goods? There is really only one realistic answer: they would have expressly provided that shippers are only liable in damages for the shipment of dangerous goods if they knew or ought to have known of the dangerousness of the goods. In that event the three parts of art. IV, r. 6 would have had to be recast to make clear that the shipper's actual or constructive knowledge was irrelevant to the carrier's right to land dangerous cargo but a condition precedent to the liability of the shippers for damages in the second part. Moreover, if this idea had been put forward for discussion the *travaux preparatoires* would no doubt have reflected the observations of carriers on such a fundamental change to their rights. The idea was never put forward. The inference must be that the framers of the Hague Rules proceeded on what was at that time an unsurprising assumption that shippers would be absolutely liable for the shipment of dangerous cargo.

In all these circumstances I am constrained to conclude that despite the decisions of the United States Courts, the best interpretation of the language of art. IV, r. 6 read with art. IV, r. 3, seen against its contextual backgrond, is that it created free-standing rights and obligations in respect of the shipment of dangerous cargo.

*Notes*

1.   In *Mediterranean Freight Services Ltd* v *BP Oil International Ltd (The Fiona)* [1994] 2 Lloyd's Rep 506 (CA), it was held that a shipowner who was in breach of the 'overriding' obligation under Art. III, r. 1 to provide a seaworthy vessel (because the tanks were contaminated by residues from previous cargoes), could not rely on Art. IV, r. 6.

2.   In *Chandris* v *Isbrandtsen-Moller Co. Inc.* [1951] 1 KB 240, Devlin J held that Art. IV, r. 6 was not to be read as implying that the shipper was *never* liable for damages if the carrier had consented to the shipment of dangerous goods. On the facts of the case, which are considered further in Chapter 9, the master had consented to the carriage of turpentine, which was in breach of the charterparty, but had not waived the shipowners' claim for damages. In these — perhaps unusual — circumstances Art. IV, r. 6 was not an obstacle to a claim by the shipowner against the shipper.

## SECTION 11: OTHER PROVISIONS

We include here, for reference, the parts of COGSA 1971 not set out above.

### Carriage of Goods by Sea Act 1971

#### 1.   Application of Hague Rules as amended

(7)   If and so far as the contract contained in or evidenced by a bill of lading or receipt within paragraph (a) or (b) of subsection (6) above applies to deck cargo or live animals, the Rules as given the force of law by that subsection shall have effect as if Article I(c) did not exclude deck cargo and live animals.

In this subsection 'deck cargo' means cargo which by the contract of carriage is stated as being carried on deck and is so carried.

#### 2.   Contracting States, etc.

(1)   If Her Majesty by Order in Council certifies to the following effect, that is to say, that for the purposes of the Rules—

(a)   a State specified in the Order is a contracting State, or is a contracting State in respect of any place or territory so specified; or

(b)   any place or territory specified in the Order forms part of a State so specified (whether a contracting State or not),

the Order shall, except so far as it has been superseded by a subsequent Order, be conclusive evidence of the matters so certified.

(2)   An Order in Council under this section may be varied or revoked by a subsequent Order in Council.

#### 4.   Application of Act to British possessions, etc.

(1)   Her Majesty may by Order in Council direct that this Act shall extend, subject to such exceptions, adaptations and modifications as may be specified in the Order, to all or any of the following territories, that is—

(a)   any colony (not being a colony for whose external relations a country other than the United Kingdom is responsible),

(b)   any country outside Her Majesty's dominions in which Her Majesty has jurisdiction in right of Her Majesty's Government of the United Kingdom.

(2)   An Order in Council under this section may contain such transitional and other consequential and incidental provisions as appear to Her Majesty to be expedient, including provisions amending or repealing any legislation about the carriage of goods by sea forming part of the law of any of the territories mentioned in paragraphs (a) and (b) above.

(3)   An Order in Council under this section may be varied or revoked by a subsequent Order in Council.

## 5.   Extension of application of Rules to carriage from ports in British possessions, etc.

(1)   Her Majesty may by Order in Council provide that section 1(3) of this Act shall have effect as if the reference therein to the United Kingdom included a reference to all or any of the following territories, that is—

(a)   the Isle of Man;

(b)   any of the Channel Islands specified in the Order;

(c)   any colony specified in the Order (not being a colony for whose external relations a country other than the United Kingdom is responsible);

(d)   any associated state (as defined by section 1(3) of the West Indies Act 1967) specified in the Order;

(e)   any country specified in the Order, being a country outside Her Majesty's dominions in which Her Majesty has jurisdiction in right of Her Majesty's Government of the United Kingdom.

(2)   An Order in Council under this section may be varied or revoked by a subsequent Order in Council.

## 6.   Supplemental

(1)   This Act may be cited as the Carriage of Goods by Sea Act 1971.

(2)   It is hereby declared that this Act extends to Northern Ireland.

(3)   The following enactments shall be repealed, that is—

(a)   the Carriage of Goods by Sea Act 1924,

(b)   section 12(4)(a) of the Nuclear Installations Act 1965,

and without prejudice to section 38(1) of the Interpretation Act 1889, the reference to the said Act of 1924 in section 1(1)(i)(ii) of the Hovercraft Act 1968 shall include a reference to this Act.

(4)   It is hereby declared that for the purposes of Article VIII of the Rules section 18 of the Merchant Shipping Act 1979 (which entirely exempts shipowners and others in certain circumstances from liability for loss of, or damage to, goods) is a provision relating to limitation of liability.

(5)   This Act shall come into force on such day as Her Majesty may by Order in Council appoint, and, for the purposes of the transition from the law in force immediately before the day appointed under this subsection to the provisions of this Act, the Order appointing the day may provide that those provisions shall have effect subject to such transitional provisions as may be contained in the Order.

## SCHEDULE

### Article IV bis

(1)   The defences and limits of liability provided for in these Rules shall apply in any action against the carrier in respect of loss or damage to goods covered by a contract of carriage whether the action be founded in contract or in tort.

(2)   If such an action is brought against a servant or agent of the carrier (such servant or agent not being an independent contractor), such servant or agent shall be entitled to avail himself of the defences and limits of liability which the carrier is entitled to invoke under these Rules.

(3)   The aggregate of the amounts recoverable from the carrier, and such servants and agents, shall in no case exceed the limit provided for in these Rules.

(4)   Nevertheless, a servant or agent of the carrier shall not be entitled to avail himself of the provisions of this article, if it is proved that the damage resulted from an act or omission of the servant or agent done with intent to cause damage or recklessly and with knowledge that damage would probably result.

## Carriage of Goods by Sea Act 1971

### SCHEDULE

**Article V**
A carrier shall be at liberty to surrender in whole or in part all or any of his rights and immunities or to increase any of his responsibilities and obligations under these Rules, provided such surrender or increase shall be embodied in the bill of lading issued to the shipper. The provisions of the Rules shall not be applicable to charterparties, but if bills of lading are issued in the case of a ship under a charter party they shall comply with the terms of these Rules. Nothing in these Rules shall be held to prevent the insertion in a bill of lading of any lawful provisions regarding general average.

**Article VIII**
The provisions of these Rules shall not affect the rights and obligations of the carrier under any statute for the time being in force relating to the limitation of the liability of owners of sea-going vessels.

**Article IX**
These Rules shall not affect the provisions of any international Convention or national law governing liability for nuclear damage.

## SECTION 12: THE HAMBURG RULES

The United Nations Convention on the Carriage of Goods by Sea, 1978 — the Hamburg Rules — took a long time to reach the requisite number of signatures for entry into force. The Convention did, however, finally come into force on 1 November 1992 and, although no major maritime country has yet ratified it, it can be expected to gain in importance in the future. The Convention breaks with the Hague Rules tradition on a number of significant points.

### UNITED NATIONS CONVENTION ON THE CARRIAGE OF GOODS BY SEA, 1978

*Preamble*

*The states parties to this convention, Having recognised the desirability of determining by agreement certain rules relating to the carriage of goods by sea, have decided to conclude a Convention for this purpose and have thereto agreed as follows:*

PART I
GENERAL PROVISIONS

## Article 1  Definitions
In this Convention:
1.    'Carrier' means any person by whom or in whose name a contract of carriage of goods by sea has been concluded with a shipper.
2.    'Actual carrier' means any person to whom the performance of the carriage of the goods, or of part of the carriage, has been entrusted by the carrier, and includes any other person to whom such performance has been entrusted.
3.    'Shipper' means any person by whom or in whose name or on whose behalf a contract of carriage of goods by sea has been concluded with a carrier, or any person by whom or in whose name or on whose behalf the goods are actually delivered to the carrier in relation to the contract of carriage by sea.
4.    'Consignee' means the person entitled to take delivery of the goods.
5.    'Goods' includes live animals; where the goods are consolidated in a container, pallet or similar article of transport or where they are packed, 'goods' includes such article of transport or packaging if supplied by the shipper.
6.    'Contract of carriage by sea' means any contract whereby the carrier undertakes against payment of freight to carry goods by sea from one port to another; however, a contract which involves carriage by sea and also carriage by some other means is deemed to be a contract of carriage by sea for the purposes of this Convention only in so far as it relates to the carriage by sea.
7.    'Bill of lading' means a document which evidences a contract of carriage by sea and the taking over or loading of the goods by the carrier, and by which the carrier undertakes to deliver the goods against surrender of the document. A provision in the document that the goods are to be delivered to the order of a named person, or to order, or to bearer, constitutes such an undertaking.
8.    'Writing' includes, inter alia, telegram and telex.

## Article 2  Scope of application
1.    The provisions of this Convention are applicable to all contracts of carriage by sea between two different States, if:
    (a)    the port of loading as provided for in the contract of carriage by sea is located in a Contracting State, or
    (b)    the port of discharge as provided for in the contract of carriage by sea is located in a Contracting State, or
    (c)    one of the optional ports of discharge provided for in the contract of carriage by sea is the actual port of discharge and such port is located in a Contracting State, or
    (d)    the bill of lading or other document evidencing the contract of carriage by sea is issued in a Contracting State, or
    (e)    the bill of lading or other document evidencing the contract of carriage by sea provides that the provisions of this Convention or the legislation of any State giving effect to them are to govern the contract.
2.    The provisions of this Convention are applicable without regard to the nationality of the ship, the carrier, the actual carrier, the shipper, the consignee or any other interested person.
3.    The provisions of this Convention are not applicable to charterparties. However, where a bill of lading is issued pursuant to a charterparty, the provisions of the Convention apply to such a bill of lading if it governs the relation between the carrier and the holder of the bill of lading, not being the charterer.

4.   If a contract provides for future carriage of goods in a series of shipments during an agreed period, the provisions of this Convention apply to each shipment. However, where a shipment is made under a charterparty, the provisions of para. 3 of this Article apply.

### Article 3   Interpretation of the Convention
In the interpretation and application of the provisions of this Convention regard shall be had to its international character and to the need to promote uniformity.

## PART II
## LIABILITY OF THE CARRIER

### Article 4   Period of responsibility
1.   The responsibility of the carrier for the goods under this Convention covers the period during which the carrier is in charge of the goods at the port of loading, during the carriage and at the port of discharge.

2.   For the purpose of para. 1 of this Article, the carrier is deemed to be in charge of the goods:

(a)   from the time he has taken over the goods from:

(i)   the shipper, or a person acting on his behalf; or

(ii)   an authority or other third party to whom, pursuant to law or regulations applicable at the port of loading, the goods must be handed over for shipment;

(b)   until the time he has delivered the goods:

(i)   by handing over the goods to the consignee; or

(ii)   in cases where the consignee does not receive the goods from the carrier, by placing them at the disposal of the consignee in accordance with the contract or with the law or with the usage of the particular trade, applicable at the port of discharge; or

(iii)   by handing over the goods to an authority or other third party to whom, pursuant to law or regulations applicable at the port of discharge, the goods must be handed over.

3.   In paras 1 and 2 of this Article, reference to the carrier or to the consignee means, in addition to the carrier or the consignee, the servants or agents, respectively of the carrier or the consignee.

### Article 5   Basis of liability
1.   The carrier is liable for loss resulting from loss of or damage to the goods, as well as from delay in delivery, if the occurrence which caused the loss, damage or delay took place while the goods were in his charge as defined in art. 4, unless the carrier proves that he, his servants or agents took all measures that could reasonably be required to avoid the occurrence and its consequences.

2.   Delay in delivery occurs when the goods have not been delivered at the port of discharge provided for in the contract of carriage by sea within the time expressly agreed upon or, in the absence of such agreement, within the time which it would be reasonable to require of a diligent carrier, having regard to the circumstances of the case.

3.   The person entitled to make a claim for the loss of goods may treat the goods as lost if they have not been delivered as required by art. 4 within 60 consecutive days following the expiry of the time for delivery according to para. 2 of this Article.

4.   (a)   The carrier is liable:

(i)   for loss of or damage to the goods or delay in delivery caused by fire, if the claimant proves that the fire arose from fault or neglect on the part of the carrier, his servants or agents;

(ii)   for such loss, damage or delay in delivery which is proved by the claimant to
have resulted from the fault or neglect of the carrier, his servants or agents, in taking all
measures that could reasonably be required to put out the fire and avoid or mitigate its
consequences.

(b)   In case of fire on board the ship affecting the goods, if the claimant or the
carrier so desires, a survey in accordance with shipping practices must be held into the
cause and circumstances of the fire, and a copy of the surveyor's report shall be made
available on demand to the carrier and the claimant.

5.   With respect to live animals, the carrier is not liable for loss, damage or delay in
delivery resulting from any special risk inherent in that kind of carriage. If the carrier
proves that he has complied with any special instructions given to him by the shipper
respecting the animals and that, in the circumstances of the case, the loss, damage or delay
in delivery could be attributed to such risks, it is presumed that the loss, damage or delay in
delivery was so caused, unless there is proof that all or a part of the loss, damage or delay in
delivery resulted from fault or neglect on the part of the carrier, his servants or agents.

6.   The carrier is not liable, except in general average, where loss, damage or delay
in delivery resulted from measures to save life or from reasonable measures to save
property at sea.

7.   Where fault or neglect on the part of the carrier, his servants or agents combines
with another cause to produce loss, damage or delay in delivery the carrier is liable only
to the extent that the loss, damage or delay in delivery is attributable to such fault or
neglect, provided that the carrier proves the amount of the loss, damage or delay in
delivery not attributable thereto.

## Article 6   Limits of liability

1.   (a)   The liability of the carrier for loss resulting from loss of or damage to goods
according to the provisions of art. 5 is limited to an amount equivalent to 835 units of
account per package or other shipping unit or 2.5 units of account per kilogramme of
gross weight of the goods lost or damaged, whichever is the higher.

(b)   The liability of the carrier for delay in delivery according to the provisions of
art. 5 is limited to an amount equivalent to two and a half times the freight payable for
the goods delayed, but not exceeding the total freight payable under the contract of
carriage of goods by sea.

(c)   In no case shall the aggregate liability of the carrier, under both sub-paras (a)
and (b) of this paragraph, exceed the limitation which would be established under
sub-para (a) of this paragraph for total loss of the goods with respect to which such
liability was incurred.

2.   For the purpose of calculating which amount is the higher in accordance with
para. 1(a) of this Article the following rules apply:

(a)   Where a container, pallet or similar article of transport is used to
consolidate goods, the package or other shipping units enumerated in the bill of
lading, if issued, or otherwise in any other document evidencing the contract of
carriage by sea, as packed in such article of transport are deemed packages or
shipping units. Except as aforesaid the goods in such article of transport are deemed
one shipping unit.

(b)   In cases where the article of transport itself has been lost or damaged, that
article of transport, if not owned or otherwise supplied by the carrier, is considered one
separate shipping unit.

3.   Unit of account means the unit of account mentioned in art. 26.

4.   By agreement between the carrier and the shipper, limits of liability exceeding
those provided for in para. 1 may be fixed.

### Article 7　Application to non-contractual claims

1.　The defences and limits of liability provided for in this Convention apply in any action against the carrier in respect of loss or damage to the goods covered by the contract of carriage by sea, as well as of delay in delivery whether the action is founded in contract, in tort or otherwise.

2.　If such an action is brought against a servant or agent of the carrier, such servant or agent, if he proves that he acted within the scope of his employment, is entitled to avail himself of the defences and limits of liability which the carrier is entitled to invoke under this Convention.

3.　Except as provided in art. 8, the aggregate of the amounts recoverable from the carrier and from any persons referred to in para. 2 of this Article shall not exceed the limits of liability provided for in this Convention.

### Article 8　Loss of right to limit responsibility

1.　The carrier is not entitled to the benefit of the limitation of liability provided for in art. 6 if it is proved that the loss, damage or delay in delivery resulted from an act or omission of the carrier done with the intent to cause such loss, damage or delay, or recklessly and with knowledge that such loss, damage or delay would probably result.

2.　Notwithstanding the provisions of para. 2 of art. 7, a servant or agent of the carrier is not entitled to the benefit of the limitation of liability provided for in art. 6 if it is proved that the loss, damage or delay in delivery resulted from an act or omission of such servant or agent, done with the intent to cause such loss, damage or delay, or recklessly and with knowledge that such loss, damage or delay would probably result.

### Article 9　Deck cargo

1.　The carrier is entitled to carry the goods on deck only if such carriage is in accordance with an agreement with the shipper or with the usage of the particular trade or is required by statutory rules or regulations.

2.　If the carrier and the shipper have agreed that the goods shall or may be carried on deck, the carrier must insert in the bill of lading or other document evidencing the contract of carriage by sea a statement to that effect. In the absence of such a statement the carrier has the burden of proving that an agreement for carriage on deck has been entered into; however, the carrier is not entitled to invoke such an agreement against a third party, including a consignee, who has acquired the bill of lading in good faith.

3.　Where the goods have been carried on deck contrary to the provisions of para. 1 of this Article or where the carrier may not under para. 2 of this Article invoke an agreement for carriage on deck, the carrier, notwithstanding the provisions of para. 1 of art. 5, is liable for loss of or damage to the goods, as well as for delay in delivery, resulting solely from the carriage on deck, and the extent of his liability is to be determined in accordance with the provisions of art. 6 or art. 8 of this Convention as the case may be.

4.　Carriage of goods on deck contrary to express agreement for carriage under deck is deemed to be an act or omission of the carrier within the meaning of art. 8.

### Article 10　Liability of the carrier and actual carrier

1.　Where the performance of the carriage or part thereof has been entrusted to an actual carrier, whether or not in pursuance of a liberty under the contract of carriage by sea to do so, the carrier nevertheless remains responsible for the entire carriage according to the provisions of this Convention. The carrier is responsible, in relation to the carriage performed by the actual carrier, for the acts and omissions of the actual carrier and of his servants and agents acting within the scope of their employment.

2.　All the provisions of this Convention governing the responsibility of the carrier also apply to the responsibility of the actual carrier for the carriage performed by him.

The provisions of paras. 2 and 3 of art. 7 and of para. 2 of art. 8 apply if an action is brought against a servant or agent of the actual carrier.

3.    Any special agreement under which the carrier assumes obligations not imposed by this Convention or waives rights conferred by this Convention affects the actual carrier only if agreed to by him expressly and in writing. Whether or not the actual carrier has so agreed, the carrier nevertheless remains bound by the obligations or waivers resulting from such special agreement.

4.    Where and to the extent that both the carrier and the actual carrier are liable, their liability is joint and several.

5.    The aggregate of the amounts recoverable from the carrier, the actual carrier and their servants and agents shall not exceed the limits of liability provided for in this Convention.

6.    Nothing in this Article shall prejudice any right of recourse as between the carrier and the actual carrier.

### Article 11    Through carriage

1.    Notwithstanding the provisions of para. 1 of art. 10, where a contract of carriage by sea provides explicitly that a specified part of the carriage covered by the said contract is to be performed by a named person other than the carrier, the contract may also provide that the carrier is not liable for loss, damage or delay in delivery caused by an occurrence which takes place while the goods are in the charge of the actual carrier during such part of the carriage. Nevertheless, any stipulation limiting or excluding such liability is without effect if no judicial proceedings can be instituted against the actual carrier in a court competent under paras. 1 or 2 of art. 21. The burden of proving that any loss, damage or delay in delivery has been caused by such an occurrence rests upon the carrier.

2.    The actual carrier is responsible in accordance with the provisions of para. 2 of art. 10 for loss, damage or delay in delivery caused by an occurrence which takes place while the goods are in his charge.

## PART III
## LIABILITY OF THE SHIPPER

### Article 12    General rule

The shipper is not liable for loss sustained by the carrier or the actual carrier, or for damage sustained by the ship, unless such loss or damage was caused by the fault or neglect of the shipper, his servants or agents. Nor is any servant or agent of the shipper liable for such loss or damage unless the loss or damage was caused by fault or neglect on his part.

### Article 13    Special rules on dangerous goods

1.    The shipper must mark or label in a suitable manner dangerous goods as dangerous.

2.    Where the shipper hands over dangerous goods to the carrier or an actual carrier, as the case may be, the shipper must inform him of the dangerous character of the goods and, if necessary, of the precautions to be taken. If the shipper fails to do so and such carrier or actual carrier does not otherwise have knowledge of their dangerous character:

　　(a)    the shipper is liable to the carrier and any actual carrier for the loss resulting from the shipment of such goods, and

　　(b)    the goods may at any time be unloaded, destroyed or rendered innocuous, as the circumstances may require, without payment of compensation.

3. The provisions of para. 2 of this Article may not be invoked by any person if during the carriage he has taken the goods in his charge with knowledge of their dangerous character.

4. If, in cases where the provisions of para. 2, sub-para. (b), of this Article do not apply or may not be invoked, dangerous goods become an actual danger to life or property, they may be unloaded, destroyed or rendered innocuous, as the circumstances may require, without payment of compensation except where there is an obligation to contribute in general average or where the carrier is liable in accordance with the provisions of art. 5.

## PART IV
## TRANSPORT DOCUMENTS

### Article 14   Issue of bill of lading

1. When the carrier or the actual carrier takes the goods in his charge the carrier must, on demand of the shipper, issue to the shipper a bill of lading.

2. The bill of lading may be signed by a person having authority from the carrier. A bill of lading signed by the master of the ship carrying the goods is deemed to have been signed on behalf of the carrier.

3. The signature on the bill of lading may be in handwriting, printed in facsimile, perforated, stamped, in symbols, or made by any other mechanical or electronic means, if not inconsistent with the law of the country where the bill of lading is issued.

### Article 15   Contents of bill of lading

1. The bill of lading must include, inter alia, the following particulars:

(a)   the general nature of the goods, the leading marks necessary for identification of the goods, an express statement, if applicable, as to the dangerous character of the goods, the number of packages or pieces, and the weight of the goods or their quantity otherwise expressed, all such particulars as furnished by the shipper;

(b)   the apparent condition of the goods;

(c)   the name and principal place of business of the carrier;

(d)   the name of the shipper;

(e)   the consignee if named by the shipper;

(f)   the port of loading under the contract of carriage by sea and the date on which the goods were taken over by the carrier at the port of loading;

(g)   the port of discharge under the contract of carriage by sea;

(h)   the number of originals of the bill of lading, if more than one;

(i)   the place of issuance of the bill of lading;

(j)   the signature of the carrier or a person acting on his behalf;

(k)   the freight to the extent payable by the consignee or other indication that freight is payable by him;

(l)   the statement referred to in para. 3 of art. 23;

(m)   the statement, if applicable, that the goods shall or may be carried on deck;

(n)   the date or the period of delivery of the goods at the port of discharge if expressly agreed upon between the parties; and

(o)   any increased limit or limits of liability where agreed in accordance with para. 4 of art. 6.

2. After the goods have been loaded on board, if the shipper so demands, the carrier must issue to the shipper a 'shipped' bill of lading which, in addition to the particulars required under para. 1 of this Article, must state that the goods are on board a named ship or ships, and the date or dates of loading. If the carrier has previously issued to the shipper a bill of lading or other document of title with respect to any of such goods, on

request of the carrier, the shipper must surrender such document in exchange for a 'shipped' bill of lading. The carrier may amend any previously issued document in order to meet the shipper's demand for a 'shipped' bill of lading if, as amended, such document includes all the information required to be contained in a 'shipped' bill of lading.

3.    The absence in the bill of lading of one or more particulars referred to in this Article does not affect the legal character of the document as a bill of lading provided that it nevertheless meets the requirements set out in para. 7 of art. 1.

**Article 16    Bills of lading: reservations and evidentiary effect**

1.    If the bill of lading contains particulars concerning the general nature, leading marks, number of packages or pieces, weight or quantity of the goods which the carrier or other person issuing the bill of lading on his behalf knows or has reasonable grounds to suspect do not accurately represent the goods actually taken over or, where a 'shipped' bill of lading is issued, loaded, or if he had no reasonable means of checking such particulars, the carrier or such other person must insert in the bill of lading a reservation specifying these inaccuracies, grounds of suspicion or the absence of reasonable means of checking.

2.    If the carrier or other person issuing the bill of lading on his behalf fails to note on the bill of lading the apparent condition of the goods, he is deemed to have noted on the bill of lading that the goods were in apparent good condition.

3.    Except for particulars in respect of which and to the extent to which a reservation permitted under para. 1 of this Article has been entered:

(a)    the bill of lading is prima facie evidence of the taking over or, where a 'shipped' bill of lading is issued, loading, by the carrier of the goods as described in the bill of lading; and

(b)    proof to the contrary by the carrier is not admissible if the bill of lading has been transferred to a third party, including a consignee, who in good faith has acted in reliance on the description of the goods therein.

4.    A bill of lading which does not, as provided in para. 1, sub-para (k) of art. 15, set forth the freight or otherwise indicate that freight is payable by the consignee or does not set forth demurrage incurred at the port of loading payable by the consignee, is prima facie evidence that no freight or such demurrage is payable by him. However, proof to the contrary by the carrier is not admissible when the bill of lading has been transferred to a third party, including a consignee, who in good faith has acted in reliance on the absence in the bill of lading of any such indication.

**Article 17    Guarantees by the shipper**

1.    The shipper is deemed to have guaranteed to the carrier the accuracy of particulars relating to the general nature of the goods, their marks, number, weight and quantity as furnished by him for insertion in the bill of lading. The shipper must indemnify the carrier against the loss resulting from inaccuracies in such particulars. The shipper remains liable even if the bill of lading has been transferred by him. The right of the carrier to such indemnity in no way limits his liability under the contract of carriage by sea to any person other than the shipper.

2.    Any letter of guarantee or agreement by which the shipper undertakes to indemnify the carrier against loss resulting from the issuance of the bill of lading by the carrier, or by a person acting on his behalf, without entering a reservation relating to particulars furnished by the shipper for insertion in the bill of lading, or to the apparent condition of the goods, is void and of no effect as against any third party, including a consignee, to whom the bill of lading has been transferred.

3. Such letter of guarantee or agreement is valid as against the shipper unless the carrier or the person acting on his behalf, by omitting the reservation referred to in para. 2 of this Article, intends to defraud a third party, including a consignee, who acts in reliance on the description of the goods in the bill of lading. In the latter case, if the reservation omitted relates to particulars furnished by the shipper for insertion in the bill of lading, the carrier has no right of indemnity from the shipper pursuant to para. 1 of this Article.

4. In the case of intended fraud referred to in para. 3 of this Article the carrier is liable, without the benefit of the limitation of liability provided for in this Convention, for the loss incurred by a third party, including a consignee, because he has acted in reliance on the description of the goods in the bill of lading.

### Article 18 Documents other than bills of lading

Where a carrier issues a document other than a bill of lading to evidence the receipt of the goods to be carried, such a document is prima facie evidence of the conclusion of the contract of carriage by sea and the taking over by the carrier of the goods as therein described.

### PART V
### CLAIMS AND ACTIONS

### Article 19 Notice of loss, damage or delay

1. Unless notice of loss or damage, specifying the general nature of such loss or damage, is given in writing by the consignee to the carrier not later than the working day after the day when the goods were handed over to the consignee, such handing over is prima facie evidence of the delivery by the carrier of the goods as described in the document of transport or, if no such document has been issued, in good condition.

2. Where the loss or damage is not apparent, the provisions of para. 1 of this Article apply correspondingly if notice in writing is not given within 15 consecutive days after the day when the goods were handed over to the consignee.

3. If the state of the goods at the time they were handed over to the consignee has been the subject of a joint survey or inspection by the parties, notice in writing need not be given of loss or damage ascertained during such survey or inspection.

4. In the case of any actual or apprehended loss or damage the carrier and the consignee must give all reasonable facilities to each other for inspecting and tallying the goods.

5. No compensation shall be payable for loss resulting from delay in delivery unless a notice has been given in writing to the carrier within 60 consecutive days after the day when the goods were handed over to the consignee.

6. If the goods have been delivered by an actual carrier, any notice given under this Article to him shall have the same effect as if it had been given to the carrier, and any notice given to the carrier shall have effect as if given to such actual carrier.

7. Unless notice of loss or damage, specifying the general nature of the loss or damage, is given in writing by the carrier or actual carrier to the shipper not later than 90 consecutive days after the occurrence of such loss or damage or after the delivery of the goods in accordance with para. 2 of art. 4, whichever is later, the failure to give such notice is prima facie evidence that the carrier or the actual carrier has sustained no loss or damage due to the fault or neglect of the shipper, his servants or agents.

8. For the purpose of this Article, notice given to a person acting on the carrier's or the actual carrier's behalf, including the master or the officer in charge of the ship, or to a person acting on the shipper's behalf is deemed to have been given to the carrier, to the actual carrier or to the shipper, respectively.

**Article 20   Limitation of actions**

1.   Any action relating to carriage of goods under this Convention is time-barred if judicial or arbitral proceedings have not been instituted within a period of two years.

2.   The limitation period commences on the day on which the carrier has delivered the goods or part thereof or, in cases where no goods have been delivered, on the last day on which the goods should have been delivered.

3.   The day on which the limitation period commences is not included in the period.

4.   The person against whom a claim is made may at any time during the running of the limitation period extend that period by a declaration in writing to the claimant. This period may be further extended by another declaration or declarations.

5.   An action for indemnity by a person held liable may be instituted even after the expiration of the limitation period provided for in the preceding paragraphs if instituted within the time allowed by the law of the State where proceedings are instituted. However, the time allowed shall not be less than 90 days commencing from the day when the person instituting such action for indemnity has settled the claim or has been served with process in the action against himself.

**Article 21   Jurisdiction**

1.   In judicial proceedings relating to carriage of goods under this Convention the plaintiff, at his option, may institute an action in a court which, according to the law of the State where the court is situated, is competent and within the jurisdiction of which is situated one of the following places:

(a)   the principal place of business or, in the absence thereof, the habitual residence of the defendant; or

(b)   the place where the contract was made provided that the defendant has there a place of business, branch or agency through which the contract was made; or

(c)   the port of loading or the port of discharge; or

(d)   any additional place designated for that purpose in the contract of carriage by sea.

2.   (a)   Notwithstanding the preceding provisions of this Article, an action may be instituted in the courts of any port or place in a Contracting State at which the carrying vessel or any other vessel of the same ownership may have been arrested in accordance with applicable rules of the law of that State and of international law. However, in such a case, at the petition of the defendant, the claimant must remove the action, at his choice, to one of the jurisdictions referred to in para. 1 of this Article for the determination of the claim, but before such removal the defendant must furnish security sufficient to ensure payment of any judgment that may subsequently be awarded to the claimant in the action.

(b)   All questions relating to the sufficiency or otherwise of the security shall be determined by the court of the port or place of the arrest.

3.   No judicial proceedings relating to carriage of goods under this Convention may be instituted in a place not specified in paras. 1 or 2 of this Article. The provision of this paragraph do not constitute an obstacle to the jurisdiction of the Contracting States for provisional or protective measures.

4.   (a)   Where an action has been instituted in a court competent under paras. 1 or 2 of this Article or where judgment has been delivered by such a court, no new action may be started between the same parties on the same grounds unless the judgment of the court before which the first action was instituted is not enforceable in the country in which the new proceedings are instituted:

(b)   for the purpose of this Article the institution of measures with a view to obtaining enforcement of a judgment is not to be considered as the starting of a new action;

(c) for the purpose of this Article, the removal of an action to a different court within the same country, or to a court in another country, in accordance with para. 2(a) or this Article, is not to be considered as the starting of a new action.

5. Notwithstanding the provisions of the preceding paragraphs, an agreement made by the parties, after a claim under the contact of carriage by sea has arisen, which designates the place where the claimant may institute an action, is effective.

### Article 22   Arbitration

1. Subject to the provisions of this Article, parties may provide by agreement evidenced in writing that any dispute that may arise relating to carriage of goods under this Convention shall be referred to arbitration.

2. Where a charterparty contains a provision that disputes arising thereunder shall be referred to arbitration and a bill of lading issued pursuant to the charterparty does not contain a special annotation providing that such provision shall be binding upon the holder of the bill of lading, the carrier may not invoke such provision as against a holder having acquired the bill of lading in good faith.

3. The arbitration proceedings shall at the option of the claimant, be instituted at one of the following places:

(a)   a place in a State within whose territory is situated:

(i)   the principal place of business of the defendant or, in the absence thereof, the habitual residence of the defendant; or

(ii)   the place where the contract was made, provided that the defendant has there a place of business, branch or agency through which the contract was made; or

(iii)   the port of loading or the port of discharge; or

(b)   any place designated for that purpose in the arbitration clause or agreement.

4. The arbitrator or arbitration tribunal shall apply the rules of this Convention.

5. The provisions of paras. 3 and 4 of this Article are deemed to be part of every arbitration clause or agreement, and any term of such clause or agreement which is inconsistent therewith is null and void.

6. Nothing in this Article affects the validity of an agreement relating to arbitration made by the parties after the claim under the contract of carriage by sea has arisen.

PART VI
SUPPLEMENTARY PROVISIONS

### Article 23   Contractual stipulations

1. Any stipulation in a contract of carriage by sea, in a bill of lading, or in any other document evidencing the contract of carriage by sea is null and void to the extent that it derogates, directly or indirectly, from the provisions of this Convention. The nullity of such a stipulation does not affect the validity of the other provisions of the contract or document of which it forms a part. A clause assigning benefit of insurance of the goods in favour of the carrier, or any similar clause, is null and void.

2. Notwithstanding the provisions of para. 1 of this Article, a carrier may increase his responsibilities and obligation under this Convention.

3. Where a bill of lading or any other document evidencing the contract of carriage by sea is issued, it must contain a statement that the carriage is subject to the provisions of this Convention which nullify any stipulation derogating therefrom to the detriment of the shipper or the consignee.

4. Where the claimant in respect of the goods has incurred loss as a result of a stipulation which is null and void by virtue of the present Article, or as a result of the omission of the statement referred to in para. 3 of this Article, the carrier must pay compensation to the extent required in order to give the claimant compensation in

accordance with the provisions of this Convention for any loss of or damage to the goods as well as for delay in delivery. The carrier must, in addition, pay compensation for costs incurred by the claimant for the purpose of exercising his right, provided that costs incurred in the action where the foregoing provision is invoked are to be determined in accordance with the law of the State where proceedings are instituted.

### Article 24   General average

1.   Nothing in this Convention shall prevent the application of provisions in the contract of carriage by sea or national law regarding the adjustment of general average.

2.   With the exception of art. 20, the provisions of this Convention relating to the liability of the carrier for loss of or damage to the goods also determine whether the consignee may refuse contribution in general average and the liability of the carrier to indemnify the consignee in respect of any such contribution made or any salvage paid.

### Article 25   Other conventions

1.   This Convention does not modify the rights or duties of the carrier, the actual carrier and their servants and agents, provided for in international conventions or national law relating to the limitation of liability of owners of seagoing ships.

2.   The provisions of arts 21 and 22 of this Convention do not prevent the application of the mandatory provisions of any other multi-lateral convention already in force at the date of this Convention relating to matters dealt within the said Articles, provided that the dispute arises exclusively between parties having their principal place of business in States members of such other convention. However, this paragraph does not affect the application of para. 4 of art. 22 of this Convention.

3.   No liability shall arise under the provisions of this Convention for damage caused by a nuclear incident if the operator of a nuclear installation is liable for such damage:

(a)   under either the Paris Convention of 29 July 1960, on Third Party Liability in the Field of Nuclear Energy as amended by the Additional Protocol of 28 January 1964, or the Vienna Convention of 21 May 1963, on Civil Liability for Nuclear Damage, or

(b)   by virtue of national law governing the liability for such damage, provided that such law is in all respects as favourable to persons who may suffer damage as either the Paris or Vienna Conventions.

4.   No liability shall arise under the provisions of this Convention for any loss of or damage to or delay in delivery of luggage for which the carrier is responsible under any international convention or national law relating to the carriage of passengers and their luggage by sea.

5.   Nothing contained in this Convention prevents a Contracting State from applying any other international convention which is already in force at the date of this Convention and which applies mandatorily to contracts of carriage of goods primarily by a mode of transport other than transport by sea. This provision also applies to any subsequent revision or amendment of such international convention.

### Article 26   Unit of account

1.   The unit of account referred to in art. 6 of this Convention is the Special Drawing Right as defined by the International Monetary Fund. The amounts mentioned in art. 6 are to be converted into the national currency of a State according to the value of such currency at the date of judgment or the date agreed upon by the parties. The value of a national currency, in terms of the Special Drawing Right, of a Contracting State which is a member of the International Monetary Fund is to be calculated in accordance with the method of valuation applied by the International Monetary Fund in effect at the date in question for its operations and transactions. The value of a national currency in terms

of the Special Drawing Right of a Contracting State which is not a member of the International Monetary Fund is to be calculated in a manner determined by that State.

2. Nevertheless, those States which are not members of the International Monetary Fund and whose law does not permit the application of the provisions of para. 1 of this Article may, at the time of signature, or at the time of ratification, acceptance, approval or accession or at any time thereafter, declare that the limits of liability provided for in this Convention to be applied in their territories shall be fixed as:

12,500 monetary units per package or other shipping unit or 37.5 monetary units per kilogramme of gross weight of the goods.

3. The monetary unit referred to in para. 2 of this Article corresponds to sixty-five and a half milligrammes of gold of millesimal fineness nine hundred. The conversion of the amounts referred to in para. 2 into the national currency is to be made according to the law of the State concerned.

4. The calculation mentioned in the last sentence of para. 1 and the conversion mentioned in para. 3 of this Article is to be made in such a manner as to express in the national currency of the Contracting State as far as possible the same real value for the amounts in art. 6 as is expressed there in units of account. Contracting States must communicate to the depositary the manner of calculation pursuant to para. 1 of this Article, or the result of the conversion mentioned in para. 3 of this Article, as the case may be, at the time of signature or when depositing their instruments of ratification, acceptance, approval or accession, or when availing themselves of the option provided for in para. 2 of this Article and whenever there is a change in the manner of such calculation or in the result of such conversion.

...

**Article 29   Reservations**
No reservations may be made to this Convention.

**Article 30   Entry into force**
1. This Convention enters into force on the first day of the month following the expiration of one year from the date of deposit of the 20th instrument of ratification, acceptance, approval or accession.

2. For each State which becomes a Contracting State to this Convention after the date of the deposit of the 20th instrument of ratification, acceptance, approval or accession, this Convention enters into force on the first day of the month following the expiration of one year after the deposit of the appropriate instrument on behalf of that State.

3. Each Contracting State shall apply the provisions of this Convention to contracts of carriage by sea concluded on or after the date of the entry into force of this Convention in respect of that State.

**Article 31   Denunciation of other conventions**
1. Upon becoming a Contracting State to this Convention, any State party to the International Convention for the Unification of Certain Rules relating to Bills of Lading signed at Brussels on 25 August 1924 (1924 Convention) must notify the Government of Belgium as the depositary of the 1924 Convention of its denunciation of the said Convention with a declaration that the denunciation is to take effect as from the date when this Convention enters into force in respect of that State.

2. Upon the entry into force of this Convention under para. 1 of art. 30, the depositary of this Convention must notify the Government of Belgium as the depositary of the 1924 Convention of the date of such entry into force, and of the names of the Contracting States in respect of which the Convention has entered into force.

isions of paras 1 and 2 of this Article apply correspondingly in respect of
o the Protocol signed on 23 February 1968, to amend the International
or the Unification of Certain Rules relating to Bills of Lading signed at
5 August 1924.

4.       ithstanding art. 2 of this Convention, for the purposes of para. 1 of this
Article, a Contracting State may, if it deems it desirable, defer the denunciation of the
1924 Convention and of the 1924 Convention as modified by the 1968 Protocol for a
maximum period of five years from the entry into force of this Convention. It will then
notify the Government of Belgium of its intention. During this transitory period, it must
apply to the Contracting States this Convention to the exclusion of any other one.
. . .

*Done at Hamburg, this thirty-first day of March one thousand nine hundred and seventy-eight,
in a single original, of which the Arabic, Chinese, English, French, Russian and Spanish texts
are equally authentic.*

## COMMON UNDERSTANDING ADOPTED BY THE UNITED NATIONS
## CONFERENCE ON THE CARRIAGE OF GOODS BY SEA

It is the common understanding that the liability of the carrier under this Convention is
based on the principle of presumed fault or neglect. This means that as a rule, the
burden of proof rests on the carrier but, with respect to certain cases, the provisions of
the Convention modify this rule.

*Notes*
*1.* The Hamburg Rules tilt the balance in favour of the cargo-owner in several
ways. Their application is not restricted to contracts covered by bills of lading,
so that they cannot be avoided by issuing non-negotiable shipping documents
instead of bills of lading. They apply to both outward *and inward* shipments,
and jurisdiction is conferred on the courts in the State where the port of loading
or port of discharge is situated as well as the courts of the State where the
defendant has his principal place of business.

The carrier's responsibility extends throughout the period during which he
is 'in charge of the goods', and liability for loss, damage or delay to the cargo is
based on 'presumed fault', i.e., the carrier is required to prove that 'he, his
servants or agents took all measures that could reasonably be required' to avoid
the loss. There is no provision corresponding to the list of exceptions in Art. IV
of the Hague-Visby Rules. In particular, the carrier will be liable under the
Hamburg Rules for negligent navigation or management of the ship.

The principles of both time and financial limits on liability have been
continued, but the limits are extended in favour of the cargo-owner.

*2.* For an interesting account of the Hamburg Rules, see Waldron, AJ: 'The
Hamburg Rules — A Boondoggle for Lawyers' *Journal of Business Law*, 1991,
pp. 305–319. Echoes of the Rules are to be found in French law (see Rodière,
*op cit*, p. 256) and their influence can be seen in the new Nordic Maritime
Code: Tiberg, H, 'The Nordic Maritime Code' *Lloyd's Maritime and Commer-
cial Law Quarterly*, 1995, pp. 527–533. See also Hetherington, S, 'Australian
Hybrid Cargo Liability Regime', Lloyd's Maritime and Commercial Law
Quarterly, 1999, pp. 12–15.

*Question*

The Alban Line issues bills of lading which provide that the contract is to be governed by English law and state that the English courts shall have exclusive jurisdiction over any disputes arising out of the contract. Nina shipped a cargo of machinery to Libreville, Ruritania on the *Alban Centurion*, owned by Alban Line. Ruritania has adopted the Hamburg Rules. Fifteen months after the machinery is delivered at Libreville, Inez, to whom Nina indorsed the bill of lading, threatens to institute proceedings in Libreville for damage to the machinery on the voyage.

What advice would you give Alban Line?

# 8 VOYAGE CHARTERPARTIES

We now turn to consider in detail the relationship between shipowner and charterer of the vessel. Under a voyage charterparty, the charterer agrees to pay freight in return for the right to load the vessel to its capacity with cargo of the agreed kind and to have that cargo carried from A to B. The charterer may be the cargo-owner/shipper, or some or all of the space on the vessel may be used for the carriage of cargo supplied by others under bill of lading contracts — see the facts of *Asfar & Co.* v *Blundell*, above, for example. (Of course, it is common for bills of lading to be issued to charterers as well in repect of their own goods, but in this case the charterparty, not the bill of lading, governs the contractual relationship, as we have seen, in Chapter 6.)

The aspect of voyage charterparties which undoubtedly gives rise to most disputes in practice is the question of laytime and demurrage, i.e., the charterparty provisions for dealing with the risks of delay beyond the control of the parties at the loading and discharging stages. (These provisions are considered in Chapter 9.) *The Johanna Oldendorff* is one of the leading cases on laytime, and the speech of Lord Diplock contains a valuable analysis of voyage charterparties generally.

### E.L. Oldendorff & Co. GmbH v Tradax Export SA
### (The Johanna Oldendorff)
#### [1974] AC 479 (HL)

LORD DIPLOCK: My Lords, this is a case about whether the charterer or the shipowner must bear the expense of unavoidable delay in the discharge of cargo at the Port of Liverpool under a voyage charterparty for the carriage of grain from North America in the familiar Baltimore form. Voyage charters have been the subject of litigation in the English courts since the 16th century. Even in those days, merchants and shipowners recognised that ship's time lost was money lost, and 16th century charterparties contained provision for payment of demurrage by the charterer if loading or discharging were prolonged beyond the agreed 'lay time', specified in the charterparty as the period during which it was to be available to the charterer for that purpose.

Despite the transformation that has taken place in shipping, in port facilities and in communications during the last four hundred years, the business nature of the adventure to which the contract between charterer and shipowner relates remains essentially the same. It is an adventure which of its nature has always been exposed to the risk of being prevented, impeded or delayed by a variety of causes beyond the control of either party. If it is known in advance how loss due to delay from any particular cause is to be borne as between charterer and shipowner, account can be taken of the risk in fixing the freight payable. What matters from a commercial point of view is not so much that the risk should be borne by one party rather than by the other, but that it should be known, at the time the charterparty is made, by which of them it will be borne.

A charterparty is a type of contract which has been the subject of minimal intervention by Parliament; nor has there been any significant alteration, at any rate since the early 19th century, in those words in a voyage charter which state the essential obligations of the parties and have been treated by the courts as determinative of the apportionment between charterer and shipowner of the risk of unavoidable delay in loading or discharging cargo. For although any standard form of modern charterparty is a document of great elaboration, it still does not spell out in express words the division of responsibility between charterer and shipowner for securing that all the various things are done that must be done to carry out the adventure. It tacitly assumes that the parties have intended this to be regulated by mercantile usage to which legal sanction has been given by decisions of the courts. It is only by reference to these decisions that the division of responsibility can be ascertained. The small print in a modern charterparty does little more than modify or elaborate what would have been the respective rights of charterer and shipowner under mercantile usage if nothing had been said about them.

*Note*

In *The Johanna Oldendorff* Lord Diplock also pointed out that the adventure contemplated by a voyage charterparty falls into four distinct stages — the loading voyage, the loading operation, the carrying voyage, and the discharging operation: after looking at some preliminary questions relating to the vessel, we will consider each of Lord Diplock's stages in turn.

## SECTION 1: THE VESSEL

When the parties enter into a charterparty agreement — usually referred to as a 'fixture' — the shipowner will give detailed particulars of the vessel. Since most of these particulars are perhaps of greater concern to a time charterer than to a charterer under a voyage charterparty they will be considered in Chapter 10, below, on Time Charters. Two matters are however of prime importance to the charterer under a voyage charterparty and we consider them here: (a) what is the vessel's cargo capacity, and (b) when will she be ready for the voyage?

*A: Cargo capacity*

Where the charterparty states that the vessel has a deadweight capacity of, e.g., 10,000 tonnes, does this mean that she is warranted to be able to lift 10,000 tonnes of the particular cargo to be carried under that charterparty?

### Robert Mackill v Wright Brothers & Co.
### (1888) 14 App Cas 106 (HL)

The *Lauderdale* was chartered at a lump sum freight of £2,200 to carry a cargo of machinery and coals from Glasgow to India. The charterparty provided: 'Owners guarantee that the vessel shall carry not less than 2,000 tons dead weight' and stated that freight was to be reduced pro rata 'should the vessel not carry the guaranteed dead weight'. The cargo tendered included more bulky pieces of machinery — locomotives (in pieces), tenders and engine turntables — than the shipowners had been told about and the vessel could only take 1,691 tons of the charterers' cargo. The charterers alleged that they expected the coal to be put among the machinery, but it was found that this would have been improper stowage without the consent of the party to whom the charterers had sold some of the coal, and this consent had not been sought. The Court of Session held that the charterers were entitled to a reduction in the freight, but the House of Lords allowed the shipowners' appeal.

LORD MACNAGHTEN: My Lords, the question turns upon the true construction of a charterparty in some respects peculiar. It is a charter for the hire of a vessel for a lump sum from Glasgow to Kurrachee. It has a note in the margin as to the description of part of the proposed cargo, and it contains this guarantee, 'Owners guarantee that the vessel shall carry not less than 2,000 tons dead weight of cargo.' In effect, the charterers say to the owners, 'We want a vessel to carry to Kurrachee a general cargo, including parcels of machinery; we give you the dimensions and number of the largest pieces; will your vessel carry 2,000 tons dead weight?' The owners say 'It will'. That is, I think, something more than a mere guarantee of carrying capacity. It is a guarantee of the vessel's carrying capacity with reference to the contemplated voyage and the description of the cargo proposed to be shipped, so far as that description was made known to the owners.

It is not disputed that the *Lauderdale* possessed a carrying capacity of more than 2,000 tons dead weight.

It is admitted that the *Lauderdale* did not, in fact, carry 2,000 tons.

It is admitted that a cargo up to but not in excess of that weight, and consisting partly of machinery and partly of coal and other goods, was tendered by the charterers.

It is not disputed that the cargo so tendered could not have been carried on the *Lauderdale*, unless the coal had been packed with the machinery.

Though not admitted by the charterers, it is, I think, clear upon the evidence, and proved even by the testimony of the charterers' witnesses, that it is not proper stowage to pack machinery and coal together. The coal is invariably crushed and injured. The machinery generally suffers too, especially if the coal be damp or the machinery of delicate construction.

Further, it seems to me that the fair result of the evidence is, that in regard to the machinery which was tendered for shipment and shipped, the cargo was not such a cargo as was contemplated by the charterparty. It contained more large pieces; it was more bulky in comparison to its weight, and it was more awkward for stowage than the terms of the charterparty would naturally have led the owners to expect.

These being the material facts of the case, the clause in the charterparty on which the question turns remains to be considered. The charterparty has this provision:— 'Should the vessel not carry the guaranteed dead weight, as above, any expense incurred from this cause to be borne by the owners, and a pro rata deduction per ton to be made from the first payment of freight.'

What is the meaning of this provision? What is the event contemplated? Is it the case of the vessel (1) not actually carrying 2,000 tons dead weight from any cause whatever; or (2) not carrying that weight from any cause not attributable to the charterers?

I think it would be unreasonable to read the provision as allowing abatement in the freight in every case of short weight. Such a construction would place the shipowners at the mercy of the charterers. They might fill the whole space at their disposal, and yet the cargo might be much under the contemplated weight, and so the shipowners would lose their full freight without any fault on their part.

I think that the provision was intended to have effect in the event of the vessel not carrying the specified weight, assuming the cargo tendered to be such a cargo as was contemplated by the charterparty, that is, an ordinary general cargo with a fair and reasonable proportion of machinery corresponding as to the largest pieces with the numbers, dimensions, and weights specified in the margin of the charterparty. In other words (to put it most favourably for the charterers), the provision was to come into effect in the event of the vessel not carying 2,000 tons dead weight from any cause not attributable to the charterers.

I think that the loss of cargo space and the short weight of the cargo carried on the *Lauderdale* were attributable to the charterers. It was their doing; I do not say it was their fault. They have committed no breach of the charterparty. They were not bound to load a full and complete cargo, and no blame, therefore, in the proper sense of the word attaches to them. But I do not think that they could take advantage of the stipulation for reduction of freight unless they tendered a cargo of the contemplated description and not in excess of the specified weight. They did tender a cargo of proper weight, but it was not of the contemplated description, and the result was that that cargo could only be stowed on board if stowed improperly. The charterers were at liberty to load the vessel with such goods as they pleased not inconsistent with the intention of the charterparty. They did not take the trouble to avail themselves of the whole space at their disposal. Why should the shipowners be fined for that?

*Note*

It may reasonably be inferred from the speeches in *Robert Mackill v Wright Brothers & Co.* that the charterers would have been held to be entitled to a reduction in freight if they had loaded the contemplated cargo. As the next case shows, however, the courts are reluctant to interpret the charterparty in that sense.

### W. Millar & Co. Ltd v Owners of SS Freden
### [1918] 1 KB 611 (CA)

SWINFEN EADY LJ: . . . The charterparty is between the plaintiffs and the defendants for the ship to carry from Durban to a port in the United Kingdom a full and complete cargo of maize in bags. Then there is a rate of freight per ton according to the port of call at which she should be directed to discharge. There are different rates for different ports, but nothing turns upon that. Then comes the clause upon which the whole contest has turned: 'The owners guarantee the ship's dead-weight capacity to be 3,200 tons and freight to be paid on this quantity.' So that in order to ascertain the amount to be paid for freight all that one has to do is to multiply the number of tons, 3,200, by the rate per ton according to the port of discharge ultimately selected. It was therefore a contract for a lump sum freight and not for freight so much per ton delivery on arrival. There is no dispute that the vessel was of a dead-weight capacity of 3,200 tons — in other words, that she would take on board a cargo to that extent without sinking the ship below her proper load-line. With regard to the particular cargo of maize she was only able to take on board 3,081 tons 560 lbs., but that was not because her dead-weight capacity was not as guaranteed, or had been in any way misrepresented. It was because the cubic capacity of the space on board was insufficient to allow of the stowage of more than 3,081 tons 560 lbs. of maize in bags. On the one hand it is said on behalf of the appellants, reading the guarantee of the capacity of the ship in connection with the cargo, that the shipowners had notice of what the cargo was to be. It was maize in bags, and it is said that the guarantee must be read as if it meant 'We guarantee that the ship on this voyage will be of a capacity to take, and will be able to carry, 3,200 tons of maize in bags.' On the other hand the respondents say 'That is not the language which is used, and that is not what we meant. What we said was, and what we adhere to is, "We guarantee that the ship shall be and is of a dead-weight capacity of 3,200 tons, and so it is".' The guarantee is a measure of the capacity of the ship, the general capacity irrespective of the particular cargo that she was to carry on this voyage.

Reading the language as it stands in the contract, the words seem to me to be free from ambiguity. 'The owners guarantee the ship's dead-weight capacity to be 3,200 tons.' They guarantee the ship's dead-weight capacity — nothing to do with what the ship will carry, nothing to do with a particular voyage, but the general capacity of the ship. Rowlatt J [1917] 2 KB 662, applying this language to the proposition which he was considering, said: 'To test it by approaching the matter from the opposite point of view: assume the parties to have decided to provide for the carriage of a cargo of maize at a freight calculated on the guaranteed dead-weight capacity of the ship in the strictest sense, would they not have written down exactly what they have written here?' That is quite a proper test to apply. In my opinion there is here a clear and definite agreement that freight was to be paid by way of a lump sum calculated upon the guaranteed dead-weight capacity of the ship, the charterers being entitled, and indeed bound, to load a full and complete cargo. I am unable to extract the construction which the appellants desire to put upon the clause from the language used according to its natural and ordinary meaning.

Reference was made to *Mackill* v *Wright* (1888) 14 App Cas 106. The dispute there was whether the cargo that was actually shipped corresponded to that which was intended, having regard to the representations made at the time the contract was entered into. But it will be observed that the language of the contract there was very different from what we have to consider here. There it was 'the owners guarantee that the vessel shall carry not less than 2,000 tons dead-weight of cargo'. Now that must have been a guarantee that the vessel should carry that amount on the voyage in question; and then there was a subsequent clause: 'and should the vessel not carry' — that is, should the vessel not carry on this particular voyage — 'the guaranteed dead-weight as above, then any expense incurred from this cause to be borne by the owners and a pro rata reduction per ton to be made from the first payment of freight'. So that there was language there pointing to a guarantee with regard to the weight of cargo to be carried on that particular voyage, and not to the general carrying capacity of the ship. Here it is the opposite. The only guarantee is with reference to the general carrying capacity of the ship — a certain dead-weight capacity.

In my opinion the appeal fails and should be dismissed.

BANKES LJ: ... The expression 'the ship's dead-weight capacity' in my opinion has reference primarily to the vessel's lifting or weight-carrying capacity in the abstract, and I find nothing either in the position in which the words are used in this charterparty or in any other of the provisions of the charterparty itself to displace that primary meaning and lead to the conclusion that the secondary meaning ought to be adopted here as contended for by the appellants. That, in my opinion, is sufficient to dispose of the appeal. But I think it is possible to go further and to say that the words themselves negative the contention, because, if I understood Mr MacKinnon's argument, it is that you ought to read into the clause in the charterparty after the words '3,200 tons' the words 'of maize'. So reading the clause it runs thus: 'The owners guarantee the ship's dead-weight capacity to be 3,200 tons of maize in bags and freight to be paid on this quantity.' Now that is just what the parties did not want. They wanted to provide that freight was not to be paid on the quantity of maize or the quantity of bags; they desired that freight should be paid on a tonnage — that is to say, the tonnage in the abstract of the vessel. I think if those words are read into the clause it negatives the argument that has been addressed to us in support of the appeal.

With reference to the case of *Mackill* v *Wright*, it seems to me that the language in that case had reference to the particular contract, which indicated on the face of it that the parties were contracting with reference to the capacity of the vessel in regard to that particular voyage, which, as indicated on the face of the charter, was one on which a certain class of cargo was to be carried. In my opinion that language has really no reference to the case we have to decide.

*Questions*

Why is it difficult to be sure of the vessel's capacity in relation to a particular cargo? Who should have the responsibility of seeing that vessel and cargo match? Is it significant that 'stowage factors' (i.e., the space occupied, in cubic metres, by one tonne (1,000 kg) of a given commodity) can only be stated as a range in many cases, e.g., cotton 1.416 to 2.833, rubber 1.481 to 2.125, barley or oats 1.558 to 2.408?

*B: The vessel's present position*

The old practice was for the shipowner to state the vessel's whereabouts at the time when the fixture was made, and for the charterer then to rely on the shipowner's express or implied undertaking to proceed with all convenient despatch to the loading port. Clearly, the parties have sharply conflicting interests here: the charterer needs to know as precisely as possible when the vessel will arrive, so that the cargo can be got ready without incurring unnecessary storage charges, but the shipowner needs as much flexibility as he can negotiate to cover himself against delay beyond his control in reaching the loading port. Because the statement of the vessel's position was so crucial to the charterer's calculations, it was treated as a contractual condition in the strict sense.

### *Behn* v *Burness*
(1863) 3 B & S 751; 121 ER 939 (Exch Ch)

The charterparty described the vessel as 'now in the port of Amsterdam'. In fact, because of severe gales, she only reached Amsterdam four days later. The charterer refused to load. The shipowner's action for damages failed.

WILLIAMS J (giving the judgment of the Court): The question on the present charterparty is confined to the statement of a definite fact — the place of the ship at the date of the contract. Now the place of the ship at the date of the contract, where the ship is in foreign parts and is chartered to come to England, may be the only datum on which the charterer can found his calculations of the time of the ship's arriving at the port of load. A statement is more or less important in proportion as the object of the contract more or less depends upon it. For most charters, considering winds, markets and dependent contracts, the time of a ship's arrival to load is an essential fact, for the interest of the charterer. In the ordinary course of charters in general it would be so: the evidence for the defendant shews it to be actually so in this case. Then, if the statement of the place of the ship is a substantive part of the contract, it seems to us that we ought to hold it to be a condition upon the principles above explained, unless we can find in the contract itself or the surrounding circumstances reason for thinking that the parties did not so intend. If it was a condition and not performed, it follows that the obligation of the charterer dependant thereon, ceased at his option and considerations either of the damage to him or of proximity to performance on the part of the shipowner are irrelevant. So was the decision of *Glaholm* v *Hays* (2 M & G 257), where the stipulation in a charter of a ship to load at Trieste was that she should sail from England on or before the 4th February, and the nonperformance of this condition released the charterer, notwithstanding the reasons alleged in order to justify the nonperformance....

*Note*

In *Bentsen* v *Taylor, Sons & Co.* [1893] 2 QB 274, the Court of Appeal applied *Behn* v *Burness* to the statement 'now sailed or about to sail from a pitch pine port to the United Kingdom'. The charterparty was made on 29 March 1892 and the parties knew that the vessel had been loading at Mobile, Alabama. In fact she did not sail from Mobile until 23 April. The statement was held to be a condition, meaning that the vessel would sail at the latest in a day or two, but on the facts the charterers were held to have waived their right to refuse to load.

### *Freeman* v *Taylor*
### (1831) 8 Bing 124

F was owner and captain of the *Edward Lombe*. He chartered her to T to proceed with all convenient speed (from London, where she then was) via Madeira and the Cape of Good Hope to Bombay, to load a cargo of cotton. The charterparty reserved the cabins and between decks for the benefit of F. After arriving at the Cape, F stayed eight days longer than he need have done and took on a cargo of cattle for Mauritius on his own account. He finally reached Bombay six or seven weeks later than he would have done if he had sailed direct. T refused to load and F sought damages. The direction to the jury was as follows:

TINDAL CJ: ... that inasmuch as the freighter might bring his action against the owner, and recover damages for any ordinary deviation, he could not, for such a deviation, put an end to the contract: but if the deviation was so long and unreasonable that, in the ordinary course of mercantile concerns, it might be said to have put an end to the whole object the freighter had in view in chartering the ship, in that case the contract might be considered at an end; and he left it to the jury to decide, whether the delay here was of such a nature as to have put an end to the ordinary objects the freighter might have had in view when he entered into the contract.

The jury found for the Defendant.

*Notes*

1. On a rule nisi to set aside the verdict in favour of the defendant, the Court approved the direction and upheld the verdict.
2. *Freeman* v *Taylor* was followed in *W.P. and R. McAndrew* v *Adams* (1834) 1 Bing (NC) 29. There, the *Swallow* was chartered on 20 October 1832 to proceed from Portsmouth, where she then was, to St Michael's in the Azores to load a cargo of oranges. The period for loading was to commence on 1 December and the charterer had the option to cancel if the vessel was not ready by 31 January. Instead of sailing directly to the Azores, the master went first to Oporto to land some troops there; he was prevented from doing so by the opposing forces, however, and returned the troops to Portsmouth, so that he did not sail for the Azores until 6 December. Although the charterers knew of the delay and the reason for it, they still loaded the cargo, but lost money because the oranges arrived in London after prices had fallen; they recovered only nominal damages for the master's 'deviation', because of their knowledge of the delay when entering into commercial commitments with regard to the oranges. Although the judges in both cases refer to 'deviation', it is clear that they do not mean this in the strict sense, but are using the word merely to describe a failure to proceed with all convenient despatch.

## SECTION 2: THE LOADING VOYAGE

The modern practice is to approach the question of the ship's readiness to load from the point of view of arrival at the load port rather than departure from present position. Commonly there is no actual statement of present position at all, merely that the vessel is 'now trading': this is then coupled with a statement of the date when the vessel is 'expected ready to load' (ERTL) under the charter. As so often happens, the issue is how such an undertaking deals with the risk of delay beyond the control of the parties.

*A: The nature and effect of the ERTL undertaking*

### Maredelanto Compania Naviera SA v Bergbau-Handel GmbH
### (The Mihalis Angelos)
[1971] 1 QB 164 (CA)

LORD DENNING MR: The material facts are these. On May 25, 1965, the shipowners let the steamer *Mihalis Angelos* to the charterers for a voyage from Haiphong, in North Vietnam, to Hamburg or other port in Europe. In the charterparty the shipowners said that she was 'expected ready to load under this charter about July 1, 1965'. The vessel was to proceed to Haiphong and then load a cargo of apatite and carry it to Europe. There was a cancelling clause in case the vessel was not ready to load by July 20, 1965.

The owners were quite wrong in saying she was expected to load on July 1 at Haiphong. They had no reasonable grounds for any such expectation. On May 25, 1965, the date of the charter, the *Mihalis Angelos* was in the Pacific on her way to Hong Kong. She was not expecting to reach Hong Kong until June 25 or 26. She would need 14 days to discharge, thus taking it to July 9 or 10. She had to have a survey of two days. That took it to July 11 or 12. She would take two days from Hong Kong to Haiphong. So she could not reasonably be expected to arrive at Haiphong until July 13 or 14. Yet the shipowners, quite wrongly, said she was expected to arrive on July 1.

In point of fact, she made up time across the Pacific, and arrived at Hong Kong on June 23: but the discharge at Hong Kong was unexpectedly prolonged. She did not complete it until July 23. Meanwhile, however, the charterers had their own troubles. They discovered there was no apatite ore available at Haiphong. They thought it was due to the war in North Vietnam. It was said that the Americans had bombed the railway line to the port. On July 17, 1965, the charterers cancelled the contract as a case of force majeure. The shipowners accepted this information as a repudiation of the contract. They did not charter the vessel to anyone else. Instead they sold her on July 29, as she lay in Hong Kong.

The arbitrators found that if the ship, after discharge at Hong Kong, had proceeded to Haiphong, the charterers would, beyond doubt, have cancelled the charter on the ground that the ship had missed her cancelling date. So the owners, in fact, lost nothing. But they claimed damages on the footing that they lost the charter on July 17, and were entitled to £4,000 damages. The arbitrators rejected the claim, but the judge allowed it.

The first point arises on the clause by which the charterers said that the vessel was 'expected ready to load … about July 1, 1965'. The charterers said that this was a condition of the contract: and that it was broken because the owners had no reasonable grounds for any such expectation. The arbitrators found that 'on May 25, 1965, the owners could not reasonably have estimated that the *Mihalis Angelos* could or would arrive at Haiphong "about July 1, 1965".' The charterers did not take this point on July 17, 1965, when they cancelled the charter. They put it on the ground of force majeure. But the owners admit that, if this point is a good one, the charterers can rely on it. The fact that a contracting party gives a bad reason for determining it does not prevent him from afterwards relying on a good one when he discovers it: see *British & Beningtons Ltd v North Western Cachar Tea Co. Ltd* [1923] AC 48, 71–72, *per* Lord Sumner.

The contest resolved itself simply into this: was the 'expected ready to load' clause a condition, such that for breach of it the charterers could throw up the charter? Or was it a mere warranty such as to give rise to damages if it was broken, but not to a right to cancel, seeing that cancellation was expressly dealt with in the cancelling clause?

Sir Frederick Pollock (*Formation of Contracts*) divided the terms of a contract into two categories: conditions and warranties. The difference between them was this: if the promisor broke a *condition* in *any* respect, however slight, it gave the other party a right to be quit of his future obligations and to sue for damages: unless he by his conduct waived the condition, in which case he was bound to perform his future obligations but could sue for the damage he suffered. If the promisor broke a *warranty* in *any* respect, however serious, the other party was not quit of his future obligations. He had to perform them. His only remedy was to sue for damages.

This division was adopted by Sir Mackenzie Chalmers when he drafted the Sale of Goods Act 1893, and by Parliament when it passed it. It was stated by Fletcher Moulton LJ in his celebrated dissenting judgment in *Wallis, Son & Wells* v *Pratt & Haynes* [1910] 2 KB 1003, 1012, which was adopted in its entirety by the House of Lords in [1911] AC 394.

It would be a mistake, however, to look upon that division as exhaustive. There are many terms of many contracts which cannot be fitted into either category. In such cases the courts, for nigh on 200 years, have not asked themselves: was the term a condition or warranty? But rather: was the breach such as to go to the root of the contract? If it was, then the other party is entitled, at his election, to treat himself as discharged from any further performance. That is made clear by the judgment of Lord Mansfield in *Boone* v *Eyre* (1777) 1 Hy Bl 273; and by the speech of Lord Blackburn in *Mersey Steel & Iron Co.* v *Naylor, Benzon & Co.* (1884) 9 App Cas 434, 443–444; and the notes to *Cutter* v *Powell* (1795) 6 Term Rep 320 (2 *Smith's Leading Cases*, 13th ed. (1929), pp. 16–18). The case of *Hongkong Fir Shipping Co. Ltd* v *Kawasaki Kisen Kaisha Ltd* [1962] 2 QB 26 is a useful reminder of this large category.

Although this large category exists, there is still remaining a considerable body of law by which certain stipulations have been classified as 'conditions' so that any failure to perform, however slight, entitles the other to treat himself as discharged.... After referring to *Behn* v *Burness*, above, Lord Denning continued:

The question in this case is whether the statement by the owner: 'expected ready to load under this charter about July 1, 1965', is likewise a 'condition'. The meaning of such a clause is settled by a decision of this court. It is an assurance by the owner that he honestly expects that the vessel will be ready to load on that date and that his expectation is based on reasonable grounds: see *Samuel Sanday & Co.* v *Keighley Maxted & Co.* (1922) 27 Com Cas 296. The clause with that meaning has been held in this court to be a 'condition' which, if not fulfilled, entitled the other party to treat himself as discharged: see *Finnish Government* v *H. Ford & Co. Ltd* (1921) 6 Ll L Rep 188. Those were sale of goods cases. But I think the clause should receive the same interpretation in charterparty cases. It seems to me that, if the owner of a ship or his agent states in a charter that she is 'expected ready to load about July 1, 1965', he is making a representation as to his own state of mind; that is, of what he himself expects: and, what is more, he puts it in the contract as a term of it, binding himself to its truth. If he or his agent breaks that term by making the statement without any honest belief in its truth or without any reasonable grounds for it, he must take the consequences. It is at lowest a misrepresentation which entitles the other party to rescind: and at highest a breach of contract which goes to the root of the matter. The charterer who is misled by the statement is entitled, on discovering its falsity, to throw up the charter. It may, therefore, properly be described as a 'condition'.

MEGAW LJ: It is not disputed that when a charter includes the words 'expected ready to load ...' a contractual obligation on the part of the shipowner is involved. It is not an obligation that the vessel will be ready to load on the stated date, nor about the stated date, if the date is qualified, as here, by 'about'. The owner is not in breach merely because the vessel arrives much later, or indeed does not arrive at all. The owner is not undertaking that there will be no unexpected delay. But he is undertaking that he honestly and on reasonable grounds believes, at the time of the contract, that the date named is the date when the vessel will be ready to load. Therefore in order to establish a breach of that obligation the charterer has the burden of showing that the owner's contractually expressed expectation was not his honest expectation, or, at the least, that the owner did not have reasonable grounds for it.

In my judgment, such a term in a charterparty ought to be regarded as being a condition of the contract, in the old sense of the word 'condition': that is, that when it has been broken, the other party can, if he wishes, by intimation to the party in breach, elect to be released from performance of his further obligations under the contract; and he can validly do so without having to establish that on the facts of the particular case the breach has produced serious consequences which can be treated as 'going to the root of the contract' or as being 'fundamental', or whatever other metaphor may be thought appropriate for a frustration case. I reach that conclusion for four interrelated reasons.

First, it tends towards certainty in the law. One of the essential elements of law is some measure of uniformity. One of the important elements of the law is predictability. At any rate in commercial law, there are obvious and substantial advantages in having, where possible, a firm and definite rule for a particular class of legal relationship: for example, as here, the legal categorisation of a particular, definable type of contractual clause in common use. It is surely much better, both for shipowners and charterers (and, incidentally, for their advisers), when a contractual obligation of this nature is under consideration, and still more when they are faced with the necessity for an urgent decision as to the effects of a suspected breach of it, to be able to say categorically: 'If a breach is proved, then the charterer can put an end to the contract,' rather than that they should be left to ponder whether or not the courts would be likely, in the particular case, when the evidence has been heard, to decide that in the particular circumstances the breach was or was not such as 'to go to the root of the contract'. Where justice does not require greater flexibility, there is everything to be said for, and nothing against, a degree of rigidity in legal principle.

Second, it would, in my opinion, only be in the rarest case, if ever, that a shipowner could legitimately feel that he had suffered an injustice by reason of the law having given to a charterer the right to put an end to the contract because of the breach by the shipowner of a clause such as this. If a shipowner has chosen to assert contractually, but dishonestly or without reasonable grounds, that he expects his vessel to be ready to load on such-and-such a date, wherein does the grievance lie?

Third, it is, as Mocatta J held, clearly established by authority binding on this court that where a clause 'expected ready to load' is included in a contract for the sale of goods to be carried by sea, that clause is a condition, in the sense that any breach of it enables the buyer to reject the goods without having to show that the dishonest or unreasonable expectation of the seller has in fact been prejudicial to the buyer. . . . If the contract says 'loading to be during July', the buyer can reject the goods if the loading was not complete until midday on August 1. He is not limited to claiming damages; he is not obliged to show that he has suffered any damage.

It would, in my judgment, produce an undesirable anomaly in our commercial law if such a clause — 'expected ready to load' — were to be held to have a materially different legal effect where it is contained in a charterparty from that which it has when it is contained in a sale of goods contract. True, in the latter case the relevant 'expectation' is that of the seller of the goods, who may himself be the charterer; whereas in the former case the relevant 'expectation' is that of the shipowner. But I do not see that that fact is sufficient to warrant the making of a distinction between the two. True, also, as was stressed by counsel for the owners, the charterparty will almost invariably include a cancelling clause; and it is argued that that fact justifies the drawing of a distinction. Again, I think not, for various reasons. One of them is that the date before which the cancelling clause cannot be exercised (this involves the argument for the owners on the second issue, to be considered hereafter) is itself normally fixed by reference to the date of expected readiness to load, and on the assumption that that is an honest and reasonable expectation.

The fourth reason why I think that the clause should be regarded as being a condition when it is found in a charterparty is that that view was the view of Scrutton LJ so expressed in his capacity as the author of *Scrutton on Charterparties*. The 10th edition (1921) of the work, for which he was personally responsible, contained the same expression of opinion as is still to be found in the 17th edition (1964) at p. 79, under the head 'Case 4', as follows:

A ship was chartered 'expected to be at X about December 15 . . . shall with all convenient speed sail to X'. The ship was in fact then on such a voyage that she could not complete it and be at X by December 15. *Submitted*, that the charterer was entitled to throw up the charter.

In the footnote to that passage reference is made to, amongst other cases, *Corkling* v *Massey* (1873) LR 8 CP 395. The facts in 'Case 4' are the facts of *Corkling* v *Massey*. In *Corkling* v *Massey* the question whether the clause operated as a condition was left undecided by a Divisional Court. Scrutton LJ, in the sentence '*Submitted* . . . ,' indicated how he would have decided it.

*Note*
A statement of estimated time of arrival (ETA) has the same effect as an ERTL statement.

*B: Meeting the ERTL date: the obligation to start in time*

The change to ERTL statements has not removed the shipowner's obligation to proceed with reasonable despatch: on the contrary, it has reinforced it by requiring the shipowner to commence the loading voyage at a date on which it can reasonably be expected that the vessel will reach the load port in accordance with the ERTL date. How the vessel is employed between the making of the charterparty and this 'start date' is a matter for the shipowner, but the entire risk of failing to meet the start date falls on him. The vessel is not expected to be kept idle waiting for the start date, but any delay arising from other employment will put the shipowner in breach if, because of it, the start date is not kept.

### *Monroe Brothers Ltd* v *Ryan*
[1935] 2 KB 28 (CA)

On 2 August 1933, M chartered the *Wythburn* to R. The vessel was stated to be expected ready to load about 11 September and was to proceed with all convenient speed to Hamburg to load a cargo of sugar and salt for carriage to Kilrush in the West of Ireland. There was an exception for 'unavoidable . . . hindrances beyond . . . owners' control'. On 31 August, M chartered the *Wythburn* to carry stone from Porthoustock in Cornwall to Felixstowe. On 5 September, M's agent in Hamburg told the shippers there that the vessel would be ready to load the sugar and salt on 14 September, but she was subsequently delayed by bad weather at Porthoustock and did not commence loading at Hamburg until 18 September. The late arrival resulted in extra charges being incurred by the charterers both in Hamburg and in Ireland. In M's action for the freight, the charterers counterclaimed for damages. M were held liable on the counterclaim and their appeal was dismissed.

GREER LJ: Here we are concerned with a charterparty where it has been found convenient to put, instead of a definite date, the words 'expected ready to load', by a given date. The charterparty says: 'It is this day mutually agreed between Messrs Monroe Brothers, managers of the good steamship called the *Wythburn* (or substitute at owner's option) expected ready to load about September 11, 1933, and Messrs A. Ryan

& Son, charterers'. It had been found in the experience of shipowners that it was a little difficult for them to undertake an exact date when the vessel would be ready to load, and this clause was invented to meet that situation. It has been explained in one or two cases, especially in the case of *Samuel Sanday & Co.* v *Keighley, Maxted & Co.* 27 Com Cas 296 by Lord Sterndale MR, where he says ibid 301: 'I think that the second is the right view, that it is to be interpreted as meaning that in view of the facts, as known to the seller at the time of his making the contract and making the statement "expected ready to load", the expectation was one which was made, as Bailhache J says in one of the cases, honestly and upon reasonable grounds'. Now it is said in that and other cases that this statement is not a mere representation; it is a contractual statement, part of the contract between the parties, but it only means that they contract that the statement is honestly made upon reasonable grounds. That does not help us very much to determine what is the date on which the ship ought to be there. It is not left alone in the charterparty, because the charterparty goes on to say: 'The said steamer being tight, staunch, strong, and every way fitted for the voyage, shall with all convenient speed proceed to Hamburg or so near thereunto as she may safely get, and there load from the said charterers a full and complete cargo,' of sugar and salt. That, I take it, means in this charterparty that the vessel will proceed at a time when it is reasonably certain that she will arrive at the loading port on or about the expected date, and the expected date in this case is on or about September 11. In the absence of evidence it is difficult to determine what the exact effect of the word 'about' is. The parties in this case in the correspondence have treated September 13 as within the area of the expected date, and I do not think we are entitled to differ from them in that respect. The charterers' complaint is: 'We do not say we suffered any damage by reason of a breach of contract in the vessel not arriving before September 14, but we do say we suffered damage by reason of a breach committed by the vessel arriving at a later date.'

The dates in this case are these: On August 31 the plaintiffs entered into another charterparty with the West of England Road-Metal Company Ltd, to carry stone from a place called Porthoustock to Felixstowe, and it is said that by doing so they broke their contract of August 2. I do not accept that argument. It must have been within the contemplation of the parties that between August 2 and September 14 the shipowners would, in fact, be using their vessel for such remunerative purposes as they could. I also think that the taking of that charter did not relieve in any way, or indeed affect the obligations of the shipowners under the charter of August 2, and by entering into that charter they took upon themselves the risk that by doing so they might be prevented from fulfilling the contract which they had made as early as August 2....

Although the shipowners in this case did not make a contract which by itself without anything more would bring about that result, they did, in fact, make a contract which in the long run did bring about the result that the vessel could not proceed with due diligence to the port of loading so as to arrive at the port of loading on or about the expected date. The only question is whether or not they were excused by reason of the exceptions in the charterparty from performing that obligation.

Now I am satisfied that there is no authority which carries the area of exceptions beyond the time when the ship starts on the agreed voyage. It is not confined to the time when she loads under the charterparty, but includes the period of time when she is steaming with all convenient speed to arrive at the loading port. ... It is an unfortunate result that people who have to make engagements in advance necessarily run the risk of the engagements clashing with one another so as to prevent the performance of one or other of their contracts, and they have to take the consequences by paying damages to the party whose contract they, in the result, have failed to perform.

I think for these reasons this appeal fails, and must be dismissed with costs.

*Note*
It was held in *Louis Dreyfus & Co.* v *Lauro* (1938) 60 Ll L Rep 94, that the same principle applied if the vessel already had an engagement for the intervening period. There the other engagement was not referred to in the charterparty; can the shipowner gain protection from the consequences of *Monroe Brothers Ltd* v *Ryan* by disclosing the vessel's intervening engagements when stating the ERTL date?

## Evera SA Commercial v North Shipping Co. Ltd
### [1956] 2 Lloyd's Rep 367 (QBD)

N chartered the *North Anglia* to E on 6 August 1953, to proceed with all convenient speed to Fort Churchill (Hudson Bay) to load grain for European ports. The vessel was at the time on a voyage to Churchill to load grain and was stated in E's charterparty to be 'now due to arrive UK to discharge about 30th August; estimating 14 days to discharge, expected ready to load under this charterparty about 27th Sept. 1953'. The *North Anglia* arrived at Churchill on 16 August, which was a little later than expected, but she loaded in two days and completed the 14½-day return voyage to Leith by 3 September. Because of congestion at the port, however, she was unable to commence discharging her cargo until 23 September. Meanwhile it had become clear that the *North Anglia* would not be able to reach Churchill before it became ice-bound, and on 18 September the charterers cancelled and engaged another vessel at a higher rate of freight. Their action for damages, being the increased freight cost, succeeded.

DEVLIN J: It is clear that there are two obligations into which the shipowner enters. He enters into the obligation of making an honest and reasonable statement about his position. That he discharged that is not questioned here. But he also entered into an obligation, which is expressed in the printed words of the charter, which I have read, that the ship 'shall with all convenient speed sail and proceed to Fort Churchill'. It is for the breach of that obligation that the ship is being sued in this case, as it was sued in the case of *Monroe Brothers Ltd* v *Ryan* [1935] 2 KB 28; and the effect of that obligation, it is submitted, combined with the statement of readiness which is made earlier on in the charter, is to impose upon the ship an absolute duty with which in this case, as in *Monroe Brothers Ltd* v *Ryan*, *sup.*, the ship has not complied. I think the best way of framing the duty, and the way which was adopted by Mr Eustace Roskill [counsel for the charterers], is to take it as it was framed by Mr Justice Branson in *Louis Dreyfus & Co.* v *Lauro* (1938) 60 Ll L Rep 94 adopting the phraseology that has been submitted to him in argument by Mr Mocatta. Mr Justice Branson, at p. 97, put it in these terms:

> In view of the combination of the expected date and of the implied term that the ship will use all convenient speed to get to her port of loading, the obligation is, as was well put by Mr Mocatta, that she shall start from wherever she may happen to be, at a date when, by proceeding with reasonable dispatch, she will arrive at the port of loading by the expected date.

Applying that to the facts of this case, Mr Eustace Roskill puts the matter in this way. The expected date of arrival was 'about' Sept. 27 (I can leave out for this purpose the effects of the word 'about'. It allows, of course, some degree of latitude, but the extent of the degree is not a matter in this case. Let me take it as being Sept. 27.) Then Mr Eustace Roskill submits that to arrive at Fort Churchill from Leith the voyage would take 14 or 15 days. Therefore, in order to comply with her obligations, she should have left Leith on about Sept. 12, and the charterparty is to be construed in just the same way as if there were an absolute obligation to leave Leith on Sept. 12. None of the exceptions in the charterparty which might excuse her once she had actually begun her voyage apply. That has been settled in a number of cases, of which *Monroe Brothers Ltd* v *Ryan*, *sup.*, is itself the latest example. Therefore, she is under an unqualified obligation to leave Leith on Sept. 12. She failed to do so, and, though it may not have been her fault that she failed to do so, she took the risk of her engagements clashing, and she is in breach of her obligation here. Thus, what *Monroe Brothers Ltd* v *Ryan*, *sup.*, does in effect is to restore the position, if I may so call it, to the simple position which appertained when shipowners did not engage their ships when they were otherwise occupied or it was contemplated they would have been occupied. In that simple position, as I have said, the relief, and the only relief, that the shipowner obtained was that if something unexpected happened in the course of the voyage to the port of loading the ship was excused. That is what still happens. Under the principle in *Monroe Brothers Ltd* v *Ryan*, *sup.*, the ship is excused if she starts out in good time but something happens on the way to the port of loading. But she is not excused if anything happens before that time which prevents her from starting out upon the expected date.

Mr Ashton Roskill's [counsel for the shipowners] first submission, though it is not his most important submission, is, I think, the one that I should take logically first. It is that there is no absolute obligation at all; that the words 'shall with all convenient speed sail and proceed to Fort Churchill' do not impose an absolute obligation. He submits that it would not matter for this purpose if a specific date were inserted on which the ship was to leave the port where she then was, for example, Sept. 12. He submits that still those words would not be words of absolute obligation and that her only duty would be to use due diligence to leave the place where she was on the prescribed day, and also, of course, not, by entering into other engagements, to do anything which would put it out of the ship's power to perform the engagement in question in this case.

I think that submission is wrong. I think that it is wrong as a matter of construction. I can see no reason why the words 'shall with all convenient speed sail and proceed' should not be given their ordinary and natural meaning. They are an unqualified undertaking. When a person agrees to do something, if he says that he shall deliver the goods, or shall do anything else under the contract, it is not without very good reason to be construed as meaning merely that he has to use due diligence to do it. I can see no reason why those words should not be given what I take to be their natural meaning, and that is an absolute undertaking, subject, of course, to any exceptions in the charterparty itself which may apply to qualify that undertaking.

I can deal shortly with this, because, in my view, even if I reached another conclusion, I should be constrained by the decision on *Monroe Brothers Ltd* v *Ryan*, *sup.*, to decide this point against the defendants. *Monroe Brothers Ltd* v *Ryan*, *sup.*, seems to me quite plainly to proceed upon the basis that the only way in which the shipowner could successfully claim to be excused from his obligation is if he could show that the exceptions in the charterparty applied, that is to say, *Monroe Brothers Ltd* v *Ryan*, *sup.*, proceeds on the basis that, subject to the exceptions in the charterparty, there is an absolute obligation. In *Monroe Brothers Ltd* v *Ryan*, *sup.*, it was held — and I do not think I have been invited to hold differently here, except for the typed words, which I will deal with by themselves — that the exceptions did not apply, and I think it follows that it was therefore decided that there was an absolute obligation.

But that, of course, does not conclude the matter. It leads indeed to what is the central point in this case. Granted that there is an absolute obligation, what is the absolute obligation? That is a matter for the construction of this particular charterparty. Mr Ashton Roskill is right, I think, in his submission that *Monroe Brothers Ltd* v *Ryan, sup.,* lays down no binding principle that would require me to construe this charterparty in any particular way. Lord Justice Greer (at pp. 36 and 181) read the clause:

> The said steamer being tight, staunch, strong, and every way fitted for the voyage, shall with all convenient speed proceed to Hamburg or so near thereunto as she may safely get, and there load . . .

— and so forth, and then went on to say:

> That, I take it, means in this charterparty that the vessel will proceed at a time when it is reasonably certain that she will arrive at the loading port on or about the expected date.

The words are substantially the same as the words here. But, as Lord Justice Greer said, 'that, I take it, means in this charterparty', and, of course, I have to look not merely at the actual words that I have to construe, but also at the whole of the charterparty and at any other words which may qualify that obligation. Mr Ashton Roskill submits that the typed words do qualify that obligation, and that the effect of reading the obligation construed in the light of the typed words is this, that the date that is set by the obligation is not such a date as would enable the ship to arrive at the loading port on the expected date; in other words, that the clause is not to be read as if, in the circumstances of this case, it said 'the 12th September', but it is to be read as inserting a date for the proceeding upon the voyage which follows on the earlier voyage that is described in the typed words in the charterparty.
. . .

Mr Eustace Roskill submits that the words are not intended for that purpose at all, and that they are to be construed quite separately as a covenant for the benefit of the charterer without impinging at all upon the shipowner's obligation to sail and proceed with all convenient speed. He submits that they are for the benefit of the charterer because, he submits, the ordinary statement of position — the ordinary statement of expected readiness to load — is put in for the benefit of the charterer, and is something that the shipowner would obviously rather not have there. He would like to be free to arrive when he can. All that is done here is to put in in that way that statement of position likewise for the benefit of the charterer. The advantage from the charterer's point of view is that he has earlier expectations which he can call in question. If, for example, he found that the ship had not arrived in the United Kingdom until, let us say, Sept. 10, he might be enabled to say there and then that 'that statement of expectation that she would discharge on Aug. 30 was one that was not made on reasonable grounds, and I here and now throw up the charter'; whereas, if the first date of expectation mentioned is Sept. 27, he might not be able to challenge it in the same way.

I think that the test by which those two contentions have to be decided is, in the end, quite a simple and well-known one. What Mr Eustace Roskill is doing is, as I think he is right in submitting, construing the charterparty — construing the clause 'shall with all convenient speed sail and proceed to Fort Churchill'. In one sense, it may be said that to read in the words 'within a reasonable time' is an implication. But it is what is sometimes called an implication of law rather than an implication of fact. The law does it automatically, and, having got those words there, then all that is necessary for Mr Eustace Roskill in his construction of the clause is to ask: 'What, in the circumstances of this case, should the Court hold to be "a reasonable time'"? I think, therefore, that he is broadly right in saying that it is a matter of construction, and that he does not need to invoke any implication of any term.

Mr Ashton Roskill does, in my judgment, need to involve the implication of a term. He needs to read in something equivalent to the words which I have indicated — 'after discharge in the United Kingdom'. The question, therefore, is simply whether he can satisfy the tests that are ordinarily applied to the implication of terms.

...

I need not trouble myself with the question as to whether or not it is necessary for the business efficacy of the contract, because I think it breaks down entirely upon the issue as to whether an implied term of that sort would, in accordance with the officious bystander test, obviously have been accepted by the charterers. In my judgment, it is not possible to say that, if the shipowner in terms had said to the charterer, 'Although I have given you all these dates, and have told you that I shall expect to be there on Sept. 20, of course you understand that if anything goes wrong with the voyage on which I am at present engaged I cannot get there until later,' that would have been accepted by the charterer. I do not think there are any grounds for thinking that a charterer would agree to that at all. Indeed, I think the charterer, even if he were disposed to consider such a proposition, would certainly ask this. He would say: 'Supposing I am content to have my date postponed until the completion of your existing voyage, what guarantee have I got that you would perform that voyage with due diligence? What guarantee have I got that it may not, albeit perhaps not through your own fault but for some other reason, be prolonged far beyond Sept. 20? I must have something to protect me here.' Then, no doubt, the shipowner would reply, as Mr Ashton Roskill has replied, 'Oh, well, I will undertake that I will perform the earlier voyage with due diligence.' That might or might not require further elaboration. It might have to be considered whether it meant due diligence in relation to the earlier voyage itself, so that if the shipowner had been minded to have protected himself in regard to that voyage with some very favourable exceptions, he could claim that he was proceeding with due diligence because he had protection under the terms of that earlier charterparty. Or it might have to be considered whether it would be a covenant to proceed with due diligence wholly irrespective of any exceptions he might have in the earlier charterparty. All those matters, I think, would have to be worked out before it could be said that there was a reasonable basis for an implication.

In short, the position is this, that if a shipowner wants to make the beginning of one voyage contingent upon the conclusion of the one before, he must say so in clear terms. There is clearly a number of things that would have to be worked out in order that such an arrangement should be made as would be fair to both sides. It may be that the shipowner had it in mind in this case that that was what he wanted. But, if he did have that in mind, he has not put it into such language as would make it plain to any reasonable charterer that the charterer was being invited to accept the risks of delay under an earlier charterparty in which that charterer was not concerned. To pass those risks on to a person who was not a party to that charter requires, in my judgment, if not express language, at least much clearer language than that which has been adopted in the present case.

I should therefore conclude that there is no ground for distinguishing this case from the principle in *Monroe Brothers Ltd v Ryan, sup.*, and that that principle applies. I construe, therefore, the obligation imposed on the shipowner by the words 'shall with all convenient speed sail and proceed to Fort Churchill' in the same way as the similar obligation was construed in *Monroe Brothers, Ltd v Ryan, sup.*, and in *Louis Dreyfus & Co. v Lauro, sup.* From that I think it follows on the authority of *Monroe Brothers Ltd v*

*Ryan, sup.*, that the exceptions, if there are exceptions in the charterparty which is disputed, cannot avail the shipowner in this case, and that he is in breach of what is in effect an absolute obligation.

### Geogas SA v Trammo Gas Ltd
### (The Baleares)
[1993] 1 Lloyd's Rep 215 (CA)

One of the issues in the case was the time at which the obligation to proceed with reasonable despatch commenced: can the shipowner be in breach before the latest start date necessary to achieve the ETA?

Here the expected ready date was 31 January. At the time of the charterparty the vessel was at Ras Tanura in the Gulf bound, ultimately, for Tarragona, which was 22 hours' steaming time from the loading port (Bethioua, in Algeria). The shipowners argued that there was no breach until 2 a.m. on 31 January, the point at which it became impossible to reach Bethioua from Tarragona in time. The Court of Appeal rejected this argument.

NEILL LJ: It seems to me that the right approach is that adopted in *Louis Dreyfus* v *Lauro* and in *The North Anglia* and indeed by the arbitrators in the present case. One looks at the combination of the expected date and the term that the ship will use all convenient speed to get to the port of loading. Both Mr Justice Branson in *Louis Dreyfus* and Mr Justice Devlin in *The North Anglia* took the view that the combined effect of the two clauses was to impose an obligation on the owners to ensure that the vessel should start from—

> . . . wherever she may happen to be, at a date when, by proceeding with reasonable dispatch, she will arrive at the port of loading by the expected date.

It is true that there are passages in the judgments in *Monroe Brothers* (sup.) *Louis Dreyfus* (sup.) and *The North Anglia* (sup.) and in the judgment in *Mitsui O.S.K. Lines* v *Garnac Grain Co. Inc* [1984] 2 Lloyd's Rep 449 which support the proposition that the duty to proceed with reasonable despatch commences at the start of the approach voyage to the loading port. It seems clear, however, that in none of these cases was the Court concerned with the problem which arises in the present case. Approaching the matter from first principles and if one leaves aside cases where there may be a right to nominate a substitute vessel, it seems to me impossible to contend that a charterer is obliged to wait until the vessel leaves the last discharge point (which might be a berth in the same port as the loading port) before he can treat the owners as being in breach. . . .

It is true that in *The North Anglia* the Court was concerned with a breach of the obligation to leave Leith in the United Kingdom in time to reach Fort Churchill on Hudson Bay by Sept. 27 (a voyage of about 14 days), but it is to be noted that in upholding the right of the charterers to rescind the charterparty on Sept. 18 Mr Justice Devlin referred at p. 372 to the fact that at the date of rescission—

> . . . there was no reasonable prospect of the ship being able to perform the contemplated voyage.

Complications may arise where the owners have the right to substitute another vessel, but for my part I can see no satisfactory basis for a rule that the owners cannot be treated as being in breach of the combined obligation before the vessel leaves the last port of discharge.

It is clear from the decision in *The Mihalis Angelos* (sup.) that a right to treat the charterparty as having been repudiated by the owners may arise before the date on which the charterers are given a contractual right to cancel. This right arises when it becomes clear that there is no reasonable prospect of the vessel being able to perform the contemplated voyage. The owners are then in breach.

*C: Cancelling clauses*

Charterparties often provide for a 'cancelling date'. The purpose of this provision is to give the charterer the option of pulling out of the contract if the vessel is not ready to load by the date stated, whatever the reason for the delay. The shipowner cannot resist cancellation on the ground that the delay is not due to any breach of the charterparty. See *Georgian Maritime Corporation plc v Sealand Industries (Bermuda) Ltd (The North Sea)* [1999] 1 Lloyd's Rep 21 (CA), at 26 (per Hobhouse LJ): '[cancellation] is not a concept of fault or acceptance of repudiation: it is the exercise of a contractual option which is exercisable even though the owner may not have been at fault.' Conversely, the charterer cannot claim damages merely because the shipowner was not ready to load by the cancelling date.

### *Smith* v *Dart & Son*
### (1884) 14 QBD 105

The charterparty for a cargo of oranges provided that 'should the steamer not be arrived at first loading port free of pratique and ready to load on or before the 15th of December next, charterers have the option of cancelling or confirming this charterparty'.

The vessel arrived off the port (Burriana) on 13 December, but because of bad weather had to take refuge in Valencia and did not return to Burriana until 17 December. Meanwhile, the charterers cancelled on 16 December. The charterparty contained an exception for dangers and accidents of the seas. It was held that the exception did not apply to the cancelling clause.

MATHEW J: ... At first I was inclined to adopt the view suggested by the learned counsel that the well known excepted perils clause applied to the clause which gave the option of cancellation if the vessel did not arrive until the 15th of December. But, on considering the point, it is clear that the clause giving the option would be practically struck out of the charter if it were to be construed 'the vessel must be ready to load by the 15th unless prevented by dangers of the sea'. That is an interpretation I should be very slow to put on a charter, and which would nullify the express provision. The next observation is that it is peculiar in this respect, viz., that it is a clause which imposes no obligation which would be the subject of an action against the shipowner. Unlike the other clauses by which the shipowner undertakes to do something, in this particular clause all that is provided is that in the event of the ship not being ready to load at the time appointed the charterers shall have the option of cancelling.

This is a charter of a vessel for importation of goods which are required in a particular season. It is important that the shipment shall be as early as possible, and such charters often contain stipulations for shipment in a particular month, and that unless the ship shall arrive at a particular time the charter shall be cancelled. On the other hand it is a contract with respect to a steamer, and charterers are apt to suppose that with a steamer all will go on well, and the shipowner might also fairly suppose that the vessel would arrive in time. In this particular case the shipowner appears to have attempted to run the time too close. He got in shortly before the 15th of December, and a storm arose and he had to put back, and it became impossible to be at the port on the 15th free of pratique and ready to load, and the charterers had their option of cancelling and exercised it, and therefore I think the rule must be discharged.

*Notes*
1.   It is settled that there is no 'anticipatory' right to cancel ahead of the cancelling date (*Cheikh Boutros Selim El-Khoury* v *Ceylon Shipping Lines Ltd, The Madeleine* [1967] 2 Lloyd's Rep 224 (Roskill J, on a time charter provision for cancellation if the vessel was not delivered by the stated date), approved by a majority of the Court of Appeal in the *Mihalis Angelos*, above).
2.   The interval between the estimated date of readiness and the date for cancellation is referred to as the laycan or laycan spread. A provision in a time charter for 'owners to narrow laycan to a 15 day spread 25 days prior to the narrowed laycan' was held to be a strict contractual condition: *Hyundai Merchant Marine Co. Ltd* v *Karander Maritime Inc (The Niizuru)* [1996] 2 Lloyd's Rep 66 (QBD, Mance J).

*Question*
A charterparty made between O, the shipowner, and C, the charterer, has a cancelling date of 1 May. On 25 April, O asks if C will wait until 5 May for the vessel to be ready. C replies 'As you are obviously not going to be ready by 1 May I cancel the charter now'. O thinks he *might* be able to have the vessel ready by 1 May but is not sure. Advise O. (*Cf. Fercometal SARL* v *Mediterranean Shipping Co. SA (The Simona)* [1989] AC 788.)

## SECTION 3: THE LOADING OPERATION AND PROVISION OF CARGO

How the physical process of loading is to be performed is a matter which the contract will determine. We are here more concerned with some wider issues in relation to the provision of a cargo, namely the scope of the charterer's duty, the effect of provision for alternative cargoes and the principles to be applied where dangerous cargo is loaded.

*A: Charterer's duty to provide a cargo*

The charterer takes the risk that the intended cargo may not be available for loading.

### Sueton D. Grant & Co. v Coverdale, Todd & Co.
### (1884) 9 App Cas 470

The *Mennythorpe* was chartered to proceed to Cardiff East Bute Dock and load a full and complete cargo of about 1,800 tons of bar or bundle iron. Laytime was to commence as soon as the vessel was ready to load, 'except in case of ... frosts ... and all other unavoidable accidents preventing the loading'. One thousand tons of the intended cargo was at the manufacturers' wharf on the Glamorganshire Canal and was to be brought to the dock by canal. After a small part had been loaded, the canal froze over and for two weeks the charterers were unable to bring the remaining cargo to the dock. In the shipowners' action for demurrage and damages for detention, the charterers relied on the exception for frosts. The Court of Appeal and the House of Lords held that the exception did not apply, and the action succeeded.

EARL OF SELBORNE LC: This exception in the contract being limited to 'accidents preventing the loading', the only question is, what is the meaning of 'loading'? and whether this particular frost did, in fact, prevent the loading. There are two things to be done — the operation of loading is the particular operation in which both parties have to concur. Taken literally it is spoken of in the early part of this charterparty as the thing which the shipowner is to do. The ship is to 'proceed to Cardiff East Bute Dock', 'and there load the cargo'. No doubt, for the purpose of loading, the charterer must also do his part; he must have the cargo there to be loaded, and tender it to be put on board the ship in the usual and proper manner. Therefore the business of both parties meets and concurs in that operation of loading. When the charterer has tendered the cargo, and when the operation has proceeded to the point at which the shipowner is to take charge of it, everything after that is the shipowner's business, and everything before the commencement of the operation of loading, those things which are so essential to the operation of loading that they are conditions sine quibus non of that operation — everything before that is the charterer's part only. It would appear to me to be unreasonable to suppose, unless the words make it perfectly clear, that the shipowner has contracted that his ship may be detained for an unlimited time on account of impediments, whatever their nature may be, to those things with which he has nothing whatever to do, which precede altogether the whole operation of loading, which are no part whatever of it, but which belong to that which is exclusively the charterer's business. He has to contract for the cargo, he has to buy the cargo, he has to convey the cargo to the place of loading and have it ready there to be put on board; and it is only when he has done those things that the duty and the obligation of the shipowner in respect of the loading arises. These words in the exception are as large as any words can be; they mention 'strikes, frosts, floods, and all other unavoidable accidents preventing the loading'. If therefore you are to carry back the loading to anything necessary to be done by the charterer in order to have the cargo ready to be loaded, no human being can tell where you are to stop. The bankruptcy, for instance, of the person with whom he has contracted for the supply of the iron, or disputes about the fulfilment of the contract, the refusal at a critical point of time to supply the iron, the neglect of the persons who ought to put it on board lighters to come down the canal for any distance or to be brought by sea, or to put it on the railway or bring it in any other way in which it is to be brought; all those things are of course practical impediments to the charterer having the cargo ready to be shipped at the proper place and time; but is it reasonable that the shipowner should be held to be answerable for all those things, and is that within the natural meaning of the word 'loading'? Are those things any part of the operation of loading? Nothing, I suppose, is better established in law with regard to mercantile cases of this kind than the maxim, 'Causa proxima, non remota, spectatur'; and it appears to me that the fact that this particular wharf was very near the Cardiff East Bute Dock can make no difference in principle if it was not the place of loading. . . .

*Note*

The traditional obligation to load a 'full and complete' cargo means that the charterer must load the vessel to the full extent of its capacity, even if a lower figure is stated in the charterparty. In *Hunter* v *Fry* (1819) 2 B & Ald 421, the vessel was stated to have a burden of 261 tons or thereabouts, but was proved to be capable of carrying 400 tons of the charterer's cargo: the charterer loaded 336 tons, but was held liable for freight on 400 tons.

Quantities stated will be subject to the tolerance implied in the *de minimis* principle, but this is applied strictly. See, for example, the decision in *Margaronis Navigation Agency Ltd* v *Henry W. Peabody & Co. of London Ltd* [1965] 2 QB 430 (CA), where the difference between 12,588 tons of maize and 12,600 tons was not *de minimis*.

*B: Alternative cargo options*

If the charterparty provides for a cargo of wheat and/or barley and the charterer is unable to load wheat (for a reason covered by an exception clause), is there an obligation to load barley instead?

### Brightman & Co. v Bunge y Born Limitada Sociedad
### [1924] 2 KB 619 (CA)

The *Castlemoor* was chartered to load a full and complete cargo of wheat and/or maize and/or rye at Rosario. Time for loading was not to count if the cargo could not be loaded 'by reason of . . . obstruction . . . beyond the control of the charterers on the railways or in the docks'. The charterers planned to load wheat, but the supply of wheat was disrupted by a 'work to rule' on the Central Argentine Railway. After two weeks had been spent loading part of the cargo of wheat, the Argentine Government banned the export of wheat. Six days later the charterers started to load maize. On a claim by the shipowners for demurrage, Bailhache J held that the charterers were obliged to load maize as soon as the export of wheat was banned. The Court of Appeal held that demurrage was not payable for the six days from the imposition of the ban until the commencement of loading of maize.

SCRUTTON LJ: . . . The charter is on the form known as the 'Chamber of Shipping River Plate Charter, 1914', which was agreed between the Chamber of Shipping and the representative body of the Argentine shippers. It contains phrases not easy to construe, as is often the case when parties with conflicting interests adopt an ambiguous form which each side dare not make precise for fear the other party should disagree with their meaning if stated precisely. . . . Bailhache J, agreeing with a previous decision of Rowlatt

J on the same charter, holds that where a charterer undertakes to load a mixed cargo of various named kinds, the fact that he is prevented from loading one ingredient of the cargo does not excuse him from loading the other ingredients which he is not prevented from loading. I agree with this view, which appears to follow from the decision of this Court in *The Rookwood* 10 Times LR 314. If when the ship arrived the loading of wheat was forbidden, I do not think the charterer could say: 'I am excused from loading any cargo, for I am prevented from loading the cargo I intended to load'. The shipowners' answer would be: 'You have contracted to load a full and complete cargo of wheat and/or maize and/or rye. If you cannot load wheat, load maize or rye, which you can load'. If the charterer failed he would have to pay dead freight. Similarly if the shipowner claims demurrage because the charterer has not loaded the cargo he has contracted to load in the agreed time, it is no answer to the charterer to say, 'I was prevented from loading one sort of that cargo'; he was not prevented from loading other kinds of that cargo. If it is said the charterer had the right to select the cargo to be put on board, and when he had selected it, it became the only chartered cargo, I can see nothing in the facts found to bind the charterer to ship only wheat. No doubt he intended to do so, but if he had changed his mind and shifted from wheat to maize how could the shipowner have objected? I disagree, therefore, with the view that because the charterers intended to ship wheat they were not bound to ship maize or rye. Of course they were not bound to ship maize if they shipped a full and complete cargo of wheat; but if they could not do this, they still had contracted to ship a full and complete cargo of wheat and/or maize and/or rye, and must make up their full cargo of goods they could ship. But I do not go the full length of Bailhache J's judgment. If the charterers were shipping a contract cargo of a particular kind, and were stopped by an excepted cause from shipping that kind of cargo, I think they are allowed as the consequence of that excepted cause a reasonable time to consider the position and change their cargo, and may say that to the extent of that time they were delayed by the cause which prevented shipment of the first kind of cargo. This must be on the assumption that they had the first kind of cargo ready for shipment but for the excepted cause; and I am not sure, in view of the fact that when the cause, prohibition, stopped they shipped only maize and not wheat, that they had wheat available; but the experienced arbitrator has found that the six days they waited was not unreasonable, and while I do not think I should have given so long, it is a question of fact on which I cannot interfere with the arbitrator. . . .

## Note

The Court of Appeal held that the exception for 'obstructions' did not apply to the work to rule because clear wording is needed to extend exception clauses to matters outside the port of loading (*cf. Sueton D. Grant & Co. v Coverdale, Todd & Co.*, above). The House of Lords affirmed the decision on the construction of the exception, but did not have to consider the effect of the alternative cargo provision, since there was no appeal against the decision on that point.

### *Reardon Smith Line Ltd v Ministry of Agriculture, Fisheries and Food*
### [1963] AC 691 (HL)

Five of the seven grain elevators at the port of Vancouver were idle from 17 February to 7 May in 1953 because of a strike. Many vessels which had been chartered to load wheat during this time were unable to do so. The charterers were the Governments of India and South Africa as well as the British Ministry of Agriculture, Fisheries and Food. The shipowners claimed demurrage and the charterers counterclaimed for despatch. Three of the cases reached the House of Lords as consolidated appeals. The appeal relating to the *Queen City* was treated as typical.

All the charterparties were on the Pacific Coast grain charter form. By clause 1 the vessel had to load 'a full and complete cargo ... of wheat in bulk, ... and/or barley in bulk, and/or flour in sacks *as below* ... freight ... 80/– ... per ton wheat'. The words 'as below', which were typed on to the printed form, referred to the following addition to the form:

> Charterer has the option of loading up to one-third cargo of barley in bulk, in which case the above rate of freight to be increased by 2/6d. ... per ton on the quantity of barley loaded. Charterer has the option of loading up to one-third cargo of flour in bags at 10/– ... per ton extra over the rate for wheat, on the quantity of flour loaded, if loaded at British Columbia, and 12/6d. ... per ton extra if loaded at US Pacific.

The *Queen City* gave notice of readiness to load on 18 February, and waited throughout the strike until it became possible to load wheat. An exception clause covered the failure to load wheat during the strike, but the shipowners argued that it remained possible to load a full alternative cargo. The Court of Appeal held that the charterers were not obliged to load barley or flour and the House of Lords dismissed the shipowners' appeal.

VISCOUNT RADCLIFFE: Having regard to what has happened and to the form of the exceptions clause, it is at first sight a little difficult, I think, to see how the shipowners can be justified in their claim to be paid demurrage for 75 days as from February 26, on which date, they say, the lay days expired, since it would seem clear that throughout the period of delay the wheat cargo was held up by the strike which is itself an excepted cause.

The owners meet this, in effect, by saying that the charterers have no right to treat their obligation under this charterparty as being simply one to provide a cargo of wheat in bulk, failing an exercise of their option to ship part alternative cargoes of barley or flour. On the contrary, they say, the obligation is essentially an obligation to provide a full and complete cargo of wheat, barley or flour (up to the permitted proportions) as the charterers may select, and the mere fact that one of these possible constituents, wheat, is the subject of delay and so within the exceptions clause does not excuse the charterers from their overriding duty to find and ship a full and complete cargo made up of such proportions of these various commodities as the prevailing conditions at Vancouver made it possible to load during the period of the strike. ...

It has been apparent throughout the case that the shipowners' argument on this particular issue depends upon the proposition that the parties' rights under the charterparty are governed by principles laid down by the Court of Appeal in 1924 in *Brightman & Co.* v *Bunge y Born Limitada Sociedad*, to which I will refer as the *Brightman* case. I think that the decision in the *Brightman* case did lay down certain principles, though not so many or so far-reaching as is sometimes supposed, but in my opinion those principles are not applicable to the relationship established by the charterparty which we are now considering. ... The decision of the court was to the effect that some demurrage was payable but not to the whole extent claimed by the owners. In arriving at this decision the principles accepted by the court which are relevant to this appeal are, in my opinion, as follows—

(1)   If a shipper has undertaken to ship a full and complete cargo made up of alternative commodities, as in the terms 'wheat and/or maize and/or rye', his obligation is to have ready at the port of shipment a complete cargo within the range of those alternatives. Consequently the fact that he is prevented from loading one of the possible types of cargo by a cause within the exceptions clause, even though that is the type that he has himself selected and provided for, is not an answer to a claim for demurrage. To protect him each of the alternatives or all the alternatives would have to be covered by an excepted cause.

(2)   Consistently with this view the shipper's selection of one of the named commodities does not convert the primary obligation to ship a full cargo in one form or the other into a simple obligation to ship a full cargo of the commodity selected. In other words, his selection is not like the exercise of an option to name a port. He may change his mind and alter his choice: he 'retains control of his powers until the final ton is put on the ship', said Atkin LJ. This may not be a full statement of the nature or consequences of the right of selection, but I have no doubt that it describes the general situation.

(3)   If a shipper finds himself stopped by an excepted cause (e.g., in that case, the government prohibition) from loading or continuing to load the type of cargo that he has provided for and genuinely intended to ship, he may still rely on delay as covered by the exceptions clause to the extent of a reasonable time 'to consider the position and change [his] cargo' as Scrutton LJ said, or to 'deal with the altered conditions' as Bankes LJ said, or, simply, 'to change over' as Atkin LJ said.

As regards this last principle, I must admit that very careful attention to the three judgments of Bankes, Scrutton and Atkin LJ has left me uncertain as to its origin or its full implications. I think that on the whole his time for adjustment is better attributed to a term derived from the general position of a shipper under such a charterparty, when confronted with such circumstances, than to a right derived from any possible construction of the exceptions clause itself. I think that the members of the court were impressed by the consideration that, unless some period of time was allowed for the change-over, they would be imposing on the shipper of mixed cargoes an obligation to have one or more sets of the permitted alternatives available at the port, if he was to be sure of avoiding demurrage. Perhaps it would have been simpler to recognise that he does undertake just this risk. For, logically, there is much to be said for the view taken by Bailhache J in the first court, though not adopted by the Court of Appeal, that, given the two assumptions that a shipper is under a primary obligation to load a full cargo of one of the permitted commodities or some combination of them and that there is no excepted cause covering the loading of all those commodities, he is in default as soon as the lay days run out and gets no help from the exceptions clause or implications of 'reasonable time'. The risk is hardly more onerous than many others that commercial men have to assume. I must add, too, that the whole idea of 'reasonable time' seems to me to remain in a good deal of uncertainty and that there is a wide and unexplored range of argument as to how long the thwarted shipper is to be allowed for the purpose of considering his position, what deployment of effort he is supposed to achieve in the pursuit of his alternative cargo, when he has decided on it, and how far he is allowed to set the time and expense of getting such a cargo to the port and, it may be, its unsuitability to his own current needs against the expected delay to the cargo originally intended.

These are all questions that we should have had actively to pursue in the present case if we had regarded the charterparty obligation as being essentially the same as that which was analysed in the *Brightman* case, and for myself, I should have found it very difficult to extract from the evidence any satisfactory conclusion.

In my opinion, however, the principle of the *Brightman* case has no application here, because there is here no primary obligation on the charterers to ship a mixed cargo. The primary obligation is to provide a cargo of wheat only, the exceptions clause covers delay in the shipping of wheat, and there is no obligation on the charterers to lose that protection by exercising their option to provide another kind of cargo that is not affected by a cause of delay, even assuming such a cargo to be readily available. Really, that seems to me to contain the whole point of the dispute. There is in this case no duty on the charterers to 'switch' from wheat to barley or flour, because their choice of loading barley or flour is unfettered and is not at any time controlled in their hands by an overriding obligation to put on board by a fixed date a full cargo which must include those commodities, if it cannot consist of wheat alone.

It comes down, then, to a question of construing the opening clause of the charterparty. Under it the vessel is to receive on board 'a full and complete cargo . . . of wheat in bulk . . . and/or barley in bulk and/or flour in sacks'. There are then added the words in typescript 'as below', and this is a qualification which both affects what has gone before and conditions the meaning of what follows, namely, the charterers' undertaking to ship their cargo. The words 'as below' can only refer to the options which are also added in typescript at the foot of the clause, an option to load up to 'one-third cargo of barley in bulk', subject to an increased rate of freight, and an option to load 'up to one-third cargo of flour in bags', also at an increased freight rate. There is no option relating to wheat: wheat is the one commodity not subject to option.

It is said for the shipowners that there is no special significance in the use of the word option in this clause. Charterers who have stipulated for and undertaken to provide mixed or alternative cargoes have an option anyway, since it is they who retain to the end the right of selecting what cargo they are actually to provide; and it is argued that the total effect of the clause is, just as in the *Brightman* case, to leave the charterers under a primary obligation to put on board at the due date a full cargo made up in one or other of the permitted ways.

I do not think that that is the right construction. I cannot agree that, just because even without mentioning an option the charterers would have had a right of choice, the word 'option', when it is expressly mentioned, means no more than this. Wheat, it is to be noted, though linked indifferently with barley and flour as one of the possible cargoes, is, unlike them, not described as the subject of an option. This supports the view that wheat is to be the basic cargo, displaced only if and as the charterers so decide; just as the rate of freight for wheat is to be the basic rate of which other rates are expressed as a variation. Indeed, if the barley and flour options are not intended to be true options in the sense that only the positive exercise of the holder's choice can ever give him any responsibility to load or the shipowners any right to call for those commodities as part of a cargo, I cannot see how the parties could have expressed the option provisions in the way that they did. For, if the language is understood as the shipowners argue that it should be, the phrases introduced by the words 'charterer has the option' convey nothing more than a restriction on the right of selection among the commodities previously mentioned by tying the range of selection down to the permitted proportions; and what is clearly introduced as a right beneficial to the charterers would amount merely to a limitation on their existing power of selection. Moreover, even a short delay in the shipping of the cargo they wanted would turn their right of choice into a burden to ship a cargo they might never require. I cannot think that this was the bargain of the parties.

This first clause is not the only place in which the charterparty speaks of options. There are, for instance, clause 10 and clause 17. In both cases it appears that the option given is intended to confer on the holder an unfettered right to take advantage of the choice if, and only if, it suits him to do so. It is pointed out by the shipowners that if the options mentioned in clause 1 were to be regarded as rights of this kind it would be natural to expect that conditions would be attached to them stipulating in what form and at what time an effective exercise of them was to be made. It is just because a right of selecting among alternative cargoes is not regarded as an option in the true sense that formal notice is not usually required to indicate its exercise, and the shipper is looked upon as at liberty to change his intentions up to the very point of shipment. In my opinion, however, there is a danger of arguing in a circle on this issue. If the charterers are indeed the holders of unfettered options in respect of barley and flour, there is no difficulty in supposing that the law would imply whatever conditions might be commercially reasonable to give effect to such a relationship. For instance, I have no doubt that in any particular case it could decide whether the permissible time for exercising the option had been exhausted, or whether a notification of intention to exercise it had become irrevocable so as to fix the terms of the charterparty cargo. There is no inherent reason why in commercial dealings a formal notice of the option's exercise, which I should expect to be roughly coincident with the vessel's notice of readiness, should be treated as revocable. It would depend on the facts of the case. But these incidents can be worked out in practice once the principle itself is established: I think that it would put the matter the wrong way round to let the principle be determined by the supposed incidents or the lack of them.

### Notes

1. Although the evidence was not conclusive, it seems unlikely that the charterers would have been able to load *any* wheat: the vessels in question were tramp ships, i.e., operating wherever there was cargo to be carried, not liners (sailing on scheduled routes) and the loading of part cargoes of wheat was restricted to liners. Since the charterparty called for at least one-third of the cargo to be wheat, the charterers could still not load a full and complete cargo.
2. The case is considered further in Chapter 9, on the meaning of 'weather working days' in the clause defining laytime.

### Question

If the interpretation in *Reardon Smith Line Ltd* v *Ministry of Agriculture, Fisheries and Food* is correct, what is left of the obligation to load 'a full and complete cargo' in the case of alternative cargo options?

### C: Dangerous cargo

Almost any cargo is dangerous unless handled properly. We are not concerned here with the detailed provisions relating to the carriage of particular hazardous substances, but with the wider issue of the extent of the shipper's liability if the cargo shipped causes damage to the vessel or to other cargo. It is now established that the shipper is strictly liable for the consequences of shipping dangerous goods, except in so far as the shipowner takes the risk of any dangers inherent in the carriage of cargo of the contract description.

### *Effort Shipping Co. Ltd v Linden Management SA*
### *(The Giannis NK)*
### [1998] 1 Lloyd's Rep 337 (HL)

The facts are stated in Chapter 7, above, in relation to Art. IV, r. 6 of the Hague Rules.

LORD LLOYD OF BERWICK: Since the shippers are in my view liable in full for the consequences of shipping the infested ground-nuts by virtue of art. IV, r. 6, the last question [i.e., that of the shipper's liability at common law] does not arise. But the question was fully argued, and although your Lordships are always reluctant to decide a point on which their views will be obiter, nevertheless it seems appropriate to make an exception in this case.

The point at issue arises because of a difference of opinion in *Brass* v *Maitland* (1856) 6 E & B 470. The facts in that case were that the plaintiffs were owners of a general ship. The defendants shipped a consignment of chloride of lime, better known as bleaching powder, on board the plaintiffs' vessel. Chloride of lime is a corrosive substance liable to damage other cargo if it escapes. The plaintiff shipowners were unaware of the dangerous nature of the cargo. They claimed damages from the defendants on two counts. The third plea by way of defence was that the defendants had bought the goods from a third party already packed, and that they had no knowledge, or means of knowledge, that the packing was insufficient, and that they were not guilty of negligence. It was held by the majority that the third plea was bad in law. Lord Campbell CJ said, at p. 481:

> Where the owners of a general ship undertake that they will receive goods and safely carry them and deliver them at the destined port, I am of the opinion that the shippers undertake that they will not deliver, to be carried in the voyage, packages of goods of a dangerous nature, which those employed on behalf of the shipowner may not on inspection be reasonably expected to know to be of a dangerous nature, without expressly giving notice that they are of a dangerous nature.

On the question whether absence of knowledge or means of knowledge on the part of the shippers is a good defence, Lord Campbell said, at p. 486:

> The defendants, and not the plaintiffs, must suffer, if from the ignorance of the defendants a notice was not given to the plaintiffs, which the plaintiffs were entitled to receive, and from the want of this notice a loss has arisen which must fall either on the plaintiffs or on the defendants. I therefore hold the third plea to be bad.

Mr Justice Crompton took a different view. He would have held that knowledge on the part of the shipper is an essential ingredient of liability. At p. 492 he said:

> I entertain great doubt whether either the duty or the warranty extends beyond the cases where the shipper has knowledge, or means of knowledge, of the dangerous nature of the goods when shipped, or where he has been guilty of some negligence, as shipper, as by shipping without communicating danger which he had the means of knowing and ought to have communicated.

A little later he said, at p. 493:

> ... where no negligence is alleged, or where the plea negatives any alleged negligence, I doubt extremely where any right of action can exist.

Mr Johnson relies heavily on the dissenting judgment of Mr Justice Crompton and the commentary in the 13th ed. (1892) of *Abbott on Shipping*, a work of great authority, where it is said that the powerful reason urged by Mr Justice Crompton rendered the decision, to say the least, doubtful. In the 14th ed. (1901) it is said, at p. 647 that Mr Justice Crompton's views are more in accordance with later authorities.

But when one looks at the later authorities, and in particular at *Bamfield* v *Goole and Sheffield Transport Co. Ltd* [1901] 2 KB 94 and *Great Northern Railway Co.* v *LEP Transport and Depository Ltd* [1922] 2 KB 742 it is the majority view which has found favour. It is suggested by Mr Johnson that *Bamfield* v *Goole* and the *Great Northern Railway* cases can be explained on the ground that the plaintiffs in those cases were common carriers. That may or may not be a relevant distinction. What matters is that in both cases the Court regarded itself as being bound by the majority decision in *Brass* v *Maitland* (1856) 6 E & B 470 which was *not* a case of a common carrier.

Mr Johnson advanced a number of more wide ranging arguments, that to hold the shippers strictly liable for shipping dangerous goods would be impracticable and unreasonable, and create an anomalous imbalance between the rights and liabilities of shippers and carriers. But equally strong arguments of a general nature can be advanced on the other side.

The dispute between the shippers and the carriers on this point is a dispute which has been rumbling on for well over a century. It is time for your Lordships to make a decision one way or the other. In the end that decision depends mainly on whether the majority decision in *Brass* v *Maitland*, which has stood for 140 years, should now be overruled. I am of the opinion that it should not. I agree with the majority in that case and would hold that the liability of a shipper for shipping dangerous goods at common law, when it arises, does not depend on his knowledge or means of knowledge that the goods are dangerous.

An incidental advantage of that conclusion is that the liability of the shipper will be the same whether it arises by virtue of an implied term at common law, or under art. IV, r. 6 of the Hague Rules.

The problems of the inherent risks of carriage of the cargo in question were considered in relation to coal — the carriage of which was said to have become something of a lost art — in *The Athanasia Cominos* [1990] 1 Lloyd's Rep 277, at p. 282 (per Mustill J, as he then was: the case was decided in 1979, though not reported until 1990) and more generally in the next case.

### *General Feeds Inc. v Burnham Shipping Corporation (The Amphion)*
[1991] 2 Lloyd's Rep 101 (QBD)

The *Amphion* was chartered for a cargo of 'anti-oxidant treated bagged fishmeal' from Peru to China. Bagged fishmeal is listed in the IMO's code for carriage of dangerous goods (IMDG): unless it is properly treated, a build-up of heat occurs with a risk of spontaneous combustion. When the cargo was being discharged at Huangpu on the Pearl River, a smell of burning was reported from No. 3 hold. Although only a very small number of bags — perhaps no more than three — had not been effectively treated, the cost of dealing with the problem came to $55,000. The arbitrators (by a majority) decided in favour of the shipowners on their claim to recover this increased cost of discharge. The award was upheld.

EVANS J: The Dissenting Reasons end by referring to the importance of the questions raised by the arbitration, expressing the hope that they will be addressed. I will therefore add some general comments about what is, in my view, the correct legal approach to matters of this sort, and I am encouraged to do so by the extensive references, both by the majority and in the dissent, to the judgment in *The Athanasia Comninos*.

That case included claims against shippers as well as charterers, but there were allegations against both that the coal that was shipped did not comply with the straightforward description 'coal' (in fact, coal from a certain source, but the difference was immaterial (p. 284)). Mr Justice Mustill dealt with the issue of conformity with the contractual description at pp. 282–284. He concluded that 'a special danger which consists of a difference in degree, rather than in kind, from the known danger' could, as a matter of principle, be 'outside the area of risk which the shipowner has contracted to bear' (p. 283), meaning, in my respectful view, that such goods would be outside the contractual description. Thus, there arose the problem of identifying the boundary between the two categories, a distinction which cannot be made, he held, merely by drawing a line based on the proper method of carriage (p. 283). This was because, so far as coal was concerned, there was an area of risk which could not be avoided even by strict compliance with the requirements of safe carriage — the so-called gap between 'safe' (guaranteed) and 'acceptable' (normal) standards which was found to exist, and the risk of which the shipowner, by agreeing to carry goods of that description, assented to bear.

This implies, in my judgment, that 'coal' is a cargo which is generally known to involve carriage risks which the carrier cannot necessarily avoid by carrying it properly. A consequence of this view is that in such cases the carrier cannot prove that the goods were non-contractual merely by proving that despite proper standards of carriage an accident occurred: whether any particular cargo is within or without this category is a question of fact, to be answered by reference to the contractual description in each case.

In *The Athanasia Comninos* this test was applied to the description 'coal' by having regard to those factors—

... from which the extent of the carrier's assent to the running of the risk can be inferred [p. 284].

The extensive reference to implied terms and collateral warranties in the present case, and to questions of risk, has tended to make the enquiry more complicated and more extensive that it need have been. When there is, as here, a charterparty obligation to load cargo of a certain description, then the cargo in fact shipped either complies with that description, or it does not. If cargo answering that description carries with it some risk for the shipowners, then by agreeing to carry it the shipowner has accepted that risk. If it does not, then the shipowner can prove prima facie that the charterer shipped a non-conform and therefore non-contractual cargo, by proving that an accident occurred despite strict compliance with the standards of proper carriage. This prima facie proof may of course be displaced by further evidence, but the issue remains the same: did the cargo shipped answer the contractual description, or not?

If a cargo of that description is not known to present any danger, if carried properly, then in the absence of further circumstances the shipowner cannot be said to have accepted any such risk. That is the corollary of finding that the charterer shipped a non-contractual cargo, and was in breach of contract. It seems to me, therefore, that ultimately the question is one of contractual description, and therefore of breach, and not of 'risk' except that (1) whether or not either party can be said to have assented to a known risk will understandably be relevant in deciding whether the contractual description has been complied with, or not; and (2) where the risk ultimately lies is a consequence rather than a pre-condition of the question whether the charterers were in breach.

In summary, therefore—

(a)   Where there is a contractual description of the cargo required to be loaded, it is a question of fact whether the goods in fact shipped complied with that description, or not.

(b)   If there is a known risk of danger to the ship, which cannot be altogether avoided by strict compliance with the rules of safe carriage, then by agreeing to carry goods of that description the shipowner may be held to have accepted that risk for himself.

(c)   Proof that the rules of safe carriage were complied with will establish prima facie that the cargo did not comply with the contractual description, unless the shipowner accepted some residual risk for himself, as in (b).

(d)   The acceptance of risk, however, is only one factor to be considered when deciding whether the goods on shipment complied with the charterparty description, or not.

(e)   In cases like the present, which are governed by the issue as to the contractual description of the goods, further questions as to implied terms and collateral warranties do not, without more, arise.

*The present case*

In my judgment, therefore, the arbitrators correctly asked themselves what risks were implicit in the agreement to load and to carry 'anti-oxidant treated fishmeal'. The majority rightly concluded, in the light of the findings, that the shipowners, although they may have accepted the residual risk of overheating occurring even in a treated cargo, properly handled, did not accept the risk from 'improperly treated fishmeal' which arose here. It followed that the cargo shipped did not comply with the charterparty description and the charterers were in breach. The majority's references to an absolute warranty of safety, and to the alleged collateral warranty, were not necessary for their decision on this issue, but despite those references their finding is, in my judgment, clear. Their finding as to owners' non-acceptance of risk has to be read as equivalent to a finding that the charterers were in breach, i.e., that the cargo was non-conform.

*Note*

In *Chandris v Isbrandtsen-Moller Co. Inc.* [1951] 1 KB 240, the facts of which are stated in Chapter 9, Devlin J had to consider whether turpentine was a prohibited cargo within the meaning of a charterparty for a cargo of 'lawful general merchandise, excluding acids, explosives, arms, ammunition or other dangerous cargo'. On the question of construction *ejusdem generis*, Devlin J said:

A rule of construction cannot be more than a guide to enable the court to arrive at the true meaning of the parties. The ejusdem generis rule means that there is implied into the language which the parties have used words of restriction which are not there. It cannot be right to approach a document with the presumption that there should be such an implication. To apply the rule automatically in that way would be to make it the master and not the servant of the purpose for which it was designed — namely, to ascertain the meaning of the parties from the words they have used. The first approach will often plainly show that the words are used far more widely than the parties could have intended; as, for example, 'all other perils' in the policy which formed the subject of the well-known decision of *Thames and Mersey Marine Insurance Co. Ltd* v *Hamilton, Fraser & Co.* (1887) 12 App Cas 484. The so-called rule is, in short, really only a recognition of the fact that parties with their minds concerned with the particular objects about which they are contracting are apt to use words, phrases or clauses which, taken literally, are wider than they intend. Under the description of ejusdem generis the principle is applied to words only. But it is not different from the principle which restricts the meaning of clauses if literally they are inconsistent with the main object of the contract, as in *Glynn* v *Margetson & Co.* [1893] AC 351....

I cannot think that Lord Macnaghten in his rather cryptic observation in *Steamship Knutsford Ltd* v *Tillmanns & Co.* [1908] AC 406, 409 or Hamilton J in *Thorman* v *Dowgate Steamship Co. Ltd* [1910] 1 KB 410, were intending to say that the rule should be applied more stringently in the case of commercial documents than in the case of settlements. If that is what these two great lawyers had in mind it would be impossible for me to differ from them. But I find that hard to credit. Legal draftsmen are all familiar with the existence of the rule, and familiar too with the proper signals to hoist if they do not want it to apply. Phrases such as 'whether or not similar to the foregoing' and 'without prejudice to the generality of the foregoing' are often employed in legal draftsmanship; and if the draftsman has read the report of *Larsen* v *Sylvester & Co.* [1908] AC 295, he will know that the addition of 'whatsoever' generally serves the same purpose. Commercial draftsmen are not usually taught these rules.

Moreover, the main argument of construction which justifies the application of the rule does not apply in commercial documents. It is that if the general words have an unrestricted meaning the enumerated items are surplusage. The presumption against surplusage is of little value in ascertaining the intention of the parties to commercial documents, as many great commercial judges have recognised. In *Burrell & Sons* v *F. Green & Co.* [1914] 1 KB 293, 303, Bailhache J said that he was unimpressed by the argument of redundancy 'because charterparties often contain many redundant words'.... Scott LJ in *Beaumont-Thomas* v *Blue Star Line Ltd* (1939) 55 TLR 850, 852, referred to the same habit, but less kindly, as 'the common and pernicious practice of cramming a contract with particular illustrations of some general stipulation, which in a legal sense are wholly unnecessary, and just because they are unnecessary often afford a pretext for limiting general words in a way that was never intended'.

Draftsmen of charterparties — whether of the printed form or of the typewritten clause, but perhaps especially of the latter — are probably not consciously familiar even with the idea of ejusdem generis. The charterparty in the present case refers, for example, to 'a full and complete cargo of wheat and/or maize and/or other lawful merchandise'. Nobody has ever, I think, suggested that by such a charterparty the merchandise has to be similar to wheat or maize; although the first question which would occur to a lawyer would be to ask himself why the parties bothered to refer to wheat or maize if they meant that the cargo might be anything from chalk to cheese, including turpentine.

I apply the principle laid down in *Anderson* v *Anderson* [1895] 1 QB 749 and so inquire whether there is anything in the text of this charterparty or in the circumstances in which it was made which would lead me to suppose that the parties intended 'other dangerous cargo' to have some limited meaning. I can find no such indication. It seems to me that the only reason why the owner is objecting to acids, explosives, arms or ammunition is because they are dangerous; and that being so he may be presumed to have the same objection to all other dangerous cargo. On this ground, therefore, I think that Mr Hodgson's contention fails.

This makes it unnecessary for me to consider the other point regarding the ejusdem generis rule. But since it was fully argued, and is a point much in dispute, I may permit myself to express shortly my view of it. If the ejusdem generis principle is a rule of automatic application, it becomes of the first importance to determine exactly what the rule is. If it is merely, as I think, an aid to ascertaining the intention of the parties, no point of controversy need arise at all. If there is something to show that the literal meaning of the words is too wide, then they will be given such other meaning as seems best to consort with the intention of the parties. In some cases it may be that they will seem to indicate a genus; in others that they perform the simpler office of expanding the meaning of each enumerated item. If a genus cannot be found, doubtless that is one factor indicating that the parties did not intend to restrict the meaning of the words. But I do not take it to be universally true that whenever a genus cannot be found the words must have been intended to have their literal meaning, whatever other indications there may be to the contrary. I see no reason why, if it accords with the apparent intention of the parties, the words should not be treated, as suggested by Lord Macnaghten in *Thames and Mersey Marine Insurance Co. Ltd* v *Hamilton, Fraser & Co.* 12 App Cas 501, as being 'inserted in order to prevent disputes founded on nice distinctions' and 'to cover in terms whatever may be within the spirit of the cases previously enumerated'.

## SECTION 4: THE CARRYING VOYAGE

The shipowner must carry the goods to the contractual destination. If the port of discharge has not been specified, but is to be nominated by the charterer from a range, the charterer is bound to nominate a safe port: this principle applies equally to time charters and is considered in Chapter 10, as is the effect of the charterer's giving non-contractual orders. The only aspect to be considered here is the effect of the so-called 'near clause', which permits the shipowner to discharge the cargo at a place other than the named port if the vessel cannot safely discharge at that port and the actual place of discharge is 'so near thereto as she may safely get and lie always afloat'.

### *The Athamas (Owners)* v *Dig Vijay Cement Co. Ltd*
[1963] 1 Lloyd's Rep 287 (CA)

SELLERS LJ: ... The question for decision is whether the claimants' vessel, the *Athamas*, fulfilled the obligations of the charterparty dated Dec. 24, 1958, into which the owners had entered with the charterers for the carriage of cement in bags from Port Sika in India to two ports, Saigon and Pnom-Penh, in the South China Sea when, in the circumstances which arose, she discharged the whole cargo at Saigon. The claim is for demurrage while completing the delivery of the cargo at that port.

The clause in the charterparty on which the claimants have relied is:

> ... and being so loaded the vessel shall proceed to one safe berth or place SAIGON, always afloat, where the vessel is to discharge part cargo, such quantity to be at the sole discretion of the Master, and to be sufficient to enable the vessel thereafter to proceed safely to, and to enter and discharge the balance of the cargo at one safe place, always afloat, PNOM-PENH, or so near thereto as she may safely get and lie always afloat and there deliver the cargo ...

The words in that clause vitally affecting this case, 'or so near thereto as she may safely get', go back possibly some 150 years to the days of sailing ships and have been in current use in relation to the carriage of goods by sea throughout the era of steamships and their modern successors.

The clause has been invoked by the claimants in these circumstances, briefly stated:

At Port Sika, the *Athamas* loaded 8,913 metric tons of cement in bags of which 2,100 metric tons were intended for Pnom-Penh, but the master, who was given by the charter-party the sole discretion as to how much cargo he should discharge at Saigon, subject to retaining enough to enable the vessel to proceed safely to Pnom-Penh, did not make a final decision on this matter at the port of loading. After the ship's arrival at Saigon on Mar. 12, 1959, the cargo originally intended for there, 6,813 metric tons, was discharged.

By Mar. 13, well before the *Athamas* was ready to leave the port, the pilotage authority for Pnom-Penh, where pilotage is compulsory, refused to take her up the River Mekong to that port. It was the low-water season, the pilotage authority insisted on a minimum speed of 10 knots, and in order to navigate the river the ship had to be so light that her propeller would be partly out of the water and in this trim such a speed could not be maintained. She seems to have been an unsuitable ship for that port at that season, but nothing now turns on that and it has been found that this requirement of a speed of 10 knots was unforeseen and could not reasonably have been anticipated. In those circumstances, the *Athamas* did not sail, and after due notice to the charterers she discharged the remainder of the cargo covered by Pnom-Penh bills of lading at Saigon. The discharge was completed on Apr. 14, 1959.

The geography of the area is to be seen on the chart and is conveniently summarised in the judgment as follows ([1962] 2 Lloyd's Rep., at p. 127):

> Saigon is in South Viet Nam; Pnom-Penh is in Cambodia. The Governments of South Viet Nam and Cambodia are wholly separate. Saigon lies about 40 miles up the Saigon River; and Pnom-Penh about 180 miles up the River Mekong. Both rivers discharge into the South China Sea. The mouth of the River Mekong which is nearest to the mouth of the Saigon River is about 28 miles distant, so that the steaming distance between Saigon and Pnom-Penh is about 250 miles. There are six bars between the mouth of the River Mekong and Pnom-Penh itself. The height of the water over the bars varies between the low water season (say January to April) and the high-water season (say mid-August to November) by over 3 ft. In both rivers and both ports pilotage is compulsory. The pilotage authorities are separate, although the head office of the Mekong pilotage authority is in Saigon. A vessel proceeding to Saigon picks up her pilot off Cap St Jacques, a promontory on her starboard side at the mouth of the Saigon River. If, on leaving Saigon, she wishes to go to Pnom-Penh, she picks up her Mekong pilot off the same Cap St Jacques, and then she must proceed to the entrance of Cua Tieu (one of the mouths of the River Mekong about 28 miles to the south-west).

The arbitrators made the following further findings:

(1)   For the *Athamas* to have proceeded farther than Cap St Jacques on a passage from Saigon to Pnom-Penh, in defiance of the refusal of a pilot, would have been illegal and would have involved actual and real danger to the ship.

(2)   The ship would have had to wait until mid-August before she could trim herself by the stern to submerge the propeller sufficiently to attain 10 knots and meet the requirements of the pilotage authority. (It was then March.)

(3)   There was nowhere on the route between Saigon and Pnom-Penh where the cargo intended for Pnom-Penh could have been discharged.

(4)   It was at no time suggested by anyone concerned that there was any third choice; discharge had to take place at Saigon or Pnom-Penh.

...

In the absence of authority which they thought precluded them, the arbitrators would have concluded that the owners had, in the unfortunate circumstances which arose, followed and complied with the rights and obligations the charterparty gave and imposed on them when they completed the discharge of the ship at Saigon.

...

The two cases which troubled and restrained the arbitrators from finding as they would have wished to find have been reviewed by Mr Justice McNair and by my brother, Lord Justice Pearson, and I do not re-state their detailed facts. The cases were aptly cited in relation to Lord Campbell CJ's much-quoted statement on the clause 'or so near thereunto as she might safely get' in *Schilizzi* v *Derry* (1855) 4 E & B 873, at p. 886:

> ... the meaning of the charterparty must be that the vessel is to get within the ambit of the port, though she may not reach the actual harbour.

The Court of Queen's Bench in *Metcalfe* v *Britannia Ironworks Company* (1876) QBD 613, accepted Lord Campbell CJ's view and that has formed the basis of the appellants' argument.

In both the cases, it is true, it was held that the obstruction which at the time prevented the vessel reaching her destination in the one case to load and in the other to discharge was of a temporary character and not of sufficient duration to bring the clause permitting an alternative place of discharge into operation. But those cases were decided on their own facts. In particular, in the Court of Appeal in *Metcalfe* v *Britannia Ironworks Company* (1877) 2 QBD 423, it was held that the obstruction of ice in the Sea of Azov between Kertch and the ship's destination, Taganrog, for the delivery of her cargo was only temporary and such as must be incident to every contract for a voyage to a frozen sea. They in no way bound the arbitrators to the extent they seem to have thought.

The principle in this matter, which has long been applied, was considered in the House of Lords in *Dahl* v *Nelson, Donkin, and Others* (1881) 6 App Cas 38, and what had been said by Lord Justice Brett in the Court below ((1879) 12 Ch D 568, at p. 593) was accepted. Lord Watson, at p. 59, said:

> ... I adopt the view of Lord Justice Brett that the shipowner must bring his ship to the primary destination named in the charterparty, 'unless he is prevented from getting his ship to that destination by some obstruction or disability of such a character that it cannot be overcome by the shipowner by any reasonable means, except within such a time as, having regard to the adventure of both the shipowner and the charterer, is, as a matter of business, wholly unreasonable.

The parties put before the arbitrators the facts affecting the adventure from their respective points of view and the arbitrators themselves would not be unmindful of the nature and extent of the business venture from both sides. On their findings, that it would be wholly unreasonable to expect the *Athamas* to wait from Mar. 21 to mid-August in order to proceed to Pnom-Penh to discharge the balance of the cargo and that what she did was, from a commercial point of view, reasonable, the arbitrators were free to hold — and on their findings should in law have held — that the shipowners had established their right to discharge as they did at Saigon. But, this is subject to the correctness of their first finding that Saigon was within the 'ambit' of Pnom-Penh or, more accurately put, I think, that in discharging the Pnom-Penh cargo at Saigon the *Athamas* was delivering the cargo as near to Pnom-Penh as she could safely get.

In the thorough and resourceful arguments of both learned Counsel we were referred, I think, to all the cases on the clause in question since 1855 and we were supplied by the appellants with an analysis of distances from the stipulated destination where it had been held that the ship had fulfilled the requirement of the charterparty in getting 'so near thereto as she may safely get' and these ranged from under half a mile to 30 miles. On the other hand, the contrary had been held in some four cases where the distances ranged from 95 miles to possibly 600 miles.

Mere mileage in itself cannot, I think, be the test. The parties to a charterparty could easily over the years, as could the particular parties to this charterparty, have put 'the nearest safe place not exceeding x miles' from the named destination. If, on the other hand, the substitute place is to be 'within a stone's throw' of the destination, it would generally give the clause no effect because obstructions both physical and legal are rarely so limited. Certainly physical bars, banks or shallows closely adjacent to a harbour are nowadays normally dealt with successfully by dredging or by maintaining a channel through them and any delay would be short or tidal or of a seasonal character which the parties to such a contract ought to have anticipated.

The clause serves to mitigate the rigidity of the bargain and by the concept of a secondary destination to permit the charterparty to be performed and to prevent it being frustrated with uncertain and perhaps harsh results for one party or the other.

The appellants' argument based on Lord Campbell CJ's 'ambit' gave the bar or bank closely adjacent to a harbour as the situation which the clause contemplated and the submission was that the clause was restricted to such circumstances or limited in some comparable way. The voyage to the named port had to be virtually completed.

... 'Ambit' is not, as far as I can discover, a word normally used, but for Lord Campbell CJ, in association with or as applicable to a port. Many ports, particularly the larger ones, have a port authority with a defined area of jurisdiction and so the port is strictly a limited and defined district. Such an area might well include more than 'the actual harbour', to use Lord Campbell CJ's words, and to apply the words 'at one safe place ... PNOM-PENH, or so near thereto as she may safely get' would appear to indicate a place outside the port area, not within it. The word 'ambit' does not seem to fit any commercial usage and is not a strict paraphrase of the clause. As Lord Blackburn said in *Dahl* v *Nelson, Donkin and Others* (1881) 6 App Cas 38, at p. 51:

... Whether the language which Lord Campbell uses is quite the most accurate to express his idea may be doubted ...

In so far as 'ambit' conveys the idea of a circuit, which at least one dictionary introduces, it may well have an adaptation, for the obligation to deliver at the nearest safe port may require an extension of the voyage north, south, east or west of a named port. It is fortuitous here that the journey was in fact shortened and that the nearest safe port was also the first port of delivery, Saigon.

Distance is relative. Ports on the South China Sea or outposts in a desert could be 'near' each other in the estimate of men, who might regard a similar distance along the English Channel or in an English county as remote, although places available for discharge along the English Channel ports would be restricted if a charterparty were in respect of one of the larger ships, and, too, the distance between Plymouth and Southampton might be regarded as relatively small if the voyage were from or to Australia. The requirement is not a near port and not the nearest port but the nearest safe port or place. Such a provision seems, of necessity, to involve consideration of a coast-line or length of river where safe facilities for loading or discharging could be found outside and away from the named port. If the River Mersey were closed, for sufficient duration, to a 10,000-ton freighter, no owner or charterer would contemplate that the River Dee or even, I think, the River Ribble would be available alternatives. The very size of the ship and her requirements might enlarge the area contemplated by the clause.

In approaching this question in the light of all the authorities and without reviewing them in all their particular facts, I would follow Mr Justice McNair's application of the views of Lord Blackburn and Lord Watson in *Dahl* v *Nelson*, *sup.*, supported as I think they are by the observations of Mr Justice Scrutton (as he then was) sitting in the Court of Appeal in 1914 in *The Fox* (1914) 83 LJ(P) 89, at p. 101.

. . .

The learned Judge is further supported, in my view, by Lord Justice Scrutton in *The Varing* [1931] P 79, in his summary (*ibid.*, at p. 87):

. . . After all, one goes back to *Dahl* v *Nelson*, *sup.*, and as I understand the decision of the House of Lords, it is this: when you are chartered to go to a discharging place and cannot get there, you are bound to wait a reasonable time before having recourse to the clause 'or as near thereto as she can safely get'. You cannot arrive and, when you find that you cannot get in on the exact day you desire, immediately go off to a place which you describe as 'as near thereto as she can safely get'. When a reasonable time has elapsed, and when there is no chance of your getting in to your discharging place within a reasonable time, the ship is at liberty to go to a reasonable discharging place — 'as near thereto as she can safely get' — and can call upon the consignee to take delivery at the substituted place. But the shipowner must make up his mind what he is going to do and give notice to the consignee, saying, 'I am going to such-and-such a place being the nearest discharging berth to which I can safely get, and you must take my cargo there'. Obviously, inasmuch as it involves the question whether the ship has waited a reasonable time, and whether a particular place is a reasonable place — 'as near thereto as she can safely get' — shipowners should always be slow before taking a decided course of that sort, and landing themselves with a lawsuit in which it will be uncertain what the result may be on the facts.

As Mr Justice McNair uses the word 'ambit' I would prefer slightly to adapt his words and say, just as Lord Blackburn and Lord Watson in *Dahl* v *Nelson*, *sup.*, that when considering the question whether an obstacle is temporary or permanent, import the element of reasonableness in relation to time, so in considering whether a substitute discharging place is within the phrase 'so near thereto as she may safely get' the Court or tribunal should apply the conception of reasonableness in relation to distance. The distance might be so great in relation to the contemplated length, duration and nature of the adventure that notwithstanding that it was the nearest safe port or place the substituted place of discharge could not be assumed to be within the contemplation of the parties as fair and reasonable men.

In the present case the arbitrators were clearly of the opinion that the *Athamas* could not get to Pnom-Penh within a reasonable time. This was based on the arbitrators' knowledge of the nature of the adventure and of all the factors involved, the period of time, the carrying and earning capacity of the ship and the expense of the delay to both the charterers who presumably wanted their cargo and the shipowners who would lose if their ship were idle. The arbitrators were further of opinion that Saigon, in those circumstances, was the appropriate substituted or alternative place of delivery under the charterparty.

I would agree with the learned Judge that the arbitrators by their findings and on an application of the true principles of law decided this issue in favour of the claimants.

The effect of the decision is that the discharge of the Pnom-Penh cargo at Saigon is a fulfilment of the voyage and of the charterparty obligations and that the demurrage claimed is therefore recoverable on the basis claimed, which, on account of the slower rate of discharge allowed for Pnom-Penh and the better facilities at Saigon, is in this respect not unfavourable to the charterers.

In this case, the shipowners get the full freight (paid in advance) for the full contemplated journey and the charterers had to incur heavy expense in lightering the cargo in question to Pnom-Penh. Lightering might have been necessary if delivery had been made at Pnom-Penh and the cost would have fallen on the charterers, but nevertheless there has been a heavy additional expense. I do not think it follows that where a clause such as this requires a substituted place of delivery the burden will always be on the charterers. In some circumstances the additional expense and delay might fall on the shipowners.

In my opinion, Mr Justice McNair answered 'Yes' correctly to Question (b), 'Whether the owners are entitled to demurrage other than that (if any) incurred at the port of loading', the only question posed for his consideration, and correctly remitted the award to the arbitrators. I would, therefore, dismiss the appeal.

*Question*
Would *Metcalfe* v *Britannia Ironworks Co.* (1877) 2 QBD 423 still be decided in the same way today?

## SECTION 5: THE DISCHARGING OPERATION

Delivery to the holder of the bill of lading provides the shipowner with a complete defence against claims by other parties to have an interest in the goods (*Glyn Mills Currie & Co.* v *The East and West India Dock Co.* (1882) 7 App Cas 591 (HL), see Chapter 6). Conversely, the shipowner who delivers the goods to anyone other than the holder of the bill of lading does so at his peril (*The Stettin* (1884) 14 PD 142 (PD); *Kuwait Petroleum Corporation* v *I & D Oil Carriers Ltd (The Houda)* [1994] 2 Lloyd's Rep 541 (CA), where the principle was applied to time charters: see further Chapter 10, below). Can this liability be avoided by an appropriately worded exception clause?

### *Sze Hai Tong Bank Ltd* v *Rambler Cycle Co. Ltd*
[1959] AC 576 (PC)

R shipped £3,000 worth of bicycle parts on Glen Line (G's) ship *Glengarry* to Singapore. The consignees were Southern Trading Co. When the goods arrived, G's agents delivered the goods to Southern without production of the bill of lading, in return for an indemnity given by SHT, Southern's bank. Southern failed to pay. R brought an action for damages against G, who brought in SHT as a third party. G did not appeal against the judgment in R's favour, but SHT did, arguing that G had a good defence in the 'cesser' clause in the bill of lading. The Judicial Committee of the Privy Council held that the clause did not protect them.

LORD DENNING: ... The shipping company's agents were quite frank about what they did. Their representative said in evidence:

In issuing delivery orders and in everything we do we act as agents for the Glen Line. It is an accepted fact that, in absence of bills of lading, goods are released on an indemnity. I agree we are supposed to deliver on the bill of lading being produced to us. I agree that, when we do not have the bill of lading produced, we cover ourselves by getting an indemnity. When it is suggested to me that we get these indemnities because we know we are doing what we should not do, I say that if no risk, we would not need indemnity. I agree we get indemnity because we are doing something we know we should not do, but it is common practice. It is an everyday occurrence. We rely on the bank's guarantee.

It is perfectly clear law that a shipowner who delivers without production of the bill of lading does so at his peril. The contract is to deliver, on production of the bill of lading, to the person entitled under the bill of lading. In this case it was 'unto order or his or their assigns', that is to say, to the order of the Rambler Cycle Company, if they had not assigned the bill of lading, or to their assigns, if they had. The shipping company did not deliver the goods to any such person. They are therefore liable for breach of contract unless there is some term in the bill of lading protecting them. And they delivered the goods, without production of the bill of lading, to a person who was not entitled to receive them. They are therefore liable in conversion unless likewise so protected.

In order to escape the consequences of the misdelivery, the appellants say that the shipping company is protected by clause 2 of the bill of lading, which says that: '. . . the responsibility of the carrier, whether as carrier or as custodian or bailee of the goods, shall be deemed to commence only when the goods are loaded on the ship and to cease absolutely after they are discharged therefrom'.

The exemption, on the face of it, could hardly be more comprehensive, and it is contended that it is wide enough to absolve the shipping company from responsibility for the act of which the Rambler Cycle Company complains, that is to say, the delivery of the goods to a person who, to their knowledge, was not entitled to receive them. If the exemption clause upon its true construction absolved the shipping company from an act such as that, it seems that by parity of reasoning they would have been absolved if they had given the goods away to some passer-by or had burnt them or thrown them into the sea. If it had been suggested to the parties that the condition exempted the shipping company in such a case, they would both have said: 'Of course not'. There is, therefore, an implied limitation on the clause, which cuts down the extreme width of it: and, as a matter of construction, their Lordships decline to attribute to it the unreasonable effect contended for.

But their Lordships go further. If such an extreme width were given to the exemption clause, it would run counter to the main object and intent of the contract. For the contract, as it seems to their Lordships, has, as one of its main objects, the proper delivery of the goods by the shipping company, 'unto order or his or their assigns', against production of the bill of lading. It would defeat this object entirely if the shipping company was at liberty, at its own will and pleasure, to deliver the goods to somebody else, to someone not entitled at all, without being liable for the consequences. The clause must therefore be limited and modified to the extent necessary to enable effect to be given to the main object and intent of the contract: see *Glynn* v *Margetson & Co.* [1893] AC 351, 357; 9 TLR 437, *G.H. Renton & Co. Ltd* v *Palmyra Trading Corporation of Panama* [1956] 1 QB 462, 501; [1956] 2 WLR 232; [1956] 1 All ER 209; [1957] AC 149, 164; [1957] 2 WLR 45; [1956] 3 All ER 957.

To what extent is it necessary to limit or modify the clause? It must at least be modified so as not to permit the shipping company deliberately to disregard its obligations as to delivery. For that is what has happened here. The shipping company's agents in Singapore acknowledged: 'We are doing something we know we should not do.' Yet they did it. And they did it as agents in such circumstances that their acts were the acts of the shipping company itself. They were so placed that their state of mind can properly be regarded as the state of mind of the shipping company itself. And they deliberately disregarded one of the prime obligations of the contract. No court can allow so fundamental a breach to pass unnoticed under the cloak of a general exemption clause: see *The Cap Palos* [1921] P 458, 471; 37 TLR 921.

The appellants placed much reliance, however, on a case which came before their Lordships' Board in 1909, *Chartered Bank of India, Australia and China v British India Steam Navigation Co. Ltd* [1909] AC 369; 25 TLR 480. There was there a clause which said that 'in all cases and under all circumstances the liability of the company shall absolutely cease when the goods are free of the ship's tackle'. The goods were discharged at Penang and placed in a shed on the jetty. Whilst there a servant of the lading agents fraudulently misappropriated them in collusion with the consignees. Their Lordships' Board held that the shipping company were protected by the clause from any liability.

Their Lordships are of opinion that that case is readily distinguishable from the present, as the courts below distinguished it, on the simple ground that the action of the fraudulent servant there could in no wise be imputed to the shipping company. His act was not its act. His state of mind was not its state of mind. It is true that, in the absence of an exemption clause, the shipping company might have been held liable for his fraud, see *United Africa Co. Ltd v Saka Owoade* [1955] AC 130; [1955] 2 WLR 13; [1957] 3 All ER 216. But that would have been solely a vicarious liability. Whereas in the present case the action of the shipping agents at Singapore can properly be treated as the action of the shipping company itself.

*Notes*

*1.* Lord Denning went on to draw an analogy with cases of fundamental breach. In so far as this was part of the reasons for the decision, it must now presumably be treated as unsound following *Photo Production Ltd v Securicor Transport Ltd* [1980] AC 827 (HL).

*2.* In *MB Pyramid Sound NV v Briese Schiffahrts GmbH (The Ines)* [1995] 2 Lloyd's Rep 144 (QBD), Clarke J applied *Sze Hai Tong Bank Ltd v Rambler Cycle Ltd* to a provision that 'the carrier has no responsibility whatsoever for the goods prior to the loading on and subsequent to the discharge from the ocean vessel' and held that the provision did not cover delivery without production of the bill of lading. Following comments in *Suisse Atlantique Société d'Armement Maritime SA v NV Rotterdamsche Kolen Centrale* [1967] 1 AC 361, 401, 434, he regarded the decision in *Sze Hai Tong Bank* as based on the principle of *Glynn v Margetson & Co* [1893] AC 351 (HL) and concluded that it was not limited to cases 'where there has been a deliberate and conscious decision of the shipowners or their agents to deliver goods without production of a bill of lading'.

*3.* In *Chartered Bank of India, Australia and China v British India Steam Navigation Co. Ltd* [1909] AC 369 (PC), the cargo was discharged into lighters on arrival at Penang. The lighters were sent to the ship by 'landing agents' whose function was to put the goods into jetty sheds and deliver them to the appropriate consignees on production of bills of lading endorsed by the ship's agents with a delivery order. The landing agents, or their servant, fraudulently released the goods to the consignees without production of the bill of lading.

The Privy Council regarded it as immaterial whether the landing agents were agents of the shipowners. The cesser clause ('the liability of the company shall absolutely cease when the goods are free of the ship's tackle, and thereupon the goods shall be at the risk for all purposes and in every respect of the shipper or consignee') was found to be 'perfectly clear' and without ambiguity. The matter was one about which the parties were 'perfectly free to make any stipulation they please'.

*Questions*
Which decision is preferable from a commercial point of view? Does the reasoning in the earlier decision no longer carry weight?

*Note*
The final problem to be considered is that of the legal principles to be applied where the cargo of two or more bill of lading holders has become mixed in such a way that the individual parcels can no longer be identified, e.g., by the obliteration of marks.

### *Spence* v *Union Marine Insurance Co. Ltd*
### (1868) LR 3 CP 427 (CP)

S insured 43 bales of cotton, shipped at Mobile for Liverpool, with UM. The vessel ran aground off Florida. Some of the total of 2,493 bales on board were lost or sold at Key West. The remainder were transhipped, but the marks of many bales had become obliterated and only two of S's 43 bales could be identified. S claimed a total loss of the 41 bales; UM offered to pay as an average loss only, i.e., 43/2493 of the cotton lost and the cotton which arrived but could not be identified. S argued that UM could not prove that any of S's 41 bales had arrived.

BOVILL CJ: It has been long settled in our law, that, where goods are mixed so as to become undistinguishable, by the wrongful act or default of one owner, he cannot recover, and will not be entitled to his proportion, or any part of the property, from the other owner: but no authority has been cited to shew that any such principle has ever been applied, nor indeed could it be applied, to the case of an accidental mixing of the goods of two owners; and there is no authority nor sound reason for saying that the goods of several persons which are accidentally mixed together thereby absolutely cease to be the property of their several owners, and become bona vacantia.

The goods being before they are mixed the separate property of the several owners, unless, which is absurd, they cease to be property by reason of the accidental mixture, when they would not so cease if the mixture were designed, must continue to be the property of the original owners; and, as there would be no means of distinguishing the goods of each, the several owners seem necessarily to become jointly interested, as tenants in common, in the bulk.

... [B]y the mixture of the bales, and their becoming undistinguishable by reason of the action of the sea, and without the fault of the respective owners, these parties became tenants in common of the cotton, in proportion to their respective interests. This result would follow only in those cases where, after the adoption of all reasonable means and exertions to identify or separate the goods, it was found impracticable to do so.

We cannot assume that the whole of the plaintiffs' forty-one bales were amongst those that were destroyed, any more than we can assume that they all formed part of the 1,645 which were brought home; and we see no means of determining the extent of the interest of the several owners, except by adopting a principle of proportion, and which would, we think, be equally applicable in determining the plaintiffs' portion of the 231 bales that were totally lost as of the 1,645 which arrived in this country, though without the marks.

. . .

Upon the main question, therefore, that was argued before us, we think that there was not an actual total loss of the plaintiffs' forty-one bales of cotton. We think also there was not a constructive total loss of those bales. We adopt the principle upon which the defendants have paid money into court; and our decision upon this question is in their favour.

*Note*

In *Frank Stewart Sandeman & Sons* v *Tyzack and Branfort Steamship Co. Ltd* [1913] AC 680 (HL), the appellants received only 494 of the 500 bales of jute covered by the bills of lading. In all there were 14 bales missing on outturn from the total of 28,002 stated to have been shipped; there were also 11 bales which could not be matched to any bill of lading. In the respondent shipowners' action for the balance of freight, the appellants counterclaimed for the value of the six missing bales. The respondents argued that the appellants were to be treated as owners in common of the 11 undelivered bales and their counter-claim reduced by the value of that share. The House of Lords rejected this argument. *Spence* v *Union Marine Insurance Co.* was distinguished: there the shipowner had delivered the whole cargo that he was bound to deliver (the remainder having been lost by a peril of the seas), but here the shipowner could not prove that any of the appellants' six bales was among those delivered and *the missing bales were not covered by any exception.*

### Indian Oil Corporation Ltd v Greenstone Shipping SA
### (The Ypatianna)
[1987] 2 Lloyd's Rep 286 (QBD)

A cargo of 69,276 tonnes of Soviet export blend crude oil was shipped at Novorossisk for carriage to India. At the time of loading the vessel already had more than 15,000 barrels of oil from previous voyages in her tanks which was then mixed with the Soviet oil. After discharge at Madras the vessel still had 9,545 barrels of pumpable oil on board. The cargo receivers claimed that this residue (worth $342,000), having been mixed with their cargo without their consent, had thereby become their property. The arbitrators rejected this claim and the receivers' appeal was dismissed. (In the arbitration the shipowners were the claimants and the receivers the respondents.)

STAUGHTON J: . . . Confusio is the Latin word for the mixing of goods belonging to two different owners, so that they cannot be separated. Where they can be separated it is commixtio (Buckland's *Text-Book of Roman Law* (3rd ed.) p. 208). The effect in English law was decided as long ago as 1594 in a case described as *Anon* Pop. 28 (or sometimes as *Stock* v *Stock*). There the decision of Chief Justice Popham and the Court of King's Bench was this:

> ... the plaintiff pretending title to certain hay which the defendant had standing in certain land, to be more sure to have the action pass for him, took other hay of his own (to wit, the plaintiff), and mixed it with the defendant's hay, after which the defendant took and carried away both the one and the other that was intermixed, upon which the action was brought, and by all the court surely the defendant shall not be guilty for any part of the hay, for by the intermixture (which was his own act), the defendant shall not be prejudiced as the case is, in taking the hay. And now the plaintiff cannot say which part of the hay is his because the one cannot be known from the other, and therefore the whole shall go to him who hath the property in it with which it is intermixed.

In the present case the claimants mixed crude oil loaded on their vessel at Novorossisk in the Soviet Union with crude oil which was their own property. At least for practical purposes the mixture could not be separated so it was a case of confusio. When the vessel came to discharge at Madras the respondents claimed delivery of the whole. Hence this dispute.

. . .

Four topics need further consideration. The first is the nature and quality of the crude oil on board before loading. To the extent that it comprised Iranian or Indonesian or other crude oils, I would infer that its specification was not exactly the same as that of Soviet export blend. But there is no finding that it was either better or worse. . . . It would have comprised on average no more than 3 per cent of the cargo discharged, so that a quality claim might well have been difficult to prove or trivial in amount. . . . I conclude that although the owners may possibly have wished to improve the quality of their crude oil by mixing it with the cargo loaded, there is no evidence that in fact they had that objective or that they achieved it. The inference which I think it fair to draw is that the crude oil loaded, and that already on board, were substantially of the same nature and quality.

The second topic is the conduct of the owners. The award finds that there was interconnection between the vessel's cargo, ballast and fuel oil systems which was a breach of the International Maritime Organisation and classification society rules. I am aware that a number of cases have recently occurred where there has been the transfer of cargo to a vessel's fuel tanks for use on the voyage, thus constituting theft as well as giving rise to danger of fire on board. So there is a hint here that these owners were going equipped for theft; but it is no more than a hint.

The awards finds that—

> During the voyage from Novorossisk to Madras there were many deliberate inter-tank transfers and there were also inter-tank leakages.

That too is a hint, but no more than a hint, of wrongdoing on the part of the owners. It is sometimes appropriate and necessary to make inter-tank transfers during a voyage, for example to correct the trim of a vessel as bunker fuel is consumed. I decline to infer that deliberate wrong doing on the part of the owners in that respect is proved. . . .

Thirdly, I must say something about a procedure called Load on Top. This has been devised in order to avoid pollution from tank washing and ballast water. After successively washing some tanks and ballasting others, the vessel ends up with all oil residues in one tank, no doubt intermingled in some degree with water. New cargo is then loaded on top in the slop tank, as well as in the other cargo spaces which are empty. The effect is described by the arbitrators as follows:

> The Load on Top procedure is widely used in the tanker business and had been for many years prior to the voyage in question. It is common usage or commonly understood in the bulk oil trade that charterers/receivers are entitled to all pumpable oil remaining in the vessel's cargo tanks after discharge when the conventional Load on Top procedure has been adopted. This may result in there being a delivery from the vessel of more oil than the bill of lading quantity loaded into the vessel although experience suggests that over delivery is not common. There is no common usage or common understanding as far as we are aware in respect of what is the practice in circumstances such as those now before us which were of an unusual nature.

The usual Load on Top procedure was not employed in this case. The existing residues were distributed among all or some of the vessel's cargo tanks as well as in the deep tanks, rather than in one cargo tank only. Although this point featured in the owners' skeleton argument, at the hearing it was not contended that the usage found in relation to the Load on Top procedure is directly applicable here. However, Mr Rokison for the receivers seeks to derive some support from that usage. If receivers are entitled to all pumpable oil when that procedure is adopted, he argues that a fortiori they should be entitled to pumpable residues when it is not. But the arbitrators' finding does not, in my judgment, form a sufficient foundation for any binding custom or practice when the pumpable oil exceeds the quantity loaded by a substantial amount. . . .

Fourthly, there is the question whether the cargo interests consented to the mixing of the crude oil loaded with that already on board. . . . It is essential to the receiver's argument that admixture took place without consent and that must mean, in my judgment, without consent of those who owned the oil at the time of loading, or of any agent acting on their behalf. It is for consideration whether the award should be remitted to the arbitrators for them to state:

. . . (3) whether in fact those who owned the oil at the time of loading or any agent acting on their behalf consented to the admixture.

The arbitrators may well be able to answer those questions sufficiently without difficulty; and if the answers are important that seems to me the best way to proceed. Perhaps there never was a snail in the ginger beer bottle. But for the present I assume that there was no relevant consent by anybody.

After dealing with the question of tolerances, and upholding the arbitrators' award that the shipped quantity would have diminished by 0.55 per cent because of water and sediment in the crude oil and vapour losses during loading and discharge, Staughton J turned to the admixture claim.

Mr Rokison's submission is as follows: Where B wrongfully mixes the goods of A with goods of his own, so that the original goods cannot be separated or identified, the whole of the mixture becomes the property of A. So it is a case of 'happy undeserving A', if not also of 'wretched meritorious B'.

Mr Pollock's submission is this: Where a wilful admixture occurs without consent, both parties have a joint interest in the whole and the innocent party is entitled to receive his full contribution from the mixture even if it has been diminished by subsequent accidental loss. Alternatively, he submits that the general rule is as above, but that the innocent party is entitled to the whole if (1) the admixture was deliberately brought about for the purpose of depriving the innocent party of his rights, or making them difficult of enforcement, and (2) it is impossible to tell with any certainty what the contributing proportions had been.

There are numerous and very distinguished authorities. But it is agreed on both sides that none of them is binding on me. In the circumstances, I do not see that I can refrain from citing all those which were put before me, even if the result is an inordinately long judgment for a case where the argument lasted rather less than two days.

Staughton J then reviewed the authorities, ranging from *Justinian's Institutes* to the American Law Institute's *Restatement of the Law of Restitution*, and including *Spence* v *Union Marine Insurance Co. Ltd* (1868) LR 3 CP 427, above, and the statement by Lord Moulton in *Frank Stewart Sandeman & Sons* v *Tyzack and Branfort Steamship Co. Ltd* [1913] AC 680, at p. 694 that 'the conclusions of the Courts in such cases, though influenced by certain fundamental principles, have been little more than instances of cutting the Gordian knot — reasonable adjustments of the rights of parties in cases where complete justice was impracticable of attainment', and Lord Moulton's 'doubt whether even the fundamental principles enunciated above would be strictly adhered to in extreme cases where they would lead to substantial injury', and concluded:

In the present case there is, as I have said, a hint that the owners were engaged in wrong doing, but on the award as a whole I do not conclude that they mixed the cargo with their own oil for some commercial motive. It would be a severe penalty to impose of them a fine $342,000 for their conduct (that being the difference between the receivers' larger claim of $388,000 and the award in respect of the shortage of some $46,000). The arbitrators who know a great deal about the business of carriage by sea, did not perceive justice in that; and neither do I. But in any event, the rule cannot, unless Lord Moulton's qualification represents the existing law, be altered to suit the circumstances of each particular case. It must be one rule for all cases. Those may vary between one where the shipowner deliberately mixes property with a view to stealing it, to another where he does so purely for convenience of carriage without any intention to harm anybody.

The other motive to be found in the cases is that of Chief Justice Coke—

... otherwise a man should be made to be a trespasser, *volens nolens*, by the taking of his goods again.

In theory there may still be cases where that reasoning is sound, for example, if a farmer wished to retake his hay from a heap where it had been wrongly mixed with that of somebody else. In practice, it is not likely to arise often and certainly not in the present case: the notion of the Indian receivers boarding the owners' vessel after the conclusion of discharge at Madras in order to retake their oil is implausible. I would not regard that argument as justification for a rule which may work substantial injustice.

In the days when corn and hay were to be found in heaps which could not be measured accurately, when such disputes were tried by jury and witnesses might be illiterate or ignorant, a rough and ready rule which Goff and Jones describe as punitive may have been the best that the law could find. But a primitive rule is no longer appropriate when modern and sophisticated methods of measurement are available. The measurement of cargoes of oil is, as I learnt in the *Amoco* case, conducted with care and precision. It will not, of course, achieve absolute accuracy. What method of measurement ever does? But for all practical purposes the quantity of the innocent party's goods which have gone into the mixture can often be ascertained with a sufficient degree of precision, as it can be in this case. Similarly, there are methods of sampling and analysis which should enable the quality of the innocent party's goods, and of the mixture, to be assessed. If doubt remains as to either quantity or quality, the principle of *Armory* v *Delamirie* (1722) 1 Stra 505 provides a solution.

Seeing that none of the authorities is binding on me, although many are certainly persuasive, I consider that I am free to apply the rule which justice requires. This is that, where B wrongfully mixes the goods of A with goods of his own, which are substantially of the same nature and quality, and they cannot in practice be separated, the mixture is held in common and A is entitled to receive out of it a quantity equal to that of his goods which went into the mixture, any doubt as to that quantity being resolved in favour of A. He is also entitled to claim damages from B in respect of any loss he may have suffered, in respect of quality or otherwise, by reason of the admixture.

Whether the same rule would apply when the goods of A and B are not substantially of the same nature and quality must be left to another case. It does not arise here. The claim based on a rule of law that the mixture becomes the property of the receivers fails.

*Note*

The principle of *Armory* v *Delamirie* (1722) 1 Stra 505 is that if the wrongdoer prevents the innocent party proving how much of his property has been taken, the wrongdoer is liable to the greatest extent that is possible in the circumstances.

# 9 LAYTIME AND DEMURRAGE

Every voyage charterparty must make provision for the time to be allowed to the charterer for performing the loading and discharging operations. This 'laytime' defines the period for which the charterer may detain the vessel without penalty, and is sometimes described as 'paid for in the freight'. If the laytime is exceeded — even for reasons beyond the charterer's control — the vessel is being detained in breach of contract and the charterer is in principle liable to pay damages for the detention. In practice, the charterparty will invariably limit the charterer's liability to the payment of demurrage, i.e., a specified (daily) amount during the period of detention, which will be less than the amount that would otherwise be recoverable as damages.

Laytime and demurrage clauses are thus in effect apportioning between the parties the risk and cost of unexpected delay at the loading and discharging stages. To a very large extent the parties must make their own rules, but the almost universal adoption of standard forms of charterparty means that certain standard formulae are in constant use and the courts put a high premium on achieving certainty in the meaning of these expressions. This tends to lead to narrow, conservative interpretations.

## SECTION 1: THE COMMENCEMENT OF LAYTIME

Unless the parties have agreed otherwise, laytime does not commence until the vessel has become an arrived ship, is (or will be) ready to load and has given notice of readiness.

### A: An arrived ship

The charterparty may specify the berth or dock to be reached, but commonly only the port is indicated. If the ship has to wait at the port for a berth to become free, so that loading or unloading may begin, is she an arrived ship? The Court of Appeal thought so in *Leonis Steamship Co. Ltd* v *Rank Ltd* [1908]

1 KB 499, but the House of Lords threw the law into confusion by holding, in *Sociedad Financiera de Bienes Raices SA* v *Agrimpex Hungarian Trading Co. for Agricultural Products (The Aello)* [1961] AC 135, that a vessel waiting at Buenos Aires 22 miles from the berth had not arrived. The House of Lords considered the matter again in 1973.

### E.L. Oldendorff & Co. GmbH v Tradax Export SA
### (The Johanna Oldendorff)
### [1974] AC 479 (HL)

LORD REID: My Lords, by a voyage charterparty of December 1, 1967, the appellants undertook that their ship the *Johanna Oldendorff* should load a bulk grain cargo in the United States and 'therewith proceed to London or Avonmouth or Glasgow or Belfast or Liverpool/Birkenhead (counting as one port) or Hull'. The charterer, the respondents duly gave instructions to proceed 'to the port of Liverpool/Birkenhead to discharge'. The charterers were informed that the vessel was due at Mersey Bar anchorage at 17.00 hours on January 2, 1968, but no berth was nominated by them. When she arrived she anchored there. The next day she proceeded to Prince's Pier landing stage, Liverpool, and cleared with the customs. She was then ordered by the port authority to leave and proceed to anchor at the bar light vessel. She did so arriving at that that anchorage at 14.40.

Meanwhile the owners gave to the charterers notice of readiness. This was received at 14.30 on January 3. The vessel lay at anchor at the bar from January 3 to 20 ready, so far as she was concerned, to discharge.

The question at issue is who is liable to pay for the delay. The owners claimed demurrage and the matter was submitted to arbitration in accordance with the charterparty. The decision was made by the umpire in the form of a special case dated April 21, 1970. He decided in favour of the owners and awarded them £7,800 with interest. The question of law stated is whether on the facts found the lay time for discharge started on January 4, or on January 20.

The argument before your Lordships turned on the time when the vessel became an arrived ship. The main contention for the owners is that she became an arrived ship when she anchored at the bar anchorage because that is within the port of Liverpool, it is the usual place where vessels lie awaiting a berth, and it was the place to which she had been ordered to go by the port authority. The reply of the charterers is that anchorage is at least 17 miles from the dock area, or commercial area of the port, that arrival at that anchorage is not arrival at the port of Liverpool/Birkenhead and that the ship did not arrive until she proceeded to her unloading berth in the Birkenhead docks.

If a berth is not available when a ship reaches her destination the ship must wait. Waiting costs money and for a very long time the question who is to pay has been a prolific source of litigation. The risk is foreseeable and no doubt in an ideal world the parties to every contract would settle the matter when they contracted. But experience shows that business is not done in that way. Parties are inclined to adopt well-tried forms leaving it to the court to determine their meanings. There appear to be three common forms of voyage charterparty where the destination is said to be a port or a dock or a berth. To say when a vessel arrives at a dock or a berth may be easy, but it is not easy when the destination is a port.

After examining the *Leonis* case and *The Aello* in detail, Lord Reid concluded:

... [I]n my judgment this is certainly a case in which this House ought to exercise its power to alter its previous decision.

But it was strenuously argued for the charterers that it is not possible to find any better or more practical test than that of Parker LJ. We cannot say that whenever a vessel anchors in the usual waiting area for a port she becomes an arrived ship because there are a great many ports where that area is well outside the port area. Glasgow and Hull are examples in this country and we were told of an American port where the usual waiting area is 50 miles from the loading area of the port. All are agreed that to be an arrived ship the vessel must have come to rest within the port.

Then it was argued that the limits of many ports are so indefinite that it would introduce confusion to hold that a ship is an arrived ship on anchoring at a usual waiting place within the port. But I find it difficult to believe that there would, except perhaps in rare cases, be any real difficulty in deciding whether at any particular port the usual waiting place was or was not within the port. The area within which a port authority exercises its various powers can hardly be difficult to ascertain. Some powers with regard to pilotage and other matters may extend far beyond the limits of the port. But those which regulate the movements and conduct of ships would seem to afford a good indication. And in many cases the limits of the port are defined by law. In the present case the umpire has found as a fact (paragraph 19) that the ship was 'at the bar anchorage, within the legal, administrative and fiscal areas of Liverpool/Birkenhead'.

On the whole matter I think that it ought to be made clear that the essential factor is that before a ship can be treated as an arrived ship she must be within the port and at the immediate and effective disposition of the charterer and that her geographical position is of secondary importance. But for practical purposes it is so much easier to establish that, if the ship is at a usual waiting place within the port, it can generally be presumed that she is there fully at the charterer's disposal.

I would therefore state what I would hope to be the true legal position in this way. Before a ship can be said to have arrived at a port she must, if she cannot proceed immediately to a berth, have reached a position within the port where she is at the immediate and effective disposition of the charterer. If she is at a place where waiting ships usually lie, she will be in such a position unless in some extraordinary circumstances proof of which would lie in the charterer. For as Donaldson J points out [1971] 2 Lloyd's Rep 96, 100:

> In this context a delay of two or three hours between the nomination of a berth and the ship reaching it is wholly immaterial because there will be at least this much notice before the berth becomes free.

If the ship is waiting at some other place in the port then it will be for the owner to prove that she is as fully at the disposition of the charterer as she would have been if in the vicinity of the berth for loading or discharge.

It follows that I would allow the appeal and answer the question of law set out in the stated case by holding that the lay time for discharge started at 08.00 on Thursday, January 4, 1968.

LORD DIPLOCK: In the case of two common types of voyage charters, berth charters and dock charters, principles had been formulated by the end of the 19th century as to how the loss occasioned by delay in loading or discharging was to be borne, when the delay was due to the place at which the vessel was obliged by the terms of the charterparty to load or discharge her cargo, being occupied by other shipping. Berth charters are those in which the place to which the vessel is to proceed and there load or discharge is a single berth, either named in the charterparty itself or nominated thereafter by the charterer in the exercise of an express power to do so. Dock charters are those in which the corresponding named or nominated place is a dock containing, it may be, several berths. So charterers and shipowners when fixing the freight under these types of charters knew where they stood as respects this risk. They knew when lay time would start to run.

But there is another common type of voyage charter, a port charter, in which the named or nominated place of loading or discharge is a port containing, it may be, several docks each with several berths. In the case of port charters the process of judicial decision as respects delay due to congestion at the port remained at the close of the century in the empirical stage. The decided cases spanned a period in which maritime commerce had been undergoing a transformation as sail gave way to steam, and it was not easy to identify a factor common to empirical solutions that had been applied to problems which had arisen in such widely differing circumstances. The decision of the Court of Appeal in *Leonis Steamship Co. Ltd v Rank Ltd* [1908] 1 KB 499, and particularly the judgment of Kennedy LJ, was regarded for 50 years thereafter as having identified this factor and settled the principle for port charters. For those 50 years, charterers, shipowners and shipbrokers entering into this type of charter thought that they knew where they stood; for what was understood to be the criterion laid down for determining when lay time started to run was one which was easy to apply to the particular circumstances of individual cases of delay due to congestion at loading or discharging ports.

However, all this was changed by the decision of the majority of this House in *The Aello* [1961] AC 135, a case of delay due to congestion at the port of Buenos Aires in circumstances which were very exceptional. All five members of this House purported to apply to these exceptional circumstances the criterion laid down in *Leonis v Rank*. But they differed as to the interpretation of the language used . . .

My Lords, the actual words used in the judgments of the two Lords Justices in *Leonis v Rank* must be read in the light of

(a)    the particular facts of that case to which their minds were primarily directed,

(b)    the previous decisions dating from as far back as the days of sailing ships which they cited and from which they were seeking to extract a consistent principle, and

(c)    the kind of ships, port facilities and methods of communication in general use in maritime commerce in 1905.

They had not and could not have had in mind the enormous changes that were to take place in these respects during the next 60 years. So in re-examining the correctness of the way in which the test as to when lay time started under a port charter was formulated by the majority of this House in *The Aello*, I would approach the problem afresh, not by a minute verbal analysis of the judgments in *Leonis v Rank*, but by a consideration of the essential characteristics of the contract embodied in a voyage charter — whether it be berth or dock or port charter.

The adventure contemplated by a voyage charter involves four successive stages. They are:

(1)    The loading voyage, viz. the voyage of the chartered vessel from wherever she is at the date of the charterparty to the place specified in it as the place of loading.

(2)    The loading operation, viz. the delivery of the cargo to the vessel at the place of loading and its stowage on board.

(3)    The carrying voyage, viz. the voyage of the vessel to the place specified in the charterparty as the place of delivery.

(4)    The discharging operation, viz. the delivery of the cargo from the vessel at the place specified in the charterparty as the place of discharge and its receipt there by the charterer or other consignee.

In all four of these stages acts of performance by the shipowner are called for; in the two voyage stages acts of performance by him alone. The actual words in the charterparty which impose on him the obligation to perform them do not differ significantly in any of the standard forms of voyage charterparty. They are short, simple and time-honoured. Omitting all that are not essential they are (in the Baltimore Form):

> ... the ... vessel ... shall proceed to '[the specified place of loading]' and there load ... '[the specified cargo]' ... and being so loaded shall therewith proceed to '[the specified place of discharge]' ... and deliver the same ...

Loading and discharging are joint operations. So the loading stage and the discharging stage call for acts of performance by the charterer as well. The essential words which impose upon the charterer the obligation to perform them are (in the Baltimore Form):

> Vessel to be loaded ... with customary ... despatch and if detained longer than '[the specified lay time]' ... Charterers to pay demurrage at '[the stipulated rate]' provided such detention shall occur by default of the charterers.... Cargo to be received at destination at '[the stipulated rate]' provided vessel can deliver at this rate, otherwise demurrage to be paid....

Charterparties originated at a period when contractual obligations were as a general rule treated as absolute. A party's obligation was to secure that anything that he warranted should be done, was done. If it was not, then, unless this was the result of some default of the other party, he was liable in damages, even though circumstances over which he himself had no control and could not even have foreseen made it impossible for it to be done. In the case of maritime carriage this rule was subject to the exception that performance was excused if it were prevented by Act of God or of the King's enemies or by inherent vice in the goods carried. At a very early date it became usual to incorporate in charterparties express exceptions for other maritime perils, and in modern charterparties these have been extended to strikes and other hindrances to performance which take place on land. But that the old rule still applies in the absence of an express exception in the charterparty is shown by the fact that when there is deviation from the chartered voyage the shipowner's liability for the safe delivery of the goods is absolute, save for the limited common law exceptions mentioned above.

The standard forms of charterparty do not usually include an exception clause for delay caused by the inability of the vessel to load or to discharge her cargo because of congestion at the place, whether berth or dock or port, specified in the charterparty as the place of loading or discharge. So any loss due to delay from this cause falls upon the party who is thereby prevented from doing timeously what, by the terms of the charterparty, he had undertaken the primary obligation to secure was done.

Herein lies the importance of the four stages into which the adventure is divided. Each must be completed before the next can begin. So until the vessel has reached the specified place of loading on the loading voyage or the specified place of discharge on the carrying voyage, the contractual obligation to bring the vessel there lies on the shipowner alone; and any loss occasioned by delay in doing so falls upon him.

This characteristic of the contract was sufficient to solve the problem in the case of berth charters. Where a single berth was specified in the charterparty as being the place of loading or of discharge, the loading voyage or the carrying voyage did not end until the vessel was at that very berth. Until then no obligation could lie upon the charterer to load the cargo, or to receive it, as the case might be. If the specified berth were occupied by other shipping, the vessel was still at the voyage stage while waiting in the vicinity of the berth until it became available, and time so spent was at the shipowner's expense.

But when the charterparty specifies as the place of loading or discharge some larger area of water, such as a dock or port, in which there was more than one berth, the solution to the problem of liability for delay caused by congestion at berths within that larger area calls for a closer analysis of the contract. Since the business purpose of the voyage stages is to bring the vessel to a berth at which the cargo can be loaded or discharged, the shipowner does not complete the loading or the carrying voyage until the vessel has come to a stop at a place within the larger area whence her proceeding further would serve no business purpose. If on her arrival within the dock or port there is a berth available at which the charterer is willing and able to load or discharge the cargo, the vessel must proceed straight there and her loading or carrying voyage will not be completed until she reaches it. But if no berth is available, the voyage stage ends when she is moored within the larger area at any convenient place from which she can get to a berth as soon as one is vacant. The subsequent delay while waiting for a berth does not fall within the voyage stage under a dock charter or port charter, but in the loading or discharging stage. In each of these two stages acts of performance are called for on the part of both shipowner and charterer — by the former on the vessel, by the latter on the shore. So the question becomes: on whom does the primary obligation lie at these two stages to secure that the cargo is loaded or discharged.

The answer reached was to treat the primary obligation as resting upon the charterer, since he was the party who played the major part in the loading and discharging stages. The loading operation cannot commence until the cargo is alongside the ship. It is the obligation of the charterer to bring it there. To do so calls for preparations to be made by him on shore before the ship's arrival, by arranging for transport of the cargo to the actual spot where it will be alongside the ship, for its storage there or at a readily accessible place to await the ship's arrival and for labour to be available to put it on board the ship. So, too, the discharging operation cannot commence until the charterer is ready to receive the cargo at the ship's side. To do so calls for preparations to be made by him on shore before the ship's arrival, by arranging for labour to be available to remove the cargo over the ship's side at the actual spot where she berths, and for the storage or onward transport of the cargo after it has been landed there. To enable the charterer to make these preparations it is necessary, in order to carry out the business purpose of the adventure with least delay, that the charterer should have the right to decide upon the actual berth within the larger area specified in the charter at which the cargo is to be loaded or discharged; for, in contrast to those of the charterer, the necessary preparations by the shipowner take place on board the ship. He must make her ready to receive or to discharge the cargo over the ship's side as soon (or what for practical business purposes may be so treated) as she reaches the actual berth within the larger area at which the charterer is ready to deliver or receive the cargo. But these are preparations which can be made once the vessel is moored in safety inside the larger area, whether already at berth or not and wherever within that larger area she is moored.

It was this practical consideration which led to its being well settled by the end of the 19th century that, under a dock charter or a port charter, the charterer had the right and corresponding duty to give to the shipowner directions as to the particular berth within the area of the named dock or the named port at which the cargo was to be loaded or discharged. As a corollary the obligation to secure that there was a berth available for loading or for discharge lay on the charterer. Once the vessel had arrived within the area of the named dock or port the obligation of the shipowner was to put the vessel at the disposal of the charterer in a state of readiness to load or discharge her cargo, and thereafter to comply with the directions of the charterer as to the particular berth at which the cargo was to be loaded or discharged. If the charterer failed to perform his obligation to secure a berth for the purpose of loading or discharging the vessel as soon as she had been put at his disposal by the shipowner he was responsible for loss occasioned to the shipowner by the delay; the loss being assessed at the agreed rate for demurrage specified in the charterparty.

It has long been the practice to incorporate in voyage charters express provision that lay time shall not start to run until some period (often the beginning of the next working period) after the shipowner has informed the charterer that the vessel is at his disposal by giving him written notice of readiness to load or readiness to discharge. This simplifies the calculation of demurrage but it does not detract from the underlying principle that once the loading or the carrying voyage has been completed and the vessel put at the disposal of the charterer in a state of readiness to load or to discharge, the charterer is liable in damages for any delay in completing the loading or discharging after the laytime has expired, except when the delay is due to some default of the shipowner.

My Lords, it was not difficult to apply this principle in cases of dock charters even in the days of sailing ships. A dock encloses a comparatively small area entered through a gate. There is no difficulty in saying whether a vessel has arrived in it. As soon as a berth is vacant in the dock a vessel already moored inside the dock can get there within an interval so short that for the practical business purpose of loading or discharging cargo it can be ignored. For such purposes she is as much at the disposal of the charterer when at her mooring as she would be if she were already at the actual berth at which the charterer will later make or accept delivery of the cargo, but is unable for the time being to do so.

The area of a port, however, may be much larger. It may sometimes be less easily determinable, because of absence of definition of its legal limits or variations between these and the limits within which the port authority in actual practice exercises control of the movement of shipping; but I do not believe that in practice it is difficult to discover whether a place where ships usually wait their turn for a berth is within the limits of a named port; or is outside those limits as is the case with Glasgow and with Hull. In the days of sailing ships, whose movements were dependent on favourable wind and weather, and even in the days of steamships before there was regular radio communication between ship and shore, a ship prevented by congestion in the port from reaching a berth on her arrival there might be compelled to moor at some place which, although it was within the limits of the port, was nevertheless one at which she could not fairly be regarded for business purposes as being already at the disposition of the charterer, because the interval which would elapse between the time when a berth did become actually available and the time when the vessel would be able to reach it in response to directions given by the charterer, might be so long that it would be of practical business significance.

...

My Lords, the application of the principle that under a port charter the vessel must be put at the disposal of the charterer before lay time for loading or discharge can start, calls for consideration of the particular circumstances of the adventure contemplated by the charterparty, and must take into account changes in the kinds of ships used in maritime commerce, in means of communication and in port facilities and the management of ports. If a port is congested so that on arrival within its limits the chartered vessel cannot proceed immediately to a berth to load or to discharge, it is of no business importance to the charterer where she waits within those limits, so long as it is a place (1) where she counts for turn if the port is one where vacant berths are allotted to waiting vessels in order of arrival; (2) where the charterer can communicate with her as soon as he knows when a berth will become available for the cargo to be loaded or discharged, and (3) from which the vessel can proceed to the available berth when she receives the charterer's communication, so as to arrive there as soon as the berth has become vacant or so shortly thereafter as not to be significant for practical purposes.

The waiting places within the limits of an extensive port which have these characteristics alter as ships become more manoeuvrable, faster or larger, and communications between ship and shore improve. It was an area of the port which embraced but did not extend beyond these places that Kennedy LJ in *Leonis v Rank* [1908] 1 KB 499, 521 called 'the commercial area of a port' which the parties to a port charter must be taken to have meant as the area in which the vessel must have arrived and come to a stop in order to complete its loading or carrying voyage. Whether these waiting places were also places at which other ships could be actually loaded or discharged, or usually were at other times, was irrelevant to the business purposes of the parties to the particular adventure if the chartered vessel itself could not.

Since it is to the interest of all concerned, of port authorities as well as charterers and shippers, that time should not be wasted by leaving berths vacant when they are available for loading or discharging cargo, the usual places for ships to wait their turn for a vacant berth are those which do possess the three characteristics that I have mentioned, if there are any such places within the limits of the port. In days of sailing ships close proximity to berths likely to become vacant may have been necessary in order that a place should possess those characteristics, but distance from the actual berth becomes of less importance as steam and diesel power replaces sail and instantaneous radio communication is available between ship and shore. In modern conditions it is possible for port authorities and charterers to know at least some hours in advance, when a berth presently occupied by a loading or discharging vessel will become vacant and available for use by the chartered vessel. Notice of similar length can be given by the charterer to the waiting vessel so as to enable her to reach the berth as soon as it becomes vacant, if she can make the journey from her waiting place to the berth within that time. And if she can she is as effectively at the disposal of the charterer for loading or discharging while at that waiting place as she would have been if waiting in the immediate vicinity of the berth.

My Lords, this no doubt is why the bar anchorage, which is within the legal limits of the Port of Liverpool and included in the area in which the port authority is entitled to control the movement of shipping, has become the usual place to which vessels are directed by the port authority to wait their turn for a berth. And the same must generally be true of usual waiting places within the limits of other ports where congestion is liable to occur. I would therefore accept as a convenient practical test as to whether a vessel has completed her loading voyage or her carrying voyage under a port charter so as to cast upon the charterer the responsibility for subsequent delay in finding a vacant berth at which her cargo can be loaded or discharged, the test as it is formulated by my noble and learned friend, Lord Reid, at the conclusion of his speech.

This practical test, which I will call the 'Reid test', is very different from the 'Parker test' as expounded in the passage in the judgment of Parker LJ in *The Aello* when it was in the Court of Appeal, that has been cited by my noble and learned friend, Lord Reid. The decision of this House in *The Aello* has generally been regarded as applying the Parker test and approving it as one of general application for determining when lay time can start to run under a port charter if, owing to congestion in the port, there is delay in loading or discharge. The reasoning by which I myself would support the Reid test leads ineluctably to the conclusion that the Parker test is wrong and irrelevant to the business purpose of the adventure. The subsequent efforts by the courts and arbitrators to apply it have only led to uncertainty in an important aspect of the law affecting those engaged in maritime trade. I therefore agree that your Lordships should now declare that the Parker test is wrong even though this may involve overruling the earlier decision of this House in *The Aello*. While it may be that the speeches of the majority of this House in *The Aello* are susceptible of a different interpretation from that which has hitherto been placed upon them, I do not propose myself to embark upon a verbal analysis of those speeches to see whether this is so or not. The resolution of the Lords of Appeal in Ordinary of 1966 *Practice Statement (Judicial Precedent)* [1966] 1 WLR 1234 asserts your Lordships' right to state the law as you believe it to be even though this does involve departing from a previous decision of this House. The instant appeal is one in which I am satisfied that this right ought to be exercised.

I would therefore allow this appeal and answer the question of law set out in the stated case by holding that lay time for discharge started at 08.00 hours on Thursday, January 4, 1968.

*Note*

In *The Johanna Oldendorff* the usual waiting place was within the port, but this is not always the case. Can the ship be an arrived ship while waiting at a place outside the port? The Court of Appeal thought so in the next case, but the House of Lords disagreed.

### *Federal Commerce and Navigation Co. Ltd* v *Tradax Export SA (The Maratha Envoy)*
### [1978] AC 1 (HL)

The *Maratha Envoy* carried a cargo of grain in bulk for 'one safe port German North Sea'. The charterers (T) eventually nominated Brake, one of the four ports on the River Weser. The only waiting area for large vessels for all Weser ports is the Weser Lightship, 25 miles out to sea from the river mouth and outside the area of the ports. The *Maratha Envoy* anchored at the Lightship on 7 December 1970, and took her turn for discharge at any of the Weser ports. On two occasions she proceeded upriver until off Brake and then returned to the Lightship. During the second such trip, on 12 December, notice of readiness was given, but she could not berth until 30 December. The shipowners (F) claimed demurrage on the basis that the *Maratha Envoy* became an arrived ship on 12 December: the Court of Appeal persuaded counsel to argue that she arrived when she first anchored at the Lightship and gave judgment on that basis. The House of Lords allowed the charterers' appeal.

LORD DIPLOCK: My Lords, the freight market for chartered vessels still remains a classic example of a free market. It is world-wide in coverage, highly competitive and sensitive to fluctuations in supply and demand. It is a market in which the individual charterers and shipowners are matched in bargaining power and are at liberty to enter into charterparties in whatever contractual terms they please.

In practice the contracts negotiated in this market by the parties or their brokers are based upon one or other of a number of printed forms of charterparties appropriate to the various kinds of use to which vessels are put. These forms incorporate numerous standard clauses to which additions, often in the form of other well-known standard clauses, and deletions are agreed in the course of the bargaining process in which agreement is also reached upon such basic terms as rate of freight, demurrage and dispatch money.

So far as the profitability of the transaction to each party is concerned, there is an inter-relationship between rates of freight, demurrage and dispatch money and clauses of the charterparty which deal with the allocation between the charterer and shipowner of those risks of delay in the prosecution of the adventure contemplated by the charterparty which, being beyond the control of either party, have been conveniently called 'misfortune risks' as distinguished from 'fault risks'. Among the most prevalent of misfortune risks is congestion at a loading or discharging port causing the vessel to wait idly until a berth falls vacant at which her cargo can be loaded or discharged. If it is to wait at the shipowner's expense he will endeavour to secure that the risk is covered in the freight rate that he charges. If it is to wait at the expense of the charterer and paid for as demurrage or by reduction in dispatch money he will expect this to be reflected in a lower freight rate charged.

No market such as a freight, insurance or commodity market, in which dealings involve the parties entering into legal relations of some complexity with one another, can operate efficiently without the use of standard forms of contract and standard clauses to be used in them. Apart from enabling negotiations to be conducted quickly, standard clauses serve two purposes. First, they enable those making use of the market to compare one offer with another to see which is the better; and this, as I have ponted out, involves considering not only the figures for freight, demurrage and dispatch money, but those clauses of the charterparty that deal with the allocation of misfortune risks between charterer and shipowner, particularly those risks which may result in delay. The second purpose served by standard clauses is that they become the subject of exegesis by the courts so that the way in which they will apply to the adventure contemplated by the charterparty will be understood in the same sense by both the parties when they are negotiating its terms and carrying them out.

It is no part of the function of a court of justice to dictate to charterers and shipowners the terms of the contracts into which they ought to enter on the freight market; but it is an important function of a court, and particularly of your Lordships' House, to provide them with legal certainty at the negotiation stage as to what it is that they are agreeing to. And if there is that certainty, then when occasion arises for a court to enforce the contract or to award damages for its breach, the fact that the members of the court themselves may think that one of the parties was unwise in agreeing to assume a particular misfortune risk or unlucky in its proving more expensive to him than he expected, has nothing to do with the merits of the case or with enabling justice to be done. The only merits of the case are that parties who have bargained on equal terms in a free market should stick to their agreements. Justice is done by seeing that they do so or compensating the party who has kept his promise for any loss he has sustained by the failure of the other party to keep his.

My Lords, in *E.L. Oldendorff & Co. GmbH* v *Tradax Export SA (The Johanna Oldendorff)* [1974] AC 479, the purpose of this House was to give legal certainty to the way in which the risk of delay from congestion at the discharging port was allocated between charterer and shipowner under a port charter which contained no special clause expressly dealing with this matter. The standard form of charterparty used in *The Johanna Oldendorff* was also that used in the instant case — the Baltimore berth grain charterparty — although in each case the destination of the carrying voyage was a port, not a berth. The allocation of this risk under this kind of charterparty depends upon when the vessel becomes an 'arrived ship' so as to enable laytime to start running and demurrage to become payable once laytime has expired. Legal certainty on this subject had been impaired by the earlier decision of this House in *Sociedad Financiera de Bienes Raices SA* v *Agrimpex Hungarian Trading Co. for Agricultural Products (The Aello)* [1961] AC 135, which had laid down a test ['the Parker test'] of what was an 'arrived ship' under a port charter. The Parker test had in the years that followed turned out in practice to be obscure and difficult to apply to the circumstances of individual cases. So *The Johanna Oldendorff* [1974] AC 479 was brought up to this House for the specific purpose of re-examining the Parker test with a view to replacing it by one which would provide greater legal certainty. In order to ensure that the matter should be fully considered this House refused to adopt the leap-frog procedure for which Donaldson J had given the necessary certificate. It required the ordinary course to be followed so that this House might have the benefit of the opinions of the members of the Court of Appeal as well. After a hearing extending over six days in the course of which the position of ports where the usual waiting place lies outside the limits of the port of discharge was fully considered and cases dealing with such ports were cited, this House substituted for the Parker test a test which I ventured to describe as the 'Reid test', which in its most summary form is stated by Lord Reid thus, at p. 535:

> Before a ship can be said to have arrived at a port she must, if she cannot proceed immediately to a berth, have reached a position within the port where she is at the immediate and effective disposition of the charterer.

My noble and learned friend, Viscount Dilhorne, stated specifically that for it to have 'arrived' the place where the vessel is waiting must be within the port. A vessel ordered to wait outside the port is not an arrived ship. In the course of my own speech I spoke throughout of a waiting place *within* the port and this qualification was a necessary consequence of the analysis of the four stages of the adventure contemplated by a charterparty which led to my acceptance of the Reid test as correct.

My Lords, I am not aware that in practice the Reid test has proved difficult of application because of any doubt as to whether the usual place where vessels wait their turn for a berth at a particular port lies within the limits of that port or not. Neither in *The Johanna Oldendorff* nor in the instant case were counsel able to provide your Lordships with an example from real life. There may be one but if such a port exists it would seem to be too little used to be likely to suffer from congestion. It would be doing a grave disservice to the shipping community if this House were to allow the legal certainty introduced by the Reid test to be undermined.

...

Lord Denning MR and Shaw LJ ... simply rejected as superfluous the requirement laid down in the Reid test, and supported by each of the other speeches in this House, that for a ship to be an arrived ship under a port charter the place where she is waiting for a berth must be within the limits of the port. They regarded the rationale of the test laid down in *The Johanna Oldendorff* [1974] AC 479 as based exclusively upon the vessel being 'as effectively at the disposal of the charterer for loading or discharging while at that waiting place as she would have been if waiting in the immediate vicinity of the berth' (p. 561) and they pointed out, quite correctly, that the ability of a vessel to satisfy this requirement does not depend upon whether the waiting place is just within or just outside the legal, fiscal, or administrative limits of the port.

My Lords, there would be much to be said for this approach if the chartering of ships had been a recent innovation instead of the charterparty being one of the earliest of commercial contracts. Its form and nearly all the phrases used in it have evolved over many years, in some cases running into centuries, in the course of which their meaning in the special context of this kind of contract has acquired legal certainty by judicial exegesis. So one starts not with a clean slate but with a palimpsest on which even some of the earliest writing may still show through. As I endeavoured to explain in *The Johanna Oldendorff* the basic nature of the adventure contemplated by a voyage charter has remained unchanged. Its four stages include two voyage stages which end either at a named port (port charter) or at a berth in a named port (berth charter); and while until *The Johanna Oldendorff* there may have been uncertainty under a port charter as to where within the named port a ship must be in order to complete the voyage stage, there was legal certainty that neither in port nor berth charter was the voyage stage brought to an end by the arrival of the ship at any waiting place short of the limits of the named port.

Where charterers and shipowners as part of their bargain have desired to alter the allocation of the risk of delay from congestion at the named port which would otherwise follow from the basic nature of their contract, they have not sought to do so by undermining whatever legal certainty had been attained as to when a voyage stage ends. Instead they have achieved the same result without altering the basic nature of the contract, by inserting additional clauses to provide that time should begin to run for the purposes of laytime or demurrage if, although the voyage stage is not yet ended, the ship is compelled to wait at some place outside the named port of destination until a berth falls vacant in that port. That is why resort is had by shipowners and charterers to the time lost clause and the standard clauses which deal specifically with individual ports where a usual waiting place for vessels waiting for a berth lies outside the limits of the port.

Charterparties are not notorious for stylistic elegance or easy intelligibility by those whose business does not lie in the freight market; but to those who operate in that market a considerable degree of certainty as to the meaning and application of standard forms and clauses has been achieved by costly litigation over the years. Your Lordships would be doing a disservice to the shipping community if, so shortly after the Reid test had been laid down by this House in *The Johanna Oldendorff*, you did not reaffirm it and insist upon its application to the instant case.

. . .

Lord Denning MR and Shaw LJ were also prepared to *imply* a term in the charterparty to the same effect as the express Weser Lightship clause. Charterparties entered into upon printed forms and adapted to the particular adventure contemplated by the parties often contain surplus phrases or clauses: but there is no ground for implying terms which are not necessary to give business efficacy to the contract and which if incorporated in the contract would alter the allocation of a misfortune risk in a way for which the parties themselves had not provided when negotiating rates of freight and provisions for demurrage. I agree with Stephenson LJ that in the instant case there is no ground for any such implication.

Finally, there is the voyage of convenience down to Brake and back. This was rejected by Donaldson J and, in the Court of Appeal, by Stephenson and Shaw LJJ. Lord Denning MR characterised it as commercial nonsense but said [1977] QB 324, 341 that he 'would swallow the commercial nonsense if it was the only way in which justice could be done'.

My Lords, I cannot swallow it, nor for reasons I have stated earlier, do I see that justice would be done if I could bring myself to do so.

I would allow the appeal and restore the judgment of Donaldson J.

*Note*

The Weser Lightship clause provides 'If vessel is ordered to anchor at Weser Lightship by port authorities, since a vacant berth is not available, she may tender notice of readiness upon arriving at anchorage near Weser Lightship, as if she would have arrived at her final loading/discharging port. Steaming time for shifting from Weser Lightship to final discharging port, however, not to count.' Similar clauses are also used in relation to Avonmouth, Glasgow and Hull, where the waiting area is also outside the port.

### Question

Why did they not include a Weser Lightship clause in the charterparty in *The Maratha Envoy*?

### B: *Express provisions shifting waiting risk to charterer*

Besides the clauses for particular ports just mentioned there are several ways in which the charterparty may seek to put the risk of losing time waiting for a berth on the charterer.

### (a)    *Wibon clauses*

This is a provision ('*Whether in berth or not*') by which time runs under a berth or dock charterparty from arrival at the port. It clearly covers delay caused by congestion, i.e., where the berths are occupied by other ships: in the next case the shipowners argued that it applied whatever the reason for the ship not being able to berth.

### *Seacrystal Shipping Ltd v Bulk Transport Group Shipping Co. Ltd (The Kyzikos)*
### [1989] 1 Lloyd's Rep 1

LORD BRANDON OF OAKBROOK: My Lords, by a voyage charterparty dated Oct. 26, 1984 the appellants ('the charterers') chartered the m.v. *Kyzikos* ('the ship') owned by the respondents ('the owners') to carry a cargo of steel and/or steel products from Italy to the US Gulf. The ship was ordered to discharge at the port of Houston. She arrived and anchored there at 06 45 on Dec. 17, 1984, and at some time before 12 00 the master gave notice of readiness to discharge. Then, and all material times afterwards, the berth at which the ship was to discharge was available for her use. She was, however, prevented from proceeding to it immediately because of fog, which resulted in the pilot station being closed. Because of this the ship did not arrive in her berth until 14 50 on Dec. 20, 1984.

A dispute arose between the owners and the charterers with regard to the liability of the latter for demurrage at the port of discharge. The owners claimed US$30,435.72 in respect of a balance of demurrage remaining unpaid. The charterers denied liability. The essential question governing the validity of the claim was whether time for discharging counted during the period for which the ship was prevented from proceeding to her berth by reason of fog.

The dispute was referred, pursuant to a London arbitration clause contained in the charterparty, to Mr Bruce Harris as sole arbitrator. By a reasoned award dated Nov. 26, 1985 the arbitrator decided that the owners' claim succeeded in full. The charterers obtained leave to appeal against the award and on July 30, 1986 Mr Justice Webster in the Commercial Court gave a reserved judgment [1987] 1 Lloyd's Rep 48 allowing the appeal and dismissing the owners' claim. The owners appealed with the leave of Mr

Justice Webster to the Court of Appeal (Lloyd and Glidewell LJJ and Sir John Megaw). That Court on May 15, 1987 gave reserved judgments [1987] 2 Lloyd's Rep 122; [1987] 1 WLR 1565 allowing the appeal and restoring the arbitrator's award. The charterers now bring this further appeal against the decision of the Court of Appeal by leave of your Lordship's House.

The charterparty was on the Gencon (Box Layout) 1974 printed form, which contains 21 boxes, each with a printed heading, followed by a series of printed clauses. Typed entries were made in the boxes and typed amendments were made to a number of the printed clauses. A large number of typed clauses were also added by the way of rider. The material provisions, with typed entries and typed amendments indicated by underlining, were as follows:

> Box 11. Discharging port or place (Cl. 1)
> 1/2 safe always afloat, always accessible berth(s) each port — 1/2 safe port(s) US Gulf excluded Brownsville and no port North of Baton Rouge.
> Box 15. Laytime allowed for loading (Cl. 5)
> See clause 17
> Box 17. Laytime allowed for discharging (Cl. 6)
> See clause 17
> Box 18. Demurrage rate (load and disch) (Cl. 7)
> USD. 3.000, — per day/pro rata . . .
> Clause 1. . . . the vessel shall proceed to the discharging port or place stated in Box 11 or so near thereto as she may safely get . . .
> Clause 5. Loading . . . Time to commence at 2 p.m. if notice of readiness to load is given before noon and at 8 a.m. next working day if notice given during office hours after noon . . . Time lost in waiting for berth to count as loading time. Time to count as per Clause 5 Wipon/Wibon/Wifpon/Wccon and master to have the right to tender notice of readiness by cable, both in the loading and discharging port(s).
> Clause 6. Discharging Cargo to be received by merchants . . . and to be discharged in the number of running working days stated in Box 17. Time to commence at 2 p.m. if notice of readiness to discharge is given before noon and 8 a.m. next working day if notice given during office hours after noon. Time lost in waiting for berth to count as discharging time.
> Clause 7. Demurrage at the rate stated in Box 18 per day or pro rata for any part of a day to be allowed at ports of loading and discharging.
> Clause 17: . . . The cargo to be loaded . . . and discharged . . . within 18 total weather working days of 24 consecutive hours, Saturdays/Sundays/Holidays excepted, unless used, in which case actual time used to count half . . .

The acronyms used in cl. 5 have the following meanings: 'wipon' — whether in port or not, 'wibon' — whether in berth or not, 'wifpon' — whether in free pratique or not, 'wccon' — whether cleared customs or not. Clause 17 is one of the additional typed clauses referred to in box 21.

Much of the argument in this case has revolved round the difference between two kinds of voyage charterparty, a port charterparty on the one hand and a berth charterparty on the other. The characteristics of a port charterparty are these. First, the contractual destination of the chartered ship is a named port. Secondly, the ship, in order to qualify as having arrived at the port, and therefore entitled to give notice of readiness to discharge, must satisfy two conditions. The first condition is that, if she cannot immediately proceed to a berth, she has reached a position within the port where waiting ships usually lie. The second condition is that she is at the immediate and effective disposition of the charterers. By contrast, the characteristics of a berth charterparty are these. First, the contractual destination of the chartered ship is a berth designated by the charterers within a named port. Secondly, the ship, in order to qualify as an arrived ship, and therefore entitled to give notice of readiness to discharge, must (unless the charterparty otherwise provides) have reached the berth and be ready to begin discharging.

... Lord Justice Lloyd who gave the leading judgment in the Court of Appeal considered [1987] 2 Lloyd's Rep 122 at p. 123; [1987] 1 WLR 1565 at p. 1568, that the appeal raised, potentially at least, two questions in relation to a voyage charterparty which it was common ground was a berth and not a port charterparty, but contained a provision allowing the ship to give notice of readiness to discharge 'whether in berth or not'. The first question was whether the ship could give a valid notice of readiness to discharge when, on her arrival in the discharging port, a berth for her was vacant but she was prevented from reaching it by bad weather, in this case fog. The second question, which only arose if the first question was answered in the affirmative, was whether the ship, in the situation postulated, could properly be said to be at the 'immediate and effective disposition of the charterers' as would be required to enable her to qualify as an arrived ship under a port charterparty.

I agree with this analysis and it will be convenient to examine what Lord Justice Lloyd described as the first question first. In doing so I shall treat the amendment to cl. 5 of the charterparty (loading) as applying also to cl. 6 (discharging). That it was intended to do so appears to have been accepted by both sides at the arbitration. The contrary view seems to have been raised, to some extent at least, before Mr Justice Webster who was not impressed by it. Before the Court of Appeal and in your Lordships' House the matter was common ground.

Two views have been advanced, at each stage of the proceedings, with regard to the meaning of the phrase 'whether in berth or not' in a berth charterparty. One view, put forward by the charterers and accepted by Mr Justice Webster is that the phrase covers cases where the reason for the ship not being in berth is that no berth is available, but does not cover cases where a berth is available and the only reason why the ship cannot proceed to it is that she is prevented by bad weather such as fog. The other view, put forward by the owners and accepted by the arbitrator and the Court of Appeal, is that the phrase covers cases where a ship is unable to proceed to a berth either because none is available or because, although a berth is available, the ship is prevented by bad weather such as fog from proceeding to it.

...

So far as the authorities are concerned, they present two aspects, one positive and the other negative. The positive aspect of the authorities is that in them the phrase 'whether in berth or not', when used in a berth charterparty, has uniformly over a long period been interpreted as relating to the availability or unavailability of a berth. In other words the phrase has been interpreted as dealing with the problem of congestion in ports, and putting on the charterers rather than the owners the risk of delay caused by such congestion.

...

In *Federal Commerce and Navigation Co. Ltd* v *Tradax Export SA (The Maratha Envoy)* [1977] 2 Lloyd's Rep 301; [1978] AC 1 the House was concerned with questions arising out of a charterparty which, although a port charterparty and not a berth charterparty, contained in relation to the commencement of laytime the phrase 'whether in berth or not'. Referring to the phrase Lord Diplock, after pointing out that it was surplusage in a port charterparty, went on to say, at pp. 308 and 14:

The effect of this well-known phrase in berth charters has been settled for more than half a century. Under it time starts to run when the vessel is waiting within the named port of destination for a berth there to become vacant.

The negative aspect of the authorities is this. The phrase 'whether in berth or not' has been used in berth charterparties at least since 1909, the date of the charterparty in *Northfield Steamship Co.* v *Compagnie L'Union des Gaz* [1912] 1 KB 434. Yet Counsel for the owners was unable to point to any reported case in which it had ever been contended that the phrase covered a case where a berth was available for a ship but she was prevented by bad weather from proceeding to it.

The inference which it seems to me to be right to draw from these two aspects of the authorities, the one positive and the other negative, is that the phrase 'whether in berth or not' has over a very long period been treated as shorthand for what, if set out in longhand, would be 'whether in berth (a berth being available) or not in berth (a berth not being available)'. There is, in my view, nothing unusual in commercial men, knowing the purpose for which a phrase is inserted into a particular type of contract, expressing their common intention in a shorthand form in this way.

I turn to the context in which the acronym 'wibon' is to be found in the charterparty here concerned. There are, as it seems to me, two significant features about that context. The first significant feature is this. The general procedure followed when making typed amendments to the printed clauses of the charterparty was to delete so much of the printed clauses as was modified or replaced by such amendments. Examples of this general procedure can be seen in cl. 2 (partial deletion of lines 25 and 26), cl. 4 (total deletion) and cl. 5 (deletion of the first two paragraphs, lines 57–67). The final line of cl. 5 as printed (line 72) reads: 'Time lost in waiting for berth to count as loading time'. The final line of cl. 6 as printed (line 80) reads: 'Time lost in waiting for berth to count as discharging time'. If the introduction of the acronym 'wibon' in the typed addition to cll. 5 and 6 had been intended to modify or replace the two final lines of those clauses to which I have referred, one would have expected those lines to have been similarly deleted. In fact, however, those lines were not deleted but left in place. The inference to be drawn is that the introduction of the acronym 'wibon' by the typed addition to cll. 5 and 6 was not intended to modify or replace the final lines of those two clauses as printed.

The second significant feature about the context in which the acronym 'wibon' is to be found is the close association in the typed addition to cll. 5 and 6 of that acronym with the three other acronyms, 'wibon', 'wifpon' and 'wccon'. These last three acronyms all seem to me to be directed at the problem of congestion in the loading or discharging port, rather than the problem of delay to the ship due to bad weather. It is therefore reasonable to infer that the acronym 'wibon' is similarly directed.

These two features of the context in which the acronym 'wibon' is to be found appear to me to support the view which I expressed earlier about the inference to be drawn from the authorities as to the effect in a berth charterparty of the phrase 'whether in berth or not'.

With great respect to Lord Justice Lloyd and the other members of the Court of Appeal who agreed with him, I do not consider, in the light of the examination which I have made of the three main matters relied on by Lord Justice Lloyd, that they provide the support for his conclusion which he regarded them as providing. On the contrary, I am of opinion, having regard to the authorities to which I referred earlier and the context in which the acronym 'wibon' is to be found in the charterparty here concerned, that the phrase 'whether in berth or not' should be interpreted as applying only to cases where a berth is not available and not also to cases where a berth is available but is unreachable by reason of bad weather.

Since I have reached that conclusion on what Lord Justice Lloyd described as the first question, what he described as the second question does not arise.

*Note and Questions*
1.   How would you answer the 'second' question, viz. whether the vessel was at the immediate and effective disposition of the charterers while waiting?
2.   As Lord Diplock pointed out in *The Maratha Envoy*, a wibon clause is meaningless in a port charterparty; from what point of the voyage could a shipowner rely on a wipon clause?
3.   A common clause having a similar effect to a wibon clause is a provision that the charterer is to nominate a berth 'reachable on arrival'. Once the vessel has reached a point, whether technically an arrived ship or not, at which she will be held up unless an immediately available berth is nominated, the risk of delay falls on the charterer: *cf. Nereide SpA Navigazione* v *Bulk Oil International (The Laura Prima)* [1982] 1 Lloyd's Rep 1 (HL). Suppose that the nominated berth is free, but the ship is prevented by fog from moving into it: is it 'reachable'? (*Cf. The Fjordaas* [1988] 1 Lloyd's Rep 336; *The Sea Queen* [1988] 1 Lloyd's Rep 500.)

(b)   *'Time lost in waiting' clauses*

### Aldebaran Compania Maritima SA v Aussenhandel AG Zürich (The Darrah)
### [1977] AC 157 (HL)

LORD DIPLOCK: Some standard forms of voyage charterparty that are in general use contain express provision as to what are to be the financial consequences to the parties if time which would otherwise be available for loading or discharging cargo is wasted because the vessel has been compelled to wait for a berth to become available. Others contain no such express provision but leave the question upon whom the loss shall fall to depend upon whether the charterparty is a berth charter or a port (or dock) charter: see *E.L. Oldendorff & Co. GmbH* v *Tradax Export SA (The Johanna Oldendorff)* [1974] AC 479. The instant appeal, which comes before your Lordships upon an award of an arbitrator stated in the form of a special case, is about the method of working out the financial consequences of delay due to this cause which is called for under the current Gencon charter by the provisions in the printed clauses relating to loading and discharging: 'Time lost in waiting for berth to count as loading time' or 'as discharging time', or, the variant that was used in the charterparty in the instant case, 'as laytime'.

The 'time lost' clauses in the Gencon form of voyage charter, though not the particular variant used in the instant case, have been the subject of consideration in a number of authorities over the last 20 years. The development of the case law on this topic, in my view, provides an object lesson in the misuse of judicial precedent in decisions upon special cases stated by commercial arbitrators.

The instant case arises out of a claim for demurrage against the charterers of the *Darrah*. She was chartered to carry a cargo of cement from Novorossisk to Tripoli in Libya. The charterparty was a port charter based upon the printed Gencon form, but with a considerable number of substitute and additional clauses. These, however, do not affect the answer to the only question raised in the stated case. It is enough for present purposes to say that the cargo was to be discharged at the rate of 625 metric tons per weather working day of 24 consecutive hours, Fridays and holidays excepted; that time was to commence at 2 p.m. if notice of readiness to discharge was given before noon and at 8 a.m. the next working day if notice given during office hours after noon; that time from noon on Thursday or noon on the day before a legal holiday until 8 a.m. the next working day was not to count; and that demurrage at discharging port was payable at the rate of US$1,000 per day or pro rata for any part of a day.

The *Darrah* completed her carrying voyage upon reaching a usual waiting place within the limits of the port of Tripoli. Under the port charter she thereupon became an arrived ship: *The Johanna Oldendorff* [1974] AC 479. She gave notice of readiness to discharge at 2 p.m. on Tuesday, January 2, 1973. So laytime started to run at 8 a.m. on Wednesday, January 3. The vessel was compelled to wait her turn for an available discharging berth. She moved into this at 8 a.m. on the following Tuesday, January 9, and discharge began immediately. It was completed by 8 a.m. on Wednesday, January 24, with such dispatch that allowing for the intervention of Fridays and public holidays between January 2 and January 24, 1973, the laytime allowed under the charterparty to the charterers for the discharging operation was not exceeded.

Nevertheless, the shipowners claimed demurrage to the amount of about $10,000. The basis of this calculation was to treat as counting against laytime the whole of the six days that had elapsed while the *Darrah* was waiting for a berth, despite the fact that they included two non-working days, a Friday and a legal holiday, and the period from noon on the day before each. The effect of this was to treat the laytime as having expired and demurrage as having started to run before discharge had been completed on January 24, and to have run continuously thereafter on Fridays and legal holidays as well as weather working days until 8 a.m. on January 24.

My Lords, it would at first sight seem startling that notwithstanding that the charterer under a voyage charter had completed the discharging operation within the laytime permitted by the charterparty and paid for in the freight, the shipowner should be enriched by an amount equivalent to 10 days' demurrage merely because the absence of a vacant berth at which the vessel's cargo could be discharged had prevented the charterer from using some of the days that would have otherwise been available to him for that purpose, though he would have been under no contractual duty so to use them provided that he could complete the discharging operation within the permitted laytime.

Before turning to the cases which are relied upon by the appellant shipowners in support of their claim, I would approach the question of the construction of the simple words 'Time lost in waiting for berth to count as laytime' or 'as loading time' or 'as discharging time' by considering the nature of the contract in which those words are used. In *The Johanna Oldendorff* [1974] AC 479, 556, I sought to analyse the maritime adventure contemplated by a voyage charter in four stages (1) the loading voyage (2) the loading operation (3) the carrying voyage and (4) the discharging operation. In consideration of the stipulated freight the charterer under such a charterparty is entitled to require the vessel to be available for use in the loading and discharging operation for such length of time as may be specified in the contract or, if not expressly specified, for such time as is reasonably required to complete the operation. The time for loading or discharging that is so specified and paid for in the freight is known as laytime. Strictly speaking laytime does not start until the vessel has completed the preceding loading voyage or carrying voyage and has become an arrived ship. Once started it does not, however, run continuously; there are generally excluded from the reckoning of permitted laytime used up, Sundays (Fridays in Muslim countries) and legal holidays and days on which work is stopped because of weather.

Under a berth charter the vessel does not complete the loading or the carrying voyage until the vessel reaches the designated berth. So any time spent waiting for the berth to become available serves only to prolong the voyage stage and in the absence of express provision to the contrary any loss occasioned to the shipowner by reason of the delay falls on him alone. Under a port charter on the other hand the voyage stage is completed upon arrival of the vessel at a usual waiting place within the limits of the port. If because of congestion the charterer cannot designate a berth to which she can proceed immediately, laytime nevertheless starts to run against the charterer and if, as a consequence of her being compelled to wait until a berth becomes available, the charterer is unable to complete the loading or discharge within the stipulated laytime he must pay demurrage for any additional time used to complete it. In the case of a port charter it is only when the carrying vessel is compelled to wait her turn at a place outside the limits of the port that the time spent waiting for a berth would operate to prolong the voyage stage and to cast the loss occasioned by the delay upon the shoulders of the shipowner.

The commercial interest of the shipowner in a voyage charter is to make profitable use of his vessel. Unlike the charterer he is not primarily concerned with the choice of ports between which she is used to carry goods, though it may be to his interest that the loading port in any voyage charter is as near as possible to the discharging port in the immediately preceding charter, and that the discharging port in the new charter is not too remote from potential loading ports for subsequent charters. But his primary concern is that his vessel should earn the stipulated freight in as short a time as possible. To the charterer, on the other hand, the identity of the particular ports between which the cargo is to be carried is vital. So if he wants his cargo to be carried to or from ports where there is risk of delay in loading or unloading cargo owing to congestion, it makes good sense commercially that, irrespective of whether it be a berth charter or a port charter, the charterer should assume the financial burden of that risk and compensate the shipowner for the additional time that his vessel has had to be employed in the adventure in the event of delay resulting from this cause.

This, as it seems to me, is what the printed clauses in the Gencon form of voyage charter, viz. 'Time lost in waiting for berth to count as loading time' and 'Time lost in waiting for berth to count as discharging time', were meant to do. The printed form is adapted to be used for port charters as well as berth charters but it was drafted before the decision of this House in *The Johanna Oldendorff* [1974] AC 479 had reduced considerably the number of occasions on which a vessel under a port charter would not already be an arrived ship in respect of which laytime would be running while she was waiting for a berth even if the clauses were omitted.

My Lords, although in the course of the argument in this House there has been much discussion about the difference between calendar time, elapsed time, conventional time, chronological time, time reckoned in broken periods, I for my part do not find the question of construction of these clauses, with or without the substitution of 'laytime' for 'loading time' or for 'discharging time', susceptible of much elaboration. 'Time lost in waiting for berth' in the context of the adventure contemplated by a voyage charter, as it seems to me, must mean the period during which the vessel would have been in berth and at the disposition of the charterer for carrying out the loading or discharging operation, if she had not been prevented by congestion at the port from reaching a berth at which the operation could be carried out. The clauses go on to say that that period is to count as loading time or as discharging time, as the case may be. That means that for the purposes of those provisions of the charterparty which deal with the time allowed to load or to discharge the vessel and how it is to be paid for (i.e., laytime and demurrage) the vessel is to be treated as if during that period she were in fact in berth and at the disposition of the charterer for carrying out the loading or discharging operation. So whatever portions of the waiting period would have been taken into account in calculating the permitted laytime used up if the vessel had in fact then been in berth and at the disposition of the charterer (e.g., weather working days) are to be treated as if they had been available for loading or discharging cargo, and whatever portions of the waiting period would not have been taken into account in that calculation (e.g., Sundays or Fridays and legal holidays and days on which working was prevented by inclement weather) are not to be treated as if they had been available for loading or discharging cargo.

In a berth charter the effect of the clauses is to put the shipowner in the same position financially as he would have been if, instead of being compelled to wait, his vessel had been able to go straight to her berth and the obligations of the charterer to carry out the loading or discharging operation had started then. In a port charter the clauses are superfluous so far as concerns time spent in waiting in turn within the limits of the port. This counts as laytime anyway; it is laytime. The clauses would however have the same effect as in a berth charter in respect of ports like Hull or Glasgow where the usual waiting place is outside the limits of the port.

How then has it come about that by judicial decision a meaning has been ascribed to those words which is not in harmony with the commercial purposes of a voyage charter and differs from that which I understand all your Lordships to think is their plain meaning? ... [A]s Roskill LJ has pointed out in a percipient introductory passage in his judgment in the instant case, one starts with an unconsidered reference by Singleton LJ in *The Radnor* [1956] 1 QB 333 to the 'time lost' clause as being 'independent' of a clause in the charterparty which, while it did contain the only stipulation as to laytime that was relevant to the question for decision in the case, viz. when laytime commenced, also contained other stipulations as to what was to be reckoned as included in permitted laytime, with which the Lord Justice was not concerned. What was intended as no more than a convenient way of stating that a provision which made notice of readiness a condition precedent to the commencement of laytime in a berth charter could have no application to the time lost clause, becomes elevated by the time *The Loucas N* [1971] 1 Lloyd's Rep 215 reached the Court of Appeal into a rule of law that 'time lost' clauses and 'laytime' clauses in a berth charter constitute two independent and unrelated codes for computing the amount of permitted laytime that has been used up.

...

In recommending your Lordships to overrule the construction of a standard clause in a much-used form of charterparty which has no doubt been accepted as correct by shipowners, charterers and maritime arbitrators for the last 10 years since the decision of McNair J in *The Vastric* [1966] 2 Lloyd's Rep 219 I am not unaware of the importance of not disturbing an accepted meaning of a clause commonly used in commercial contracts upon which the parties to such contracts have relied in regulating their business affairs. But this is a consideration which in my view carries little weight in the case of the 'time lost' clauses in the Gencon form of voyage charters. In the first place, the results of ascribing to the clauses the meaning accepted since 1966 do not make commercial sense; it gives to the shipowner the chance of receiving a bonus dependent upon whether (a) his ship is lucky enough to be kept waiting for a berth and (b) is so kept waiting during a period which includes time which would not have counted against permitted laytime if the ship had been in berth. In the second place, I do not think that the chance of obtaining such a bonus is likely to have influenced the freight or demurrage rates charged. In the third place, the effect of using the variant 'counted as laytime' in place of 'counted as loading time' and 'counted as discharging time', as has been done in the instant case, has never previously been the subject of judicial decision.

Shipowners and charterers would not go to the trouble of altering the printed words in the standard form of 'time lost' clause, unless they wished the clause to bear some other and more commercially sensible meaning than that which has been ascribed by judicial decision to the clause in its printed form. For my own part, as I have already said, I do not think that the alteration makes any difference to the meaning of the clauses, but I have little doubt that if you gave to the clause in the version which appears in the charter the effect which I have ascribed to it and to the printed clauses alike your Lordships would be carying out the intentions of the parties when they entered into the charter.

For these reasons I would dismiss the appeal.

*Question*

A charterparty provides 'Time lost in waiting for berth to count as used laytime'. The laytime allowed is '12 days Fridays and holidays excluded unless used'. The vessel has to wait for a berth for three days which fall in the Muslim Eid-al-Fitr holiday. How much laytime is left? (*Cf. Huyton SA* v *Inter Operators SA* (*The Stainless Emperor*) [1994] 1 Lloyd's Rep 298 (QBD).)

*C: Notice of readiness*

At common law reasonable notice of readiness was required at the loading port, but there was no requirement of notice at the port of discharge. At the present day the normal practice is to require notice to be given at both ports.

How much notice of readiness is to be given, and how and when it is to be given, are matters for the charterparty to determine. It is a clear legal requirement that the ship must be ready in fact to load or discharge when the notice is given, but it is commercially sensible for notice to be given in advance of the moment when loading or discharge could physically begin. The problem is to determine how much latitude to allow the shipowner, whose interest is obviously to give notice of readiness at the earliest possible moment and start laytime running.

### *Compania de Naviera Nedelka SA* v *Tradax Internacional SA*
### *(The Tres Flores)*
### [1974] 1 QB 264 (CA)

LORD DENNING MR: In October 1970 the *Tres Flores* was chartered for a voyage to go to Varna in Bulgaria, there load a cargo of maize in bulk and carry it to Famagusta in Cyprus. The charterparty was on the Synacomex form and dated in Paris, on October 27, 1970. The arbitration clause provided for disputes to be referred to arbitration in Paris, but subsequently the parties expressly agreed that the arbitration on this dispute should be held in London. Two commercial arbitrators in London, without legal assistance, agreed on their award, but they stated it in the form of a special case. Mocatta J [1972] 2 Lloyd's Rep 384 has upset their award. Now there is an appeal to this court. It is about the lay time at the loading port.

On November 22, 1970, the vessel arrived in the roads at the port of Varna. Once she was in the roads she had arrived within the terms of the charterparty. Clause 21 said:

At loading port, time to commence, whether vessel be in berth or not, whether in free pratique or not, whether in port or not, at 2 p.m. if written notice is given during usual office hours before noon and at 8 a.m. next working day if notice is given during usual office hours after noon. Master is allowed to give the notice of load readiness by telegram when ship is arrived on the road of loading port.

The vessel arrived at the port of Varna at 05.00 hours on Sunday, November 22, 1970: but no berth was available, so she anchored in the roads. At 10.00 hours on that Sunday morning, the master gave notice of readiness in these terms:

...I...master of M/S: *Tres Flores*, arrived on road of Varna today at 05.00, hereby declared that the above ship under my command is ready in all aspect to load a completely cargo of about 6,900 M/T mais in bulk, in accordance all terms, conditions and exceptions to the charterparty issued at Paris and dated October 27, 1970.

On Monday, November 23, 1970, the charterers had the cargo of maize, 6,500 tons, in the port of Varna ready for loading on the vessel. But the vessel could not be inspected at that time. She was in the roads. There was heavy weather, so that the inspectors of shipping at Varna could not get out to the vessel for some days. They did not get out to her until Friday, November 27. On that day they inspected her and gave their certificate:

... at the survey, made on November 27, 1970, of the hatches of M/V *Tres Flores*, arrived for loading of maize, it was found that there are pests in the hatches. It was ordered by the inspection to be done a fumigation before loading.

The fumigation took place not on that Friday. It was not done until the following Monday, November 30, 1970. It took four and a half hours. Then and then only did the charterers accept the notice of readiness. They accepted it on Tuesday, December 1. Even then there was no berth available for some days. The vessel berthed on December 7 and then loading commenced at 11.00 hours on that day. Loading was completed at 10.00 hours on December 13, 1970.

The charterparty [clause 6 as amended] contained this provision as to laytimes:

At both ends from Saturday noon or local equivalents or from 5 p.m. on days preceding holidays, until following working day at 8 a.m., time not to count even if used. Any time lost in fitting the shifting boards or other material not to count as laytime. Before tendering notice master has to take necessary measures for holds to be clean, dry, without smell and in every way suitable to receive grain to shippers/charterers' satisfaction.

The dispute is whether laytime commenced at the time for which the master gave his notice of readiness, that is, 14.00 hours on Monday, November 23, or only at the time when the vessel had been fumigated and was suitable to receive the cargo, that is, at 14.00 hours on Tuesday, December 1, 1970.

It seems to me that this dispute is really covered by the specific sentence in the charterparty which I have already read but which I will repeat now:

Before tendering notice master has to take necessary measures for holds to be clean, dry, without smell and in every way suitable to receive grain to shippers/charterers' satisfaction.

That lays down a condition precedent to the validity of a notice of readiness to load. That condition precedent was not fulfilled until the fumigation had been completed on November 30, and therefore the notice of readiness could not validly be given until that time.

That is sufficient for the decision of this case; but, as the contrary has been discussed before us, it may be desirable for the members of the court to give their views upon it.

One thing is clear. In order for a notice of readiness to be good, the vessel must be ready at the time that the notice is given, and not at a time in the future. Readiness is a preliminary existing fact which must exist before you can give a notice of readiness: see per Atkin LJ in *Aktiebolaget Nordiska Lloyd* v *J. Brownlie & Co. (Hull) Ltd* (1925) 30 Com Cas 307, 315.

The next question, when can a ship be said to be ready? Conversely, if some things are yet to be done, what are the things which make her unready to receive cargo?

The leading case is *Armement Adolf Deppe* v *John Robinson & Co. Ltd* [1917] 2 KB 204, where the hatch covers had not been removed at the time when the notice of readiness was given. It would be necessary for them to be removed before discharging could take place. The notice of readiness was held to be good. Then there is *Sociedad Financiera de Bienes Raices SA* v *Agrimpex Hungarian Trading Co. for Agricultural Products, The Aello* [1961] AC 135, where a police permit was necessary before a ship could be loaded. It was held that the absence of a police permit did not prevent the *Aello* from being 'ready to load' while at the anchorage: see per Lord Radcliffe at pp. 174–175. And finally *Shipping Developments Corporation* v *V/O Sojuzneftexport (The Delian Spirit)* [1972] 1 QB 103, where the vessel had not obtained free pratique and would need it before she could load. It was held that she was entitled to give notice of readiness.

In considering the cases, it seems to me that the submission which Mr MacCrindle put forward was correct. In order to be a good notice of readiness, the master must be in a position to say 'I am ready at the moment you want me, whenever that may be, and any necessary preliminaries on my part to the loading will not be such as to delay you.' Applying this test it is apparent that notice of readiness can be given even though there are some further preliminaries to be done, or routine matters to be carried on, or formalities observed. If those things are not such as to give any reason to suppose that they will cause any delay, and it is apparent that the ship will be ready when the appropriate time arrives, then notice of readiness can be given.

In the present case there were pests in the hold such as to make the ship unready to receive cargo. Fumigation was not a mere preliminary, nor a routine matter, nor a formality at all. It was an essential step which had to be taken before any cargo could be received at all. Until the vessel had been fumigated, notice of readiness could not be given. It has always been held that, for a notice of readiness to be given, the vessel must be completely ready in all her holds to receive the cargo at any moment when she is required to receive it. It was said by Lopes J in *Groves, Maclean and Co.* v *Volkart Brothers* (1884) 1 TLR 92, and accepted in *Noemijulia Steamship Co. Ltd* v *Minister of Food* [1951] 1 KB 223 by Devlin J, as a clear rule, at p. 227, and by Tucker LJ at p. 235. So on this ground also the condition of the holds meant that the notice of readiness could not be given.

So, both under the specific clause and at common law, I am of opinion that the presence of pests in the hold invalidated the notice of readiness. I think the decision of Mocatta J was right and I would dismiss this appeal.

ROSKILL LJ: ... Mr Mustill sought to substitute for a requirement of entire physical readiness at the time of giving notice a more limited requirement of potential physical readiness, the sufficiency of that readiness being measured by whether the matters which remained to be done to the vessel to make her completely ready could be carried out without causing the charterers any delay.

Quite apart from the special provisions of clause 6 of this charterparty (to which I shall return later), Mr Mustill's argument is in my opinion wrong for a number of reasons.

First, it has long been accepted in this branch of the law that a vessel which presents herself at a loading port must be in a position to give the charterer unrestricted access to all her cargo spaces before she can give a valid notice of readiness. This state of readiness must be unqualified. It is not open to the shipowner to say: 'Here is my ship; she is not quite ready yet but I confidently expect to be able to make her ready by such time as I consider it likely that you will in fact need her.' The charterer has contracted for the exclusive and unrestricted use of the whole of the vessel's available cargo space, and he is entitled to expect that that space will be placed at his disposal before he can be called upon to accept the vessel as having arrived and thereafter being at his risk and expense as regards time.

Secondly, I do not think that this principle is in any way weakened by the decision in *Armement Adolf Deppe* v *John Robinson & Co. Ltd* [1917] 2 KB 204, nor did Scrutton LJ in the passage relied on by Mr Mustill, at p. 212, intend to weaken it. All that that case decided was (i) that there was no need as a condition precedent to the giving of a valid notice of readiness for a shipowner to incur useless expenditure by opening hatches or engaging stevedores at a time when they could not be used, and (ii) that a ship was ready to load or discharge when all that remained to be done to enable cargo work to begin was the carrying out of such work as the opening of hatches or the rigging of cargo gear, as would in practice be necessary whenever a ship loads or discharges cargo. In my judgment the essential distinction between the present case, on the one hand, and *Armement Adolf Deppe* v *John Robinson & Co. Ltd* and *The Delian Spirit* [1972] 1 QB 103, on the other, is that in those latter cases the matters which remained to be done before the vessel could begin to discharge or load were in the nature of normal and usual preliminaries which would require to be carried out in every case, whereas the fumigation in the present case could not so be described.

Thirdly, the adoption of the test contended for by Mr Mustill would introduce an unwelcome element of uncertainty into this area of the law. In a case such as *Armement Adolf Deppe* v *John Robinson & Co. Ltd* [1917] 2 KB 204, some slight delay may occur after the vessel has berthed and before cargo operations can begin, but it is delay which is to be expected as normal and is predictable within narrow limits. The charterer can safely accept the vessel's notice of readiness knowing that he can act upon it because, apart from the usual preliminaries, the vessel will be fully available to him as soon as she berths. Such a position would not obtain if Mr Mustill's proposition were accepted. In a case such as the present a statement in the notice of readiness that the ship was ready would be factually incorrect and that statement could only become correct (if at all) at some future date which could not be accurately predicted and of which a shipowner's honest prediction might well be subsequently falsified by intervening events.

A ship in order to be ready and thus entitled to give valid notice of readiness must be ready to obey the charterer's orders whenever they are given. In the present case the ship was not in a position to do this since at the time when she gave notice she could only be made ready by fumigation of then unknown extent at some future time. The fallacy in the owners' argument was (if I may say so) aptly pointed out by Cairns LJ during yesterday's argument when he said that if the argument be right, a charterer might have to pay demurrage as liquidated damages for failing to load when the ship was in fact unfit to load. That is not and never has been the law.

...

If it be said that the maintenance of an absolute rule of this kind (subject only to questions of de minimis) may work hardship on shipowners or lead to unjust results, the answer is that the parties are always free to modify the common law rule. In the present case that rule might have been modified by a 'time lost waiting for berth' provision. But in this class of case, where questions not only of lay time and demurrage arise, but also of the right of a charterer to cancel because a ship is not ready by a stated date, it is of crucial improtance that the basic principle must be able to be simply applied to the given facts of a particular case. Certainty is essential in commercial matters and certainty is more important than that there may be hardship in a particular case because the application of the principle may cast the incidence of liability one way rather than the other. One has only to take this example. If Mr Mustill's contention be right, what would be the position where there was only a short interval of time between the geographical arrival of the vessel and the cancelling date and notice of readiness was given in the expectation that a particular defect making the ship immediately unfit to load might be remedied within a matter of hours, but this prediction was falsified in the event? What is the position of the parties to be if that defect has not in the event been remedied before the cancelling date? Is the notice of readiness, prima facie good on Mr Mustill's argument, suddenly to become retrospectively bad because of an unexpected turn of events? The complications of such a situation are endless. The sure way of avoiding such complications is to have a rule which can be applied with absolute certainty.

*Notes and Questions*

1.  In *Antclizo Shipping Corporation* v *Food Corporation of India (The Antclizo) (No. 2)* [1992] 1 Lloyd's Rep 558 (CA), it was held that notice of readiness could validly be given after 'final entry' at Customs in Bombay but before the grant of an 'entry inwards order' by the Preventive Officer. The possibility that the grant of the order might be unexpectedly delayed did not prevent the notice being valid. In the words of Parker LJ: '... in *The Delian Spirit* there was a possibility that at an inspection some reason might have been found not to grant free pratique. Furthermore, in the case of the ship's tackle or hatches there is always the possibility that some unforeseen accident will occur which will result in a delay. Those possibilities cannot in my judgment affect the validity of a notice of readiness. If they do, no notice of readiness could, as it seems to me ever be given.'

2.  The *Three Flowers* is an elderly ship. Her winches are steam driven and use 20 tons of fresh water a day. On arrival at the port of discharge she has only 15 tons of fresh water on board and the cargo will take several days to unload. Max, the master, gives notice of readiness immediately on arrival. Is it valid? (*Cf. Unifert International SAL* v *Panous Shipping Co. Inc. (The Virginia M)* [1989] 1 Lloyd's Rep 603 (QBD).)

3.  In *Transgrain Shipping BV* v *Global Transporte Oceanico SA (The Mexico I)* [1990] 1 Lloyd's Rep 507 (CA), notice of readiness to discharge was given at a time when the cargo was 'overstowed' by other cargo. The notice was thus invalid. The charterers conceded that, although no further notice was given, laytime commenced when actual discharge began. The shipowners' contention, that the anticipatory notice was a 'delayed action device' effective to start laytime automatically as soon as the vessel *became ready* to discharge the cargo, was rejected. This was applied in *TA Shipping Ltd* v *Comet Shipping Ltd (The Agamemnon)* [1998] 1 Lloyd's Rep 675 (QBD, Thomas J): notice given before the vessel reached the point specified ('arrival at or off the port of loading/ discharging or so near thereto as she may be permitted to approach') was

ineffective and lay time only began to run with commencement of loading, not when the vessel reached the Baton Rouge anchorage, the specified point.

4.	The charterparty requires notice of readiness to be given between the hours of 06.00 and 17.00. Notice is given at 18.00 by fax. Is it a valid notice? If so, at what time does it take effect? (*Cf Galaxy Energy International Ltd* v *Novorossiysk Shipping Co. (The Petr Schmidt)* [1998] 2 Lloyd's Rep 1 (CA)).

5.	It is not uncommon for charterparties to provide that notice may be given at a time when the vessel will not in fact be ready to load, with sometimes tortuous consequential provisions for any actual delay caused by unreadiness: see e.g., *Cobelfret NV* v *Cyclades Shipping Co Ltd (The Linardos)* [1994] 1 Lloyd's Rep 28 (QBD, Colman J) and *United Nations/Food and Agriculture Organisation* v *Caspian Navigation Inc (The Jay Ganesh)* [1994] 2 Lloyd's Rep 358 (QBD, Colman J, on the Worldfood charterparty).

## SECTION 2: THE AMOUNT OF LAYTIME

Laytime may be 'fixed' or left to be determined according to the custom of the port and what is reasonable in the particular case. The latter was the normal approach in the 19th century but is rarely, if ever, employed today.

*A: Laytime not fixed*

### Pantland Hick v Raymond & Reid
[1893] AC 22 (HL)

LORD HERSCHELL LC: My Lords, this action was brought by the appellant, who is a shipowner, against the respondents, who were consignees and holders of the bills of lading of a cargo carried on board the plaintiff's steamship *Derwentdale*, to recover damages for the detention of the vessel during her discharge at the port of London. By the bills of lading the cargo was to be delivered in good order and condition 'at the port of London'.

On the 14th of August, 1889, the vessel arrived in the Millwall Dock and was reported to the Custom House. The discharge of the wheat, of which the cargo consisted, commenced on the 16th of August. On the 20th of August a strike of dock labourers began in the port of London, and some of the labourers engaged in the discharge of the *Derwentdale* then ceased to work. A few days after the strike became general, and no work was done in the discharge of the vessel until the 16th of September, when it was recommenced and finished on the 18th.

Evidence was given that apart from the strike the discharge of the vessel would have been completed in six days. The dock company were employed by the respondents to discharge the vessel. Only the trimming of the cargo was to be the work of the shipowner, otherwise the entire obligation to discharge the vessel rested on the consignees.

...

I think it must be taken that throughout the whole of the time during which the discharge ceased, and the dock company were unable to supply labour to effect it, it was not possible for the respondents either to find any other person to provide the labour or themselves to obtain the necessary labour in any other way. If the terms of the bills of lading had required the discharge to be effected in any particular number of days, it is quite clear that the burden of the delay caused by the difficulty of obtaining labour would have fallen upon them, and it would have been no answer to a charge that they had failed to fulfil their obligation, to say that the circumstances had rendered it impossible for them to do so.

The bills of lading in the present case contained no such stipulation, and, therefore, in accordance with ordinary and well-known principles the obligation of the respondents was that they should take discharge of the cargo within a reasonable time. The question is, has the appellant proved that this reasonable time has been exceeded? This depends upon what circumstances may be taken into consideration in determining whether more than a reasonable time was occupied.

The appellant's contention is, that inasmuch as the obligation to take discharge of the cargo, and to provide the necessary labour for that purpose, rested upon the respondents, the test is what time would have been required for the discharge of the vessel under ordinary circumstances, and that, inasmuch as they have to provide the labour, they must be responsible if the discharge is delayed beyond that period.

The respondents on the other hand contend that the question is not what time would have been necessary or what time would have been reasonable under ordinary circumstances, but what time was reasonable under existing circumstances, assuming that, in so far as the existing circumstances were extraordinary, they were not due to any act or default on the part of the respondents.

My Lords, there appears to me to be no direct authority upon the point, although there are judgments bearing on the subject to which I will presently call attention. I would observe, in the first place, that there is of course no such thing as a reasonable time in the abstract. It must always depend upon circumstances. Upon 'the ordinary circumstances' say the learned counsel for the appellant. But what may without impropriety be termed the ordinary circumstances differ in particular ports at different times of the year. As regards the practicability of discharging a vessel they may differ in summer and winter. Again, weather increasing the difficulty of, though not preventing, the discharge of a vessel may continue for so long a period that it may justly be termed extraordinary. Could it be contended that in so far as it lasted beyond the ordinary period the delay caused by it was to be excluded in determining whether the cargo had been discharged within a reasonable time? It appears to me that the appellant's contention would involve constant difficulty and dispute, and that the only sound principle is that the 'reasonable time' should depend on the circumstances which actually exist. If the cargo has been taken with all reasonable despatch under those circumstances I think the obligation of the consignee has been fulfilled. When I say the circumstances which actually exist, I, of course, imply that those circumstances, in so far as they involve delay, have not been caused or contributed to by the consignee. I think the balance of authority, both as regards the cases which relate to contracts by a consignee to take discharge, and those in which the question what is a reasonable time has had to be answered when analogous obligations were under consideration, is distinctly in favour of the view taken by the Court below.

*Note*

An obligation to load in the time which is reasonable in the circumstances does not modify the charterer's obligation to provide a cargo: *Ardan Steamship Co.* v *Andrew Weir & Co.* [1905] AC 501 (HL), where no laytime was fixed but the loading operation, at Newcastle, NSW, was prolonged by the charterers' inability to obtain the full cargo immediately. The charterers were held liable for detention of the vessel.

*B: Fixed laytime*

At the present day laytime is defined by reference to periods of days (or hours): the principal issues which must be addressed in drafting laytime clauses of this kind are the position of non-working days, the risk of bad weather interruptions and whether to link the time allowance to a stated quantity of cargo (un)loaded in the chosen unit of time. In this section we consider some of the standard solutions to these problems.

(a)    *The meaning of 'days'*

### Reardon Smith Line Ltd v Ministry of Agriculture, Fisheries and Food
### [1963] AC 691 (HL)

The facts are stated in Chapter 8. The case also involved a claim for despatch by the charterers which depended on the construction of the laytime clause: 'Clause 15. Lay days. *Six weather* working lay days (Sundays, holidays, and rainy days not to be counted as lay or working days . . .), to commence twenty-four hours after the receipt by charterers' agents at loading port of the Captain's written notice of readiness . . .'.

LORD DEVLIN: . . . In the beginning a day was a day — a Monday, a Tuesday or a Wednesday, as the case might be. Work began, one may suppose, some time in the morning and ended in the evening, the number of hours that were worked varying from port to port and in different trades. But whatever the number was, at the end of the Monday, one lay day had gone and at the end of the Tuesday another; and if the work went into Wednesday, that counted as a whole day because of the rule that a part of a day was to be treated as a day. For this reason the charterer was not obliged to use a 'broken' day. If notice of readiness was given during the day he could, if he chose, wait till the following day so that he could start with a whole day; see *The Katy* [1895] P 56, 63; 11 TLR 116 CA, *per* Lord Esher MR. But this general rule had to yield to any inference to be drawn from the provisions of the particular charterparty. The most common of such provisions is the stipulation about the commencement of the lay days. In *Leonis SS Co. Ltd* v *Rank (Joseph) Ltd (No. 2)* (1908) 13 Com Cas 161, 163; 24 TLR 280 the charterparty provided that time for loading should commence 12 hours after written notice had been given on working days between 9 a.m. and 6 p.m. 'That, in my opinion', Bigham J said, 'alters the construction that would otherwise have been put upon the clause, and it makes the loading time commence at an hour during the 24 to be reckoned with reference to the notice given by the captain.' Thus there came into existence the artificial or conventional day, as it is now called, of 24 hours, starting from the time when the notice of readiness expired, replacing the calendar day from midnight to midnight. If Sundays and holidays were excepted, the excepted day, running from midnight to midnight, had to be cut out; see *Hain Steamship Co. Ltd* v *SA Comercial de Exportacion e Importacion (Louis Dreyfus & Co. Ltd)* (1934) 49 Ll L R 86, 88, *per* MacKinnon J
      The next question that arose was whether when you were dealing with an artificial day the rule that a part of a day — or a part of a period of 24 hours — counted as a whole day continued to apply. In *Verren* v *Anglo-Dutch Brick Co. (1927) Ltd* (1929) 34 Ll L R

56, 58; 45 TLR 404 Roche J held that it did not. In the Court of Appeal Scrutton LJ (1929) 34 Ll L R 210, 213; 45 TLR 556, CA reserved the point. Nevertheless it is now the general practice, so your Lordships were told, to treat a part of an artificial day as a fraction. Your Lordships were not told of any generally agreed method by which the fraction is calculated.

(b)  *Non-working days*
This was the main issue in *Reardon Smith Line Ltd* v *Ministry of Agriculture, Fisheries and Food*: are Saturdays working days? Lord Devlin said:

... It appears at one time to have been argued that Saturday came in whole or in part within the term 'holiday'. The contrary was, I think, clearly decided in *Love & Stewart Ltd* v *Rowtor Steamship Co. Ltd*, and before your Lordships the only contention was that Saturday was not in whole or in part a 'working day'. The facts are not in dispute, an agreement having been reached in the following terms: 'The normal working hours in the port of Vancouver were for the grain elevator operators a 5 day, Monday to Friday, 40-hour week and for the longshoremen a 5½ day, Monday to Saturday morning inclusive, 44-hour week. The labour of both these bodies of employees was essential to the operation of loading grain.' The evidence showed that both classes of men were prepared to work overtime, if necessary to get a ship out, at time and a half on Saturdays and double time on Sundays.

The claim which your Lordships have to consider is a claim for dispatch money by the charterers, the amount of which depends on whether Saturday does or does not count in whole or in part as a lay day....

After dealing with an argument that the word 'working' in the expression 'weather working days' referred to weather, not days (see (c) below), Lord Devlin turned to the meaning of 'working days' and continued:

... As I have said, the term has been in use for a very long time. I think that originally it may have been used to exclude Sundays and holidays before it became usual to exclude those days specifically. Thus, in *Cochran* v *Retberg* (1800) 3 Esp 121, 123, Lord Eldon LC held, having regard to the usage in the Port of London, 'the fourteen days mentioned in the bill of lading mean working days, that is a construction which excludes Sundays and holidays'. In *Nelson & Sons Ltd* v *Nelson Line (Liverpool) Ltd (No. 3)* (1907) 12 Com Cas 185, 193 Channell J said that where the charterparty says 'working days', the mention of Sundays and holidays would be unnecessary as those days would not be working days. But there may, of course, be days in some ports, such as the Mahomedan Friday, which are not working days and yet cannot well be described as Sundays or holidays. There is a comprehensive definition by Hamilton J in *British & Mexican Shipping Co. Ltd* v *Lockett Brothers & Co. Ltd* [1911] 1 KB 264, 273 (his decision was reversed in the Court of Appeal but on another point) as follows:

'working day' in this charterparty means something contradistinguished from days which are not working days, a day of work as distinguished from days for play or rest; and I think it is immaterial whether the days for play or rest are so for secular or religious reasons, and whether they are so by the ancient authority of the Church or by the present authority of the State.

From this it appears that 'working' is a description of a type of day. Prima facie it is a calendar day of 24 hours just as Sundays and holidays are days of 24 hours, which, when excepted, are taken out of the lay days. They are taken out as a whole because, as Lord

Sumner said in *Love & Stewart Ltd* v *Rowtor Steamship Co. Ltd* [1916] 2 AC 527, 536 the exception of holiday is based on days and not on parts of days. The charterers' contention runs counter to this. They say that a working day is not just a description of a type of calendar day, but is to be contrasted in terms of time with the calendar day. It is the working part of the day made up of the hours constituting the normal working day as distinct from the 24 hours which make up the calendar day. This was the view adopted by the Court of Appeal in the *Rubystone* [1955] 1 QB 430; Lord Goddard CJ said ibid. 445 that the word 'working' qualifies the word 'day' and cuts it down. He said that it meant that part of the day during which work is carried on and was to be ascertained by determining what are the usual ordinary hours that are worked either at a particular place or in a particular trade. If this is its true meaning, the ground is laid for the charterers to contend that the test whether a Saturday is a working day or not is not to inquire whether it is some sort of a holiday (which it is conceded it is not) but to inquire whether it is a day on which normal hours at normal rates are worked in the port. The question is whether 'working' is descriptive of a whole day or definitive of a part of it: or, to put the point another way, whether a working day consists of a number of working hours.

... I conclude, with respect, that it is contrary to all authority before 1955 to say that a working day is a calendar day cut down. 'Working' does not define a part of a day but describes the character of the day as a whole. Secondly, I conclude that the character of a day as a working day cannot be determined by inquiring whether on that day or on a part of it work was done at standard rates. There is no established authority for that view which I think stems from the misconception that the 'working day' of the lay time clause has something to do with the hours of the day during which the ship can be compelled to work. Thirdly, I conclude that the general rule that a part of a day counts as a day prevails unless there is something in the charterparty which is inconsistent with it or there is present some factor such as the weather which must naturally break up the day.

The question for your Lordships is whether Saturday is wholly or in part not a working day. The conclusions I have stated compel me to reject the argument that because for an essential trade, namely, the elevator men, Saturday does not form part of the normal working week, therefore it is a non-working day. I should reach the same conclusion if no one at all at the port worked at standard rates on Saturday afternoon, and therefore I reject the alternative argument that Saturday afternoon should be treated as a non-working part of a day. I reject this alternative also for the reason that the charterparty contains nothing to justify splitting the working day into fractions. On the contrary, if the parties had not wanted Saturday afternoon to count, they would, I believe, do as was done in the *Rubystone* and include it among the exceptions. The whole basis of the argument before your Lordships, however well it may be disguised, is that Saturday should be treated either as a whole or as a half holiday. If it had been put in that form without disguise it would have offended not only against Lord Sumner's decision which I have cited from *Love & Stewart Ltd* v *Rowtor Steamship Co. Ltd* [1916] 2 AC 527 but also against *Robert Dollar Co. (The)* v *Blood, Holman & Co.* (1920) 4 Ll L Rep 343, 350; 36 TLR 843 and *'Z' Steamship Co. Ltd* v *Amtorg, New York* (1938) 61 Ll L Rep 97, 102 both of which were, I think, on this point rightly decided. But that is what the argument really amounts to. Accordingly, I think that the charterers' contention that Saturday does not count in whole or in part as a working day should fail and that the appeal to that extent should succeed.

*Question*
If loading actually takes place on a Sunday or holiday, does that day then count as a lay day?

(c)  *The risk of interruption by bad weather*
Although the state of the weather was not in fact significant in *Reardon Smith Line Ltd* v *Ministry of Agriculture, Fisheries and Food*, the House of Lords gave detailed consideration to the meaning of 'weather working days'. Lord Devlin said:

The argument for the charterers, who say that Saturday is not a lay day has to proceed in two stages. First, they have to show that the lay days consist only of working days. . . .
   The first question depends on whether 'six weather working days' means six calendar days on which the weather is fine or six working days on which the weather is fine. . . .
   The expression 'weather working day' has been in use for some time, but there is no English case (other than the decision of the Court of Appeal in 1955 which we are asked to review) which authoritatively determines its meaning. Mr Roche relied on the dictum of Walton J in *Bennetts & Co.* v *Brown* [1908] 1 KB 490, 497; 24 TLR 199; 13 Com Cas 110 to the effect that it meant a day on which the work is not prevented by bad weather. But this does not really help because the learned judge was not directing his mind to the question whether 'day' meant working day or calendar day. There is an obiter dictum by Buckley LJ in *Nelson & Sons Ltd* v *Nelson Line (Liverpool) Ltd, In re Same* [1907] 2 KB 705, 722 CA, based on what the learned Lord Justice took to be the grammatical meaning of the words, and in favour of the charterer's view, that a weather working day must be a working day.
   I do not think that a grammatical analysis is decisive in the case of a term which was obviously first devised as a shorthand phrase. I am more impressed by two considerations. The first is that the expression 'working day' has been in use for very much longer than 'weather working day' and 'working day' was introduced, as I shall show when I come to consider its meaning more precisely, to describe a class of day which was more limited than a calendar day. I think, therefore, that if business men had intended 'weather working day' to include days that were not working days, they would have used some different phraseology. Secondly, although there is no clear English authority, there are two decisions, both by United States circuit courts of appeal, *The India* (1891) 49 Fed Rep 76 and *NV Zuid-Hollandsche Sheepvaart Maatschappij of Rotterdam* v *Pensacola Maritime Corpn* (1932) 2 AMC 1552 which decide that a weather working day must be a working day. On such a point as this, these authorities are of the highest value and I think that your Lordships ought to follow them.
   . . . A weather working day started like a working day as a description of a day. A wet Monday on which no work could be done was for the purpose of the lay days an excepted day just like a Sunday or a holiday. The Monday had to fit into one description or the other; it had to be wet or fine. There was no investigation to see to what extent the weather actually prevented work. If that was what was wanted, if the weather was to be treated as if it were an excepted peril excusing work only when it was actually operating, words could, of course, be found to do it. In *Stephens* v *Harris & Co.* (1887) 57 LJQB 203 CA, the Court of Appeal held that the phrase 'weather permitting' in the lay time clause had that effect. I see no reason to doubt the authority of that decision although there has been some controversy about it. But at any rate there can be no doubt that a formula can be found; see, for example, *Burnett Steamship Co. Ltd* v *Danube & Black Sea Shipping Agencies* [1933] 2 KB 438; 49 TLR 553, CA. It is well established that whether a day is a weather working day or not depends on the character of the day and not on whether work was actually interfered with. The authorities on this point have recently been reviewed by Pearson J in *Compania Naviera Azuero SA* v *British Oil & Cake Mills Ltd* [1957] 2 QB 293; [1957] 2 WLR 997; [1957] 2 All ER 241, and neither side challenged the correctness of his decision.

It must now be a matter for speculation as to why commercial men wanted the day to count as a whole since weather so often affects a day intermittently. Possibly they wanted to make up their minds at the beginning of the day whether it was to be treated as a working day or not so that if it was not the crew need not stand by but might have shore leave. At any rate, the time came when it was felt to be unreasonable to treat the day as a whole. Lord Russell of Killowen CJ thought so in the *Branckelow* case [1897] 1 QB 570 to which I have referred. The answer might have been that if the parties did not want the day treated as a whole they could use a phrase like 'weather permitting'. But Lord Russell's answer was that the day could be cut in half. He said ibid. 573: 'I think, however, that the most equitable view is to charge half a day against the charterers where substantial work is done, though not amounting to half a day, and to charge a full day against them where substantially a full day's work, though not amounting to twelve hours, is done; no smaller fraction than half a day should, however, be taken into consideration, and if the time worked is quite insignificant it should not be charged at all'. In *Bennetts & Co.* v *Brown* [1908] 1 KB 490, 496 Walton J said that the phrase weather working day 'might refer to half a day'. Since then it appears that in practice the rough division of the day into halves has been replaced by some more precise method of calculating the fraction. But no case has been cited which takes the matter any further until the *Rubystone* [1955] 1 QB 430. It was then decided for the first time that the fraction must be based on normal working hours.

My Lords, I cannot, with the greatest respect, think that this latest development is a satisfactory one or one that is warranted by any reasonable construction of the ordinary charterparty. How do you ascertain what are normal hours? I should agree that there is no way of answering that except by inquiry what hours are paid for at normal rates. But I think that answer to be quite unrealistic. Overtime in ports is the rule rather than the exception; and collective bargaining in the labour market often produces a rise in wages by means of a reduction in normal hours. In *Maatschappij (NV) Zeevart* v *M. Friesacher Soehne* [1962] 1 WLR 534; [1962] 2 All ER 511 Elwes J was bound by the *Rubystone* to decide that a working day was a period of 9 hours although there was a practice in the port to work 24.

Then there is the question, which arose in the present case, whether normal hours means normal hours in the port or in the trade. On this point there was a division of opinion in the courts below. If it means in the trade, the grain trade or whatever else it may be (the view taken by McNair J [1960] 1 QB 439 and Sellers and Donovan LJJ [1962] 1 QB 42), what happens if there is a cargo of general merchandise? This would make the lay days difficult if not impossible to compute. If the working day means the number of hours normally worked in the port, computation would be difficult if there is a number of different loading ports with different standard hours, or if the lay days are reversible. Even in the case of one trade, such as the grain trade, certainty is not achieved, for it appears that the longshoremen work at normal rates on Saturday morning and the elevator men do not. If the parties use the phrase 'working hours' the court must do the best it can with it, though the parties would be well advised to be more precise. But I can see no justification for the court, unless there is something which in the charterparty demands it, turning the working day into a number of working hours.

. . .

If your Lordships are of the same opinion as I am, then the House will approve the decision in the *Rubystone* that a weather working day is a species of working day but disapprove the decision in that case that a working day is composed of the number of hours paid for at standard rates. Since weather is not a factor in the present case, that is all that in strictness it is necessary to say about the meaning of weather working days. But I think it would be unsatisfactory if your Lordships were to leave your consideration of the *Rubystone* without expressing an opinion upon how weather working days should be computed in relation to the weather. Should fractions be permitted and, if so, how should they be calculated?

On the first part of that question there is something to be said on both sides. There is nothing in the charterparty to displace the prima facie rule unless it be found in the word 'weather' itself. It can be argued that weather is so changeable and unpredictable that it can be used only too infrequently to characterise the day as a whole and that the parties must have intended to have contracted with that in mind. I do not say that I could have acepted that as a matter of construction if it were now being put forward for the first time. But I accept it as established by the *Branckelow* case [1897] 1 QB 570 with which I think your Lordships ought not now to interfere.

The second part of the question raises matters of great difficulty. Should it be a fraction of the 24 hours that compose the calendar day, or a fraction of some part, and if so, what part of the day? My Lords, I am not, with respect, so startled as were McNair J and the Court of Appeal in the *Rubystone* case by the thought that, if the fraction is based upon the full calendar day, the charterer might conceivably be debited with only a third of a day when in fact the day's work had not been interfered with at all. If the night is wet and the day is fine, that is what may happen. But this sort of artificiality is inherent in the conception of the weather working day. If, as in the present case, there can be no loading anyway because the elevators cannot be worked, the weather cannot matter at all, but admittedly the lay days still have to be computed according to whether or not they are wet. If the charterer can obtain relief for the whole of a wet day which he is not using, why should he not obtain a portion of that relief for a wet night which he is not using? If the parties want to keep closer to reality, they should use 'weather permitting' or some other phrase of exception. And if it is uncertain how many of the 24 hours are going to be used — and, after all, working in shifts around the clock is not uncommon — they might well be content with a simple calculation based on the whole day.

If the matter were free of authority, I should have been tempted to find a solution in that way. But this sort of solution was decisively negatived in 1955 and to the extent that the *Rubystone* rejected for this purpose the 24-hour day (though not to the extent of the alternative the Court of Appeal there proposed) it was based on the *Branckelow* case. Lord Russell of Killowen there clearly supposes that the day is to be split up into wet or fine according to that part of it that was being or might, but for the weather, have been used which he took, presumably on evidence that is not recorded, to be 12 hours. It is true that the *Rubystone* is not an authority of long standing, but I do not think it would be right now to return to an entirely different method of calculation which since 1955 has probably been discarded, if it was not discarded before on the authority of *Branckelow*. On the other hand, I can see no justification as a matter of construction for taking 'weather working day' as being limited to the hours paid for at normal rates, and for the reasons I have given I do not think it to be a method that would produce a satisfactory result.

I think that the best that can be done by way of expansion of the phrase 'weather working days' is to infer that it is intended by it that a reasonable apportionment should be made of the day — Lord Russell of Killowen based his decision on an 'equitable view' — according to the incidence of the weather upon the length of day that the parties either were working or might be expected to have been working at the time. The matter must be at large for the arbitrator or other judge of fact; and at the risk of constantly repeating mysef, I say again that if the parties want an exact measurement to be made of the actual effect of weather upon the work, they have only to say so. I do not mean that the arbitrator must deal in half days or even quarter days if he has the material before him that will enable him to do better. If the work is actually being carried on subject to interruptions from bad weather, he should not have much difficulty in determining what part of the day was in use; whether or not some of it was overtime seems to me to be immaterial. If no work is being done at all, his task may not be so easy. But an experienced arbitrator will probably know from the number of the lay days, the amount of cargo to be loaded and the rate of loading to be expected at the port, how much of the day was expected to be used; and he would naturally assume that work would be done so far as possible during normal hours at standard rates and after that, if necessary, during the hours in which overtime was most likely to be worked. I should regard such an apportionment as entirely a question of fact and should not, as at present advised, be prepared to recognise any principle of law that would allow the court to interfere with it.

There is one concluding observation I should like to make. Much of the difficulty in settling disputes about lay time arises from the fact that commercial men have taken to increasingly complicated methods of calculation without substantially altering the simple terms in which the lay time clause was originally expressed. The practice has changed but the words have not. Your Lordships have been told of methods of calculation which are said to be in constant use, but which it is extremely difficult to justify by reference to the words of the charterparty or by any authorised interpretation of them. I should not wish the House to dictate to commercial men how they should frame their documents, but they must appreciate that in the end disputes have to be determined according to the language used. However liberal a court of law may be in giving effect so far as it can to practice, usage and custom, it is the words in the charterparty that must ultimately determine the issue. The confusion that has been created by the divergence between practice and language appears to me to be now so great as to call for some reconsideration of the terms in which the lay time clause is usually expressed.

*Note*
Part of the difficulty with clauses referring to the state of the weather is to determine whether they not only apply to the (real) effect of the weather on loading or discharging which is actually taking place, but also apply notionally to periods when laytime is running but loading/discharging cannot actually be done for some other reason, for example, where the vessel is not yet in berth but the lay days have started under a wibon clause.

### *Dow Chemical (Nederland) BV v BP Tanker Co. Ltd*
### *(The Vorras)*
### [1983] 1 Lloyd's Rep 579 (CA)

SIR JOHN DONALDSON MR: This appeal concerns demurrage and the meaning and effect of '72 running hours, weather permitting' in the Beepeevoy 2 form of charterparty.

*Vorras* was chartered—

... to proceed One port Algeria or so near thereunto as she may safely get ...

to load a cargo of petroleum products for carriage—

... to One or two ports United Kingdom, Continent (Bordeaux-Hamburg) range.

This was therefore a port, as contrasted with a berth, charterparty.

The vessel arrived at the nominated loading port of Skikda, Algeria, on Dec. 15, 1980, and tendered notice of readiness. There was a special provision that laytime should not commence before Dec. 19, 1980. Loading was not completed until Jan. 13, 1981, when the vessel sailed for Rotterdam. Disputes have arisen as to the amount of demurrage payable, but these disputes can be settled amicably if one point of principle can first be resolved. In order to understand that point, it is necessary to explain in outline what caused the delay at the loading port.

When *Vorras* arrived, the loading berth was occupied by another vessel, *Brese Jarl*. That vessel left on the evening of Dec. 16, 1980, but within a very short time the port was closed due to bad weather. This closure was maintained until the afternoon of Dec. 20 when another vessel, *Skikda*, occupied the loading berth. She eventually left on the morning of Dec. 26, but her loading was interrupted by bad weather and it seems that at one time the weather was such that she had to leave the berth temporarily. After she left finally, the port was again closed due to bad weather and *Vorras* only went on the berth on Dec. 28, 1980. Thereafter her loading was continually delayed by bad weather.

Against this background the point of principle can be simply stated. Under this charterparty laytime takes some account of weather, but demurrage time does not. Bad weather was a major, albeit intermittent, feature of the vessel's visit to the loading port. Once laytime expired, the risk of delay for any reason, including bad weather, lay on the charterers. Accordingly it is no surprise to find the owners arguing that laytime expired very soon after the vessel's arrival and the charterers arguing that the effect of bad weather was to postpone its expiry for a very substantial period. Put more precisely, the owners say that laytime is only extended if the weather at the berth is such as to prevent the loading of *Vorras* and that this could not happen when she was not on the loading berth and another vessel was there. The charterers, for their part, say that laytime is extended if the weather was such as to prevent loading at the berth, whether *Vorras* or another vessel or no vessel at all was on the berth.
. . .

Authority apart, the charterers' case is simplicity itself. They say: 'Clause 15 says that we *shall* be allowed 72 running hours during which the weather permits loading before the vessel comes on demurrage. If laytime expires at midnight on Dec. 21/22, as the owners say it did, we have been robbed, because during none, or virtually none, of the previous three days could anyone have loaded a vessel. If the weather had been suitable for loading, but we could not get the vessel to the berth because another vessel was there, that would be our bad luck. But if the owners are right, whatever the weather we are only entitled to three days' laytime unless we can actually get the vessel on to the berth. This is not what the charter says'.

The owners' case can be equally simply stated. They say: 'We agreed a rate of freight which allowed you 72 free hours for loading. It was up to you to make sure that the berth was free. The only qualification which we accepted was that if you could not use some of those hours because of the weather, the time would be extended. You had your 72 hours and the weather did not prevent your loading. What prevented your loading was the fact that another vessel was on the berth'.

Authority apart, I would have no doubt that the charterers were right. As Mr Justice Parker pointed out in *Gebr. Broere BV* v *Saras Chimica SpA* [1982] 2 Lloyd's Rep 436, the owners' construction can lead to a very surprising result. Assume that two tankers arrive on successive days and each has a laytime of 72 running hours weather permitting. The first gets into the berth and bad weather prevents loading for the next 21 days, after which she loads in 72 hours. Her charterers will neither pay demurrage nor receive dispatch. The second, which arrived next day, has to wait 20 days for the weather to improve and then three days for the other vessel to load. She then herself loads in three days. Her charterers are liable to pay 23 days' demurrage. Yet for only three of those days did it matter that she could not get into the berth. If she had been able to do so, she could not have loaded because of the weather. One would have expected the second tanker to be liable for three days' demurrage, not 23 days'.

In this field, however, it is indeed rare for any point to be free from authority and it is to the authorities that I must now turn.

In *Stephens v Harris* (1887) 57 LJQB 203, '400 tons per weather working day, weather permitting' was allowed for loading. The vessel was to load ore and duly reached her loading berth, lying under the spouts. The ore itself was to come from five miles away and bad weather delayed the bringing of it to the vessel. There was also a strike. As Mr T.E. Scrutton, for the shipowners, tersely put it before he was stopped by the Court:

> ... Neither the weather nor the strike affected the loading, but only the transit to the ship prior to the loading.

The Court held that the running of laytime was not interrupted, because the weather did not affect the loading of the vessel. This might be thought to assist the owners' argument. However the Court was considering a case in which the vessel was at the loading berth and the effect of the weather was not. It did not consider the converse case in which the effect of the weather was at the loading berth and the vessel was not.

After referring to *The Glendevon* [1893] P 269, Sir John Donaldson MR quoted the comments of Lord Devlin on 'weather permitting' in *Reardon Smith Line Ltd v Ministry of Agriculture, Fisheries and Food*, above (which he later refers to as the *Vancouver Strikes* case) and continued:

Undoubtedly Lord Devlin was saying that 'weather permitting' is a 'phrase of exception' which requires regard to be had to the actual effect which weather is having on the loading process and he was basing himself on the Court of Appeal decision in *Stephens v Harris*. But regard can be had to the actual effect of the weather in two different ways. You can look to see whether the loading process is in fact prevented by the weather or you can look to see whether it is the weather which is the actual cause of the particular vessel not being loaded. In *Stephens v Harris* and in the *Vancouver Strikes* case, both questions would have received the same answer. In neither case was the loading process affected by the weather. The loading process was at a standstill because there was no cargo (*Stephens v Harris*) and because the elevators could not be worked (*Vancouver Strikes*). The particular vessel was not prevented from loading by the weather but by the absence of cargo (*Stephens v Harris*) and the failure of the elevators to work (*Vancouver Strikes*). Lord Devlin did not have to consider a case in which (a) weather was the sole cause of the loading process being at a standstill or not available, and (b) there was a different or additional reason why the particular vessel was not able to be loaded, namely that she was not in the berth.

There matters rested until Mr Justice Brandon had to consider laytime defined as—

> ... 750 metric tons per day of 24 consecutive hours per weather permitting working day [in *The Camelia and The Magnolia* [1978] 2 Lloyd's Rep 182].

The charterparties in that case also had a special clause reading:

> Berth occupied: when no grain berth available on arrival roads, Master will cable ... date and time of arrival roads to the Agents and this time will be treated as if the vessel has tendered notice of readiness alongside the berth and time will count accordingly.

The learned Judge said at p. 184L:

> There are, it seems to me, two questions to be considered. The first question is —
> what is the effect of the words 'per weather permitting working day' in relation to
> actual laytime after the ship is in berth? The second question is — what is the effect of
> the same words in relation to notional laytime before the ship is in berth? With regard
> to the first question, it was contended for the charterers that the expression 'weather
> permitting working day' had the same effect as the expression 'weather working day',
> that is to say it meant a day on which work was permitted by the weather whether it
> would in fact have been carried out or not (see *Compania Naviera Azuero SA* v *British
> Oil & Cake Mills Ltd* [1957] 1 Lloyd's Rep 312; [1957] 2 QB 293). It was contended
> for the shipowners on the other hand that the expression meant the same as the
> expression 'working day weather permitting', that is to say that it meant a working day
> which counted unless work was actually prevented by the weather — a day on which
> work would have been done but for the weather preventing it (see *Stephens* v *Harris*
> (1887) 57 LJQB 203). The contention for the charterers involves treating the words
> as words of description: the contention for the shipowners involves treating them as
> words of exception. The language of the charterparty is not very happy. Line 61 has
> printed on the original form the expression 'per weather working day'. An additional
> word 'permitting' has been typed in the margin with a line showing that it is to be
> inserted between the word 'weather' and the words 'working day'. In my view, the
> intention was to produce the same result as would be produced by the words 'working
> day weather permitting'. Accordingly, I prefer, in relation to this first question the
> contention for the shipowners to that for the charterers.

Turning to the second question, the learned Judge held, on the authority of *The
Darrah* [1976] 2 Lloyd's Rep 359; [1977] AC 157, that the object of the berth occupied
clause was—

> . . . to put both parties in the same position when a berth is not available as they would
> have been in if it had been available [p. 185L].

This decision undoubtedly supports the owners to some extent but its weight depends
upon the correctness of the learned Judge's reliance upon *Stephens* v *Harris*. For my part
I regard *Stephens* v *Harris* as inconclusive. The vessel was in the berth and the weather
did not affect either the loading process or her loading. Accordingly whether the
expression 'weather permitting' was one of description or exception, the answer would
have been the same.

The latest case in which the words 'weather permitting' were considered is *Gebr.
Broere BV* v *Saras Chimica SpA* [1982] 2 Lloyd's Rep 436. Mr Justice Parker upheld the
charterers' contention that—

> . . . there must be excluded from the computation of laytime used up any periods
> during which, had the vessel berthed on arrival, weather would have prevented
> loading which would otherwise have taken place.

I refrain from setting out the learned Judge's reasoning or commenting upon it, since the
matter arose upon a preliminary point in an arbitration which is still proceeding.

This leaves only *The Darrah* [1976] 2 Lloyd's Rep 359; [1977] AC 157. It appears to
have played a decisive part in the judgment of Mr Justice Bingham, but it has to be
remembered that there is no transcript of his judgment which was given in Chambers.
For my part I do not understand its relevance. It was a weather working day case in
which it was agreed that 'time lost waiting for berth to count as laytime'. It is authority

for the proposition that a time lost clause is immaterial in a port charterparty, at least after the vessel has arrived, since in such circumstances time lost waiting for berth *is* laytime. No such clause occurs in the charterparty with which we are concerned.

In the absence of authority, other than the decision of Mr Justice Brandon which was, I think, based upon a misreading of *Stephens* v *Harris*, I have to construe the words used in their natural meaning. The words are '72 hours, weather permitting'. The essence of the owners' argument is that this phrase means '72 hours, unless the weather prevents the vessel from loading'. There would be something to be said for this if the antonym for 'permitting' was 'preventing'. But it is not. It is 'prohibiting'. If the phrase is to be inverted, it reads '72 hours unless the weather prohibits loading'. In my judgment the weather prohibited any vessel of this general type from loading and it is nothing to the point that owing to the presence of another vessel in the berth, the prohibition was not the operative cause which prevented the vessel from loading. I would construe '72 hours, weather permitting' as meaning '72 hours when the weather was of such a nature as to permit loading'.

There have been attempts to classify laytime provisions as either 'descriptive' or 'exceptive', the latter importing a causative connection with the delay. I am not sure how much this adds to clarity. Prima facie, any clause defining laytime is descriptive and any clause providing that time shall not count against laytime so defined (see for example cl. 17 of this charterparty) is exceptive. If it matters, I would classify the expression '72 running hours, weather permitting' as descriptive.

*Questions*
1.   How would Lord Devlin have decided *The Vorras?*
2.   If *The Vorras* is correct, what is the difference between 'weather working days' and 'weather permitting'?

(d)    *Laytime calculated according to an assumed rate of loading/discharge*

By a formula of this kind laytime is expressly related to the actual quantity of cargo to be handled.

### *William Alexander & Sons* v *Aktieselskabet Dampskibet Hansa*
[1920] AC 88 (HL)

VISCOUNT FINLAY: My Lords, this is a claim by shipowners for demurrage under a charterparty. The Lord Ordinary decided in favour of the pursuers (now respondents), and the Second Division affirmed his decision. The questions arising on this appeal from their affirmance are two: (1) as to the general nature of the obligation imposed upon a charterer by a clause providing for discharge in a fixed number of days; and (2) as to the meaning and effect of the words at the end of the marginal note in this charterparty: 'Always provided steamer can load and discharge at this rate.'

The appellants are the charterers and the respondents the owners of the steamship *Hansa*. By the charterparty the vessel was to load at Archangel a cargo of timber and proceed with it to Ayr. The third clause in the charterparty so far as material is as follows: 'The cargo to be loaded and discharged *at the rate of not less than 100 standards per day, counting from steamer's arrival at the respective ports, and notice of readiness given in writing during business hours, and permission to load granted, whether berth available or not, always provided that steamer can load and discharge at this rate. . . .*' The words in italics form the marginal note, and there is a provision in the charter that 'should the steamer be detained beyond the time stipulated as above for loading or discharging, demurrage shall be paid at 70*l.* per day and pro rata for any part thereof.' If the discharge at Ayr had been carried out at the rate of 100 standards per day the time occupied would have been six and one-third days. Owing to a scarcity of labour at the port, the discharging, which began on November 17, was not completed until 6 p.m. on December 2. By the custom of the port the discharge was a joint operation. It was the duty of the shipowners to put the cargo on the quay and of the charterers to remove it thence. Both the shipowners and the charterers employed the same stevedore for this work, and, as he could not get enough men, delay took place alike as regards the placing of the cargo on the quay and its removal thence. The appellants, having been sued by the respondents for demurrage at the stipulated rate, urge that they are not liable, as the ship was not in a position to put the cargo on to the quay at the stipulated rate, owing to the same cause, scarcity of labour, which prevented the appellants from removing it. Lord Hunter, the Lord Ordinary, rejected this contention. He said: 'It is well settled that where a merchant has undertaken to discharge a ship within a fixed number of days he is liable in demurrage for any delay of the ship beyond that period unless such delay is attributable to the fault of the shipowner or those for whom he is responsible. The risk of delay from causes for which neither of the contracting parties is responsible is with the merchant.' The Second Division, consisting of the Lord Justice-Clerk, Lord Dundas, Lord Salvesen and Lord Guthrie, were unanimously of the same opinion. Lord Dundas said that in view of the authorities, if Mr Sandeman's appeal for the appellants was to succeed, it must be in the House of Lords.

On this appeal a great many cases were cited laying down the rule that if the charterer has agreed to load or unload within a fixed period of time (as is the case here, for certum est quod certum reddi potest), he is answerable for the non-performance of that engagement, whatever the nature of the impediments, unless they are covered by exceptions in the charterparty or arise through the fault of the shipowner or those for whom he is responsible. I am here adopting in substance the language used by Lord Justice Scrutton in his work upon *Charterparties and Bills of Lading* art. 131. Of the authorities I will mention only *Budgett & Co.* v *Binnington & Co.* [1891] 1 QB 35, and I refer specially to the judgment in that case given by Lord Esher. Although no authority upon the point was cited which would in itself be binding upon your Lordships' House, there has been such a stream of authority to the same effect that I think it would be eminently undesirable to depart in a matter of business of this kind from the rule which has been so long applied, even if your Lordships felt any doubt as to the propriety of these decisions in the first instance. I myself have no doubt as to their correctness, and I understand that this is the opinion of all your Lordships. It seems to me that the appeal on this point must fail.

With regard to the construction of the concluding words of the marginal note, the motive of the charterers for desiring the insertion of these words is immaterial; the question is: what is the true meaning of the words themselves? As regards all mechanical facilities and appliances the steamer was equipped for delivery at the rate mentioned in the charterparty. It was owing to the shortage of labour that she was unable so to deliver. It was forcibly contended that it was for the ship to provide the labour as well as the appliances; that appliances without labour are of no use, and that it is a condition of the charterer's liability in terms of the marginal note that the steamship should be in a position to discharge at the stipulated rate, having men and appliances alike. I do not think that this meaning should be read into the words of this proviso. The Court of Appeal in the case of *Northfield Steamship Co.* v *Compagnie L'Union des Gaz* [1912] 1 KB 434 took the view that such words should be read as referring merely to the physical capacity of the ship for discharging, and that where the inability to discharge was due to want of labour without fault on the part of the shipowner or of his servants, the charterer would not be protected by such words. I think they were right. If it had been intended that mere liability on the part of the ship to find labour should excuse the charterer, much clearer words would have been employed. The terms used are not sufficient to work such a departure from the well-established rule that the charterer is excused from delivery in the stipulated fixed time only when he is prevented from doing his part by the default of the shipowner. He is not excused by the fact that the shipowner, as well as himself, was prevented, without any fault on his part, from doing his share of the work. I think that this appeal should be dismissed with costs.

*Note*

A common refinement of the rate of loading/discharge approach is to define laytime by the time needed to load/unload '*x* tons per available workable hatch'. Although not entirely free from ambiguity, this is generally taken to mean that the total number of days permitted is the number required to complete the loading/unloading of the largest (or 'longest') hold at the stated rate, it being assumed that other holds will be worked at the same time. The next case provides an object lesson in the hazards of tampering with an established formula.

***President of India*** v ***Jebsens (UK) Ltd***
***(The General Capinpin)***
[1991] 1 Lloyd's Rep 1 (HL)

LORD GOFF OF CHIEVELEY: My Lords, these appeals are concerned with the construction of a laytime clause which (with immaterial variations) was used in three charterparties sharing the common feature that in each case the charterer was the President of India who, as is well known, is the world's largest charterer of dry cargo vessels. The first appeal is concerned with a charterparty dated May 25, 1983, under which *General Capinpin* was chartered for the carriage of a cargo of wheat from the US Gulf to the east coast of India. The second is concerned with a charterparty dated Dec. 16, 1983, under which *Free Wave* was chartered for the carriage of a cargo of wheat from Argentina to the west or east coast of India. The third is concerned with a charterparty dated June 25, 1984 under which *Proteus* was chartered for the carriage of a cargo of fertiliser from the US Gulf to the west coast of India. The Courts below were also concerned with a fourth charter of a vessel called the *Dinara*. However the point now in question has ceased to be material in that case, and so the appeal in that case was not pursued before your Lordships' House.

In the *General Capinpin* charter, the laytime clause in question is cl. 14. The relevant part is cl. 14(a), which reads as follows:

> Cargo to be discharged by consignees' stevedores, free of risk and expense to vessel at the average rate of 1,000 metric tons basis five or more available workable hatches pro rata, if less number of hatches, per weather working day of 24 consecutive hours Saturday afternoon, Sundays and holidays excepted, even if used, always provided the vessel can deliver at this rate.

It is to be observed that cl. 14(a) did not, in its original form, contain the words—

... basis five or more available workable hatches pro rata, if less number of hatches.

Those words were added in a marginal note to cl. 14(a) in this particular charter. By the date of the *Free Wave* charter, the words had been incorporated in the body of the clause (in that charter numbered 19(a)); and similar words were likewise incorporated in cl. 19(b), concerned with deep tanks and wing tanks (a point which seems to have been overlooked in cl. 14(b) of the *General Capinpin* charter). Almost identical words are to be found in the laytime clause (cl. 28) of the *Proteus* charter.

It is the effect of those words which lies at the heart of the dispute between the parties in these three appeals. The owners contend that the laytime clause expressly provides for an overall rate for the ship, i.e., 1,000 tonnes per weather working day. The effect of the added words is not to substitute a rate per hatch for the overall rate, but is to qualify the provision for an overall rate in two respects. First if, when the vessel commences discharging, less than five workable hatches are available, the overall rate will be reduced pro rata. Second if, in the course of discharging, any of the vessel's hatches should cease temporarily to be available, the relevant period (to the extent that it has an impact upon the laytime) shall not count towards the laytime used. However the mere fact that the discharging of any particular hatch is completed does not itself effect the computation of laytime, because the rate of discharging is not a rate per hatch, but an overall rate for the vessel.

The charterer adopts a different approach. He contends that the expression 'available workable hatch' has acquired, in law, a well established meaning. In *Cargill Inc.* v *Rionda de Pass Ltd (The Giannis Xilas)* [1982] 2 Lloyd's Rep 511 at p. 513, Mr Justice Bingham said that the effect of the expression:

> Is not to distinguish a cargo hatch from any other kind of hatch but to denote a hatch which can be worked either because under it there is a hold into which cargo can be loaded or a hold out of which cargo can be discharged, in either event being a hatch which the party responsible for loading or discharging is not for any reason disabled from working.

On this approach, if a hatch is not in this sense available workable, whether at the commencement of loading or discharge (as the case may be), or by reason of any temporary impediment during the operation of loading or discharge, or by reason of the loading or discharge of the hatch having been completed, time shall not count in respect of that hatch. This leads to the practical result that, if this approach is adopted in respect of the form of clause under consideration in the present appeals, it will have the same effect as if the clause had provided for a dischraging rate per available workable hatch — a well established formula for the computation of laytime, which the charterer says must have been intended by choosing a clause in this form which adopts the available workable hatch as its basis. The owners riposte that the form of clause now under consideration does not provide for a rate per hatch but for an overall rate for the whole vessel, and that if it had been intended to provide for a rate per hatch that could easily have been done, in accordance with well established precedent. Indeed Mr Young for the owners was able to point out that, on the charterer's approach, the laytime for discharging would never be calculated with reference to an average rate for the vessel of 1,000 tonnes per day, unless there was an equal quantity of cargo under each hatch, which was in practical terms an inconceivable eventuality. It was the owners' approach which was accepted by the arbitral tribunal in all three cases. On appeal, the Judge (Mr Justice Webster) preferred the approach of the charterer; but the Court of Appeal reversed his decision, and restored the decision of the arbitral tribunal in each case. It is against the decision of the Court of Appeal that the charterer now appeals to your

Lordships' House, with the leave of your Lordships (though on special terms as to costs).

The rival contentions in these appeals are, in my opinion, best approached by first examining the form of clause considered in previous authorities, which provides for an average rate of loading or discharge per working or workable or available workable hatch per day. Here, of course, the rate of loading or discharge is expressly related to each hatch. The effect of such a clause was first considered in *The Sandgate* — *'Sandgate' (Owners)* v *W.S. Partridge & Co.* (1929) 35 Ll L Rep 9. The clause in that case provided for cargo to be taken from alongside 'at the average rate of 125 tons per working hatch per day', with a proviso that 'consignees shall not be obliged to take cargo from alongside . . . at a higher rate than 500 tons per day'. The owners submitted that the expression 'working hatch' was intended only to distinguish cargo hatches from other hatches, such as bunker hatches; and that as soon as the number of cargo hatches was ascertained, the rate of discharge was fixed — two hatches, 250 tons per day, three hatches, 375 tons per day, and four or more hatches, 500 tons per day (the proviso limiting the discharging rate to a maximum of 500 tons per day). The Divisional Court rejected this contention. They held that the expression 'working hatch' meant more than 'cargo hatch'; it denoted a hatch which can be worked because there is cargo underneath it waiting to be discharged. It followed that if, during discharge of a ship with four working hatches, discharge of one hatch was completed before the others, that hatch would cease to be a working hatch; the obligation in relation to the remaining three hatches would still be to discharge at a rate of 125 tons per day per hatch — a total rate of 375 tons per day instead of 500 tons per day when all four hatches were working hatches.

At the end of his judgment, Mr Justice Hill adverted to the manner of calculation of the laytime under a clause of this kind. He said (at pp. 12–13):

> As to the suggested difficulty of the shipowner in knowing what the lay days are going to be, there is nothing in it at all, because it appears from the charterparty that a bill of lading was to be issued and presumably was issued specifying the quantity of tons in each of the respective holds. I suppose worked out most accurately you would take these several quantities and start with 500 and go on reducing to 375, reducing to 250 and finally to 125; but you get exactly the same result, and the shipowner would have no difficulty in doing the arithmetic if he took the quantity in the hold which contains the largest quantity and divided that by 125, then that would give you the period in which the discharge had to be carried out, and you would then take into account Sundays and holidays.

The decision of the Divisional Court in that case was affirmed by the Court of Appeal (see (1929) 35 Ll L Rep 151; [1930] P 30). The leading judgment was delivered by Lord Justice Scrutton. He first pointed out that the function of the word 'average' in the clause was to ensure that there was no obligation to discharge any particular amount on any particular day. He then, like the Divisional Court, rejected the owners' contention that a working hatch meant simply a cargo hatch; it meant a hatch which can be worked because there is cargo underneath it.

The analysis of the clause was carried further by Mr Justice Devlin in *Compania de Navigacion Zita SA* v *Louis Dreyfus & Compagnie (The Corfu Island)* [1953] 2 Lloyd's Rep 472; [1953] 1 WLR 1399. The clause there provided for loading—

> . . . at an average rate of not less than 150 metric tons per available workable hatch per weather working day (Sundays and holidays excepted) . . .

The charterers contended that, in accordance with the approach of Mr Justice Hill in *The Sandgate*, the laytime for loading should be calculated by dividing by 150 the largest quantity of cargo loaded into any one of the hatches. The owners' contention was that it should be calculated by looking at the actual time occupied in loading, reducing the rate of loading as and when the loading of each hatch was completed. Mr Justice Devlin preferred the approach of the charterers, because on the owners' construction the number of laydays would depend on the way in which the charterers chose to load the vessel. The laytime clause was not prescribing a method of loading, but was setting a standard; it was drawing a notional line above which there would be a bonus and below a penalty. However, Mr Justice Devlin pointed out that the effect of interruptions in loading must of course be considered with reference to the actual events on the ship. Unavailability was outside the formula and a matter for separate calculation. An interruption in the loading which renders a hatch temporarily unavailable may or may not have the effect of extending the laytime, depending on the circumstances. Prima facie, the longest hatch is the critical hatch. Any interruption which prolongs the loading of that hatch will therefore prolong the laytime. But an interruption which affects the length of time for loading another hatch will only prolong the laytime if it so prolongs the loading of that hatch as to render it the critical hatch. If that happens, then the laytime will be calculated with reference to that hatch, instead of the longest hatch.

It will be observed that Mr Justice Devlin gave independent meaning to the words 'workable' and 'available' in this context. On his approach, a workable hatch is one which has cargo under it for discharge, or into which cargo has to be loaded; an available hatch is one which is not rendered unavailable by reason of the party responsible for loading or discharge being disabled from working it. In *The Giannis Xilas* [1982] 2 Lloyd's Rep 511 at p. 513. Mr Justice Bingham treated the expressions 'working hatch' and 'available workable hatch' as having the same meaning. In *Cargill Inc. v Marpro Ltd (The Aegis Progress)* [1983] 2 Lloyd's Rep 570, 576–577, Mr Justice Hobhouse stated that he was unpersuaded that to introduce the word 'available' into either the clause or the judicial discussion adds anything of substance. This point does not however trouble your Lordships in the present case, since both adjectives appear in the clauses under consideration.

Such are the authorities on the construction of the form of clause which provides for a rate per available workable hatch. This form of clause is to be contrasted with the well-known form of clause which provides for an overall rate for the whole ship. Both forms of clause have their virtues. Under the clause which provides for an overall rate for the ship, a quick, if rough and ready calculation can be made which will enable the parties to calculate how much laytime is prima facie available to the charterers for discharging; all they have to do for this purpose is to divide the bill of lading quantity by the specified rate. This calculation must be to some extent rough and ready, because it does not take account of the incidence of weekends or of bad weather, or of the impact of any other contractual exception; even so, it should provide a very helpful guide to charterers, bearing in mind that provisions in laytime clauses for weekends and weather generally favour the charterer. On the other hand, a laytime clause which provides for a rate per hatch — in particular, a rate per available workable hatch — is a more highly tuned clause which takes account of the fact that loading or discharge of one particular hatch may take longer than another, and that the completion of loading or discharge of the whole ship may well be governed by the amount of cargo under the longest hatch. This is likely to be of special importance where there is a substantial discrepancy between the volumes of the cargo spaces in the ship (taking account of the number of hatches per cargo space). The impact of such a clause on the calculation of the laytime, if taken in isolation, is likely to favour the charterer, because he will be protected by it from prolongation of the loading or discharge by reason of the existence of comparatively long hatches. I say 'in isolation', because if a clause is perceived to favour one or other party, its inclusion in the charter may be reflected in the freight rate. Moreover, it is not to be forgotten that the relative sizes of a ship's cargo spaces and the number of her hatches may be obvious to the charterer from the type of ship, and anyway can be ascertained by the charterer at the time of the fixture; and if it appears that there are significant differences in the sizes of the holds, the charterer can bargain for more favourable terms, either in relation to the freight rate or in relation to the rate of loading or discharge, or indeed by requesting a laytime clause which expressly specifies a rate per hatch.

This latter point is of some significance in the present case. In the course of argument, your Lordships' attention was focused upon the practical impact of the parties' respective approaches to the construction of the clauses under consideration, and it was revealed that the owners' approach, favouring an overall rate per ship, led to remarkable differences in the amount of cargo to be discharged per day under the three charters under consideration by your Lordships. For, if the owners' approach was correct, the daily rate of discharge required from the longest hatch in the cases of *General Capinpin* and *Proteus* was 252 and 278.72 tonnes respectively, whereas in the case of *Free Wave* a daily rate of 431.79 tonnes was required. This startling difference was due to the fact that *Free Wave* had two small cargo spaces (holding 1,045 and 1,600 tonnes respectively) and two large cargo spaces (holding respectively 5,344 and 6,071 tonnes). By proceeding on the basis of an overall discharging rate for the vessel of 1,000 tonnes per day, the effect of these disproportionately small and large spaces was that a very fast discharging rate was required from the longest hatch to complete the discharge of the vessel within the laytime. At first I was impressed by this point; but the more I thought about it, the less was the importance which I felt should be attached to it. First of all, the disproportionate sizes of the cargo spaces in *Free Wave* may, for all I know, be most unusual in this trade, and I hesitate therefore to attach much importance to this particular ship.... I turn to the construction of the clause, and to the resolution of the problem in these cases, which is essentially whether the clause should be given effect to as expressly providing for an overall rate of discharge for the whole ship, the reference to 'basis five or more available workable hatches' being treated only as qualifying that provision in the respects proposed by the owners, or whether that reference should be treated as overriding the provision for an overall rate of discharge, substituting for it a rate per available workable hatch. In truth the point is a short one, and it derives from the fact that the clause, which retains from its original form an overall rate of discharge which is then qualified by the words 'basis five or more available workable hatches', has built into it a tension between two different kinds of discharging rate. This gives rise to a problem which has to be solved as a matter of construction, but the meaning of the clause must also be to some extent a matter of impression. In this connection it is of some interest that, in all three cases, the construction favoured by the owners appears to have been unanimously adopted by the arbitrators. In the case of *General Capinpin* the arbitrator appointed by the charterer was Mr Clifford Clark, and in the cases of *Free Wave* and *Proteus* the arbitrator so appointed was Mr Cedric Barclay, both of them commercial men and arbitrators of exceptional distinction and experience. Although there was disagreement between the arbitrators in the case of the *Proteus*, it is legitimate to infer (since Mr Cedric Barclay was also the charterer's arbitrator in the case of *Free Wave*, where there was an agreed award) that the disagreement in the case of the *Proteus* must have been on another point....

... No great issue of principle arises in this case, which is concerned with the construction of an amended clause; though doubtless the clause in the present form has been employed by the charterer in a considerable number of cases, with the result that the present appeals are of importance to him. I can see no good reason for departing from the conclusion of the arbitrators in these three cases ...

*Note*
Lord Templeman dissented on the ground (*inter alia*) that 'a formula which defines laytime by reference to the total cargo produces results which are unfair to the charterer'. How important a consideration is that?

*C: Exclusions from laytime*
Time which would otherwise count as laytime may be excluded by a special provision in the charterparty; but exceptions formulated in general terms will not normally be applied to laytime unless the intention that they should apply is clear: see, for example, *Sametiet M/T Johs Stove v Istanbul Petrol Rafinerisi A/S (The Johs Stove)* [1984] 1 Lloyd's Rep 38 (QBD).

Time is also excluded if the inability of the vessel to load/discharge is due to the fault of the shipowners. See, e.g., *Gem Shipping Co. v Babanaft (Lebanon) SARL (The Fontevivo)* [1975] 1 Lloyd's Rep 339 (QBD): vessel left port because of fear of air raids.

## SECTION 3: DEMURRAGE

Demurrage is the agreed payment to compensate the shipowner for the charterer's breach in detaining the vessel beyond the permitted laytime. The principles of law are clear, though the results of their application may sometimes be surprising at first sight.

*A: The nature of demurrage*

### Chandris v Isbrandtsen-Moller Co. Inc.
[1951] 1 KB 240 (KB)

Under a voyage charterparty for a cargo of 'lawful general merchandise, excluding acids, explosives ... or other dangerous cargo' the charterer loaded 1,546 tons of turpentine, which was a dangerous cargo. The master consented to the shipment but did not waive the shipowner's rights in respect of it. After the vessel began to discharge her cargo at Liverpool, she was ordered to leave the dock, because of the dangerous nature of the turpentine, and discharge in the river into lighters. As a result discharge took 16 days longer than it otherwise would have done. The shipowner claimed damages, put at over £7,500, for detention of the ship for this period: the charterers argued that their liability was to pay the agreed rate of demurrage (£100 per day) and no more. The arbitrator found for the shipowner but the charterers' appeal was allowed.

DEVLIN J: A demurrage clause is merely a clause providing for liquidated damages for a certain type of breach. It is presumably the parties' estimate of the loss of prospective freight which the owner is likely to suffer if his ship is detained beyond the lay days. The demurrage rate in this case appears to have been a good deal lower than the freight market rate; and I suppose I need not shut my eyes to the fact that a sum produced by demurrage is generally less than damages for detention, which are presumably assessed by reference to the market rate of freight at the time of the breach. To this extent a demurrage clause may be in practice a concession to the charterer. But I am not, and I do not think I could be, invited to consider it as different in its nature from an ordinary liquidated damage clause.

At first sight it would appear that a demurrage rate should be as applicable to dangerous cargo as to any other sort of cargo. If the discharge of the dangerous cargo takes longer, the demurrage will be larger. Mr Mocatta has argued, however, that the shipment of dangerous cargo often results in the necessity for paying danger money or some other sort of bonus to officers and crew; and so, if the contract had covered dangerous cargo, a higher rate of freight and of demurrage might well have been demanded. The arbitrator thought so too; so let it be accepted. It seems to me that it is just because it may well be that neither the demurrage clause nor any other clause of the contract was originally intended to apply to the new situation created by a wrongdoer, that the aggrieved party is given his choice whether he desires them to apply or not. If he thinks that the freight and demurrage rates provided by the contract are insufficient to compensate him, he can rescind and sue on an implied contract for an adequate remuneration.

*Notes*
1.    In *Novorossisk Shipping Co.* v *Neopetro Co. Ltd (The Ulyanovsk)* [1990] 1 Lloyd's Rep 425, Steyn J pointed out (at p. 431) that some legal systems adopt a different theory of demurrage, namely as additional freight paid by the charterer, which may arguably be 'the sounder theory and more in tune with the way the market views demurrage'.
2.    A demurrage clause limits the damages payable even where the charterer deliberately slows down the loading and discharging operations, so as to reduce the number of voyages performed — and thereby reduce the liability for freight — under a charterparty for two years' consecutive voyages: *Suisse Atlantique Société d'Armement Maritime SA* v *NV Rotterdamsche Kolen Centrale* [1967] 1 AC 361 (HL).

*Question*
The *Ella Rose* was chartered to load a full and complete cargo of 850 standards of deal at Archangel for carriage to Manchester. Laytime was 10 days for loading and demurrage was fixed at £500 a day. When the *Ella Rose* arrived at Archangel there was still time to load a full summer cargo, but because of delay in obtaining the cargo, she became subject to winter cargo limits before completing loading and sailed with only 500 standards. The shipowners are claiming dead freight on 350 standards (£14,000) but the charterers say that they are only liable to pay demurrage for 10 days, the time by which they exceeded the laytime at the loading port. What should the arbitrator's decision be? (*Cf. Aktieselskabet Reidar* v *Arcos Ltd* [1927] 1 KB 352 (CA).)

*B: 'Once on demurrage, always on demurrage'*

This somewhat cryptic phrase expresses the principle that when laytime has expired and the vessel has gone on to demurrage, *prima facie* all time counts for

demurrage, even Sundays, holidays and any other period which is excluded
from the calculation of laytime, unless the charterparty shows a clear intention
to the contrary. General exceptions, even laytime exceptions, will be taken not
to cover demurrage unless the intention to apply them is clearly shown.

### Dias Compania Naviera SA v Louis Dreyfus Corporation
### (The Dias)
[1978] 1 Lloyd's Rep 325 (HL)

LORD DIPLOCK: My Lords, this appeal is about a dispute between shipowners and
charterers which arose under a voyage charter for the carriage of 26,500 tons of wheat
from the United States to China. As is generally the case with charterparties, the subject
of the dispute is laytime and demurrage; and the answer to the question that is involved
is to be found by applying well-established principles of construction to the particular
clauses of the charterparty.

The charterparty, dated Aug. 10, 1973, was a berth charter on the Baltimore berth
grain charterparty printed form. The place of discharge was 'one or two safe berths, one
or two safe ports, China'. The clauses, numbered 12 to 17, relating to arrival and
discharge of the cargo at its destination, were not in standard form. They were
type-written and special to the charterparty; they included a 'time lost' clause, viz.

Time lost in waiting and/or shifting for berth and/or discharge to be counted as
discharging time.

The clause which lies at the heart of the dispute is cl. 15:

At discharging, Charterers/Receivers have the option at any time to treat at their
expense ship's holds/compartments/hatchway and/or cargo and time so used to not
count. The Master to co-operate with the Charterers/Receivers or their representative
with a view to the treatment being carried out expeditiously.

It is common ground that 'treat' in this clause means fumigate and that fumigation is
an operation that has to be performed while the cargo is still on board or at any rate
before it has been fully discharged.

What happened was that the vessel was ordered to Hsinkang as the discharging port.
She anchored in the roads waiting her turn for a berth. Laytime expired on Oct. 26,
1973. A fortnight later on Nov. 9 fumigation started. It continued for 16 days six hours
until Nov. 25. Discharge into lighters started on Nov. 30 and at berth on Dec. 6. So no
additional delay was caused by the work of fumigation.

The only question in this appeal is whether demurrage is payable for the period of 16
days six hours during which fumigation was being carried out. So the laytime involved
in the dispute is laytime for discharge. The dispute between the parties, which at that
time was more extensive, went to arbitration in London, under the Centrocon
arbitration clause included in the charterparty. The umpire, in an award in the form of
a special case, held that demurrage was payable for that period. Mr Justice Mocatta
agreed (see [1976] 2 Lloyd's Rep 395): so did Lord Justice Browne in the Court of
Appeal, but his was a dissenting judgment. The majority of the Court (Lord Denning
MR, and Sir John Pennycuick) both held that demurrage was not payable, though their
reasons for doing so were not the same (see [1977] 1 Lloyd's Rep 485).

My Lords, the principles that apply to laytime and demurrage under voyage
charterparties are clear. What 'laytime' and 'demurrage' mean was stated succinctly by

Lord Guest (with the substitution of 'lay days' for 'laytime') in *Union of India* v *Compania Naviera Aeolus SA* [1962] 2 Lloyd's Rep 175; [1964] AC 868 at pp. 191 and 899:

> Lay days are the days which parties have stipulated for the loading or discharge of the cargo, and if they are exceeded the charterers are in breach; demurrage is the agreed damages to be paid for delay if the ship is delayed in loading or discharging beyond the agreed period.

For the purposes of the adventure in four stages contemplated by a voyage charterparty, laytime is that period of time, paid for by the charterer in the freight, for which the shipowner agrees to place the ship at the disposition of the charterer for carrying out the loading operation or the discharging operation. Laytime for discharging is generally based upon an estimate of the time which will be needed to carry out the operation with reasonable diligence if everything else goes well. With dry cargoes the actual discharging of the cargo is not an operation that can be carried on continuously for 24 hours in each successive day, but only intermittently, as weather and working days at the port permit. So the length of time for which the vessel will need to be at the disposition of the charterer for this operation in order to enable him to complete it within the stated period by the exercise of reasonable diligence on his part, is not predictable in advance. It can only be a matter of subsequent calculation by the application of an agreed formula to events that have occurred.

The formula states at what point of time laytime will start and what period of time thereafter shall be excluded from the calculation and so prevent its running continuously. These excluded periods are sometimes expressed as exceptions, e.g., 'Sundays and holidays excepted', sometimes by some such phrase as that time used for a stated purpose is 'not to count as laytime [or discharging time]' or simply 'not to count'. Similarly, the formula may state that there shall be included in the calculation periods of time spent by the ship in some way or other, which would otherwise not form part of the laytime because during the period so spent the ship had not yet become an arrived ship at the place for loading or discharge, e.g., a 'time lost' clause. The commonest way of expressing this is to say that time so spent is 'to count as laytime' or simply 'to count'.

As Mr Justice Mocatta, a Judge of great experience in these matters, said in his judgment in the instant case:

> ... In my experience, so far as it goes, phrases like 'to count' or 'not to count' are generally used in charters in reference to laytime.

If laytime ends before the charterer has completed the discharging operation he breaks his contract. The breach is a continuing one; it goes on until discharge is completed and the ship is once more available to the shipowner to use for other voyages. But unless the delay in what is often, though incorrectly, called redelivery of the ship to the shipowner, is so prolonged as to amount to a frustration of the adventure, the breach by the charterer sounds in damages only. The charterer remains entitled to continue to complete the discharge of the cargo, while remaining liable in damages for the loss sustained by the shipowner during the period for which he is being wrongfully deprived of the opportunity of making profitable use of his ship. It is the almost invariable practice nowadays for these damages to be fixed by the charterparty at a liquidated sum per day and pro rata for part of a day (demurrage) which accrues throughout the period of time for which the breach continues.

Since demurrage is liquidated damages, fixed by agreement between the parties, it is possible by apt words in the charterparty to provide that, notwithstanding the continuance of the breach, demurrage shall not be payable in respect of the period when some event specified in the charterparty is happening; but the effect of such an agreement is to make an exception to the ordinary consequences that would flow in law from the charterer's continued breach of his contract, viz. his liability in damages. As was said by Lord Justice Scrutton in a passage in his work on charterparties that was cited by Lord Reid in the *Union of India* case (ubi sup), at pp. 180 and 879:

> When once a vessel is on demurrage no exceptions will operate to prevent demurrage continuing to be payable unless the exceptions clause is clearly worded so as to have that effect.

This is but an example of the general principle stated by Lord Guest in the same case in continuation of the passage that I have already cited:

> . . . an ambiguous clause is no protection. 'If a party wishes to exclude the ordinary consequences that would flow in law from the contract that he is making he must do so in clear terms'. [*Szymonowski & Co.* v *Beck & Co.* [1923] 1 KB 457 at 466 per Lord Justice Scrutton.]

With these principles in mind I turn to the clause (cl. 15) principally relied upon by the charterers as excluding the accrual of demurrage during the period while fumigation, which did not commence until after the expiration of laytime, was being carried out. Appearing as it does in a set of six clauses dealing with the discharging operation, laytime allowed for it, and demurrage, my immediate reaction, like that of Mr Justice Mocatta, is that the answer to the question: 'for what purpose is time used in fumigation "not to count"?' would be: 'for the purpose of calculating laytime'. These words do not seem to me to be an apt way of saying that the time so used is not to be taken into account in assessing the damages payable by the charterer for breach of contract for failing to complete the discharging operation within the stipulated time. Reliance was placed by the charterers on the fact that the words at the beginning of the clause 'at any time' entitled the charterer to carry out the fumigation not only before laytime began to run and while it was running, but also after laytime had run out. For my part, I am unable to attach any significance to this, although Sir John Pennycuick thought it to be decisive. As I have pointed out, the charterers' breach of contract in failing to complete discharge within the laytime sounds in damages only, it does not deprive the charterer of his right to require the shipowner to continue performing his part of the contract. In this respect, the right of the charterer to fumigate after laytime has run out is no different from his right to complete the discharging of the cargo. In the remaining typewritten clauses of the charterparty, the expression 'time so used to count' or 'not to count' appears in cll. 12, 16 and 17, in contexts in which, as Lord Justice Browne pointed out, it is plain that it can only mean time to count or not to count as laytime, though the express words 'as laytime' are used only in cl. 17. In cl. 13, which includes the time lost clause that I have already cited, the words 'time to count' appear in the last sentence, also in a context in which, in my view, they can only mean to count as laytime.

For my part, I think that when construed in the light of established principles, cl. 15 is unequivocal. It means that time used in fumigation is not to be taken into account only in the calculation of laytime. The provision that time is 'not to count' has no further application once laytime has expired. But even if I were persuaded that the clause was in some way ambiguous, this would not be enough to save the charterers from their liability to pay demurrage during the period while fumigation was being carried out after laytime had expired. For these reasons, and in agreement with Mr Justice Mocatta and Lord Justice Browne I would allow this appeal.

## Union of India v Compania Naviera Aeolus SA
[1964] AC 868 (HL)

The shipowners, Aeolus, appealed against a decision of the Court of Appeal granting the charterers, Union of India, a declaration that they were not liable to pay demurrage for the period during which discharge was held up by a strike.

LORD REID: My Lords, the appellants are the owners of the *SS Spalmatori*. Under a charterparty of February 20, 1957, the vessel proceeded to Tacoma in the State of Washington, USA, and there loaded a cargo of 9,950 tons of wheat, belonging to the respondents, the Union of India. The bill of lading incorporated the provisions of the charterparty and that document provided that the provisions of the strike clause of the well-known Centrocon charterparty should apply. The decision of this appeal depends on the proper construction of that strike clause.

The vessel duly arrived at Bombay to discharge this cargo. The lay time expired at 13.56 hours on July 2, 1957. Discharge was still proceeding and admittedly from that time onwards the respondents were in breach of contract and demurrage at the rate of £200 per day became payable by them. Then discharge was interrupted by a strike which lasted from 07.00 hours on July 5 to 17.00 hours on July 13. The question in this case is whether demurrage ceased to be payable for the period of the strike.

. . .

I think that this case must be decided on the proper construction of the Centrocon strike clause taken by itself. It was not suggested that we could look at it in its original context in the Centrocon charterparty, and I find nothing in the provisions of the charterparty or bill of lading in this case which would throw any clear light on the present question.

The clause is a single clause not divided into paragraphs, but it has been treated, I think rightly, as consisting of four parts, and for convenience I set it out so as to show this division.

If the cargo cannot be loaded by reason of riots, civil commotions, or of a strike or lock-out of any class of workmen essential to the loading of the cargo or by reason of obstructions or stoppages beyond the control of the charterers on the railways, or in the docks or other loading places or if the cargo cannot be discharged by reason of riots, civil commotions or of a strike or lock-out of any class of workmen essential to the discharge, the time for loading or discharging, as the case may be, shall not count during the continuance of such causes.

Provided that a strike or lock-out of the shippers' and/or receivers' men shall not prevent demurrage accruing if by the use of reasonable diligence they could have obtained other suitable labour at rates current before the strike or lock-out.

In case of any delay by reason of the before-mentioned causes, no claim for damages or demurrage shall be made by the charterers, receivers of the cargo, or owners of the steamer.

For the purpose, however, of settling despatch rebate accounts any time lost by the steamer through any of the above causes shall be counted as time used in loading.

. . .

The substantial dispute in this case is as to the meaning of the third part of the clause. The respondents say that it operates independently of the rest of the clause and that they clearly come within its words. There was delay. The delay was by reason of a

before-mentioned cause, that is, a strike. The appellants are owners claiming demurrage. The clause says there shall be no claim for demurrage if there has been any such
delay. What more can you want? But I do not think that the case is as simple as that. The
whole clause — all four parts — must be read together, and moreover the third part itself
requires closer examination.

The first question which occurs to me on reading the clause as a whole is this. If the
third part was intended to operate independently of the rest of the clause why was it
sandwiched into the middle of the clause? If it was intended like the second and fourth
parts to be ancillary to the first part there is no difficulty. It is fairly obvious that the third
part is not an original part of the clause but is a later addition: I cannot imagine even the
least legally minded draftsman drafting the clause as a whole in its present form. We
were informed that the cases show that 50 years ago the clause was in use without this
third part, but I prefer to base my conclusions on the clause as it stands now.

Perhaps I should make good my statement that the second and fourth parts are only
ancillary to the first part. The second part is in the form of a proviso to the first part, and
the normal function of a proviso is to qualify what precedes it. . . . I think that the same
applies to the fourth part. Suppose a case where the lay time is six days and a strike
interrupts the lay time for four days. The first part then provides that the lay time is not
to expire until the tenth day. But suppose that in spite of the strike the work is completed
in nine days. Then without the fourth part the operation of the first part would give rise
to a claim for dispatch rebate. The fourth part prevents that, but clearly it can have no
application to a case where a strike occurs after demurrage has begun to accrue.

So the position is that the first, second and fourth parts can only apply in cases where
a strike occurs before the end of the stipulated lay time, but the respondents maintain
that there is no such limitation as regards the third part because it can be taken
independently of the rest of the clause. I must therefore now examine the third part to
see whether it can be treated as independent.

The first difficulty is that pointed out by McNair J [1960] 1 WLR 297, 303. If you
read the provision literally, then if there were one day's delay by reason of a strike but
ten days demurrage there could be no claim at all for the demurrage. That might be got
over by substituting for the initial words 'In case of any delay' the words 'In respect of
any delay'. But the second part, the proviso, creates a much more serious difficulty. One
of the 'before-mentioned causes' of the third part is 'a strike or lock-out of any class of
workmen essential to the loading of the cargo'. Even if I make the alteration in the third
part which I have just suggested, the third part taken independently provides that there
shall be no claim for demurrage in respect of any delay by reason of such a strike. But
the proviso provides that there shall be a claim for demurrage if other suitable labour was
available. It seems to me impossible to adopt a construction which would produce such
a flat contradiction between two parts of the same clause.

. . .

It is never satisfactory to construe a commercial document purely on a meticulous
examination of its language and I would not regard what I have just said as decisive. But
it does at least throw doubt on the validity of the simple method of construction for
which the respondents contend. And that doubt appears to me to be increased by
another consideration. If the third part is read as standing by itself it covers every
possible case to which the first part could apply as well as many others. In other words,
it virtually supersedes the first part and becomes the leading provision of the clause. I
find it almost incredible that those who added the third part to the original clause
intended it to have such a far-reaching effect.

So now I must consider what are the difficulties if the third part is regarded as merely
ancillary to the first part. It would still have an important part to play. As I said when

dealing with the first part, that part does not cover two kinds of case (1) where the strike does not stop work but merely slows down the loading or unloading and (2) where the after-effects of the strike stop or slow down the work. The third part may well have been intended to cover such cases: it is unnecessary to decide whether or not it does so.

...

The real question is how one should interpret 'the before-mentioned causes'. Clearly there are some instances in which the draftsman of the third part has not used language accurately, and this phrase may well mean strikes, etc., of the kind with which the earlier parts of the clause are dealing, that is, strikes, etc., occurring during the lay time. It is true that on this interpretation one possible case is not provided for. A strike may end before the lay time begins but leave such congestion that work during the lay time cannot proceed in the ordinary way. But the loose drafting of this part of the clause leads one to suppose that inadequate consideration was given to it and this case may well not have been foreseen.

So in my view the case stands in this position. There is no wholly satisfactory interpretation or explanation of the third part of the clause and one must choose between two almost equally unsatisfactory conclusions. In a case like this where a clause in common use has simply been copied one cannot try to find what the parties intended. They almost certainly never thought about things happening as they did. So I must fall back on the rule which I have already quoted from the work of Scrutton LJ. I do not think that it is an arbitrary rule for this reason. If a strike occurs before the end of the lay time neither party can be blamed in any way. But if it occurs after demurrage has begun to accrue the owner might well say: true, your breach of contract in detaining my ship after the end of the lay time did not cause the strike, but if you had fulfilled your contract the strike would have caused no loss because my ship would have been on the high seas before it began: so it is more reasonable that you should bear the loss than that I should. So it seems to me right that if the respondents are to escape from paying demurrage during this strike they must be able to point to an exceptions clause which clearly covers this case. And in my judgment they cannot do that. I am therefore of opinion that this appeal should be allowed, and the judgment of McNair J restored.

*Notes*

*1.* Lord Cohen and Lord Morris of Borth-y-Gest dissented. Is it not difficult to disagree with Lord Morris when he says: 'If the parties had intended that after the words "the before-mentioned causes" there should be words to the effect "always provided that such causes occurred during the time for loading or discharging" they would surely have said so?'

*2.* The principle of the above cases was applied to a mutual exception of restraint of princes in *Ellis Shipping Corporation* v *Voest Alpine Intertrading (The Lefthero)* [1992] 2 Lloyd's Rep 109 (CA, reversing Evans J).

*3.* Demurrage is not payable where the delay is due to the fault of the shipowner: *Blue Anchor Line Ltd* v *Alfred C. Toepfer International GmbH (The Union Amsterdam)* [1982] 2 Lloyd's Rep 432 (QBD). There the vessel grounded by the negligence of the pilots; the charterparty incorporated the negligent navigation exception from the US Carriage of Goods by Sea Act 1936. At the time of the grounding the vessel was moving into berth and was already on demurrage. Parker J rejected the shipowners' argument that 'fault' in this context meant only actionable fault and held that demurrage was not payable during the delay caused by the grounding.

# 10 TIME CHARTERS

Under a voyage charterparty the relationship between the shipowner and the charterer is based on a legal framework which puts most of the financial risk of the venture on the shipowner unless the parties agree otherwise. In the case of time charters, the position is reversed: the underlying principle is that risks in general fall on the charterer unless the contract puts them on the shipowner. Moreover, the time charterer is paying, in principle, for the unrestricted use of the vessel's services and the master must obey the charterer's orders throughout the term — limitations on the charterer's power to give orders must be found in the contract, either expressly or (exceptionally) by implication.

For these reasons the contract is all important. However, the issues which need to be addressed have little in common with those facing the draftsman of a voyage charterparty. In this chapter, after looking at some judicial definitions of time charters, we will examine the following aspects of them: the description of the vessel, orders for employment, the safe port limitation, the effect of requiring the master to sign bills of lading 'as presented', provisions for payment of hire and withdrawal of the vessel for non-payment, 'off-hire' clauses and the problem of the overrunning last voyage.

## SECTION 1: JUDICIAL DEFINITIONS OF A TIME CHARTER

### *Sea and Land Securities Ltd* v *William Dickinson & Co. Ltd*
[1942] 2 KB 65 (CA)

MACKINNON LJ: ... The rights and obligations of the parties to a time charterparty must depend on its written terms, for there is no special law applicable to this form of contract as such. A time charterparty is, in fact, a misleading document, because the real nature of what is undertaken by the shipowner is disguised by the use of language dating from a century or more ago, which was appropriate to a contract of a different character then in use. At that time a time charterparty (now known as a demise charterparty) was an agreement under which possession of the ship was handed by the shipowner to the charterer for the latter to put his servants and crew in her and sail her for his own benefit. A demise charterparty has long been obsolete. The modern form of time charterparty is, in essence, one by which the shipowner agrees with the time charterer that during a certain named period he will render services by his servants and crew to carry the goods which are put on board his ship by the time charterer. But certain phrases which survive in the printed form now used are only pertinent to the older form of demise charterparty. Such phrases, in the charterparty now before the court, are: 'the owners agree to let', and 'the charterers agree to hire' the steamer. There was no 'letting' or 'hiring' of this steamer. Then it is in terms provided that at the end of the period the vessel shall be 'redelivered' by the time charterers to the shipowners. 'Redelivery' is only a pertinent expression if there has been any delivery or handing over of the ship by the shipowner to the charterer. There never had been any such delivery here. The ship at all times was in the possession of the shipowners and they simply undertook to do services with their crew in carrying the goods of the charterers. As I ventured to suggest quite early in the argument, between the old and the modern form of contract there is all the difference between the contract which a man makes when he hires a boat in which to row himself about and the contract he makes with a boatman that he shall take him for a row.

*Note*
Demise (or 'bareboat') charters are certainly not obsolete at the present day, whatever may have been the position in 1942. Demise charterers are virtually in the position of shipowners for the period of the charter, as they have possession and control of the vessel. See Scrutton, pp. 59–63.

### *Scandinavian Trading Tanker Co. AB v Flota Petrolera Ecuatoriana (The Scaptrade)*
[1983] 2 AC 694

The facts are stated in section 6, below.

LORD DIPLOCK: A time charter, unless it is a charter by demise, with which your Lordships are not here concerned, transfers to the charterer no interest in or right to possession of the vessel; it is a contract for services to be rendered to the charterer by the shipowner through the use of the vessel by the shipowner's own servants, the master and the crew, acting in accordance with such directions as to the cargoes to be loaded and the voyage to be undertaken as by the terms of the charterparty the charterer is entitled to give to them. . . .

*Note and Questions*
1.   Neither of the above definitions mentions payment. Is this because it is not important, or because time charters are no different from other charterparties in this respect?
2.   Although many time charters *are* for a 'certain named period', the period may also be defined as a voyage, e.g., 'one round trip UK — West Africa': the time charter format can thus be used for a venture that could equally well be undertaken in the voyage charterparty format. Why might the parties choose one rather than the other?

*3.* A trip charter commonly includes an estimate of duration, e.g., '70/80 days without guarantee': the estimate must be made in good faith, i.e., genuinely believed, but it is immaterial whether or not it is reasonable or based on reasonable grounds: *Continental Pacific Shipping Ltd* v *Deemand Shipping Co. Ltd (The Lendoudis Evangelos II)* [1997] 1 Lloyd's Rep 404 (QBD, Longmore J: an argument for the owners that the effect should be the same as an estimated ready to load provision in a voyage charterparty was rejected as giving no meaning to 'without guarantee').

## SECTION 2: DESCRIPTION OF THE VESSEL

We have already dealt with statements as to the cargo capacity of a chartered vessel in relation to voyage charterparties (Chapter 9). Time charterers have a more immediate interest in other aspects of the vessel's performance, notably speed and fuel consumption. Since no two ships are identical in every detail, they also want to be sure that the vessel placed at their disposal is the one they contracted to take.

### Reardon Smith Line Ltd v Hansen-Tangen
### *(The Diana Prosperity)*
### [1976] 1 Lloyd's Rep 621 (HL)

LORD WILBERFORCE: My Lords, these appeals arise out of a charterparty and a sub-charterparty both relating to a medium sized newbuilding tanker to be constructed in Japan. By the time the tanker was ready for delivery the market had collapsed, owing to the oil crisis of 1974, so that the charterers' interest was to escape from their contracts by rejecting the vessel. The ground on which they hoped to do so was that the vessel tendered did not correspond with the contractual description.

Both charterparties were on the well known form Shelltime 3. The result of the appeal depends primarily upon the view taken of the sub-charterparty between the appellants in the first appeal ('Reardon Smith') and the respondents in that appeal ('Hansen-Tangen'), but, for the issue to be understood, it is necessary first to state some dates.

In 1972 the respondents in the second appeal ('Sanko'), a Japanese company, formed the 'Sanko plan' which was a project for the construction in Japanese yards of some 50 tankers of about 80,000 tons each which would be placed on charter by Sanko. At this time the market was strong. Before any vessels were actually built or even started Sanko arranged a number of charters — called 'fixtures' — defining the contractual terms of hire, the actual ships covered by each of them to be nominated later by Sanko. One such charter was that between Sanko and Hansen-Tangen (referred to in these proceedings as the 'intermediate charter'). It was dated Aug. 15, 1972. Clause 41 contained the following (emphasis supplied):

This Charter Party, subject to what is hereinafter stated, is for a motor tank vessel *to be built at a yard in Japan to be declared by Owners, (s.c. Sanko) together with the applicable Hull number for the vessel* within 30 June 1973 ...

Clause 42 conferred an option (not exercised) to nominate a slightly smaller vessel

... owners to declare name of shipyard and Hull number ... at the time such option ... is exercised.

The description of the vessel — warranted by the owners — was (as provided by cl. 24) set out in form B which is a standard form giving very detailed particulars about the ship, its equipment and performance. It is to be assumed for the purposes of these appeals that the vessel tendered complied in all respects with these requirements, and that therefore the charterers got precisely the kind of ship they wanted to precisely the 'description' stipulated.

On Mar. 28, 1973, by which time progress had been made with the plan, Sanko as charterers entered into a charterparty with a Liberian company called Sculptor as 'owners' for 'the good newbuilding tank vessel called Osaka Shipbuilding Co. Ltd. Hull No. 354 at Osaka Zosen' or 'built by Osaka Shipbuilding Co. Ltd and known as Hull No. 354 until named'. This charterparty also contained a form B in the same form as in the intermediate charter. Osaka Shipbuilding Co. Ltd is a substantial and reputable Japanese shipbuilding company with a yard at Osaka, which, however, could not build ships exceeding 45,000 tons. (The vessel contracted for was of about 88,000 tons.) So at this point, as the document shows, the vessel to be taken by Sanko, and passed on by Sanko to charterers from Sanko had gained an identity, not a physical identity, since construction had not yet started, but an identity in contracts and in order books.

Following on this, Sanko nominated the vessel to perform the intermediate charter. This was done by an addendum to that charterparty dated Aug. 10, 1973, which also altered the duration of the intermediate charter and the hire payments to be made under it. The nomination was made in the following terms:

With reference to Clause 41 and 42 of [the intermediate charter] the vessel to perform this Charter is to be built by Osaka Shipbuilding Co. Ltd and known as Hull No. 354 until named and shall have a deadweight of about 87,600 ... (other details follow).

Soon after this, on Oct. 12, 1973, the sub-charter between Hansen-Tangen and Reardon Smith was signed. I set out the preamble having emphasised the words which were added to the printed form.

It is this day agreed between H.E. Hansen-Tangen of Kristiansands, Norway (hereinafter referred to as 'Owners') being *Disponent* Owners of the good *Japanese flag (subject to Clause 41) Newbuilding motor tank vessel called Yard No. 354 at Osaka Zosen* [— Zosen = shipbuilding —] (hereinafter described as 'the vessel') described as per Clause 24 hereof and Reardon Smith Line Limited of Cardiff (*Sir William Reardon Smith and Sons Ltd of Cardiff — Managers*) (hereinafter referred to as Charterers').

The charterparty contained a cl. 24 and form B similar to the intermediate charter.

Parallel with these charter agreements were a number of contracts and arrangements concerning the building of the vessel. It is not necessary to specify these in detail. Osaka Shipping Co. Ltd ('Osaka') was, as I have mentioned, unable to build a vessel of 80,000 tons in its Osaka yard so it set about arranging for a new yard to be built at Oshima, which is on the island of Kyushu about 300 miles from Osaka. The method chosen was for Osaka to enter into a joint venture with two companies of the powerful Sumitomo group followed by the formation of a new company called Oshima Shipbuilding Ltd

('Oshima') in which Osaka had a 50 per cent interest and two Sumitomo companies the other 50 per cent. Oshima took over responsibility for building the new yard.

A series of contracts was entered into by which the Liberian company Sculptor ordered the vessel from a Sumitomo company, which agreed to build it by subcontract with Osaka; the Sumitomo company placed a shipbuilding contract with Osaka; and Osaka placed a shipbuilding (sub-) contract with Oshima. As mentioned above it was Sculptor from whom Sanko chartered the vessel on Mar. 28, 1973. As regards Oshima, a large part of its work force and a preponderant part of its expert managerial staff was provided on secondment from Osaka. The vessel to be constructed was to be numbered 004 in Oshima's books but also 354 in Osaka's books and in export documents. The chain, therefore, was (1) Oshima agreed to construct the vessel under contract with Osaka, (2) Osaka contracted with a Sumitomo company to build and deliver the vessel, (3) the Sumitomo company agreed to build the vessel by Osaka and to sell it to Sculptor, (4) Sculptor agreed to hire it to Sanko, (5) Sanko agreed to hire it to Hansen-Tangen, (6) Hansen-Tangen agreed to hire it to Reardon Smith. In all these contracts the vessel was described as no. 354 in connection with Osaka.

These being the background facts, the whole case, as regards the first appeal, turns, in my opinion, upon the long underlined passage in the sub-charter set out above which, for convenience of reference I repeat.

> ... (the good) Japanese flag (subject to Clause 41) Newbuilding motor tank vessel called Yard No. 354 at Osaka Zosen.

I shall refer to this as the 'box' since it appears enclosed in a typed box on the document.

The contract is in the English language and (cl. 40) is to be construed in accordance with English law. But it has been sought to introduce, as an aid to construction, a considerable amount of evidence as to Japanese usages and practice, some of which was in fact taken into account by the Court of Appeal. To decide how far this is legitimate one must make a distinction. When it comes to ascertaining whether particular words apply to a factual situation or, if one prefers, whether a factual situation comes within particular words, it is undoubtedly proper, and necessary, to take evidence as to the factual situation. Thus once one has decided what is meant by 'Yard No. 354', or 'to built at a Yard' it is proper by evidence to establish the characteristics of particular yards, the numbering used at those yards, and the 'building' which may have been done, in order to answer, yes or no, the question whether the contractual requirements have been met. There is no difficulty, in law, about this part of the case.

It is less easy to define what evidence may be used in order to enable a term to be construed. To argue that practices adopted in the shipbuilding industry in Japan, for example as to sub-contracting, are relevant in the interpretation of a charterparty contract between two foreign shipping companies, whether or not these practices are known to the parties, is in my opinion to exceed what is permissible. But it does not follow that, renouncing this evidence, one must be confined within the four corners of the document. No contracts are made in a vacuum: there is always a setting in which they have to be placed. The nature of what is legitimate to have regard to is usually described as 'the surrounding circumstances' but this phrase is imprecise: it can be illustrated but hardly defined. In a commercial contract it is certainly right that the Court should know the commercial purpose of the contract and this in turn presupposes knowledge of the genesis of the transaction, the background, the context, the market in which the parties are operating.

...

It is often said that, in order to be admissible in aid of construction, these extrinsic facts must be within the knowledge of both parties to the contract, but this requirement should not be stated in too narrow a sense. When one speaks of the intention of the parties to the contract, one is speaking objectively — the parties cannot themselves give direct evidence of what their intention was — and what must be ascertained is what is to be taken as the intention which reasonable people would have had if placed in the situation of the parties. Similarly when one is speaking of aim, or object, or commercial purpose, one is speaking objectively of what reasonable persons would have in mind in the situation of the parties. It is in this sense and not in the sense of constructive notice or of estopping fact that judges are found using words like 'knew or must be taken to have known' ...

... [W]hat the Court must do must be to place itself in thought in the same factual matrix as that in which the parties were. All of these opinions seem to me implicitly to recognize that, in the search for the relevant background, there may be facts, which form part of the circumstances in which the parties contract in which one, or both, may take no particular interest, their minds being addressed to or concentrated on other facts, so that if asked they would assert that they did not have these facts in the forefront of their mind, but that will not prevent those facts from forming part of an objective setting in which the contract is to be construed. I shall show that this is so in the present case.

So I ask what was the commercial purpose of these charterparties and what was the factual background against which they were made? The purpose is clear: it was to make available to (1) Hansen-Tangen and (2) to Reardon Smith a medium sized tanker suitable for use as such, this tanker not being in existence, or even under construction at the date of either charter, and, at the date of the intermediate charter not even the subject of contracts made by the supplying company. The vessel was to be constructed in a Japanese yard and made available on charter to Sanko as part of a programme. At the date of the subcharter the vessel was identified in contracts for its construction in Japan and had a serial number. In order to ensure that the tanker was suitable for its purpose a detailed specification was drawn up — by way of a warranted description with which of course the vessel must strictly comply.

In addition, since at the time of either charterparty the vessel was not in existence or under construction, some means had to be agreed upon for identifying the particular vessel — one out of a programme — which would form the subject matter of the charters. This was indispensable so as to enable those committing themselves to hire and vessel, to sub-hire it, if they wished, and if necessary to arrange finance. This necessary identification was to be effected by nomination, by Sanko in the first place and then by Hansen-Tangen.

The text of the charterparties confirms beyond doubt that this was what was intended and done. The preamble, in the Shelltime 3 form, provides for the insertion of a name — 'being owners of the good ... tank vessel called ...'. The box insertion in the sub-charter was made in this place — 'called Yard No. 354 at Osaka Zosen'. The intermediate charter, entered into before Sanko had nominated any vessel, provided in its preamble — instead of 'called ...' for declaration by the owners together with the hull number, and the addendum, entered into after Sanko had nominated, provided 'to be built by Osaka Shipbuilding Co. Ltd and known as Hull No. 354 until named'. What is vital about each of these insertions is that they were simple substitutes for a name, serving no purpose but to provide a means whereby the charterers could identify the ship. At the dates when these insertions were made no importance could have been attached to the matters now said to be so significant — they were not a matter of negotiation, but of unilateral declaration. What is now sought is to elevate them into strict contractual terms in the nature of 'conditions'.

The appellants sought, necessarily, to give to the 'box' and the corresponding provision in the intermediate charter contractual effect. They argued that these words formed part of the 'description' of the future goods contracted to be provided, that, by analogy with contracts for the sale of goods, any departure from the description entitled to other party to reject, that there were departures in that the vessel was not built by Osaka Shipbuilding Co. Ltd, and was not hull no. 354. I shall attempt to deal with each of these contentions.

In the first place, I am not prepared to accept that authorities as to 'description' in Sale of Goods cases are to be extended, or applied, to such a contract as we have here.... But in case it does not appeal to this House, I am also satisfied that the appellants fail to bring the present case within the strictest rules as to 'description'.

In my opinion the fatal defect in their argument consists in their use of the words 'identity' or 'identification' to bridge two meanings. It is one thing to say of given words that their purpose is to state (identify) an essential part of the description of the goods. It is another to say that they provide one party with a specific indication (identification) of the goods so that he can find them and if he wishes sub-dispose of them. The appellants wish to say of words which 'identify' the goods in the second sense, that they describe them in the first. I have already given reasons why I can only read the words in the second sense.

The difference is vital. If the words are read in the first sense, then, unless I am right in the legal argument above, each element in them has to be given contractual force. The vessel must, as a matter of contract, and as an essential term, be built by Osaka and must bear their yard no. 354 — if not the description is not complied with and the vessel tendered is not that contracted for.

If in the second sense, the only question is whether the words provide a means of identifying the vessel. If they fairly do this, they have fulfilled their function. It follows that if the second sense is correct, the words used can be construed much more liberally than they would have to be construed if they were providing essential elements of the description.

The two significant elements (whether in the 'box' or in the intermediate charter) are (i) the yard no. 354, (ii) the expression 'built by Osaka Shipbuilding Ltd'. [These words do not appear in the 'box' but I will assume, very much in the appellants' favour, that the 'box' has the same meaning as if the word 'built' were used.] The appellants at one time placed great stress on the yard no. provision. They contended that by using it the 'owners' assumed an obligation that the vessel should bear a number which would indicate that it would be constructed in the yard, where that number was appropriate, in sequence after vessels bearing earlier yard numbers (350–353). But this argument broke down in face of the fact, certainly known to Sanko which used and introduced the number into the charterparties, that the sequence through 354 was the sequence used at Osaka Shipbuilding Co.'s yard at Osaka, which yard could not construct the vessel. Thus the use of the yard no. for the contracted vessel must have had some other purpose than indicating construction at a particular yard. This turns the argument against the appellants — for it shows the words to be 'labelling' words rather than words creating an obligation.

So the question becomes simply whether, as a matter of fact, it can fairly be said that — as a means of identification — the vessel was yard no. 354 at Osaka Zosen or 'built by Osaka Shipping Co. Ltd and known as Hull No. 354 until named'. To answer this, regard may be had to the actual arrangement for building the vessel and numbering it before named.

My Lords, I have no doubt, for the reasons given by the Court of Appeal that an affirmative answer must be given. I shall not set out the evidence which clearly makes this good. The fact is that the vessel always was Osaka Hull no. 354 — though also Oshima no. 4 — and equally it can fairly be said to have been 'built' by Osaka Shipbuilding Co. Ltd as the company which planned, organised and directed the building and contractually engaged with Sculptor to build it, though also it could be said to have been built by Oshima Co. Ltd. For the purpose the identificatory clause, the words used are quite sufficient to cover the facts. No other vessel could be referred to: the reference fits the vessel in question.

There are other facts not to be overlooked. (1) So long as the charterers could identify the nominated vessel they had not the slightest interest in whatever contracting or subcontracting arrangements were made in the course of the building, a fact which no doubt explains the looseness of the language used in the 'box'. (2) In making the arrangements they did for building the vessel Osaka acted in a perfectly straightforward and open manner. They cannot be said to be substituting one vessel for another; they have not provided any ground upon which the charterers can claim that their bargain has not been fulfilled. The contracts all down the chain were closely and appropriately knitted into what Osaka did. (3) If the market had risen instead of falling, it would have been quite impossible for Osaka or Sculptor, or Sanko, to refuse to tender the vessel in accordance with the charters on the ground that it did not correspond with that contracted for. No more on a falling market is there, in my opinion, any ground on which the charterers can reject the vessel. In the end I find this a simple and clear case.

*Notes*

*1.* At common law a statement of the vessel's classification was held to imply no guarantee that the classification would be maintained beyond the date of making the charterparty (*French* v *Newgass* (1878) 3 CPD 163 (CA)).

*2.* By contrast, there *was* an implied undertaking by the shipowner that the flag would not be changed, because to do so 'would materially affect the ship as the subject-matter of the charterparty'; it would affect not only the status of the ship but also determine 'the nationality and therefore to some extent the discipline and morals of the crew' (*per* Rowlatt J in *M. Isaacs & Sons Ltd* v *William McAllum & Co. Ltd* [1921] 3 KB 377, at p. 386).

*3.* In *Cosmos Bulk Transport Inc.* v *China National Foreign Trade Transportation Corp. (The Apollonius)* [1978] 1 Lloyd's Rep 53 (QBD), the vessel was stated to be capable of steaming 14.5 knots. Between signing and delivery, she had spent seven weeks at Whampoa, where her bottom became encrusted with molluscs (this was not foreseen, as molluscs prefer saltwater and the water at Whampoa is fresh or slightly brackish). As a result, she achieved less than 11 knots on the charter trip from Japan to the Argentine. Mocatta J held, not following the view of Atkinson J in *Lorentzen* v *White Shipping Co. Ltd* (1942) 74 Ll L Rep 161, that for 'overwhelming' commercial reasons the shipowners' undertaking as to the vessel's speed applied to the time of delivery. (The decision relieving the charterers of liability to pay hire for the additional steaming time required to complete the trip was based on the off-hire clause in the charter: the fouling of the bottom was an 'other accident'.)

*4.* Time charters usually require the shipowner to use due diligence to maintain the vessel's performance and contain detailed provision for adjustment of the hire if the vessel falls below or exceeds the stated performance. For an example of what Bingham LJ charitably called a clause 'of commercial rather than legal draftsmanship', see *Didymi Corp.* v *Atlantic Lines and Navigation Co. Inc. (The Didymi)* [1988] 2 Lloyd's Rep 108.

## SECTION 3: ORDERS FOR EMPLOYMENT

*A: 'Employment, agency and other arrangements'*

The effect of the traditional phrase that 'the master shall be under the orders and direction of the charterer as regards employment, agency and other arrangements' is to exclude matters of navigation from the right of the charterer to decide where and how the vessel shall be employed.

### *Larrinaga Steamship Co. Ltd* v *The King*
[1945] AC 246 (HL)

In 1939 the *Ramon de Larrinaga* was requisitioned by the Crown on time charter terms. The charter provided that the master was to be under the orders and direction of the charterer (i.e., the Crown) 'as regards employment, agency or other arrangements'. While discharging a cargo of military transport at St Nazaire, then a British war base, on 13 October, the ship received written orders from the Sea Transport Officer at St Nazaire to proceed immediately to Quiberon Bay on completion of discharge to join a convoy to be escorted to the British Channel for off-survey to Cardiff. The first officer then had a personal interview with the Sea Transport Officer (the master was ill) and objected that conditions were too dangerous for the voyage that evening, but the Sea Transport Officer insisted that the ship could not stay in the berth overnight. The ship was then taken by pilot to an anchorage down channel; soon afterwards the weather worsened and the pilot advised returning to St Nazaire. While attempting to do so, the ship grounded on a sand bank and sustained damage costing nearly £42,000 to repair. The shipowners claimed that the cost of repairs should be borne by the Crown as the damage arose as a result of carrying out the charterer's orders. The House of Lords affirmed the decision of the Court of Appeal in favour of the Crown.

LORD WRIGHT: ... I merely add a few observations on the important question of principle which is raised by the appellants' claim to an indemnity under cl. 9 of the charterparty. I find myself with all deference unable to take the same view as in the Court of Appeal MacKinnon LJ took, and out of respect to his authority I think I ought to state briefly, in my own words, my reasons for differing from him. The central point of contest is what is meant by the words 'employment, agency and other arrangements' occurring as they do in cl. 9. The opposed views are, on the one hand, that they mean 'employment of the ship' or, on the other hand, that they mean 'employment of persons, stevedores, agents, pilots, tug owners or other persons'. To my mind the former is the sense in which the 'employment' is used in this context. It couples up with the words 'to be employed in such lawful trades' in cl. 1. It also fits in with the words 'agency or other arrangements' with which it is directly associated. All three words have a reference to the general management of the ship's business and affairs under the charterparty. 'Employment' means employment of the ship to carry out the purposes for which the charterers wish to use her; 'agency' deals with another aspect of the conduct of the ship's affairs. The shipowner is entitled in the ordinary course to decide to what firm or person in each port the ship in the course of the charterparty is to be consigned as agent. The selection is here left to the charterers. That is an important matter because of the multifarious duties and responsibilities which may fall to be discharged according to mercantile law by the ship's agents. 'Arrangements' is a wider term. It is also used in this charterparty in cl. 3. There it refers to disbursements which have to be made for services in connexion with operating the ship, and I think it has a similar scope in cl. 9. In this way the three words in question have a kindred significance and are used as referring to the general conduct of the business of the ship under the charterparty, while the 'employment of persons' would introduce a different and incongruous element. It is true that lower down in cl. 9, in a separate paragraph, there are the words 'other qualified persons' employed by the charterers. But there the ambit of the word 'employed' is clearly limited and defined by the word 'persons'. It is a different matter when it is used simpliciter in the first paragraph of the clause, in a context in which prima facie the employment of persons is alien. Such authority as there is goes to support the view that 'employment' means 'of the ship'. In *Weir* v *Union Steamship Co. Ltd* [1900] AC 525, 532, 533, Lord Davey has some observations on a somewhat similar clause in the charterparty there in question, but he seems to assume that the words referred to the vessel's employment, which he distinguished from any incident of navigation. The other Law Lords do not refer to the clause which in that charterparty was numbered cl. 4. Since then two very experienced commercial judges have accepted the construction that 'employment' meant employment of the ship. Greer LJ in *Lensen Shipping Co. Ltd* v *Anglo-Soviet Shipping Co. Ltd* 40 Com Cas 320, 329 and Roche J in *Portsmouth Steamship Co. Ltd* v *Liverpool and Glasgow Salvage Association* (1929) 34 Ll L Rep 459. What they say does at least indicate how it struck them that the word in the context should be construed.

In my opinion the 'employment' referred to is 'employment of the ship'. This opinion, based on the words, seems to me to be confirmed by looking at the structure and scheme of the charterparty as a whole. But I can best consider that when I have indicated what is, I think, meant by 'orders and direction of the charterer as regards employment' of the ship. Atkinson J (1943) 168 LT 203, 205 seems to have thought that it included what he described as 'sailing orders to Quiberon Bay to be obeyed forthwith in the dark and in bad weather with a falling glass and insisted upon after protest'. He accordingly gave an enlarged scope to the indemnity. But I think the word 'employment' in cl. 9 has the same meaning as in cl. 1, and means the services which the ship is ordered to perform, such as the voyages to or from particular ports, with particular cargoes or in ballast. In this particular case the order as to employment was the order to go to Cardiff for the off-survey. The order to go to Cardiff for the off-survey was, in my opinion, an order as to employment within cl. 9 of the charterparty. No point is made in regard to the directions in writing given under cl. 11. They were at once properly destroyed and their exact tenor is not clear. The view of the judge was that what he desribed as the 'sailing orders to Quiberon Bay to be obeyed forthwith' (I have already quoted his words), were orders as to employment within cl. 9. With the greatest respect, I cannot agree with that view. These sailing orders which the judge found were given were, in my opinion, merely dealing with matters of navigation, in regard to carrying out the orders to proceed to Cardiff. It was the duty of the master to exercise his judgment in such matters of navigation. The master was the servant of the shipowner. Lord Davey in *Weir* v *Union Steamship Co. Ltd* was of opinion that the clause he was considering had 'nothing whatever to do with navigation or any incident of navigation'. That is even more obvious when the general scheme of the charterparty now in question is considered. Not only is the charterparty not a demise, but the shipowner is expressly made liable inter alia for all services in connexion with the navigation of the ship. Under the later paragraphs of cl. 9 the charterers are not to be held responsible for damage caused by the negligence of masters, officers or crews, and the owners are not relieved from responsibility for safe and proper stowage. The whole scheme of the charterparty was to place liability for sea perils on the shipowners who were to be responsible for insurance, other than that for war risks. The appellants did not, in fact, insure against marine risks, but the position must be considered as if they had, and if they had, the judgment of Atkinson J would have had the result that the marine underwriters, on paying the loss caused by the stranding, would have been entitled by subrogation to pass the loss on to the charterers, who would thus have been compelled to bear a marine loss of a type which was never intended, according to the plain meaning of the contract, to fall on them. Further, if the indemnity in cl. 9 applies in this case, it must be because the loss was a consequence of the ship complying with an order or direction as to the employment of the ship. It would follow on that view that generally every marine casualty which affects the ship when sailing under charterers' orders would be a consequence of her employment and of the orders or directions of the charterers under cl. 9. I cannot accept this conclusion. In this aspect the peculiar features of the case, such as the objections of the master, are not material. The strange results which would follow from the decision of Atkinson J would, it is true, be avoided by the construction adopted by the Court of Appeal, but I am unable to adopt that construction. The construction which I adopt gives, I think, a natural meaning to the words of the charterparty and does not involve a departure from its business scheme. I have not thought it necessary to consider whether the orders on which the judge based his judgment were or were not given by the Sea Transport Officer in his capacity as harbour master or port official. Indeed, the evidence on this point is insufficient. I concur in the motion proposed.

### Newa Line v Erechthion Shipping Co. SA
### (The Erechthion)
[1987] 2 Lloyd's Rep 180 (QBD)

The *Erechthion* was let on a time charter trip from Flushing to West Africa. The charterers ordered her to Port Harcourt in Nigeria. On arrival, as her draught was too deep for the river, she was ordered by the harbour authority to proceed to Dawes Island anchorage to lighten. When approaching the anchorage she ran aground and during attempts to refloat was damaged by striking a solid submerged object. Neither the master nor pilot was negligent. Arbitrators upheld the shipowners' claim to an indemnity in respect of the damage. The charterers obtained leave to appeal.

STAUGHTON J: It was not argued for the owners that the order, admitted to have been given by or on behalf of the charterers, for the vessel to proceed to Port Harcourt was in itself the cause of the casualty. Likewise it has not been argued that the advice of Pilot Okonkwo amounted to orders given by or on behalf of the charterers. What the owners do say is that between those events there occurred the instructions of the harbour authority to proceed to the Dawes Island anchorage. It is that order which is said to have qualified, directly or indirectly, as the charterers' order for the purposes of the implied indemnity.

In theory at any rate, it is the right of the charterer of a time chartered vessel to give all orders as to the vessel's employment — where she shall load, what cargo she shall carry, and where she must discharge it. That is emphasised in the present case by cl. 9 of the charterparty:

> The Captain (although appointed by the Owners) shall be under the orders and directions of the Charterers as regards employment . . .

But in practice, at many if not most ports in the world, it is the harbour authority which decides when and where a vessel shall discharge her cargo. Until the harbour authority has allocated a discharging place, the charterer is unable to give any effective orders. Once a discharging place has been allocated by the harbour authority, it would be an ideal formality for the charterer to issue confirmation in the shape of an order to the vessel to go there. I suppose that a pedantic charterer might expressly reserve to himself the right to give the order; or an eccentric charterer might even countermand the harbour authority's instruction and tell the master to wait in the roads rather than proceed to the berth allocated. But that again is theory. In practice, so far as the vessel was concerned at this port, it is manifest that the charterers left it to the harbour authority to instruct the vessel where to go in order to discharge the cargo. If the master had refused to comply until those orders had been confirmed by the charterers, I have no doubt that they would have reproached him for wasting time at their expense.

One analysis of the owners' argument is that so far as they were concerned, the harbour authority was the charterers' agent to give orders. For my part, I prefer the way that it was put in argument by Mr Mocatta in *Stag Line Ltd* v *Ellerman & Papayanni Lines Ltd* (1949) 82 Ll L Rep 826 as recorded by Mr Justice Morris at p. 835:

> . . . Mr Mocatta, I think submits further that even though the orders to go to a particular berth were the orders of the military, they were in effect the orders of the charterers because the charterers had ordered their master to Naples and presumably to go then to the particular berth to which he was directed by the military. Mr Mocatta points to Clause 3 of the charterparty and says that it is for the charterers to arrange for unloading . . .

Mr Justice Morris did not find it necessary to rule on that argument. I consider it well-founded. Applied to the present case, it means that the charterers' order to go to Port Harcourt meant to go to such discharging place on arrival there as the harbour authority should designate.

. . .

It is well settled that the orders which a charterer is entitled to give, and an owner bound to obey, are orders as to the employment of the vessel. They do not include orders as to navigation, which remains in the control of the owner through his master — at any rate in the absence of special and unusual terms. It follows that a charterer, again in the absence of such terms, is only bound to indemnify the owner against the consequences of orders as to employment, and not of orders as to navigation. That is established by *Weir* v *The Union Steamship Company Ltd* [1900] AC 525, *Larrinaga Steamship Co. Ltd* v *The King* (1945) 78 Ll L Rep 167; [1945] AC 246, the *Stag Line* case, *Scrutton on Charterparties* (19th ed.) p. 376, *Carver on Carriage by Sea* (13th ed.) par. 669, *Wilford on Time Charters* (2nd ed.) pp. 197 to 198.

The question here is whether the order to proceed to Dawes Island anchorage was an order as to employment or as to navigation. Seeing that the manifest intention was for the vessel to lighten there by discharging part of her cargo, I am of opinion that it was plainly an order as to employment. By contrast the advice of the pilot as to precisely where the vessel should anchor, if it had been an order and if (which is not suggested) it had been given on behalf of the charterers, would have been an order as to navigation.

*Notes*
1.   The case was remitted to the arbitrators to make a finding as to the proximate cause of the casualty, since the indemnity only applies if the order to proceed to the anchorage is the proximate cause. The shipowners' claim was subsequently rejected: see *Triad Shipping Co.* v *Stellar Chartering & Brokerage Inc (The Island Archon)* [1994] 2 Lloyd's Rep 227, at 235, per Evans LJ.
2.   Navigation includes choice of route, so that charterers' instructions to follow the (shorter) northern great circle route from Vancouver to Yokkaichi and Shiogama respectively, as opposed to the more southerly rhumb line route, were not orders as to employment and the owners were not in breach of the charter because the master took the longer route, which he considered safer: *Whistler International Ltd* v *Kawasaki Kisen Kaisha Ltd (The Hill Harmony)* [1998] 2 Lloyd's Rep 367 (QBD, Clarke J, affirmed (CA), *The Times*, 25 May 1999.). An argument that the master had failed to 'prosecute his voyage with the utmost despatch' (cl. 8 of the charter) foundered on the exclusion of errors of navigation (cl. 16, and Art. IV, r. 2(a) of the Hague-Visby Rules, which were incorporated into the charter).

*B: Compliance with orders*

### Kuwait Petroleum Corporation v I&D Oil Carriers Ltd
### (The Houda)
[1994] 2 Lloyd's Rep 541 (CA)

NEILL LJ: This is an appeal by I & D Oil Carriers Ltd (whom I shall call 'the owners') from the order of Mr Justice Phillips first made on Oct. 8, 1992 and perfected on Jan. 12, 1993. By his order Mr Justice Phillips granted a declaration that the owners' vessel (*Houda*) was off-hire for a substantial part of the period between Aug. 8, 1990 and Sept. 27, 1990. The declaration was made at the instance of Kuwait Petroleum Corporation (whom I shall call 'the charterers') to whom the owners had chartered *Houda* under a time charter-party dated Apr. 2, 1990 on the Shelltime 4 form. The Judge's judgment is reported [1993] 1 Lloyd's Rep 333.
. . .

*The facts*
On Aug. 2, 1990 Iraq invaded Kuwait. On that day *Houda* was loading oil at Mina Al Ahmadi. On the announcement of the invasion *Houda* sailed part loaded. Before her departure blank bills of lading had been issued pursuant to the early departure procedure, but these bills of lading were left behind in Kuwait. The bills of lading named the charterers as the shippers of the cargo and stated that the cargo was to be delivered at the port of Ain Sukhna to the order of the charterers. The master had signed the bills of lading but it had been arranged that the charterers would complete the documents when the amount of cargo was known. By the time of sailing about 150,000 tonnes of crude oil had been loaded. The bills of lading have disappeared.

By Aug. 8, 1900 *Houda* had proceeded to an anchorage off Fujairah, which lies just outside the Gulf. The charterers do not complain about this deviation from the orders given on Aug. 3 to proceed to Dubai.

Before the invasion of Kuwait *Houda* was operating under standing instructions which had been issued by the charterers in these terms:

> All instructions relating to the voyages of your vessel will be issued by Kuwait Petroleum Corp. in Kuwait.

After the invasion the management of the charterers was moved to London. It was from the charterers' office in London that the orders were given on which the charterers rely in the present proceedings.

At 16.45 GMT on Aug. 8 the charterers sent a telex through Davies and Newman, the brokers who had fixed the vessel, to the owners' managers in Athens instructing the vessel to proceed to the Red Sea for orders. The telex was in these terms:

> Vessel now to proceed Red Sea for orders. Intention Ain Sukhna. Possibility that vessel will top up Yanbu however this is extremely private and should not be reported. Please request Master to advise ETA basis Aden, Yanbu and Ain Sukhna urgently to D & N.

At 17.15 GMT a similar message was sent stressing the urgency of the matter.

. . .

In the course of the next few days further messages passed between the parties. Meanwhile the charterers sent instructions to SGS in Dubai to carry out a cargo survey on the cargo aboard *Houda*. The owners however were unwilling to permit a survey to be carried out until they were satisfied that the charterers' London office had authority to act for the charterers in the matter. The SGS surveyors were therefore told by the master that they could board the vessel to carry out a survey only if they could prove that they had the charterers' authority. By this time the parties had instructed solicitors.

. . .

The parties' solicitors, however, were unable to reach agreement. On Aug. 16, 1990 the charterers applied to Mr Justice Steyn for interlocutory relief. They sought an order permitting a surveyor to survey the cargo and to restrain the owners from using *Houda* otherwise than in accordance with the charter-party and orders from the charterers. Mr Justice Steyn declined to grant this relief but adjourned the matter to the following day on an undertaking from the owners that *Houda* would not sail from its present position and that they would not seek to terminate the charter-party.

On Aug. 17 the application by the charterers was restored before Mr Justice Morland. By this time the charterers' position had been strengthened because they had received information which led them to believe that *Houda* had sailed from Fujairah in breach of the undertaking by the owners. It subsequently transpired that the vessel had had to stand clear from Fujairah for safety reasons. However that may be, Mr Justice Morland made an order that the owners should permit an SGS surveyor to board *Houda* forthwith to carry out inspections and measurements. In addition Mr Justice Morland granted an injunction restraining the owners from causing, permitting or ordering the vessel to sail to anywhere other than Ain Sukhna or such other place as the charterers might direct save with the consent of the charterers. The order also included an undertaking by the charterers in these terms:

> Not to seek delivery of the cargo aboard the vessel *Houda* without either: (a) the consent of [the owners]; or (b) an order of this court.

On Aug. 18 *Houda* returned to an anchorage off Fujairah and on Aug. 19 the surveyors boarded the vessel and carried out an inspection.

*Houda* sailed for Ain Sukhna on Aug. 21 where she arrived at 08.00 GMT on Sept. 4, anchoring about 12 miles off the Sumed pipeline. The Judge, however, limited the period during which he held the vessel to be off hire off Fujairah to a period of 11 days and 12 minutes because (a) he allowed a period of 24 hours for a cargo survey at Fujairah; and (b) he fixed 16.57 GMT on Aug. 20 as the conclusion of the off-hire period because the charterers wished the vessel to remain at Fujairah until Aug. 21 so that cargo insurance could be arranged.

. . .

On Aug. 22 charterers offered to provide a letter of indemnity in the owners P & I Club form incorporated in the charter-party countersigned by a bank, but this was coupled with a request that owners issue a further set of bills of lading. These terms were not accepted by owners.

On Sept. 5, charterers wrote offering a letter of indemnity countersigned by a bank subject to a 12 month limit on the bank's liability. On Sept. 7 Shaw & Croft wrote repeating this offer and calling upon the owners to agree a variation of Mr Justice Morland's order to enable the cargo to be discharged. The owners did not agree to this.

On Sept. 10 the charterers gave an order to Captain Fantomas to proceed to discharge at Ain Sukhna. The master's response was that this was not an order that charterers were entitled to give having regard to the terms of their undertaking to Mr Justice Morland.

All this while the parties had been preparing for a speedy hearing of this action in the Commercial Court. On Sept. 27, however, a without prejudice agreement was concluded under which discharge was effected, with the result that this action has been able to follow a more leisurely progress. *Houda* resumed performing the service required by the charterers at 17.30 GMT on Sept 27.

The writ in these proceedings was issued by the charterers on Aug. 20, 1990. The points of claim were served on Sept. 7, 1990 to which the owners responded with points of defence served on Sept. 11, 1990.

The pleadings have been subsequently amended on more than one occasion but it is unnecessary to refer to them in detail. In summary the charterers' case is that they were deprived of the use of the vessel in August and September, 1990 by reason of the owners' refusal to comply with the orders which were lawfully given. The owners' case on the other hand is that they were entitled to seek further information before they complied with any orders and that moreover they were under no duty to discharge the cargo otherwise than on presentation of one of the sets of the bills of lading.

. . .

On Oct. 10, 1991 Mr Justice Saville ordered that the trial should take place in two stages and that at the first stage all issues should be dealt with save 'the reasonableness issues'. Accordingly when the hearing took place before Mr Justice Phillips in February, 1992 it was his task to determine any issue which was capable of resolution without deciding whether or not the conduct of the owners was reasonable.

. . .

### The charter-party

The charter-party was in the Shelltime 4 form and contained the following relevant provisions:

> 12.   the charterers shall from time to time give the master all requisite instructions and sailing directions. . .

13.   (as amended by clause 50) The master (although appointed by owners) shall be under the orders and directions of charterers as regards employment of the vessel, agency and other arrangements and shall sign bills of lading as charterers or their agents may direct (subject always to clauses 35(a) and 40) without prejudice to this charter.

Charterers hereby indemnify Owners against all consequences or liabilities that may arise from the master, charterers or their agents signing bills of lading or other documents or from the master otherwise complying with charterers' or their agents' orders (including delivery of cargo without presentation of Bills of Lading, or at port(s) different from the port(s) shown on the Bills of Lading) as well as from any irregularities in papers supplied by charterers or their agents. Letter of indemnity to owners' P & I club wording to be incorporated in this charter-party.

21(a)   On each and every occasion that there is loss of time (whether by way of interruption in the vessel's service, or from reduction in the vessel's performance, or in any other manner) ... (ii) due to industrial action, refusal to sail, breach of orders or neglect of duty on the part of the master, officers or crew; or ... the vessel shall be off-hire from the commencement of such loss of time until she is again ready and in an efficient state to resume her service from a position not less favourable to the charterers than that at which such loss of time commenced, provided, however, that any service given or distance made good by the vessel whilst off-hire shall be taken into account in assessing the amount to be deducted from her.

. . .

*In what circumstances can owners be excused for not complying immediately with charterers' orders?*
It was argued on behalf of the owners that the Judge made an error of law in finding that *Houda* was off hire between Aug. 8 and 20. During this time, it was said, the owners were asking repeated questions as to the ownership of the cargo and as to the authority of the persons purporting to give orders on behalf of the charterers. In addition the owners expressed their concern as to whether the orders which were given were lawful, having regard to the imposition of sanctions against Iraq by the United Nations. It was therefore contended that the owners had not refused to obey the charterers' order but were acting reasonably in seeking clarification of the matters which gave them cause for concern. The question whether they had acted reasonably in the circumstances would fall to be determined at the second stage of the trial.

It was argued on behalf of the charterers on the other hand, that subject to three exceptions, the owners and the master were obliged to obey the charterers' orders immediately, or at any rate as soon as practicable. Counsel for the charterers identified these exceptions as follows: (1) where obedience to an order might involve a significant risk of endangering the vessel or its cargo or crew; (2) where it was necessary to seek clarification of an ambiguous order; and (3) where the owners had knowledge of circumstances which were not known to the charterers but which might, if known, affect their orders, and the owners needed confirmation that the orders were to stand. It was submitted that there was no room for the implication of a general term whereby the owners were allowed a reasonable time in which to seek confirmation of the authority of those giving the orders or of the lawfulness of the orders. Furthermore, it was submitted that on the facts of this case the owners' conduct amounted not to delayed compliance but to a refusal to comply with the charterers' orders.

It is clear therefore that it is common ground between the parties that a master is entitled to delay in executing an order if to comply would threaten to expose the ship and cargo to a potential peril or if the circumstances otherwise fall within one of these three exceptions. We were referred to four authorities in support of that proposition. I propose to consider these authorities to see whether one can detect any wider principle on which a right to pause before complying with an order can be founded.

In *Pole* v *Cetcovitch* (1860) 9 CB (NS) 430 the master of an Austrian vessel declined to comply immediately with an order to sail from Falmouth to Copenhagen. He relied on the fact that war had broken out between France and Austria and therefore the voyage might expose his vessel to capture by a French cruiser. The Court of Common Pleas upheld a direction to the jury that if they considered that in the circumstances the master was justified in pausing before complying with the order they should find that he was not in breach.

The next case to which we were referred was the decision of the Privy council in *The Teutonia* (1872) LR 4 PC 171. In giving judgment Lord Justice Mellish said at p. 179:

> It seems obvious that, if a Master receives credible information that, if he continues in the direct course of his voyage, his ship will be exposed to some imminent peril, as, for instance, that there are pirates in his course, or icebergs or other dangers of navigation, he must be justified in pausing and deviating from the direct course, and taking any step which a prudent man would take for the purpose of avoiding the danger.

The reference to 'credible information' is of importance because the information which the master had received was premature in the sense that war between France and Prussia was not formally declared until three days later. Counsel for the charterers treated this case as one where the master had some additional information and where there was a risk of danger to the ship or cargo.

A year later the Privy Council gave judgment in a similar case — *The San Roman* (1873) LR 4 PC 301. In the course of a voyage to Europe *San Roman* put in to Valparaiso for repairs. The repairs were completed on or about Sept. 23, 1870 but the vessel delayed sailing until Dec. 23 because war had broken out between France and Prussia and it was believed that if the vessel sailed there was a risk of capture by the French Navy. In the course of the judgment Sir Montague Smith said at p. 306:

> ... the question their Lordships have to determine is entirely a question of fact, namely, whether the German master had during that time such an apprehension of capture founded on circumstances calculated to affect his mind — he being a man of ordinary courage, judgment, and experience — as would justify delay; and their Lordships agree with the judge in the court below that there was a sufficient risk of capture to justify this delay.
>
> This is not a case where the master has refused to perform the contract at all. No doubt, if the voyage had been abandoned, then it would have been necessary to show that he had been actually prevented from performing it; but this is merely a question of whether there was a reasonable cause for delay.

It was held that the fact that the cargo was an English cargo made no difference. Sir Montague Smith continued at p. 307:

> If their Lordships were to look upon this case as a case in which the cargo was German as well as the ship, or a case in which both ship and cargo belonged to the same person, and then were to ask the question: Would a man of reasonable prudence, under such circumstances, have set sail or waited? It appears to their Lordships most clearly that a man of reasonable prudence would have waited.

The fourth case in this quartet was the decision of Mr Justice Donaldson in *Midwest Shipping Co.* v *D. I. Henry (Jute) Ltd* [1971] 1 Lloyd's Rep 375.
. . .

In the present case Mr Justice Phillips was referred to these four cases other than *The San Roman* (sup.).
. . .

The Judge continued at p. 345:

> As a matter of business efficacy — and on the authorities — I can see justification for the right of owners and their master to delay in obeying an order when it is reasonably necessary in the interests of the safety of the ship, cargo and crew. I can see scope, as a matter of business efficacy, for the requirement of some term — express or implied — as to the manner in which charterers' orders are to be conveyed to owners. But I do not consider that any principle of law or business efficacy requires that owners be entitled to delay in obeying a lawful order so long as it is reasonably necessary to satisfy themselves that the order is authorised, or lawful under the charter-party, or that in discharging the cargo pursuant to that order they are not infringing the rights of the owners of that cargo. It is for the charter-party to provide what orders the charterers can lawfully give and for the charterers to ensure that their orders are lawful. If they give a lawful order, but the owners have doubts about its legality, it seems to me that the owners' delay in complying with that order must be at their own peril.
>
> . . .

In the course of the argument in this Court Counsel for the charterers introduced what might be regarded as a fourth category of exception. Thus he accepted that the owners and a master might pause and seek further information if they knew or had reasonable cause to suspect that the instructions had not been given by the charterers. It was not enough, however, it was said, to justify delay if the owners and the master had merely a vague apprehension.

I am unable to accept that the right, or indeed the duty, to pause can safely be confined to specific categories of cases. I consider that it is necessary to take a broad and comprehensive view of the duties and responsibilities of the owners and the master and to ask, as was suggested in *The San Roman* (sup.): How would a man of reasonable prudence have acted in the circumstances? Thus, for example, the delivery of a cargo pursuant to an order given by the agent of an invading army may pose just as much a threat to cargo and those who have legitimate rights to it as an iceberg or a foreign frigate. It will depend on the circumstances.

In the present case, as Mr Justice Phillips noted at p. 336, prior to the invasion of Kuwait *Houda* was operating under standing instructions issued by the charterers which provided:

> . . . all instructions relating to the voyages of your vessel will be issued by Kuwait Petroleum Corp. in Kuwait.

The orders which form the basis of the charterers' case in these proceedings emanated from London. It is not of course for this Court to decide whether on the facts the owners had reasonable grounds to pause, but I am satisfied that in a war situation there may well be circumstances where the right, and indeed the duty, to pause in order to seek further information about the source of and the validity of any orders which may be received is capable of arising even if there may be no immediate physical threat to the cargo or the ship.

In the course of my consideration of this matter I have had the advantage of reading the comment of Mr Brian Davenport on this case ([1993] *Lloyds Maritime and Commercial Law Quarterly* 40). In his article he pointed out that the question whether Carl-Zeiss-Stiftung of Jena or Carl-Zeiss-Stiftung of Heidenheim was entitled to the name of the original foundation established in 1891 in the Grand Duchy of Saxe-Weimar—

> ... was tried in the courts of over fifty countries and was argued in England for twenty four days before the House of Lords as a preliminary point.

Though the present facts are very different it seems to me that it is at least possible that where a country has been invaded prudent owners may be entitled to guard against the risk that their orders may have come from the 'wrong' side.

It is of course true that by their solicitor's letter dated Feb. 12, 1992 the owners conceded that the charterers had authority to give the orders. I am not persuaded, however, that this later concession affects the reasonableness of the stance taken by the owners in August 1990.

I would therefore allow the appeal on this point and order that the reasonableness of the owner's delay and the period for which they were entitled to delay be determined as part of the second trial ordered by Mr Justice Saville.

*Notes*

1.   The Court of Appeal also confirmed, contrary to the view of Phillips J, that the master cannot be required to deliver the cargo otherwise than on presentation of the bill of lading, there being no distinction in this respect between a voyage charterer and a time charterer.

2.   When considering the master's duty to obey orders in *Midwest Shipping Co. Ltd Inc.* v *D. I. Henry (Jute) Ltd* [1971] 1 Lloyd's Rep 375, Donaldson J commented: ... it is important to remember that the master of a merchant ship occupies a civilian post. He is not the captain of a naval vessel who might well be expected to comply instantly with an order and seek verification or reconsideration afterwards. Furthermore, he is not receiving the instruction from somebody who is his professional superior, as would be the case in the services. He is the representative of his owners and also to some extent of the charterers. He occupies a post of very great responsibility, and he occupies that post by virtue of long training and experience. If he was the type of man who would immediately act upon any order from charterers without further consideration, he would probably be unfitted for that post. It seems to me that against that background it must be the duty of the master to act reasonably upon receipt of orders. Some orders are of their nature such that they would, if the master were to act reasonably, require immediate compliance. Others would require a great deal of thought and consideration before a reasonable master would comply with them.'

3.   Where the employment is more than usually hazardous, the master should follow the instructions without undue question 'within the limits of obviously grave danger', per Roche J in *Portsmouth Steamship Co. Ltd* v *Liverpool & Glasgow Salvage Association* (1929) 34 Ll L Rep 459, where the vessel was chartered to take cargo off a ship which had run aground off the Cape Verde Islands. The cargo included leaking barrels of palm oil and mahogany logs

weighing up to 8 tons each, which were very difficult to handle and caused damage to the chartered vessel. The shipowners were held to be entitled to an indemnity. On the right to an indemnity, see further Section 6, below.

## SECTION 4: MASTER TO SIGN BILLS OF LADING 'AS PRESENTED'

The underlying purpose of time charters is generally for the charterers to have the services of the vessel in order to engage in the business of carriage of goods by sea, a business which is likely to involve the issue of bills of lading to shippers (*cf.* Saville J in *Kuwait Maritime Transport Co.* v *Rickmers Linie KG (The Danah)* [1993] 1 Lloyd's Rep 351, at p. 353). Bills of lading signed by, or on behalf of the master, impose contractual liabilities upon the shipowner. 'Master to sign bills of lading as presented' clauses, which are found in voyage charterparties also, are designed to give the charterer control of what bills of lading are to be issued within the overall limits set by the charterparty. There is an obligation on the charterer to indemnify the shipowner if any liability is imposed upon the latter contrary to the other terms of the charterparty. Although the master may refuse to sign a bill which does not conform with the requirements of the charterparty, his failure to exercise the right of refusal does not in itself deprive the shipowner of the right to an indemnity.

### Krüger & Co. Ltd v Moel Tryvan Ship Co. Ltd
### [1907] AC 272 (HL)

LORD LOREBURN LC: ... My Lords, this case raises a novel point.

The respondents, shipowners, chartered their vessel under a charterparty which relieved them from liability for negligence of the master, and with the following clause: 'The master to sign clean bills of lading for his cargo, also for portions of cargo shipped (if required to do so) at any rate of freight, without prejudice to this charter, but not at lower than chartered rates, unless the difference is paid to him in cash before signing bills of lading.'

The vessel was under the terms of the charterparty to proceed to Rangoon, and there load from the charterers a cargo of rice and thence proceed to Rio. She went to Rangoon and loaded the rice. Charterers' agents then presented bills of lading to the master. These bills of lading contained the words 'freight for the said goods and all other conditions as per charterparty', but did not incorporate the exception contained in the charterparty exempting the shipowners from liability for negligence of the master. Accordingly, under these bills of lading, the owner was in law liable to whosoever might have the right to sue on them for the consequences of this negligence. The agents did not realise this, nor did the master, who duly signed the bills. Both were mistaken in law, and both acted in good faith. Unfortunately the cargo was lost through the negligence of the master, and the owners were compelled to pay the value of the cargo in an action brought by the indorsees of those bills of lading. Having paid it, they brought this action against the charterers, claiming to be indemnified.

In my view the cardinal fact which ought to govern our decision is that under this charterparty the shipowners are not to be liable for losses caused by the master's negligence in navigating the vessel. When bills of lading are given they may give rise to rights in persons other than the charterers and on conditions other than those contained in the charterparty; and therefore it is the duty of the charterers who have to present these bills, to provide that they shall not expose the shipowners to risks from which by contract they are to be exempt. Nothing has occurred that disentitles the shipowners to this protection. The master, who signed the bills of lading under an excusable error of law, did not waive his principals' right to be so protected, nor did his principals waive it. It is not a case of warranty. It is a case in which, by contract, the shipowners undertook to carry a cargo on the footing that they were not to be liable for the master's negligent navigation, and the charterers have made them so liable by the bills of lading. Hence arises a duty to give adequate indemnity.

Accordingly I move your Lordships to dismiss this appeal.

LORD JAMES OF HEREFORD: That the bills of lading came into existence for the convenience and business purposes of the charterers is also clear. Shipowners have only to carry. They care not for whom, and have nothing to do with the terms upon which the charterers deal with their goods.

But to the charterers it is all-important that they should obtain bills of lading which they can indorse over and so transfer the property in the cargo. Of the terms of such transfer the shipowner knows nothing, and thus from the nature of things and from the course of business the charterers prepare the bills of lading and tender them to the master of the vessel for signature. And so it comes that the charterers, who are controlled by the charterparty and acting under it, have cast upon them the primary duty of tendering to the master bills of lading in accordance with the terms of that document. They had no right to ask the master to sign a bill of lading in any way deviating from the charterparty.

*Note*
The master may refuse to sign bills of lading which are in the prescribed form but have blanks not filled in: *Garbis Maritime Corp.* v *Philippine National Oil Co. (The Garbis)* [1982] 2 Lloyd's Rep 283 (per Robert Goff J). On the other hand, if the bill of lading as presented is in accordance with the charterparty, the master may not insist on having further clauses added to it: 'what the captain is to sign are the bills of lading presented to him and not some bills of lading of his own devising' (per Mustill J in *Gulf Steel Co. Ltd* v *Al Khalifa Shipping Co. Ltd (The Anwar Al Sabar)* [1980] 2 Lloyd's Rep 261 (QBD)).

## SECTION 5: THE SAFE PORT OBLIGATION

The charterer may only order the vessel to a port within the trading limits specified in the charter. Usually there will be an express term requiring the ports nominated to be safe ports, and this will be implied if the charter is silent. It is now settled law that the charterer's obligation is to nominate a port which is prospectively safe at the time of nomination, but there is no undertaking implied that the port will remain safe while the vessel is there.

### *Kodros Shipping Corp. of Monrovia* v *Empresa Cubana de Fletes (The Evia) (No.2)*
[1983] 1 AC 736 (HL)

The appellants chartered the *Evia* to the respondents on 12 November 1979 for 18 months, two months more or less in charterers' option, vessel to be employed 'between good and safe ports'. In March 1980 she was ordered to load a cargo of cement and building materials in Cuba for Basrah in Iraq. She berthed in Basrah on 20 August, but by the time she had completed discharge of the cargo on 22 September the *Evia*, along with many other ships, was trapped in the Shatt-al-Arab waterway by the outbreak of the Iran-Iraq war.

The umpire held that the charterparty was frustrated and rejected the shipowners' claim that the charterers were in breach of the safe port clause. This decision was reversed by Goff J, but restored by the Court of Appeal. The House of Lords dismissed the shipowners' appeal.

LORD DIPLOCK: My Lords, I agree with the speech to be delivered by my noble and learned friend, Lord Roskill, and with the detailed reasons that he will give for dismissing this appeal.

For my part, I would regard the nature of the contractual promise by the charterer that a chartered vessel shall be employed between safe ports ('the safe port clause') as having been well settled for a quarter of a century at the very least. It was correctly and concisely stated by Sellers LJ in *Leeds Shipping Co. Ltd* v *Société Francaise Bunge (The Eastern City)* [1958] 2 Lloyd's Rep 127 in a classic passage which, in its reference to 'abnormal occurrence', reflects a previous statement in the judgment of Morris LJ in *Compania Naviera Maropan SA* v *Bowaters Lloyd Pulp and Paper Mills Ltd (The Stork)* [1955] 2 QB 68, Sellers LJ said, at p. 131:

> a port will not be safe unless, in the relevant period of time, the particular ship can reach it, use it and return from it without, in the absence of some abnormal occurrence, being exposed to danger which cannot be avoided by good navigation and seamanship . . .

It is with the prospective safety of the port at the time when the vessel will be there for the loading or unloading operation that the contractual promise is concerned and the contractual promise itself is given at the time when the charterer gives the order to the master or other agent of the shipowner to proceed to the loading or unloading port.

What are the respective rights and duties of charterer and shipowner under a voyage charter if the port becomes prospectively unsafe by reason of some abnormal occurrence actually occurring (whether or not to the knowledge of either of them) during the period of the loading or unloading voyage is not a matter that arises in the instant appeal and I think it would be unwise for your Lordships to express any view about it. In the case of the time charter, however, under which the charterer has power to substitute for his original order to the master to proceed to a particular port and there undertake the loading or unloading operation a fresh order to proceed elsewhere, so long as such fresh order is given at a time when it is possible for the vessel to comply with it, the contractual promise is a continuing one and if an occurrence which at the time of the original order could properly be regarded as abnormal has actually occurred and has rendered the port prospectively unsafe, the charterer could not rely upon the exception of 'abnormal occurrence' in Sellers LJ's statement of the effect of the safe port clause.

So great is the variety of ports to which chartered vessels are ordered to go that it is not surprising that disputes should arise as to whether damage sustained by a particular vessel in a particular port on a particular occasion was caused by an 'abnormal occurrence' rather than resulting from some normal characteristic of the particular port at the particular time of year. In cases of this kind, judges, particularly at first instance with their minds directed solely to the particular facts of the case they are deciding, may, not infrequently, in expressing the reasons for their decision, state a proposition of law on which they rely as relevant to the particular case in general terms which omit qualifications to that proposition that would be relevant to other cases, but are not relevant to the case under decision.

The heresy that, in the last decade or so, has been embraced by judges in the commercial court in the course of several judgments at first instance, culminating in that of Mustill J in *Transoceanic Petroleum Carriers* v *Cook Industries Inc. (The Mary Lou)* [1981] 2 Lloyd's Rep 272, 277, would have the effect of eliminating the exception based upon abnormal occurrence in Sellers LJ's statement of the effect of the safe port clause. These judgments, which are analysed by Lord Roskill in his speech, afford in my view a classic example of the danger of assembling together isolated statements contained in judgments at first instance, each dealing with the facts of a particular case, and using such statements to build up some novel principle of law, inconsistent with an existing principle which carries with it the authority and approval of an appellate court.

LORD ROSKILL: My Lords, I propose to consider first the question which arises on clause 2. It will be convenient to quote again those few words in that clause which are relevant — 'The vessel to be employed ... between good and safe ports....' Learned counsel were unable to offer any suggestion what in this context the word 'good' added to the word 'safe'. Your Lordships are, I think, all of the like mind. So I will consider only the eight words 'The vessel to be employed ... between ... safe ports....' The argument for the appellants is simple. The relevant restriction during her employment is to safe ports. Her employment took her to Basrah. Basrah, though safe when nominated, on September 22, 1980, became, and thereafter remained, unsafe. The *Evia* was trapped. Those eight words applied. The respondents were therefore in breach.

... [T]he first question is whether, apart from authority, these words are to be construed in the manner suggested. In order to consider the scope of the contractual promise which these eight words impose upon a charterer, it must be determined how a charterer would exercise his undoubted right to require the shipowner to perform his contractual obligations to render services with his ship, his master, officers and crew, the consideration for the performance of their obligation being the charterer's regular payment of time charter hire. The answer must be that a charterer will exercise that undoubted contractual right by giving the shipowner orders to go to a particular port or place of loading or discharge. It is clearly at that point of time when that order is given that that contractual promise to the charterer regarding the safety of that intended port or place must be fulfilled. But that contractual promise cannot mean that that port or place must be safe when that order is given, for were that so, a charterer could not legitimately give orders to go to an ice-bound port which he and the owner both knew in all human probability would be ice-free by the time that vessel reached it. Nor, were that the nature of the promise, could a charterer order the ship to a port or place the approaches to which were at the time of the order blocked as a result of a collision or by some submerged wreck or other obstacles even though such obstacles would in all human probability be out of the way before the ship required to enter. The charterer's contractual promise must, I think, relate to the characteristics of the port or place in question and in my view means that when the order is given that port or place is prospectively safe for the ship to get to, stay at, so far as necessary, and in due course, leave. But if those characteristics are such as to make that port or place prospectively safe in this way, I cannot think that if, in spite of them, some unexpected and abnormal event thereafter suddenly occurs which creates conditions of unsafety where conditions of safety had previously existed and as a result the ship is delayed, damaged or destroyed, that contractual promise extends to making the charterer liable for any resulting loss or damage, physical or financial. So to hold would make the charterer the insurer of such unexpected and abnormal risks which in my view should properly fall upon the ship's insurers under the policies of insurance the effecting of which is the owner's responsibility under clause 3 unless, of course, the owner chooses to be his own insurer in these respects.

After an exhaustive review of the authorities, Lord Roskill concluded that decisions such as *The Mary Lou* [1981] 2 Lloyd's Rep 272, imposing an undertaking that the nominated port would continue to be safe, were unsound and continued:

> My Lords, on the view of the law which I take, since Basrah was prospectively safe at the time of nomination, and since the unsafety arose after the *Evia's* arrival and was due to an unexpected and abnormal event, there was at the former time no breach of clause 2 by the respondents, and that is the first ground upon which I would dismiss this appeal.
>
> But, my Lords, since the Court of Appeal gave leave to appeal in order that this branch of the law should be fully explored, I think your Lordships may wish further to consider whether, notwithstanding the rejection of the views of Mustill and Robert Goff JJ and of Ackner LJ, there is a residual obligation upon a charterer, whether for time or voyage, given that he has fully complied with his obligation at the time of nomination. My Lords, unless there is something unusual in the relevant express language used in a particular charterparty, the charterer's obligation at the time of nomination which I have been discussing must, I think, apply equally to a voyage charterer as to a time charterer. But in considering whether there is any residual or remaining obligation after nomination it is necessary to have in mind one fundamental distinction between a time charterer and a voyage charterer. In the former case, the time charterer is in complete control of the employment of the ship. It is in his power by appropriate orders timeously given to change the ship's employment so as to prevent her proceeding to or remaining at a port initially safe which has since it was nominated become unsafe. But a voyage charterer may not have the same power. If there is a single loading or discharging port named in the voyage charterparty then, unless the charterparty specifically otherwise provides, a voyage charterer may not be able to order that ship elsewhere. If there is a range of loading or discharging ports named, once the voyage charterer has selected the contractual port or ports of loading or discharge, the voyage charterparty usually operates as if that port or those ports had originally been written into the charterparty, and the charterer then has no further right of nomination or renomination. What, then, is the contractual obligation of such charterers whether for time or voyage if the nominated port becomes unsafe after it was nominated?
>
> My Lords, in the case of a time charterer, I cannot bring myself to think that he has no further obligation to the owner even though for the reasons I have given earlier he is not the insurer of the risks arising from the unsafety of the nominated port. Suppose some event has occurred after nomination which has made or will or may make the nominated port unsafe. Is a time charterer obliged to do anything further? What is a voyage charterer to do in similar circumstances? My Lords, this problem seems never to have been judicially considered in any detail; indeed, as I have already stated, in *The Houston City* [1956] AC 266 the Privy Council expressly declined to consider it.
>
> In my opinion, while the primary obligation of a time charterer under clause 2 of this charterparty is that which I have already stated, namely, to order the ship to go only to a port which, at the time when the order is given, is prospectively safe for her, there may be circumstances in which, by reason of a port, which was prospectively safe when the

order to go to it was given, subsequently becoming unsafe, clause 2, on its true construction, imposes a further and secondary obligation on the charterer.

In this connection two possible situations require to be considered. The first situation is where, after the time charterer has performed his primary obligation by ordering the ship to go to a port which, at the time of such order, was prospectively safe for her, and while she is still proceeding towards such port in compliance with such order, new circumstances arise which render the port unsafe. The second situation is where, after the time charterer has performed his primary obligation by ordering the ship to go to a port which was, at the time of such order, prospectively safe for her, and she has proceeded to and entered such port in compliance with such order, new circumstances arise which render the port unsafe.

In the first situation it is my opinion that clause 2, on its true construction (unless the cause of the new unsafety be purely temporary in character), imposes on the time charterer a further and secondary obligation to cancel his original order and, assuming that he wishes to continue to trade the ship, to order her to go to another port which, at the time when such fresh order is given, is prospectively safe for her. This is because clause 2 should be construed as requiring the time charterer to do all that he can effectively do to protect the ship from the new danger in the port which has arisen since his original order for her to go to it was given.

In the second situation the question whether clause 2, on its true construction, imposes a further and secondary obligation on the time charterer will depend on whether, having regard to the nature and consequences of the new danger in the port which has arisen, it is possible for the ship to avoid such danger by leaving the port. If, on the one hand, it is not possible for the ship so to leave, then no further and secondary obligation is imposed on the time charterer. This is because clause 2 should not be construed as requiring the time charterer to give orders with which it is not possible for the ship to comply, and which would for that reason be ineffective. If, on the other hand, it is possible for the ship to avoid the new danger in the port which has arisen by leaving, then a further and secondary obligation is imposed on the time charterer to order the ship to leave the port forthwith, whether she has completed loading or discharging or not, and, assuming that he wishes to continue to trade the ship, to order her to go to another port which, at the time when such fresh order is given, is prospectively safe for her. This is again because clause 2 should be construed as requiring the time charterer to do all that he can effectively do to protect the ship from the new danger in the port which has arisen since his original order for her to go to it was given.

My Lords, what I have said with regard to these further and secondary obligations under clause 2 of this charterparty will apply to any other similarly worded 'safe port' clauses.

My Lords, for the reasons I have given I find it much more difficult to say what are the comparable obligations under a voyage charterparty at any rate where there is no express right to renominate. The well known decision in *Duncan* v *Köster (The Teutonia)* (1872) LR 4 PC 171 — a case decided long before the doctrine of frustration assumed its modern form — has always presented difficulties and voyage charterparties today almost invariably contain war and strike clauses which give the shipowners and their masters the right sometimes to require another nomination and sometimes an unfettered right in any event to proceed elsewhere. I think, therefore, in a case where only a time charterparty is involved, that it would be unwise for your Lordships to give further consideration to the problems which might arise in the case of a voyage charterparty, and for my part, I would leave those problems for later consideration if and when they arise.

My Lords, on the basis that time charterers were potentially under the further and secondary obligations which I have held that clause 2 may impose on them, it cannot avail the appellants against the respondents since the events giving rise to the unsafety did not occur until after the *Evia* had entered Basrah, and an order to leave the port and proceed to another port could not have been effective.

*Notes*

1. Denning LJ in the Court of Appeal ([1982] 1 Lloyd's Rep 334, at 338) gave the following definition of a safe port: 'To my mind it must be reasonably safe for the vessel to enter, to remain, and to depart without suffering damage so long as she is well and carefully handled. Reasonably safe, that is, in its geographical configuration on the coast or waterway and in the equipment and aids available for her movement and stay. In short, it must be safe in its set-up as a port. To elaborate a little, every port in its natural state has hazards for the ships going there. It may be shallows, shoals, mudbanks, or rocks. It may be storms or ice or appalling weather. In order to be a 'safe port', there must be buoys to mark the channel, lights to point the way, pilots available to steer, a system to forecast the weather, good places to drop anchor, sufficient room to manoeuvre, sound berths, and so forth. In so far as any of these precautions are necessary — and the set-up of the port is deficient in them — then it is not a 'safe port'.

Once the set-up of the port is found to be deficient — such that it is dangerous for the vessel when handled with reasonable care — then the charterer is in breach of his warranty and he is liable for any damage suffered by the vessel in consequence of it ... On the other hand, if the set-up of the port is good but nevertheless the vessel suffers damage owing to some isolated, abnormal or extraneous occurrence — unconnected with the set-up — then the charterer is not in breach of his warranty. Such as when a competent berthing-master makes for once a mistake, or when the vessel is run into by another vessel, or a fire spreads across to her, or when a hurricane strikes unawares. The charterer is not liable for damage so caused.'

2. The safe port clause sometimes takes the form of an obligation to exercise due diligence to ensure that the vessel is only employed between safe ports. The precise effect of this variation, which, as it is coupled with an express statement that the charterers do not warrant the safety of any port, seems to have been drafted with *The Mary Lou* in mind, has not yet been finally determined. The charterparty contained such a clause in *K/S Penta Shipping A/S v Ethiopian Shipping Lines Corporation (The Saga Cob)* [1992] 2 Lloyd's Rep 545 (CA) but the port of Massawa was found not to be prospectively unsafe in spite of an attack on the vessel by Eritrean guerillas, as the risk of such attack had not become a normal characteristic of the port, so that the question of due diligence did not arise. Nevertheless, Parker LJ, giving the judgment of the court, stated that due diligence is the same as reasonable care and added: 'There is in our judgment at least a strong argument that the test should be expressed thus — 'if a reasonably careful charterer *would* on the facts known have concluded that the port was prospectively unsafe'.

Parker LJ also commented that a port will not be regarded as unsafe 'unless the political risk is sufficient for a reasonable shipowner or master to decline to send his vessel there'. In *Pearl Carriers Inc. v Japan Line Ltd* (*The Chemical Venture*) [1993] 1 Lloyd's Rep 508 (QBD), Gatehouse J found this part of the judgment 'puzzling' and doubted whether the Court of Appeal was suggesting that the established test of safety needed modification or that the shipowner need call evidence from a reasonable shipowner or master. If the port is unsafe and the facts are known to the charterer 'the case [of failure to exercise due diligence] is one of *res ipsa loquitur* unless the charterer adduces evidence to justify his order' (ibid. at p. 519).

3. In *Dow Europe SA v Novoklav Inc* [1998] 1 Lloyd's Rep 306 (QBD), the *Acina* was loading condensate at Arzew (Algeria) when a fire occurred causing considerable damage to the vessel. The arbitrators held that the berth was unsafe because there was no emergency shutdown system to stop the flow of condensate. The charterers (Novoklav) had delegated the nomination of a safe berth to the port authority. It was held that the due diligence clause in the charter (Shelltime 4, cl. 4) did not protect them from liability. Timothy Walker J said (at 309): 'The standard construction of a due diligence provision is that the obligation is one of due diligence 'by whomsoever it may be done' even if the obligation is delegated to an independent contractor (see *The Muncaster Castle* [1961] 1 Lloyd's Rep 57; [1961] AC 807), unless this is ousted by clear words restricting the obligation to one of personal want of due diligence. There are well known examples in the trade of forms of charter-party which do achieve this result (e.g., the Baltime form considered by Mr Justice McNair in *The Brabant* [1965] 2 Lloyd's Rep 546). The form these experienced commercial arbitrators were considering was not one of them.'

If a prospectively unsafe port is nominated, the master may refuse the order and may call for an alternative nomination. If the master does comply, however, the charterer remains liable to indemnify the shipowner if damage occurs.

### Motor Oil Hellas (Corinth) Refineries SA v Shipping Corporation of India
### (The Kanchenjunga)
#### [1990] 1 Lloyd's Rep 391

The *Kanchenjunga*, a 272,000 ton crude carrier, was chartered to the appellants for eight consecutive voyages. In performance of a sub-charter the appellants nominated Kharg Island as the loading port for the last voyage in November 1980. The shipowners instructed the master to proceed to Kharg Island. He arrived on 23 November and gave notice of readiness. On 1 December, while the *Kanchenjunga* was still waiting to berth, Iraq bombed Kharg Island; the master immediately proceeded away from Kharg Island to a place of safety. It was found that Kharg Island was not prospectively safe when nominated. Agreeing with the lower courts, the House of Lords held that the shipowners had waived their right to object to the nomination.

LORD GOFF OF CHIEVELEY: . . . The arbitrators' finding that Kharg Island was, at the time of its nomination by the charterers, prospectively an unsafe port was not, and indeed could not be, challenged. Kharg Island was not therefore a port which, under the terms of the charter, the charterers were entitled to nominate. It followed that the nomination was a tender of performance which did not conform to the terms of the contract; as such, the owners were entitled to reject it. Even so, by their nomination of Kharg Island the charterers impliedly promised that that port was prospectively safe for the vessel to get to, stay at, so far as necessary, and in due course, leave (see *Kodros Shipping Corporation of Monrovia* v *Embresa Cubana de Fletes (The Evia) (No. 2)* [1982] 2 Lloyd's Rep 307 at p. 315; [1983] AC 736 at p. 757, per Lord Roskill). Accordingly if the owners, notwithstanding their right to reject the nomination, complied with it and their ship suffered loss or damage in consequence, they would be entitled to recover damages from the charterers for breach of contract, though the ordinary principles of remoteness of damage and causation would apply to any such claim: see *Compania Naviera Maropan SA* v *Bowaters Lloyd Pulp and Paper Mills Ltd (The Stork)* [1955] 1 Lloyd's Rep 349; [1955] 2 QB 68, and *Reardon Smith Line Ltd* v *Australian Wheat Board (The Houston City)* [1956] 1 Lloyd's Rep 1; [1956] AC 266.

This is not, however, a case in which the owners have complied with an order to proceed to an unsafe port, and their ship has proceeded there and suffered damage in consequence. This is a case in which the owners have complied with the charterers' orders to the extent that the vessel has proceeded to the unsafe port and given notice of readiness there, but then the master, having tasted at first hand the danger inherent in the port's unsafety, has persuaded them not to persist in loading there but to sail away. Here the crucial question is whether, before the vessel sailed away, the owners had, by their words or conduct, precluded themselves from rejecting the charterers' nomination as not complying with the contract. . . .

It is a commonplace that the expression 'waiver' is one which may, in law, bear different meanings. In particular, it may refer to a forbearance from exercising a right or to an abandonment of a right. Here we are concerned with waiver in the sense of abandonment of a right which arises by virtue of a party making an election. Election itself is a concept which may be relevant in more that one context. In the present case, we are concerned with an election which may arise in the context of a binding contract, when a state of affairs comes into existence in which one party becomes entitled, either under the terms of the contract or by the general law, to exercise a right, and he has to decide whether or not to do so. His decision, being a matter of choice for him, is called in law an election. Characteristically, this state of affairs arises where the other party has repudiated the contract or has otherwise committed a breach of the contract which entitles the innocent party to bring it to an end, or has made a tender of performance which does not conform to the terms of the contract. But this is not necessarily so. An analogous situation arises where the innocent party becomes entitled to rescind the contract, i.e., to wipe it out altogether, for example because the contract has been induced by a misrepresentation; and one or both parties may become entitled to determine a contract in the event of a wholly extraneous event occurring, as under a war clause in a charterparty. Characteristically, the effect of the new situation is that a party becomes entitled to determine or to rescind the contract, or to reject an uncontractual tender of performance; but, in theory at least, a less drastic course of action might become available to him under the terms of the contract. In all cases, he has in the end to make his election, not as a matter of obligation, but in the sense that, if he does not do so, the time may come when the law takes the decision out of his hands, either by holding him to have elected not to exercise the right which has become available to him, or sometimes by holding him to have elected to exercise it. . . .

There are numerous examples of the application of this principle of election in English law. Perhaps the most familiar situation is that which arises when one contracting party repudiates the contract. The effect is that the other contracting party then has a choice whether to accept the repudiation (as it is called) and bring the contract to an end; or to affirm the contract, thereby waiving or abandoning his right to terminate it. If, with knowledge of the facts giving rise to the repudiation, the other party to the contract acts (for example) in a manner consistent only with treating that contract as still alive, he is taken in law to have exercised his election to affirm the contract.

The present case is concerned not so much with repudiation as with an uncontractual tender of performance. Even so, the same principles apply. The other party is entitled to reject the tender of performance as uncontractual; and, subject to the terms of the contract, he can then, if he wishes, call for a fresh tender of performance in its place. But if, with knowledge of the facts giving rise to his right to reject, he nevertheless unequivocally elects not to do so, his election will be final and binding upon him and he will have waived his right to reject the tender as uncontractual.

. . .

Because the arbitrators did not approach the issue of election correctly, they failed to consider the correct questions. In particular, they did not ask themselves whether there had been the necessary unequivocal representation by the owners. It is true that they did ask themselves whether there had been the necessary 'clear and unequivocal promise' when considering the alternative principle of equitable estoppel; they held that there was not, on the basis that the mere acceptance of orders without protest does not amount to such a promise. As a general proposition, this is no doubt correct; and it would equally be true if made with reference to the question whether there had been an unequivocal representation by the owners that they were waiving their right to reject the nomination as uncontractual. Moreover, if the relevant evidence had related only to the communications passing between the parties before the vessel arrived at Kharg Island, the question would have arisen whether, on these communications (set of course in their factual context), there had been such an unequivocal representation. But the matter does not stop there, because on arrival at Kharg Island the master proceeded to serve notice of readiness. Thereafter, as the Judge pointed out, the owners were asserting that the vessel was available to load; they were also calling upon the charterers to arrange priority berthing, and referring to the fact that laytime was running. In these circumstances, the owners were asserting a right inconsistent with their right to reject the charterers' orders. The right which they were asserting was that laytime had started to run against the charterers at Kharg Island, with the effect that the charterers had become bound to load the cargo there within the laytime fixed by the charter and, if they failed to do so, to pay demurrage to the owners at the contractual rate. In these circumstances, on the principle stated by Lord Diplock in the *Kammins Ballrooms* case [1971] AC 850, at pp. 882–883, the owners must be taken in law to have thereby elected not to reject the charterers' nomination, and so to have waived their right to do so or to call for another nomination. Accordingly, in my opinion, Mr Justice Hobhouse and the Court of Appeal were fully entitled in these circumstances to substitute their view of the case on this point for that of the arbitrators. There was no question of their reversing the arbitrators on an issue of fact; they were deciding, and in my opinion rightly deciding, that the arbitrators had failed to draw an inference of law which on their findings of fact they were bound to draw.

No doubt the master was entitled to refuse to endanger his ship and crew in the circumstances in which he found himself; but that did not excuse the owners from their breach of contract, after they had elected not to reject the charterers' nomination of Kharg Island in the knowledge of the facts rendering it prospectively unsafe. Furthermore this is not a case in which a new situation had developed at Kharg Island, or some other danger already existed there. If the known danger had become significantly different; or if a new and different danger and developed; or if some other danger, hitherto unknown, already existed at the port — in such circumstances as these, other questions might have arisen. But your Lordships are not troubled with any such questions in the present case. The arbitrators found as a fact that the safety or unsafety or Kharg Island was not changed in any way by the attack on Dec. 1. This was a finding which they were fully entitled to make, and which cannot be challenged.

Having waived their right to object to the nomination of Kharg Island, the shipowners had put themselves in breach of the charterparty by not loading there. They successfully relied on the 'WAR RISKS' clause in the charterparty to defeat the charterers' claim for damages for this breach. Lord Goff of Chieveley said:

I turn then to the charterers' appeal which related to the effect of cl. 20(vi) of the charter. Clause 20(vi) reads, so far as relevant, as follows:

> WAR RISKS  (a) If any port of loading or of discharge named in this charterparty or to which the vessel may properly be ordered pursuant to the terms of the bills of lading be blockaded, or (b) if owing to any war, hostilities, warlike operations ... entry to any such port of loading or of discharge or the loading or discharge of cargo at any such port be considered by the master or owners in his or their discretion dangerous or prohibited ... the charterers shall have the right to order the cargo or such part of it as may be affected to be loaded or discharged at any other safe port of loading or of discharge within the range of loading or discharging ports respectively established under the provisions of the charterparty (provided such other port is not blockaded or that entry thereto or loading or discharge of cargo thereat is not in the master's or owner's discretion dangerous or prohibited) ...

Both the Judge and the Court of Appeal held that this clause was effective to protect the owners from liability in damages, though it did not render the charterers liable in damages in the events which had happened. With this conclusion I agree; I shall therefore deal with the point briefly.

Three arguments were advanced on behalf of the charterers. The first was that, on its true construction, all that the clause did was to confer an option on them. It was simply a charterers' option clause, which conferred no rights or protection on the owners in the events specified in the clause. This argument was rejected both by the Judge and by the Court of Appeal, on the basis that it would deprive the clause of all meaning and effect if it were held that it did not protect the owners in the event of their deciding, in their discretion, that the port was dangerous or prohibited and that they would not therefore load or discharge cargo there, as the case might be. With this conclusion I agree. The clause expressly refers to the discretion which the owners and master are entitled to exercise in a situation of danger and must, in my opinion, impliedly recognise that in the exercise of that discretion they may decline to load or discharge at the relevant port. This is precisely what happened in the present case. It was not argued that, on its true construction, the clause only applied to named ports or ports properly nominated under the charterparty. This cannot be right because, in the event of an improper nomination being made by the charterers, owners' acceptance of the nomination would have the effect that all the relevant contractual provisions applied, including cl. 20(vi). Finally, it was suggested that the owners, by waiving their right to reject the charterers' nomination as uncontractual, thereby also waived their right to rely upon cl. 20(vi). Again, I cannot agree. The owners, presented by the charterers with an uncontractual nomination, had in the end to decide whether or not to reject it, and they elected not to do so. I cannot see that this election had any effect upon cl. 20(vi), and indeed in the course of argument the charterers virtually abandoned the point.

*Note*

This was, of course, a voyage charterparty, but it is clear that on the question of orders for employment there is no relevant distinction between voyage charterparties and time charters: *cf.* Hobhouse J in *Batis Maritime Corp.* v *Petroleos del Mediterraneo SA* (*The Batis*) [1990] 1 Lloyd's Rep 345 (QBD). Here the charterers ordered the vessel to Hormuz, but there was congestion there and after arrival and notice of readiness given the charterers ordered the vessel to Lavan Island instead. It was held that the giving of the order for Lavan was a breach of the charterparty, there being no power to change the instructions after they had been carried out, and the shipowners were entitled on a quantum meruit to the additional cost of proceeding to Lavan (which included an additional war risk premium of $68,000).

The scope of a clause giving the shipowner or master the right to decline the nomination of a port 'which he or they consider dangerous' was considered in the next case.

### Abu Dhabi National Tanker Co. v Product Star Shipping Ltd (The Product Star) (No. 2)
[1993] 1 Lloyd's Rep 397 (CA)

LEGGATT LJ: . . . Where A and B contract with each other to confer a discretion on A, that does not render B subject to A's uninhibited whim. In my judgment, the authorities show that not only must the discretion be exercised honestly and in good faith, but, having regard to the provisions of the contract by which it is conferred, it must not be exercised arbitrarily, capriciously or unreasonably. That entails a proper consideration of the matter after making any necessary inquiries. To these principles, little is added by the concept of fairness: it does no more than describe the result achieved by their application.

. . .

In my judgment, Mr Longmore is right on behalf of the charterers to emphasise the circumstances prevailing when the charterparty was entered into. Telex messages exchanged immediately before it was signed showed that the owners were well aware of what they called the charterers' 'intended trade pattern'. That was why special arrangements were made to take out war risk insurance in order to cover voyages to UAE ports for which the charterers were to pay on delivery. For the purpose of construing 'dangerous' in cl. 40 the common intention that the vessel should trade to UAE ports is relevant to the reasonableness of refusal by the owners to proceed there. Clause 10 gave the charterers the right to order the vessel to Ruwais. Since cl. 40, even though strictly speaking not an exceptions clause, was a provision for the owners' benefit, it was, as is accepted, for them to show that they were entitled to invoke it. Although at the time when the charterparty was made the whole of the Gulf, including UAE waters, constituted a war risk zone, the owners were, by the combination of cll. 10,

40(2) and 50, accepting that in the circumstances prevailing at the date of the charterparty the risks of proceeding to UAE ports and loading there were not such as they would consider 'dangerous', so as to render the discretion under cl. 40(2) exercisable.

In consonance with the construction, the owners undertook four voyages to the Gulf before September, 1987. They did so because they were obliged to, and not because, though they were entitled to object, they refrained from doing so. They were only entitled to object in the event that the risks had so far increased that in their discretion they considered such voyages to have become dangerous. That any increase in the nature or extent or the risks might be difficult to perceive, define or prove goes only to the difficulties besetting owners under this charter if they wished to invoke cl. 40(2) successfully.

### Owners' refusal to proceed

Master and owners may be moved by different considerations to conclude that a port or the approach to it is dangerous. The fact that their perceptions of risk will necessarily be different does not mean that they are applying different standards. Here there is no suggestion that the master considered either to be dangerous; and he was not consulted by the owners. The assessment of risk by owners may be expected to be more educated than that of the person who is directly exposed to it; and to take account of circumstances such as the immunity from attack enjoyed by ships which were proceeding to load or had loaded at UAE ports. So far as material, what has to be dangerous is approach or entry to the loadport or the operation of loading there. The state of hostilities elsewhere in the Gulf is not of direct relevance, and even in UAE waters it is relevant only in so far as ships which load there are attacked.

As Mr Longmore pointed out, in appraising the validity of owners' refusal several factors are pertinent. The owners had made no attempt to consult the master, who without demur was expecting to go to Ruwais; the refusal was made at short notice, attributing it inexplicably to 'the most recent development in waters adjacent to Ruwais'; no attack had been made at any material time on a ship trading to or from the UAE; and no explanation has ever been offered why the three directors of IMI, the managers of the vessel, should have suffered to trade in the Gulf between Sept. 15 and 25, 1987 a vessel called the *East Star*, which they also managed through IMI. The same three directors were also directors of the two one-ship companies which respectively owned *Product Star* and *East Star*. In my judgment, this factor is of such moment as to undermine, if not invalidate, the owners' reasons for declining to proceed. That in turn calls in question the owners' good faith, and in any event strongly suggests that their refusal was arbitrary.

. . . It was plain from Mr Gallagher's evidence that he was almost entirely ignorant of the previous history of hostilities in the Gulf and of the geography of the region. It might have been supposed that, if not every schoolboy, then every owner or manager of a vessel trading to the Gulf who might have to decide whether to allow a vessel to proceed to Ruwais would know the geographical relationship between Bahrain and Ruwais. Not so Mr Gallagher; he did not know, even by the time that he gave evidence, whether Ruwais was to the north, south or east of Bahrain. But above all, Mr Gallagher had failed to acquaint himself with information about whether or not vessels trading to ports in the UAE were subject to attack. The withdrawal of a vessel in that trade by a person so ignorant of the gravity of risks to which she might be subject is bound to wear a capricious air unless there had in fact been a real and substantial increase in the risks before the decision was made.

. . .

... The Judge applied to the issue of whether the owner's decision was not unreasonable, the test of whether there was—

... a sufficient degree of danger in proceeding to Ruwais in September, 1987 that a reasonable owner, informed of the relevant facts, could reasonably have considered reaching the port to be dangerous in the sense in which this word is used in cl. 40.

That test relies on a more objective standard than I think appropriate. But whether the owners' decision was unreasonable can itself be tested by considering what view a reasonable owner could have formed. The Judge concluded that—

... there was no material on which a reasonable owner could reasonably have considered that the risk of proceeding to Ruwais in September, 1987 was a different risk from that which already existed at the date of the charter.

That was a conclusion to which the Judge was entitled to come, and it is, in my judgment, fatal to the owners' contention that though they did not consider whether the risk was greater, the discretion should be held to have been validly exercised if they bona fide focused in September 1987 on the actual dangers which were in fact greater than they had been at the time when the charterparty was made.

## SECTION 6: THE RIGHT TO INDEMNITY

The charter may contain express provision for the charterer to indemnify the owner against the consequences of carrying out the charterer's orders. The question of an *implied* right of indemnity, and its extent, was addressed in the next case.

### *Triad Shipping Co.* v *Stellar Chartering & Brokerage Inc.*
### *(The Island Archon)*
### [1994] 2 Lloyd's Rep 227 (CA)

EVANS LJ: As long ago as Mar. 30, 1979, the owners of the Island Archon chartered her to the appellants for a term of 36 months on the New York Produce Exchange form of time charter-party.

In the course of her employment under the charter-party, the vessel was ordered on a voyage from European ports to Iraq. Cargo claims were asserted by the Iraqi receivers. The orders were given by German sub-charterers, but they have become insolvent. The shipowners, who are the present respondents, had to provide security before the ship was allowed to leave Basrah, the Iraqi port in question, and this gave rise to some delay. The shipowners claim an indemnity against their losses from the time charterers, who are the appellants.

The only issue raised by this appeal is whether the shipowners are entitled to succeed in their claim for an indemnity, which in the absence of any express undertaking in the charter-party must be based on an implied term.

...

The facts giving rise to the claim for an indemnity are unusual. In Basrah, the State Enterprise for Maritime Agency (SEMA) was the only agent that could be employed on behalf of the ship. SEMA were also the owners' P. & I. Club correspondents. When cargoes were discharged, the port authorities issued certificates allegedly showing short-landing and/or damage. The arbitrator found:

> These were frequently, viewed objectively, of highly dubious reliability. Nonetheless, they would be produced in Iraqi Courts in support of claims for shortage or damage and the Courts accepted them effectively as conclusive evidence against the carrier.

Moreover, whenever shortage or damage claims were intimated against a ship that was in the course of discharging — and this happened frequently, if not invariably — the agents (SEMA) would require the provision of security to cover possible cargo claims before the ship sailed (award para. 33). The local Courts assumed jurisdiction over such claims, because SEMA were regarded as an Iraqi party, and the Courts—

> ... then inevitably issued judgments based on the short-landing/damage certificates [para. 33].

The arbitrator described this as 'the Iraqi System' and his findings include the following:

> At the relevant time — and this was well-known in shipping circles — chaos was prevalent in Iraqi Ports, and in all aspects of their operation including the handling and supervision of cargoes and the pursuit of cargo claims ... put shortly, any ship ordered to discharge general cargo in Iraq was almost bound to have cargo claims made against it and to have those claims taken to court locally, leading to adverse judgments, regardless of whether there was any actual shortage or damage, or otherwise any other liability on the ship under the Bills of Lading [paras 32-33].

...

The relevant express terms of the charter-party were these. The vessel was—

> ... to be employed, in carrying lawful cargo (see Clause 62) ... in such lawful trades, between safe ports ... always within Institute Warranty Limits excluding Cuba, Israel, Vietnam, Cambodia, North Korea, and Angola including Cabioda, Namibia, Nigeria, Cyprus, Churchill ... as the Charterers or their Agents shall direct, on the following conditions ... [Lines 25-35].

The charter period, as stated above, was 36 months, two months more or less at charterers' option. Clause 8 was slightly amended to read:

> 8.   That the Captain shall prosecute his voyages with the utmost despatch, and shall tender all customary assistance with the ship's crew and boats. The Captain (although appointed by the Owners), shall be under the orders and directions of the Charterers as regards employment and agency; and Charterers are to load, stow, trim, *secure and discharge* the cargo at their expense under the supervision of the Captain, who is to sign Bills of Lading for cargo, as presented, in conformity with Mate's or Tally Clerk's receipts.

By cl. 38—
> ... the U.S. Clause Paramount. Canadian Clause Paramount, ... C.S.U.K. Paramount ... deemed to form part of this Charterparty and U.S.A. & Canadian Clauses Paramount to be incorporated in all Bills of Lading.

This was a typed clause, in other words, a specially agreed term, as was cl. 45:

> 45.   Notwithstanding the provisions of Clause 8, Master and Owners authorised Charterers, Sub-Charterers or their agents to sign Bills of Lading for and on behalf of

the Masters, in accordance with Mate's receipts, if so required by Charterers who shall indemnify vessel and Owners from all consequences arising therefrom.

If the claim had been presented on the basis that the bills of lading, which required the ship-owners to deliver the cargo in Basrah, had exposed them to a liability towards the cargo receivers which the charter-party did not require them to bear, then the claim would largely have been governed by cll. 8 and 45 of the charter-party, and by a substantial number of authorities in similar bill of lading cases. These were recognised as a separate category in *The Nogar Marin* [1988] 1 Lloyd's Rep 412 (see p. 417) although, in my judgment, no different principles are involved from other cases where an indemnity is claimed.

Under cll. 8 and 45, if bills of lading were signed by time charterers or their agents, then there was an express indemnity against the consequences of so doing (cl. 45). The only remaining issue would be whether the ship-owner's liability to the cargo receivers, as established by the judgment of the Iraq Courts, was a consequence of that act. If bills of lading were signed by the master pursuant to cl. 8, then there was no express indemnity and the question would arise whether a promise to indemnify the shipowners would be implied. In such circumstances I would have little difficulty in holding that there was an implied term. This would be justified by the weight of legal authority to which I have referred and by the further practical consideration that if there was no implied indemnity when bills of lading were presented to the master for his signature, but an express indemnity when they were signed by charterers or their agents, then the liability to indemnify might depend upon the accidental circumstances whether the master's signature could be obtained before the vessel sailed, or not.

It should be noted, however, that the implied indemnity under cl. 8 would not be as wide as the express indemnity under cl. 45. The former would not include the consequences of the master's failure to perform his duty of checking the accuracy of the bill as presented, extending at least to the apparent good order and condition of the cargo shipped: see *The Nogar Marin*, at p. 422.

However, the claim in the present case is not put forward on this basis. I mention it only because it is relevant to the issues which do arise, as will appear below.

What is said is that the loss suffered by the shipowners, in the form of the payments which they were required to make, first as security for cargo claims and then in order to satisfy the order of the Iraqi Courts even though no shortage or damage to cargo in fact had occurred, was a direct consequence of the charterers' order to the vessel to proceed to Basrah and deliver the cargo there. The arbitrator so found:

... there was an unbroken chain of causation between the orders to discharge in Iraq and the owners' liability to indemnify SEMA or pay the receivers ... [para. 35].

This was against the background of his earlier findings in paras 32 and 33 that no significant loss or damage to the cargo could be said to have occurred in fact.

The plaintiffs therefore rely on an implied undertaking to indemnify them against the consequences of the charterers' order to the vessel to proceed to Iraq. It matters not for this purpose whether the order was given expressly, as probably it was, or impliedly by means of presenting bills of lading which named Basrah as the destination of the voyage.

The learned Judge upheld this claim, applying principles which he deduced from the authorities ...

With regard to cl. 8 of the N.Y.P.E. form, he cited the following passage from the judgment of Mr Justice Mustill, in *The Athanasia Comninos* (reported in [1990] 1 Lloyd's Rep 277 though decided in December 1979):

It has long been established that a provision in this form impliedly requires the charterer to indemnify the shipowner against the consequences of complying with an order as to the employment of the ship. [p. 290]

Mr Glennie QC for the time charterers submits that this was wrong, or at least too broadly stated. He contends that no promise to indemnify can be implied if the order was one which the charterer was entitled to give. Conversely, that in order to recover an indemnity the shipowners have to establish that the charterers gave the order in breach of the charter. He relies in particular on the passage from the judgment of Mr Justice Bingham in *The C. Joyce* [1986] 2 Lloyd's Rep 285 which was quoted in part with approval in the Court of Appeal's judgment in *The Nogar Marin* per Lord Justice Mustill (p. 420). After considering the three leading cases (*Krüger & Co.* v *Moel Tryvan Steamship Co.* [1907] AC 272, *Elder Dempster & Co.* v *C. G. Dunn & Co. Ltd* (1909) 15 Com Cas 49 and *Dawson Line Ltd* v *Aktiengesellschaft 'Adler' Fuer Chemische Industrie AG* (1931) 41 Ll L Rep 75; [1932] 1 KB 433), Mr Justice Bingham, said this at p. 290.

... the first ground of liability depends on a finding that the charterers were in breach of contract in tendering bills for signature which conflicted with their obligations under the charter-party. Crucial to both grounds of decision was the finding of disparity between the bills which the charterers were under the charter-party entitled to present and the bills which they did present. From this finding the conclusion naturally follows, and it matters little whether the owners claim damages for breach of contract of which an indemnity will be the measure, or an indemnity arising from the loss which they have suffered from complying with the charterers' request to do something which they were not obliged to do under the charter-party.

Those authorities were concerned, therefore, with a situation where the charter did not permit the charterers to present bills of lading to the master for signature in the form in which they did; that was itself a breach of the charter-party. Therefore, Mr Glennie submits, no implied indemnity can arise unless the charterers were in breach, and here they were not in breach if they were entitled to give the order which they did. Basrah was within the (effectively) world-wide trading limits in this charter-party and was not an unsafe port, and the contrary is not suggested by the shipowners.

The question of principle thus raised by this appeal is whether a promise to indemnify the shipowners against the consequences of complying with an order as to the employment of the ship can be implied when the order was lawfully given; when it was an order which the charterer was entitled to give. It is common ground that any such implication—

... is not automatic. It must always depend on the facts of the individual case, and on the terms of any underlying contractual relationship ... [*The Nogar Marin* at p. 422]

but it is not suggested that any special facts, whether supporting or rebutting the alleged implication, arise here. The 'underlying contractual relationship' was that the shipowner and time charterer under a long-term time charter on NYPE terms which save as regards bills of lading signed by the charterers or their agents (cl. 45) is silent as regards any right of the shipowner to be indemnified against the consequences of obeying orders which the time charterers were entitled to give. In such circumstances, it is submitted, no such implication can properly be made. Mr Glennie relied upon the established rule that no term can be implied unless it is necessary for the business efficacy of the contract, in other words, to make the contract work, or unless the parties would have agreed with an officious bystander that 'of course' the term was part of their bargain, though not expressed. If they had agreed it, or thought that it was agreed between them, in the course of negotiating a charter-party (a 'complex and compound bargain' per Mr Justice Kerr in *Mareva Navigation Co. Ltd* v *Canaris Armadora SA* [1977] 1 Lloyd's Rep 368, p. 380), then they would have expressed it, as they did on a more limited basis in cl. 45.

Far from being 'long established' (*The Athanasia Comninos* at p. 290), Mr Glennie submitted that there is no authority which supports an implied indemnity on a time charter where the charterer is not shown to have committed a breach; where he has done no more than he was entitled to do.

This is a formidable submission and requires consideration of authorities dating back to the beginning of the present century when time charter-parties became more common or at least more frequently the subject of dispute in the Courts. The reason for this may have been the fact that shipping movements could be predicted more reliably with steamships than with sail, and this led to charterers being more willing to pay hire for the use of the ship's services throughout an agreed period. Whatever the reason was, the question of an implied indemnity soon arose for decision in *Kruger* v *Moel Tryvan* under a time charter made in 1903, and it was held that the charterers were in breach of contract when they presented bills of lading for signature which gave rise to liabilities under the bill of lading contracts which were excepted under the charter-party.

As an alternative ground of decision, the shipowners were held to be entitled to be indemnified against the liabilities which they incurred to third parties, the bill of lading holders, as the result of complying with the charterers' request to sign bills of lading in that form. This was an application of the general principle founded on *Sheffield Corporation* v *Barclay* [1905] AC 392 and recently affirmed in *Stanley Yeung Kai Yung* v *Hong Kong Shanghai Banking Corporation* [1981] AC 787. It has been held to be applicable in bill of lading cases, not only in *Krüger* v *Moel Tryvan* but since then in *Strathlorne Steamship Co. Ltd* v *Andrew Weir & Co.* (1934) 1 Ll L Rep 185 and in *The Sagona* [1984] 1 Lloyd's Rep 194 (see p. 204). In both later cases the charterer directed the master to deliver cargo to a person who was unable to present the bill of lading and therefore was not contractually entitled to receive it. This order could be said to have been given in breach of the charter-party, as it clearly was in breach of the bill of lading contract, but it may also be regarded as extra-contractual so far as the charter-party was concerned, and Mr Glennie recognises this as a second kind of situation where an implied right to an indemnity may arise. He submits, however, that such a right does not support the implication of a general right of indemnity in the charter-party itself.

Essential to the reasoning in all the authorities is the tri-partite relationship between shipowners, charterers and cargo interests. Legal relations between shipowner and charterer are governed by their contract contained in the charter-party. When a bill of lading is issued or is transferred to the owner or person entitled to possession of the cargo, who is not the charterer, then it contains or evidences a separate contract between the shipowner and that other person. If the shipowner's liability under the bill of lading is more onerous than under the charter-party, then the extent to which, if at all, he can recover an indemnity against the excess from the charterer is governed by the charter-party, or it may arise under the general principles of law recognised in *Kruger* v *Moel Tryvan* as a consequence of the master's compliance with the charterers' request.

The terms of the bll of lading as presented for signature may be different from those 'required' by the charter-party (per Lord Justice Scrutton in *Dawson Line Ltd* v *Adler* (1931) 41 Ll L Rep 75 at p. 78, col. 2; [1932] 1 KB 433 at p. 439) and in such cases a breach of contract is established from the fact of presentment alone, as in *Kruger* v *Moel Tryvan* itself. Conversely, if the bill of lading is in a form which is required by the charter-party, even though its terms are different from those of the charter-party itself, then it is difficult to imply a promise that the charterer will indemnify the shipowner against the consequences of doing what the charter required him to do. If no promise is implied, the effect is that the shipowner has agreed to the charter terms as between himself and the charterer, and other terms with the holders of the bill of lading; and this was held to be the true construction of the charter-party contract in *The C. Joyce* (above).

The intermediate case, which arises for consideration in the light of Mr Glennie's submissions, is where the charter-party permits the charterer to present and to require the master to sign a bill of lading whose terms and conditions of carriage differ from those found in the charter-party itself. In these circumstances, there is no breach of charter-party by the charterer, nor can the charterer's direction or request to the master be said to lie outside the charter-party; it is permitted by the charter-party and he is entitled by contract to act as he has done.

The particular issue, thus defined, has not been specifically addressed in any of the authorities to which we have been referred. . . .

The matter therefore must be considered as an issue of principle.

Again, the historical background is relevant. At the time of *Krüger* v *Moel Tryvan* in 1907, although time charters included such phrases as 'Master to sign bills of lading as presented', or 'without prejudice to this charter-party', it was possible to hold that presenting a bill of lading containing different terms from those of the charter-party itself was a breach of contract: see the *Kruger* decision itself. But in modern conditions the situation is entirely changed. This may be as a result of the widespread standardisation of bill of lading terms by international conventions and of national legislation which makes such terms compulsory as between shipowner and bill of lading holder, though not (usually) between shipowner and charterer: e.g., the Carriage of Goods by Sea Acts 1924 and 1971, in the United Kingdom. The current situation was described by Lord Wilberforce in *The Nanfri* [1971] 1 Lloyd's Rep 201, at p. 206, col. 1; [1979] AC 757 at p. 777, where the charter-parties were in Baltime form and therefore contained an express indemnity:

> It is important in this connection to have in mind that the present charters are time charters, the nature and purpose of which is to enable the charterers to use the vessels during the period of the charters for trading in whatever manner they think fit. The issue of bills of lading in a particular form may be vital for the charterers' trade, and indeed in relation to this trade, which involved c.i.f. or c. & f. contracts the issue of freight pre-paid bills of lading is essential if the trade is to be maintained. Furthermore, cl. 9, as is usual in time charters, contains an indemnity clause against all consequences or liabilities arising from the master signing bills of lading. This underlines the power of the charterers, in the course of exploiting the vessel, to decide what bills of lading are appropriate for their trade and to instruct the masters to issue such bills, the owners being protected by the indemnity clause.
>
> Then what limitations are there upon this power? It must be clear that the owners cannot require bills of lading to be claused so as to incorporate the terms of the time charter: such a requirement would be contrary to the whole commercial purpose of the charterers.

The situation therefore may often arise, where, far from the charterers being in breach by reason of presenting for signature a bill of lading containing different terms and conditions of carriage from the charter-party, the master would place the shipowners in breach of contract if he refused to sign, assuming only that the bill is accurate as to the apparent condition of the cargo loaded and is not in terms which can be said to be outside the scope of any which were contemplated by the charter-party. Does the implied right to be indemnified arise in such a case?

In my judgment, there is no reason in principle why it should not do so in accordance with the general rule founded on *Sheffield Corporation* v *Barclay* [1905] AC 392. If the rule applies when the charterer makes a request outside the terms of the charter-party, as Mr Glennie concedes that it does, then why should it not also apply when the same request has been contemplated by the charter itself? The fact that the request is a direction which the master is under a contractual duty to obey does not mean that the rule cannot operate: see *The Nogar Marin* at p. 417. In such circumstances, the correct legal analysis in my judgment is that the right to an indemnity exists under an implied term of the charter-party. Nor is there any reason why the implied term should be limited to the consequences of complying with one kind of direction only, that is, to sign bills of lading in a particular form.

Support for the existence of an implied right of indemnity in general terms in a time charter can be found in *The Erechthion* [1987] 2 Lloyd's Rep 180 where the parties agreed through Counsel, and Mr Justice Staughton accepted, though perhaps in terms which registered some doubt, that there was an implied obligation to indemnify against consequences caused by compliance with the charterers' lawful orders as to employment of the vessel (p. 183). On the other hand, in *The Paros* [1987] 2 Lloyd's Rep 269 Mr Justice Hobhouse, held at p. 273 that:

> . . . if it is a contractual and proper bill of lading then there is no cause for complaint and therefore no ground for claiming damages for breach of contract or an indemnity . . .

. . .

Finally, the leading text books (*Scrutton* 19th ed.) Art. 178; *Carver* (13th ed.) para. 668 and *Time Charters* (3rd ed.) by Wilford, Coghlin and Kimball) all support the existence of an implied term though without referring expressly to the issue raised by Mr Glennie in the present case.

He has demonstrated, in my judgment, that there is no authority which explicitly supports the implied right to an indemnity in a case where the charter-party entitled the charterer to act as he did and the shipowner was bound to obey. This was partly because the particular issue was never raised for decision. Nevertheless, when Mr Justice Mustill said in *The Athanasia Comninos* in 1979 that this 'has long been established', without suggesting that the right was limited to cases where the charterer's order was given in breach of contract, or was extra-contractual in the sense that the shipowner or master was not under a duty to obey it, he was referring to a long-held general belief among maritime lawyers including, and perhaps especially, maritime arbitrators that no such qualification was necessary. Although not expressly decided in any reported case, the view was supported by leading text-book writers, as it has continued to be. In my judgment, he correctly stated the law.

For these reasons, I would reject Mr Glennie's submission and hold that the shipowners are entitled to rely upon an implied right to be indemnified against the consequences of complying with the time charterers' order to proceed to Basrah and deliver cargo there, notwithstanding that it was an order which the time charterers were entitled to give and the shipowners were bound to obey. There is an express finding that the losses claimed were the direct consequence of complying with the order and on this basis the shipowners are entitled to succeed and the appeal should be dismissed.

The implications of this conclusion are, however, potentially far-reaching and these should be considered before this case is finally disposed of.

Orders as to the employment of the ship which the master is bound by cl. 8 to obey include orders to load a particular cargo from the range of lawful cargoes permitted by the charter-party (lines 24–25 and cl. 62) and to proceed to a named safe port within the limits provided for in lines 31–35.

These liberties do not, of course, entitle the charterers to load non-contractual or dangerous cargoes, or to order the ship to an unsafe port. If they were to give such an order, then the master could refuse to obey, but if he complied with the order then, unless he had exposed the ship to obvious dangers, the shipowners would be entitled to recover damages for breach of contract and it is clear that they could recover an indemnity also.

But if the order is lawful, whether as to the cargo to be carried or the port to which the vessel is to proceed, and damage results, and if there is an implied indemnity in general terms then the charterers will always be liable for such damage, notwithstanding that the cargo was permitted by the charter-party and the port was safe. This would make it unnecessary to consider whether the charterer's order was given in breach of the charter-party, so as to found a claim in damages, because the charterers would be liable in any event.

It is clear, however, that even when there is an express indemnity, time charterers are not liable for all consequences which may result from compliance with their order. First, the shipowners may themselves have been at fault: see *The Nogar Marin* at p. 417. This exception, however, may be more apparent than real, because the intervening fault can readily be seen to have broken the chain of consequences flowing from the charterers' order, in accordance with established general principles. Secondly, it has been held that the shipowner remains responsible for the safe navigation of the ship; see *Larrinaga* v R (above) and *The Erechthion* (above) where this factual issue was remitted to the arbitrators (and, we were told by Counsel, the arbitrators rejected the shipowners' claim; this must have been on the basis that, applying the law as stated by Mr Justice Staughton, they found that the port authority's orders to the vessel, which led to her being at the place where she was damaged, broke the chain of causation flowing from the charterers' order to proceed to the port — see pp. 186–188). Similarly, in *A/B Helsingfors Steamship Co.* v *Rederiaktiebolaget Rex (The White Rose)* [1969] 2 Lloyd's Rep 52 Mr Justice Donaldson at p. 59 held that:

> ... it is necessary in every case to establish an unbroken chain of causation ...

...

If the vessel is damaged at a port to which she has been properly ordered by time charterers, then it is difficult to rebut a claim that the damages was a consequence of her being there at the material time, and therefore of the time charterer's orders to proceed there. This analysis was adopted by Mr Justice Mustill, in *The George C. Lemos* where time charterers were held liable:

> It seems to one perfectly possible to have a loss which is caused by the shipment of a cargo having certain properties, even if the properties of the cargo in question are no different from those of other cargoes of the same description. In the present case, if one asks the question (eliminating the possibility of fault on the part of the shipowner) 'Why was there an explosion?' the answer is — 'Because there was methane in the hold'. And if one goes on to ask 'Why was there methane in the hold?' the answer is — 'Because the Time charterers called on the vessel to load coal'. This answer is in my opinion sufficient to found an indemnity without proof that the coal was in any way unusual [[1990] 1 Lloyd's Rep at p. 296].

If this straightforward test of causation was applied in cases where the vessel is damaged at a port to which the charterers ordered her, then it would become unnecessary to determine whether the port was unsafe at the time of the order; if it was, then the orders were given in breach of contract; if it was not, then the shipowners are entitled to an indemnity.

This clearly is not the law, and in my judgment the reason is to be found in the following passage from the judgment of Mr Justice Lloyd, in *The Aquacharm* [1980] 2 Lloyd's Rep 237.

...

It is of course well settled that owners can recover under an implied indemnity for the direct consequences of complying with the charterers' orders. But it is not every loss arising in the course of the voyage that can be recovered. For example, the owners cannot recover heavy weather damage merely because had the charterers ordered the vessel on a different voyage, the heavy weather would not have been encountered. The connection is too remote. Similarly, the owners cannot recover the expenses incurred in the course of ordinary navigation, for example, the cost of ballasting, even though in one sense the cost of ballasting is incurred as a consequence of complying with the charterers' orders: see *Weir* v *Union Steamship Co. Ltd* [1900] AC 525. The same considerations apply in the present case. The costs of transhipment were an ordinary expense incurred in the course of navigation.

Claims under an express indemnity failed in two cases where the vessel suffered a loss which resulted, not from the charterer's orders, but from navigational risks to which she was exposed in the course of carrying them out: *Larrinaga Steamship Co.* v *The Crown* (1945) 78 Ll L Rep 167 (HL) and *Stag Line Ltd* v *Ellerman & Papayanou Lines Ltd* (1949) 82 Ll L Rep 826 (Mr Justice Morris, see pp. 835–837).

...

The authorities show, therefore, that time charterers may be held liable under an express indemnity for the consequences of ordering the chartered vessel to load a particular cargo or to proceed to a named port, even though the order is one which the charterer is entitled to give and the master is bound to obey. But the consequences for which the charterer is liable do not include two categories of loss. First, the loss may be regarded as caused in law by some subsequent or intervening event. An act of negligence may often, but not invariably, break the chain of causation in this sense: *Portsmouth Steamship Co. Ltd* v *Liverpool & Glasgow Exchange Association* (1929) 34 Ll L Rep 459 (Mr Justice Roche), and *The White Rose* at p. 59. Secondly, the loss although a consequence 'in a broad sense' (Wilford p. 241) may have arisen from a risk which the shipowner has agreed to run, hence the exclusion of navigation risks and also the distinction which has been held to exist between time and voyage charter-parties (per Mr Justice Devlin, in *The Ann Stathatos* and Mr Justice Mustill, in *The Georges C. Lemos* (3rd party proceedings) [1991] 2 Lloyd's Rep 107).

This does not mean that a rigid distinction between time and voyage charters must always be made. If the question is whether the shipowner has accepted the risk to which in the event the vessel has been exposed, there could be voyage charters giving the charterer a wide range of options to choose a cargo or port where it would be 'reasonable' for the shipowner to expect the indemnity to apply, and conversely, time charters with a narrow range e.g., charters for the period of a specified voyage or 'trip', where it would not.

Applying the same analysis to the facts of the *White Rose*, the shipowners could be said to have accepted the normal incidents of loading cargo at a United States port, including the risk of liability under the local State law to an injured stevedore when the shipowners themselves were not at fault, but this would not bar them from recovering an indemnity from the time charterers if the local law was 'unusual', as contemplated by Mr Justice Donaldson, in the passage quoted above.

What risks the shipowner has agreed to bear must depend upon the true construction of the charter-party and therefore upon the situation when the charter-party was entered into. If there had been a finding in the present case that the 'Iraqi system' was notorious at the date of the charter-party in March, 1979 then there might be substance in the charterers' contention that the shipowners had consented to bear the consequences of ordering the vessel to discharge at an Iraqi port, which they could have excluded from the agreed limits if they had sought to do so. But the findings are that the Iraqi system was well known only when the vessel was ordered there in June/July 1980, and the Iran/Iraq war which may have been responsible for the problem did not begin until September 1980. In these circumstances, the shipowners' failure to guard against the difficulties over a year before cannot provide grounds for barring their claim.

This leads back to the basic issue whether an indemnity should be implied where the shipowner places the master under the orders of the charterer, but no corresponding express indemnity is given. As Mr Glennie rightly submits, it is insufficient to justify an implied term that it would be 'reasonable' for the shipowner to stipulate for an express indemnity. Nevertheless, the implication is justified, in my view, first by 'business efficacy' in the sense that if the charterer requires to have the vessel at his disposal, and to be free to choose voyages and cargoes and bill of lading terms also, then the owner must be expected to grant such freedom only if he is entitled to be indemnified against loss and liability resulting from it, subject always to the express terms of the charter-party contract; and secondly by the legal principle underlying the 'lawful request' cases such as *Sheffield Corporation* v *Barclay*; in other words, an implication of law.

In my judgment, therefore, the award and the judgment in the present case in favour of the shipowners are consistent with the authorities and justified by the relevant principles of law. The right to be indemnified may be implied, but it is subject to the same restrictions as regards consequences as have been held to apply to an express right, and in both cases the right is subject to the shipowners' acceptance of risk, including the risk of liabilities to third parties, as between himself and the charterers on the true construction of the charter-party itself. I would dismiss this appeal.

*Notes*

1. In *Naviera Mogor SA* v *Société Metallurgique de Normandie (The Nogar Marin)* [1988] 1 Lloyd's Rep 412 (CA) the charterparty required the Captain to sign bills of lading '. . . as presented without prejudice to this Charterparty'. A cargo of wire rods in coils was shipped at Caen for Tampa. The coils had been stored in the open at the quay and some were rusty when shipped. The master signed a mate's receipt which did not refer to the condition of the goods. On the strength of this the ship's agents (Sogena) issued clean bills of lading. The shipowners had to compensate the holders of the bills of lading for the damage to the cargo and sought an indemnity from the charterers. Staughton J's decision in the charterers' favour was affirmed by the Court of Appeal.

2. In *Trade Star Line Corporation* v *Mitsui & Co Ltd (The Arctic Trader)* [1996] 2 Lloyd's Rep 449 (CA), the cargo of salt was so contaminated that the mate's receipts should have been claused, but they were not and clean bills of lading were issued in reliance on the mate's receipts. The charterers complained that the resulting delay at the discharging port in Nigeria disrupted their planned

trading programme for the vessel. It was held that the owners were not under an implied duty to the charterers to clause the mate's receipts.

## SECTION 7: PAYMENT OF HIRE

It is of the greatest importance for the shipowner to ensure that hire is paid punctually. Standard forms of time charter make detailed provision for payment and confer on the shipowner the right to withdraw the vessel if there is any failure in punctual payment.

### Mardorf Peach & Co. Ltd v Attica Sea Carriers Corp. of Liberia
### (The Laconia)
### [1977] AC 850 (HL)

LORD WILBERFORCE: My Lords, the appellants are the owners of the ship *Laconia* which they chartered, in January 1970, to the respondents on a time charter for 3 months 15 days more or less in charterers' option. The charterparty, on a New York Produce Exchange form, provided that the hire was to be paid in cash in US currency semi-monthly in advance.

> to the owners . . . into their account with First National City Bank of New York, 34, Moorgate, London, E.C.2 to the credit of O.F.C. Account No. 705586.

and that 'failing the punctual and regular payment of the hire' the owners should be at liberty to withdraw the vessel.

The seventh and final instalment became due on Sunday, April 12, 1970. It was conceded by the charterers, and this case has been conducted on the footing, that, as London banks are closed on Sunday and Saturday, the due date for payment of this instalment was Friday, April 10, 1970. It was not paid on that day but was tendered or paid to the owners' bank (this will be discussed later), about 3.00 p.m. on Monday, April 13, 1970. At 6.55 p.m. on the same day the owners withdrew the vessel. The question is whether they had the right to do so. In accordance with the charterparty the matter went to arbitration. The arbitrators found in the owners' favour, but, on request, stated their award in the form of a special case which asked whether, as a question of law, the owners were entitled so to withdraw the *Laconia*. This was answered affirmatively by Donaldson J but in the negative in the Court of Appeal (Lord Denning MR and Lawton LJ, Bridge LJ dissenting).

The result of this appeal turns, in my opinion, upon the answer to two and only two questions. First, what is the meaning of the withdrawal clause. Second, whether the owners have waived the default of the charterers in not making punctual payment. These questions are, in themselves, comparatively simple, but they attract in their wake some others with which I shall have to deal.

The clause which regulates the payment of hire and the right to withdraw is, in full, as follows:

> 5. Payment of said hire to be made in New York in cash in United States currency, semi-monthly in advance, and for the last half month or part of same the approximate amount of hire, and should same not cover the actual time, hire is to be paid for the balance day by day, as it becomes due, if so required by owners, unless bank guarantee or deposit is made by the charterers, otherwise failing the punctual and regular

payment of the hire, or bank guarantee, or on any breach of this charterparty, the owners shall be at liberty to withdraw the vessel from the service of the charterers, without prejudice to any claim they (the owners) may otherwise have on the charterers.

The provision as to payment was altered by a typed addendum (clause 52) which produced the results I have previously stated.

My Lords, I cannot find any difficulty or ambiguity in this clause. It must mean that once a punctual payment of any instalment has not been made, a right of withdrawal accrues to the owners. Conversely, it is incapable of meaning that a charterer who has failed to make a punctual payment, can (unless the owners have waived the default) avoid the consequences of his failure by later tendering an unpunctual payment. He would still have failed to make a punctual payment, and it is on this failure and by reason of it that the owners get the right to withdraw. That this was so was decided, on this same clause, in *The Brimnes* [1973] 1 WLR 386; [1975] QB 929 in which powerful judgments were given by Brandon J and by the Court of Appeal (Edmund Davies, Megaw and Cairns LJJ), a decision which, in my opinion, was, on this point, unquestionably correct.

. . .

This leaves the second question, which is whether the right of withdrawal was waived by the owners. The submission of the charterers was that on Monday, April 13, 1970, before the owners purported to withdraw the ship, they accepted the charterers' late payment of the instalment and so affirmed the contract. The arbitrators found that there had not been any waiver, so that the charterers must undertake the task of showing that, upon the facts found, the only possible conclusion must have been there had.

In order to understand the argument, it is necessary to go into the facts in some detail. At about 3 p.m., at which time London banks closed for the day, a messenger from the Midland Bank, acting for the charterers, delivered to the owners' bank, the First National City Bank, 34, Moorgate, London ('F.N.C.B.'), a 'payment order' for the amount of the seventh instalment. A payment order is a document issued by one bank to another under a scheme (L.C.S.S.) by which banks maintain dollar suspense accounts in which they credit or debit each other with sums in dollars and make periodical settlements. As between banks, a payment order is the equivalent of cash, but a customer cannot draw upon it. The amount must first be credited to his account, but he can, of course, make special arrangements for earlier drawing. At about 3.10 or 3.15 p.m. the payment order was received and stamped in the sorting office of F.N.C.B. It was then taken to the transfer department. There an official called an editor wrote on the face of the order the formula CR ADV & T.T. Lausanne, an instruction (to be carried out elsewhere in the bank) meaning 'credit advice and telegraphic transfer Lausanne'. Not perhaps quite simultaneously, but at about the same time, another official telephoned to the owners' agents and said that the bank had received a payment order for the amount of the hire: this was in accordance with instructions received by the bank earlier in the day from the owners' agents. This official was immediately told to refuse the money and to return it. Thereupon the editor deleted the annotation he had made on the payment order and wrote on it. 'Beneficiary has refused payment. Advise remitter by phone.' There was no direct evidence that this was done but such may be presumed. The next day F.N.C.B. sent to the Midland Bank a payment order for the same amount as that which the Midland Bank had sent the previous day.

My Lords, much ingenuity and effort was used in order to show that this series of actions, or some part of it, constituted acceptance and waiver by the owners of the right to withdraw. But in my opinion it did not approach success. Although the word 'waiver', like 'estoppel', covers a variety of situations different in their legal nature, and tends to be indiscriminately used by the courts as a means of relieving parties from bargains or the consequences of bargains which are thought to be harsh or deserving of relief, in the present context what is relied on is clear enough. The charterers had failed to make a punctual payment but it was open to the owners to accept a late payment as if it were punctual, with the consequence that they could not thereafter rely on the default as entitling them to withdraw. All that is needed to establish waiver, in this sense, of the committed breach of contract, is evidence, clear and unequivocal, that such acceptance has taken place, or, after the late payment has been tendered, such a delay in refusing it as might reasonably cause the charterers to believe that it has been accepted.

My Lords, if this is, as I believe, what would have to be proved in order to establish a waiver in the situation under review, it must be obvious that the facts in the present case do not amount to it. Looked at untechnically, the facts were that the money was sent to the bank, taken into the banking process or machinery, put in course of transmission to the owners, but rejected by the latter as soon as they were informed of its arrival and as soon as they were called upon, or able, to define their position. Put more technically, the bank, though agents of the owners, had a limited authority. It is not necessary to decide whether, in general, and in the absence of specific instructions, bankers in such situations as these have authority to accept late payments — on this matter I regard *The Brimnes* [1975] QB 929 as a special case where an inference to this effect may have been justified on the facts and the observations of the Lords Justices (in particular of Cairns LJ at p. 972) as directed to that situation. But here it is clear that the bankers had no such authority and still less any authority to make business decisions as to the continuance or otherwise of the charterparty but that per contra they had express instructions to refer the matter to the owners' agents. On this basis they receive the order (they clearly had no right to reject it out of hand), and, while provisionally starting to process it into the owners' possession, at the same time seek the owners' directions in accordance with the owners' previous instructions. On those directions, they arrest the process and return the money. The acts of the editors — the annotation on the payment order — were internal acts (Brandon J, of a similar situation in *The Brimnes* [1973] 1 WLR 386, 411 called them 'ministerial', i.e., acts done without any intention or capacity to affect legal relations with third parties), not irrevocable, but provisional and reversible acts, consistent with an alternative decision of the customer which might be to accept or reject. The customer chose to reject, he did so as rapidly as the circumstances permitted, and he could have given no ground to the charterer for supposing that the payment had been accepted. The charterer did not act upon any such supposition.

The pattern of action is to me so clear that I do not find it necessary to decide the rather technical question whether, as regards the owners, there was payment 'in cash' as required by the charterparty, or not. Whatever it was it was not punctual payment, and not accepted in waiver of the unpunctuality. I think then that there is no basis on which the arbitrators' finding against waiver can be attacked.

The result of my conclusions on these two points leaves the matter as follows:

1.   Under the withdrawal clause, as under similar clauses, including the Baltime clause properly interpreted, a right of withdrawal arises as soon as default is made in punctual payment of an instalment of hire. Whether or not this rule is subject to qualification in a case of punctual but insufficient payment as some authorities appear to hold, is not an issue which now arises and I express no opinion upon it.

2.   The owners must within a reasonable time after the default give notice of withdrawal to the charterers. What is a reasonable time — essentially a matter for arbitrators to find — depends on the circumstances. In some, indeed many cases, it will be a short time — viz. the shortest time reasonably necessary to enable the shipowner to

hear of the default and issue instructions. If, of course, the charterparty contains an express provision regarding notice to the charterers, that provision must be applied.

3. The owners may be held to have waived the default, inter alia, if when a late payment is tendered, they choose to accept it as if it were timeous, or if they do not within a reasonable time give notice that they have rejected it.

I believe that these rules, which essentially represent the law as it was before *The Georgios C* [1971] 1 QB 488, can be easily applied by arbitrators, and that they avoid the necessity for minute and technical inquiries into the exact times of payments and actions by banks (*cf. The Brimnes* [1975] QB 929). They do not remove the need for charterers to prove that they have paid punctually, and there may be some niceties here, but, if the market has turned so greatly in favour of owners, it is reasonable to expect of charterers a greater margin of care.

### Notes

1. The House of Lords overruled the decision in *The Georgios C* [1971] 1 QB 488, on which the Court of Appeal had relied.
2. In *Tropwood AG* v *Jade Enterprises Ltd (The Tropwind)* [1982] 1 Lloyd's Rep 232, at 234, Lord Denning MR famously commented 'when market rates are rising, the shipowners keep close watch on payments of hire. If the charterer makes a slip of any kind — a few minutes too late or a few dollars too little — the shipowners jump on him like a ton of bricks.'
3. Payment 'in cash' means that what the creditor receives must be 'the equivalent of cash, or as good as cash' (per Lord Bridge of Harwich in *A/S Awilco* v *Fulvia SpA Di Navigazione (The Chikuma)* [1981] 1 Lloyd's Rep 371 (HL), where a credit to the shipowners' account would, if drawn on, have involved them in paying interest to the bank for the first four days: this was held not to be payment in cash).
4. It is for the shipowner to show that the right of withdrawal has been properly exercised according to its terms.

### Afovos Shipping Co. SA v R. Pagnan and F. lli
### (The Afovos)
[1983] 1 Lloyd's Rep 335 (HL)

LORD HAILSHAM OF ST MARYLEBONE LC: My Lords, on June 18, 1979, in circumstances hereafter to be described, the appellants as shipowners purported to withdraw the ship *Afovos* from a time charter date Feb. 8, 1978, on the New York Produce Exchange form by which she was let to the respondents as charterers for two years three months more or less at charterer's option from delivery date on Feb. 14, 1978. The purported ground was a right of withdrawal conferred by a clause in the charter. The formal question in this appeal is whether the appellant were entitled so to act, and whether their action was effective to achieve its purpose.

The commercial reality is, as happens not seldom, somewhat different. By a without prejudice agreement the ship remained on charter to the respondents for the rest of the charter period. The real question in dispute is whether the hire is to be at the original rate of US $1.97 ½ per ton, or an enhanced rate reflecting the market at the time of the purported withdrawal. The difference is about US $2 ½ million.

The result of the appeal depends upon the construction of two clauses in the charter, and the effect to be given to the purported notice of withdrawal. It will be convenient to deal first with the terms of the two clauses to be construed, and then to recite the facts, of which the purported notice of withdrawal was one.

The arrangements for payment and the right of withdrawal were contained in cl. 5 of the charter which provided as follows:—

> 5.   Payment of said hire to be made in London, to the FIRST NATIONAL BANK OF CHICAGO ... London EC3P 3DR, for the credit of ANGELICOUSSIS SHIPHOLDING GROUP, LIMITED ... in cash in United States Currency, semi-monthly in advance ... otherwise failing the punctual and regular payment of the hire ... the Owners shall be at liberty to withdraw the vessel from the service of the Charterers ...

This is the first of two clauses which falls to be construed. The severity of the right of the withdrawal contained in the last phrase was mitigated by an 'anti-technicality clause' contained in cl. 31 of the charter. This anti-technicality clause was in the following terms:—

> 31.   When hire is due and not received the Owners, before exercising the option of withdrawing the vessel from the Charterparty, will give Charterers fortyeight hours notice, Saturdays, Sundays and Holidays excluded and will not withdraw the vessel if the hire is paid within these fortyeight hours.

This is the second clause to be construed.

In the events which happened, the hire was punctually paid up to and including June 11, 1979, when there occurred a chapter of accidents, for so only can it be described, which gave rise to the present dispute. On that date the respondents gave instructions in good time to their bankers, the Padua branch of the Credito Italiano, to pay the instalment then currently due for payment on or before June 14, 1979, in accordance with the charter to the London branch of the First National Bank of Chicago for the credit of Angelicoussis Shipholding Group Ltd. This the Padua bank purported to do by telex on June 13. Both banks were in funds and were in account with one another. But for one unfortunate circumstance there was no reason why the transaction should not have been completed in due time.

The London branch of the Chicago bank had originally possessed three telex call numbers, the last two digits of which were respectively 16, 17 and 18. But that numbered 18 had been abandoned in 1975 and by 1979 had been allotted to a third party. Nevertheless, in the relevant directories for 1976, 1977 and 1978 the old call number had continued to be recorded under the name of the Chicago bank, and as at June 14, 1979, the Padua bank was using the 1978 edition. By a singular mischance the Padua branch tried first to connect with 16 and 17 and found, in the first case, that there was no reply and, in the second, that the number was engaged. The third time the Padua bank connected with the number 18 and there was a reply from the third party; and though the answering call was wrong the Padua bank transmitted the telex to the third party and the error was not discovered and corrected until June 19 when the payment of the instalment was admittedly overdue.

In the meantime, on June 14, 1979, which was the last day for paying the instalment, the appellants had purported to exercise their rights under cl. 31. At 16 40 hours

(London time) on that day, which was a Thursday, they sent to the respondents through their London agents the following telex:—

> Owners have instructed us that in case we do not receive the hire which is due today, to give charterers notice as per cl. 31 of the Charterparty for withdrawal of the vessel from their service.

The telex, we were told, was received five minutes later. Allowing for the intervening Saturday and Sunday, 48 hours from the receipt of this telex would have expired at 16 45 hours on Monday, June 18. At 19 20 hours on that day the appellants sent to the respondents a telex purporting to withdraw the vessel from their service.

This resulted in a dispute giving rise to the present proceedings commenced by writ by the appellants as plaintiffs claiming on a specially indorsed statement of claim a declaration that they were entitled to withdraw the vessel. At first instance Mr Justice Lloyd decided in their favour (see [1980] 2 Lloyd's Rep 469), but his judgment was reversed by the Court of Appeal (see [1982] 1 Lloyd's Rep 562), and so the matter comes before your Lordships' House for final disposal by leave of the Appeal Committee.

A number of questions arose for debate at one time or another. Only a small number of these were still alive by the time of the appeal before your Lordships, and, in my view, the case can be disposed of by considering only two, viz:—

(1)  At what point of time on June 14, 1979, apart from the mitigation of cl. 31, would the right of withdrawal have arisen under cl. 5 of the charter?

(2)  On the assumption that, at 16 40 or 16 45 hours on June 14, 1979, the point of time indicated by the answer to the first question had not been reached, were the appellants entitled to send a notice exercising their option under cl. 31 in advance of that point of time?

Of the two questions which must be decided, the second appears to me to be plain beyond argument. Both the grammatical meaning of cl. 31 and the policy considerations underlying the contract require that the moment of time at which the 48 hours notice must be given did not arise until after the moment of time at which, apart from the clause, the right of withdrawal would have accrued. I agree with the judgments of the Court of Appeal that both the expression 'due and received' and the reference to the right as an 'option', really only admit of this sense. The argument which appealed to the learned Judge that notice could be given at any time during the last day available for payment of the instalment (i.e., at any time after midnight on June 13/14 or alternatively at some point of time when it was unlikely that the instalment would be paid timeously) failed to make any impression on me at all. The notice can only be given 'when hire is due and not received', which cannot arise before the time postulated by the answer given to the first question (whatever that answer may be), and the notice can only be given when there is (or apart from cl. 31 would be) already in existence, an 'option' capable of exercise of 'withdrawing the vessel from the charter party', and that option can only be exercised after the arrival of the same point of time.

Even if the point of cl. 31 were ambiguous, which in my judgment it is not, I would be greatly impressed by the view of the Court of Appeal. Quite obviously the clause was inserted in order to save the charterer, who may (as in this case) be quite innocent even of the knowledge that his payment had not been received, from the extremely onerous effects (in this case a cost of $2 ½ million) of cl. 5, and equally obviously if the appellants' arguments be accepted a premature notice would have the effect of allowing the shipowner to reduce the effective period of 48 hours notice by anything up to 24 hours. . . .

In the result, I conclude that the crux of this case depends upon the answer given to the first of the two questions I have posed. This was: at what point of time apart from the mitigation of cl. 31 would the right of withdrawal under cl. 5 of the charter have arisen? To put the question in ther terms of cl. 5: At what point of time can the charterers be said to have been 'failing the punctual and regular payment of the hire'? Since the punctual payment of only one instalment is in question, for the purpose of the present appeal one need only ask the question in the simpler form 'What is the latest point of time on June 14, 1979, which would have constituted punctual payment of the instalment?' To this question I believe that, in principle, only one answer is possible, namely at midnight on the last day available to them for the due and punctual payment of the hire, i.e., June 14. I take it to be a general principle of law not requiring authority that where a person under an obligation to do a particular act has to do it on or before a particular date he has the whole of that day to perform his duty. No doubt as the hours pass it becomes less and less probable that he will be able to do it. That is the risk he runs. But he is not actually in default until the time arrives. . . . In my view, in his judgment at first instance Mr Justice Lloyd allowed himself to be deflected from his application of the present rule to the construction of cl. 5 of the charter by an analysis of the actual probability of the charterer being in default if his telex were received after counter hours in the bank, after 16 40 hours in the afternoon, or even later before midnight. But that, to my mind, is a false analysis probably based on a false analogy which, indeed, in the course of discussion, Counsel for the appellant invited us to draw. The question is not when the charterer would cease to be likely to pay in time but when, to quote cl. 5, 'punctual payment' would have failed. In my opinion this moment must relate to a particular hour, and is not dependent on the modalities of the recipient bank. It is the hour of midnight to which the general rule applies.

To escape from this meaning, Counsel for the appellant sought to rely on the doctrine of anticipatory breach. But this is not the basis on which cl. 31 stood to be invoked, or upon which an actual breach of cl. 5 can be said to have occurred. No doubt if there had been a total repudiation of the whole contract the appellants could have elected to treat the contract as at an end. But then they would not have required to invoke cl. 31 to do so or to give 48 hours notice of their election. A breach of cl. 5 occurred, and could only occur, at a particular moment of time, and it was only on the occurrence of that breach that, on the true construction of the charter, notice could be given under cl. 31. There is no reason, in my judgment to place the moment of time at which 'punctual payment' ceased to be possible at any moment earlier than midnight on June 14, 1979, in accordance with the general rule to which I have referred. . . .

*Question and Note*

1.   Joel Shipping chartered the *Lucy May* to Sam Enterprises. An instalment was due, but not paid, on Friday 1 June. The charter provides that the owners will give 48 hours' notice before withdrawing the vessel for non-payment of hire and will not withdraw the vessel if hire is paid within the 48 hours. At 23.40 on 1 June Joel sent a telex to Sam reading 'Please be notified of withdrawal of the *Lucy May*.' Is the notice effective? (see *Schelde Delta Shipping BV* v *Astarte Shipping Ltd (The Pamela)* [1995] 2 Lloyd's Rep 249 (QBD, Gatehouse J).

2.   Provided the shipowner exercises the right of withdrawal in accordance with the contract, that is an end of the matter: there is no equitable jurisdiction to grant relief to the charterer.

## Scandinavian Trading Tanker Co. AB v Flota Petrolera Ecuatoriana (The Scaptrade)
### [1983] 2 AC 694 (HL)

LORD DIPLOCK: My Lords, in this appeal between the appellant ('the charterers') and the respondent ('the owners') of the tanker *Scaptrade*, your Lordships have heard argument upon one question only: 'Has the High Court any jurisdiction to grant relief against the exercise by a shipowner of his contractual right, under the withdrawal clause in a time charter, to withdraw the vessel from the service of the charterer upon the latter's failure to make payment of an instalment of the hire in the manner and at a time that is not later than that for which the withdrawal clause provides?' I call this the jurisdiction point.

...

The time charter concerned was on the standard printed 'Shelltime 3' form with typed additions that are not material to the question that your Lordships have to decide. This form of charterparty is expressed to be governed by the law of England, and to be subject to the jurisdiction of the English court. The relevant wording of the payment of hire clause, which, as is usual in most standard forms of time charter, incorporated the withdrawal clause, was:

> Payment of the said hire shall be made in New York monthly in advance ... In default of such payment owners may withdraw the vessel from the service of charterers, without prejudice to any claim owners may otherwise have on charterers under this charter.

The charter had become by extension a three-year charter. In July 1979 when it had still a year to run the freight market was rising steeply. The charterers were unfortunate enough, through some slip-up in their own office, to fail to pay on July 8, 1979, the instalment of hire due upon that date. Four days later, on July 12, the owners gave notice to the charterers withdrawing the vessel. Tender of the overdue hire was made on the following day but was refused. After negotiations had taken place, the vessel was rechartered by the owners to the charterers on a 'without prejudice' agreement of the usual kind, the rate of hire (i.e., charter rate or market rate) to abide the result of litigation, which in the event came before Lloyd J.

...

My Lords, the judgment of the Court of Appeal [1983] QB 529, delivered by Robert Goff LJ, on the jurisdiction point was the first direct decision by any English court, given after hearing argument, upon the question that I have set out at the beginning of this speech. For reasons admirably expressed, and which, for my part, I find convincing, the Court of Appeal held that there was no such jurisdiction. The argument that there was jurisdiction in the court to grant relief against the withdrawal of the vessel from the charterer's service for default in punctual payment of an instalment of hire pursuant to the terms of the withdrawal clause in a time charter could, however, be supported by certain obiter dicta to be found in speeches in this House; in particular that of Lord Simon of Glaisdale in *Mardorf Peach & Co. Ltd* v *Attica Sea Carriers Corporation of Liberia (The Laconia)* [1977] AC 850, 873–874. Since such large sums of money may be at stake when rights to withdraw a vessel under a time charter are exercised at a time of rising freight rates (which, except where insolvency of the charterer is feared, is normally the only time when such rights are exercised), it seemed desirable to the Appeal Committee of this House that leave to appeal should be granted to the charterers, not, I must confess, with any great expectation that fuller consideration would show that on the jurisdiction point the Court of Appeal had got it wrong, but in order that a matter of such practical importance to the shipping world should, by a decision of the highest appellate court, be put beyond reach of future challenge.

Apart from a throw-away sentence in the speech of Lord Uthwatt in *Tankexpress A/S v Compagnie Financière Belge des Petroles SA* [1949] AC 76, 100, in which he said: 'Courts of equity, indeed, in appropriate cases relieve against failure to pay on a stipulated day . . .' but did not suggest that the operation of a withdrawal clause in a time charter provided a case that was 'appropriate', the origin of what I will, proleptically at this stage, describe as a beguiling heresy, which the Court of Appeal rejected in the instant case, is to be found in Lord Simon of Glaisdale's speech in *The Laconia* [1977] AC 850. In *The Laconia* itself the availability of equitable relief had not been raised in the courts below; and since it had not occurred to anyone to invite the judge to exercise a discretion to grant relief, the House had ruled that the point could not be taken in argument in the appeal.

I need not cite the passages in Lord Simon of Glaisdale's speech that gave encouragement to future charterers to claim equitable relief against withdrawal of the vessel under a withdrawal clause in a time charter, except to note that after referring to a possible analogy to relief against forfeiture for non-payment of rent under leases of real property he says, at p. 874:

> in any case, English law develops by applying an established rule of law to new circumstances which are analogous to the circumstances in which the established rule was framed: . . .

Nor need I cite the passages in the speeches of Lord Wilberforce and Lord Salmon in which the analogy with leases of real property is decried.

After defining a time charter in the terms quoted in section 1, above, Lord Diplock continued:

> . . . Being a contract for services it is thus the very prototype of a contract of which before the fusion of law and equity a court would never grant specific performance: *Clarke* v *Price* (1819) 2 Wils 157; *Lumley* v *Wagner* (1852) 1 De GM & G 604. In the event of failure to render the promised services, the party to whom they were to be rendered would be left to pursue such remedies in damages for breach of contract as he might have at law. But as an unbroken line of uniform authority in this House, from *Tankexpress* [1949] AC 76 to *A/S Awilco of Oslo* v *Fulvia SpA di Navigazione of Cagliari (The Chikuma)* [1981] 1 WLR 314, has held, if the withdrawal clause so provides, the shipowner is entitled to withdraw the services of the vessel from the charterer if the latter fails to pay an instalment of hire in precise compliance with the provisions of the charter. So the shipowner commits no breach of contract if he does so; and the charterer has no remedy in damages against him.
>
> To grant an injunction restraining the shipowner from exercising his right of withdrawal of the vessel from the service of the charterer, though negative in form, is pregnant with an affirmative order to the shipowner to perform the contract; juristically it is indistinguishable from a decree for specific performance of a contract to render services; and in respect of that category of contracts, even in the event of breach, this is a remedy that English courts have always disclaimed any jurisdiction to grant. This is, in my view, sufficient reason in itself to compel rejection of the suggestion that the equitable principle of relief from forfeiture is juristically capable of extension so as to grant to the court a discretion to prevent a shipowner from exercising his strict

contractual rights under a withdrawal clause in a time charter which is not a charter by demise.

My Lords, Lloyd J, who, as counsel for the charterers in *The Laconia* [1977] AC 850, had been prevented from arguing the point, was enabled to return to the charge when there came before him as judge of the Commercial Court *The Afovos* [1980] 2 Lloyd's Rep 469, in which the question of jurisdiction to grant relief against the operation of a withdrawal clause *was* argued. That case also ultimately reached this House where it was decided on the ground that upon the true construction of a 'non-technicality clause' included in a time charter in New York Produce Exchange form, the shipowner's notice of withdrawal was invalid. This made it unnecessary to refer in the speeches in this House to that part of Lloyd J's judgment where he had discussed the jurisdiction to grant a charterer relief from the operation of a withdrawal clause. In this House that was a question that was never reached.

In dealing with the jurisdiction point in *The Afovos* Lloyd J, in addition to adopting Lord Simon of Glaisdale's suggested analogy in *The Laconia* between re-entry on leasehold premises for non-payment of rent and withdrawal of a ship for non-payment of hire (an analogy which I reject for the reasons that I have already given), sought to extract from the speech of Lord Wilberforce in *Shiloh Spinners Ltd* v *Harding* [1973] AC 691 a more general proposition that wherever a party to a contract was by its terms given a right to terminate it for a breach which consisted only of non-payment of a sum of money and the purpose of incorporating the right of termination in the contract was to secure the payment of that sum, there was an equitable jurisdiction to grant relief against the exercise of the right of termination.

My Lords, *Shiloh Spinners Ltd* v *Harding* was a case about a right of re-entry upon leasehold property for breach of a covenant, not to pay money but to do things on land. It was in a passage that was tracing the history of the exercise by the Court of Chancery of its jurisdiction to relieve against forfeiture of property that Lord Wilberforce said, at p. 722:

> There has not been much difficulty as regards two heads of jurisdiction. First, where it is possible to state that the object of the transaction and of the insertion of the right to forfeit is essentially to secure the payment of money, equity has been willing to relieve on terms that the payment is made with interest, if appropriate, and also costs. . . .

That this mainly historical statement was never meant to apply generally to contracts not involving any transfer of proprietary or possessory rights, but providing for a right to determine the contract in default of punctual payment of a sum of money payable under it, is clear enough from Lord Wilberforce's speech in *The Laconia* [1977] AC 850. Speaking of a time charter he said, at p. 870: 'It must be obvious that this is a very different type of creature from a lease of land.'

Moreover, in the case of a time charter it is not possible to state that the object of the insertion of a withdrawal clause, let alone the transaction itself, is essentially to secure the payment of money. Hire is payable in advance in order to provide a fund from which the shipowner can meet those expenses of rendering the promised services to the charterer that he has undertaken to bear himself under the charterparty; in particular the wages and victualling of master and crew, the insurance of the vessel and her maintenance in such a state as will enable her to continue to comply with the warranty of performance.

This, the commercial purpose of obtaining payment of hire in advance, also makes inapplicable another analogy sought to be drawn between a withdrawal clause and a penalty clause of the kind against which courts of law, as well as courts of equity, before the Judicature Acts had exercised jurisdiction to grant relief. The classic form of penalty clause is one which provides that upon breach of a primary obligation under the contract a secondary obligation shall arise on the part of the party in breach to pay to the other party a sum of money which does not represent a genuine pre-estimate of any loss likely to be sustained by him as the result of the breach of primary obligation but is substantially in excess of that sum. The classic form of relief against such a penalty clause has been to refuse to give effect to it, but to award the common law measure of damages for the breach of primary obligation instead. Lloyd J in *The Afovos* [1980] 2 Lloyd's Rep 469 attached importance to the majority judgments in *Stockloser v Johnson* [1954] 1 QB 476 which expressed the opinion that money already paid by one party to the other under a continuing contract prior to an event which under the terms of the contract entitled that other party to elect to rescind it and to retain the money already paid might be treated as money paid under a penalty clause, and recovered to the extent that it exceeded to an unconscionable extent the value of any consideration that had been given for it. Assuming this to be so, however, it is incapable of having any application to time charters and withdrawal notices. Moneys paid by the charterer prior to the withdrawal notice that puts an end to the contract for services represent the agreed rate of hire for services already rendered, and not a penny more.

All the analogies that ingenuity has suggested may be discovered between a withdrawal clause in a time charter and other classes of contractual provisions in which courts have relieved parties from the rigour of contractual terms into which they have entered can in my view be shown upon juristic analysis to be false. Prima facie parties to a commercial contract bargaining on equal terms can make 'time to be of the essence' of the performance of any primary obligation under the contract that they please, whether the obligation be to a pay a sum of money or to do something else. When time is made of the essence of a primary obligation, failure to perform it punctually is a breach of a condition of the contract which entitles the party not in breach to elect to treat the breach as putting an end to all primary obligations under the contract that have not already been performed. In *Tankexpress A/S v Compagnie Financière Belge des Petroles SA* [1949] AC 76 this House held that time was of the essence of the very clause with which your Lordships are now concerned where it appeared in what was the then current predecessor of the Shelltime 3 charter. As is well-known, there are available on the market a number of so-(mis)called 'anti-technicality clauses', such as that considered in *The Afovos*, which require the shipowner to give a specified period of notice to the charterer in order to make time of the essence of payment of advance hire; but at the expiry of such notice, provided it is validly given, time does become of the essence of the payment.

My Lords, quite apart from the juristic difficulties in the way of recognising a jurisdiction in the court to grant relief against the operation of a withdrawal clause in a time charter there are practical reasons of legal policy for declining to create any such new jurisdiction out of sympathy for charterers. The freight market is notoriously volatile. If it rises rapidly during the period of a time charter, the charterer is the beneficiary of the windfall which he can realise if he wants to by subchartering at the then market rates. What withdrawal of the vessel does is to transfer the benefit of the windfall from charterer to shipowner.

The practical objections to any extension to withdrawal clauses in time charters of an equitable jurisdiction to grant relief against their exercise are so convincingly expressed by Robert Goff LJ in the judgment of the Court of Appeal [1983] QB 529, 540–541 in the instant case that I can do no better than to incorporate them in my own speech for ease of reference:

Parties to such contracts should be capable of looking after themselves: at the very least, they are capable of taking advice, and the services of brokers are available, and are frequently used, when negotiating terms. The possibility that shipowners may snatch at the opportunity to withdraw ships from the service of time charterers for non-payment of hire must be very well known in the world of shipping: it must also be very well known that anti-technicality clauses are available which are effective to prevent any such occurrence. If a prospective time charterer wishes to have any such clause included in the charter, he can bargain for it. If he finds it necessary or desirable to agree to a charter which contains no such clause, he can warn the relevant section of his office, and his bank, of the importance of securing timeous payment. But the matter does not stop there. It is of the utmost importance in commercial transactions that, if any particular event occurs which may affect the parties' respective rights under a commercial contract, they should know where they stand. The court should so far as possible desist from placing obstacles in the way of either party ascertaining his legal position, if necessary with the aid of advice from a qualified lawyer, because it may be commercially desirable for action to be taken without delay, action which may be irrevocable and which may have far-reaching consequences. It is for this reason, of course, that the English courts have time and again asserted the need for certainty in commercial transactions — for the simple reason that the parties to such transactions are entitled to know where they stand, and to act accordingly. In particular, when a shipowner becomes entitled, under the terms of his contract, to withdraw a ship from the service of a time charterer, he may well wish to act swiftly and irrevocably. True, his problem may, in any particular case, prove to be capable of solution by entering into a without prejudice agreement with the original time charterer, under which the rate of hire payable in future will be made to depend upon a decision, by arbitrators or by a court, whether he was in law entitled to determine the charter. But this is not always possible. He may wish to refix his ship elsewhere as soon as possible, to take advantage of a favourable market. It is no answer to this difficulty that the ship may have cargo aboard at the time, so that her services cannot immediately be made available to another charterer ... For one thing, the ship may not have cargo on board, and for another she can be refixed immediately under a charter to commence at the end of her laden voyage. Nor is it an answer that the parties can immediately apply to arbitrators, or to a court, for a decision, and that both maritime arbitrators and the Commercial Court in this country are prepared to act very quickly at very short notice. For, quite apart from the fact that some delay in inherent in any legal process, if the question to be decided is whether the tribunal is to grant equitable relief, investigation of the relevant circumstances, and the collection of evidence for that purpose, cannot ordinarily be carried out in a very short period of time.

For all these reasons I would dismiss this appeal. I do so with the reminder that the reasoning in my speech has been directed exclusively to time charters that are not by demise. Identical considerations would not be applicable to bareboat charters and it would in my view be unwise for your Lordships to express any views about them.

## SECTION 8: OFF-HIRE PROVISIONS

Prima facie the hire has to be paid whatever happens, but standard forms of time charter contain provisions relieving the charterer from the liability to pay hire for periods when, broadly speaking, the services of the vessel are not available to him. It is for the charterer to show that an event has happened which puts the vessel off-hire. Clearly, everything turns on the wording of the clauses in question, which generally apply one or both of the concepts of a *period* for which a specified condition is satisfied and the *time lost* for the specified reason.

'Loss of time' is usually the governing idea, although period clauses are easier to apply.

### Canadian Pacific (Bermuda) Ltd v Canadian Transport Co. Ltd
### (The H.R. Macmillan)
### [1974] 1 Lloyd's Rep 311 (CA)

LORD DENNING MR: ... The vessel *H.R. Macmillan* was built in Japan. She was specially designed for carrying timber and steel and so forth. She was fitted with three huge gantry cranes called Munck cranes. These ran on rails along the whole length of the ship. They had extending arms which could pick up timber or steel from the quay and lift it into the holds. The cranes were no good for bulk cargoes such as grain or ore, which are sucked into the hold. She was Canadian, owned by the Canadian Pacific (Bermuda) Ltd. They let her on a long time charter for eight years to Canadian charterers, the Canadian Transport Co. Ltd. This time charter contained many clauses in usual form, but it also contained a special clause to cover a breakdown of the Munck cranes. The parties wish to know what is the correct interpretation of the clause. It is important to them because, besides this ship, there are two sister ships on similar time charters. Each of the charters has some years to run.

The incident which illustrates the problem took place on Apr. 9, 1968. The vessel was at Tilbury discharging her cargo. The trolley of no. 1 crane fell from its gantry on to the quay. Two men were killed. Much damage was done. The master ordered no. 2 and no. 3 cranes to be stopped and examined. Those two cranes were out of service for two days, but then started discharging again. But no. 1 crane had to be removed from the ship. Pending its replacement the vessel went on a voyage with the two other cranes. She loaded at three ports in Vancouver Island and finally returned to discharge at Tilbury. Whilst there, on July 22, 1968, no. 1 crane was replaced. So it was out of action for 3 ½ months.

That incident sparked off several problems. I will dispose of a small question at once. I agree with the arbitrators that there was a breakdown by disablement of no. 1 Munck crane, but not of the no. 2 and no. 3 Munck cranes. So we have to deal with the breakdown of one crane only. It was out of action for 3 ½ months. These questions arise on it.

First: Were the charterers relieved of paying hire because of the breakdown?

Second: Could the charterers recover damages from the owner because of the breakdown?

These questions depend, of course, on the clauses of the charterparty. The arbitrators thought that the charterers were relieved of a small portion of the hire, and had no claim for damages beyond it. The Judge held that the charterers were relieved of a considerable portion of the hire and also had a claim for any additional damage they could establish. The owners appeal to this Court only on the question of the hire. The owners accept the Judge's ruling on the other point, which was this: If the charterers can establish a breach of contract by the owners in failing to maintain the cranes, they will be entitled to damages for that breach, but in assessing the damages they will have to give credit for any reduction in hire to which they are entitled.

So we have to deal with this principal point. If any of the three cranes break down, are the charterers entitled to a reduction of hire on that account? and if so, to what extent? The first clause to be considered is the 'off-hire' clause. It is cl. 15, which says (so far as material):

> That in the event of loss of time from ... breakdown ... to ... machinery or equipment, ... or by any other cause preventing the full working of the vessel, the payment of hire shall cease for the time thereby lost ...

Taking that clause by itself, it would mean that, if one crane broke down, there would have to be an inquiry as to the time lost thereby. That would be a most difficult inquiry to undertake. For instance, if one broke down and the other two cranes were able to do, and did do, all the work that was required, there would be no 'time lost thereby'; and there would be no cessation of hire. But if there was work for three cranes, and there was some loss of time owing to the one crane breaking down, there would have to be an assessment of the amount of time lost. In that event, as the Judge pointed out, the question would have to be asked: How much earlier would the vessel have been away from her port of loading or discharge if three Munck cranes, instead of two, had been available throughout?' The Judge called that a 'net loss of time' clause.

The next clause to be considered is the special cl. 38. It says:

> With reference to Clauses 15 and 23, in the event of a breakdown of Munck crane or cranes by reason of disablement or insufficient power, the hire to be reduced pro rata for the period of such inefficiency in relation to the number of cranes available ...

The first thing to be noticed is that cl. 38 replaces cl. 15 in the event of a breakdown of a crane. The second thing is that cl. 38 does away with any inquiry into 'the time lost thereby'. It replaces it by an inquiry into 'the period of such inefficiency'. Thus if one crane broke down during loading and the other two were able to do all that was required, there would be no 'time lost thereby' (within cl. 15); but there would be a 'period of inefficiency' (within cl. 38) until the one crane was repaired. The hire would be reduced by one-third during the time that the one crane was out of action, even though no time had been lost by it. The Judge called that a 'period clause' because the reduction of hire started at a given moment and continued until the crane was again in an efficient state.

But here comes the problem: How is the 'period of inefficiency' to be calculated? A simple example is when one crane breaks down during loading at 9 a.m. on Monday and is out of action for two hours until 11 a.m. on the same day. The period of inefficiency is two hours. The hire is reduced by one-third for two hours. But now suppose that that one crane was out of action for two days and is not repaired until 9 a.m. on the Wednesday. The arbitrators would say that the 'period of inefficiency' would not include night time or lunch time, but would be only the number of working *hours* lost. That is Monday (9 00–12 00 and 13 00–17 00), Tuesday (8 00–12 00 and 13 00–17 00); and Wednesday (8 00–9 00), making in all 16 hours lost. But the Judge would say that the 'period of inefficiency' was two days. I prefer the Judge's view, for this reason: The hire is payable per day. If all *three* cranes had been out of action for two days, the charterers would have lost two days use of the vessel. They would be relieved of two days hire, not of 16 hours hire. So also if one crane is out of action for two days, they should be relieved of one-third of two days hire. If the period of inefficiency was two days and two hours, the hire should be reduced accordingly — not for 18 hours — but for two full days and two hours.

Now suppose that on the Tuesday it rained all day or there was no cargo available to be loaded. So that no work was done on the Tuesday by any of these cranes, but only one was out of action. Both the arbitrators and the Judge would have included that Tuesday as part of the 'period of inefficiency'. The difference would be that the arbitrators would count it as eight hours and the Judge would count it as one day of 24 hours. I prefer the Judge's view. And I would say the same if the stevedores were on strike for that one day. The reason in all these cases is because the inefficiency remained throughout the whole of the Tuesday. The one crane was out of action all that day. The charterers were entitled to have that crane at their disposal for that Tuesday. Clause 23 said:

> ... all cranes to be at Charterers' disposal during loading and discharging day and night as required ...

True it is that, owing to the rain, or a strike, or lack of cargo, no time was lost. No cranes were working. So the one that broke down made no difference. But that is not the point. The crane should have been at the disposal of the charterers for that Tuesday and it was not. The period of inefficiency includes that day.

Next suppose that the crane took longer to repair and that it was out of order for a week from one Monday to the following Monday. No cargo would have been loaded on the Saturday afternoon or the Sunday. The arbitrators would not have included Saturday afternoon and Sunday in the 'period of inefficiency'. But the Judge would have done so. I prefer the Judge's view. If the crane had not broken down but had been in operation all the week, the loading might have finished on the Friday and the ship might have sailed and lost no days. By reason of the breakdown she was detained over the Saturday and Sunday and lost the use of those two days.

Lastly, suppose that on the Tuesday the ship had had to be shifted to a new berth: and the shifting took two hours. The arbitrators would have counted those two hours as part of the 'period of inefficiency', but the Judge would not have done so. I prefer the Judge's view. The time taken in shifting is on the same footing as the time spent at sea. The vessel is engaged on a task to which the cranes have no relevance. The charterers ought to pay the full hire for those two hours, just as for the time at sea. Similarly if the charterers had a party on board during which loading was stopped: or used the vessel as a floating warehouse: the time spent on the party or warehouse would not count as part of the 'period of inefficiency'. The vessel was being used in a task to which the cranes had no relevance. So also if the charterers loaded a bulk cargo of grain or iron ore by suction. The time spent would not count as part of the 'period of inefficiency', because the task was one to which the cranes had no relevance.

We were told that, even with a bulk cargo, the cranes would be needed to remove the big hatch covers and replace them. The time spent in removing them and replacing them would count as part of the 'period of inefficency', but the time spent in sucking in or out the cargo would not.

Bring together those examples, it seems to me that the 'period of inefficiency' includes the whole of the time during which the task in hand, for which the charterers were using the ship, required the use of a Munck crane or cranes, such time to run continuously, except when the charterers put the vessel to use for another task which did not require the use of cranes. The position is similar to that in *Hogarth* v *Miller* [1891] AC 48, when a ship's engine broke down. It was held that the hire ceased when the vessel was at sea — a task which required the use of the engine — but became payable when she was lying alongside the wharf to discharge her cargo — a task which did not require the use of the engine. Similarly in *Tynedale* v *Anglo-Soviet SS Co.* (1936) 41 Com Cas 206; (1936)

Ll L Rep 341, when a mast broke in half, bringing down a derrick, it was held that hire was payable when the vessel was at sea — a task which did not require the use of the derrick — but ceased when she was discharging — a task which required the use of the derrick.

I find myself in agreement with the Judge on all the points argued before us except on the question of a strike. I think the 'period of inefficiency' continues throughout notwithstanding that there is no loading actually being done owing to a strike. It is on the same footing as rain. The vessel is still required for use for loading even though it is temporarily suspended for rain or a strike.

Subject to this variation, I would dismiss the appeal.

*Note*
Even a loss of time clause may, in effect, be governed by a 'period' concept.

### *Vogemann* v *Zanzibar Steamship Co. Ltd*
(1902) 7 Com Cas 254 (CA)

On a voyage from Hamburg to the US, the vessel sustained damage on 22 November and had to put back to Queenstown for repairs. Repairs were completed on 22 December, but she only reached the point on the voyage at which the accident had occurred on 29 December. The relevant clauses in the charterparty read: '5. That the charterers shall provide and pay for all the coals . . . 14. That in the event of loss of time from deficiency of men or stores, breakdown, or damage of machinery or damage to rudder or propeller, grounding, *but not in river*, detention by average accidents to ship or cargo, or by other cause preventing the full working of the vessel (loading and/or discharging cargo), the payment of hire shall cease for the time *exceeding twenty-four hours* thereby lost.'

The shipowners accepted that the vessel was off-hire until 22 December. The charterers claimed that she was off-hire also until 29 December and that the shipowners should pay for the coal used from 22–29 December. Phillimore J and the Court of Appeal found in favour of the shipowners.

COLLINS MR: . . . The question is, whether the charterer is relieved from paying for the hire of the ship during the time which elapsed between her sailing from Queenstown after repairing and her arrival at the place where the accident, which necessitated the repairs, took place. The solution of the question depends on the construction of the charterparty, and what we have to do is to construe that which the parties have, in fact, said, and not to surmise what they may have meant to say. By the charterparty in question the steamship *Zanzibar* was chartered by the owners (the respondents) to the appellant for two or three round voyages. There are provisions as to the respective liability of the shipowners and the charterer: and clause 14 is the important clause as to the cesser of hire.

The ship sailed from Queenstown and met with an average accident, which caused her to put back to Queenstown for repairs. After the repairs were completed she started again on her voyage. The charterer contends that he is excused from the payment from the time of the accident, until the ship got back, after repairing, to the place where the accident occurred.

On the other hand, the shipowner contends that she came on hire again as soon as the ship was in full working order at Queenstown.

Phillimore J decided in favour of the latter contention, and I think he was right. The charterparty seems to me to be fairly clear. The object of the clause in question is to provide for a possible loss of time; and the question is how much time was provided for. In my opinion only such time was provided for as might elapse until the vessel was once more in full working order. When the accident ceased to prevent the full working of the vessel, the hire became again payable. This is the natural construction of the clause, and any other construction would involve intricate calculations as to the time which had been lost. I think Phillimore J was right as to the cesser of the hire, and also as to the liability to pay for the coal during the time in dispute, and the appeal must therefore be dismissed. (© Times Newspapers Ltd 1902.)

*Note*
Some standard forms of time charter now expressly provide that in such a case the vessel is off-hire, e.g., 'until she is again in the same or equidistant position from the destination and the voyage resumed therefrom': NYPE 93, cl. 17.

*Question*
Tess chartered the *Star of the Sea* for 18 months and ordered her with a cargo of crude oil to Nagoya. Soon after commencing to discharge, on 1 September, the *Star of the Sea* began to experience boiler trouble and discharge was interrupted. At the same time the weather was deteriorating as a typhoon approached and the harbour master ordered the *Star of the Sea* to leave the berth. The boiler problem was located and remedied by 8 September but the weather did not improve enough for her to return to berth until 15 September. Under the relevant clause of the charterparty, 'On each and every occasion that there is loss of time (i) due to ... breakdown (whether partial or total) of ... boilers ... then ... the vessel shall be off-hire from the commencement of such loss of time until she is again ready and in an efficient state to resume her service ...' For what period is the vessel off-hire? (*Cf. International Fina Services AG* v *Katrina Shipping Ltd (The Fina Samco)* [1994] 1 Lloyd's Rep 153 (QBD)).

*Note*
Charterparties commonly include a provision for the vessel to be off-hire if 'other' causes prevent full or efficient working, but provisions of this kind do not give the charterer as wide a protection as might appear at first sight.

### *Actis Co.* v *Sanko Steamship Co.*
### *(The Aquacharm)*
### [1982] 1 Lloyd's Rep 7 (CA)

LORD DENNING MR: In 1974 the owners of *Aquacharm* let her to Japanese charterers on a time charter. She was to carry a cargo of coal on a trip from Baltimore to Tokyo. This necessitated her passing through the Panama Canal. The charterers ordered her to load up to the draught 'permissible by the Panama Canal Company of 39 feet 6 inches TFW'. TFW stands for tropical fresh water.

The master took on board 43,000 tons of coal. That was too much for safety through the canal. When a vessel is in transit through the Panama Canal she has to sail through a lake called Gatun Lake. It is a fresh water lake. Now, when a vessel passes from salt water into fresh water, there is a tendency for the bow to go down relative to the stern. The master knew this, but he did not allow for it when he loaded at Baltimore. He was at fault in loading the vessel. She was already down by the head when she reached Cristobal, at the entrance to the canal. This gave rise to a risk that, when her bow went down on entering the Gatun Lake, she might touch bottom. He ought to have loaded less cargo so as to allow for the tendency of the bow to go down.

When the vessel arrived at the entrance to the canal, the Panama Canal Co. refused to allow her to go through. They said that she exceeded the permitted draught as prescribed by their regulations. To get over the difficulty, it was decided to discharge 636 tons of coal into another vessel called *Mini Lux*. She followed *Aquacharm* through the canal. The 636 tons were then reloaded at the other end.

This delay held up the vessel for eight days 23 hours and 45 minutes. Nine days all but a quarter of an hour. The hire for that period came to $86,344.99. The charterers refused to pay. They invoke the 'off-hire' clause to excuse them from paying.

The total cost of transhipment came to $71,740. The owners claim to recover this cost from the charterers under an express or implied term of the charter.

### 1. *Off-hire or not?*
The charterparty was on the New York Produce Exchange form, but with arbitration in London instead of New York. The 'off-hire' cl. 15 said that—

. . . in the event of loss of time . . . by any other cause preventing the full working of the vessel, the payment of hire shall cease for the time thereby lost.

The umpire (Mr Staughton, QC) and the commercial Judge (Mr Justice Lloyd (see [1980] 2 Lloyd's Rep 237)) held that the vessel was still on hire for those nearly nine days. She was not off-hire. I agree with them. In seeing whether cl. 15 applies, we are not to inquire by whose fault it was that the vessel was delayed. We are to inquire first whether the 'full working of the vessel' has been prevented. Only if it has, do we consider the 'cause'. I do not think the lightening of cargo does 'prevent the full working of the vessel'. Often enough cargo has to be unloaded into a lighter — for one reason or another — to get her off a sandbank — or into a basin. The vessel is still working fully, but she is delayed by the need to unload part of the cargo. It is rather like *Court Line Ltd* v *Dant & Russell Inc.* (1939) 64 Ll L Rep 212; (1939) 44 Com Cas 345. The vessel was still working fully, but she was delayed by the boom across the Yangtse River. This vessel was, therefore, still on hire for nearly nine days.

### 2 *The master's fault*
Seeing that the cause of all the trouble was the master's fault in overloading the vessel, the question is whether the charterers can recover damages from the owners. Such damages being the hire they have to pay to the owners for the nearly nine days.

The answer depends on whether the vessel was seaworthy or not when she left Baltimore for her trip through the Panama Canal to Japan. If she was *unseaworthy*, the shipowners would be liable. They would not be able to prove that they exercised due diligence. The shipowners would be liable under arts. III(1)(a) and IV of The Hague Rules. If she was *seaworthy*, the shipowners would not be liable. They would be exempted from liability by reason of art. IV(2)(a) because the loss arose from the neglect of the master in the 'management' of the ship.

Both the umpire and the Judge found that this vessel was seaworthy. I agree with them. I think the word 'seaworthy' in The Hague Rules is used in its ordinary meaning, and not in any extended or unnatural meaning. It means that the vessel — with her master and crew — is herself fit to encounter the perils of the voyage and also that she is fit to carry the cargo safely on that voyage — see *Scrutton on Charterparties* (18th ed.), p. 83. This vessel was so fit. It may be that she had to be lightened to pass through the Panama Canal, but that did not make her unfit. It is quite unlike *Ciampa and Others* v *British India Steam Navigation Co. Ltd* [1915] 2 KB 774. The vessel there was unfit to carry the cargo safely because she had to be fumigated. So also in *The Madeleine* [1967] 2 Lloyd's Rep 224. As the Judge said, there is no case in which a ship has been held to be unseaworthy merely because she has to lighten in order to get into port. So also if she has to lighten in order to get through the canal.

I hold, therefore, that the charterers cannot recover damages for having to pay the hire.

*Notes and Question*

1.   Clause 15 has been considered in a number of cases. It has been held that it does not cover 'extraneous' causes such as the wholly unexpected and unforeseeable interference by the authorities at Chittagong in *Andre & Cie SA* v *Orient Shipping (Rotterdam) BV (The Laconian Confidence)* [1997] 1 Lloyd's Rep 139 (QBD, Rix J) where the presence of 15.75 tonnes of rejected residue sweepings after discharge of over 10,000 tonnes of bagged rice led to the vessel being delayed for nearly 18 days. It would have been different if the clause had been amended, as it often is, by the addition of 'whatsoever' after 'cause': *ibid.*
2.   Ordinary, normal cleaning of tanks is part of the service to be provided and the tanker is not off-hire during it: *Sig Bergesen DY & Co.* v *Mobil Shipping and Transportation Co. (The Berge Sund)* [1993] 2 Lloyd's Rep 453 (CA).
3.   If the charterer has a claim against the shipowner which is not covered by an off-hire provision, may he nevertheless set it off against future payments of hire?

### Federal Commerce and Navigation Co. v Molena Alpha Inc. (The Nanfri)
[1978] QB 927 (CA)

LORD DENNING MR: At one time it was common to describe the sums payable under a time charterparty as 'freight'. Such description is to be found used by judges and textbook writers of great distinction. But in modern times a change has come about. The payments due under a time charter are usually now described as 'hire' and those under a voyage charter as 'freight'. This change of language corresponds, I believe, to a recognition that the two things are different. 'Freight' is payable for carrying a quantity of cargo from one place to another. 'Hire' is payable for the right to use a vessel for a specified period of time, irrespective of whether the charterer chooses to use it for carrying cargo or lays it up, out of use. Every time charter contains clauses which are quite inappropriate to a voyage charter, such as the off-hire clause and the withdrawal clause. So different are the two concepts that I do not think the law as to 'freight' can be

applied indiscriminately to 'hire'. In particular the special rule of English law whereby 'freight' must be paid in full (without deductions for short delivery or cargo damage) cannot be applied automatically to time charter 'hire'. Nor is there any authority which says that it must. It would be a mistake to suppose that the House of Lords had time charter hire and so forth in mind when they decided *The Aries* [1977] 1WLR 185 or the *Nova (Jersey) Knit Ltd* v *Kammgarn Spinnerei GmbH* [1977] 1 WLR 713, or that anything said in those cases can bind this court. Many of us, I know, in the past have assumed that the rule as to 'freight' does apply: and some judges have said so. But now, after full argument, I am satisfied that the 'freight' rule does not apply automatically to 'time charter' hire: and we have to consider the position on principle.
. . .

So I turn to the problem here. A shipowner has contracted to give a charterer the right to use the vessel for a period of time — six years in fact. In return the charterer has agreed to pay a stated sum of hire monthly in advance. Then let us suppose that, after the charterer has paid his month's hire in advance, the shipowner wrongly declines to allow the charterer to have the use of the vessel for some days during the ensuing months. He may put the vessel perhaps to some more profitable use. He, by his conduct, deprives the charterer of part of the consideration for which the hire was paid. I should have thought it plain that the charterer should in fairness be able to recoup himself by making a deduction from the next month's hire — so as to compensate him for the loss of use for those days — equivalent to the hire of those lost days. Likewise if the shipowner has been guilty of some other wrongful conduct which has deprived the charterer of the use of the ship during some days — or prejudiced the charterer in the use of the ship — then the charterer should in fairness be able to recoup himself by making a deduction from the next month's hire. If the charterer quantifies his loss by a reasonable assessment made in good faith — and deducts the sum quantified — then he is not in default. The shipowner cannot withdraw his vessel on account of non-payment of hire nor hold him guilty at that point of any breach of contract. If it subsequently turns out that he has deducted too much, the shipowner can of course recover the balance. But that is all. . . .

I would as at present advised limit the right to deduct to cases when the shipowner has wrongly deprived the charterer of the use of the vessel or has prejudiced him in the use of it. I would not extend it to other breaches or default of the shipowner, such as damage to cargo arising from the negligence of the crew. . . .

It follows that I find myself differing from the view of Donaldson J in *Seven Seas Transportation Ltd* v *Atlantic Shipping Co. SA* [1975] 2 Lloyd's Rep 188 and Mocatta J in *Steelwood Carriers Inc. of Monrovia, Liberia* v *Evimeria Compania Naviera SA of Panama (The Agios Giorgis)* [1976] 2 Lloyd's Rep 192, 201 and the views expressed in *Carver, Carriage by Sea*, 12th ed. (1971), vol. 1, para. 402 and *Scrutton on Charterparties*, 18th ed. (1974), p. 358.

### Note and Question
On appeal to the House of Lords ([1979] AC 757) the present point was not in issue. Set-off has been allowed subsequently at first instance (e.g., *Santiren Shipping Ltd* v *Unimarine* [1981] 1 Lloyd's Rep 159 (QBD) but contrast *Leon Corporation* v *Atlantic Lines and Navigation Inc (The Leon)* [1985] 2 Lloyd's Rep 470 (QBD, Hobhouse J) where the cross-claim involved nothing 'which could be identified as depriving the charterers of the use of the vessel or prejudicing or hindering that use') but has yet to be confirmed by higher authority. Why is the *Dakin* v *Oxley* principle of no set-off against freight (see Chapter 6) not applicable here as well?

## SECTION 9: THE LAST VOYAGE

Every time charter (other than a trip charter) provides for a date by which the charterer must 'redeliver' the vessel. This date is now generally referred to as the 'final terminal date'. Until the final terminal date the charterer has the right to the use of the vessel's services at the rate of hire agreed in the charterparty. Problems arise, however, because the orders for the last voyage must in the nature of things be given before the final terminal date: in particular, what is the shipowner's position if it seems possible, when the order is given, that the voyage will not be completed by the final terminal date; and, if the order is accepted but the voyage does overrun, what payment is due from the charterer?

### *Hyundai Merchant Marine Co. Ltd* v *Gesuri Chartering Co. Ltd*
### *(The Peonia)*
### [1991] 1 Lloyd's Rep 100 (CA)

BINGHAM LJ: By a charterparty on the New York Produce Exchange form dated Apr. 3, 1987 Hyundai Merchant Marine Co. Ltd as disponent owners chartered their vessel *Peonia* to Gesuri Chartering Co. Ltd as charterers. The charterparty provided

> [Line 13] . . . the said Owners agree to let, and the said Charterers agree to hire the said vessel, from the time of delivery, for
> [Line 14] about minimum 10 months maximum 12 months time charter, Exact duration in Charterers option
> [Line 15] Charterers have further option to complete last voyage within below mentioned trading limits.

Hire was to continue until the hour of the day of the vessel's redelivery to the owners within specified areas.

The vessel was delivered to the charterers on June 11, 1987 (thus the 10 month period expired on Apr. 11 and the 12 months period on June 11, 1988). On May 6, 1988 the charterers concluded a voyage sub-charterparty to carry soya beans from the river Plate to Singapore and Butterworth. Had the sub-charterparty fixture been performed the vessel (then discharging at Ravenna) would have been redelivered to the owners no earlier than about July 19, 1988. On May 11 the owners protested, contending that the proposed voyage was illegitimate. They asked for voyage orders which would enable the vessel to be redelivered within 45 days, namely by June 25, thereby giving effect to the expression 'about' in line 14. On May 17 the owners called for voyage orders which would enable the vessel to be redelivered within the charter period or alternatively for payment of hire at an enhanced rate for the duration of the voyage outside the charter period. The charterers accepted neither condition and the vessel was withdrawn by the owners from the service of the charterers.

. . .

The immediate legal background to the dispute is not now controversial. A time charterparty such as this is a contract by which the shipowner agrees with the time charterer that during a certain named period he will render services by his servants and crew to carry the goods which are put on board his ship by the time charterer (*Sea and Land Securities Ltd* v *William Dickinson and Co. Ltd* (1942) 72 Ll L Rep 149 at p. 162, col. 2; [1942] 2 KB 65 at p. 69). It is for the time charterer to decide, within the terms of the charterparty, what use he will make of the vessel. References to delivery and redelivery are strictly inaccurate since the vessel never leaves the possession of the shipowner, but the expressions are conventionally used to describe the time when the period of the charter begins and ends (*The Berge Tasta* [1975] 1 Lloyd's Rep 422 at p. 424). Where a time charterparty stipulates a definite date for the termination of the charter period without any express margin or tolerance the Courts imply a reasonable margin or tolerance to allow for the exigencies of maritime business (*Gray & Co.* v *Christie & Co.* (1889) 5 TLR 577; *Watson Steamship Co.* v *Merryweather & Co.* (1913) 18 Com Cas 294; *The London Explorer* [1971] 1 Lloyd's Rep 523; [1972] AC 1; *The Dione* [1975] 1 Lloyd's Rep 115). Where the parties have expressly agreed a margin or tolerance (as by agreeing a minimum and maximum period for the charter or a 'more or less' provision) such implication will not be made (*Watson* v *Merryweather*, sup.; *The Dione*, sup.). In the present case the words 'minimum 10 months maximum 12 months' which, standing alone, would ordinarily be effective to exclude the implication of any additional margin or tolerance are prefaced by the word 'about', which is effective to provide for such an additional margin or tolerance. It is not, however, suggested that even this additional margin or tolerance could be effective to cover the five week period between June 11, 1988, when the 12 months maximum period of the charter ended, and July 19 when, on the facts assumed for purpose of the arbitrators' award, the vessel would at the earliest have been redelivered had she performed the sub-charterparty voyage fixed by the charterers to Singapore and Butterworth via the river Plate.

It would seem to me (although challenged by the charterers) that every time charter must have a final terminal date, that is a date by which (in the absence of an exonerating cause) the charterer is contractually obliged to redeliver the vessel. Where the law implies a margin or tolerance beyond an expiry date stipulated in the charterparty, the final terminal date comes at the end of such implied extension. When the parties have agreed in the charterparty on the margin or tolerance to be allowed, the final terminal date comes at the end of such agreed period. But the nature of a time charter is that the charter is for a finite period of time and when the final terminal date arrives the charterer is contractually bound (in the absence of an exonerating cause) to redeliver the vessel to the owner. I shall hereafter use the expression 'final terminal date' to mean the final contractual date for redelivery, after the expiry of any margin or tolerance which the parties may agree or the law imply.

The cases and books draw a distinction between two cases which have become known as 'the illegitimate last voyage' and 'the legitimate last voyage'. In the former case the charterer gives orders for the employment of the vessel which cannot reasonably be expected to be performed by the final terminal date. He is therefore seeking to avail himself of the services of the vessel at a time when the owner had never agreed to render such services. It is accordingly an order which the charterer is not entitled to give (just as an order to visit a prohibited port would be) and in giving it the charterer commits a breach of contract (perhaps a repudiatory breach but that we need not decide). The owner need not comply with such an order, because he has never agreed to do so. Alternatively, he may comply with the order although not bound to do so: if he does comply, he is entitled to payment of hire at the charterparty rate until redelivery of the vessel and (provided he does not waive the charterer's breach) to damages (being the difference between the charter rate and the market rate if the market rate is higher than the charter rate) for the period between the final terminal date and redelivery. In the further alternative, if (which we do not decide) the charterer's breach is repudiatory, the owner may accept the repudiation, treat the charter as at an end and claim damages. In this first case, the charterer's order is illegitimate because he was not contractually entitled to give it, and the voyage (whether performed or not) is stigmatised as illegitimate because it is one the charterer could not under the charterparty lawfully require the owner to perform.

In the contrasting case of the legitimate last voyage the charterer gives orders for the employment of the vessel which can reasonably be expected to be performed by the final terminal date. These are orders which the charterer is entitled to give, and so legitimate. If the parties' reasonable expectations are fulfilled and the voyage is performed by the final terminal date no difficulty of course arises. If the voyage is not performed by the final terminal date through some fault by the owner, whether strictly a breach of contract or not, again there is no legal difficulty: the owner cannot complain of the charterer's failure to redeliver by the final terminal date if he is himself the cause of that failure. For similar reasons the position may be clear where the charterer fails to redeliver by the final terminal date for reasons within his own area of responsibility: he cannot rely on acts or omissions for which he is responsible to excuse his failure to redeliver by the final terminal date. But what if, the orders for the last voyage being legitimate in the sense defined above, the charterer fails to redeliver by the final terminal date for reasons (such as bad weather) for which neither party is responsible?

To this question the parties give different answers. In an admirably lucid and persuasive argument for the charterers Mr Glennie answers that there is in that event no breach of contract by the charterer; he remains liable to pay hire at the charter rate until the moment of actual redelivery but, there being no breach of contract, he has no liability in damages and thus no liability to pay the market rate of hire (if it is higher than the charter rate) for the period between the final terminal date and redelivery. Mr Rix, QC, to whose equally cogent argument for the owners the Court is also much indebted, answers that in this situation the charterer is in breach of contract and accordingly liable for damages in respect of the period between the final terminal date and redelivery. (But Mr Rix accepts that the charterer's breach in such a situation is not of a term going to the root of the contract: the owner's right is to damages only: the contract does not automatically terminate and he has no right to treat the contract as at an end so as to entitle him to cease to perform, a course which in mid-voyage is likely to be impracticable anyway.)

These differing answers lie at the root of the issue to be decided in this appeal, which concern the legal effect to be given to the 'further option' contained in line 15 of the charterparty quoted above. The owners construe that provision as protecting the charterers against the ordinary consequences of breach of contract if they should fail to redeliver by the final terminal date on a legitimate last voyage, at any rate unless the breach is caused by their own act or omission. The charterers contend that the provision cannot be understood as having that effect, since if (through no fault of their own) the charterers fail to redeliver by the final terminal date on a legitimate last voyage they are not in breach of contract anyway and thus have no need for contractual protection in that eventuality. But the 'further option' in line 15 is to be construed as conferring some contractual benefit on the charterers which they would not otherwise enjoy. It is therefore, the charterers argue, to be understood as entitling the charterers to order what they could not lawfully order without this provision, namely performance of what but for this provision would be an illegitimate last voyage, with no liability beyond a liability to pay hire at the charter rate until the time of actual redelivery, notwithstanding that the voyage has extended beyond the final terminal date, as it was reasonably expected by the parties to do.

The standard form of time charterparty is of course a complex bundle of interlocking rights and obligations to which special rules apply. But if one tests the differing answers of the parties to the question posed above against the rules applied in English law to contracts generally it seems to me that the owners' answer is to be preferred. If A agrees to paint B's portrait or to build a house for B he is, in the absence of special contractual provision, in breach of contract if he does not do so by whatever the law may regard as the final terminal date for performance. If A's failure to perform is caused by B's failure to attend for sittings or by B's failure to obtain planning permission when he has undertaken to do so, A is not in breach. But it does not in the ordinary way and in the absence of any frustrating event avail A to establish that he could not obtain colours or canvass or was unavailable to paint, or that he could not obtain building materials or hire labour, or that he had so much work he could not fit in the work for B.

Nor, in the ordinary way and in the absence of any frustrating event, does it avail A to show that he used his best endeavours or acted with due diligence to paint the portrait or build the house. The law of contract concentrates on A's deeds, not his thoughts, motives or intentions. He either does what he agreed to do by the time he agreed to do it, or he breaches the contract and pays the consequence in damages.

The charterers submit that whatever the validity of these general observations they have no application to a charterer's duty to redeliver, which is (they say) more akin to a best endeavours obligation. The redelivery date in the charterparty is a reference point, not a deadline. For this proposition, as for their answer to the question quoted above, the charterers rely on a number of authorities....

In *Watson Steamship Co.* v *Merryweather & Co.*, sup., a charter was expressed to continue until '15/31 October 1912'. Hire was to continue—

> ...from the time specified for terminating the charter until her redelivery...between 15th and 31st October 1912.

On Oct. 18 the charterers sent the vessel on a voyage which could not, as they knew, be performed in time to permit the vessel to be redelivered at the place specified by Oct. 31. She was not in fact redelivered until Nov. 20. By the end of October the market rate of hire had risen above the charter rate. In the arbitration which followed the owners contended that the charterers were bound to redeliver the vessel by Oct. 31, that they were in breach of contract in failing to do so and that they were accordingly liable in damages. The charterers argued that they were not bound to redeliver by Oct. 31 but were entitled to retain her until the expiration of any voyage on which they had reasonably sent her. They claimed that the voyage in question was such a voyage and relied on *Gray* v *Christie* sup. The umpire accepted the owners' contention and awarded damages accordingly. On a special case, Mr Justice Atkin upheld the umpire's award, construing the charterparty to require redelivery by Oct. 31 as the final terminal date. The decision is probably authority only for the proposition that where in a charterparty the parties agree a range of dates between which a vessel should be redelivered the Courts will not imply any further tolerance. It is further plain that the voyage in question was what would now be called an illegitimate last voyage. There was, however, as the Judge pointed out, no finding by the umpire that the voyage in question was not a reasonable voyage or that the period of 20 days overrun was an unreasonable period. It therefore seems to me that the owners recovered damages simply because the charterers did not redeliver by the final terminal date. That is consistent with the Judge's earlier observation, made with reference to a charterparty requiring redelivery within a reasonable time of a stipulated date, that if redelivery were not made within such time—

> I think there would be a breach of contract in respect of which the Owners would be entitled to recover damages [p. 300].

I read this decision as supporting the owners' argument in this case.
. . .

*The London Explorer*, sup., is a decision of central importance and both parties relied on it strongly. The charter was for '12 months 15 days more or less in charterers' option'. Clause 4 of the charterparty provided, as here, for hire to continue until the hour of the day of the vessel's redelivery. She was delivered to charterers on Dec. 29, 1967 so the charter period ended on the anniversary of that date in 1968 or, at latest, 15 days later on Jan. 13, 1969. In October, 1968 the charterers sent the vessel on what was intended to be her last voyage, there being no reason to suppose that the voyage could not be performed and the vessel redelivered well before the final terminal date. As a result of strikes at two discharge ports the vessel was not redelivered until Apr. 24, 1969. The owners claimed hire at the charter rate until redelivery. The charterers resisted this, no doubt because the market rate in early 1969 was lower than the charter rate. They accordingly contended that no contractual hire had been due after Dec. 29, that they had been in breach of contract in failing to redeliver by the final terminal date, that the charter had as a result come to an end and that the market rate, not the charter rate, was the measure of the damages which they were liable to pay. This argument of the charterers did not find favour with the arbitrators, the commercial Judge or the Court of Appeal but the charterers appealed to the House of Lords. There was a further issue concerning interest which is not germane to the present appeal.

On the main issue I have identified, Lord Guest and Lord Donovan agreed with the speech of Lord Morris. Lord Morris rejected the charterers' argument on the ground that under cl. 4 of the charter the obligation to pay hire at the charter rate continued until actual redelivery—

... whether or not there was a breach by the charterers in failing to redeliver when they should have done. [p. 529, col. 2; p. 19E].

In so ruling he was acceding, almost in terms, to the first submission of Mr Lloyd QC (as he then was) for the owners (p. 525, col. 1; p. 10B). But Lord Morris did not stop there. He went on to hold (1) that Jan. 13, 1969 was not to be regarded as the final terminal date under the charterparty and a reasonable extension of time was to be allowed for redelivery (p. 530, col. 2; p. 20C–D), (2) that if a charterer failed to redeliver within the period of such reasonable extension he might be in breach of contract and so liable to apply damages (the difference between the charter rate and the market rate if the latter were higher) for the period from the final terminal date to the time of actual redelivery (p. 530, col. 2; p. 20D–F). (3) that there was no finding of breach against the charterers, and no finding that the date of redelivery was in the circumstances not a reasonable one and the last voyage was one on which the vessel was reasonably sent (p. 530, col. 2; p. 20G–H).

The owners naturally relied on these points, particularly (2), which are (I think) strictly to be regarded as alternative ratio and not as obiter dicta, although (1) has not been generally treated as authoritative since.

Lord Cross agreed with Lord Reid, who described the nature of a time charter and rejected the notion that failure by the charterer to redeliver on time—

... if the completion of the last voyage is delayed beyond a particular date, by some cause for which neither is responsible ... [p. 526, col. 1; p. 14B]

would have the effect of bringing the charter to an end and leaving the owner free to use the vessel as he chooses. This view of Lord Reid and Lord Cross is accepted by both parties to this appeal, but was directly relevant to the charterers' argument before the House. Lord Reid then analysed *Gray & Co.* v *Christie & Co.*, sup. in terms which I have already quoted. He went on to distinguish two questions. The first was whether the last voyage was one on which the charterers were entitled to send the vessel, on which he observed that there must be reasonable flexibility in the concluding date in the absence of clear agreement to the contrary (p. 526, col. 2; p. 527, col. 1; p. 15A, B). The second was whether unexpected delays on a legitimate voyage were to be paid for at the charter rate, to which he answered that in the absence of contrary agreement—

> ... it must be presumed because it is businesslike that the charter is intended to continue in operation until the end of a legitimate last voyage — unless of course one of the parties was responsible for the delay [p. 526, col. 2; p. 527, col. 1; p. 15A, D].

The charterers naturally rely on this answer. On the charterparty in question Lord Reid assumed, without deciding, that the language used ousted any presumption of flexibility that the law might otherwise make (p. 527, col; p. 16B) and added:

> That means that it would have been a breach of contract if the charterers had sent the vessel on a voyage expected to end on January 14 or any later date. But it does not mean, as the [charterers] argue, that [they] were necessarily in breach of contract by failing to redeliver the vessel on or before January 13. If what I have said earlier is right there still remains the separate presumption that the parties intended that, if unexpected delays on the last legitimate voyage caused redelivery to be delayed beyond the agreed date, the charter should nonetheless continue in operation until the end of the voyage.

Lord Reid found this presumption to be fortified by other provisions of the charterparty, particularly cl. 4, which showed that hire was to be payable until redelivery at the charter rate. He also, therefore, dismissed the charterers' appeal on this issue.

It is in my view plain that Lord Reid's observations support the charterers' argument in this appeal. I do not, however, think that to the extent that they differ from those of Lord Morris they can be said to carry the authority of the House.

*The Dione* [1975] 1 Lloyd's Rep 115 is another important case, containing in Lord Denning's judgment the most detailed consideration of legitimate and illegitimate last voyages in any of the authorities. The charter was—

> ... for a period of 6 months 20 days more or less in charterers' option.

The vessel was delivered to the charterers on Mar. 8, 1970 so that the period of six months and 20 days expired on Sept. 28. On Aug. 2, 1970 the charterers sent the vessel on a voyage which they could not reasonably expect the vessel to accomplish in time for redelivery before mid-October. In fact, contrary to reasonable expectation, the vessel was redelivered on Oct. 7, a delay (after Sept. 28) of 8.416 days. The charterers paid the contractual rate of hire until redelivery but (the market having risen) the owners claimed damages at the difference between the charter rate and the market rate for 8.416 days.

The first issue for decision was whether, on the wording of the charterparty, six months and 20 days was to be regarded as the final terminal date for redelivery or whether a further reasonable tolerance was to be implied. The arbitrators and Mr Justice Mocatta ([1974] 1 Lloyd's Rep 86) held in favour of the charterers that a further reasonable tolerance was to be implied. In the Court of Appeal Lord Justice Orr took the same view, regarding the Court as bound by the majority view of the House of Lords in *The London Explorer* (which itself, on this point, followed the view of an unanimous Court of Appeal). Lord Denning MR however, held that the charterparty language provided a final terminal date and left no room for any implied margin or allowance. He described the observations of Lord Morris in *The London Explorer* as 'made by the way' (p. 118) and preferred the view of Lord Reid. Lord Justice Browne discussed this aspect of the case at some considerable length and came to the same conclusion. The majority of the Court therefore proceeded on the basis that Sept. 28, was the final terminal date for redelivery under the charterparty.

The second issue in that appeal was whether, as the owners argued, the charterers' failure to redeliver by the final terminal date was in itself a breach of contract entitling the owners to damages. On this issue the conclusion of Lord Justice Browne seems to me clear. At p. 121 he said:

> Unless the authorities compel me to decide otherwise, I should, therefore, hold that in the present case the charterers' express obligation was to redeliver the ship at least on September 28; that it is impossible to imply any further tolerance; that they were in breach of contract in failing to do so; and that the owners are entitled to succeed.

He went on to hold that authority did not compel him to decide otherwise and accordingly found for the owners on this ground (p. 123).

Lord Denning, MR considered the case (not, as he held, the case before him) where the parties had expressed or impliedly agreed in the charterparty that there was to be no margin or allowance in the date for redelivery:

> In such a case the charterer must ensure that the vessel is redelivered within the stated period. If he does not do so — and the market rate has gone up — he will be bound to pay the extra. That is to say, he will be bound to pay the charter rate up to the end of the stated period, and the market rate thereafter ... [p. 117].

Lord Denning next considered the case (which was on his ruling, the case before him) where the parties expressly agreed what margin or allowance there should be:

> In that case the charterer must ensure that the vessel is redelivered within the permitted margin or allowance. If he does not do so — and the market rate has gone up — he will be bound to pay the extra. That is to say, he will be bound to pay the charter rate up to the end of the expressly permitted margin or allowance, and the market rate for any overlap thereafter ... [p. 117].

His Lordship referred to *Prebensens Dampskibsselskabet A/S* v *Munson SS Line* (1919) 258 Fed R 227 where the United States Circuit Court of Appeals for the Second Circuit upheld that principle.

Applying this principle, Lord Denning concluded on this issue:

> But having expressed that margin, it was the duty of the charterers to redeliver the vessel by the '20 days more', that is by Sept. 28, 1970. Not having done so, they must pay the charter rate up to that date and the market rate thereafter ... [p. 118].

This is, as I understand, entirely in accord with the view of Lord Justice Browne (Lord Justice Orr dissenting because he did not regard Sept. 28, as the final terminal date). It is also in accord with the owners' submission on this appeal.

The third issue in that appeal was whether, as the owners also argued, the charterers were in breach in sending the vessel on an illegitimate last voyage and were accordingly liable in damages (even though, contrary to expectation, the vessel had in the event been redelivered within the implied tolerance period, if, contrary to the owners' submission, there was one). Lord Justice Orr rejected this argument on the ground that the arbitrators had not found the voyage in question to be illegitimate or unreasonable (p. 119). Lord Justice Browne agreed with him (p. 123).

Lord Denning analysed the distinction between illegitimate and legitimate last voyages and said (at pp. 117–118):

(d)   If the charterer sends the vessel on a legitimate last voyage — that is, a voyage which it is reasonably expected will be completed by the end of the charter period, the shipowner must obey the direction. If the vessel is afterwards delayed by matters for which neither party is responsible, the charter is presumed to continue in operation until the end of that voyage, even though it extends beyond the charter period. The hire is payable at the charter rate until redelivery, even though the market rate may have gone up or down [see *The London Explorer*] ...

(e)   if the charterer sends the vessel on an illegitimate last voyage — that is, a voyage which it cannot be expected to complete within the charter period, then the shipowner is entitled to refuse that direction and call for another direction for a legitimate last voyage. If the charterer refuses to give it, the shipowner can accept his conduct as a breach going to the root of the contract, fix a fresh charter for the vessel, and sue for damages. If the shipowner accepts the direction and goes on the illegitimate last voyage, he is entitled to be paid — for the excess period — at the current market rate, and not at the charter rate, see *Meyer* v *Sanderson* (1916) 32 TLR 428. The hire will be payable at the charter rate up to the end of the charter period, and at the current market rate for the excess period thereafter.

He reached this conclusion (at p. 118):

It follows also that it was illegitimate for the charterers to send her on the third voyage, seeing that they could not reasonably expect the vessel to complete it by the permitted margin, that is, by September 28, 1970.

He plainly regarded the owners are entitled to damages on that ground also.

This latter conclusion of Lord Denning, although a minority view, seems hard to challenge given the majority conclusion on the first issue. One sees force in Lord Justice Browne's view that the second and third issues were closely related (p. 123). But it is par. (d) quoted above on which the charterers principally rely in this appeal and it was, I think, this paragraph which led the arbitrators to accept the charterers' submissions on what the parties' rights would have been had the charterparty not contained line 15. They said in par. 20 of their award:

Our understanding of the '*London Explorer*' and the '*Dione*' is that if orders are given for a legitimate last voyage and the vessel is delayed by matters for which neither party is responsible, then hire will be payable at the charter rate beyond the latest redelivery date.

I do not think this understanding is to be derived from the majority decision in *The London Explorer*, although it does reflect the minority view of Lord Reid and Lord Cross. It also reflects the view of Lord Denning as expressed in par. (d). In my opinion, it does not reflect the majority decision of Lord Denning and Lord Justice Browne on the second issue in *The Dione*, which did not depend on a finding that the voyage was illegitimate. Nor can I reconcile Lord Denning's opinon at (d) with the earlier extracts from p. 117 of his judgment which I have quoted or with his decision on the second issue. It is perhaps enough to say that par. (d) plainly did not found the decision of a majority of the Court since, had it done so, Lord Justice Browne could not have omitted to decide whether the voyage was legitimate or illegitimate, as he expressly declined to do.

After referring to *The Mareva AS* [1977] 1 Lloyd's Rep 368 and *The Matija Gubec* [1983] 1 Lloyd's Rep 24, Bingham LJ continued:

... The majority decisions in *The Dione* and, perhaps, *The London Explorer* are, as I read them, authority binding on us in support of the owners' argument. They also seem to me to accord with general contractual principle. But whether or not the law is settled in the sense contended for by the owners, I certainly cannot accept that it is settled in the sense contended for by the charterers. Mr Glennie is, I think, on stronger ground in submitting that even if the law is not settled in the charterers' sense there is a general perception that it is. The later authorities give force to that contention. It is not, however, a perception which, as I infer, was shared by these highly experienced arbitrators, or by Mr Justice Saville himself. I think it would be rash to approach this charterparty on the basis of any assumption as to what the parties to it perceived the law to be.

So I turn at last to the construction of line 15, of course in the context of the clause and the charterparty as a whole. I think it plain that 'option' in line 15 is to be read as meaning 'choice' or 'right to elect'. That is how the word is used in line 14 and how it is generally used in charterparties. 'Further' conveys that the option in line 15 is additional to the option in line 14. 'Complete' must in my view bear its ordinary meaning of 'finish' and it cannot be appropriately used save in relation to some thing which has already started or begun. In the absence of any contrary indication I would incline to read 'last voyage' as meaning 'last voyage under the charterparty'.

I do not regard the language of line 15 as at all apt to convey the meaning for which the charterers contend. The facts of the present case and of other decided cases make clear that when a charterer orders a vessel on a voyage which cannot reasonably be expected to be performed in time to permit redelivery by the final terminal date, the owner objects there and then, whether he refuses to comply or agrees to perform reserving all his rights. This is what one would expect, since the owner is probably as well able to calculate time as the charterer and may well have made commitments with reference to the final terminal date. What the charterers are really claiming is not an option to complete, since no one doubts that a voyage once begun must in any ordinary circumstances be completed. What they are really claiming is a right to require the owners not to complete but to embark on an illegitimate last voyage. That is by definition a last voyage which is not under the charterparty but outside it. If the charterers in truth sought the right they now claim I cannot find that intention expressed in line 15.

I do not find line 15 very apt to express the owners' suggested meaning either. They say that line 15 gives the charterers a right to complete a legitimate last voyage at the charter rate, that is, free of any liability to pay damages in respect of the period between the final terminal date and redelivery. 'Complete' can on this reading at least be understood as applying to something already begun, although the construction is subject to the objection that line 15 makes no reference to rate of hire. While neither construction is satisfactory, the less unsatisfactory of the two is in my view the owners: line 15 gives the charterers the right, additional to the right in line 14, to require the owners to complete a legitimate last voyage free of any liability in damages in repect of the period between the final terminal date and redelivery, at any rate unless the unexpected delay were caused by the charterers' breach of contract.

I am fortified in preferring this reading by the very surprising results which could flow from the charterers' alternative construction. The charterers accepted before the arbitrators that their construction was extraordinarily favourable to them and extraordinarily unfavourable to the owners.

> The Charterers could, in theory, wait until just before the expiry of the 12 months' charterparty period and then send the vessel on what would essentially be a round the

world voyage. The charterparty would therefore be for an almost indeterminate period. Whilst recognising that such an entitlement for a charterer would not comply with what, commercially, most parties would have intended to agree, if in this particular charterparty that was the effect of what the parties had agreed, then we had no alternative other than to give affect to that agreement ... [par. 8 of the award summarising the charterers submission].

While it is true that a somewhat similar art of commercial absurdity advanced by Mr Scrutton in *Dene Steam Shipping Co. Ltd* v *Bucknall Brothers* (1900) 5 Com Cas 372 was rejected by Mr Justice Bigham, I would need clear and compelling language to persuade me that the parties intended to disturb in such a radical manner the ordinary rule whereby risk of delay under a time charterparty (in the absence of breach by the owner) falls on the charterer. I find no such clear and compelling language here.

The owners accepted before the arbitrators that line 15 must be understood as conferring on the charterers some right which they would not enjoy without it. On the reading I prefer it does so. I do not, however, think that it is a safe approach, if one were to accept (as the arbitrators did, although I do not) that the authorities considered above settled the law in the sense contended for by the charterers, one would have to consider whether line 15 had the effect of stating the relevant principle on the face of the charterparty or of conferring the additional and extraordinary right which the charterers claim. I should prefer the former alternative. It would be wrong to approach as complex a contract as the standard form of charterparty on the assumption that none of the provisions would be implied if they were not express. The presumption against surplusage or tautology, if it exists, is weak. There are many reasons (of which avoiding argument is one) why parties may think it desirable to state expressly what they believe would be the position anyway. I would therefore favour the owners' construction even if I accepted the charterers' argument on the authorities.

I agree with the conclusion of the Judge and would accordingly dismiss this appeal.

*Notes*

1.   Slade LJ pointed out that in the statement of Lord Denning MR in *The Dione* that the hire is 'payable at the charter rate until redelivery, even though the market may have gone up or down', the words 'up or' were inserted *per incuriam*.

2.   Bingham LJ, with whose judgment the other Lord Justices agreed, proceeds on the basis that the *giving* of the order for an illegitimate last voyage is a breach by the charterer, but refrains from deciding whether it is a repudiatory breach. This aspect was re-examined by the House of Lords in the next case.

The House also had to consider whether the legitimacy of the last voyage was to be judged at the time of the giving of the order or at the time of commencement of the voyage.

### *Torvald Klaveness A/S* v *Arni Maritime Corporation*
### *(The Gregos)*
### [1995] 1 Lloyd's Rep 1 (HL)

LORD MUSTILL: My Lords, in merchant shipping time is money. A cargo ship is expensive to finance and expensive to run. The shipowner must keep it earning with the minimum of gaps between employments. Time is also important for the charterer, because arrangements must be made for the shipment and receipt of the cargo, or for the performance of obligations under sub-contracts. These demands encourage the planning and performance of voyages to the tightest of margins. Yet even today ships do not run precisely to time. The most prudent schedule may be disrupted by regular hazards such as adverse weather or delays in port happening in an unexpected manner or degree, or by the intervention of wholly adventitious events.

Where the charter-party is for a period of time rather than a voyage, and the remuneration is calculated according to the time used rather than the service performed, the risk of delay is primarily on the charterer. For the shipowner, so long as he commits no breach and nothing puts the ship off-hire, his right to remuneration is unaffected by a disturbance of the charterer's plans. It is for the latter to choose between cautious planning, which may leave gaps between employments, and bolder scheduling with the risk of setting aims which cannot be realised in practice.

This distribution of risk holds good for most of the chartered service. As the time for redelivery approaches things become more complicated. (The word 'redelivery' is inaccurate, but it is convenient, and I will use it). If the market is rising, the charterer wants to have the use of the vessel at the chartered rate for as long as possible. Conversely, the shipowner must think ahead to the next employment, and if as is common he has made a forward fixture he will be in difficulties if the vessel is retained by the charterer longer than had been foreseen. This conflict of interest becomes particularly acute when there is time left for only one more voyage before the expiry of the charter, and disputes may arise if the charterer orders the ship to perform a service which the shipowner believes will extend beyond the date fixed for redelivery.

. . .

The facts of the [present] dispute were as follows. *Gregos* was chartered by Arni Maritime Corporation (hereafter 'the owners') to Torvald Klaveness A/S ('the charterers') on terms which, so far as material, were as follows:

> WITNESSETH, That the said Owners agree to let and the Charterers agree to hire the said vessel, from the time of delivery, for about 50 to maximum 70 days . . . Vessel . . . to be employed in carrying lawful merchandise . . . in such lawful trades . . . between safe port and . . . as the charterers or ports shall direct, on the following conditions: . . .
> 8. THAT the Captain shall prosecute his voyages with the utmost despatch . . . The Captain (although appointed by the Owners) shall be under the orders and directions of the Charterers as regards employment and agency . . .
> THAT the Charterers shall furnish the Captain from time to time with all requisite instructions and sailing directions . . .

. . .

The charterers' original contemplation was to employ the vessel first by ballasting her from Antwerp to Trombetas in Brazil to carry a cargo of bauxite to Matanzas, a port in Venezuela on the Orinoco River. Thence the vessel was to proceed up river in ballast to Puerto Ordaz where she would load a cargo of iron ore for Italy, prior to redelivery. Later, this plan was revised in two respects. First, the charterers interposed a second voyage from Matanzas to Trombetas in ballast with a return leg to Matanzas with bauxite, between the first bauxite voyage and the final voyage to Europe. Secondly, this final voyage was now to be from Palua, also on the Orinoco, with iron ore for Fos. The first element of this changed schedule was notified to the owners and complied with. The vessel did lift a second bauxite cargo. The other element, namely the substitution of a laden voyage from Palua to Fos, was notified by the charterers to the master of the vessel on Feb 9, 1988. If judged when the order was given, compliance with the order could reasonably have been anticipated to allow redelivery by Mar 18, the last permissible date.

Three days later things began to go wrong. Another vessel grounded with unusual severity in the Orinoco, causing delays to river traffic which led the owners to warn the charterers that if the plan was adhered to *Gregos* could not be redelivered in time. As the arbitrator was later to find, this warning was justified. Even if all had gone well thereafter there would have been a late redelivery of between two and four days. The vessel nevertheless proceeded on the very short ballast leg to Palua from Matanzas. On Feb. 25, 1988 the owners advised the charterers that they declined to perform the laden voyage from the Orinoco to Fos, and called upon the charterers to give revised orders for the final voyage. No such orders were given, and a dispute arose, the charterers insisting and the owners denying that the order of Feb 9 for a voyage from Palua to Fos remained valid. While the impasse continued the owners began to negotiate a replacement fixture with a concern named Navios involving a rate of freight higher than that provided for under the instant charter, coupled with a bonus to reflect the fact that the vessel was in place at the intended loading port under the substitute employment and did not have to perform a ballast voyage. In the event, the deadlock was broken by a without prejudice agreement between the owners and the charterers. The terms were not before the House, but it was explained in argument that the agreement provided for the performance of the laden voyage to Fos on terms that if in subsequent proceedings it was held that the owners were justified in refusing to perform the voyage they would be entitled to a sum reflecting the difference between the chartered rate of hire and the more advantageous terms of the proposed substitute fixture with Navios. Pursuant to the without prejudice agreement the vessel loaded the cargo of iron ore and prepared to sail from Palua, but her departure was further delayed because another vessel grounded in the river ahead of her. In the event, the last laden voyage was not completed until Mar 23, and the actual redelivery took place on Mar 26 — eight days late.

On these facts the matter went to arbitration. The clear and thorough reasons given by the arbitrator for his award reflected a distinction drawn in the arguments before him, and still drawn in the submissions before the House, between two issues. 1. Should the validity of the order for the final voyage be judged as at the time when it was given or as at the time when it fell to be complied with; or on some other date? 2. If the validity of the order was to be judged in the light of matters as they stood on Feb 25, so that the voyage was not one for which a legitimate order could be given, what was the effect of (a) the charterers having given the order, and (b) their refusal to replace it by another? Two decisions by the arbitrator are no longer challenged. First, that the wording of the charter left no room for a margin beyond the end of the stipulated 70 days. Second, as regards the order for the voyage from Palua to Fos, his conclusion was that if judged as at Feb 9 the order was reasonable but that due to the intervening delays by Feb 25 this was no longer the case. On the issues which are still in dispute the arbitrator reasoned as follows. Essentially on the ground of common sense, he rejected an argument for the owners that proper voyage instructions could not be given until the vessel was free of her previous cargo, for that would have left only (in the present case) the 1 ½ hours of the ballast leg to Palua during which the next voyage could be nominated. On the other hand, if it were the law that the order could be given weeks or even months in advance (and the charterers did not suggest a limitation on how in advance it could be given) it would not be sensible to allow the charterers to shelter behind the apparent reasonableness of an order given at a time when it must be anticipated that practical problems were likely to render the theoretical scheduling of the vessel wholly unrealistic.

The arbitrator thus concluded that the time for evaluating the propriety of an order previously given was when the voyage was to be commenced. Quite apart from his own reasoning, the arbitrator considered himself bound to arrive at this conclusion by *Marbienes Compania Naviera SA* v *Ferrostaal A.G. (The Democritos)* [1976] 2 Lloyd's Rep 149. On this basis, the arbitrator held that the order originally given on Feb 9, and on which the charterers were continuing to insist, had by Feb 25 become invalid. The arbitrator then turned to the question whether the giving of the illegitimate order constituted a repudiation of the contract. Given that the anticipated overrun was only a few days he would, in the absence of authority, have considered that there was no repudiation, but regarded himself as compelled by authority to the opposite view. The arbitrator then proceeded to damages, and arrived at an award of US$299,791.25, comprising the difference between the charter hire and the hire obtainable on the alternative fixture with Navios, plus the bonus which Navios would have paid to recognise the immediate availability of the ship.

This award was upheld on appeal by Mr Justice Evans. On the first question the learned Judge concluded that the time for deciding whether the owner was bound to perform the order was when the time for performance arrived. He relied principally on practical considerations but stated that the weight of authority supported his conclusion. As to repudiation he had two reasons for upholding the award. First, that timely redelivery was a condition of the contract, and that ordering the vessel on a voyage which would involve a breach of condition must of necessity have been a wrongful repudiation. Secondly, the charterers' persistence with an order for an illegitimate voyage, and the resulting failure to give a lawful order with which the vessel could comply, was in itself a wrongful repudiation.

In the Court of Appeal [1993] 2 Lloyd's Rep 335 two reasoned judgments were delivered. After a careful discussion of the reported cases in this field which, in the event, he concluded were indecisive Lord Justice Hirst analysed the first issue principally in terms of convenience and concluded, at p. 346, that:

> ... the legitimacy of the last voyage order has to be established at the date when it is given, having regard not only to the reasonableness at that date of the estimate of the expected duration of the voyage, but also to the reasonableness at that date of making an estimate at all ...

Regarding the second issue, Lord Justice Hirst dealt only with the question whether timely redelivery was a condition of the contract, since he considered that the certified question of law did not extend to the alternative possibility that the giving of an order for an illegitimate voyage was in any event repudiatory. Holding that timely redelivery was not a condition of the contract, Lord Justice Hirst concluded that an order which if complied with would involve some degree of lateness could not in itself be an actual breach of condition or a repudiatory breach.

...

I begin with the first issue, concerning the date for judging the validity of the charterer's order. Here, it seems to me that the enquiry has been led astray by concentrating too much on the order and too little on the shipowner's promise to furnish the services of the vessel, which is what the contract is about. Initially, the practical implications of the promise are undefined, since they depend on how in the future the charterer decides to employ the vessel; but they are not unlimited, being constrained from the start as to duration, nature and extent by express terms in the charter (concerning for example the types of cargo to be carried and the geographical limits of trade) and also by important implied terms. Later, when the time for performance has arrived, this broad promise is converted to a series of specific obligations by the charterer's orders for employment, but the constraints expressly or impliedly accepted by the charterer in the original contract continue to apply. Whatever the charterer may order, a service which falls outside the range encompassed by the owner's original promise is not one which he can be compelled to perform; and this is so as regards not only the duration of the chartered service, but also all the other limitations imposed by the charter-party on the charterer's freedom of choice. There is thus to be a measuring of the service called for against the service promised. As a matter of common sense, it seems to me that the time for such measurement is, primarily at least, the time when performance falls due.

My Lords, I have qualified this statement with the words 'primarily at least', because in practice the interests of both parties demand that the charterer is entitled to give orders in advance of the time for performance, and this must entail at least a provisional judgment on the validity of the order. If it can be seen at this early stage that compliance will involve a service which lies outside the shipowner's undertaking the latter can say so at once, and reject the order. But if the order is apparently valid its validity is no more than contingent, since the time for matching the service against the promise to serve does not arrive until the nature of the service is definitively known; and this will not usually be until the service is due to begin, or in some instances until it is already in progress. Thus, if and for so long as the service required conforms with those which the shipowner promised in advance to render the specific order creates a specific obligation to perform them when the time arrives. But only for so long as that state of affairs persists. If circumstances change, so that compliance with the order will call for a service which in the original contract the shipowner never undertook, the obligation to comply must fall away. As I see it, the charterer's order in advance amounts to a continuing requirement, the validity of which may change with the passage of time.

My Lords, this much I conclude simply by considering the general nature of a time charter-party. The conclusion must however be tested by recourse to the authorities and (with appropriate caution) to its practical implications. On the former I need not dwell. Great care has properly been taken in the Courts below to see whether there can be found in the decided cases any judicial pronouncement which points unequivocally to a conclusion. For my part I can find none.

. . .

Turning to the practicalities, I entirely share the opinion of Mr Justice Saville (in *The Peonia* [1991] 1 Lloyd's Rep 100 at p. 102) that questions of this kind are better decided by looking at what the contract says than by speculating on the practical outcome of preferring one solution to another. Naturally, no Judge will favour an interpretation which produces an obviously absurd result unless the words used drive him to it, since it is unlikely that this is what the parties intended. But where there is no obvious absurdity, and simply assertions by either side that its own interpretation yields the more sensible result, there is room for error. The difference of opinion in the present case is an illustration. It is an essential part of the charterers' argument that an order given at a time when it is reasonably anticipated that compliance will not infringe the restrictions imposed by the contract has an immutable contractual effect. Even if circumstances change both parties are committed to the ordered employment unless released by mutual consent. The present charterers must be arguing for this, for if a charterer is free to recall his original order and substitute another the inference is irresistible that he ought to make such a substitution if changed circumstances cause the performance to break the bounds of the shipowner's original promise. What is the commercial convenience of such an interpretation? Undeniably, there is this to be said for it, that the parties will have a firm projection of future employment on the basis of which they can both make plans. But powerful considerations point the other way. First, if the charterers are right an order given long in advance will lock both parties into a set of contractual obligations [which] may well be compromised by the passage of time, as regards both commercial desirability and physical practicability. This can be in nobody's interest. The only escape would be to hold, as the Court of Appeal has held, that the order cannot be given before it is reasonable to do so, thus diminishing the likelihood of unexpected events. My Lords, with respect I cannot accept this solution for I cannot see how, even after the event, a Court or arbitrator could set the criteria for deciding whether an order was premature or apply them to the facts. Still less, in my opinion, should a shipowner be expected in the press of the moment to decide in the light of such criteria, whether to reject the order — a rejection which, if subsequently held by an arbitrator to have been ill-founded, would in all probability be a wrongful repudiation by the shipowner. Secondly, if the order is irrevocable the shipowner may find himself, if circumstances change, obliged to perform a service which he never agreed to undertake. This consequence, unacceptable enough in the context of an order prolonging the service beyond the time stipulated in the contract, could be even more serious when related to some other restriction imposed by the charter-party to which, if the argument is sound, it must equally apply. Furthermore, if the order is irrevocably binding on both sides (which is the logic of the argument) it must follow that a charterer who has reasonably given an order which is later falsified by events is compelled to proceed with a voyage which will inevitably be a breach of contract on his part. This can hardly be in the interests of commerce.

Thus, if the matter is to be decided according to balance of convenience the owners' argument appears to have much the better of it. But I prefer to concentrate on the charter-party itself; and here, for the reasons stated, the analysis leads directly to the conclusion that, as the arbitrator and Mr Justice Evans decided, the correct date for assessment was Feb 25. By then, an order originally permissible had become illegitimate.

I turn to the issue of repudiation. Although the appeal is concerned with an invalid order for a final voyage this is only a special case of an order issued for the performance of a service which lies outside the scope of the shipowner's promise. Since orders for employment and compliance with them lie at the heart of a time charter the question is of general importance, and the solution arrived at should hold good for all types of order. The analysis is not straightforward. There are three different grounds upon which it might be said that where a charterer calls on a shipowner to perform an extra-contractual service the shipowner is entitled to treat himself as discharged. First, the giving of an invalid order is by its nature a repudiatory breach. Second, redelivery after the final date is a breach of contract, and has the character of a breach of condition, entitling the shipowner to treat himself as discharged. It follows, so the argument runs, that an order for a voyage which according to a reasonable prediction will lead to late redelivery must necessarily be a repudiatory breach. Third, the persistence of the charterers in an illegitimate order was conduct 'evincing an intention no longer to be bound' by the contract, and hence a repudiation of it.

When considering the first of these arguments it is necessary to distinguish between two propositions: that the charterer is obliged at the appropriate time to give a valid order for the employment of the ship, and that he is obliged never to give an invalid order. At first sight this distinction may seem mere wordplay, but for present purposes it is essential, as may be seen from the example of a charterer who gives a series of orders, all of them invalid and hence ineffectual. The former proposition entails that since an ineffectual order is the same as no order at all the charterer becomes in breach only when the time for giving an order for the employment of the vessel has come and gone with no valid order having been given. The consequence of the latter is different, namely that every invalid order is in itself a breach of contract, giving the shipowner an immediate and distinct cause of action on each occasion. In company with Lord Justice Simon Brown I have difficulty in accepting the latter proposition. Certainly, if the shipowner acts on the order and suffers damage he should have an implied right of indemnity at common law. But if he rejects the order and does nothing, to say that he has suffered an actionable breach of contract by the mere receipt of the message seems to introduce an unnecessary complication, and if the matter were free from authority I would hesitate to take this step. There are however a number of judgments, concerned with unsafe ports as well as final voyages, which assert or assume that an illegitimate order is in itself a breach (see, for example, *Hyundai Merchant Marine Co. Ltd* v *Gesuri Chartering Co. Ltd (The Peonia)* [1991] 1 Lloyd's Rep 100; *Motor Oil Hellas (Corinth) Refineries SA* v *Shipping Corporation of India (The Kanchenjunga)* [1989] 1 Lloyd's Rep 354; *Batis Maritime Corporation* v *Petroleos del Mediterraneo SA (The Batis)* [1990] 1 Lloyd's Rep 345) and since the proposition appears to have been conceded in the Court of Appeal I will assume it to be correct. It is however quite another matter to say that the duty never to give an invalid order is so fundamental to the working of the contract that the giving of such an order must in every case entitle the shipowner to treat the contract as at an end, even if by rejecting the order he can ensure that it causes him no damage at all. My Lords, although it is well established that certain obligations under charter-parties do have the character of conditions I would not for my part wish to enlarge the category unduly, given the opportunity which this provides for a party to rely on an innocuous breach as a means of escaping from an unwelcome bargain. In the present instance I can see no commercial necessity to hold that the issuing of an invalid order is an automatic ground of discharge, and every reason for holding that it does not. I would therefore reject the first of the shipowners' arguments.

I turn to the second argument which concentrates, not on the rejected order itself, but on the hypothetical consequences which would have been likely to ensue if it had been obeyed. It runs as follows. The timely redelivery of the vessel is a condition of the contract; an actual late redelivery, whether long or short, would therefore enable the shipowner to treat the contract as terminated; the invalid order actually given, if obeyed, would probably have caused the vessel to be redelivered late; the breach of condition which this would have entailed must be referred back to the invalid order, even though in fact it was not obeyed. At first sight this argument appears to lead straight to the law on anticipatory breach, and in particular to the discussion in *Federal Commerce & Navigation Co. Ltd* v *Molena Alpha Inc (The Nanfri)* [1979] 1 Lloyd's Rep 201; [1979] AC 757 of the situation where the threatened breach is not of a fundamental character. On reflection however I question whether this analysis is sound, for I am not convinced that the shipowner can at the same time treat the charterer as evincing an intention to commit a breach in the future and yet ensure, by rejecting the order, that no such breach ever takes place.

Quite apart from this however I find it hard to accept that timely redelivery is a condition of the contract. The classification of an obligation as a condition or an 'innominate' term is largely determined by its practical importance in the scheme of the contract, and this is not easily judged in relation to the obligation to redeliver, since the occasions for the cancellation of a charter on the ground of a few days' delay at the end of the chartered service are likely to be few. If the ship is laden when the final date arrives the shipowner will often have obligations to third party consignees which make it impossible for him to cut short the voyage, quite apart from the improbability that he will go to the trouble and expense of arranging for the discharge and receipt of the cargo at an alternative destination, just to save a few days' delay. These problems will not arise if the vessel is ballasting to the redelivery port, but even if the shipowner really wants the vessel back on time, rather than a few days late, he will not usually need to have recourse to a cancellation, since the charterer will have no motive to keep the charter in being, with its obligation to pay hire for an empty ship. Even acknowledging the importance given in recent years to time clauses in mercantile contracts (see, for example, *Bunge Corporation New York* v *Tradax Export S.A. Panama* [1981] 2 Lloyd's Rep 1; [1981] 1 WLR 711 and *Compagnie Commerciale Sucres et Denrées* v *C. Czarnikow Ltd (The Naxos)* [1991] 1 Lloyd's Rep 29; [1990] 1 WLR 1337) I would incline to the view that this particular obligation is 'innominate' and that a short delay in redelivery would not justify the termination of the contract. For this additional reason therefore I would reject the owners' second argument. It is however unnecessary to express a firm conclusion upon it, given my opinion on the owners' third argument, to which I now turn.

This argument depends, not on the invalid order which was given, but on the valid order which was not. The original order having become ineffectual the charterers were obliged by cl. 11 to replace it with one which they were entitled to give. Whether at the time of the cancellation they had committed an actual breach of this obligation is debatable, but at all events the breach was not final, since (if I correctly understand the arbitrator's reasons) there would have been time if all else failed for the charterers to ballast the vessel back to the redelivery area before the final date, or conceivably to issue an order for a revised laden voyage. But it is plain from the facts stated by the arbitrator that the charterers had no intention of doing this, and that the critical time would pass without any valid orders being given. This is the significance of the changed circumstances which rendered the original order invalid. Not that the order constituted a repudiation in itself, but that the charterers' persistence in it after it had become invalid showed that they did not intend to perform their obligations under the charter. That is to say, they 'evidenced an intention no longer to be bound' by the charter. This was an anticipatory breach, which entitled the owners to treat the contract as ended.

My Lords, although differently expressed this reasoning accords with that of Mr Justice Evans. Rather than call up a secondary obligation to give a new order once the old one has failed I prefer to envisage a continuing primary obligation to give a valid order; but this distinction is largely a matter of terminology and has no practical significance.

. . .

In conclusion I must notice a feature of the award which troubled the arbitrator himself, which Lord Justice Hirst relied upon in support of his conclusion that there had been no repudiation, and which was the subject of comment in a valuable article by B. J. Davenport QC and M. White — Last Voyage Orders — again (*The Gregos*) [1994] *LMCLQ* 154. This was what Lord Justice Hirst called the 'windfall damages' attached to the repudiation, a large multiple of those which would have been awarded simply in respect of a few days' late redelivery. At first sight, this apparently anomalous result is a good reason for questioning whether the claim for repudiation was soundly based. On closer examination, however, the anomaly consists, not so much in the size of the damages, but in the fact that damages were awarded at all. Imagine that the without prejudice agreement had not been made, and that the owners, having treated the charter as wrongfully repudiated, had accepted a substitute fixture with Navios. If one then asked what loss had the repudiation caused the owners to suffer, the answer would be — None. On the contrary, the charterers' wrongful act would have enabled the owners to make a profit. Even if they had not accepted the substitute employment they might very well have suffered no loss, since they would have been in the favourable position of having their ship free in the right place at the right time to take a spot fixture on a rising market. In neither event would the owners ordinarily recover any damages for the wrongful repudiation. Yet the arbitrator awarded a large sum. The reason was, I believe, that what the arbitrator did was not to award damages but to enforce the terms of the without prejudice agreement, and to remunerate the owners for performing a voyage from which, in consequence of the charterers' wrongful act, they would otherwise have been free. This purely technical distinction would have been of no interest but for the stress laid on the size of an award of some US$300,000 for the anticipatory repudiation of a contract which, if performance had gone ahead, would have led to a breach yielding a mere US$35,000 in damages. For the reasons just stated, this comparison is inaccurate. The point really to be made is that if the conduct of the charterers was repudiatory the consequence that they were left without a ship to lift their sub-charterers' cargo may seem out of proportion to the comparatively minor breach which their order, if performed, would have entailed. There is force in this, but not enough to overcome the contractual logic. The fact is that in a volatile market, of which merchant shipping is by no means the only example, a contract breaker may find that the consequences of a breach are multiplied to a surprising degree by adventitious factors. Here, the charterers chose to stand their ground in circumstances where, if they were mistaken, the owners would have the upper hand. I believe that they were mistaken and must suffer the consequences, harsh as they may seem.

For these reasons I would allow the appeal and restore the award of the arbitrator.

*Notes*
1.   *Pace* Lord Templeman (at p. 3) and the headnote in Lloyd's Reports, Fos, which lies west of Marseilles, is in France, not Italy.
2.   In the next case the Court of Appeal considered the effect of an express overrun clause which was differently worded from that in *The Peonia*.

### Chiswell Shipping Ltd and Liberian Jaguar Transports Inc. v National Iranian Tanker Co. (The World Symphony and World Renown)
### [1992] 2 Lloyd's Rep 115 (CA)

The charterparty in respect of the *World Renown*, in the Shelltime 3 form, provided in clause 3: 'Owners agree to let and Charterers agree to hire the vessel for a period of six months fifteen days more or less in Charterers' option commencing from the time and date of delivery of the vessel for the purpose of carrying crude oil . . . The vessel shall be delivered by Owners at Hormuz at Owners' option and redelivered to Owners at a safe anchorage off Oman at Charterers' option.' Clause 18 provided: '. . . Notwithstanding the provisions of clause 3 hereof, should the vessel be upon a voyage at the expiry of the period of this charter, Charterers shall have the use of the vessel at the same rate and conditions for such extended time as may be necessary for the completion of the round voyage on which she is engaged and her return to a port of redelivery as provided by this charter.' The final terminal date was 24 December 1988. On 4 October, while the vessel was on a voyage from Sirri Island in the Gulf to Rotterdam, the charterers instructed the master to return to Sirri after discharge in Rotterdam and load a further cargo for Rotterdam and Milford Haven. The shipowners complied with the order and, as a result, the vessel was not redelivered until 18 January 1989. The shipowners claimed damages and the charterers relied on cl. 18. Hobhouse J's decision in favour of the charterers was affirmed by the Court of Appeal.

LORD DONALDSON OF LYMINGTON MR: This is an appeal by shipowners against a decision of Mr Justice Hobhouse that on the true construction of cll. 3 and 18 of the Shelltime 3 charterparty, the charterers were entitled to order the vessel to undertake a round voyage which on no view would end before the expiration of the period of the charter mentioned in cl. 3. The Judge outlined the facts, reviewed the authorities and explained his reasons for reaching this conclusion in a judgment of outstanding clarity, which has been reported in [1991] 2 Lloyd's Rep 251. This enables me to express my views much more succinctly than would otherwise be the case.

Mr Justice Hobhouse accepted, on the authority of *Hyundai Merchant Marine Co. Ltd v Gesuri Chartering Co. Ltd (The Peonia)* [1991] 1 Lloyd's Rep 100, that in the present case if cl. 3, which defines the charter period in terms of 'six (6) months fifteen (15) days more or less in charterers' option', had stood alone, the charterers would have been in breach of the time charter in two separate respects. First, they would have been in breach of contract in ordering the master to proceed on a voyage the undertaking of which would inevitably result in the vessel being redelivered after the expiration of the period specified in cl. 3, i.e. after 22 50 hours on Dec. 24, 1988. It would not have been a legitimate order. Second, they would have been in breach of the independent obligation to redeliver the vessel by that date.

In *Hyundai* and in *The Black Falcon* [1991] 1 Lloyd's Rep 77 the vessels were chartered on the New York Produce Exchange form of charterparty, the definition of the charter periods being slightly different. In *Hyundai* it was—

... for about minimum 10 months maximum 12 months time charter, exact duration in charterers' option. Charterers have further option to complete last voyage within below mentioned trading limits.

In *The Black Falcon* it was—

... for about 9 months, charterers' option 3 months, charterers' option further 3 months, 15 days more or less on final period. Charterers having option to complete last round voyage under performance prior to delivery at charterparty rate.

In each case it was held that the last part of the clause applied and negatived any breach of contract by the charterers if when the order for the last voyage or last round voyage was given (assuming the order to have been given at the appropriate time) it was a voyage which could reasonably have been expected to result in redelivery before the expiration of the primary period of the charter, notwithstanding that, due to circumstances for which the charterers were not responsible, there was in the event a 'late' redelivery. However in *Hyundai* (this Court) and in *The Black Falcon* (Mr Justice Steyn as he then was) the Courts rejected the submission that these words entitled the charterers to order the vessel to undertake a last voyage or last round voyage which could not be expected to permit of redelivery within the primary period of the charter.

Mr Justice Hobhouse then referred to *Bucknall Brothers v Murray* (1900) 5 Com Cas 312 (Mr Justice Mathew) and *Dene Steam Shipping Co. Ltd v Bucknall Brothers* (1900) 5 Com Cas 372 (Mr Justice Bigham) in which the relevant words were:

Should the vessel be upon a voyage at the expiration of the within named period, the charterers are to have the use of the steamer at the same rate and conditions for such extended time as may be necessary for the completion of their contemplated voyage, and in order to bring the steamer to a port of delivery as provided.

Mr Justice Mathew suggested and Mr Justice Bigham held that on this wording the charterers were entitled to order the vessel to undertake a voyage which would prevent redelivery before the expiration of 'the within named period', provided that the orders were given and the voyage begun before that expiration.

Against this background Mr Justice Hobhouse pointed to the fact that owners and charterers were free to make, and did make, contracts which might not be classic voyage or time charterparties, but were hybrids and cautioned against Judges attaching too much importance to what they might think was or was not a businesslike contract, contrasting the views expressed in the *Hyundai* case and in *The Black Falcon* with those of Mr Justice Kennedy in the matter of an arbitration between *The Owners of the Istok and Drughorn* (1901) 6 Com Cas 220 at p. 225. He also pointed out that neither *Bucknall* nor *Dene* had been expressly overruled by any subsequent decision, including *The Dione* [1975] 1 Lloyd's Rep 115, a decision of this Court, which he regarded as concerned with 'broader principles' and *Hyundai*, again a decision of this Court, where *Dene* was mentioned in the judgment of Lord Justice Bingham with surprise rather than clear disapproval.

Mr Justice Hobhouse's conclusion was summed up in the following passage from his judgment:

> The actual wording of the clause uses the phrase 'at the expiry of the period of this charter' and expressly provides that the charterers shall have 'the use of the vessel' for the 'extended time'. It is on the natural meaning of the wording an 'extension of the period clause' so as to add to the calendar period an extended period defined by reference to the time it takes to complete the round voyage upon which the vessel is engaged at the expiry of the calendar period. In this charterparty this conclusion is further supported by the insertion at the commencement of the relevant sentence of the words 'notwithstanding the provisions of clause 3 hereof'. This indicates that the relevant sentence is intended to qualify the period provision in the first line of cl. 3 and that cl. 3 is not to prejudice the right given under cl. 18.

I accept unreservedly that owners and charterers are free to make any contract which in their view meets their commercial needs. I also accept, equally unreservedly, that arguments based upon apparent commercial absurdity need to be regarded with caution not least because, whilst Judges of commercial experience are in a position to make some evaluation of the benefits and burdens of liberties and limitations contained in a charterparty, they are unlikely to be able to evaluate the countervailing burden or benefit of a particular rate of hire or length of charter, which depends upon current market conditions and because the alleged absurdity of a particular provision has to be judged in the context of the whole package. Maritime arbitrators in day to day contact with the market place are in a different position.

However it is for the parties to give expression to the terms of their bargain and this has always to be done against a background of general law and accepted principles, such as that prima facie the risk of loss by delay in performance under a time charterparty falls upon the charterer.

Here the general principles are not, I think, in doubt in the light of *The Dione* and *Hyundai*. They are that: 1. A charter for a fixed period will have a small implied tolerance or margin in its duration. 2. A charter for a fixed period with an expressed tolerance or margin — in this case '15 days more or less' — will have no further implied tolerance or margin. 3. In either of these cases, in the absence of a 'last voyage' clause, charterers will be in breach of contract if the vessel is redelivered after the expiry of the fixed period extended by the implied or expressed tolerance or margin, unless the late delivery arises out of a cause for which the owners are responsible. 4. A 'last voyage' clause is needed and will protect the charterer if he orders the vessel to undertake a last voyage which can reasonably be expected to enable the vessel to be redelivered punctually, but without fault on his part in the event such redelivery proves impossible. 5. If a 'last voyage' clause is to protect a charterer from being in breach by late redelivery in circumstances in which he has ordered a voyage which is likely to or must have this result, the intention to provide this protection must be clearly expressed.

Putting on one side the crucial words 'notwithstanding the provisions of clause 3 hereof' in cl. 18 of the Shelltime 3 charterparty, I consider that the effect of the clause would be to entitle a charterer to order the vessel to undertake a last voyage which could be expected to lead to punctual redelivery and to protect him if, in the event, redelivery was late. It would not, however, extend to authorising a last voyage which was likely or doomed to result in late redelivery or to excuse the resulting lateness. The use of the words 'extended time' would be equally appropriate in either case. In so far as *Dene* and *Bucknall* decide the contrary. I do not think that they can stand with *The Dione* and *Hyundai* and should be regarded as overruled. To this extent I respectfully disagree with Mr Justice Hobhouse and do so with a full awareness of the undesirability of risking disturbance of longstanding market assumptions as to the meaning of charterparty clauses.

I turn therefore to the words 'notwithstanding the provisions of clause 3 hereof'. Mr Bernard Eder QC, appearing for the owners, makes two submissions. First he submits that they add nothing. He says that cl. 18 undoubtedly qualifies cl. 3 and this phrase does no more than record the fact. I am unable to accept this explanation. Tautology on the part of those who draft and amend charterparties may well be a way of life, but this should not lead Courts to disregard the possibility that the use of particular words is in fact intended to have some effect. There is a fundamental difference between a clause which qualifies another clause and one which is inconsistent with and overrides that other clause. A clause which makes provision for what is to happen if, through the fault of no one, the period of hire is exceeded is no more than an exceptions clause. By contrast a clause which overrides the terms of another clause — in this case by (to use Mr Gee's colourful phrase) 'bolting on' a round trip charter on to one for a fixed term — plainly involves an inconsistency. It is only the latter type of clause which calls for introductory words acknowledging the inconsistency and specifying which is paramount.

Mr Eder's second submission is that, even if cl. 18 would be an answer to a claim for damages for late redelivery which had been caused by the deliberate act of the charterers, it does not address the question of whether the charterers are entitled to order the vessel on a voyage which is doomed to give rise to such late redelivery. It does not address the legitimacy of the order. This argument I would also reject. Either cl. 18 is or it is not concerned with late redelivery caused by the charterers ordering the master to undertake a voyage which makes such late redelivery likely or inevitable. If it is so concerned, by necessary implication it authorises the giving of orders which will have that result.

I am reinforced in this view by the commercial desirability, if not necessity, of cl. 18 of the Shelltime 3 charterparty receiving the same construction worldwide and by the fact that cl. 11 of the Texacotime 2 charterparty, which is in all relevant respects in identical terms, has been so construed in *The Pacific Sun* [1983] AMC 830 which incidentally pre-dates this charterparty, and in *The Narnian Sea* [1990] AMC 274. *The Pacific Sun* report is also of interest for its review in this context of seven different standard time charterparties and for the arbitrators' refusal to express a view on whether the Beepeetime 2 charterparty which is identical with Shelltime 3 with the omission of the words 'notwithstanding the provisions of clause 3 hereof' would achieve the result contended for by the charterers in this case on the authority of *Dene* (see p. 838).

I would dismiss the appeal.

## Question
Why should a shipowner agree to a clause like cl. 18 in the Shelltime 3 form?

# INDEX